MCSE Guide to
Microsoft® Windows®
Server 2003
Active Directory, Enhanced

Michael Aubert
Brian McCann

THOMSON

COURSE TECHNOLOGY

Australia • Canada • Mexico • Singapore • Spain • United Kingdom • United States

THOMSON

COURSE TECHNOLOGY

MCSE Guide to Microsoft® Windows® Server 2003 Active Directory, Enhanced
is published by Course Technology

Managing Editor:
William Pitkin III

Product Manager:
Nick Lombardi

Production Editors:
Daphne Barbas
Cathie DiMassa

Developmental Editors:
Ralph E. Moore
Jill Batistick

Quality Assurance/Technical Edit:
Marianne Snow
Danielle Shaw
Christian Kunciw

Associate Product Managers:
Mirella Misiaszek
David Rivera
Sarah Santoro

Editorial Assistant:
Jenny Smith

Manufacturing Coordinator:
Melissa Hulse

Marketing Manager:
Guy Baskaran

Text Designer:
GEX Publishing Services

Compositor:
GEX Publishing Services

Cover Design:
Steven Deschene

BRIEF Contents

TABLE OF

Contents

CHAPTER SIX
Active Directory Physical Design

CHAPTER SEVEN
Active Directory Replication

Introduction

Welcome to *MCSE Guide to Microsoft Windows Server 2003 Active Directory, Enhanced*. This book is designed to prepare you for the 70-294 exam, Planning, Implementing, and Maintaining a Microsoft Windows Server 2003 Active Directory Infrastructure, as well as a career in Microsoft network implementation and management using Microsoft's enterprise-level directory service, Active Directory. This book provides in-depth coverage of planning, implementing, maintaining, and troubleshooting an Active Directory infrastructure. Through the use of detailed explanations, real-world examples, and interactive activities that reinforce key concepts, you will gain the in-depth knowledge you need. This book provides pointed review questions to reinforce the concepts introduced in each chapter. In addition to the review questions, detailed activities let you experience firsthand the processes involved in Active Directory configuration and management. Finally, to put a real-world slant on the concepts introduced in each chapter, case studies are provided at the end of each chapter to prepare you for typical situations you may encounter when managing in a live networking environment.

Intended Audience

MCSE Guide to Microsoft Windows Server 2003 Active Directory, Enhanced is intended for people who have some experience administering and supporting Windows 2000 Server- or Windows Server 2003-based networks. To best understand the material in this book, you should have a background in basic computer concepts and have worked with the material presented in Course Technology's *MCSE Guide to Microsoft Windows XP Professional, Enhanced* and *MCSE Guide to Managing a Microsoft Windows Server 2003 Environment, Enhanced*.

New to This Edition

- Appendix B provides detailed lab setup instructions to assist instructors in preparing their labs for class.

- Appendix C features expanded and more comprehensive chapter summaries to assist students in reviewing the material covered in each chapter.

- Two new Practice Exams are provided. One is located in the back of the textbook and is printed on perforated pages so that it can be handed in as a homework assignment or test. The second is posted on *www.course.com* in the password protected Instructor's

Resource section, along with the Solutions to both exams. The questions on these Practice Exams are modeled after the type of questions students will see on the actual MCSE 70-294 certification exam. In addition to helping students review what they have learned, they have the added benefit of preparing them for the certification exam.

- Our CoursePrep ExamGuide content is now included in PDF format on the CD that accompanies this textbook. This content features key information, bulleted memorization points, and review questions for every exam objective in an easy-to-follow two-page-spread layout. This is an excellent resource for self-study before taking the 70-294 certification exam.

Chapter Descriptions

There are fourteen chapters in this book.

Chapter 1, "Introduction to Active Directory," provides an overview of Active Directory and introduces the role of a directory service in a modern network, important Microsoft networking and Active Directory concepts, and the components or "building blocks" of Windows Server 2003 Active Directory. In addition, new Active Directory features and capabilities in Windows Server 2003 are introduced.

Chapter 2, "Name Resolution and DNS," emphasizes the importance of name resolution for correct operation of Active Directory. This chapter describes the different types of names in use on Microsoft networks—focusing on the Domain Name System (DNS) and how it is used by Active Directory. The chapter also shows how to install and configure the DNS server included with Windows Server 2003 to support Active Directory.

Chapter 3, "Active Directory Design Philosophy," outlines the importance of considering the "big picture" of how Active Directory will operate in your network. Various viewpoints or philosophies are described and information is provided about how Active Directory design decisions made early in the process can affect the life of your project.

Chapter 4, "Active Directory Architecture," explores the underlying components of Active Directory including the Extensible Storage Engine (ESE), the schema, and the various types of partitions. The chapter provides an "under the hood" look at how Active Directory data is actually stored.

Chapter 5, "Active Directory Logical Design," details the design decisions you must make when implementing the logical structure of Active Directory. Topics include how to choose a DNS name, determine the number of forests and domains, implement trust relationships, and choose an organizational unit hierarchy. A section on upgrading from Windows NT Server 4.0- and Windows Server 2000-based networks is also included.

Chapter 6, "Active Directory Physical Design," details the design decisions you must make when implementing the physical structure of Active Directory. Whereas Chapter 5 looked at logical objects such as forests and domains, this chapter covers the implementation of physical objects such as sites, site links, and the placement of domain controllers.

Chapter 7, "Active Directory Replication," provides a step-by-step explanation of the Active Directory replication process, how intra-site and inter-site replication topologies are generated, and how the frequency of Active Directory replication can be controlled. A section on monitoring and troubleshooting replication is also included. Whereas Chapter 4 covered Active Directory data storage in detail, this chapter provides an "under the hood" look at how Active Directory data is replicated.

Chapter 8, "Active Directory Operations Masters," describes the different forest-wide and domain-wide roles a domain controller can hold. Although most Active Directory operations are multi-master, there are some operations that necessitate a single point of control.

Chapter 9, "Active Directory Authentication and Security," describes security concepts in Active Directory, as well as how to control access to objects in the directory. It also focuses on how to use audit settings to monitor access to objects, and how users are authenticated and authorized on a Windows Server 2003 network.

Chapter 10, "Managing Users, Groups, Computers, and Resources," focuses on creating and managing the objects commonly found in Active Directory, and their key properties. In addition, how to publish resources and organize objects in the directory is also explored.

Chapter 11, "Group Policy for Corporate Policy," outlines how to use Group Policy to enforce corporate settings in your network. Topics include how to restrict desktop settings, redirect folders, apply scripts, set account policies, and more. A section on how to troubleshoot Group Policy problems is also included.

Chapter 12, "Deploying and Managing Software with Group Policy," outlines how to use Group Policy to distribute and maintain software. This chapter covers all phases of an application life cycle from preparation and installation to maintenance and removal. A section on how to troubleshoot software installation problems is also included.

Chapter 13, "Monitoring and Optimizing Active Directory," explores the tools available to monitor and optimize Active Directory performance. Additionally, the chapter describes how to move the Active Directory database and log files for optimal performance. The chapter concludes with a section on working with application directory partitions.

Chapter 14, "Disaster Recovery," explains the purpose of Active Directory backups and how to create a disaster recovery plan. This chapter also takes a look at the utilities and methods that you can use to recover or restore Active Directory in the event of catastrophic failures or unintentional object deletion.

Features and Approach

MCSE Guide to Microsoft Windows Server 2003 Active Directory, Enhanced differs from other networking books in its unique hands-on approach, its attention to the important details, and its orientation to real-world situations and problem solving. To help you comprehend how Microsoft Windows network management concepts and techniques are applied in real-world organizations, this book incorporates the following features:

- **Chapter Objectives**—Each chapter begins with a detailed list of the concepts to be mastered. This list gives you a quick reference to the chapter's contents and is a useful study aid.

- **Activities**—Hands-on Activities are incorporated throughout the text, giving you practice in setting up, managing, and troubleshooting a network system. The activities give you a strong foundation for carrying out network administration tasks in the real world. Because of this book's progressive nature, completing the hands-on activities is essential before moving on to the end-of-chapter projects and subsequent chapters. Additionally, if you elect to use the lab manual associated with this text, it is important that you complete the lab manual activities after the activities in this text but before progressing on to the next chapter of this text. For example, after completing activities in Chapter 1 of this text, you should then complete the activities in Chapter 1 of the lab manual. Once you have completed the activities in Chapter 1 of both texts, you can then complete the activities in Chapter 2 of this text followed by Chapter 2 of the lab manual. In order for the labs in the lab manual to work correctly, you must complete the activities in this order.

- **Chapter Summary**—Each chapter's text is followed by a summary of the concepts introduced in that chapter. These summaries provide a helpful way to recap and revisit the ideas covered in each chapter.

- **Key Terms**—All of the terms within the chapter that were introduced with boldfaced text are gathered together in the Key Terms list at the end of the chapter. This provides you with a method of checking your understanding of all the terms introduced.

- **Review Questions**—The end-of-chapter assessment begins with a set of review questions that reinforce the ideas introduced in each chapter. Answering these questions will ensure that you have mastered the important concepts.

- **Case Projects**—Each chapter closes with a section that proposes certain situations. You are asked to evaluate the situations and decide upon the course of action to be taken to remedy the problems described. This valuable tool will help you sharpen your decision-making and troubleshooting skills, which are important aspects of network administration.

- **Tear-Out Practice Exam**—A 50-question tear-out practice exam is included in the back of the text. The questions are modeled after the actual MCSE certification exam and are on perforated pages so students can hand them in as an assignment or an exam. The answers to the Practice Exam are included as part of the Instructor Resources.

- **On the CD ROM**—The CD-ROM includes CoursePrep® test preparation software, which provides sample MCSE exam questions mirroring the look and feel of the MCSE exams. The CD also contains a complete CoursePrep ExamGuide workbook in PDF format. It devotes an entire two-page spread for every exam objective, featuring bulleted memorization points and review questions for self-study before exam day.

Text and Graphic Conventions

Additional information and exercises have been added to this book to help you better understand what's being discussed in the chapter. Icons throughout the text alert you to these additional materials. The icons used in this book are described below.

TIP

Tips offer extra information on resources, how to attack problems, and time-saving shortcuts.

NOTE

Notes present additional helpful material related to the subject being discussed.

CAUTION

The Caution icon identifies important information about potential mistakes or hazards.

ACTIVITY

Each Activity in this book is preceded by the Activity icon.

CASE PROJECTS

Case Project icons mark the end-of-chapter case projects, which are scenario-based assignments that ask you to independently apply what you have learned in the chapter.

Instructor's Resources

The following supplemental materials are available when this book is used in a classroom setting. All of the supplements available with this book are provided to the instructor on a single CD-ROM.

Electronic Instructor's Manual. The Instructor's Manual that accompanies this textbook includes additional instructional material to assist in class preparation, including suggestions for classroom activities, discussion topics, and additional activities.

Solutions. Solutions are provided for the end-of-chapter material, including Review Questions, and, where applicable, Hands-On Activities and Case Projects. Solutions to the Practice Exams are also included.

ExamView®. This textbook is accompanied by ExamView, a powerful testing software package that allows instructors to create and administer printed, computer (LAN-based), and Internet exams. ExamView includes hundreds of questions that correspond to the topics covered in this text, enabling students to generate detailed study guides that include page references for further review. The computer-based and Internet testing components allow students to take exams at their computers and also save the instructor time by grading each exam automatically.

Practice Exam. A second 50-question Practice Exam is included as part of the Instructor Resources. Like the Tear-Out Practice Exam in the text, the questions are modeled after the actual MCSE certification exam. The answers to this exam are also included as part of the Instructor Resources.

PowerPoint presentations. This book comes with Microsoft PowerPoint slides for each chapter. These are included as a teaching aid for classroom presentation, to make available to students on the network for chapter review, or to be printed for classroom distribution. Instructors, please feel at liberty to add your own slides for additional topics you introduce to the class.

Figure files. All of the figures and tables in the book are reproduced on the Instructor's Resource CD, in bitmap format. Similar to the PowerPoint presentations, these are included as a teaching aid for classroom presentation, to make available to students for review, or to be printed for classroom distribution.

Minimum Lab Requirements

- **Hardware:**

  All hardware should be listed on Microsoft's Hardware Compatibility List for Windows Server 2003.

Component	Requirement
CPU	Pentium III 550 or higher
Memory	128 MB RAM (256 MB RAM recommended)
Disk Space	Minimum of two 4-GB partitions (C and D), with at least 1 GB of free space left on the drive
Drives	CD-ROM (or DVD-ROM) Floppy Disk
Networking	All lab computers should be networked. Students will work in pairs for some lab exercises. A connection to the Internet via some sort of NAT or Proxy server is assumed.

- **Software:**

  Microsoft Windows Server 2003 Enterprise Edition for each computer

  The latest Windows Server 2003 Service Pack (if available)

- **Set Up Instructions:**

  To successfully complete the Activities, set up classroom computers as listed below:

  1. Install Windows Server 2003 onto drive C: of the instructor and student servers. The following specific parameters should be configured on individual servers during the installation process:

Parameter	Setting
Disk Partitioning	Create two 4-GB NTFS partitions during the installation process, C and D. Ensure that at least 1 GB of free space is left on the hard disk for student exercises.
Computer Names	Instructor (first server), ServerXX (subsequent student servers)
Administrator Password	Password01
Components	Default Settings
Network Adapter	IP Address: 192.168.1.X. The instructor computer should be allocated a unique IP address on the same subnet as client computers. The suggested IP address for the Instructor machine is 192.168.1.100. Subnet Mask: 255.255.255.0 DNS: The IP address of the Instructor computer. Default Gateway: The IP address for the classroom default gateway. If the Instructor computer will be used to provide Internet access via ICS or NAT, it will require a second network adapter card or modem.
Workgroup Name	Workgroup

In the preceding table, "X" or "XX" should represent a unique number to be assigned to each student. For example, student "1" would be assigned a computer name of Server01 and an IP address of 192.168.1.1.

2. Once the installation process is complete, use Device Manager to ensure that all devices are functioning correctly. In some cases, it may be necessary to download and install additional drivers for devices listed with a yellow question mark icon.

3. Create a new folder named Source on drive D: of all classroom servers. Copy the entire contents of the Windows Server 2003 CD to this folder on all servers.

4. Create a new folder named Shared on drive D: of the Instructor computer only. Share this folder using the shared folder name Shared, and ensure that the Everyone group is granted the Full Control shared folder permission. This folder will be used to store any supplemental files that may need to be made available to students during the course.

5. Run dcpromo.exe on the Instructor computer to install Active Directory and DNS. Name the new domain (the first in a new forest) supercorp.net, ensure that both nonsecure and secure dynamic updates are allowed, and accept all other default options.

6. On the Instructor computer's DNS server create a reverse lookup zone for 192.168.1.x and accept all the default options.

7. Student servers should remain member servers in the workgroup named Workgroup. The Active Directory, Enhanced structure in the classroom once this is complete is illustrated in the the following figure:

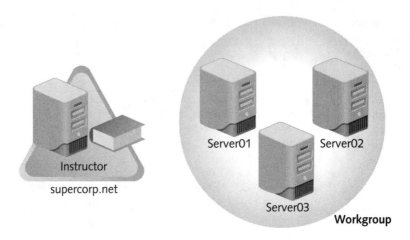

8. On each student server, use the Computer Management console to add a user account named AdminXX, where XX corresponds to the server number assigned to each server. The password associated with this account should be Password01. Also be sure to set up the account so that the password never expires. This account should be added to the Administrators group on the local server.

ACKNOWLEDGMENTS

This text is the product of the talents of many individuals. First, I wish to thank the staff at Course Technology for an enjoyable experience writing a networking textbook on Windows Server 2003. More specifically, I wish to thank my Project Manager, Nick Lombardi, for his patience and insight, my Production Editor, Cathie DiMassa, for her ability to keep everyone on track, as well as my Developmental Editor, Ralph Moore, for his cheerfulness and wit while working this text into its current state. As well, I wish to thank Moirag Haddad at Digital Content Factory and Dan DiNicolo for their advice and guidance.

Thanks also to the reviewers, Patty Gillilan: Associate Professor, Sinclair Community College; Norwood Nutting: Professor of Computer Engineering Technology, Valencia Community College; and Ron Houle: President, Brainerd Information Technology and Training Solutions. Their insightful comments were of invaluable assistance in the creation of this text.

I must take this time to thank my mother Lori for her love, support, encouragement, and patience during the time it took to write this book and while I continue to pursue a career I enjoy. I must also thank all my family and friends without whom I would not be in a position to write this book. Last, but most certainly not least, to my best four-legged friend Magic, thank you for 21 wonderful years.

I hope you will find this text to be enlightening and of benefit in your educational journey. Readers are encouraged to e-mail comments, questions, and suggestions regarding *MCSE Guide to Microsoft Windows Server 2003 Active Directory, Enhanced* to the author:

Michael Aubert: mike@2000trainers.com

CHAPTER 1

INTRODUCTION TO ACTIVE DIRECTORY

After reading this chapter, you will be able to:

♦ Describe the roles of a directory service
♦ Describe the different security models available and the roles Windows Server 2003 can perform in each
♦ Describe the core components of Active Directory
♦ Identify new Active Directory features in Windows Server 2003

As a core service for networks that use Windows Server 2003 as their **network operating system (NOS),** Active Directory provides a central repository for the information available on a network. Active Directory was introduced in the Windows 2000 Server product family and has been improved in Windows Server 2003 to include additional performance, scalability, and management features that make it easier to manage complicated network environments. It also offers greater flexibility in designing, deploying, and managing an organization s directory, which is increasingly significant as more directory-enabled applications are developed.

A **directory service (DS)**, such as Microsoft's **Active Directory (AD)**, is a network service that allows users or computers to look up information such as other users, e-mail addresses, phone numbers, or the location of network **resources**. In this chapter, you will learn more about directory services in general and the role Active Directory plays in a Windows network. This chapter also covers the basic components of Active Directory such as domains, forests, and sites. Finally, the chapter looks at some new features of Active Directory in Windows Server 2003.

To become a successful Microsoft Certified Systems Engineer (MCSE), you need practical, hands-on experience with products like Microsoft Windows Server 2003. This text includes numerous hands-on activities and case studies to help ensure that you not only understand the theory behind the concepts covered, but also that you feel comfortable carrying out common Active

Directory administration tasks. To help simulate a real-world network environment, all of the activities in the text relate to a fictitious multinational organization called Super Management Corporation, a company that provides staffing and management services with a head office based in Atlanta. For the purpose of the activities and case projects, you have been hired by Super Management Corporation as a network engineer, responsible for deploying and managing Active Directory for the organization. The scenarios presented are designed to help you relate the concepts that you learn to tasks typically carried out by a system engineer in a corporate Windows Server 2003 environment.

DIRECTORY SERVICES PLANNING AND IMPLEMENTATION

Though "directory service" is a generic term, most NOS vendors have a name for the service used in their own networks. Microsoft chose the name Active Directory (AD) for the directory service that was introduced in the Windows 2000 Server family. Since then, Microsoft has made improvements to Active Directory in the Windows Server 2003 family.

To further understand what a directory service is, think of the directory assistance service offered by most telephone companies. Even if you don't know the phone number of a person you want to contact, you probably know the name and perhaps some other identifying information, such as a street address or city. You can then call a special number, such as 411, and ask the directory operator to look up the person's number. You will probably get one of three replies: you receive the person's phone number; you are told it can't be found; or you are told that the number is unlisted, meaning you don't have the required permission to access the information. A directory service for a NOS is very similar. Its first function is to provide information about objects in the directory, including users and resources such as file shares, printers, or e-mail mailboxes.

However, Active Directory is more important than a simple phone book because the information contained in Active Directory is crucial for the correct and secure operation of the network. The security information stored in Active Directory includes user accounts, which act as the identification of users on the network; and it also includes groups, which represent a collection of user accounts that require access to the same resources. Active Directory also defines security policies that include how passwords are handled and when data should be encrypted on the network.

There are many facets to Active Directory, and the following sections cover how the exam objectives for the 70-294 exam *Planning, Implementing, and Maintaining a Microsoft Windows Server 2003 Active Directory Infrastructure* correlate to the skills you need to successfully plan, implement, and maintain Active Directory. The following sections also provide notes on where associated topics can be found in later chapters.

Planning and Implementing an Active Directory Infrastructure

The most crucial step in any Active Directory deployment is planning. A network that has the fastest hardware available may perform poorly if careful consideration is not given to the design of the Active Directory infrastructure. Factors such as network bandwidth, location of users and resources, and the types of operations being performed are all factors that can influence an Active Directory design. Additionally, in many cases a pre-existing network is already in place and must be taken into consideration when performing a migration.

NOTE

Because planning and implementing an Active Directory infrastructure covers many topics, Chapters 2 through 8 cover this area.

Managing and Maintaining an Active Directory Infrastructure

Once Active Directory has been deployed, it is often necessary to make small changes to optimize the performance of the network. In addition, it may be necessary to modify and make additions to the directory as time progresses. Regular maintenance must also be performed to ensure that data is secure and that performance has not degraded over time. Finally, problems may arise after the deployment of Active Directory that require trouble-shooting to identify the malfunction.

NOTE

Chapter 13, "Monitoring and Optimizing Active Directory," and Chapter 14, "Disaster Recovery," contain more information on managing and maintaining an Active Directory infrastructure in addition to the information covered in Chapters 2 through 8.

Planning and Implementing User, Computer, and Group Strategies

Today, security is more of a concern than ever before. The first step in securing a network is **authentication**, which is the process of identifying a user to the network and making sure the user is who they say they are. In Active Directory, the user account contains the identification of the user and the information needed to authenticate the user. When planning a user account strategy, the level of security required by the organization and the data the network is protecting are the primary influences on the design. Password length, complexity, and at what times accounts can be used are all issues that should be decided on when planning a user account strategy.

Once a user has been authenticated to the network, he or she can be granted or denied access to such resources as file shares and printers. This process of allowing or denying access to resources is referred to as **authorization**. In other words, once the network knows who a particular user is, authorization controls what the user can and can't do on the network. To make managing user access to resources easier, users can be added to groups, which are in turn given access to resources. Designing a group strategy is a complex subject, and such factors as who controls the resource and where the user accounts are located affect the strategy.

Chapter 9, "Active Directory Authentication and Security," and Chapter 10, "Managing Users, Groups, Computers, and Resources," contain more information on planning and implementing user, computer, and group strategies.

Planning and Implementing Group Policy

Group Policy is used to manage the way workstations, servers, and user environments behave. Corporate policies can be implemented that require all communications between clients and servers to be encrypted, control how the user's desktop appears, perform maintenance tasks, and much more. Group Policy can also be used to deploy applications to computers or users throughout the network. User requirements, corporate policies, the network design, and who manages the policies are all factors that influence a Group Policy design.

Managing and Maintaining Group Policy

Once a Group Policy design has been implemented, changes to policies and troubleshooting the result of policies may be required. Additionally, applications are often updated and these updates must be applied to computers and users that had the application installed via Group Policy.

Chapter 11, "Group Policy for Corporate Policy," and Chapter 12, "Deploying and Managing Software with Group Policy," contain more information on planning, implementing, managing, and maintaining Group Policy.

WINDOWS NETWORKING CONCEPTS OVERVIEW

Before looking at Active Directory in more detail, it is important to understand the differences between the workgroup and domain security models as well as the roles that a server can hold. The two different security models used in Windows network environments are known as the workgroup model and the domain model. Although most midsize and large organizations use the domain model, and in turn Active Directory, the workgroup model is often implemented in smaller environments. As part of understanding a Windows network, you should be familiar with both models, including the benefits and limitations of each.

When a Windows Server 2003 system is deployed, it can participate on the network in one of three major roles. These roles include being configured as a stand-alone server, member server, and domain controller. The decision as to which role a server should be configured in is a function of the network model in use (workgroup or domain), as well as the types of tasks that the server will be handling. In the following sections, you'll learn more about both of the Windows networking models, as well as each Windows Server 2003 server role.

Workgroups

A Windows **workgroup** is a logical group of computers characterized by a decentralized security and administration model. In a workgroup, every computer holds its own security database, known as the local **Security Accounts Manager (SAM) database**, as shown in Figure 1-1. Because computers in a workgroup do not share a common security database, each computer must authenticate users independently. To authenticate users, a set of credentials that typically consist of a user name and password combination are used. In Activity 1-1, you will use a local user account to log on to your server and access resources in a workgroup security model.

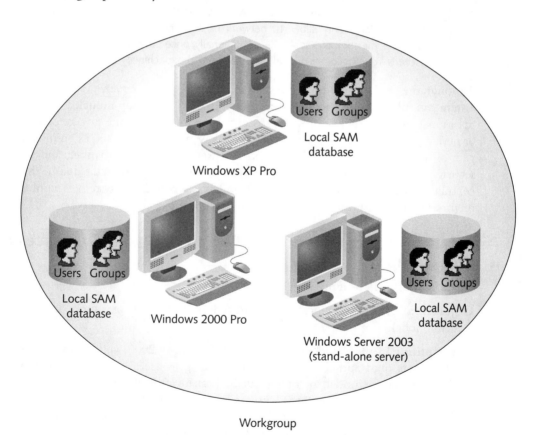

Figure 1-1 Workgroup security model

One of the major benefits of the workgroup model is that it is simple, and does not explicitly require a server—users can share resources directly from their desktop systems as necessary. However, workgroups can be time consuming to manage. If a user that is logged on to one computer wants to access resources on another computer, the user must have an account on the computer hosting the resource that matches the user name and password with which they are currently logged on. Alternatively, the user can provide alternate credentials to authenticate to the computer hosting the resource, if the user does not have an account with a matching user name and password on the remote computer. In either event, the administrator must create and manage user accounts on multiple computers. For example, if a user wants to change their password on one system, they must also change their password on all other computers on the network individually. Another issue is that individual users effectively manage their own systems in the workgroup model, which can lead to potential security issues.

 NOTE   Microsoft recommends that a workgroup be no larger than 10 computers, because operating systems such as Windows 2000 Professional and Windows XP Professional only allow 10 network users to be connected at a time to resources the computer is sharing. Additionally, once the number of computers exceeds 10, it becomes difficult to manage all the machines individually.

Although the workgroup model does not explicitly require a server, a Windows Server 2003 system can still be made part of a workgroup. In the workgroup model, a server is used for traditional purposes, such as providing a centralized location for the storage of user data files, or perhaps to act as an e-mail server. However, a Windows Server 2003 system configured as part of a workgroup does not authenticate users in a central manner, and configuring security settings (such as file and folder permissions) is more difficult due to the lack of a centralized security database. When a Windows Server 2003 system is configured as a member of a workgroup, it is properly referred to as a stand-alone server.

 ACTIVITY

Activity 1-1: Logging on Locally and Accessing Resources in a Workgroup

Time Required: 10 minutes

Objective: Perform the local logon procedure and access resources in a workgroup security model.

Description: In the Windows Server 2003, Windows 2000, and Windows XP product families, users must authenticate before they can gain access to the local computer. In a workgroup security model, the only security database available for authentication is the one local to the particular computer the user is logging on at. This type of logon is referred to as "logging on locally" because the local security database is being used. In a workgroup, once a user has been authenticated on the machine where they are physically located, the user must then be authenticated by any additional computers they access over the network. The following user accounts have already been created on each server:

Account Name   Password

AdminXX   Password01

(where *XX* corresponds to the server number)

1. Start your computer and ensure that all users are logged off.

2. When the computer first starts, the Welcome to Windows screen appears. If you wish, you can click **Help** for more information about the Ctrl+Alt+Delete key sequence.

3. Press **Ctrl+Alt+Delete** to bring up the Log On to Windows dialog box.

4. Clicking the **Options** command button toggles the display of all available options. Ensure that all options are displayed by clicking **Options**. Observe that the text characters on the **Options** button change slightly to indicate when the full set of options is shown, and when they are not.

NOTE

The Shut Down button is grayed out because, by default, you must be logged on as an administrator to shut down a computer running Windows Server 2003.

5. Log on to the machine by typing **AdminXX** (where *XX* is the server number of your server) for the user name and **Password01** (note the capitalized *P*) for the password. Notice that your password is not visible, but hidden as a series of dots, as shown in Figure 1-2.

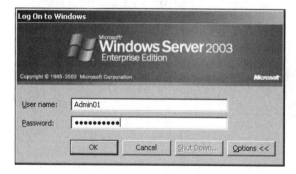

Figure 1-2   Logging on locally

CAUTION

The passwords used in these projects are for demonstration purposes only. To protect an administrative account from unauthorized access, you should change your password to one that only you know and that is not easily guessable. A more secure password should consist of numbers, letters, and special characters such as !, $, ?, or #. Windows passwords are case sensitive (meaning that the lowercase *a* is considered different from the uppercase *A*).

TIP   A common trick to building a strong password is to think of a phrase and use the first letter from each word. For example, the phrase "Magic is the sweetest cat in Niceville" could make it easy to remember the password "MitsciN", and is much harder to guess than using just a pet's name. Another trick is to substitute symbols or numbers for letters that they resemble or sound like. For example "h0mel@nd" is a more secure password than "homeland."

6. Click **OK**.

7. Once the desktop has loaded, the Manage Your Server window appears by default. To prevent this window from opening each time you log on to this computer, check the **Don't display this page at logon** check box.

8. Close the Manage Your Server window.

9. Once you close the Manage Your Server window, the Start menu automatically opens if this is the first time you have logged on using this account. If necessary, click the **Start** button on the task bar, and then click **Run** to open the Run dialog box.

10. In this project, you will be accessing the hidden administrative share C$ on your partner's server. This share is created automatically by Windows Server 2003 and shares the root of the C: drive. Type **\\SERVERXX\C$** (where *XX* is the server number of your partner's server) in the Open combo box.

11. Click **OK**.

NOTE   Because you are currently logged on as Admin*XX* (where *XX* is the number of your server) and your partner's server does not have an account in its local security database with a matching user name and password, you are prompted for alternative credentials as shown in Figure 1-3.

Figure 1-3   Providing alternative credentials

12. In the Connect To SERVER.XX (where *XX* is the server number of your partner's server) window, enter **AdminXX** (where *XX* is the server number of your partner's server) for the user name and **Password01** for the password. This account and password combination has already been created on your partner's server and the account has permission to view the C$ share.

13. Click **OK**. A window displaying the hidden administrative share C$ for your partner's server appears.

14. Close the window that displays the administrative share C$ for your partner's server.

15. Click **Start** on the task bar and then click **Log Off**.

16. In the Log Off Windows message box, click **Log Off**.

Domains

In contrast to a workgroup, a **domain** is a logical group of computers characterized by centralized authentication and administration. In the domain security model, all domain computers use a centralized security database, as shown in Figure 1-4. Special computers known as domain controllers (DC) are responsible for managing the security database and authenticating users on the domain. In Windows Server 2003, domain controllers store security information needed to authenticate users in Active Directory rather than a stand-alone security database. While the directory conceptually centralizes both authentication and administration, Active Directory is stored on one or more computers configured as domain controllers. In a Windows Server 2003 environment, a domain controller can be a server running Windows Server 2003 or Windows 2000 Server. In order to function as a domain controller, a server must explicitly be configured to hold this role.

NOTE A server running Windows NT Server 4.0 can also participate as a domain controller. However, it does not actually store a copy of Active Directory. If Windows NT Server 4.0 domain controllers exist as part of a Windows 2000/ 2003 domain, the NT 4.0 Servers only store security information in their SAM database (in the exact same way as if the domain was strictly running Windows NT 4.0). Windows NT Server 4.0 domain controllers are limited to performing domain functions such as user authentication—they cannot do anything regarding Active Directory queries.

Once a user has been authenticated to the domain by a domain controller, individual computers known as "domain members" or "member servers" can authorize access to a particular resource based on the domain authentication. In Activity 1-2, you will learn how to join your server to the domain—making it a member server. The obvious benefit of this model is that a user requires only a single account to be created to gain access to the entire network, rather than an account in the SAM database of many different workstations. This feature is also known as **single sign-on**. By extension, this model also facilitates easier management of the network, given that users and their properties can be managed centrally.

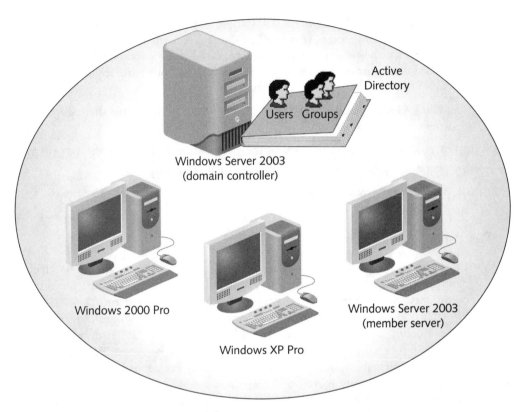

Figure 1-4   Domain security model

In Activity 1-3, you will use a domain user account to log on to your server and access resources in a domain security model.

NOTE

Computers that join a domain and become domain members or member servers still have access to their local security database in addition to the domain database. User accounts that are stored in the domain database are referred to as domain accounts, whereas user accounts that are stored in the computer's local security database are called local accounts. Local accounts are only accessible on the computer on which they are created.

The domain model is highly recommended in any environment that consists of more than 10 users or workstations. One drawback of the model is that it requires at least one server configured as a domain controller, which means additional expense. Optimally, a domain environment consists of a minimum of two domain controllers for the purpose of fault tolerance and load balancing. Later in this chapter, you'll learn more about Windows Server 2003 domains, and specifically Active Directory.

Activity 1-2: Joining a Domain

Time Required: 10 minutes

Objective: Explain and perform the steps needed to join a computer to a domain.

Description: In order for a computer to participate in a domain and become a domain member it must first join the domain. Each computer can be a member of only one domain at a time.

1. Log on locally to your server using the user name **AdminXX** (where *XX* is the server number of your server) and the password **Password01**.

2. Click **Start**, select **Control Panel**, and then click **System**. The System Properties window appears.

3. Click the Computer Name tab in the System Properties window.

4. On the Computer Name tab, click the **Change** button. The Computer Name Changes window appears.

5. In the Member of area, select the **Domain** option button.

6. In the text box below the Domain option, enter **supercorp.net** as shown in Figure 1-5. The supercorp.net domain has already been created on your instructor's server.

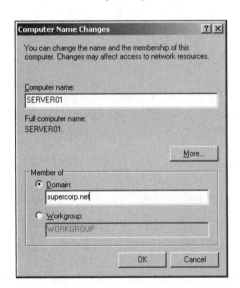

Figure 1-5 Computer Name Changes window

7. Click **OK**.

8. A window appears that prompts you for a user name and password for an account that has permission to join computers to the domain. Enter the user name **Administrator**, the password **Password01**, and then click **OK**. This account has already been created in the supercorp.net domain and has permission to add computers to the domain.

9. If the computer was successfully joined to the domain, a message box appears welcoming you to the supercorp.net domain as shown in Figure 1-6. Click **OK**.

Figure 1-6   Welcome to domain message box

10. Another message box then appears, informing you that the computer must be restarted before the changes can take effect. Click **OK**. The Computer Name Changes window closes.

11. On the System Properties window, click **OK**.

12. The System Settings Change message box appears and asks if you want to restart the computer now or at a later time. Click **Yes** to restart the computer now.

Activity 1-3: Logging on to a Domain and Accessing Domain Resources

Time Required: 10 minutes

Objective: Perform the domain logon procedure and access resources in a domain security model.

Description: Once a computer has joined a domain, users can log on to the computer using a domain user account. When the user provides credentials and selects a domain to log on to, instead of the local computer authenticating the user, the request for authentication is sent to a domain controller. If the domain controller successfully authenticates the user, the local computer then allows the user to log on to the workstation or server. As the user connects to additional resources on other domain member computers, re-authenticating to each computer is not necessary because the authentication originally done by the domain controller is used.

The exact process of how authentication occurs between a workstation and domain controller depends on the authentication protocol in use. Authentication is covered in more detail in Chapter 9, "Active Directory Authentication and Security."

1. Wait for your computer to restart after the last exercise, if necessary, and ensure that all users are logged off.

2. At the Welcome to Windows screen, press **Ctrl+Alt+Delete** to bring up the Log On to Windows dialog box.

3. If all options are not displayed, click the **Options** button. After joining your computer to a domain, you should see an additional drop-down list box labeled Log on to.

4. Type **Administrator** for the user name and **Password01** as the password. This account has already been created in the supercorp.net domain as an administrator.

5. In the Log on to list box, select **SUPERCORP** as shown in Figure 1-7.

Figure 1-7 Logging on to a domain

 Notice that the SERVER*XX* (this computer) option is still available. If you selected the SERVER*XX* (this computer) option, you would be logging on locally to the computer and not to a domain.

NOTE

 Notice that the name of the domain in the Log on to list box is shown as SUPERCORP and not supercorp.net. For backwards compatibility with older versions of Windows such as NT 4.0, the NetBIOS name SUPERCORP is used instead of the Domain Name System (DNS) name supercorp.net. For the moment, do not worry about this difference; the next chapter covers NetBIOS and DNS names in detail.

NOTE

6. Click **OK**.

7. Once the desktop has loaded, the Manage Your Server window appears by default. To prevent this window from opening each time you log on to this computer, check the **Don't display this page at logon** check box.

8. Close the Manage Your Server window.

9. Once you close the Manage Your Server window, the Start menu automatically opens if this is the first time you have logged on using this account. If necessary, click the **Start** button on the task bar, and then click **Run** to open the Run dialog box.

10. In this project, you will be accessing the hidden administrative share C$ on your partner's server. This share is created automatically by Windows Server 2003 and shares the root of the C: drive. Type **\\SERVERXX\C$** (where *XX* is the server number of your partner's server) in the Open combo box as shown in Figure 1-8.

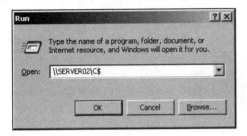

Figure 1-8   The Run dialog box

11. Click **OK**. A window displaying the hidden administrative share C$ for your partner's server appears.

Because you have authenticated using a domain user account, you are not prompted to provide any additional credentials when accessing another computer that is also a domain member—the authentication that was done by the domain controller is used. This is referred to as single sign-on because the user only needs to provide credentials once.

NOTE

12. Close the window that displays the administrative share C$ for your partner's server.

13. Click **Start** on the task bar, and then click **Log Off**.

14. In the Log Off Windows message box, click **Log Off**.

Member Servers

A **member server** is a Windows Server 2003 system that has a **computer account** in a domain, but is not configured as a domain controller. Member servers are typically used for a wide variety of functions including file, print, and application services. Member servers also commonly host network services such as the Domain Name Service (DNS), Dynamic Host Configuration Protocol (DHCP), and others. Each of the four Windows Server 2003 editions can be configured in the role of a member server in a domain environment.

For a description of the editions of Windows Server 2003 available, please see the page titled "Introducing the Windows Server 2003 Family" currently located at: *www.microsoft.com/windowsserver2003/evaluation/overview/family.mspx.*

NOTE

Domain Controllers

While still a member of a domain, a **domain controller** is a Windows Server 2003 system explicitly configured to store a copy of the Active Directory database, and is responsible for servicing user authentication requests and queries about domain objects. While many companies choose to dedicate servers to the role of a domain controller exclusively, other companies use their domain controllers to also provide file, print, application, and networking services on the network. The main considerations when deciding which additional roles a domain controller should take on are the current utilization of the server, as well as whether sufficient resources (such as memory) are available to handle those roles. Of the four Windows Server 2003 editions, only Windows Server 2003 Web Edition cannot be configured as a domain controller.

INTRODUCTION TO WINDOWS SERVER 2003 ACTIVE DIRECTORY

Active Directory is the native directory service included with Windows Server 2003 operating systems. Active Directory provides the following services and features to the network environment:

- A central point for storing, organizing, managing, and controlling network objects, such as users, computers, and groups
- A single point of administration of objects, such as users, groups, and computers, and Active Directory-published resources, such as printers or shared folders
- Logon and authentication services for users
- Delegation of administration to allow for decentralized administration of Active Directory objects, such as users and groups

The Active Directory database is stored on all Windows Server 2003 servers that have been promoted to the role of domain controller. Each domain controller on the network has a writeable copy of the directory database. This means that you can make Active Directory changes to any domain controller within your network, and those changes are replicated to all of the other domain controllers. This process is called **multi-master replication**, and provides a form of fault tolerance. If a single server fails, Active Directory does not fail because replicated copies of the database are available from other servers within the network.

Active Directory uses DNS to maintain domain-naming structures and to locate network resources. What this means to a network designer is that all Active Directory names must follow standard DNS naming conventions. An example of a standard DNS naming convention would be *supercorp.net*. A child domain of *supercorp.net* would add its name as a prefix, such as *europe.supercorp.net*.

Active Directory Objects

Active Directory stores a variety of objects within the directory database. An **object** represents network resources such as users, groups, computers, and printers. When an object is created in Active Directory, various attributes are assigned to it to provide information about the object. For example, Figure 1-9 illustrates creating a new user object and the ability to add various attributes, such as First name, Last name, and User logon name. If you need to locate information about an object in Active Directory, you can perform a search on specific attributes relating to the object.

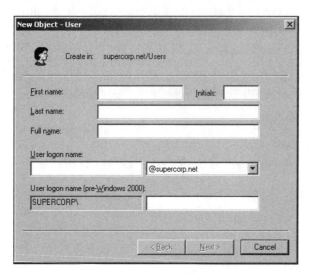

Figure 1-9   Creating a new user object

Active Directory Schema

All of the objects and attributes that are available in Active Directory are defined in the **Active Directory schema**. In Windows Server 2003, the schema defines the objects for the entire Active Directory structure. This means that there is only one schema for a given Active Directory implementation, and this schema is replicated among all domain controllers within the network.

The Active Directory schema consists of two main definitions: **object classes** and **attributes**. Object classes define the types of objects that can be created within Active Directory, such as user objects and printer objects. All object classes consist of various attributes that describe the object itself. For example, the user and printer object classes may both have an attribute called "description," which describes the use of the object. Attributes are created and stored separately in the schema and can be used with multiple object classes to maintain consistency.

The Active Directory database stores and replicates the schema partition to all domain controllers in an Active Directory environment. Storing the schema within the Active Directory database provides the ability to dynamically update and extend the schema, as well as provides instant access to information for user applications that need to read the schema properties.

Active Directory Logical Structure and Components

Active Directory is made of several components that provide a way to design and administer the hierarchical, logical structure of the network. The logical components that make up an Active Directory structure include:

- Domains and Organizational Units
- Trees and Forests
- Trusts

To ensure efficient maintenance and troubleshooting within Active Directory, it is essential that you understand these logical components. The next few sections discuss each component in greater detail.

Domains and Organizational Units

A Windows Server 2003 domain is a logically structured organization of objects, such as users, computers, groups, and printers that are part of a network and share a common directory database. Each domain has a unique name and is organized in levels and administered as a unit with common rules and procedures such as common password policies for all domain user accounts. Windows Server 2003 domains provide a number of administrative benefits including the ability to configure unique security settings, decentralize administration (if necessary), and control replication traffic. By default, members of the Administrators group are only allowed to manage the objects within their own domain. All domain controllers within a single domain store a copy of the Active Directory database, and domain-specific information is only replicated between the domain controllers of the same domain.

An **organizational unit (OU)** is a logical container used to organize objects within a single domain. Objects such as users, groups, computers, and other organizational units can be stored in an organizational unit container. For example, you may want to organize your users based upon the department in which they work. You might create a Sales organizational unit to store all of your sales department users and objects. You might also create a Marketing organizational unit to store all of your Marketing Department users and objects. Not only does this make it easier to locate and manage Active Directory objects, but it also allows you to apply Group Policy settings to define more advanced features such as software deployment or desktop restrictions based upon department, job function, or perhaps geographic location. Figure 1-10 illustrates an example of a domain with several organizational units.

Another main advantage of using an organizational unit structure is the ability to delegate administrative control over organizational units. For example, you may want to give a group of users the right to add or remove new users within the Sales organizational unit. You do not have to provide the group with full administrative rights to accomplish this task because Active Directory allows you to delegate very specific tasks, if necessary.

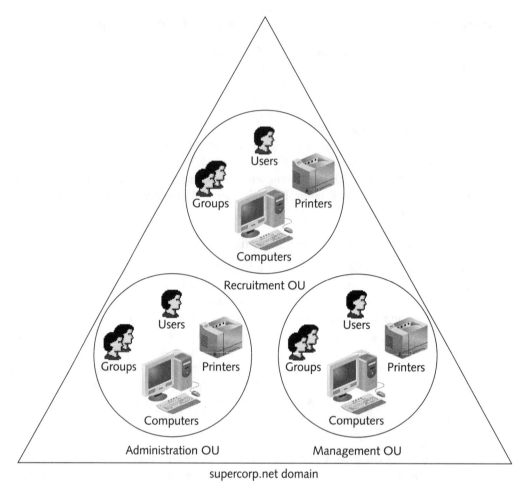

Figure 1-10   An Active Directory domain and organizational unit structure

Trees and Forests

When designing a Windows Server 2003 network infrastructure, there might be times when you are required to create multiple domains within an organization. Reasons for doing this include the following:

- Divisions within the company may be administered on a geographic basis. To make administration easier, a separate domain is created for each division.

- Different divisions within an organization require different password policies.

- An extraordinarily large number of objects need to be defined.

- Replication performance needs to be improved.

Although domains are replication boundaries, replication can also be controlled using site objects. Site objects are discussed later in this chapter and covered in more detail in Chapter 6, "Active Directory Physical Design."

1

The first Active Directory domain created in an organization is called the **forest root domain**. When multiple domains are needed, they are connected to the forest root to form either a single **tree** or multiple trees, depending upon the design of the domain name structure. A tree is a hierarchical collection of domains that share a contiguous DNS namespace. For example, Super Management Corporation has its head office in Atlanta with a forest root domain called *supercorp.net*. Super Corp has two divisions, one located in London and the other located in Hong Kong. Because of geographic and administrative differences, you might decide to create a distinct domain for each division. Two child domains can be created off of the forest root domain. The London domain can be named *europe.supercorp.net*, which follows the contiguous DNS namespace design. Similarly, the Hong Kong domain can be called *asia.supercorp.net*. Figure 1-11 illustrates an example of this structure. In Activity 1-4, you will create a new child domain in the supercorp.net domain tree.

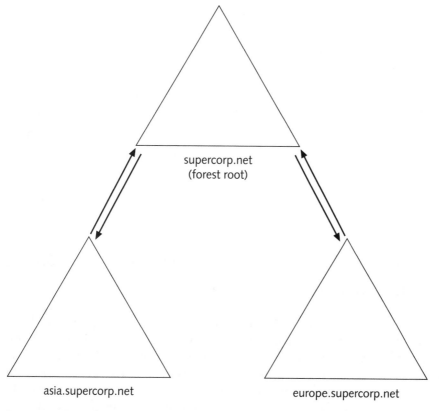

Figure 1-11   The supercorp.net domain tree

A **forest** is a collection of trees that do not share a contiguous DNS naming structure. For example, Super Management Corporation purchases a large international company called Fast IT Staffing, an information technology staffing organization. It may not make sense to make the Fast IT domain a child of *supercorp.net* because of the renaming required to maintain a contiguous naming convention based on *supercorp.net*. Instead, you could create a new tree and allow Fast IT to start its own contiguous naming hierarchy. Both trees make up an Active Directory forest. See Figure 1-12 for an illustration. Although the term "forest" implies a number of trees, an Active Directory forest might consist of only a single domain.

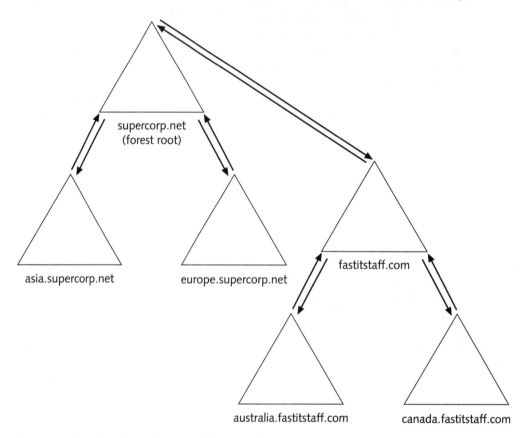

Figure 1-12   Creating an Active Directory forest

Even though the trees within a forest do not share a common namespace, they do share a single Active Directory schema, which ensures that all object classes and attributes are consistent throughout the entire structure. A special group called Enterprise Admins is also created, which allows members to manage objects throughout the entire forest. The Enterprise Admins group is created within the initial forest root domain and has a scope throughout the entire forest. In addition to the schema, another component that is shared throughout the forest is a **global catalog**. The global catalog is covered later in this chapter.

Trusts

Whenever a child domain is created, a two-way, transitive trust relationship is automatically created between the child and parent domains. Similarly, when a new tree is created, a two-way, transitive trust relationship is automatically created between the forest root domain and the root of the new tree. A **transitive trust** means that all other trusted domains implicitly trust one another. For example, because *europe.supercorp.net* trusts the *supercorp.net* forest root domain, Europe also implicitly trusts the *asia.supercorp.net* domain via the *supercorp.net* domain. Additionally, *europe.supercorp.net* also implicitly trusts *fastitstaff.com*, *australia.fastitstaff.com*, and *canada.fastitstaff.com* via the *supercorp.net* domain. These two-way, transitive trusts allow for resource access anywhere throughout the Active Directory structure. Windows Server 2003 also allows explicit trusts to be created between domains in the same forest, as well as between forests if necessary.

Chapter 5, "Active Directory Logical Design," covers the design of a logical Active Directory structure in more detail.

NOTE

Activity 1-4: Creating a Child Domain in an Existing Domain Tree

ACTIVITY

Time Required: 20 minutes

Objective: Promote a member server to a domain controller for a new child domain in an existing domain tree.

Description: The process of creating a new domain controller is referred to as promotion. Both member servers and stand-alone servers can be promoted to domain controllers for a new domain or an existing domain. To promote a server to a domain controller, the Active Directory Installation Wizard is used and is accessible by running the DCPROMO command or using the Configure Your Server Wizard located on the Start menu under Administrative Tools. The goal of this project is to become more familiar with the promotion process—later chapters will cover the options available in more detail.

1. Log on to the supercorp.net domain using the NetBIOS name **SUPERCORP**, the user name **Administrator**, and the password **Password01**.

2. Click **Start** and then click **Run**.

3. When the Run dialog box opens, type **DCPROMO** in the **Open** combo box and then click **OK**. The Welcome to the Active Directory Installation Wizard window appears.

4. Click **Next**. The **Operating System Compatibility** window appears.

5. Click **Next**.

6. On the Domain Controller Type window, ensure that the **Domain controller for a new domain** option button is selected, and click **Next**.

7. In the Create New Domain window, select the **Child domain in an existing domain tree** option button, as shown in Figure 1-13, and click **Next**.

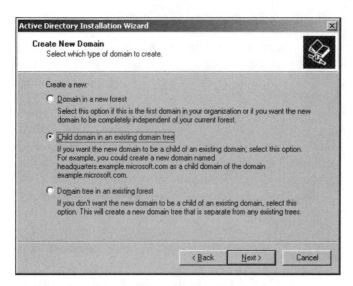

Figure 1-13   Create New Domain window

8. In the Network Credentials window, enter **Administrator** as the user name and **Password01** as the password. This account has already been created in the supercorp.net domain.

9. Click **Next**.

10. In the Child Domain Installation window, enter **childXX** (where *XX* is the server number of your server) in the Child domain text box, as shown in Figure 1-14. Notice that the Complete DNS name of new domain text box is updated to show the combination of the new domain's name and its parent. If multiple parent domains existed, you would click the **Browse** button to select a different parent domain.

11. Click **Next**.

12. The NetBIOS Domain Name window appears. Leave the default **Domain NetBIOS name CHILDXX**, and click **Next**.

13. In the Database and Log Folders windows, accept the default locations for the database and log folders, and click **Next**.

14. In the Shared System Volume window, accept the default location for the SYSVOL folder, and click **Next**.

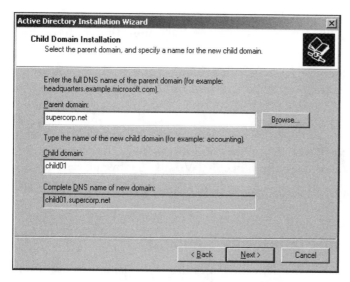

Figure 1-14   Child Domain Installation window

15. The Active Directory Installation Wizard now tests whether DNS is configured. Because your server has already been configured to use your instructor's server for DNS name resolution, the DNS Registration Diagnostics window should look similar to Figure 1-15. Click **Next**.

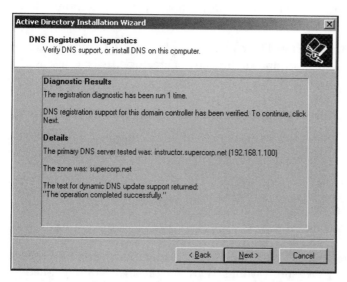

Figure 1-15   DNS Registration Diagnostics window

16. In the Permissions window, leave the default option **Permissions compatible only with Windows 2000 or Windows Server 2003 operating systems** selected. Click **Next**.

17. In the Directory Services Restore Mode Administrator Password window, type **Password01** in the Restore Mode Password and Confirm password text boxes.

18. Click **Next**.

19. The Summary window then displays a summary of the options you chose in the wizard. Click **Next** to start the promotion process. Once the promotion process ends, the Completing the Active Directory Wizard window appears. Click **Finish**.

20. A message box prompts if you want to restart now or at a later time. Click **Restart Now**.

Active Directory Communications Standards

As mentioned previously, Active Directory uses the DNS naming standard for hostname resolution and for providing information on the location of network services and resources. For example, if you need to locate a server called *mail.supercorp.net*, your workstation first queries a DNS server to resolve the IP address of the e-mail server. Once the IP address is known, a direct communication session can take place.

The same process occurs when you need to log on to the domain. Your workstation queries DNS to find a domain controller to perform authentication. Once the location of a domain controller is known, then the authentication process can take place, thus allowing a user access to network resources.

When users need to access Active Directory, the **Lightweight Directory Access Protocol (LDAP)** is used to query or update the Active Directory database. Just as a DNS name contains a specific naming convention (for example, *supercorp.net*), LDAP also follows a specific naming convention. LDAP naming paths are used when referring to objects stored within the Active Directory. Two main components of the naming paths include:

- *Distinguished name*—Every object in Active Directory has a unique **distinguished name (DN)**. For example, the *supercorp.net* domain component has a user object with a common name (CN) of Carolyn Commander that is stored within the Management OU. The distinguished name for the object would be CN=Carolyn Commander,OU=Management,DC=supercorp,DC=net.

- *Relative distinguished name*—A portion of the distinguished name that uniquely identifies the object within the container is referred to as the **relative distinguished name**. For example, the distinguished name OU=Management, DC=supercorp,DC=net would have a relative distinguished name of OU=Management. For the distinguished name CN=Carolyn Commander, OU=Management,DC=supercorp,DC=net, the relative distinguished name would be CN=Carolyn Commander.

Chapter 4, "Active Directory Architecture," covers the underlying Architecture of Active Directory in more detail.

NOTE

Active Directory Physical Structure

The Active Directory physical structure relates to the actual connectivity of the physical network itself. Because the Active Directory database is stored on multiple servers, you need to make sure that any modification to the database is replicated as quickly as possible between domain controllers. You must also design your topology so that replication does not saturate the available network bandwidth. One replication problem that you may encounter is when domain controllers are separated over a slow WAN connection. In this scenario, you likely want to control the frequency and the time that replication takes place.

In addition to replication, you may also want to control logon traffic. Referring back to the previous scenario, you generally would not want any user authentication requests to have to cross slow WAN links during the logon process. Optimally, users should authenticate to a domain controller on their side of the WAN connection.

Keep in mind that the physical structure of Active Directory is totally separate from the logical structure. The logical structure is used to organize your network resources, whereas the physical structure is used to control network traffic.

NOTE

You can control Active Directory replication and authentication traffic by configuring sites and site links. An Active Directory **site** is a combination of one or more Internet Protocol (IP) subnets connected by a high-speed connection, which is typically considered to be 10 Mbps or faster. It is assumed that domain controllers that belong to the same site all have a common network connection. It is also assumed that any connection between sites that is not reliable at all times must have replication controlled through replication schedules and frequency intervals.

A **site link** is a configurable object that represents a connection between sites. Site links created using the Active Directory Sites and Services snap-in are the core of Active Directory replication. The site links can be adjusted for replication availability, bandwidth costs, and replication frequency. Windows Server 2003 uses this information to generate the replication topology for the sites, including the schedule for replication. Figure 1-16 shows an example of a site structure within a single domain. Each site contains domain controllers that share a high-speed connection. Because of a slower WAN connection between Atlanta, Hong Kong, and London, sites and site links have been defined to better control replication and logon traffic.

Replication within a site takes place based on a change notification process. If any change is made within Active Directory, the server waits 15 seconds and then announces the changes to another domain controller. In cases where a domain controller has multiple replication

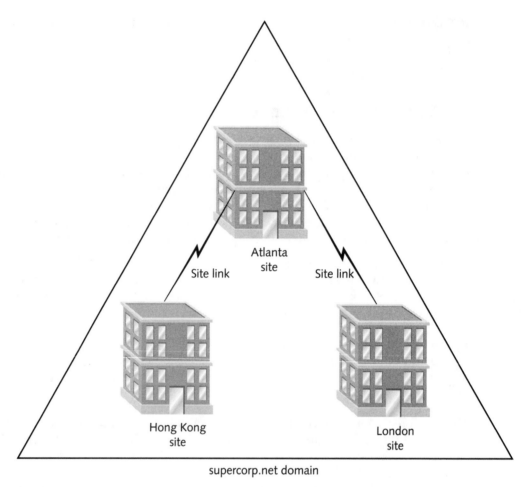

supercorp.net domain

Figure 1-16   The site structure for the supercorp.net domain

partners within a site, changes are sent out to additional domain controllers at three-second intervals. Even if no changes have been made, replication takes place once an hour by default. Replication between sites is initially set at every three hours by default, but can easily be changed by editing the properties of the site link object.

Global Catalog

A global catalog is an index and partial replica of the objects and attributes most frequently used throughout the entire Active Directory structure. Some of the common attributes that are stored in a global catalog include a user's first and last names, logon name, or e-mail address. A global catalog is replicated to any server within the forest that is configured to be a global catalog server.

A global catalog is used primarily for four main functions:

- Enables users to find Active Directory information from anywhere in the forest.

- Provides universal group membership information to facilitate logging on to the network. During the logon process in a multiple-domain environment, a global catalog server is contacted to provide universal group membership information.

- Supplies authentication services when a user from another domain logs on using a **User Principal Name (UPN)**. (A UPN is a representation of a user's logon credentials in the form user@domain.com. When a UPN is used, a domain name does not need to be explicitly specified in the Log on to drop-down box—the box is grayed out and unavailable.)

- Responds to directory lookup requests from Exchange 2000/2003 and other applications.

The first domain controller in Active Directory automatically becomes a Global Catalog server. To provide redundancy, additional domain controllers can easily be configured to also be Global Catalog servers. Multiple Global Catalog servers can improve user query and logon authentication performance, especially in Active Directory environments that include geographically distant sites connected by WAN links. Microsoft recommends that each Active Directory site be configured with at least one domain controller acting as a Global Catalog server.

In cases where placing a global catalog at a site is not practical (possibly because of slow WAN links between locations), Windows Server 2003 Active Directory provides a new feature known as Universal Group Caching. Universal Group Caching allows the domain controllers within a particular site to query a Global Catalog server in another location for a user's Universal Group membership information, and then cache that information locally for use in subsequent logons.

Chapter 6, "Active Directory Physical Design," covers the design of a physical Active Directory structure in more detail.

NOTE

New Active Directory Features in Windows Server 2003

Although Active Directory is not new, Windows Server 2003 brings new features and capabilities to Active Directory in the areas of deployment, management, security, performance, and dependability. These enhancements have two primary benefits—they make Active Directory more flexible and lower the total cost of ownership (TCO). For a better understanding of the individual enhancements, the following sections point out some of the new features of Active Directory in Windows Server 2003.

Deployment and Management

In very large enterprises with multiple forests, domains, and sites, Windows Server 2003 makes configuring and managing Active Directory easier for the administrator. For easier deployment, Windows Server 2003 adds the ability to rename domains and has improved migration tools for migrating from earlier versions of Windows. After Active Directory is deployed, new management features such as multi-object selection, better drag-and-drop capabilities, and improvements in Group Policy help the administrator to be more productive.

Active Directory Migration Tool (ADMT) 2.0

The second major release of the Active Directory Migration Tool (ADMT 2.0) makes migrating to Active Directory even easier. The new version of ADMT now allows passwords to be migrated from Windows NT 4.0 to Windows 2000 and Windows Server 2003 domains.

Domain Rename

Once a domain was created in Windows 2000, no method existed for renaming it, other than removing the domain and recreating it. Windows Server 2003 adds support for renaming both the Domain Name System (DNS) and NetBIOS names of existing domains. This makes administration much easier, because decisions that were once final are now reversible. Organizations that are restructuring or merging can now redesign their Active Directory deployment without losing previous work.

Schema Redefine

The Active Directory schema has been made more flexible by adding the ability to deactivate and then redefine class definitions and attributes. If an error is made in a class or attribute definition, it can now be redefined to correct the error.

Security

Windows Server 2003 adds several new features that make managing security in a multi-forest environment easier. A new type of trust, the cross-forest trust, provides a new way of managing the relationship between two forests—making administration of cross-forest authentication and authorization much simpler. With a cross-forest trust, users can access resources in other forests, while still keeping the benefits of easier administration and single sign-on by having only one user name and password. Plus, the new Credential Manager allows for the secure storage of passwords and certificates. Windows Server 2003 also adds a new software restriction policy that allows an administrator to restrict what software can and can't be run on a system.

Cross-forest Trust

A cross-forest trust is created between the root domains of two forests, and allows for secure access to resources when the user account and computer account are not in the same forest. While still keeping the benefits of easier administration and single sign-on by having only one user name and password stored in the user's home forest, a cross-forest trust allows a user to be authenticated securely in another forest. Additionally, a cross-forest trust makes authorization easier for administrators by allowing selection of users and groups in a trusted forest when setting permissions on resources or setting group memberships.

Credential Manager

The Credential Manager increases the usefulness of single sign on by providing for secure storage of passwords and certificates. When a user attempts to access a line-of-business application that requires authentication, the user is prompted to provide the credentials the first time he or she accesses the application. After the user authenticates for the first time, the credentials are securely stored and associated with the requesting application. From this point forward, requests for authentication by the same application uses the saved credentials instead of prompting the user.

Software Restriction Policies

Software restriction policies now allow the administrator to restrict what software can and can't run on a system. By restricting the use of unknown or untrusted software, the administrator can better protect the network environment. Policies can be set up that either allow or disallow unknown software to run by default, with additional rules added that make exceptions for individual applications.

Performance and Dependability

With improvements in replication and synchronization, Windows Server 2003 is more efficient at propagating updates to Active Directory. An administrator now has better control over the types of information that domain controllers replicate within a domain as well as between multiple domains. Additionally, by replicating only the changes to groups rather than the entire group membership list, network bandwidth and processor usage are decreased.

Universal Group Caching

In Windows Server 2003, branch offices with only a Windows Server 2003 domain controller can now use cached credentials to log users on without having to contact a Global Catalog server. Caching user credentials improves reliability, because the loss of a WAN link between a branch office and global catalog no longer affects a user's ability to log on. Additionally, logon performance is increased by not having to wait for a global catalog to respond—while at the same time WAN bandwidth utilization is lowered.

Application Directory Partitions

Certain portions of information stored in Active Directory do not need to be available on all domain controllers across the entire forest. Application directory partitions allow an administrator to configure the location of replicas and the scope of replication. This allows information for applications to be stored where it is needed while impacting the network performance as little as possible. The DNS Server in Windows Server 2003 is one of the first applications/services to take advantage of this new feature.

Install Replica from Media

When creating a new domain controller in an existing domain or forest, one of the most network-intensive steps is the initial replication, where existing Active Directory information is copied to the new domain controller. A new feature in Windows Server 2003 allows initial replication to be sourced from a backup of an existing domain controller or global catalog. This saves network bandwidth because only changes from the time the backup was taken must be replicated. Additionally, for branch offices with slow links, sourcing from media can save a considerable amount of time in creating a domain controller.

NOTE

For more information on the new features in Windows Server 2003, please see the page titled "What's New in Windows Server 2003" currently located at: *www.microsoft.com/windowsserver2003/evaluation/overview/technologies/*.

CHAPTER SUMMARY

- A directory service provides a way to locate objects and resources on a network. Specifically, Active Directory is the directory service for networks running Windows Server 2003 or Windows 2000 Server network operating systems. Active Directory is the single point of management for a network, providing search mechanisms and enabling single sign-on for users.

- Windows networks use one of two models to logically group computers. A workgroup is a model characterized by decentralized authentication and administration, and is typically used on small networks. A domain provides centralized authentication and administration, and is more common in larger environments.

- When a server running Windows Server 2003 is part of a workgroup, it can perform the role of a stand-alone server. When a server running Windows Server 2003 is a member of a domain, it can perform the role of either member server or domain controller.

- Active Directory stores a variety of objects within the directory database that includes users, groups, computers, and printers. All objects in Active Directory are defined by the schema, which consists of object classes and attributes.

❑ The logical components of Active Directory include domains, organizational units, trees, forests, and trusts. The physical components of Active Directory include domain controllers, sites, and site links.

❑ When users need to access Active Directory, the Lightweight Directory Access Protocol (LDAP) is used to query or update the Active Directory database.

❑ Many improvements have been made to Active Directory in Windows Server 2003. Some of these improvements include the ability to rename domains, cross-forest trusts, Universal Group caching, and application directory partitions.

Key Terms

Active Directory (AD) — Microsoft's directory service included with Windows Server 2003 that provides a single point of administration, and storage for user, group, and computer objects.

Active Directory schema — Contains the definition of all object classes and attributes used in the Active Directory database.

attributes — Used to define the characteristics of an object class within Active Directory.

authentication — The process of identifying a user by using a set of credentials. Typically a user name and password are provided as credentials.

authorization — Determines if a user is allowed access to a particular resource. Authorization can only occur after a user has been identified through authentication.

computer account — An account that is stored in the domain database and provides a way for a domain member computer to securely identify itself to the domain.

directory service (DS) — A network application or database, usually integrated as a core component of a network operating system, that provides information about users, computers, resources, and other network elements.

distinguished name (DN) — An LDAP component used to uniquely identify an object throughout the entire LDAP hierarchy by referring to the relative distinguished name, domain name, and the container holding the object.

domain — A logically structured organization of objects, such as users, computers, groups, and printers, that are part of a network and share a common directory database. Domains are defined by an administrator and administered as a unit with common rules and procedures.

domain controller — A Windows Server 2003 system explicitly configured to store a copy of the Active Directory database, and service user authentication requests or queries about domain objects.

forest — A collection of Active Directory trees that do not necessarily share a contiguous DNS naming convention but do share a common global catalog and schema.

forest root domain — The first domain created within the Active Directory structure.

Global catalog — An index of the objects and attributes used throughout the Active Directory structure. It contains a partial replica of every Windows Server 2003 domain within Active Directory, enabling users to find any object in the directory.

Group Policy — The Windows Server 2003 feature that allows for policy creation that affects domain users and computers. Policies can be anything from desktop settings to application assignment to security settings and more.

Lightweight Directory Access Protocol (LDAP) — An access protocol that defines how users can access or update directory service objects.

member server — A Windows Server 2003 system that has a computer account in a domain, but is not configured as a domain controller.

Multi-master replication — A replication model in which any domain controller accepts and replicates directory changes to any other domain controller. This differs from other replication models in which one computer stores the single modifiable copy of the directory and other computers store backup copies.

network operating system (NOS) — A computer operating system that is designed primarily to support workstations on a local area network (LAN).

object — A collection of attributes that represent items within Active Directory, such as users, groups, computers, and printers.

object classes — Define which types of objects can be created within Active Directory, such as users, groups, and printers.

organizational unit (OU) — An Active Directory logical container used to organize objects within a single domain. Objects such as users, groups, computers, and other organizational units can be stored in an organizational unit container.

relative distinguished name — An LDAP component used to identify an object within the object's container.

resources — Any shared piece of equipment or information made available to users on the network, such as file shares and printers.

Security Accounts Manager (SAM) database — The local security and account database on a Windows Server 2003 stand-alone or member server.

single sign-on — The concept that a user only has to identify himself or herself with a single set of credentials once to access all resources that he or she has been authorized to use throughout the entire network.

site — A combination of one or more Internet Protocol (IP) subnets connected by a high-speed connection.

site link — A low-bandwidth or unreliable/occasional connection between sites. The site links can be adjusted for replication availability, bandwidth costs, and replication frequency. They enable control over replication and logon traffic.

stand-alone server — A Windows Server 2003 system that is configured as part of a workgroup.

tree — A group of one or more domains in a forest that have a contiguous DNS namespace.

User Principal Name (UPN) — A user-account naming convention that includes both the user name and domain name in the format user@domain.com.

workgroup — A logical group of computers characterized by a decentralized security and administration model.

REVIEW QUESTIONS

1. Which of the following is a logical group of computers characterized by a decentralized security and administration model?

   a. Forest

   b. Domain

   c. Workgroup

   d. Directory

2. What is special about a domain controller?

   a. It is the only role in which a Windows Server 2003 computer can participate.

   b. It stores a copy of the Active Directory database.

   c. It can only be configured on Windows Server 2003, Web Edition.

   d. It stores some attributes for every object in the forest.

3. What is the name of the first domain installed within the Active Directory database?

   a. Master root domain

   b. Tree root domain

   c. Forest root domain

   d. Default root domain

4. What is the difference between authentication and authorization?

   a. Authentication identifies the user and authorization determines if that user has access to a given resource.

   b. Authorization identifies the user and authentication determines if that user has access to a given resource.

   c. Authentication only occurs in the domain security model.

   d. A user must be authorized before they can be authenticated.

5. What is the advantage of single sign-on?

   a. Users only have to authenticate once during their work session.

   b. It can be used in a workgroup security model.

   c. Users don't need to use a password as long as they always use the same workstation.

   d. It is only available when all domain controllers are running Windows Server 2003.

6. Assuming a user name of John Doe with a user account located in the Marketing OU of the domain *supercorp.net*, what would be the object's distinguished name?

   a. CN=John Doe

   b. OU=Marketing, CN=John Doe

   c. DC=net, DC=supercorp, OU=Marketing, CN=John Doe

   d. CN=John Doe, OU=Marketing, DC=supercorp, DC=net

7. Assuming a user name of John Doe with a user account located in the Marketing OU of the domain *supercorp.net*, what would be the object's relative distinguished name?

   a. CN=John Doe

   b. OU=Marketing,CN=John Doe

   c. DC=net,DC=supercorp,OU=Marketing,CN=John Doe

   d. CN=John Doe,OU=Marketing,DC=supercorp,DC=net

8. In an Active Directory domain, users need a different password for each domain controller. True or False?

9. When logging on locally, what is used to authenticate the user?

   a. The local SAM database

   b. The local Active Directory database

   c. A domain controller in the local site

   d. A global catalog in the local site

10. Which edition of Windows Server 2003 cannot be configured as an Active Directory domain controller?

    a. Windows Server 2003, Web Edition

    b. Windows Server 2003, Standard Edition

    c. Windows Server 2003, Enterprise Edition

    d. Windows Server 2003, Datacenter Edition

11. In the domain security model, what are accounts stored in the domain database called?

    a. Local accounts

    b. Domain accounts

    c. Directory accounts

    d. Shared accounts

12. Which of the following domain controllers will become global catalog servers by default?

    a. First domain controller in all domains

    b. All domain controllers in the forest root domain

    c. First domain controller in the forest root domain

    d. No global catalog servers are created by default

13. Which of the following statements best describes an Active Directory tree?

    a. A collection of organizational units

    b. A collection of users with common settings

    c. A collection of domains with different schemas

    d. A collection of domains that share a contiguous DNS namespace

14. How are domains, trees, and forests related?
    a. A domain is made up of one or more forests.
    b. A tree is made up of one or more domains.
    c. A domain can belong to multiple trees.
    d. A domain can belong to multiple forests.

15. How are objects, classes, and attributes related?
    a. A class has many objects, but only one attribute.
    b. A list of attributes that are all equal is called a class.
    c. A class defines the attributes that make up an object.
    d. An object has many classes and attributes.

16. Which of the following logical Active Directory components is created mainly for the delegation of administrative authority and the implementation of Group Policy?
    a. Forest
    b. Tree
    c. Domain
    d. Organizational unit

17. In Windows Server 2003, a two-way, transitive trust relationship is maintained between which of the following?
    a. Child and parent forests
    b. Child and parent groups
    c. Child and parent domains
    d. None of the above

18. Replication between domain controllers within a site is triggered by a change notification process initiated how many seconds after the change occurs?
    a. 5
    b. 10
    c. 15
    d. 20

19. How often does Active Directory replication between sites take place by default?
    a. Every hour
    b. Every two hours
    c. Every three hours
    d. Once a day

20. Which group exists within the forest root domain only, but has administrative privileges in all forest domains by default?

a. Administrators

b. Root Admins

c. Domain Admins

d. Enterprise Admins

CASE PROJECTS

Case Project 1-1: Workgroup Woes

Alice Smith is the new accounting manager at the Atlanta office. Her new computer is constantly asking her for a password and she sometimes has to use different passwords to access different file shares. She also reports a great deal of trouble printing. She would like to access the color printer and high-speed laser printer, but doesn't know which server they are connected to. When she shows you how she logs on, you notice that she is not able to select the company's domain on her logon screen. What is the most likely cause of this problem? How would you resolve the problem?

Case Project 1-2: Assessing Super Management Corporation's Active Directory Implementation

Super Management Corporation has recently implemented Windows Server 2003 and Active Directory. Super Corp's network consists of three main locations with offices in Atlanta, Hong Kong, and London. The Atlanta location is the head office and connects to London via a 512-Kbps Frame Relay link. The Atlanta location is also connected to Hong Kong via a 128-Kbps Frame Relay link. Super Corp has recently considered opening new offices in Seattle and Dallas, which would both have a dedicated WAN connection to the Atlanta location. Additionally, a WAN connection between the new Seattle office and Hong Kong would be added. While the Atlanta, Seattle, and Dallas locations will use a common password policy, the Hong Kong and London locations will both require their own password policies. A junior network administrator will be available at both the Seattle and Dallas locations, but administrative authority will still remain at the Atlanta office. Based on what you know of Windows Server 2003 thus far and the information provided above, the IT manager has asked you to assess Super Management Corporation's Active Directory design by answering the following questions.

1. Of the factors listed in the scenario, which would influence the logical design of Super Corp's Active Directory implementation?

2. What type of domain structure would you suggest for Super Corp?

3. Based on Super Corp's current and future locations, what would be the best naming strategy for their Active Directory domain structure?

1

4. How many sites would likely be configured as part of Super Corp's Active Directory implementation once the Seattle and Dallas offices open, and how many site links would be required?

5. Once the Seattle and Dallas offices are opened, how many Global Catalog servers should be implemented on the network to ensure adequate performance?

CASE PROJECTS

Case Project 1-3: Diagramming Your Work

The IT manager likes what you have recommended and has asked you to create some diagrams that illustrate your recommendations. He would like you to create a diagram showing the logical structure of Super Management Corporation's Active Directory. Additionally, he would like a diagram that illustrates the sites and site links required.

2

NAME RESOLUTION AND DNS

After reading this chapter, you will be able to:

♦ Describe and identify valid NetBIOS and DNS names

♦ Understand and describe how DNS resolves names

♦ Install and configure the Microsoft DNS Server Service to work with Active Directory

In Chapter 1, you learned about the role of directory services—particularly Active Directory—in a modern computer network. You also learned about the two types of security models available in Windows networks and the fundamental concepts and components of Active Directory.

In this chapter, you will learn about the name resolution process, focusing on the **Domain Name System (DNS)**. Name resolution is the process of resolving a human-friendly name into a number that a computer can use to contact another computer on a network. In Windows Server 2003, the primary service that provides name resolution is DNS—the same system that is used on the public Internet. Additionally, to locate domain controllers that are running Active Directory or a server that is running a given service, client computers can query DNS and retrieve the addresses of one or more servers running the requested service.

While DNS is the primary system for naming computers in Windows 2003, it is not the only naming system available. For backwards compatibility with **down-level client** operating systems prior to Windows 2000, such as Windows NT 4.0 and Windows 98, NetBIOS name resolution is still available. To better understand the differences between NetBIOS and DNS, the first section in this chapter provides a general overview of the name resolution process in a Windows network.

Once you have an understanding of the different methods for resolving names and locating services on a network, this chapter then focuses in more detail on DNS. Because Active Directory requires DNS to function correctly, it is important that you understand the concepts of DNS. You will learn how DNS resolves names and the function of the different record types. In the last section of this chapter, you will learn hands-on skills in configuring the Microsoft DNS server that ships with Windows Server 2003.

It is important to note an essential difference between a classroom and a production business environment. In a classroom or testing lab, it doesn't really matter if a system is not online constantly or if it is not running in the most efficient way possible. Because you are learning and testing, errors and problems are possible, and they are tolerated. You can "play with" a system in a nonproduction environment, and try out different options, just to see what they do. This wouldn't be acceptable on a live network, often called a production environment, on which an enterprise is depending. In a production environment, it is crucial to the success of an Active Directory deployment that you design, plan, and test before leaping into installation.

NAME RESOLUTION

For humans, remembering a name such as *www.microsoft.com* is much easier than remembering a number such as 207.46.249.222. On the other hand, for a computer, the name *www.microsoft.com* does not directly give the computer any information it needs to contact one of Microsoft's servers. To contact a Microsoft server, a computer needs a number such as 207.46.249.222, which in this case is an Internet Protocol (IP) address used on the Internet. Unlike the name *www.microsoft.com*, an IP address contains the information needed to contact a remote system on an IP network. The IP address is used to determine on which network a particular computer is located and for which computer (also known as a host) on that network the data is destined.

Simply put, name resolution is the process of converting a human-friendly name (for example, *www.microsoft.com*) into a number that computers can use to locate one another (for example, 207.46.249.222). Name resolution is also used because it allows names to stay relatively constant, while numbers such as IP addresses can change from time to time—typically when the computer is moved.

In a Windows network, there are two primary naming systems in use, both of which can resolve their respective names to IP addresses. NetBIOS, which stands for Network Basic Input Output System, was introduced back in the Windows 3.x and Windows NT 3.x families of operating systems. Today, NetBIOS is only provided for backwards compatibility with operating systems and older applications that require the use of NetBIOS names. Because of limitations with NetBIOS and the growth of the Internet, NetBIOS has been replaced by the Domain Name System (DNS) starting with Windows 2000 and continued in Windows Server 2003. However, NetBIOS is still not completely gone, and understanding how it works can help in troubleshooting name resolution issues. The following section covers NetBIOS and its limitations in more detail.

2

The primary naming system in use on a Windows Server 2003 network is DNS. In a small workgroup network, DNS name resolution is not required for the network to function correctly. However, networks using Active Directory require that a DNS infrastructure be in place due to Active Directory's heavy reliance on DNS for locating servers and services. Because Active Directory requires DNS, this chapter places a much stronger focus on DNS and related concepts.

If a computer needs to resolve a name to an IP address, and it is unable to determine if the name is a NetBIOS or a DNS name, Windows 2000 Server and Windows Server 2003 computers first attempt to resolve the name using DNS, and then by using NetBIOS name resolution. This is in contrast to such operating systems as Windows NT 4.0 and Windows 98, which attempt to resolve a name using NetBIOS first, and then DNS.

NetBIOS

A NetBIOS name is a 16-character name, with the first 15 characters available for the name and the 16th character reserved to describe a particular service or functionality. A NetBIOS name can consist of letters, numbers, and the following special characters:

! @ # $ % ^ & ( ) - _ ` { } . ~

NetBIOS names, however, must be unique and cannot contain spaces or any of the following special characters:

\ * + = | : ; " ? < > ,

NetBIOS names are not case sensitive, which means *A* is equivalent to *a*. Some examples of valid NetBIOS names include SUPERCORP, SERVER01, and INSTRUCTOR.

In a NetBIOS name, the reserved 16th character is typically expressed as a hexadecimal number surrounded by angle brackets at the end of the name. For example, the NetBIOS name SUPERCORP<1C> would represent a request for the SUPERCORP domain controllers. When a user tries to access a given service, manually appending a NetBIOS suffix at the end of the name is not necessary as Windows does this automatically. Additionally, when setting the NetBIOS name on a domain or computer, it is entered without the 16th character—because a single NetBIOS name can be used to represent many different services on the same system.

NOTE

Keep in mind while the 16th character of a NetBIOS name is expressed as a hexadecimal number surrounded by angle brackets, in actuality the 16th character is a single ASCII character with a value from 0 to 255. The reason the number is expressed in hexadecimal and not as a character is because some characters, such as the line feed and tab, don't have an equivalent "printable character" that is visible when displayed on the screen. Additionally, the angle brackets are only written to help distinguish the 16th character from the rest of the name and are not actually part of the name.

Another characteristic of NetBIOS names is that all names are at the same level—a concept referred to as a "flat" namespace. In other words, all NetBIOS names are in one big "pool," without any identification as to what part of the network the name belongs. For example, SERVER01 and SERVER02 are both valid NetBIOS names, but by looking at the names, it is impossible to tell that SERVER01 is a member of the domain CHILD01 and SERVER02 is a member of CHILD02. Because of the flat name structure used by NetBIOS, it becomes much more difficult to manage a large network environment.

Resolving NetBIOS Names

The simplest way for a computer to resolve a NetBIOS name to an IP address is to send a network broadcast—which is a message destined for all computers on a given network. The broadcast message includes the NetBIOS name a computer is looking for, the type of service (represented by the 16th character), and the IP address of the computer sending the broadcast, such that the computer with the requested NetBIOS name can respond to the request. If a computer with a matching NetBIOS name and service type receives the broadcast message, it responds directly to the computer that sent the broadcast message with its IP address.

NOTE NetBIOS is (for the most part) a Session layer protocol that provides name resolution and session management between computers. NetBIOS on its own does not provide the capabilities to transport data between computers—it relies on a lower-level protocol such as TCP/IP to perform that function. In order for NetBIOS to work on top of TCP/IP, NetBIOS over TCP/IP (NetBT) is used. NetBT is enabled by default, but can be disabled on the WINS tab in the Advanced TCP/IP Settings of a network connection (shown in Figure 2-2).

For example, Figure 2-1 illustrates using a broadcast to resolve the NetBIOS name Workstation02 for Workstation01. In the first step, Workstation01 sends out a broadcast requesting the IP address of Workstation02. As shown in the figure, the message is sent to all computers on the network. In the second step, Workstation02 responds directly to Workstation01 with its IP address. Workstation03, after looking at the request, does not respond to the request because its NetBIOS name does not match the name Workstation01 is looking for.

Once the two computers know each other's IP addresses, they can then communicate directly with one another. Additionally, in order to improve performance and reduce network traffic, IP addresses associated with resolved NetBIOS names are cached for 10 minutes by default.

2

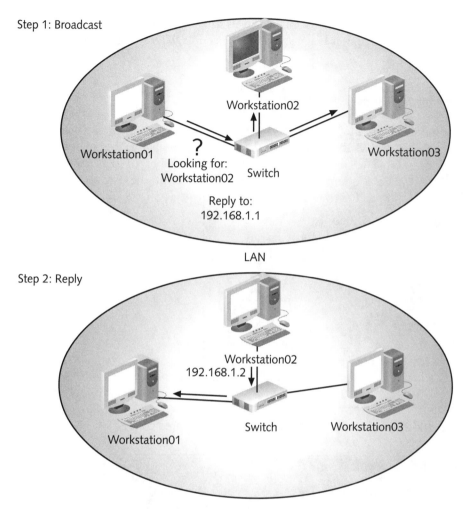

Step 1: Broadcast

Workstation02

Workstation01

?
Looking for:
Workstation02   Switch

Workstation03

Reply to:
192.168.1.1

LAN

Step 2: Reply

Workstation02
192.168.1.2

Switch   Workstation03

Workstation01

Figure 2-1   NetBIOS name resolution using broadcast

While using broadcasts to resolve NetBIOS names is simple, it is certainly not efficient. Also, network devices such as routers—which are used to separate different networks—do not forward broadcasts by default. This means that two computers on different physical networks separated by a router would be unable to resolve each other's NetBIOS names. To overcome some of these problems, Microsoft introduced the Windows Internet Naming Service (WINS).

WINS is simply a database with which all the computers on a network register their NetBIOS names. In order for computers to register with WINS, they must be configured with the IP address of one or more WINS servers on the network, as shown in Figure 2-2. By default, when a computer needs to resolve a NetBIOS name to an IP address, it sends a request directly to a WINS server instead of sending a broadcast to the entire network. If the

WINS server finds a matching name in its database, it responds to the request with the IP address of the computer being sought. An example WINS registration database is shown in Figure 2-3.

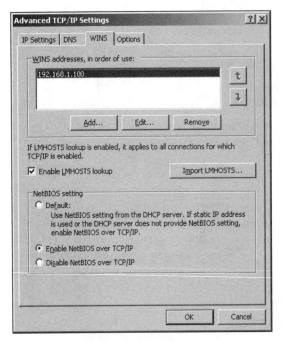

Figure 2-2   Advanced TCP/IP Settings on a local area connection

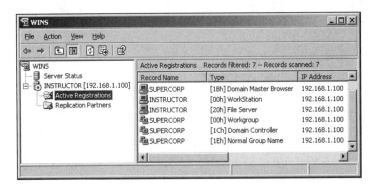

Figure 2-3   Example WINS database

While WINS resolves issues such as excessive broadcasts and the inability of broadcasts to cross routers, the issues associated with having a flat namespace are still apparent. Even with WINS, it is still impossible to assign authority for part of the namespace to different administrators. Additionally, it is impossible to split the WINS database into multiple smaller pieces—the entire WINS database has to be stored on and replicated to every WINS server.

This means that a branch office that has a WINS server has to store and replicate records from all other branch offices, even if the office only accesses servers at the main office. To overcome these issues, and to account for the larger role the Internet plays in today's networks, Microsoft decided to switch to DNS as the primary name resolution system on Windows networks starting with Windows 2000, and this has continued in Windows Server 2003.

Setting up and configuring a WINS server is outside the scope of this text and the 70-294 exam.

NOTE

Domain Name System

Unlike NetBIOS, the Domain Name System is a hierarchical naming system most commonly known because of its use on the Internet. DNS resolves **Fully Qualified Domain Names (FQDNs)** such as *www.microsoft.com* and *SERVER01.child01.supercorp.net* to IP addresses such as 207.46.249.222 and 192.168.1.1. Because DNS is a hierarchical system, control over different parts of the namespace can be given to different organizations or administrators. Additionally, DNS allows for different parts of the namespace to be located on different servers.

Once a computer has resolved the FQDN of another system, the computers can then pass information back and forth using IP addresses. DNS can also be used to provide **reverse lookup** services, which is the ability to identify a host's name by knowing its IP address. This is useful for logging and reporting, analysis, and configuring certain types of security.

DNS can provide name services for private networks; however, it is most commonly known for its role in the operation of the public Internet. DNS works well on the Internet because it is a distributed system that scales well (it currently holds millions of names and IP addresses).

NOTE

An FQDN is actually made up of two parts—a hostname such as www or hostABC, and a DNS domain suffix such as microsoft.com or supercorp.net. All possible FQDNs are contained in what is sometimes called the **DNS namespace**. Figure 2-4 shows a simplified view of this namespace concept. For compatibility with all DNS servers, an FQDN can consist of letters, numbers, and the hyphen (-). In addition, FQDNs can also contain periods (.), but only as a separator between the different levels in the FQDN. An FQDN is restricted to 63 bytes for the host name and each domain level—which are referred to as labels—and 255 bytes for the entire FQDN including the trailing period. Each label in an FQDN must begin and end with either a letter or a number. FQDNs are not case sensitive.

The reason to use bytes and not characters directly in measuring sizes is that the Microsoft DNS server included with Windows 2000 and Windows Server 2003 supports the use of UTF-8 character encoding. While ASCII characters only use one byte per character, some UTF-8 characters use more than one byte, which makes it impossible to determine size strictly based on the number of characters.

TIP

TIP When you create an Active Directory domain, several subdomains are added to the DNS structure, such as _msdcs. Within these subdomains, DNS records are added that Active Directory and client computers can use to locate servers that are domain controllers, global catalogs, or other services. Because of the additional depth required for these subdomains, a domain controller's FQDN can't be any longer than 155 bytes. Member servers and workstations can still have a 255-byte FQDN.

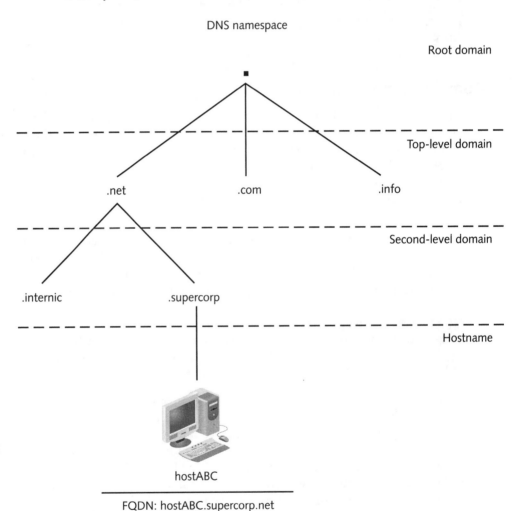

Figure 2-4   Conceptual view of the DNS namespace

NOTE Like all Internet standards, the operation of DNS is defined by a set of documents collected by the Internet Engineering Task Force (IETF). No one person or company invented DNS, but all properly working DNS software follows the same set of basic rules. It is beyond the scope of this book to discuss in detail the standards development process, but if you are interested in learning more, you can visit the IETF at *www.ietf.org* or download the DNS standard from *www.ietf.org/rfc/rfc1034.txt*.

The entire DNS namespace is represented by a single period (.)—which is called the **root domain**. The period is located at the end, or rightmost position of an FQDN, but is often not entered at all (and instead just assumed). For example, *www.microsoft.com* and *www.microsoft.com.* represent the same FQDN. After the root domain, the next level of categorization is a **top-level domain (TLD)**, which is the rightmost part of an FQDN if the period representing the root domain is not entered. For example, the TLD for the FQDN *www.microsoft.com* is com, and the TLD for the FQDN hostABC.supercorp.net is net. There are many other TLDs, which are divided into two categories: **country code TLDs (ccTLD)** and **generic TLDs (gTLD)**. The next two sections of the chapter will look at each of these top-level domains.

Following the TLD is the second-level domain (SLD), which is a **subdomain** of a TLD. For example, microsoft is the SLD of the FQDN *www.microsoft.com* and a subdomain of the com TLD. As another example, in the FQDN *hostABC.supercorp.net*, supercorp is the SLD that is a subdomain of the net TLD.

The leftmost name in an FQDN represents the host—which is nothing more than an IP address, and sometimes multiple IP addresses, assigned to the particular FQDN. For example, in the FQDN *www.microsoft.com*, www has been assigned one or more IP addresses that correlate to the server hosting Microsoft's Web site.

In some cases, you will come across FQDNs that are deeper than just a TLD, SLD, and hostname. For example, in the FQDN *SERVER01.child01.supercorp.net*, *child01* would be a third-level domain name and a subdomain of the *supercorp.net* domain. Additionally, SERVER01 would be the host name and have one or more IP addresses associated with it. Once an FQDN is deeper than the third-level domain, any additional domains are referred to as just subdomains. However, practically speaking, once you have a third-level domain or one level below a third-level domain, it is a good idea to avoid going any deeper in the naming hierarchy. Otherwise, FQDNs start to get too long and will be harder to remember.

Because an IP address can be assigned at any level of the DNS hierarchy, most SLD operators have IP addresses assigned to their SLD directly that points to their Web site, such as *microsoft.com* (a host called microsoft in the com TLD). In theory, an IP address could even be assigned directly to a TLD, and in the past there have been Web sites such as http://cc or http://tv. In practice, however, an FQDN has at least two parts and typically three.

DNS domains and traditional Windows domains are not the same thing, although they may share the same namespace. To avoid confusion, this book uses the term "domain," if used alone, to refer to a Windows domain, and the terms "top-level domain," "TLD," or "subdomain" to refer to a DNS domain.

TLD by Country

Each country has been assigned a two-letter TLD, such as .ca for Canada and .uk for the United Kingdom. These are called country code TLDs (ccTLDs). Each national government defines the rules for its own ccTLD. Some, like Tuvalu (.tv) and Micronesia (.fm) have sold rights to their ccTLD namespace to corporate entities to gain much needed capital. Other countries may do the same. Although not as commonly used, there is a .us ccTLD.

The ccTLD abbreviation for each country is assigned by the Internet Assigned Numbers Authority (IANA), and is based on the list of country codes maintained by the International Standards Organization (ISO). Ranging from *.ac* for Ascension Island to .zw for Zimbabwe, the complete list of ccTLDs and policies concerning their assignment is located at *www.iana.org/cctld/cctld.htm*.

Generic TLD

Generic TLDs are termed as such because they are not tied to any one particular country, and include very common TLDs, such as .com, .net, and .org.

New gTLDs have recently been defined. Some of the newer ones include .info, .biz, and even .museum. Each of these TLDs has specific criteria governing who can register names within it. For example, only U.S. military entities exist in .mil. The most exclusive TLD is probably .int, which allows only entities created by multinational treaties to register. Current examples include worldbank.int and nato.int. Although there are a number of proposals for new gTLDs as of this writing, the current list is as follows: .aero, .biz, .com, .coop, .edu, .gov, .info, .int, .mil, .museum, .name, .net, .org, and .pro. You can read more about gTLDs at *www.iana.org/gtld/gtld.htm*.

There is one additional TLD, known as the .arpa domain, which is used to provide reverse lookup services. IANA calls it an "infrastructure TLD," and states that the abbreviation means "address and routing parameter area." It is worth noting, however, that the Defense Advanced Research Projects Agency (DARPA) developed the first networks that became the Internet, and was commonly called ARPA. The forerunner of the Internet, in the late 1960s, was known as the ARPANET.

TLD Registrars

Each TLD is operated by a registrar who collects and manages information from those who register in it, usually for a fee. If a network operator were to set up a DNS server and establish his own *microsoft.com* subdomain without regard to the registration process, the Domain Name System would be unable to function properly within that network. The rest of the world would carry on operations, but users of that DNS server would not be able to reach the Microsoft Web site correctly.

In most cases, this is not desirable. However, it is one way to deliberately block access to certain sites (but only by name, not by IP address). It is also a way to create a private DNS structure that will not be exposed to any user or service outside a private network. For this reason, some DNS servers have information about fictitious TLDs or subdomains, such as .local or .private. However, all subdomains within a public TLD should be registered with that TLD's registrar. In other words, a private DNS structure under .net, such as supercorp.net, should be registered with the net TLD registrar. If not, problems could arise later if someone else registers your fictitious subdomain. In Activity 2-1, you will learn how to examine the registration for a subdomain of the .com TLD.

TIP

The IANA pages mentioned for gTLD and ccTLD information also include the name and contact information for the registrars or operators of each TLD.

ACTIVITY

Activity 2-1: Examining the Registration of a Second-level Domain

Time Required: 5 minutes

Objective: To practice looking up the registration information of a DNS second-level domain that has been publicly registered.

Description: If you decide to use a public DNS domain name for your Active Directory structure (you will look at using public and private DNS domain names later in this chapter), it is important to check if the name you intend to use is properly registered to you or your organization.

1. If necessary, start your server and log on using the **AdminXX** account in the **CHILDXX** domain (where *XX* is the number of your server).

2. If necessary, close the Manage Your Server window.

3. Click the **Start** menu, point to **All Programs** and click **Internet Explorer**. A dialog box will inform you of Microsoft Internet Explorer's Enhanced Security Configuration.

4. Check the **In the future, do not show this message** check box and click **OK**.

5. In the Address bar, enter **www.internic.net** and click **Go**.

6. Click **Whois** on the menu near the top of the page.

7. Type **microsoft.com** in the text box on the Whois search form. Then click **Submit**. A message box informs you about sending information over the Internet.

8. Click **Yes**. The basic information will be shown in the result page, including the names of registered DNS name servers for the subdomain. Because there are now multiple registrars, you may also see a line labeled **Referral URL**.

9. If desired, browse to the Referral URL and search for more detailed information such as the administrative and technical contacts.

10. Log off your server if you do not intend to immediately continue to the next project. Otherwise, stay logged on.

TIP

The Internet is dynamic, and each registrar is responsible for its own Web site. You may have to explore a bit to find the detailed information.

UNDERSTANDING THE DOMAIN NAME SYSTEM

With an understanding of how DNS is organized, you can examine how a computer actually finds an address for a given FQDN. Just as certain computers keep a copy of the Active Directory database and are known as domain controllers, certain computers store parts of the DNS database and are called DNS servers. Often, domain controllers are also DNS servers, but DNS servers also commonly run on UNIX/Linux platforms or dedicated Windows servers. The purpose of a DNS server is to answer queries presented by clients or other DNS servers about FQDNs and related addressing information.

Each piece of DNS information, such as the address for a particular host, is called a Resource Record (RR). There are several types of RRs in the Domain Name System. The most common is an **address (A) record** that records the IP address of a host. Other important RR types include the **mail exchanger (MX) record** that directs e-mail to the correct server, the **name server (NS) record**, and **start of authority (SOA) records**.

RRs are kept in either a text file or a database and are collected or grouped into DNS zones. A **zone** normally includes all the RRs for a subdomain, but a single zone could include a subdomain and any number of other subdomains within the same contiguous naming hierarchy. For example, the RRs for mydomain.com and subdivision.mydomain.com could be kept in one zone, or divided into two zones. Zones are administrative divisions that allow you to manage how DNS information is replicated between DNS servers. Zones also allow you to control which DNS servers provide information about which DNS subdomains. To put it another way, a zone contains all the information about a DNS domain, except for any parts of that DNS domain that are delegated elsewhere (such as another level of subdomain).

2

Zones are sometimes referred to as "zone files" because in most non-Windows implementations, the RRs are stored in text files. The most common DNS server software used on the Internet is called BIND. BIND is an acronym for Berkeley Internet Name Domain. (It is no longer developed at Berkeley, and it used to be called a "Naming Daemon," but its acronym has now become its name in almost all common uses.) Originally designed for UNIX, versions of BIND are also available for Windows. BIND uses zone files and because of its popularity, BIND terminology permeates the industry. Zone or zone data are better terms than zone file, because DNS servers can use databases, Active Directory, or even the Windows registry to store RRs.

No single DNS server could possibly hold all of the RRs used on the Internet. Rather, when a DNS server is configured, its administrators decide which DNS subdomains that particular server will provide information about. The administrators then make sure that the server has copies of the zone information for those DNS subdomains. For example, a host called *nameserver1.mydomain.com* could be the DNS server for the *mydomain.com* subdomain. Nameserver1 would then be configured to store all of the RRs relating to *mydomain.com* in a zone. A second server, nameserver2, could also be created to share the workload and to keep a redundant copy of the zone in case nameserver1 were to go offline or fail.

Authoritative Servers

When a DNS server has a zone containing a particular subdomain, it is said to be authoritative for that subdomain. In other words, a DNS server that knows all there is to know about that subdomain without asking any other name server is an "authority" on the subject. A DNS server never asks another server about a subdomain for which it is authoritative. This means that if a DNS server has a zone file for a particular subdomain, it never asks any other DNS server about that zone. When troubleshooting a DNS or name resolution problem, it is important to remember that the request does not go to any other servers after an authoritative server has processed the request. If a given record is on one server but not on another, this almost always results in an error (except in the special case called "split DNS," discussed in Chapter 5), and can be difficult to troubleshoot.

When an SLD is registered, the registrar collects information about the person or organization registering the SLD. From a technical standpoint, the most important information gathered includes the names and IP addresses of at least two authoritative DNS servers that will answer queries about the new SLD. The registrar enters NS records into the TLD zone so that the TLD DNS servers can refer queries to the SLD's name servers. This is called delegation. For example, the .com TLD has delegated the authority for *microsoft.com* to the server DNS1.CP.MSFT.NET and four other DNS servers. The root domain has delegated authority for an SLD to a DNS server operated by the SLD. The TLD usually delegates authority for each SLD to DNS servers that have FQDNs in the given SLD.

As you will see in the next section, this process of delegation that begins at the root domain and follows down through all subdomain levels is fundamental to the operation of DNS.

Most DNS servers for the root domain and for TLDs refer queries only to other DNS servers that provide more specific answers—that is, most TLD DNS servers do not provide answers themselves (unless there are hosts in the TLD itself). This is because the root and TLD servers must answer hundreds of millions of queries in the fastest possible time.

Prior to the advent of Active Directory, changes to RRs in a zone could only be made at one DNS server. This DNS server with a read-write copy of the zone is called a **primary name server**. Any other DNS servers with read-only copies of the zone are called **secondary name servers**, as shown in Figure 2-5. In this example, ns1 is the primary name server, while ns2 and ns3 are the secondary name servers. In a properly configured environment, the secondary name servers receive updated information and new RRs from the primary name server. A common misconfiguration occurs when two (or more) primary servers are accidentally created for the same zone, which results in changes not being propagated to all of the authoritative servers.

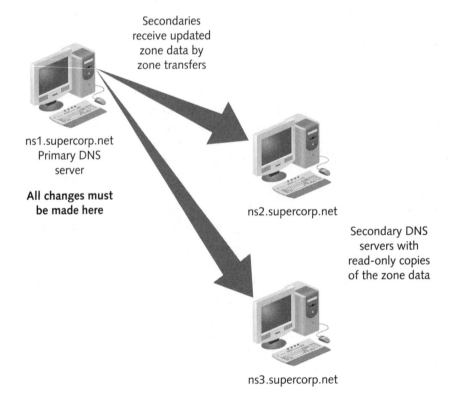

Figure 2-5   Primary and secondary name servers

Alternatively, using the Microsoft DNS server that is shipped with all versions of the Windows Server 2003 family can eliminate the need for primary and secondary servers. The Microsoft DNS server can be configured to store zone information in Active Directory, where multimaster replication can be used to synchronize updates between domain controllers.

Transferring Information

Zone information is transferred from a primary DNS server to a secondary DNS server using a process called **zone transfer**, which is shown in Figure 2-5. Traditional DNS servers copied the entire zone whenever a change was made, no matter how small the change.

To make the process of updating secondary DNS servers more efficient, modern DNS servers, including Microsoft DNS, support **incremental zone transfers**. Incremental zone transfers are more efficient because they send only new or changed information across the network, which decreases traffic. Traditionally, a secondary DNS server had to poll its primary DNS server to check for changes. Newer servers, including Microsoft DNS, can be configured so that the primary DNS server notifies the secondary DNS servers as soon as a change occurs. This reduces the time it takes for all authoritative servers to receive the correct information. Information about the current version of the zone is stored in the Start of Authority (SOA) resource record and is kept in all copies of the zone.

Primary Does Not Mean Authoritative

Many people mix and match DNS terms incorrectly. It may be confusing at first, but a primary DNS server and an authoritative DNS server are not the same. Many organizations publicly register only secondary servers, because their primary server is behind a firewall. An example of this arrangement is pictured in Figure 2-6. In this case, the TLD and other hosts on the Internet know that the secondary DNS servers are authoritative, but know nothing about the primary server. Inside the organization, however, the primary server is still an authoritative server because it has a copy of the zone.

The DNS Name Resolution Process

A computer workstation that accesses the Internet uses an IP address to identify its preferred DNS server. If the workstation has been configured manually, an administrator has entered the DNS server's IP address. If the workstation is configured automatically with Dynamic Host Configuration Protocol (DHCP), then a DNS server's IP address is usually provided by the DHCP server. When the workstation needs to look up an IP address, perhaps because the user wishes to browse a Web site, the workstation uses the IP address for its DNS server to send a query to the DNS server.

There are two kinds of queries that can be issued to a DNS server: recursive and iterative (or nonrecursive). Recursive queries are the default, and indicate that the client wants the address resolved if at all possible, or an error if it cannot be resolved. The client does not want to ask any other DNS server, but wishes the DNS server to find an address, even if it has to

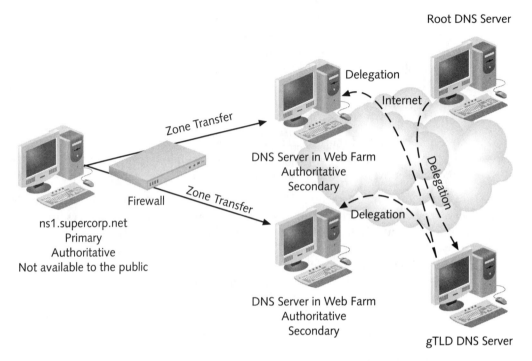

Figure 2-6   A typical DNS scenario

ask another DNS server. Conversely, an iterative (or nonrecursive) query indicates that the client wants the DNS server to respond only with information from that particular DNS server. It expects a resolved address, an error, or a referral to another server.

It is this ability to issue referrals that makes the Domain Name System both highly scaleable and geographically dispersed. This is very useful if ns1 doesn't have zone information about the microsoft.com SLD, but knows where to find it. Figure 2-7 illustrates the process that typically occurs when a client requests the IP address for an FQDN.

A client workstation mydesk.supercorp.net needs to resolve an IP address for *www.microsoft.com* so the user can read about the latest server products available from Microsoft. The workstation has been configured manually to use 192.168.10.25 (the host ns1.supercorp.net) as its DNS name server, so the workstation issues a recursive request to the name server ns1 to resolve *www.microsoft.com* (1).

The DNS server first checks its own zones. It quickly determines that it is not authoritative for microsoft.com (2). If it did have a copy of the microsoft.com zone, it would immediately return the entry for www, or an error if it did not exist. The name server then looks at its cache of recently retrieved records (2). Because the name server has not looked this entry up before, it finds no match.

2

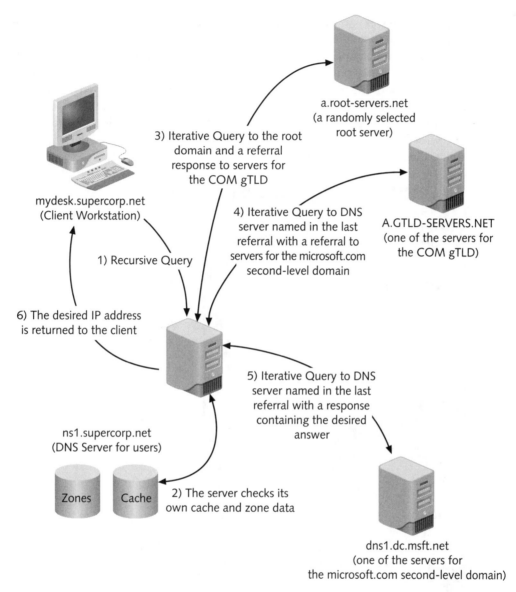

a.root-servers.net
(a randomly selected
root server)

3) Iterative Query to the root
domain and a referral
response to servers for
the COM gTLD

mydesk.supercorp.net
(Client Workstation)

4) Iterative Query to DNS
server named in the last
referral with a referral to
servers for the microsoft.com
second-level domain

A.GTLD-SERVERS.NET
(one of the servers for
the COM gTLD)

1) Recursive Query

6) The desired IP address
is returned to the client

5) Iterative Query to DNS
server named in the last
referral with a response
containing the desired
answer

ns1.supercorp.net
(DNS Server for users)

Zones   Cache   2) The server checks its
own cache and zone data

dns1.dc.msft.net
(one of the servers for
the microsoft.com second-level domain)

Figure 2-7   Resolving a DNS query

Ns1 has no information about the desired host, but it knows where to look. Name servers that perform recursion have entries in their databases that point to the servers for the root DNS domain. These entries are called root hints, and are shown in Figure 2-8. The name server picks one of the root servers and sends it an iterative (nonrecursive) query for the desired record (3). The root name server, a.root-servers.net in this example, checks its own zones and cache.

Because microsoft.com is not in the root DNS domain, the root name server checks to see if it has NS records delegating authority for the gTLD or ccTLD (in this case, a gTLD). Because .com is a common gTLD, it finds several records pointing to authoritative servers for .com and sends these NS records back to the requesting server (3). Ns1 now knows something about the .com domain. To avoid the need to resolve the IP address for the next name server, the records returned include the IP addresses for the delegated name servers. The name server that sent the query (ns1) caches this information for future use, so a new query for any host in any .com subdomain does not need to go to the root server, and the name server skips this step in the future.

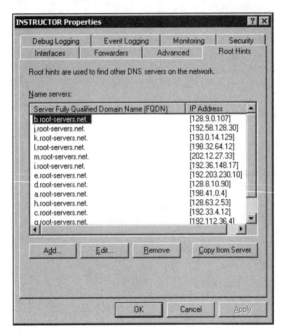

Figure 2-8   Root hints in Microsoft DNS server

In production environments, the root servers are rarely queried because the TLD referrals are cached, usually for 48 hours or longer.

TIP

The process repeats again, this time by sending an iterative query to one of the name servers included in the records returned from the root (4). Name server referrals are usually returned in a round-robin order to divide up the work. The next name server up in the round-robin order for .com happens to be a.gtld-servers.net. Like the root name servers, TLD name servers are usually operated by larger organizations that are geographically dispersed. The TLD server a.gtld-servers.net checks its zone information and its cache, but does not have a record for the requested host. It does, however, have NS records delegating authority for the SLD microsoft.com, and returns the names and IP addresses of those authoritative servers (4).

2

Ns1 now caches the information for future use and keeps it for the length of time specified in the NS record's Time to Live (TTL) value. The name server submits the query to dns1.dc.msft.net (5). Microsoft Corporation operates this machine, which checks its zone information and finds that it is authoritative for microsoft.com, and that it has multiple A Records for the desired host. It returns the IP addresses to the requesting name server (5).

Finally, ns1 has collected all of the required information, cached it for future use, and can now send the answer back to the client's workstation, complete with an IP address (6). The user's browser can now retrieve the Web pages, allowing the user to read up on the latest offerings from Microsoft. In Activity 2-2, you will manually perform this process to resolve the FQDN *www.google.com*.

Written out, this seems like a lengthy process, but it is very efficient. This process uses the User Datagram Protocol (UDP), not the Transmission Control Protocol (TCP), in order to avoid the overhead required to set up and tear down TCP connections. Caching the results improves performance and eliminates all but a few trips to the root server (and many trips to the gTLD servers). You can work through these steps manually using the Nslookup utility included with Windows.

ACTIVITY

Activity 2-2: Tracing DNS Name Resolution

Time Required: 10 minutes

Objective: To trace DNS name resolution and referrals from the root servers to the destination.

Description: When DNS is not working correctly it is typically due to human error. The DNS name resolution process may fail completely, work correctly for some FQDNs but not others, or may return incorrect results. In any of these situations, it is necessary to locate what is causing the problem. To help in the troubleshooting process, Windows Server 2003 includes a tool called Nslookup, which can be used to query DNS servers. In this exercise, you will manually perform the name resolution process from both the client computer and local DNS server's perspectives by performing both recursive and iterative queries. First, you will resolve the FQDN *www.google.com* by using iterative queries to simulate the same process a DNS server would use to resolve an FQDN. You will then switch back to the local DNS server and perform a recursive query on a local DNS server as a client computer typically would.

1. If necessary, start your server and log on using the **AdminXX** account in the **CHILDXX** domain (where *XX* is the number of your server).

2. Click the **Start** menu, then click **Command Prompt**.

3. At the command prompt, type **NSLOOKUP** and press **Enter**. Your default server should display as instructor.supercorp.net with an IP address of 192.168.1.100. This indicates that requests entered are sent to the DNS server on instructor.supercorp.net for DNS name resolution.

4. By default, Nslookup makes recursive queries to DNS servers. To turn off recursive queries and have Nslookup make iterative queries, type **set norecurse** and press **Enter**.

NOTE   If you receive an error that the server name cannot be found for 192.168.1.100 because of a non-existent domain, don't worry. This error means that your server attempted to do a reverse lookup on 192.168.1.100 and was unable to find the FQDN associated with that IP. The most likely reason for this error is that a reverse lookup zone is not set up for 192.168.1.x or a pointer record does not exist for that specific IP address.

TIP   For all the options and commands supported by Nslookup, type a question mark (?) and press Enter.

TIP   Some servers, such as the root name servers, are configured not to perform recursive queries—only iterative. If you use Nslookup to make a recursive query to a root name server, the server responds only with the address of another server that knows more about the requested subdomain (which is the same information returned with an iterative query). Because the root servers receive so much traffic, this is necessary to prevent the servers from being slowed down by recursive queries.

5. Next, type **server A.ROOT-SERVERS.NET** and press **Enter**. Nslookup can now send all queries to A.ROOT-SERVERS.NET instead of instructor.supercorp.net. Your screen should look similar to Figure 2-9.

NOTE   If you are unable to connect to A.ROOT-SERVERS.NET (for example, you receive a "Server Failed" error message), try using another root server such as B.ROOT-SERVERS.NET or C.ROOT-SERVERS.NET.

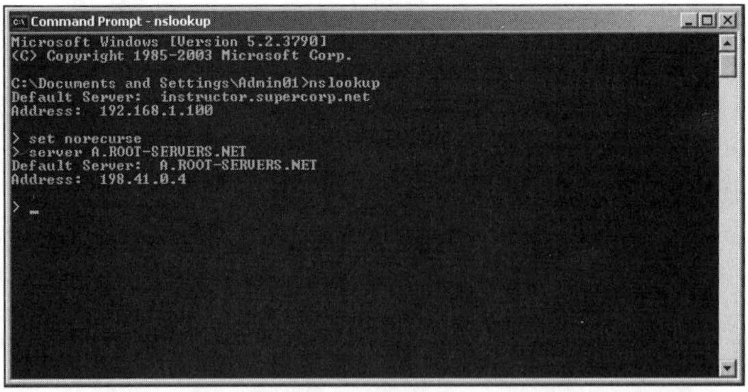

```
Command Prompt - nslookup                                        _|□|x|
Microsoft Windows [Version 5.2.3790]
(C) Copyright 1985-2003 Microsoft Corp.

C:\Documents and Settings\Admin01>nslookup
Default Server:  instructor.supercorp.net
Address:  192.168.1.100

> set norecurse
> server A.ROOT-SERVERS.NET
Default Server:  A.ROOT-SERVERS.NET
Address:  198.41.0.4

> _
```

Figure 2-9   Setting the recursion option and default server in Nslookup

TIP You can also use the **root** Nslookup command to change to a root DNS server.

2

6. Type **www.google.com** and press **Enter**. A list of the name servers that are authoritative for the .com TLD are returned by A.ROOT-SERVERS.NET.

7. Type **server A.GTLD-SERVERS.NET** and press **Enter**. A.GTLD-SERVERS.NET is now the DNS server used for any queries entered.

8. Type **www.google.com** and press **Enter**. A list of the name servers that are authoritative for the google.com SLD are returned by A.GTLD-SERVERS.NET as shown in Figure 2-10.

```
Command Prompt - nslookup                          _|□|x|
> server A.GTLD-SERVERS.NET
Default Server:  A.GTLD-SERVERS.NET
Address:  192.5.6.30

> www.google.com
Server:  A.GTLD-SERVERS.NET
Address:  192.5.6.30

Name:     www.google.com
Served by:
- ns2.google.com
          216.239.34.10
          google.com
- ns1.google.com
          216.239.32.10
          google.com
- ns3.google.com
          216.239.36.10
          google.com
- ns4.google.com
          216.239.38.10
          google.com
>
```

Figure 2-10 Servers that are authoritative for google.com as returned by A.GTLD-SERVERS.NET

9. Type **server ns2.google.com** and press **Enter**. ns2.google.com is now the DNS server used for any queries entered.

10. Type **www.google.com** and press **Enter**. ns2.google.com responds with the IP address for the FQDN *www.google.com*.

NOTE You have now performed the same iterative queries a DNS server uses to look up an IP address. While it is important to understand the underlying process, performing each step of the name resolution process is typically not required. What you typically do is make recursive queries to your local DNS server or to another DNS server that in turn performs a set of iterative queries to resolve the name.

11. To clear out the settings that have been changed and to get back to the local default server and settings, the easiest thing to do is exit out of Nslookup and then start again. In order to exit Nslookup, type **exit** and press **Enter**.

12. To start Nslookup again, type **NSLOOKUP** and press **Enter**. Because instructor.supercorp.net has been configured as your server's primary DNS server, it is automatically set as the default server.

13. Type **www.google.com** and press **Enter**. instructor.supercorp.net performs the needed iterative queries and then returns the IP address for the FQDN *www.google.com*. Note that instructor.supercorp.net returns a nonauthoritative answer because it is not authoritative for the google.com SLD, as shown in Figure 2-11.

NOTE   Because *www.google.com* is actually multiple Web servers with the same FQDN, you may receive a different IP address in Step 14 then you did in Step 11. This is normal and to be expected for large Web sites that have multiple Web servers.

```
Command Prompt - NSLOOKUP                                    _ | □ | x |
Default Server:  ns2.google.com
Address:  216.239.34.10

> www.google.com
Server:  ns2.google.com
Address:  216.239.34.10

Name:     www.google.com
Address:  216.239.53.99

> exit

C:\Documents and Settings\Admin01>NSLOOKUP
Default Server:  instructor.supercorp.net
Address:  192.168.1.100

> www.google.com
Server:  instructor.supercorp.net
Address:  192.168.1.100

Non-authoritative answer:
Name:     www.google.com
Address:  216.239.39.99

>
```

Figure 2-11   Performing a recursive query on a local DNS server

14. Type **exit** and press **Enter** to exit Nslookup.

15. Type **exit** and press **Enter** to close the command prompt.

16. Log off your server if you do not intend to immediately continue to the next project. Otherwise, stay logged on.

Common Errors and Misconceptions About DNS

DNS is complex, and as a result, configuration errors can occur, particularly in large networks. Most errors occur in one of three areas:

- *Resource record errors*—Resource record errors are greatly reduced by using modern software and graphical tools. Manual editing of resource records is an advanced skill and is not usually necessary.

- *Delegation errors*—To avoid delegation errors, plan carefully and document the configuration of all servers involved. Make sure that any contractors used, such as ISPs and domain registrars, are well versed in DNS and understand how NS and SOA records are used.

2

- *Weak authorities*—Weak authority is a general term used to describe a situation in which a machine that is supposed to be authoritative isn't, or a machine that isn't supposed to be authoritative thinks it is. Imagine that you have your public DNS hosted at your ISP, and your ISP suddenly ceases operations. All of the root and gTLD name servers will delegate authority for your domain to servers that no longer exist. You quickly arrange to have new DNS service provisioned elsewhere, but it takes longer than expected to get the delegation changed through your registrar. During this time, your new DNS services do not have the delegated authority that they need for the public to access your networks.

Conversely, imagine that someone chooses to set up a zone for microsoft.com on a DNS server on his own network. All of the workstations on this network use this DNS server for lookups. None of these clients will receive correct DNS information from Microsoft's servers. This could be some sort of deliberate attack or blockade against Microsoft (although not very effective unless done on the servers of a large ISP), but more likely, a misinformed administrator thought this would improve caching performance, which is simply incorrect. You can avoid weak authority situations by planning, documenting, and ensuring that adequate redundancy exists for your critical services.

Most client software, including Windows 2000 and Windows XP, can be set so that more than one DNS server is able to resolve names. For example, ns1 and ns2 could both be available to all clients on the LAN. However, the client applications only send queries to the second server if the first server is not available. A common misconception is that if the first server doesn't find a record, the query is tried on the second. This is not the case. If the first server replies but cannot find the record, the second server is not queried.

Remember that a server that is authoritative for a subdomain never recurses or otherwise asks another name server for entries in that subdomain (except for delegations). If a zone for a DNS subdomain exists on a DNS name server, only records from that file are returned in answer to queries. In rare cases, this can be a good thing, especially if you are trying to keep certain resource records private. More often, someone has made a mistake when configuring the DNS servers involved.

DNS Suffixes

Probably the most misunderstood concept in DNS name resolution has to do with hostnames and DNS suffixes. The first thing to remember is that DNS servers do not resolve hostnames (that is, by themselves) to IP addresses—they resolve FQDNs to IP addresses. For example, there are multiple hosts with the hostname *www*. If you try and submit a query to a DNS server for *www*, the server assumes you mean the top-level domain named *www* and will most likely return an error that the domain does not exist. Because DNS names are hierarchical, it is impossible to tell if you are looking for *www.microsoft.com* or *www.supercorp. net* without the full FQDN of the host—which are just two examples of hosts with the hostname *www*.

The above example assumes there is no subdomain named *www*, but in that case *www* would be an FQDN even though it is only one level.

NOTE

To use another example, say you want to view the shared folders on a server named *DevFileSrv*—so you type \\DevFileSrv\ in the Run window, and click OK on a client computer. Because the name is less than 16 characters and contains characters that are valid for both DNS and NetBIOS names, it is impossible for Windows to determine if the name is a DNS or NetBIOS name. Because the default is to use DNS name resolution, DNS resolution is attempted first. However, as seen in the previous example, sending a request to the DNS server to resolve *DevFileSrv* will not work—DNS assumes *DevFileSrv* is a top-level domain.

In order to overcome this problem, Windows appends one or more DNS suffixes to the hostname. By default, the primary DNS suffix is first appended to the hostname and the resulting FQDN is sent to the DNS server for resolution. The primary DNS suffix is set by default to be the same as the DNS name of the domain the computer joins—although you can change the primary DNS suffix by opening the System applet in Control Panel, clicking Change on the Computer Name tab, and then clicking More. Appending the same DNS suffix to the hostname that is used by the client computer first makes sense, because in most cases the server and client are going to be in the same domain.

In this example, it is important to remember that DNS suffixes are only used when attempting to resolve a hostname. If you entered an FQDN such as \\DevFileSrv.development.supercorp.net\, no DNS suffixes would need to be appended. The FQDN would be sent to a DNS server for resolution by the client as is.

NOTE

The primary DNS suffix for a computer defines part of the computer's FQDN. The primary DNS suffix should only be changed when you need to change a computer's FQDN—it should not be changed to solve name resolution issues.

NOTE

To continue with the same example, say the client computer was a member of a Windows Server 2003 domain with the DNS name of *research.supercorp.net*. When attempting to resolve *DevFileSrv*, the client first would send a request to resolve *DevFileSrv.research. supercorp.net* to a DNS server. Now from this point, one of two things is going to happen. If there is a host with the FQDN *DevFileSrv.research.supercorp.net*, the DNS server will return the IP address for the file server and the client will then attempt to connect to the server. On the other hand, if there is no host with the FQDN *DevFileSrv.research.supercorp.net*, the DNS server will return an error to the client and the client must try additional step(s) to resolve the name.

If trying the client's primary DNS suffix appended to the hostname does not resolve to an IP address, the client will then attempt to remove labels from the primary DNS suffix one by one (that is, it will try the parent subdomains one by one). The client will then resubmit the shortened FQDN(s) to a DNS server for resolution until only two labels are left in the suffix. For this example, what this means is that the client will remove the research part of the primary DNS suffix and then resubmit the FQDN *DevFileSrv.supercorp.net* for resolution. If the FQDN *DevFileSrv.supercorp.net* does not resolve to an IP address, the client would then stop trying to remove additional labels from the primary DNS suffix because there are only two labels left (*supercorp* and *net*).

TIP You can use ipconfig /all to view the primary DNS suffix as well as the list of DNS suffixes that will be used when attempting to resolve hostnames (called the DNS Suffix Search List).

In many cases, if a client is unable to resolve a hostname by appending the primary DNS suffix (or one of its parent subdomains), DNS name resolution fails because no additional suffixes have been specified. If no other DNS suffixes are specified, the client then attempts to use NetBIOS name resolution to resolve the name. However, you can specify additional DNS suffixes in the Advanced TCP/IP Properties of a network connection—which the client will attempt to append to the hostname before attempting NetBIOS name resolution.

CAUTION The Append primary and connection specific DNS suffixes, Append these DNS suffixes, and Append parent suffixes of the primary DNS suffix options are global to all connections that use TCP/IP. Although you may make changes to these settings in one network connection, the settings will be changed on all connections that use TCP/IP.

There are several options that control how DNS suffixes are appended, as shown in Figure 2-12.

The first option you have is if you want to use the Append primary and connection specific DNS suffixes or Append these DNS suffixes option. If you use the Append primary and connection specific DNS suffixes option, the first suffix a client attempts to append to a hostname is its own primary DNS suffix. If the client is unable to resolve the name using the primary DNS suffix, it then tries any connection specific DNS suffixes.

NOTE Connection specific DNS suffixes are designed to allow you to have multiple FQDNs for a single host when the host has multiple network connections. A connection-specific DNS suffix is entered in the DNS suffix for this connection text box.

Once the primary DNS suffix and any connection-specific DNS suffixes have been appended, the Append parent suffixes of the primary DNS suffix check box determines if the client attempts to try the parent subdomains of the primary DNS suffix as previously described. Note that this option is only applicable to the primary DNS suffix—the client does not try the parent subdomains of a connection-specific DNS suffix (just the full connection-specific DNS suffix).

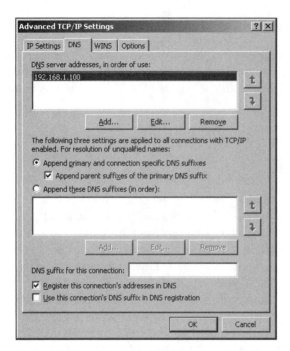

Figure 2-12   DNS tab of Advanced TCP/IP Settings

In contrast to the Append primary and connection specific DNS suffixes option, the Append these DNS suffixes option allows you to specify a list of DNS suffixes that will be appended when attempting to resolve hostnames. When the Append these DNS suffixes option is selected, only the suffixes that you enter are appended to hostnames—the primary DNS suffix and any connection-specific DNS suffixes are not automatically appended (although you can add them to the list manually).

Continuing with the example, say *DevFileSrv* is a member of the *development.supercorp.net* domain and has an FQDN of *DevFileSrv.development.supercorp.net*. Using the Append these DNS suffixes option, the list of DNS suffixes could be configured as in Figure 2-13. In this configuration, the client first asks a DNS server to resolve *DevFileSrv.research.supercorp.net,* then *DevFileSrv.supercorp.net,* and is finally successful when it tries *DevFileSrv.development.super corp.net.* Note that if you want to search parent subdomains, you must explicitly specify them (as shown in this example by having supercorp.net in the list)—they are not automatically tried like the primary DNS suffix.

This is actually not uncommon—one parent domain (supercorp.net) with two or more child domains (research.supercorp.net and development.supercorp.net). Because a client only attempts to append DNS suffixes based on its own primary DNS suffix, by default it may become necessary for you to manually specify (or use DHCP) a list of DNS suffixes. Alternatively, you could always use FQDNs instead of hostnames when attempting to access resources.

2

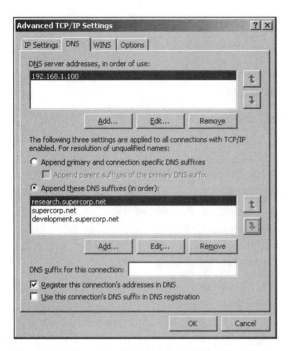

Figure 2-13   Specifying a list of DNS suffixes

NOTE

The above example regarding DevFileSrv assumes the computer attempting to access the list of shares (that is, the client) is running Windows 2000, Windows Server 2003, or Windows XP Professional. However, keep in mind that the steps to modify DNS suffixes are written and tested only for Windows Server 2003 and may be slightly different for Windows 2000 and Windows XP.

INSTALL AND CONFIGURE DNS FOR ACTIVE DIRECTORY

Active Directory requires a much deeper understanding of DNS issues than do older Windows server products. With Windows NT networks, all that was required was the ability for a client to find a working name server to surf the Web, and perhaps an A or MX record for inbound mail or Web services. In many cases, these services were provided by the company's ISP, and were rarely changed.

The release of Windows 2000 and Active Directory altered the picture considerably. A solid DNS is an essential foundation for a proper Active Directory deployment. Windows 2000 and Windows XP clients rely on DNS for name resolution within the LAN as well as on the Internet. These clients can also dynamically update their own resource records in DNS.

There are three essential functions of DNS that affect Active Directory:

- Defining the namespace
- Locating services
- Resolving names to IP addresses

After covering these functions, Microsoft DNS Server installation in Windows Server 2003 is discussed.

Defining the Namespace

Active Directory domains use the same namespace as DNS. This does not mean that an Active Directory domain and a DNS domain are equal, but it does mean that they use the same hierarchical system. There is a one-to-one relationship between Active Directory domains and DNS domains. Because selecting a name is an important step, Chapter 5 will cover the selection of a namespace in more detail.

Locating Services

The netlogon service running on a domain controller is responsible for registering a number of records in DNS, as long as the DNS servers support dynamic updates. If the DNS server does not support Dynamic DNS (DDNS), then an administrator must make the entries manually. Each domain controller registers an A record for the name of the domain. This allows a client to resolve the name of the domain (for example, mydomain.mycorp.com) to an IP address, making that IP address the address of a domain controller. Usually, an A record links a host or machine to a specific IP number, but in this case it allows the domain to be resolved without a hostname. Because a domain normally has several domain controllers, the name of the domain will resolve to several IP addresses, each representing a domain controller.

In addition to this A record, Active Directory clients make extensive use of a comparatively new type of RR called a **service locator (SRV) record**. An SRV record allows a client to send a DNS query specifying the type of service that it is looking for, and the DNS server will return the name of a computer providing that service. SRV records are created to allow clients to locate a domain controller in a particular domain, a domain controller in a particular site in a particular domain, the domain controller acting as the PDC Emulator for a particular domain, a Global Catalog server for a forest, or a particular domain controller based on its own unique identifier.

SRV records are also created to assist clients in the Kerberos authentication process, the Kerberos password-changing process, and general Lightweight Directory Access Protocol (LDAP) lookups. (Kerberos is discussed in detail in Chapter 9.) Although DNS would support these records as they point to any hosts, in practice, it is rare that they point to anything other than a Windows Active Directory domain controller. When a server is acting as a Windows Active Directory domain controller, its netlogon service will create numerous SRV records, and some A records.

When a client computer running Windows 2000, Windows Server 2003, or Windows XP software needs to use one of these services, perhaps during the logon process or to search the global catalog, the system first tries to locate the desired resource using a DNS query. The client issues a DNS query for the appropriate SRV record. For example, to find a Global Catalog in the default site of the supercorp.net forest, a query is issued for an SRV record matching _gc._tcp.Default-First-Site-Name._sites.supercorp.net. After looking up the SRV record, the client could look up the address record for the host named in the SRV record, but to avoid another round-trip, the DNS server usually returns the IP address as well, though only the name is stored in the SRV record.

To support pre-Windows 2000 configurations, these clients can try NetBIOS name resolution, but if your DNS configuration is wrong, Active Directory will not function properly and a host of problems may become evident.

Resolving Names to IP Addresses

As with any host on the Internet, clients participating in an Active Directory domain will use DNS to resolve host names to IP addresses. In addition to traditional Internet use, the process extends to hosts on the internal LAN as well as hosts on extranets or intranets. This name resolution follows the process discussed in the last section, although it is often the case that the first name server queried will have information about the target subdomains without having to go back to the root servers.

Installing Microsoft DNS Server in Windows Server 2003

Any DNS server software that supports the functions required by Active Directory can be used. It is sometimes believed that only Microsoft DNS can be used with Microsoft Active Directory, but this is not the case. You can use recent versions of BIND under UNIX or Windows, as well as other third-party servers. If you choose to use a different DNS server, it must support SRV records, and it is recommended that you use a server that supports incremental zone transfers and dynamic updates. In the BIND product, for example, version 4.9.7 is the oldest tested and supported version; however, version 8.2.2 or newer is recommended.

The Microsoft DNS server that ships with all versions of the Windows Server 2003 family was specifically designed to support the needs of Active Directory. It can handle a large workload and is much easier to administer than most third-party software, including BIND. The advantage to using the Microsoft DNS server is its ability to store zone data in Active Directory. Under Windows 2000, DNS information was stored in the domain directory partition, but with the Windows Server 2003 family, zone data can be stored in an application partition, allowing more flexibility regarding which domain controllers can be DNS name servers for which zones. (Active Directory partitions are discussed in detail in Chapter 4.) Zones stored in Active Directory are called **Active Directory integrated zones**, not primary or secondary zones. The Microsoft DNS server can run on any Windows Server 2003 family system, but only DNS servers running on domain controllers can use Active Directory integrated zones.

Storing zone data in Active Directory ensures that the DNS servers can handle zone transfers effectively. The Active Directory replication process makes a copy of the zone data available to all domain controllers running DNS. The zone data can be changed by sending a DDNS update to any DNS server or by using the DNS administrative tool for any of the DNS servers, and it will be automatically updated on the others.

During the installation of Active Directory, the installation wizard examines the computer's DNS settings and contacts the DNS servers. If it does not find an existing DNS server that supports SRV records, DDNS, and incremental transfers, it allows the installation of the DNS server components as part of the Active Directory domain controller creation, or allows the administrator to research and correct the error. The DNS server components can also be installed separately, either before or after promoting a machine to a domain controller, or on a machine that will not be a domain controller. In Activity 2-3, you will learn how to manually install the Microsoft DNS Server Service. You will then learn how to configure your DNS server to forward name resolution requests to another DNS server in Activity 2-4.

ACTIVITY

Activity 2-3: Installing the Microsoft DNS Server Service

Time Required: 10 minutes

Objective: To install the Microsoft DNS Server Service on a Windows Server 2003 computer.

Description: The Microsoft DNS Server Service provides a full-featured DNS server for use on Windows-based platforms, including the Windows Server 2003 family. You will now install the service on your computer so that it can function as a DNS server on the network. You could use third-party software, such as BIND, but the Microsoft service included with Windows is simpler to operate and integrates with Active Directory.

1. If necessary, start your server and log on using the **AdminXX** account in the **CHILDXX** domain (where *XX* is the number of your server).

2. Click the **Start** menu, select **Control Panel**, and then click **Add or Remove Programs**.

3. Once the Add or Remove Programs window is displayed, click **Add/Remove Windows Components**.

4. Once the Windows Components Wizard is displayed, click **Networking Services** in the list box. (Do not click the check box; click the words themselves.)

5. Click **Details**.

6. Click the **Domain Name System (DNS)** check box as shown in Figure 2-14.

7. Click **OK** on the Networking Services window.

8. Click **Next** on the Windows Components Wizard window.

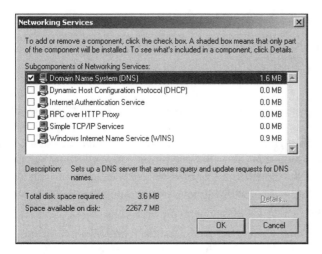

Figure 2-14   Networking Services window

9. Wait for the Windows Components Wizard to copy files and configure the system. If your classroom has been configured dynamically with DHCP, you will receive a warning and be given the opportunity to change the IP address. If this occurs, please consult your instructor. Additionally, you may be prompted for the Windows Server 2003 CD in order to copy files from it. If prompted for the CD, select the D:\Source\I386 folder, or use an alternate location if one is provided by your instructor.

10. Once the wizard is done copying files, click **Finish**.

11. Close the Add or Remove Programs window.

12. To confirm that the DNS Server Service has been installed on your server, click **Start**, select **Administrative Tools**, and then click **DNS**.

13. In the left tree pane, expand **SERVERXX** (where *XX* is your server number).

14. Expand both the **Forward Lookup Zones** and **Reverse Lookup Zones** folders and note names of any zones that appear.

NOTE

There should be at least one zone when you perform Step 14. If you do not see any zones, you may need to close the DNS console, wait a few minutes, and then reopen the console. It takes a small amount of time for the DNS records stored in Active Directory to replicate to your server. If you wish, you can complete Activity 2-4 and then check again.

15. Close the DNS console and log off your server if you do not intend to immediately continue to the next project. Otherwise, stay logged on.

ACTIVITY

Activity 2-4: Configuring Forwarders

Time Required: 10 minutes

Objective: To configure your DNS server to forward name resolution requests to another server.

Description: In an Active Directory network, it is very common to have child domains forward name resolution requests to parent DNS servers. When a DNS server is configured to forward requests, instead of trying to resolve names using the methods described earlier in this chapter, a DNS server forwards the name resolution request to another DNS server for any domains to which it is not authoritative or does not have any information cached. In this project, you will configure your DNS server to forward name resolution requests to the supercorp.net DNS server.

1. If necessary, start your server and log on using the **AdminXX** account in the **CHILDXX** domain (where *XX* is the number of your server).

2. Click **Start**, select **Administrative Tools**, and then click **DNS**. In the left tree pane, right-click **SERVERXX** (where *XX* is the number of your server) and click **Properties**.

3. In the SERVERXX Properties window, click the **Forwarders** tab.

4. In the DNS domain list box, make sure **All other DNS domains** is selected.

5. In the Selected domain's forwarder IP address list text box, enter **192.168.1.100**, which is the IP address of your instructor's server. Your instructor will inform you if the IP address you need to use is different.

6. Click **Add**. Your screen should look like Figure 2-15.

7. Click **OK**.

8. Close the DNS console and log off your server if you do not intend to immediately continue to the next project. Otherwise, stay logged on.

Each time you create a new domain, you have the option to create the DNS forward lookup zone ahead of time, or allow the Active Directory Installation Wizard to create the zone for you. In Activity 2-5, you will learn how to manually create a new DNS zone on your server to store DNS records for the childXX.supercorp.net subdomain.

In the last chapter when you promoted your server to a domain controller in a new domain, your server had its DNS server set to instructor.supercorp.net or 192.168.1.100. Because a zone for supercorp.net already existed on that DNS server, the Active Directory Installation Wizard used the existing zone and added an additional subdomain to the zone. While it is possible to store the DNS records for all zones on the DNS servers in the forest root domain, it's not practical or efficient in a large Active Directory forest. To solve this problem, you can move your subdomain from the supercorp.net DNS zone into a zone on the DNS server in your domain by using delegation. In Activity 2-6, you will learn how to delegate authority for the subdomain you create in Activity 2-5 to your DNS server. Finally, in Activity 2-7, you will configure your server to resolve FQDNs itself.

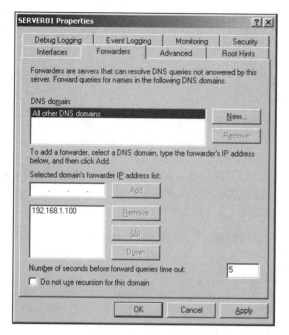

Figure 2-15 Setting up a DNS forwarder

NOTE While having to divide a DNS zone into multiple smaller zones is not the end of the world, it can effect network connectivity until domain controllers reregister their DNS records in the new DNS zone. Therefore, it is a good idea to plan out your DNS infrastructure before you start creating domains rather then reorganizing afterwards. Keep in mind that the following projects can also be used before you create an Active Directory domain.

Activity 2-5: Creating Zones on the DNS Server

Time Required: 10 minutes

Objective: To create a zone to hold the DNS records for your child domain.

Description: In the domain controller promotion process, you can allow the Active Directory Installation Wizard to create a zone automatically. However, you can also manually create the DNS zone before you promote the first domain controller in a new domain. In addition, if you want to reorganize your DNS structure, you must create the new zone or zones. Over the next several projects, you will see how to move a child domain's DNS records to a separate DNS zone. The first step in this process is creating the new zone on the child domain's DNS server(s).

1. If necessary, start your server and log on using the **AdminXX** account in the **CHILDXX** domain (where *XX* is the number of your server).

2. Click **Start**, select **Administrative Tools**, and then click **DNS**. If necessary, in the left tree pane, expand **SERVERXX** (where *XX* is the number of your server).

3. Right-click **Forward Lookup Zones** and click **New Zone**. The first window of the New Zone Wizard is displayed.

4. Click **Next**.

5. In the Zone Type window, ensure that the default option button **Primary zone** is selected and the **Store the zone in Active Directory** check box is checked.

6. Click **Next**.

7. In the Active Directory Zone Replication Scope window, leave the default option button, **To all domain controllers in the Active Directory domain child*XX*.supercorp.net**, selected. This places the DNS data in the child*XX*. supercorp.net domain directory partition of Active Directory.

8. Click **Next**.

9. In the Zone name text box, enter **child*XX*.supercorp.net** (where *XX* is the number of your server and child domain), and click **Next**.

10. In the Dynamic Update window, leave the default option button, **Allow only secure dynamic updates**, selected. Secure dynamic updates prevent unknown computers from registering and modifying records in DNS.

11. Click **Next**.

12. In the Completing the New Zone Wizard window, click **Finish**.

13. In the right pane of the DNS console, the new zone you have just created is displayed as shown in Figure 2-16.

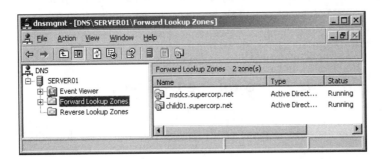

Figure 2-16   New zone created in DNS

14. Close the DNS console and log off your server.

Activity 2-6: Delegating DNS Authority for a Subdomain

Time Required: 10 minutes

Objective: To delegate the authority for your subdomain from the classroom DNS server instructor.supercorp.net to a DNS server running on your server.

2

Description: Once you have the subdomain created, you must delegate control of the subdomain to your DNS server. If the subdomain of your Active Directory domain is a second-level domain name, the domain registrar of the top-level domain will set up all the delegations that are necessary. However, if you have additional subdomains that are stored in different zones, you must add delegations to DNS that point the subdomain to the appropriate servers that are authoritative for the zone. In this project, you will add a delegation to the supercorp.net second-level domain that delegates the subdomain child*XX*.supercorp.net to your DNS server.

1. If necessary, start your server and log on using the **Administrator** account in the **SUPERCORP** domain.

2. Click **Start**, select **Administrative Tools**, and then click **DNS**. In the left tree pane, right-click **DNS** and then click **Connect to DNS Server**.

3. Select **The following computer** option button and enter **INSTRUCTOR** in the text box. Click **OK**.

4. Once the INSTRUCTOR DNS server is added to the DNS console, expand **INSTRUCTOR**, then expand **Forward Lookup Zones**, and then select **supercorp.net**. The details for the **supercorp.net** zone are shown in the right pane as shown in Figure 2-17.

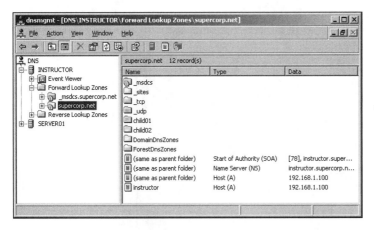

Figure 2-17   supercorp.net zone details

5. In the right pane, right-click **child*XX*** (where *XX* is the number of your server and child domain) and click **Delete**. Do *not* delete any other records or subdomains.

6. In the message box that asks if you are sure you want to delete child*XX*, click **Yes**. If the message box displays the wrong subdomain, click **No** and then repeat Step 5—ensuring you select the correct subdomain.

TIP If a subdomain already exists, you must delete the subdomain in the existing zone before you can create a delegation for that same subdomain in that same zone.

7. In the left tree pane, right-click **supercorp.net** and then click **New Delegation**.

8. When the New Delegation Wizard welcome message appears, click **Next**.

9. In the Delegated domain text box, enter **childXX** (where *XX* is the number of your server and child domain).

10. Click **Next**.

11. In the Name Servers window, click **Add**. This is where you add NS records for the DNS servers that are authoritative for the subdomain.

12. In the Server fully qualified domain name (FQDN) text box, enter **SERVERXX.childXX.supercorp.net** (where *XX* is the number of your server and child domain).

13. In the IP address text box, enter **192.168.1.XX** (where *XX* is your server's number—without any leading zeros—or an alternative number provided by your instructor), and click **Add**.

14. Click **OK** on the New Resource Record window. The DNS server you just added now appears in the **Name servers** list box as shown in Figure 2-18.

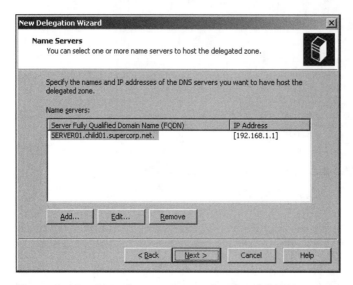

Figure 2-18   List of name servers for the child*XX*.supercorp.net subdomain

15. Click **Next**.

16. In the Completing the New Delegation Wizard window, click **Finish**. The new DNS delegation for the subdomain now appears in the left tree pane.

17. Close the DNS console and log off your server.

Activity 2-7: Configuring Your Server to Resolve DNS Itself

Time Required: 5 minutes

Objective: To configure your computer to use its own DNS Server Service to resolve DNS queries.

Description: Now that your computer has an installed, working, and configured DNS Server Service running, there is no need for queries from your own server to first go to another DNS server. This procedure will set your server to use its own DNS Server Service to resolve DNS queries.

1. If necessary, start your server and log on using the **AdminXX** account in the **CHILDXX** domain (where *XX* is the number of your server).

2. Click **Start**, select **Control Panel**, select **Network Connections**, and then click **Local Area Connection**.

3. In the Local Area Connection Status window, click **Properties**.

4. In the This connection uses the following items list box, select **Internet Protocol (TCP/IP)**. Be sure to select the text and not the check box.

5. Click **Properties**.

6. If the **Use the following DNS server addresses** option button is not selected, select it.

7. In the Preferred DNS server text box, enter **192.168.1.XX** (where *XX* is your server's number or an alternative number provided by your instructor). The Preferred DNS server and IP address should now match each other.

8. Click **OK**.

9. In the Local Area Connection Properties window, click **Close**.

10. In the Local Area Connection Status window, click **Close**.

11. Log off your server.

CHAPTER SUMMARY

- In a real-world environment, develop a complete plan and test it in an offline test or lab environment that is not connected to your live production network before starting the installation.

- NetBIOS is a flat name system that is provided in Windows Server 2003 for backwards compatibility with operating systems prior to Windows 2000.

- The Domain Name System (DNS) is a distributed, scalable, hierarchical system that provides name resolution services (lookup of IP numbers from names, or vice versa) for the Internet and private networks.

- DNS is defined by multivendor standards coordinated by the IETF.

- The DNS namespace is organized into divisions called domains and subdomains. The namespace hierarchy begins at the root domain, represented by a single period. The next level, containing top-level domains, consists of generic top-level domains and country-code top-level domains.

- TLDs are further divided into second-level domains. Most second-level domains are registered to companies, individuals, or organizations, and authority for those SLDs is delegated to servers maintained and operated by the registrants or their ISPs.

- Subdomains can be divided into more subdomains.

- DNS data is organized into resource records. Important RR types include address (A), name server (NS), start of authority (SOA), mail exchanger (MX), and service locator (SRV) records.

- RRs are grouped into zones. Zones include all of the information for a domain or subdomain that is not delegated to another name server. Zone data can be stored in text files, databases, the Windows registry, or Active Directory, depending on the DNS server software used.

- A common implementation of DNS server software is called BIND, which has become a de facto industry standard. With all operating systems in the Windows Server 2003 family, Microsoft supplies a DNS server that is well-suited to general use and to supporting Active Directory.

- A DNS name server that has zone data for a given subdomain is authoritative for that subdomain.

- Authority can be delegated from a TLD or subdomain to another name server.

- Names are resolved to IP addresses using either iterative or recursive queries. With a recursive query, the DNS server returns the best result it can find. With an iterative query, the DNS server only returns records for which it itself is authoritative, a referral to another name server, or a "not found" message.

- Configuration errors can occur in the DNS structure. This often prevents Active Directory from working properly.

❏ Active Directory uses DNS to define the namespace, to locate various services by using SRV records, and to look up IP numbers for FQDNs.

❏ A large number of SRV records are registered dynamically in DNS by the netlogon service on domain controllers. These SRV records are used by clients or other servers to locate particular domain services.

❏ The Microsoft DNS server can be installed from Windows 2003 server setup, from the control panel, or automatically during Active Directory installation.

Key Terms

Active Directory integrated zones — A DNS zone in which data is stored as objects in Active Directory. Available only on Microsoft DNS servers running on domain controllers.

address (A) record — An address (A) resource record maps a hostname to an IP address.

country code TLD (ccTLD) — A top-level domain assigned by ISO country codes on a geo-political basis, such as .us for the United States.

DNS namespace — The entire map of valid names in the domain name system.

Domain Name System (DNS) — A highly available, scalable, and dispersed system that provides name resolution on the Internet or private networks.

down-level client — Clients older than the current operating system that lack some functionality. Usually refers to Windows products released prior to Windows 2000.

Fully Qualified Domain Names (FQDN) — A host name that includes all parts necessary to resolve a name to an IP address from the host name to the root domain, including any subdomains or TLDs, such as myhost.mysubdomain.mycompany.com.

generic TLDs (gTLD) — A top-level DNS domain that is not assigned to a specific country, and is directly delegated by the root servers .aero, .biz, .com, .coop, .edu, .gov, .info, .int, .mil, .museum, .name, .net, .org, and .pro.

incremental zone transfer — A process whereby a secondary DNS server can request changes made only to zone data, not the entire zone.

mail exchanger (MX) record — A mail exchanger (MX) resource record specifies the host that can receive SMTP mail for the subdomain.

name server (NS) record — A name server (NS) resource record is used to delegate authority for a subdomain to another zone or server.

primary name server — The only DNS server where changes can be made to zone data.

reverse lookup — The process of looking up a host's FQDN using its IP address, which is the reverse of the normal process.

root domain — The top of the DNS hierarchy, which delegates authority for all TLDs.

secondary name server — An authoritative DNS server that has a read-only copy of zone data that has been transferred from a primary name server.

service locator (SRV) record — The service locator (SRV) resource record provides a method to locate servers offering specific services in specific sites by using the Domain Name System.

start of authority (SOA) records — A start of authority (SOA) resource record provides information about the zone data.

subdomain — A subdivision of a DNS domain name.

top-level domain (TLD) — A division of the DNS namespace that is divided directly off the root domain. It includes ccTLDs and gTLDs.

zone — A file or database containing DNS records for a subdomain.

zone transfer — The process by which a primary DNS server sends copies of the zone data to secondary DNS servers.

REVIEW QUESTIONS

1. A fully qualified domain name can resolve to more than one IP address in DNS. True or False?

2. Which statement is most accurate?

   a. Active Directory only works with BIND DNS servers.

   b. Active Directory only works with Microsoft DNS servers.

   c. Active Directory will not work with BIND servers before version 4.9.

   d. Active Directory can use NetBIOS name resolution if no DNS server is configured.

3. When resolving a name that Windows Server 2003 is unable to identify, which of the following will it do?

   a. First, attempt to use NetBIOS name resolution and then use DNS.

   b. First, attempt to use DNS name resolution and then use NetBIOS.

   c. Only use NetBIOS name resolution.

   d. Only use DNS name resolution.

4. When resolving a name that Windows NT 4.0 is unable to identify, which of the following will it do?

   a. First, attempt to use NetBIOS name resolution and then use DNS.

   b. First, attempt to use DNS name resolution and then use NetBIOS.

   c. Only use NetBIOS name resolution.

   d. Only use DNS name resolution.

5. The root domain of DNS is represented as which of the following?

   a. .local

   b. .root

   c. .com

   d. a period (.)

6. Which of the following is a valid FQDN?

   a. domain..com

   b. domain.com.

   c. domain!.com

   d. -domain.com

7. Which statement concerning ccTLDs is most accurate?

   a. A ccTLD can only be used by a host in a particular country.

   b. A ccTLD cannot be divided into subdomains.

   c. Policies regarding ccTLDs are set by the country concerned, and therefore vary.

   d. ccTLDs will not be used once all of the new gTLDs are established.

8. Anyone can register a subdomain in any TLD if they are willing to pay the prescribed fee. True or False?

9. A Windows domain and a DNS domain are exactly equal and synonymous. True or False?

10. A host called server1 belongs to Microsoft Corporation and is a member of the Windows domain referred to as Redmond. If we know that Redmond is a subdomain (or child domain) of ds.microsoft.com, then this machine's fully qualified domain name is most likely which of the following?

   a. redmond.microsoft.com

   b. server1.microsoft.com

   c. server1.ds.microsoft.com

   d. server1.redmond.ds.microsoft.com

11. The Microsoft DNS server offers choices for how zone data is stored, including zone files or which of the following?

   a. an application partition

   b. a system partition

   c. a DNS partition

   d. a data partition

12. If an authoritative server for a particular zone cannot find any entries for a particular host in that zone, which of the following will it do?

   a. return a random IP number

   b. return a result indicating failure

   c. send a recursive query to its own secondary servers

   d. send a recursive query to the root domain

13. It is not necessary to register your subdomain name with a public registrar under which of the following circumstances?

    a. when it is a subdomain of a TLD, such as .com or .us

    b. when you have a public Web site in that subdomain

    c. when your DNS server is behind a firewall

    d. when it is a subdomain of a private TLD, such as .private or .local

14. What reduces network traffic by transferring only changes to the zone data, not the entire zone?

    a. incremental zone transfer

    b. partial zone transfer

    c. change zone transfer

    d. complete zone transfer

15. Which of the following is the one DNS server in which changes are made for a particular zone and then propagated to other DNS servers.

    a. authoritative DNS server

    b. head DNS server

    c. primary DNS server

    d. top DNS server

16. A DNS server can be primary for one zone and secondary for another. True or False?

17. The default type of query issued by a client workstation locating a Web site is which of the following?

    a. automatic query

    b. recursive query

    c. iterative query

    d. destination query

18. Most DNS servers for TLDs and the root name servers accept recursive queries. True or False?

19. Every DNS lookup involves a trip to the root servers. True or False?

20. Active Directory creates a great number of which types of resource records in DNS to allow clients to locate domain controllers?

    a. server

    b. service

    c. section

    d. provider

CASE PROJECTS

Case Project 2-1: Name Resolution Nightmare

2

At Super Corp's Atlanta location, a problem has come to light. Most of the LAN clients use Windows 2000 Professional or Windows XP Professional, but about 10% use a variety of other operating systems. Recently, all DNS servers have been migrated from UNIX to Microsoft DNS, which run on three machines, each using Windows Server 2003 for their operating system. These machines are not domain controllers.

Although there are three DNS server machines, statistics show that almost all traffic is going to the host called DNS1, while DNS2 and DNS3 are practically idle. All three DNS servers have copies of the zone data. Everyone would like to see the load split more evenly among these three machines.

Why do you think this load is being handled by just one machine? What can you do to even it out?

Case Project 2-2: Not Resolving Names

After reconfiguring the clients in the Atlanta office, one large group of users reports that they can no longer access many Web sites. You suspect that one of the three DNS servers is configured incorrectly. So that you can troubleshoot the issue, the users experiencing the problem have provided you with the Web site addresses they can't access. What tool or tools could you use to determine which DNS server is causing the problem? How do you troubleshoot the issue?

Case Project 2-3: Finding Contacts

The IT manager for Super Corp has decided that he would like to obtain super.com for the company's Internet presence. He would like you to check if that domain name is already registered and if it is to find out who the administrative contact is.

How would you go about determining if a .com second-level domain has already been registered? If the name is registered, how can the administrative contact information be located? Who is currently the administrative contact for the super.com second-level domain?

3

ACTIVE DIRECTORY DESIGN PHILOSOPHY

> **After reading this chapter, you will be able to:**
> ♦ Choose an appropriate design philosophy
> ♦ Describe the roles of service owners and data owners
> ♦ Determine which individuals should be given access to Active Directory
> ♦ Make the proper Active Directory design decisions
> ♦ Understand the importance of a shared vision for an Active Directory design project

You may be surprised to find the term "philosophy" in a technical book, as many network administrators focus on the hands-on, practical work that pervades day-to-day operations. In this chapter, however, you will examine the bigger picture—how to approach a large-scale Active Directory project.

The approach taken by a design team or an individual designer is based on their design philosophy. As with most areas of work, individual viewpoints, team dynamics, and corporate attitudes all play a role in shaping the philosophy and thus the end result. This chapter discusses some of the elements of design philosophy and presents some issues that should be considered when choosing how to approach the project.

INTRODUCING DESIGN PHILOSOPHY

Active Directory has many roles to play as the directory service in a network. As discussed in Chapter 1, Active Directory is the primary directory service for the Windows Server 2003 operating system (OS), supporting security and routine network operations for large and small networks. Networking has evolved over the past few years, especially as more and more computers are connected to the Internet, wide area networks (WANs), and multiple local area networks (LANs). This level of interconnectivity leads to increased demands for all sorts of directory structures and directory services. Some of the roles for which organizations are deploying Active Directory include the following:

- The directory service for the operating system
- An enterprise-wide directory (of both people and resources)
- An e-mail directory (of internal users or external contacts)
- A "white pages" directory (external users looking up internal addresses)
- An e-commerce authentication system

The particular roles that Active Directory will be deployed to perform affects the design of that Active Directory structure. However, all deployments need to follow some sound Active Directory design principles. In Activity 3-1, you will gather information and identify how you can use Active Directory in an organization.

ACTIVITY

Activity 3-1: Identifying Roles for Active Directory

Time Required: 10 minutes

Objective: Identify ways that Active Directory can be used in an organization.

Description: In this activity, you will begin pulling together information from some of the case studies to see how each potential Active Directory deployment might differ. Also, Matt, the IT manager from Super Management Corporation, has set up an appointment to discuss the potential uses of Active Directory in the company. You may choose to complete this project individually, with a partner, or as a class group.

1. Prepare for your meeting by reviewing the information in the client's file (represented by the Case Projects in Chapters 1 and 2).

2. From the list of the roles preceding this activity, record the ones that would be well-suited to an Active Directory deployment at Super Management Corporation.

3. List any additional directory service functions or roles you believe the company will require.

Note that Active Directory is an infrastructure for a business enterprise, just like roads and bridges are for a transportation system, or water and pipes are for a city sewage system. Because of its nature as an essential infrastructure, Active Directory is involved in issues that cross many boundaries.

First, an Active Directory deployment crosses the boundary between technology and business. A good Active Directory deployment is unlikely to happen in an enterprise where the technical leadership (technicians, engineers, programmers, or analysts) can't speak the same language as the business management and executives.

Second, Active Directory also crosses boundaries between departments and divisions within an enterprise. If the decision is made to operate separate Active Directory forests in a properly designed, planned, and deployed environment, that decision should be made after consultation. A successful Active Directory design process requires conversations, consultations, and consensus between and among many parties in an enterprise. You first want to determine the key roles that departments, groups, or staff will play in the new Active Directory installation.

OWNERSHIP ROLES

Because of the way Active Directory crosses boundaries within the organization, it is often necessary to determine or define owners for parts of the directory. While every object in Active Directory has an **object owner**, a design team must also consider ownership on a much broader scale—including the sense of responsibility and accountability for the operation of the directory service and for the data that it contains. Microsoft documentation uses two terms to describe different types of ownership: **data owner** and **service owner**.

Data owners, also called object owners, are responsible for the contents of the directory. They create, modify, delete, and manage objects in the directory, such as users. The data owner may also be responsible for defining policies for the network they control. Active Directory supports this through the application of Group Policy. You will learn about Group Policy and its application in Chapter 10, but for now you should be aware that data owners are often well-positioned in their organization in order to determine how Group Policy should be applied to the objects they manage or own. In Activity 3-2, you will use organizational information to identify potential data owners.

Service owners, sometimes called directory owners or directory administrators, are responsible for the operation of the directory service itself. This role includes creating or removing domains, implementing changes to the schema, installing and managing domain controllers, creating the site topology, and monitoring the health of the domain controllers. In Activity 3-3, you will use organizational information to identify potential service owners.

As an example of how these roles might be played out in real life, consider a Human Resources (HR) Department that is the data owner for part or all of the Active Directory structure. In this role, HR staff members have been given permissions that allow them to create, delete, and modify the attributes of users. In other words, they are responsible for the contents—the information—in the directory. However, they are not the service owners. They do not have the ability to create new domains, to back up the directory, or to determine the location of domain controllers (these functions are performed by the staff of a central IT group).

Activity 3-2: Identifying Data Owners

Time Required: 10 minutes

Objective: Identify potential data owners for the Super Management Corporation Active Directory system.

Description: Matt from Super Corp has faxed over an organizational chart of the company. He noted that it is a bit dated, and that he heard significant growth is soon expected. In this activity, you will review this corporate information and consider possible role assignments. You may choose to complete this project individually, with a partner, or as a class group.

Examine the organizational chart in Figure 3-1. Think about who in the organization will be responsible for creating or deleting users, who will decide which resources a user is allowed to access, who will need to act immediately if an employee is terminated for cause, and who has the most vested interests in the people and resources represented by objects in Active Directory. Your instructor may play the role of the client, if you wish to clarify roles shown on the chart.

Remember that although users are probably the most common object, resources, groups, contacts, or other objects may need to be managed as well.

1. List any questions you might ask Matt to help determine potential data owners.

2. Identify and list prospective data owners.

Activity 3-3: Identifying Service Owners

Time Required: 10 minutes

Objective: Identify potential service owners for the Super Management Corporation Active Directory system.

Description: Matt also faxed a block diagram of Super Corp's network. In this activity, you will review corporate information about the computers and networks at the company and consider possible role assignments. You may choose to complete this project individually, with a partner, or as a class group.

1. Examine the block diagram of the Super Management Corporation network, as shown in Figure 3-2.

2. Review the diagrams and the other information you have about the company.

3. List any additional questions you might ask Matt to help determine potential service owners.

4. Identify and list prospective service owners.

This division of ownership between those who own the data and those who own the infrastructure is a key concept in the forest and domain design in a Microsoft Active Directory network. Microsoft promotes the use of this **split administration model**, which

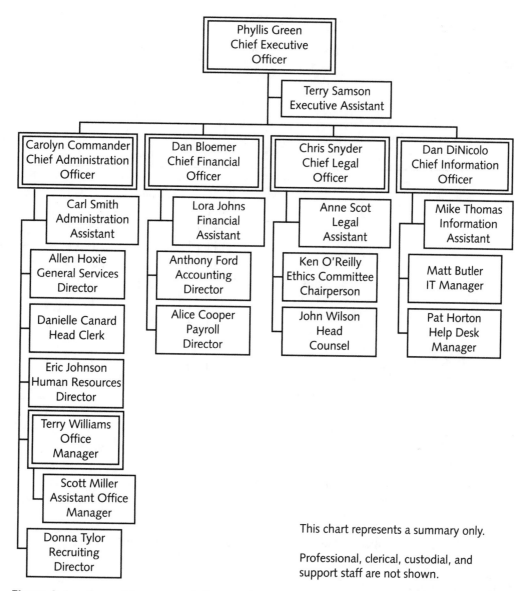

Figure 3-1   Super Management Corporation organizational chart

leverages granular security settings in Active Directory to allow people to do their jobs without giving them more authority than they need. It can also help you avoid arguments and allow the design team to come to a consensus quicker, because data owners don't need to give up ownership and control of "their" data. It also allows more flexibility than the Windows NT domain model, in which being an administrator was much more of an all-or-nothing proposition.

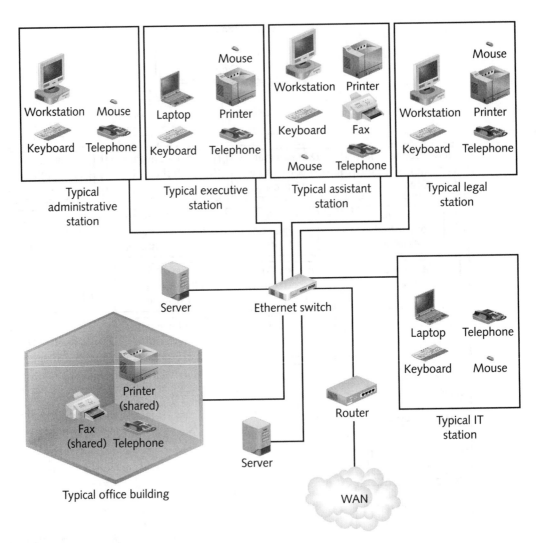

Figure 3-2   Super Management Corporation computer systems

A QUESTION OF TRUST

In today's world, the security of a company's computers and the information they contain is crucial. Administrators are constantly receiving updates and newsletters filled with descriptions of denial-of-service attacks, virus outbreaks, malicious actions by users, and security breaches resulting from security gaps that should have been closed. It is very important that all of your design decisions—from the first idea through to final implementation—give consideration to security.

3

Throughout any discussion of Active Directory design, the word "trust" appears in its normal definition as well as in the context of how credentials from one domain or forest can be used in another (trusts are discussed in Chapter 5). When you set up a technical trust, you should also trust the person or organization in the traditional sense. It is good practice to allow computers and networks to trust each other when the people involved also trust each other.

Any administrator of a domain controller or anyone who is given membership to the administrative groups of a domain or a forest is being explicitly trusted with very valuable assets of the enterprise. A domain controller often stores information from other domains (in the configuration partition or in the global catalog), and it might be possible for an unscrupulous (but highly skilled) administrator to misuse this information or to attack the network from within the organization.

Microsoft wrote about one such possibility in its Knowledge Base article 289243, which stated: "Exploiting this vulnerability would be a challenge. At a minimum, an attacker would need administrative privileges on the trusted domain, and the technical wherewithal to modify low-level operating system functions and data structures." In other words, this scenario is unlikely and difficult, but still possible.

Finally, remember that anyone who can gain physical control of a domain controller can eventually compromise it. Part of your Active Directory planning should include proper physical security of domain controllers. When considering physical security, don't neglect servers, especially domain controllers in remote sites where building security may not be as obvious and the servers may not be in a dedicated computer room.

MAKING ACTIVE DIRECTORY DESIGN DECISIONS

A joke circulating among trainers who teach Active Directory courses states that no matter what the question, the only correct answer to any Active Directory design question is "It depends." There is so much variation between one Active Directory deployment and the next that it is sometimes a formidable task to even get started. With so many variables, options, and possibilities, how can a stable and reliable Active Directory structure ever emerge?

Active Directory design is the process of creating a structure around the objects to be stored in the Active Directory database. Your first step is to realize that it is a process, not a one-size-fits-all answer. Because each organization is different, each Active Directory deployment is also different, and each design team must consider the following issues.

Design to Support the Organization's Goals

First and foremost, the design of an enterprise's directory service needs to support the goals of the organization. What does the organization want to accomplish by using Active Directory (or, for that matter, any other directory service)? A for-profit company, by definition, has the ultimate goal of making money. But each business chooses its own way of being profitable and its own way of doing business. In most large companies, business goals are already defined; however, in small businesses, they may need to be discussed or documented before planning the Active Directory structure.

When Active Directory is used in government, military, educational, or nonprofit settings, the goals may not always be as clear, and they may be very different than those pursued by a for-profit organization. In either case, it is essential to determine the organization's business goals so that the directory can support them, not hinder them. Any large organization will have many people and many departments or divisions, some of which will have conflicting goals. As the design team works to achieve a common vision, trade-offs are likely, even if the goals are defined. If the goals have never been defined, chaos can easily ensue.

Gaining Executive Sponsorship with Documented Value

Early on in the project, and throughout its life, executive management should be involved. This ensures that business goals are well represented and avoids a waste of resources by making sure that the power exists to see that the resulting design is implemented. To gain executive sponsorship and justify the costs that will be incurred for planning, testing, and employment, you must be able to identify the value of Active Directory to the executives within your organization (see Activity 3-4). To reach a consensus, you may need to show the value of the design in concrete terms.

ACTIVITY

Activity 3-4: Identifying Executives Who Can Sponsor the Project

Time Required: 10 minutes

Objective: Emphasize the importance of gaining the support of senior management within the organization.

Description: In this activity, you will review the organizational chart for Super Management Corporation and consider which executives need to sponsor the project to ensure its success. You may choose to complete this project individually, with a partner, or as a class group.

1. Refer back to Figure 3-1 to identify the key members of the executive and management levels.

2. Identify and list some of the potential managers and executives who need to be involved in the Active Directory deployment project.

3. Prepare a brief explanation for each of your choices, including any assumptions you made.

Designing for the Future and the Present

An Active Directory design should have long-term value and validity. The right choices for DNS names, the number of forests and domains, and the organizational unit structure (each discussed in Chapter 5) are driven by the organization's current needs, as well as what its future needs might be. For example, is your organization expected to grow by acquisition? Does your company work intimately with a partner agency on a project basis that changes from month to month? Are your company's organizational charts redrawn as a quarterly exercise? Is the number of staff expected to change significantly? Using Activity 3-5 as a guide, consider these kinds of questions as you design your Active Directory deployment.

Activity 3-5: Considering Corporate Change

Time Required: 10 minutes

Objective: Understand the need to include the known and predictable future in your design plans.

Description: Matt just called to tell you that Super Management Corporation will eventually be merging with another project management company, creating a much larger organization. He does not yet have all the details, but felt that it might affect the Active Directory plans. In this activity, you will act on information provided by Super Management Corporation and consider the impact of future plans on your design vision. You may choose to complete this project individually, with a partner, or as a class group.

1. Consider this new information and list or state how the amalgamation might affect the recommendations made during earlier activities.

2. State whether you believe this would be a reason to put the project on hold.

3. If the project will not be put on hold, identify any added elements or constraints created by this new information.

Designing to Support the Delegation of Authority

One of the strengths of Active Directory is its ability to delegate authority and permissions on a granular basis. When combined with the ability to separate ownership of data from ownership of service, it becomes very powerful.

You should make design choices that support the ability to delegate authority. This means that services and service owners should most often be grouped together, while resources owned (or managed) by the same people should probably be placed in the same organizational unit or domain in Active Directory. Delegation of authority and permissions are discussed in Chapter 9.

Designing to Support the Application of Group Policy

Group Policy allows an organization to define rules or policies and allows the system to enforce them automatically. Group Policy can also be used to distribute software or lock down systems. A good Active Directory design groups objects so that they are subject to the same policies in the same organizational unit. For example, if all of the desktops in the Finance Department must log on using smart cards for security purposes, it makes sense to locate the computer objects representing the finance computers in one organizational unit. An Active Directory design that doesn't consider Group Policy makes administration more complex, requires the needless duplication of Group Policy objects (GPOs), and may result in longer logon times as inefficient policies are processed.

Parts of your organization with similar policy needs should be grouped together in your Active Directory design. Why? Because doing so allows you to administer one (or a few) GPOs that apply to one organizational unit, rather than managing several GPOs scattered throughout the forest.

The application of Group Policy becomes particularly relevant as choices regarding organizational units are made, because Group Policy Objects can only be linked to a domain, a site, or an organizational unit.

 In Chapter 11, the role of Group Policy is examined in detail.

NOTE

Justifying the Design

Every forest, every domain, and every organizational unit in a proposed design should serve a particular purpose. Do not create these structures just for the sake of doing so. Do not even create them to fill in the organizational chart. Some designs are based on geography (continents, regions, even cities); some designs are based on the administrative organization of an enterprise (departments, divisions); and others are based on a functional model (what people do in their jobs, regardless of which part of the organization they work in). None of these models are wrong, but none of them are necessarily right either. What makes them correct is that the design team has considered the issues and is able to justify why the choice was made in terms of value, business goals, and business requirements.

STARTING A DESIGN PROJECT

Sometimes the terminology surrounding a project or deployment can be confusing. Different schools of thought will also use different terms that mean essentially the same thing. Many companies have established processes or frameworks that they use consistently. This is more likely to be the case in large organizations with well-established, central IT

Departments. Other companies, especially small ones, may not have any guidelines. Regardless of the size of the company for which you are working, resist the urge to just jump in and start changing configurations and installing software. Instead, rely on a disciplined, logical approach to apply a consistent design philosophy.

Over the past few years, Microsoft has examined the long-standing processes used by successful IT firms to manage change or projects. Microsoft combined this wisdom and documented it in models—or frameworks—that its customers can use to increase their success rate while lowering costs. Other companies publish similar frameworks, and your company may already use one of them. Some adventurous companies have established their own framework through years of developing policy and procedures.

Two of the most common frameworks are the **Microsoft Solutions Framework (MSF)** and the **Microsoft Operations Framework (MOF)**. MSF is suited to the creation of new software or a new computer infrastructure. MOF is suited to the day-to-day operations of complex computer systems. The larger the organization, the more value is brought by using these formally defined processes.

Microsoft Solutions Framework (MSF)

MSF is ideally suited to the business of creating and publishing software. A project managed with the philosophy of MSF goes through a number of stages leading to a product's release. The common MSF stages are envisioning, planning, developing, stabilizing, and deploying. Older versions of the MSF model may combine stabilizing and deploying. These five stages can also be applied to an Active Directory project. The following sections outline how each stage can be applied to such a project.

Envisioning Phase

To begin, the project needs a vision and scope. This is the stage in which a project team is assembled and definition of common goals based on business objectives is achieved. Risks and specific requirements should also be identified. You will learn more about the envisioning phase in the next section of this chapter.

Planning Phase

Next, you need to create a detailed plan of exactly what the resulting Active Directory structure will look like, starting with the vision. While the vision has broad goals, now is the time to generate specifics. The planning phase ends with the creation of a document called the **functional specification**, which contains detailed, low-level specifications and a project schedule.

Developing Phase

The developing phase takes the results of planning—the functional specification—and creates the components required to make it a reality. In a software project, this is where the coders do a great deal of work. However in a project like an Active Directory deployment, the code is already written. Despite this, domain controllers probably need to be purchased and configured, and depending on the complexity of the installation, some customization or third-party add-ons may need to be developed or purchased. Testing is usually extensive during the developing phase, although "proof-of-concept" tests may be done as part of the planning stage (or even earlier), and testing may also continue into the stabilizing phase, especially if pilot projects are used.

Stabilizing Phase

While testing may continue into this phase, the key difference between developing and stabilizing is that the features of the product (in the case of software) or the details of the design (in the case of a project like Active Directory) are complete. For example, in the case of an Active Directory project, any changes to be made to the schema are known and finalized. At the end of this phase, the project is deemed ready for use, and control of the new project moves from the designers and builders to those who will operate and support it.

Deploying Phase

At long last you are ready to deploy the system. Your project goes into full production status, and the organization starts reaping the benefits. There may be some overlap between phases, particularly if you already have a live network and are migrating to a new Active Directory environment.

NOTE Active Directory does not always fit precisely into the MSF process, but many organizations are familiar with MSF and choose to use it—perhaps modified slightly—to lend the needed structure and discipline to creating their Active Directory deployment. MSF is designed to be flexible, allowing organizations to use the parts of the model that assist them.

TIP The Microsoft Windows Server 2003 Deployment Kit contains detailed deployment and technical resources for deploying Windows Server 2003. The kit's guidelines and recommended processes for deploying Windows Server 2003 are based on the Microsoft Solutions Framework. To download the Windows Server 2003 Deployment Kit, visit the Windows Server 2003 section of the Microsoft Web site at: *www.microsoft.com/windows2003* and then see the technical resources section.

Microsoft Operations Framework (MOF)

While MSF is designed around the creation of software, MOF is designed around the operation of the IT infrastructure. MOF consists of a series of guidelines, **best practices**, and how-to guides that maximize the availability and performance of a network and its components. In short, MSF deals with the creation of new software and new systems, while MOF deals with the effective management of existing systems, particularly core Microsoft enterprise offerings.

A detailed analysis of MOF and MSF is outside the scope of this book, and outside the published exam objectives of the Microsoft Certification Exams on Active Directory. However, it will benefit you to be familiar with some of their terms and concepts.

3

THE NEED FOR A VISION

Before leaving the topic of design philosophy, consider some of the specifics of what should occur in the envisioning stage. The choices made early in a project—that is, those that are largely governed by the design philosophy—have lasting impact throughout the deployment process and the life of the directory service.

At the beginning of an Active Directory project, the designer and other project team members should gain a shared vision of the end result. It is important that all key stakeholders have the same goals for the big picture. Who are the key stakeholders? How are they represented? That will, of course, depend on the organization. Some stakeholders can include:

- Executive management, owners, or shareholders

- Functional management, especially those responsible for the people and budget being used to implement the project

- Employees (including managers), especially those whose jobs will change as a result of the project

- The IT Department, especially if it will be the service owner and responsible for making sure the system runs reliably

- Customers or the public, especially in government projects or in projects that involve systems interacting directly with customers

The relative importance of each of these stakeholders can only be considered along with the business goals of the organization. The ideal is for your Active Directory system to help an organization reach its business goals.

Business goals are as varied as the organizations that use computers. A business is ultimately concerned with profit—creating value for owners and shareholders. Therefore, most for-profit organizations have business goals centered on lowering costs, increasing profits, and serving customers in faster or better ways. The stakeholders will want to see a return on investment (ROI) for the project, including the time spent planning and testing.

Even nonprofit organizations have business goals. Most organizations of this type have a burning desire to make a difference. Their stakeholders might be any number of groups from the disadvantaged to the alumni of a prestigious college. Instead of owners, stakeholders may worry about donors, and making sure that the money given to them is not wasted. Planning and testing is not wasting money.

In the government sector, stakeholders might include politicians and the public that elects them. The pressure for accountability and to stretch every dollar to its furthest is no less in government than in business.

In addition to identifying the stakeholders as a broad group, the owners of the project must also be identified at the beginning of a project. In other words, everyone involved must know who is responsible for the project. Rarely is a project completed by only one or two people; there is usually a project team. The best teams include representation from all of the relevant stakeholders. Outside help, such as contractors or consultants, may also be part of an Active Directory project team. As the team is being put together, it is important to ensure the following:

- Business goals have been defined and communicated to the design team.

- Everyone on the design team has an awareness of the "big picture" and the design philosophy, even if they will only be working on a small part of the project.

- The design team understands the ownership roles of both services and data, and key data owners are either members of the design team or are regularly involved in conversations.

- The role of Active Directory as infrastructure is understood by the design team and key contacts.

- Executive management is either actively represented on the team, or is supportive, involved, and sponsoring the project.

Activity 3-6: Building the Team

Time Required: 10 minutes

Objective: Identify project team members and practice assembling a project team.

Description: In this activity, you will review the Super Management Corporation information and consider who should be included on a project team. You will need to look back at the information provided in Figures 3-1 and 3-2, and consider your earlier decisions. You may be instructed to complete this project individually, with a partner, or as a class group.

1. Refer back to Figures 3-1 and 3-2 and the earlier Super Management Corporation activities.

2. Identify and list potential project team members, keeping in mind the following:

   - Who did you identify as data owners, and should they be included on the project team?

   - Who did you identify as service owners, and should they be included on the project team?

   - Who did you identify as potential executive sponsors? What would you expect their involvement to be?

- Are there other key stakeholders? Should they be represented on the team?

- Does Super Corp have internal staff with adequate experience to successfully complete a project like this? If so, who do you see filling the role of project owner? If not, how could you address the situation?

3. Prepare a list of your team and a brief explanation of its composition. Be prepared to present your team's makeup to your partner and your instructor, and to discuss your choices.

CHAPTER SUMMARY

- Active Directory can play many different roles in modern networks. The type of role that is chosen will affect the design, but all design projects should follow sound principles.

- Active Directory is an infrastructure, and because of its importance to the entire organization, design issues cut across political and departmental boundaries. The design team should be broadly based and seek consensus by collaboration and conversation with all key stakeholders.

- Active Directory allows networks to be managed with a split administrative style that divides data ownership from service ownership.

- Data owners are responsible for the contents of the directory. They create, modify, delete, and manage objects in the directory, such as users.

- Service owners are responsible for the operation of the directory service itself, including domain controllers.

- When you set up a trust relationship between forests (or to a Windows NT domain), you are also trusting a person or an organization and letting them into parts of your network. Therefore, careful consideration should always be given so that this trust is not misplaced.

- Any administrator in a domain or forest is being trusted with the valuable assets of the enterprise. The enterprise should have full confidence in the trustworthiness of its network administrators.

- Domain controllers should always be physically secured.

- Active Directory design is the process of creating a structure around the objects to be stored in the Active Directory database. It is a process, not a one-size-fits-all answer.

- Active Directory design decisions should be based on defined business goals or requirements.

- Executive management should be involved with and sponsoring the Active Directory design project. This may require documentation of the value of Active Directory to the company.

- A good Active Directory design allows for growth and reasonable amounts of change in the business.

❏ A good Active Directory design supports delegation of control to data owners and the application of Group Policy in a logical, consistent way.

❏ The design team or architect should be able to justify design decisions and trade-offs in terms of value, business goals, and business requirements.

❏ Documenting the value of Active Directory in business terms helps in gaining executive support.

❏ Microsoft recommends following a philosophy called the Microsoft Solutions Framework (MSF) for project management during development of new software or network infrastructure. A project using MSF has five stages: envisioning, planning, developing, stabilizing, and deploying.

❏ Microsoft also publishes a framework called the Microsoft Operations Framework (MOF) to promote high-availability operations of network infrastructure.

❏ During the envisioning stage, a project team is created and a common vision is built around business goals and the needs of stakeholders.

KEY TERMS

best practices — A preferred way of doing something, defined either by an authority or by common practice in well-run companies.

data owner — A person or team responsible for managing the content of a part of the directory, not maintaining the directory service itself. Data owners usually create objects and edit their attributes.

functional specification — The document created at the end of the planning stage that describes the Active Directory design.

Microsoft Operations Framework (MOF) — A set of documents, guidelines, and models developed by Microsoft to help companies increase reliability, availability, and ease of management and support. MOF provides guidance for the operation of systems, particularly Microsoft infrastructure systems in large enterprises. Visit *www.microsoft.com/mof*.

Microsoft Solutions Framework (MSF) — A set of documents, guidelines, and models developed by Microsoft to help companies improve the effectiveness of software or infrastructure development projects. Visit *www.microsoft.com/msf*.

object owner — Specifically, each object in the directory has an identified owner. More generically, sometimes used to mean data owner.

service owner — A person or team responsible for maintaining and operating the directory service as a whole. The service owner manages domain controllers and the site structure.

split administration model — The concept that service ownership and data ownership can be divided.

REVIEW QUESTIONS

1. The _____ owner is responsible for the proper operation of the directory service system.

2. The _____ owner is responsible for the content of the directory, such as creating new users.

3. Active Directory can be used as a public e-mail directory to allow your clients to find staff e-mail addresses on a Web page. True or False?

4. In which of the following roles can Active Directory be found? (Choose all that apply.)
   a. Enterprise-wide directory (of people and resources)
   b. E-mail directory (of internal users or external contacts)
   c. White pages directory (external users looking up internal addresses)
   d. E-commerce authentication and authorization

5. No matter in what role Active Directory is used, all Active Directory designs use the same domain structures. True or False?

6. The deployment of Active Directory is a technological issue only of concern to technologists, such as the IT Department. True or False?

7. Active Directory is part of your company's network _____ , just like water and pipes are part of a city's sewer system.

8. Put the following in the order they would occur under the Microsoft Solutions Framework philosophy of deployment.
   a. The functional specification is complete.
   b. The first domain controller running Active Directory is installed on the live production network.
   c. The envisioning phase begins.
   d. The planning stage begins.

9. Each object in the Active Directory database has an object _____ .

10. An Active Directory design should be forward-thinking enough to allow for _____ in the enterprise or business environment.

11. The division between service owners and data owners is called the _____ .

12. Which person or team would install and configure a new domain controller?
   a. Service owner
   b. Data owner
   c. Either
   d. Neither

13. You should always plan to create trusts between your forest and those in all subsidiaries or other departments of your company. True or False?

14. Which statement is most correct?

    a. Executive management should become involved as soon as the functional specification is complete.

    b. Documenting the value of Active Directory in business terms helps in gaining executive support.

    c. Executive management does not need to be involved in the planning process.

    d. Executive management is the best choice for the service owner role.

15. How does projected future growth in your company affect the Active Directory design process? Choose the best response:

    a. Designs should be reevaluated every six months.

    b. Additional forests should be created if the company grows by more than 10%.

    c. The designs should be forward-thinking enough to allow for predictable change.

    d. It is impossible to predict the future, so designs reflect the current needs only.

16. Should every department or division shown on the organizational chart have its own organizational unit in Active Directory?

    a. Always

    b. Never

    c. Only when doing so is warranted by data ownership roles

    d. Only if the department or division is a service owner

17. Nonprofit agencies and for-profit businesses may both use Active Directory to help accomplish their unique business or organizational goals. True or False?

18. Delegation of _____ means that data owners can be given permissions to manage their own objects in the directory.

19. A good design supports the logical application of _____ to enforce rules or policies defined by the organization.

20. MSF is used to manage projects that develop new software or new infrastructure, while following the procedures in the _____ may help maximize the availability of your infrastructure.

CASE PROJECTS

For the following case projects, you will be in the role of a consultant working for Super Management Corporation, the fictitious company introduced in Chapter 1. As your knowledge of Active Directory grows, your employer is calling on you to provide input into Active Directory situations arising with customers.

Case Project 3-1: Identifying Service and Data Owners

Consider a company that has about 1,000 staff members, with qualified and competent people working in both the Human Resources (HR) and Information Technology (IT) departments. Currently, IT maintains an Active Directory forest for the company. The IT staff creates and deletes users in the directory on receipt of written instructions (by memo) from the HR Department. The instructions from HR are not reviewed or questioned. The company would like to find a way to reduce the delay sometimes caused by this process.

Describe how the roles of data owner and service owner might apply in this situation.

Case Project 3-2: Negotiating on Cross-departmental Issues

You have been asked to coordinate a design team working on a new Active Directory forest plan for a legal services firm. In early meetings, there is resistance from the HR Division and the Commercial Litigation Division, neither of which have participated in a central directory service before. HR is concerned that it will have to spend a lot of time and effort chasing down information and coordinating with the IT Department when people are hired and fired. The Commercial Litigation lawyers do not want to put their file server in the forest, because they do not want the "busybodies in the Real Estate Division nosing about" in their confidential files.

What roles and concerns do you see being played out here? What are some possible solutions?

Case Project 3-3: Working with a Customer

You have been asked to install a domain controller for a new client, a mid-sized hotel in the same city as your office. When you arrive on site, they show you the domain controller computer and tell you that they would like to have their new domain working by the end of the day. With a quick, "We'll leave you to it, then!" they leave you alone in the equipment room. In what stage of the design project do you think this firm is currently? How would you proceed?

4

ACTIVE DIRECTORY ARCHITECTURE

After reading this chapter, you will be able to:

♦ Describe the underlying database of Active Directory

♦ Describe the Active Directory schema and how it can be extended

♦ Describe the different Active Directory partitions and their functions

In the last chapter, you learned about choosing a design philosophy and how to build a team for an Active Directory deployment project. While it is important to be able to take a step back and look at a deployment in abstract terms, you must also have a deep technical understanding of Active Directory in order to perform a successful deployment project. This chapter focuses on the architecture of Active Directory—what's going on under the hood.

To fully understand the underlying architecture of Active Directory, you need to be part network engineer, part database administrator, and part programmer. The topics you will learn about in this chapter include the underlying database used to store the directory, the schema that describes the objects that you can create in the directory, and the different partitions that are used to break Active Directory into separate pieces.

ACTIVE DIRECTORY PHYSICAL DATABASE STORAGE

At its core, Active Directory is made up of several layers, which together provide the directory service. The layers include the **Extensible Storage Engine (ESE)**, the **Database layer**, and the **Directory Service Agent (DSA)**. Additional components, such as LDAP, that run on top of these three layers provide communication to other services. The division of these functional layers is shown in Figure 4-1.

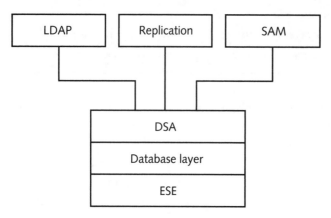

Figure 4-1   Active Directory layers

The Extensible Storage Engine is at the lowest level and is directly responsible for manipulating the database files—known as the **Active Directory store**—that hold the objects in Active Directory. At this layer, all objects are stored in nonhierarchical form as rows in a database table—allowing the object hierarchy to be abstracted from the actual storage. While the ESE deals with objects in a nonhierarchical form, it is the Database layer's responsibility to provide an object-oriented hierarchical view of the objects contained in the Active Directory store. Because the Database layer is a set of unpublished application programming interfaces (APIs), it is not discussed further in this chapter.

The Directory Service Agent is the third layer and is responsible for enforcing the semantics—or "the rules"—that govern how objects in Active Directory are created and manipulated. For example, the DSA is responsible for ensuring that an object has all the required attributes when it is created, or that writing to a given attribute does not exceed the attribute's maximum length. The rules that the DSA follows are defined in the Active Directory schema, which is covered in more detail later in this chapter.

Keep in mind that only the adjacent layers communicate with one another. That is, the ESE is the only layer that accesses the Active Directory store directly. Similarly, the Database layer is the only layer that communicates with the ESE, and the DSA is the only layer that communicates with the Database layer. Other components such as LDAP can communicate only with the DSA, and none of the other layers below the DSA. By requiring all additional components to work with the DSA, the integrity of the Active Directory database is ensured, because the DSA does not allow modifications that violate the semantics of objects in Active Directory.

Extensible Storage Engine

4

The Active Directory store is a transactional database that is based on the Extensible Storage Engine. Each addition, modification, or deletion to the Active Directory store is called a **transaction**. As these transactions are made to the database, they are first logged to a file for recovery purposes before the actual change is made to the data.

When data is needed from the Active Directory store it is first pulled from the hard disk and then loaded into memory. For example, when viewing the properties of a user account, if the user account is not already in memory, ESE loads the data for the user account from the hard disk and places it into memory. When a transaction is performed, the first thing that happens is the operation is logged to the hard disk. Because logging only requires recording that a given transaction took place, it can be done very quickly. Once the transaction is logged, the modification the transaction performs is made to the in-memory copy of the data—not the copy of the data on the hard drive. Because manipulating the in-memory copy of the data is so much faster than having to modify the copy of the data stored on the hard disk, the database can perform much faster.

Least Recently Used

Although working with the in-memory copy of data is much faster, it brings up several issues. First, there is only a finite amount of memory available. Because the Active Directory store can be many gigabytes in size, storing the entire database in memory is not practical, and there needs to be a way to move data that is no longer needed and write the changes back to the hard drive. To solve this issue, ESE writes the data stored in memory back to the hard disk using a least recently used algorithm when memory is running low or the system is at a period of low activity. This means that data that has not been accessed or modified recently is the first to be written back to disk.

Transactions

Writing the least recently used data back to disk solves the memory issue outlined. However, there is still another issue regarding system failures. Continuing with the last example, consider what would happen if several modifications were made to the user account's properties. The first thing that happens is the changes are logged, and then the in-memory copy is updated. But what happens if a badly written driver crashes the system, or a UPS fails and the system loses power before the in-memory copy of the data is written back to disk? Because ESE writes all transactions to a log before they are made to the in-memory copy, the next time the domain controller starts ESE can use the transactions recorded in the log to reapply the changes to the copy of the data stored on the hard disk. This is called recovering the database and is done without user intervention.

Checkpoints

One final issue still remains, however. To recover the database, how much of the transaction log must ESE reapply in order for the data in the Active Directory store to be consistent? Data that is constantly being updated is theoretically never written back to disk, based on the recently used algorithm ESE uses. This means that the transaction log could be huge, and would require that all transactions from the very beginning be reapplied in order to bring the data into a consistent state. To shorten recovery times and reduce the amount of hard drive space the logs take up, **checkpoints** are performed. When a checkpoint occurs, completed transactions are written back to disk, and the fact that transactions up to a given point (the point at which the checkpoint started) were successfully written back to the hard drive is noted. By noting which transactions have been successfully written back to disk, ESE only needs to reapply transactions from the point of the last checkpoint and not the entire transaction log if the data needs to be recovered. Additionally, once a checkpoint occurs, the transactions that have been written to disk are no longer needed and can be deleted from the log.

NOTE   When a domain controller is shutdown correctly, a checkpoint occurs and ESE notes the shutdown in the transaction log. The next time the server is started, ESE checks the log for the shutdown record, and if present, does not need to perform a recovery. However, if the shutdown record is not present, ESE performs the necessary recovery.

Active Directory File Structure

As shown in Figure 4-2, the Active Directory store and the other files needed by ESE to maintain data integrity are:

- NTDS.DIT
- EDB.LOG
- EDB*XXXXX*.LOG
- EDB.CHK
- RES1.LOG and RES2.LOG
- TEMP.EDB

NTDS.DIT

The NTDS.DIT file is the actual Active Directory store. It stores all objects and their attributes in Active Directory. By default, this file is located in the %SYSTEMROOT%\NTDS folder on domain controllers. The size of the database file may vary between domain controllers because of the way changes are replicated, and because each domain controller may hold replicas of a different set of partitions.

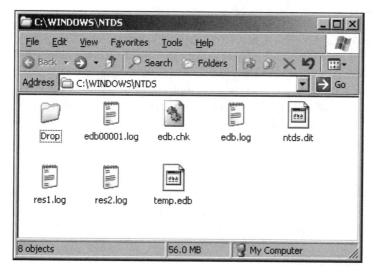

Figure 4-2   Active Directory files

%SYSTEMROOT% is a placeholder (or variable) that represents the path to your Windows Server 2003 installation, such as C:\windows.

NTDS.DIT is made up of three tables: the schema table, the data table, and the link table. The schema table stores information on the types of objects you can create, including the optional and mandatory attributes for each type of object. The data table stores the objects and the values for their attributes in Active Directory. The link table contains linked attributes that point to other objects in Active Directory. For example, group membership is linked to both the group and to the user object in Active Directory.

EDB.LOG

EDB.LOG is the current transaction log file. All changes to Active Directory are noted first in the transaction log file. The updates are then written to the in-memory copy of the Active Directory store, and finally NTDS.DIT when system resources are available. Following a system failure, transactions that are written to the log can be applied to Active Directory after the domain controller restarts.

The size of EDB.LOG is always 10 MB, even when it is first created. When a variable-sized file is expanded, it takes a small amount of time. Keeping EDB.LOG a consistent size allows changes to be written to disk faster because expanding the log each time a change is made is not required.

EDB*XXXXX*.LOG

By default, when EDB.LOG is filled, it is renamed to EDB*XXXXX*.LOG, where *XXXXX* is a number increased by one each time a new log file is created. For example, EDB00001. LOG, EDB00002.LOG, EDB00003.LOG, and so on (this is a hexadecimal number). A new transaction log file named EDB.LOG is then created. Every 12 hours, a garbage-collection process runs that deletes old EDB*XXXXX*.LOG log files that contain completed transactions that have been written to disk.

EDB.CHK

EDB.CHK is the checkpoint file used by ESE to keep track of what data in the transaction log(s) has been written to the database. If the system needs to recover from a failure, it uses the EDB.CHK file to determine what transactions still need to be written to the database and what transactions have already been written.

RES1.LOG and RES2.LOG

RES1.LOG and RES2.LOG are placeholder files that reserve disk space. If the domain controller runs out of free disk space, the space reserved by these two 10 MB files can be used. This prevents updates to Active Directory from being lost due to insufficient disk space. When installing Active Directory, it is important that you include additional free space to store the Active Directory database as it grows.

TEMP.EDB

TEMP.EDB is a temporary storage space. ESE uses this file to hold large transactions while they are in process, and during some maintenance operations.

LDAP

While there are several components that work directly with the DSA, the primary protocol that you will use to work with objects in active directory is LDAP. Because LDAP is used extensively with Active Directory, it is vital that you understand how to use LDAP naming paths. If you remember back to Chapter 1, you learned what a distinguished name (DN) and a relative distinguished name (RDN) are.

To review, every object in Active Directory has a unique DN that describes exactly where the object is located in the object hierarchy. The DN is made up of the name of the object and all of the parent objects above it in the hierarchy. In contrast, an object's RDN identifies the object within its container (that is, its parent object). The RDN contains only the name of the object—none of the parent objects.

In Active Directory, there are three acronyms you must know in order to refer to an object's name. They are:

- DC (Domain Component)—part of a domain name
- OU (Organizational Unit)—name of an organizational unit
- CN (Common Name)—name of most objects

NOTE Because CN is used to refer to the name of a container, it is a common mistake to think that CN stands for container—it does not. CN is used to refer to most objects' names in Active Directory, with the primary exception being organizational units.

When referring to objects in Active Directory, you will use DC to specify part of the domain name, OU to represent the name of any organizational units, and CN to represent the name of other objects. For example, a user named Lori Thompson located in the *dev.supercorp.net* domain in the Research organizational unit would have a DN of:

CN=Lori Thompson,OU=Research,DC=dev,DC=supercorp,DC=net

Similarly, Lori's RDN would be:

CN=Lori Thompson

As another example, take a printer object. In Windows 2000 and Windows Server 2003, printer objects are automatically added to Active Directory so users can search for printers. By default, printer objects are added as a child object under the print server's (that is, the computer that is sharing the printer on the network) computer account object. If a computer named PS1 in the Computers container shared a printer called Sales Color in the *supercorp.net* domain, the default DN of the printer object would be:

CN=Sales Color,CN=PS1,CN=Computers,DC=supercorp,DC=net

Similarly, the printer's RDN would be:

CN=Sales Color

ACTIVE DIRECTORY SCHEMA

As outlined in Chapter 1, all of the objects and attributes that are available in Active Directory are defined in the Active Directory schema. The schema sets out exactly what kind of objects are represented in Active Directory, what properties or attributes are required or optional for each object, and even what types of values are acceptable for each attribute. Because modifying the schema is not something that you should do without careful consideration, the tool needed to modify the schema is not available by default. Activity 4–1 shows how the Active Directory Schema snap-in can be registered on a domain controller.

There are many issues to consider before extending the schema. If not planned and tested properly, adding new classes to the schema can result in reduced performance for the entire network.

CAUTION

Activity 4-1: Registering Active Directory Schema Console

ACTIVITY

Time Required: 10 minutes

Objective: Register the Active Directory Schema snap-in so you can view and modify the schema.

Description: Super Corp is developing a new application to help the company manage its available outsourcing staff. The development team has created an application that uses Active Directory as its data store. They have asked you to modify the schema on Super Corp's development network so that they can test their application in a larger environment. In order to modify the schema for the development department, you must first register the Active Directory Schema snap-in on one of Super Corp's servers.

1. If necessary, start your server and log on using the **AdminXX** account in the **CHILDXX** domain (where *XX* is the number of your server).

2. Click **Start** and then click **Run**.

3. In the Open combo box, type **regsvr32.exe %systemroot%\system32\schmmgmt.dll**

4. Click **OK**. A message box is displayed indicating that schmmgmt.dll was registered successfully, as shown in Figure 4-3.

Figure 4-3   schmmgmt.dll registration confirmation message box

5. Click **OK**. The Active Directory Schema snap-in has been registered on the server.

6. To access the newly registered snap-in, click **Start** and then click **Run**.

7. In the Open combo box, type **mmc** and then click **OK**. An empty Microsoft Management Console displays.

8. On the File menu, click **Add/Remove Snap-in**.

9. On the Add/Remove Snap-in window, click **Add**.

10. On the Add Standalone Snap-in window, select **Active Directory Schema** from the list of available snap-ins, as shown in Figure 4-4.

Figure 4-4   Add Standalone Snap-in dialog box

11. Click **Add** to add the snap-in to the console, and then click **Close**.

12. Click **OK** to close the Add/Remove Snap-in window. The Active Directory Schema snap-in now appears in the left tree pane.

13. On the File menu, click **Save** to save the console.

14. In the Save in list box, choose the **C:** drive.

15. Navigate to the **C:\Documents and Settings\All Users\Desktop** folder.

16. In the File name combo box, enter **Schema.msc** and then click **Save**. This saves the console so it is available on all user's desktops when they log on to this server.

17. Close the Schema console you have just created.

18. When finished, log off your server.

You can also install the Windows Server 2003 management tools, including the Schema snap-in, on a computer running Windows XP Professional. To do so, copy the file %systemroot%\system32\adminpack.msi from a Windows Server 2003 computer to a Windows XP Professional computer and then run adminpack.msi.

NAMING

Every object class and attribute in the schema must have a unique common name, an LDAP display name, and an Object Identifier (OID). To create a common name for a class or attribute, use the following rules:

- Start the name with the registered DNS name of the company and separate each level of the DNS name with hyphens (-) instead of periods.

- Add another hyphen (-) at the end of the company's name, enter the current year, and then follow the year with another hyphen (-).

- Choose a product-specific prefix that is unique within your company and that identifies the product or application of the class or attribute. This name should begin with an uppercase letter with additional letters using the capitalization of your choice.

- Follow the product-specific prefix with a hyphen (-) and then enter the name of the class or attribute separated by hyphens.

To create a class's or attribute's LDAP display name, use the following rules:

- Start with the common name you have already created for the class or attribute.

- Make the first character of the product-specific prefix lowercase. Characters following the first character may be uppercase or lowercase.

- Make every character in the class or attribute part of the name that is preceded by a hyphen (-) uppercase.

- Remove all hyphens (-) after the product-specific prefix.

Table 4-1 shows a common name (attribute: cn) and the corresponding LDAP display name (attribute: LDAPDisplayName).

Table 4-1   Example common names and LDAP display names

Common Name	LDAP Display Name
Supercorp-Com-2004-CRM-Attribute-1	Supercorp-Com-2004-crmAttribute1
Supercorp-Com-2004-CRM-Class-1	Supercorp-Com-2004-crmClass1

While a common name and LDAP display name can be created based on a company's registered DNS domain name, an OID space must be obtained separately. The two primary ways you can obtain an OID space are through Microsoft or an International Standards Organization (ISO). By obtaining an OID space instead of just randomly choosing an OID, classes and attributes created in the Active Directory schema by different organizations' products will not conflict with one another. An example OID is 1.2.840.113556.1.4.786, which is the OID for the SMTP-Mail-Address attribute.

If you are working in a production environment and need to extend the Active Directory schema, you should go ahead and obtain an OID space. You can find more information on obtaining an OID space at *msdn.microsoft.com/ library/en-us/netdir/ad/obtaining_an_object_identifier.asp*.

Object Classes

4

Each item of data stored in Active Directory is called an object. The definition of each type of object is called an object class. An object class is like a template, or blueprint, from which objects are created. For example, the User object class defines how a User object is implemented.

Consider an analogy from architecture: a builder has a blueprint for a house, but he doesn't have a house. After the house is created, he still has the blueprint, and he also now has an existing house. He can then make another house from the same blueprint. If he needs to build a grocery store, he needs to have a blueprint for a grocery store before it can be built. An object class is like the blueprint, and an object is like the physical house or store. You could also say that the schema as a whole is like a bound set of all blueprints used to construct an entire subdivision. The important part of a class definition is that it specifies the attributes that are stored for each object.

Creating an object from a class definition is referred to as **instantiation**.

Inheritance

An important concept to understand is that object classes in Active Directory support inheritance—which is also sometimes called derivation. Inheritance is the ability for a new class to derive and expand the set of attributes of an existing object class. For example, consider an object class called Point that was made up of an X attribute and a Y attribute. By creating a Point object from the *point* object class, you can represent a point anywhere on a two dimensional plane. By creating a new class called Rectangle that inherits from (also referred to as "deriving" from) the Point class, the new class automatically inherits the X and Y attributes from Point. You could then add additional attributes to the Rectangle class, such as *height* and *width*, which allow you to represent a rectangle. Similarly, you could create a Circle object class that derives from the *point* object class and adds an additional *radius* attribute. While these examples only show a single level of inheritance, the inheritance hierarchy can be multiple levels deep, if required.

All classes in Active Directory inherit from a class called *top*—either directly or indirectly.

NOTE

Class Types

In the Active Directory schema, there are actually four types of object classes: Structural classes, Abstract classes, Auxiliary classes, and 88 classes.

Structural classes are the only classes that can have an instance of an object instantiated from them. That is, to create an object in Active Directory, the object class from which the object is instantiated must be a Structural class. A Structural class can be derived from another Structural class or from an Abstract class and can include zero or more Auxiliary classes in its definition. An example of a Structural class would be a House or Store class, because in order to create an object directly from these classes, they must be Structural classes. In Activity 4-2, you will create a new Structural class so that a custom application can store its data in Active Directory.

Abstract classes are used as templates for Structural classes and other Abstract classes. Objects in the directory cannot be instantiated directly from an Abstract class—they can only be instantiated from a Structural class that inherits from the Abstract class. An Abstract class can only be derived from another Abstract class, but can include zero or more Auxiliary Classes in its definition. For example, a Building Abstract class may be created that has an attribute for the address, with the House and *store* Structural classes inheriting from the Building Abstract class. Although you can't instantiate an object from the *building* class, you can instantiate a House or Store object, both of which will have the address attribute.

Auxiliary classes are a little different from Structural classes and Abstract classes. While a Structural class can inherit from only one other Structural class (or one Abstract class), Structural classes and Abstract classes can contain zero, one, or multiple Auxiliary classes in their definitions. Structural classes and Abstract classes are not derived from Auxiliary classes. Rather, Auxiliary classes contain a list of attributes that are included in another classes' definition. Objects cannot be instantiated from Auxiliary classes, but new Auxiliary classes can be derived from other Auxiliary classes.

If you are familiar with programming, think of an Auxiliary class as an "include" file—or an "interface" if you are familiar with object-oriented programming.

TIP

88 classes are designed for backwards compatibility, with the X.500 1988 specification. The X.500 specification did not define the three different types of classes until the X.500 1993 specification (on which Active Directory is based). For compatibility with classes created before the 1993 specification, classes that do not specify their type default to the 88 class.

Active Directory will not return an error when it encounters an 88 class—instead, it uses looser semantic checking then the 1993 specification requires.

> When you define a new object class in the schema, you must use one of the three class types defined in the X.500 1993 specification. You cannot create an 88 class.

NOTE

4

Possible Superiors

Active Directory is a hierarchy of objects with objects containing other objects. For example, an organizational unit object may hold 15 user objects, 10 computer objects, 5 group objects, and 1 printer object. Now it would not make much sense if a printer object contained 15 user objects, 10 computer objects, and five group objects. To control which types of objects a new object can be instantiated or moved under, classes contain a list of **possible superiors**. The user object, for example, allows an organizational unit as one of its possible superiors. Because a printer is not listed as a possible superior for a user object, a user object cannot be created (or moved) under a printer object.

Activity 4-2: Creating a Structural Class

ACTIVITY

Time Required: 10 minutes

Objective: Learn how to extend the Active Directory schema to include additional classes.

Description: Super Corp's development team has provided you with a list of modifications that need to be made to the schema. The first modification on the list is the addition of a new class to represent available outsourcing staff. This new class inherits from the existing contact class. The development team's new application creates these objects as necessary to store outsourcing staff information.

1. If necessary, start your server and log on using the **Administrator** account in the **SUPERCORP** domain.

> Because modifying the schema has consequences across all domains in the entire forest, only members of Schema Admins have permission to modify the schema by default. Schema Admins is a group located in the forest root domain. The default Administrator account in the forest root domain is automatically a member of Schema Admins.

CAUTION

2. On the desktop, double-click the **Schema** console you created in Activity 4-1.

3. In the left tree pane, expand the **Active Directory Schema** node.

4. In the left tree pane, right-click **Classes**, select **New**, and then click **Class**. A message box is displayed informing you that schema objects cannot be deleted once they are created—they can only be disabled.

5. Click **Continue**. The Create New Schema Class window opens.

NOTE

In Chapter 5, you will look at how the forest functional level can be raised to allow classes to be redefined after a class has been disabled.

6. In the Common Name text box, enter **Supercorp-Com-2004-MAN-Staff-XX** (where *XX* is the number of your server).

7. In the LDAP Display Name text box, enter **Supercorp-Com-2004-manStaffXX** (where *XX* is the number of your server).

8. In the Unique X500 Object ID text box, enter **1.2.840.113556.1.5.7000.111.28688.28684.8.87986.XX.1** (where *XX* is the number of your server, without any leading zeros).

9. In the Description text box, enter **Outsourcing Staff**.

10. In the Parent Class text box, enter **Contact**.

11. Ensure that **Structural** is selected in the **Class Type** drop-down list. Your screen should look like Figure 4-5.

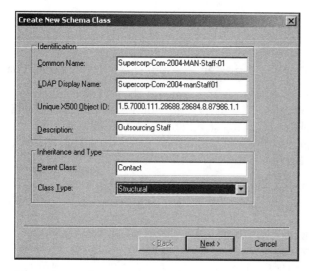

Figure 4-5   Creating a new class

12. Click **Next**. The next window lets you add mandatory and optional attributes to the class.

CAUTION

Be aware that once you create a class, you cannot add or remove mandatory attributes to the class—you can only add or remove optional attributes to or from a class. If the class you are creating must contain mandatory attributes that are not already created, you must create the attributes before creating the class.

13. Click **Finish**. The new class has been created.

14. In the left tree pane, expand the **Classes** node.

15. In the left tree pane, right-click **Supercorp-Com-2004-manStaffXX** and then click **Properties**. The Supercorp-Com-2004-manStaffXX Properties window appears.

> If you select a class in the left pane, you can see a list of all its attributes in the right details pane. The details show from where the attribute was inherited (if at all), and if the attribute is mandatory or optional.

TIP

16. Click the **Relationship** tab.

17. Click **Add Superior**.

18. In the Select Schema Object window, locate **organizationalUnit** in the **Select a schema object** list box, and then click **OK**. This allows Supercorp-Com-2004-manStaffXX objects to be instantiated under only organizationalUnit objects. Your screen should look similar to Figure 4-6.

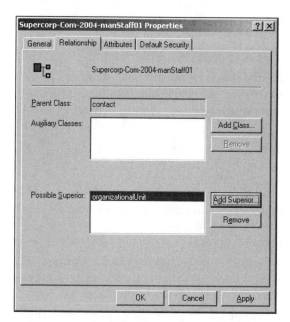

Figure 4-6   Adding a Possible Superior

19. Click **OK**.

20. Close the Schema console you created in Activity 4-1. If you are prompted to save changes to the console, click **No**.

21. When finished, log off your server.

ATTRIBUTES

The schema contains a list of all possible attributes. From this list, a class is assigned both mandatory and optional attributes. An attribute can be used in more than one class definition. When an object is created from the class definition, all of the mandatory attributes are needed, but optional ones are optional, as the name suggests. It is also worth noting that some objects may have attributes that other objects do not.

For example, the User object has an optional attribute to hold a telephone number. Some users will have this attribute populated with a value, but the system does let you create a User object without a telephone number. However, the Printer object does not have this attribute at all, because it wouldn't make sense to phone a printer.

NOTE

Attributes are sometimes called "properties," but the term "attributes" is used when discussing Active Directory.

In a philosophical sense, an object is the sum of its attributes. Given enough of an object's attributes, you can define that object. If an acquaintance tells you that he has an object of the Vehicle class in his driveway, the statement is not very unique or descriptive. But when he lists some of its attributes, you get a much clearer picture: color=red, make=BMW, model year=2003, model name=M5, interior state=spotless. As in Active Directory, there are additional attributes that can identify this person's vehicle. For example, if he specified an attribute for the license plate number, you would be able to uniquely identify his vehicle. In Activity 4-3, you will learn how to create an attribute. Then, in Activity 4-4, you will learn how to add an attribute to an existing class as an optional attribute.

Syntaxes

Each attribute has a **syntax** that defines the data type the attribute can store. For example, an attribute called *active* may use the Boolean data type, which can store the value TRUE or FALSE. Attempting to enter the string "MAYBE" into the *active* attribute would fail, because the value that was entered was not TRUE or FALSE. This helps to ensure that data entered for attributes is valid and logically makes sense. Table 4-2 lists some of the more common data types available and the type of data each can hold.

NOTE

You can only use the predefined syntaxes—you cannot add new syntaxes.

Table 4-2   List of common syntaxes

4

Name	Description
Boolean	A Boolean value of either TRUE or FALSE
Integer	Whole numbers from -2,147,483,648 to 2,147,483,647 (32 bits)
LargeInteger	Whole numbers from -9,223,372,036,854,775,808 to 9,223,372,036,854,775,807 (64 bits)
String(Numeric)	A string that contains only digits (0 to 9)
String(Object-Identifier)	A string used to hold an OID; can contain digits (0 to 9) and decimal points (.)
String(Octet)	Array of bytes used to store binary data
String(Printable)	A case-sensitive string which can hold characters from the printable character set
String(Sid)	A string used to hold a security identifier (SID)
String(Unicode)	A case-insensitive Unicode string
String(Generalized-Time)	Used to store time values in Generalized-Time format
Object(Distinguished Name)	A string that contains a distinguished name; automatically updated by Active Directory if object moves or is renamed

TIP

You do not need to memorize Table 4-2.

While an attribute can hold a single value by default, an attribute can also be marked as **multi-valued**. When an attribute is marked as multi-valued, the attribute can hold multiple values of the same syntax. For example, if an *authorizedDrivers* attribute (using the object syntax) was added to the *vehicle* class, it could be marked as multi-valued so that multiple drivers could be specified.

Indexes

Consider an example where you want to search for a user account with the telephone number 555 555 5555. To perform the search, Active Directory logically starts with the first user account, checks the telephone number, and then returns the user account if the telephone numbers match. If the telephone numbers do not match, Active Directory keeps trying subsequent user accounts until a match is found, or until all user accounts have been searched. Statistically, Active Directory has to search at least one half of the user accounts and possibly all the user accounts in order to find the user account with the telephone number for which you are searching. This is neither efficient nor quick, and is a very resource-intensive procedure when you have tens of thousands of user accounts that must be searched.

To solve this issue, Active Directory allows attributes to be indexed, which improves performance of queries for that attribute. Indexes are similar in concept to the index in the back of the book. They work by storing the values (in order) for all objects that have a given attribute. So instead of having to scan each user account one by one, Active Directory can quickly look up a telephone number in the index and return the user account(s) with that number.

NOTE   Keep in mind that indexes apply to attributes and not classes. When an attribute is indexed, the attribute is indexed for all classes that include the attribute—not just a particular class.

Although indexes can speed up queries, they slow down the creation of objects and updating of attributes. When an object is created, any attributes it contains that are indexed must be added to the index. Additionally, updating an attribute that is indexed means the index must also be updated. Because adding indexes means slower write operations, it is recommended that you only create indexes on attributes when the benefit of faster queries outweighs the slower creation/modification time. Also keep in mind that indexes take additional hard drive space to store.

NOTE   Multivalued attributes can also be indexed, but they require more processing time for creation of or modifications to attributes. They also require additional storage space on the hard drive.

When deciding what attributes to index, choose attributes that have highly unique values. That is, choose attributes where many objects do not share the same value. For example, indexing a *doors* attribute used in the Vehicle class would not be the best choice because there are not very many unique values—mainly two or four. However, indexing a *plateNumber* attribute used by the Vehicle class would be a good choice because the values contained by that attribute are going to be highly unique between the different *vehicle* objects. While an index on the *doors* attribute could eliminate about 50% of possible objects, the *plateNumber* could eliminate over 99% of all possible objects.

A rule of thumb is that if the index can eliminate 90% or more of the objects with a given attribute, it would make a good index.

TIP

Activity 4-3: Creating an Attribute

4

ACTIVITY

Time Required: 10 minutes

Objective: Learn how the Active Directory schema can be extended to include additional attributes.

Description: After creating the outsourcing staff class, a member of the development team calls and asks you to add an additional optional attribute to the outsourcing staff class. This new attribute supports a new feature the team just added to the staff management application. The development team's custom application will read from and write to this attribute in order to store additional information about outsourcing staff.

1. If necessary, start your server and log on using the **Administrator** account in the **SUPERCORP** domain.

2. On the desktop, double-click the **Schema** console you created in Activity 4-1.

3. In the left tree pane, expand the **Active Directory Schema** node.

4. In the left tree pane, right-click **Attributes**, and then click **Create Attribute**. A message box opens and informs you that schema objects cannot be deleted once they are created—they can only be disabled.

5. Click **Continue**. The Create New Attribute Window opens.

6. In the Common Name text box, enter **Supercorp-Com-2004-man-Stat-XX** (where *XX* is the number of your server).

7. In the LDAP Display Name text box, enter **Supercorp-Com-2004-manStatXX** (where *XX* is the number of your server).

8. In the Unique X500 Object ID text box, enter **1.2.840.113556.1.5.7000.111.28688.28684.8.87165.XX.1** (where *XX* is the number of your server, without any leading zeros).

9. In the Description text box, enter **Outsourcing Staff Status**.

10. In the Syntax drop-down list, select **Unicode String**.

11. In the Minimum and Maximum text boxes, enter **2**. This will require that any string entered (in this case, a status code) must be two characters in length. Your screen should look like Figure 4-7.

Figure 4-7   Creating a new attribute

12. Click **OK**. The new attribute has been created.

13. In the left tree pane, if necessary, select the **Attributes** node to show a list of all attributes in the right pane. Scroll down until you locate the Supercorp–Com–2004–manStat*XX* attribute, as shown in Figure 4-8.

14. Close the Schema console you created in Activity 4-1. If you are prompted to save changes to the console, click **No**.

15. Log off your server if you do not intend to immediately continue to the next project. Otherwise, stay logged on.

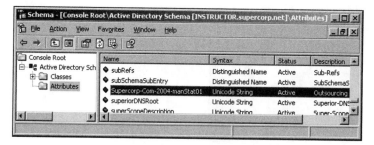

Figure 4-8   Supercorp-Com-2004-manStatXX attribute

Activity 4-4: Adding an Optional Attribute to a Class

Time Required: 5 minutes

Objective: Learn how to add additional attributes to a class.

Description: Now that you have created the new attribute to hold the status of outsourcing staff, you must add it to the outsourcing staff class.

1. If necessary, start your server and log on using the Administrator account in the SUPERCORP domain.

2. On the desktop, double-click the **Schema** console you created in Activity 4-1.

3. In the left tree pane, expand the **Active Directory Schema** node.

4. In the left tree pane, expand the **Classes** node.

5. In the left tree pane, right-click **Supercorp-Com-2004-manStaffXX** (where *XX* is the number of your server), and then click **Properties**. The Supercorp-Com-2004-manStaffXX Properties window appears.

6. Click the **Attributes** tab.

7. Click **Add**.

8. In the Select Schema Object window, locate **Supercorp-Com-2004-manStatXX** (where *XX* is the number of your server) in the Select a schema object list box, and then click **OK**. This adds the Supercorp-Com-2004-manStatXX attribute as an optional attribute to the Supercorp-Com-2004-manStaffXX class, as shown in Figure 4-9.

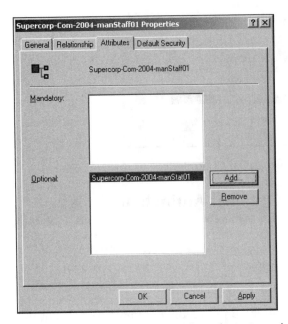

Figure 4-9   Adding an optional attribute to a class

9. Click **OK** to close the Supercorp-Com-2004-manStaffXX Properties window.

10. Close the Schema console you created in Activity 4-1. If you are prompted to save changes to the console, click **No**.

11. When finished log off your server.

ACTIVE DIRECTORY PARTITIONS

To effectively manage the replication of Active Directory, the database is divided into groups called **partitions**, or **naming contexts**. Although all of the naming contexts are stored in one big file on the domain controller, each naming context is replicated independently of the others. This makes sense because some information changes more frequently than other information, and different partitions are stored on different domain controllers. You should be aware of the following types of partitions: the schema partition, the domain partition, the configuration partition, and the application partition. An example of where these partitions would be located is shown in Figure 4-10.

4

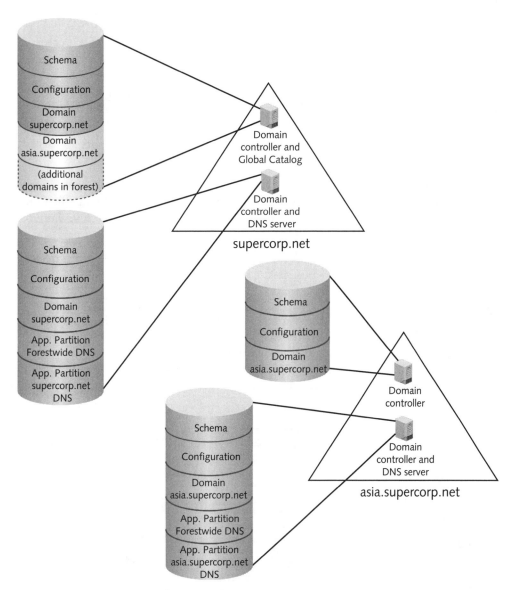

Figure 4-10   Partitions on various domain controllers

Active Directory replication is covered in Chapter 7.

NOTE

A snap-in called ADSI Edit, which is included with the Windows Server 2003 Support Tools, can be used to view and modify objects in the various Active Directory partitions. Activity 4-5 shows how the Windows Server 2003 Support Tools can be installed.

Activity 4-5: Installing Windows Support Tools

Time Required: 10 minutes

Objective: Learn how to install the Windows Server 2003 Support Tools on a domain controller.

Description: You need to view all the naming contexts that exist in Super Corp's network. However, you have decided to use ADSI Edit, which is not currently installed on the server from which you are working. You must install the Windows Server 2003 Support Tools so you can use the ADSI Edit snap-in.

1. If necessary, start your server and log on using the **AdminXX** account in the **CHILDXX** domain (where *XX* is the number of your server).

2. Click **Start** and then click **My Computer**.

3. The contents of the Windows Server 2003 CD have already been copied to a folder called Source on the D: drive of your server. Locate the Windows Server 2003 Support Tools by navigating to **D:\Source\SUPPORT\TOOLS** (your instructor will inform you if the files are located in an alternate location), as shown in Figure 4-11 (note that your screen may appear slightly different if the default folder view settings have been changed).

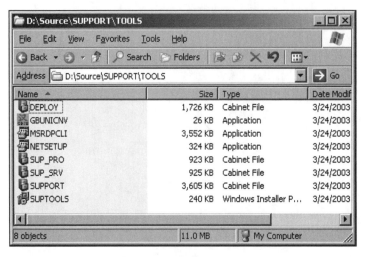

Figure 4-11   Windows Server 2003 Support Tools folder

4. Double-click **SUPTOOLS**. The Welcome screen of the Windows Support Tools Setup Wizard is displayed.

5. Click **Next**.

6. In the End User License Agreement window, select the **I Agree** option button and then click **Next**.

7. In the User Information dialog box, enter **Super Corp** in the Name and Organization text boxes, as shown in Figure 4-12.

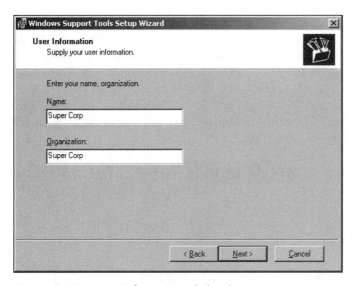

Figure 4-12   User Information dialog box

8. Click **Next**.

9. In the Destination Directory dialog box, leave the default location to install the support tools and then click **Install Now**.

10. Once the tools are installed, the Completing the Windows Support Tools Setup window is displayed. Click **Finish** to close the wizard.

11. Close the D:\Source\SUPPORT\TOOLS Explorer window.

12. Log off your server if you do not intend to immediately continue to the next project. Otherwise, stay logged on.

Schema

Active Directory stores the schema in its own partition called the schema partition. This partition contains the definitions of all the classes and attributes in the entire forest. It is replicated to all domain controllers in the forest, and the content is the same throughout the forest. Every domain controller in a forest has a read-only copy of the schema partition.

Although Active Directory is a multi-master technology, there are a few operations that must be guaranteed in order to complete (or abort) without the possibility of having to resolve a conflict. To ensure that this happens correctly, one domain controller is designated as an operations master for these less frequent operations (such as changing the schema). Operations masters are discussed in Chapter 8, but you should be aware that the schema operations master is the only domain controller with a writeable copy of the schema partition.

Configuration

The configuration partition stores information about the replication topology used in the forest. This replication topology information specifies how a domain controller determines with which other specific partners it replicates. This partition also contains information about every other domain in the forest, the names and configuration of sites, and service-specific information, such as the information used by certificate servers if you are using a Public Key Infrastructure (PKI). This partition is also found on all domain controllers and is the same throughout the forest. In Activity 4-6, you will learn how to use ADSI Edit to view objects in the configuration partition.

ACTIVITY

Activity 4-6: Using ADSI Edit to View the Configuration Partition

Time Required: 10 minutes

Objective: Learn how to view the configuration naming context for a forest using ADSI Edit.

Description: Now that the ADSI Edit snap-in is installed on your server, you need to view all the naming contexts in Super Corp's Active Directory forest. You can do so by viewing the configuration partition for the forest.

1. If necessary, start your server and log on using the **AdminXX** account in the **CHILDXX** domain (where *XX* is the number of your server).

2. Click **Start** and then click **Run**.

3. In the Open combo box, type **mmc** and then click **OK**. An empty Microsoft Management Console opens.

4. On the File menu, click **Add/Remove Snap-in**.

5. On the Add/Remove Snap-in window, click **Add**.

6. On the Add Standalone Snap-in window, select **ADSI Edit** from the list of available snap-ins, as shown in Figure 4-13.

Figure 4-13 Add Standalone Snap-in dialog box

7. Click **Add** to add the snap-in to the console, and then click **Close**.

8. Click **OK** to close the Add/Remove Snap-in dialog box. The ADSI Edit snap-in now appears in the left tree pane.

9. Right-click the **ADSI Edit** node in the left tree pane, and then click **Connect to**.

10. In the Connection Point section of the Connection Settings dialog box, ensure that the **Select a well known Naming Context** option button is selected.

11. In the Select a well known Naming Context list box, choose **Configuration**, as shown in Figure 4-14.

12. Click **OK**.

13. If necessary, expand the ADSI Edit node. A Configuration node appears under the ADSI Edit node. Expand the **Configuration** node.

14. Double-click the **CN=Configuration,DC=supercorp,DC=net** node in the left tree pane. Note the objects and their class in the right pane.

15. Click the **CN=Partitions** node in the left tree pane to show the objects it contains in the right details pane.

16. In the right details pane, right-click **CN=CHILD*XX*** (where *XX* is the number of your server) and then click **Properties**.

17. In the Attributes list box, locate the whenCreated attribute and note the date and time your domain partition was created.

18. Click **Cancel** on the CN=CHILD*XX* Properties window to discard any changes.

19. Close the console window. When prompted to save the console, click **No**.

20. When finished, log off your server.

Figure 4-14 Connection Settings dialog box

Domain

When people talk about objects in Active Directory, they are usually talking about objects contained in the domain partition. This is the naming context that contains the users, computers, groups, and organizational units created in a Windows domain. This naming context is replicated to all domain controllers in the domain. It is often a large amount of data, and it is usually the partition that changes the most frequently as users are added, deleted, and modified. Each domain controller is, by definition, a member of a domain and has a copy of this naming context for its own domain. You cannot choose to replicate only part of a domain partition between domain controllers in that domain. Every domain controller has a full copy of the domain partition for its own domain.

If a domain controller is a Global Catalog server, it also has partial replicas of the domain partitions for all of the other domains in the forest. These partial replicas from other domains contain only selected attributes of each object.

Application

Application developers can create an application partition and control where it is replicated. Application partitions cannot contain security principals (users, groups, or computers), but they can be replicated to many different domains in the forest without necessarily being included on all domain controllers. An application partition is used when the developer of an Active Directory-aware application wants to store information in Active Directory, but either wishes to control exactly where it is replicated, or needs to have it replicated beyond one domain.

For example, the Windows DNS server that shipped with Windows 2000 could store information in Active Directory, and have Active Directory replicate it between domain controllers. However, it was stored in the domain naming context, so to make it available across domains, standard secondary zones had to be used. Also, the DNS information was stored on every domain controller, regardless of whether that domain controller was also a DNS server. The introduction of application partitions in Windows Server 2003 allows DNS information to be replicated to DNS servers running on domain controllers in any domain in the forest (by using the ForestDnsZones partition). Application partitions can also prevent DNS information from being replicated to domain controllers that are not DNS servers (by using a DomainDnsZones partition).

4

CHAPTER SUMMARY

- At its core, Active Directory is made up of several layers: the Extensible Storage Engine (ESE), the Database layer, and the Directory Service Agent (DSA).

- Each addition, modification, or deletion to the Active Directory store is called a transaction.

- By logging all transactions, ESE can reapply the transactions in the event of a system failure and bring the data back to a consistent state.

- The NTDS.DIT file is the actual Active Directory store. It stores all objects and their attributes in Active Directory.

- EDB.LOG is the current transaction log file. All changes to Active Directory are written first to the transaction log file.

- All of the objects and attributes that are available in Active Directory are defined in the Active Directory schema.

- Every object class and attribute in the schema must have a unique common name, an LDAP display name, and an Object Identifier (OID).

- Each item of data stored in Active Directory is called an object. The definition of each type of object is called an object class. An object class is like a template, or blueprint, from which objects are created.

- Structural classes are the only classes that can have an instance of an object instantiated from them.

- The schema contains a list of all possible attributes. From this list, a class is assigned both mandatory and optional attributes.

- To effectively manage the replication of Active Directory, the database is divided into groups called partitions. The four types of partitions are: the schema partition, the domain partition, the configuration partition, and the application partition.

- Active Directory stores the schema in its own partition, called the schema partition.

- ❏ The configuration partition stores information about the replication topology used in the forest, the domains in the forest, and other service-specific information.

- ❏ The domain partition is the naming context that contains the users, computers, groups, and organizational units created in a Windows domain.

- ❏ An application partition is used when the developer of an Active Directory-aware application wants to store information in Active Directory, but either wishes to control exactly where it is replicated, or needs to have it replicated beyond one domain. Application partitions cannot contain security principals (users, groups, or computers).

KEY TERMS

Abstract classes — Used as templates for Structural classes and other Abstract classes, but cannot be directly instantiated.

Active Directory store — The NTDS.DIT database file in which all Active Directory objects are stored. The Active Directory store is a transactional database based on the Extensible Storage Engine (ESE).

Auxiliary classes — Contains a list of attributes that are included in another classes' definition.

checkpoints — An event where ESE writes all completed transactions to the copy of the Active Directory store on the hard drive. Checkpoints shorten the amount of time needed to recover the Active Directory store, because ESE only needs to reapply the transactions that were made after the last checkpoint.

Database layer — A functional layer of Active Directory that provides an object-oriented hierarchical view of the objects contained in the Active Directory store. It presents a set of application programming interfaces (APIs) to the Directory System Agent (DSA) so that DSA does not communicate directly with the Extensible Storage Engine (ESE).

Directory Service Agent (DSA) — A functional layer of Active Directory that is responsible for enforcing the semantics that govern how objects in Active Directory are created and manipulated.

Extensible Storage Engine (ESE) — The Active Directory database engine; it is based on an improved version of the Jet database engine that Microsoft Exchange Server 5.5 uses. ESE uses transactions to ensure that data can be recovered even in the event of an unexpected system failure.

instantiation — The process of creating an instance of an object from an object class.

multi-valued — An attribute that can hold multiple values of the same syntax.

naming contexts — A category or division of information within Active Directory. Each naming context is replicated separately.

partitions — See naming contexts.

possible superiors — A list of other classes in which a given class's objects can be contained.

Structural classes — Classes that can have objects instantiated from them. A Structural class can be derived from other Structural classes or an Abstract class.

syntax — Defines the type of data an attribute can store.

transaction — A modification to the Active Directory store including the creation and deletion of objects or the modification of attributes.

REVIEW QUESTIONS

4

1. The Active Directory store is based on which of the following?
   a. The Expandable Storage Engine
   b. The Extensible Storage Engine
   c. The Exclusive Storage Engine
   d. The Data Storage Engine

2. Which layer of Active Directory provides an object-oriented hierarchical view of the objects contained in the Active Directory Store?
   a. Database layer
   b. Data layer
   c. Object Presentation layer
   d. Object Persistence layer

3. Which layer of Active Directory is responsible for enforcing the semantics, or rules, defined in the schema?
   a. Directory System Agent
   b. Directory Data Agent
   c. Directory Service Agent
   d. Directory Schema Agent

4. The Active Directory store is a _____ database.

5. The Extensible Storage Engine uses a _____ algorithm when it needs to free memory that is being used.

6. Which of the following does the Extensible Storage Engine use to shorten recovery times and reduce the amount of hard drive space logs take up?
   a. checkpoints
   b. syncpoints
   c. transactpoints
   d. cuepoints

7. All of the objects and attributes that are available in Active Directory are defined in the Active Directory _____ .

8. Each instance of a class in Active Directory is called a(n) _____ .

9. An object _____ is like a template, or blueprint, from which objects are created.

10. Which of the following defines the classes in which a given classes' objects can exist?

    a. possible containers

    b. possible superiors

    c. possible parents

    d. possible owners

11. _____ is the process of creating an instance of an object from an object class.

12. Once classes are added to the schema, they can never be deactivated. True or False?

13. Which type of classes can be used as templates for Structural classes and Abstract classes?

    a. Structural classes

    b. Abstract classes

    c. Auxiliary classes

    d. Attribute classes

14. Which is the only type of class from which objects can be directly instantiated?

    a. Structural classes

    b. Abstract classes

    c. Auxiliary classes

    d. Attribute classes

15. The _____ of an attribute defines the type of data the attribute can hold.

16. Attributes that can hold multiple values are called which of the following?

    a. Multiattributed

    b. Multistore

    c. Multivariable

    d. Multivalued

17. The Active Directory database is divided into groups called _____ or _____ .

18. Which naming context holds information about the replication topology?

    a. schema partition

    b. configuration partition

    c. domain partition

    d. application partition

19. In what naming context can a Windows 2000 DNS server store DNS information?

    a. schema partition

    b. configuration partition

    c. domain partition

    d. application partition

20. A Global Catalog server holds a partial replica of what naming context for every domain in a forest?

    a. schema partition

    b. configuration partition

    c. domain partition

    d. application partition

CASE PROJECTS

Case Project 4-1: Follow the Data

So that junior network administrators can have a better idea of what is going on under the hood of Active Directory, Super Corp's IT manager has asked you to make a short write-up on how the Extensible Storage Engine deals with data. For the example, he wants you to describe the steps that take place when a user's account properties are opened and modified once. He would also like you to describe what happens if the domain controller crashes immediately after making the modification (assume that the server will be rebooted).

Case Project 4-2: Identify Index Candidates

Super Corp's IT manager has asked you to identify which attributes on a new *manager* class would be good candidates for indexes. He has provided you with a list of attributes that will be commonly searched on and a description of the data each holds.

Gender—Identifies the gender of the manager

Employee Number—The manager's employee number

Preferred Shift—Describes the shift the manager prefers to work (morning/evening/night)

CASE
PROJECTS

Case Project 4-3: Explain Naming Contexts

Super Corp is planning to add two new domain controllers: an additional domain controller in the supercorp.net domain and a domain controller in a new domain named dev.super corp.net. Neither domain controller will have a DNS server installed; however, the new dev.supercorp.net domain controller will be configured as a Global Catalog server.

1. What naming contexts will the additional domain controller in the supercorp.net domain contain? Are any of these naming contexts new?

2. What naming contexts will the domain controller in the new dev.supercorp.net domain contain? Are any of these naming contexts new?

CHAPTER
5

ACTIVE DIRECTORY LOGICAL DESIGN

After reading this chapter, you will be able to:

♦ Choose the best DNS name for a domain

♦ Make Active Directory forest design decisions

♦ Make Active Directory domain design decisions

♦ Understand the roles and describe the characteristics of trusts

♦ Describe the role and characteristics of organizational units

♦ Understand the different functionality levels of Active Directory and how to upgrade Windows NT and 2000 domains

Chapter 1 defined the basics of Active Directory; Chapter 2 looked at name resolution. In Chapter 3, you learned about the "big picture" of Active Directory, including how your design philosophy might affect your choices. Chapter 3 introduced you to the Microsoft Solutions Framework (MSF), a multistage approach to managing software or infrastructure creation. Finally, Chapter 4 reviewed the underlying architecture of Active Directory—how data is structured and stored.

During the second phase of an MSF project—the planning phase—you translated the goals and visions from the envisioning phase into specific, actionable plans. You tested your design to ensure it worked. While the design philosophy guides the approach to designing and configuring Active Directory, the team must also make implementation decisions for each installation. You will learn about those decisions in this chapter.

You will first look at how the Active Directory namespace interacts with DNS, and some choices regarding DNS and Active Directory. You will then learn about situations that might require creating more than one forest in an organization. Then you will learn how to select from different configurations of domains within a forest as well as choices for arranging the organizational units within the domain. You will also learn how a forest or domain can interact with other forests and domains using a trust relationship. The chapter will finish with a look at the different domain and forest functional levels as well as the different migration paths from Windows NT 4.0 and Windows 2000.

CHOOSING A DNS NAME FOR ACTIVE DIRECTORY

As you already learned, DNS defines the namespace used by Active Directory. Choosing the DNS name of a domain is not a decision to take lightly or to put off until the last minute. The DNS name is used extensively throughout the domain and affects every member of the domain. Changing the domain name after the domain has been created can be complicated, time consuming, and expensive. If a DNS name is widely circulated, a company may be reluctant to change it once people have started using it.

What Makes a Good DNS Name?

Avoid unnecessary expense and trouble by choosing a good DNS name for your domain at the beginning of the process. A good DNS name for your Active Directory domain should be meaningful and scalable—that is, it should represent your entire business and support current and future plans. You also need to consider the difference between a DNS name used for a public Internet presence and one used just to support Active Directory.

Making the Name Meaningful and Scalable

The DNS name chosen for the first domain created in a tree will be a part of the DNS names for all the **child domains** in that tree, the same way that *supercorp.net* is contained in *asia.supercorp.net*. Because a domain name can be difficult, impractical, or even impossible to change, your DNS name should be both meaningful and scalable. It needs to represent the whole of the enterprise, not just part of it, and allow for future growth. The issue of domain renaming is discussed in more detail later in this chapter.

Take the fictitious case of Billy Bob's Seafood Restaurant—a small, but growing chain of specialty dining establishments. Rushing in to an Active Directory deployment, it chose *bbseafood.com* as the DNS name for its domain. However, the IT Department didn't consider its wholly owned subsidiary, JoJo's Fine Coffees, the arm of the business that procures coffee for its own restaurants and also resells it to other establishments. The DNS name it selected does not represent its entire enterprise; therefore, it is not a good, long-term choice.

Two Common Uses for DNS: Internet Presence and Active Directory

Most companies using Active Directory will have two uses for DNS. The first (and of most consequence to this book) is to define the namespace used by Active Directory and thus how resources are located within the network. The second is to provide a way for the rest of the world to contact the enterprise—via e-mail, the company Web site, or an e-commerce initiative. This role—a company's public address on the Internet—is sometimes called its Internet presence. For example, Microsoft Corporation uses *microsoft.com* for its corporate **Internet presence**. Its main Web site is *www.microsoft.com*, and e-mail is addressed as follows: *username@microsoft.com*. However, microsoft.com is not the namespace used by its corporate Active Directory implementation.

5

Choosing How DNS Names for Internet and Active Directory Are Related

The relationship between a DNS name used for an Internet presence—such as e-mail and a Web site—and the DNS name used for an Active Directory domain can be complicated. You have several choices:

- Use the same DNS name for both.
- Use completely different names altogether.
- Delegate a subdomain from your Internet name for Active Directory.

The next few sections will examine each of these possibilities.

Using the Same DNS Name for Active Directory and Internet Presence

The problem with using the same name for both Active Directory and the Internet presence is that it requires complicated steps to prevent confidential data from being made available publicly, and is therefore not recommended. Crackers and hackers love to discover the details of systems implementation within a company. Every bit of knowledge they gain adds to their ability to attack the network or socially engineer additional information from unsuspecting employees. Even learning the names and IP numbers of important hosts on your network, such as the domain controllers, increases their probability for success. For these reasons, it is not recommended that your SRV records or unnecessary hostnames be publicized.

When you use the same name on the Internet as used internally, all of your resource records are publicly available (which is not desirable), unless you use a technique called split DNS. Split DNS, as seen in Figure 5-1, gives internal DNS servers complete zone data, including all SRV records, and gives external DNS servers only the public records for that same zone. You must maintain that public zone data manually, and always take care to ensure that internal clients connect only to internal servers (because the external ones won't be able to handle their requests) and that external clients only connect to the external servers.

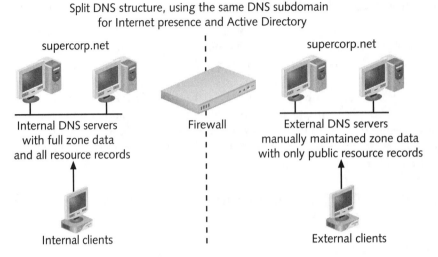

Figure 5-1   Using a split DNS configuration with Active Directory

Using split DNS is even more complicated if internal users start connecting from the outside, perhaps over a virtual private network (VPN). There is nothing inherently wrong with this approach, but it is complex to administer. The more complex something is, the greater the chance for error. It also requires additional hardware, as the internal and external zones cannot be hosted on the same DNS servers. There is no particular benefit to this arrangement that offsets the great amount of work required to maintain it, so it is rarely recommended.

Using Completely Different Names for Active Directory and Internet Presence

In a scenario where the Active Directory DNS name is completely removed from the Internet presence DNS name, there is no possibility of conflict between them. Management of the names and hosts for the Internet is completely separate from Active Directory. The Active Directory DNS name may be completely private, such as a name ending with .local or .private. As an example, consider *supercorp.private* used for Active Directory and *supercorp. com* used for the Internet presence. Of course, a variation on the same approach would be to have the Active Directory DNS name registered separately with a TLD registrar, such as *supercorp.net* for Active Directory and *supercorp.com* for the Internet presence as shown in Figure 5-2.

In the type of design shown in Figure 5-2, the designers must ensure that internal clients can resolve both internal names to support Active Directory and external names to access Internet resources. To accomplish this, clients can query the internal servers using a forwarder or recursion to resolve external names. The potential downfall of this design is that if an internal client is not correctly set to use an internal name server, it cannot receive a referral unless the internal subdomain name is also within a public TLD and registered with

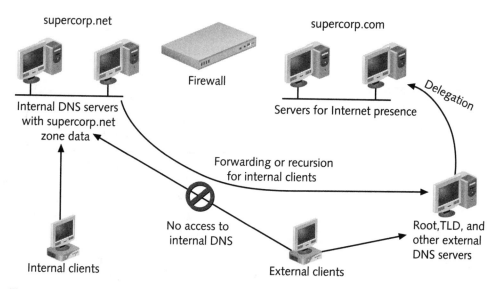

Figure 5-2 Using completely different names for Active Directory and Internet presence

the TLD's registrar. In small organizations, the private and public zones could be hosted on the same DNS servers, but in most cases they are separated. Public DNS servers are often located with the Web servers, while the internal DNS usually runs on the domain controllers.

Delegating a Subdomainfrom the Internet PresenceSubdomain for Active Directory

This solution also uses separate zones to keep Active Directory and the Internet presence apart, but rather than creating a new name, a subdomain is delegated from the existing Internet presence name. For example, ad.supercorp.com is a delegated subdomain of *supercorp.com*. This design is simple to administer and is extremely palatable to organizations with a large existing investment in DNS infrastructure, or existing DNS servers running BIND or other UNIX software.

Setting up the delegation is a simple matter of the existing DNS administrators entering the delegation records to point all queries related to Active Directory to the correct servers. It is not necessary to reconfigure clients, as any client that can find a working DNS server can find the address for the DNS servers providing resolution for the Active Directory subdomain. (Usually, most external clients would still be blocked by a firewall from making a connection.) This example is shown in Figure 5-3.

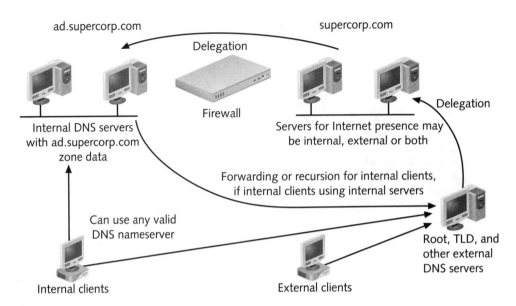

Figure 5-3   Delegating a subdomain from the Internet presence subdomain for Active Directory

Recall that you learned the skills to delegate a subdomain in Chapter 2.

NOTE

Best Practices for Choosing a DNS Name

Microsoft recommends a delegated subdomain as a best practice for DNS design with Active Directory in organizations that already have an existing DNS structure. Even in organizations without existing DNS implementations, Microsoft recommends creating a new registered DNS name with a delegation to a zone dedicated to Active Directory. The zones created to support Active Directory should be configured as Active Directory integrated zones.

In Windows 2000 Server, Microsoft recommended that all domain controllers act as DNS servers—and this recommendation made sense. Because the DNS server in Windows 2000 stores Active Directory integrated zones in the domain partition, the DNS data was replicated to all domain controllers in the domain—regardless if the domain controller was also a DNS server or not. It made sense to go ahead and configure all domain controllers as DNS servers because they already contained the DNS data locally. In other words, the DNS data was going to be replicated to a domain controller even if it was or was not a DNS server, so it might as well act as a DNS server.

NOTE In a mixed environment where both Windows 2000 Server and Windows Server 2003 DNS servers exist, you should follow the recommendations for Windows 2000 when placing DNS servers. This is because Windows 2000 DNS servers only support storing Active Directory integrated zones in the domain partition. Windows 2000 DNS servers can't use the DomainDnsZones and ForestDnsZones Active Directory application partitions.

For the most part, the recommendation that all domain controllers act as DNS servers holds true in Windows Server 2003. However, the introduction of the DomainDnsZones Active Directory application partition in Windows Server 2003 can affect DNS server placement. Unlike storing the Active Directory integrated zones in the domain partition (where the data is replicated to all domain controllers in the domain), the DomainDnsZones application partition is only replicated to domain controllers that are also DNS servers for the domain. This can reduce replication traffic because only servers that are designated as DNS servers need to replicate DNS data.

NOTE When deciding where to place DNS servers, it is important to remember that Active Directory relies heavily on DNS for name resolution. If DNS becomes unavailable, Active Directory will not work correctly—even if one or more domain controllers are still available.

For example, in a small remote office (that is connected to a larger main office via a WAN) with only one domain controller, you *could* choose not to setup a Windows 2003 DNS server. The benefit of this configuration is that replication traffic related to the DomainDnsZones application partition does not have to cross the WAN. However, there are two major downsides to not placing a DNS server at this small office. First, DNS name resolution traffic must cross the WAN to be resolved by a DNS server in another office. This not only takes up WAN bandwidth, but is probably much slower than accessing a DNS server that is local to the remote office. Second, if the WAN link becomes unavailable, DNS would also become unavailable and in turn Active Directory would not work correctly—even though the office has a local domain controller. Because of these reasons, in this situation it would be best to configure the domain controller as a DNS server also.

As another example, assume that a medium-sized office has two domain controllers. If this is the only office with no WAN links, then obviously both domain controllers should run DNS in order to provide fault tolerance. However, what if there are WAN links to other offices that already have domain controllers? In this situation, it is theoretically possible to get away with only one DNS server. If the WAN connection fails, the local DNS server can be used. Or if the local DNS server fails, a DNS server in another office can be contacted over the WAN. In other words, the only situation where a DNS server would be unavailable is if both the WAN connection and the local DNS server failed.

While it is unlikely that both the DNS server and the WAN would fail at the same time, in most cases it would be best to make both domain controllers at the office DNS servers. The first reason for making both domain controllers DNS servers has to do with how data is replicated in Active Directory. The exact details of how replication is controlled and works is covered in the next couple of chapters, but for now be aware that the data in the DomainDnsZones partition would only need to be replicated across the WAN link to one of the two domain controllers in this example. The second domain controller would then replicate updates from the first domain controller. This means that adding a second DNS server to the office location does not add any additional WAN traffic—only LAN traffic. Because LAN bandwidth is not nearly as much of a concern as WAN bandwidth, the extra replication traffic generated typically is not an issue.

Finally, the other reason to make both domain controllers DNS servers in this example is an issue of speed and capacity. If the office only had a single DNS server and the DNS server failed, DNS name resolution would probably take much longer because the request must cross a WAN link. Additionally, by utilizing two DNS servers, the client load can be spread across the servers. Again, because of these reasons, in this situation it would be best to configure both domain controllers as DNS servers also.

So far you have looked at two examples where the recommendation of making every domain controller a DNS server applies. While in the majority of situations you will configure all domain controllers as DNS servers, in extremely large domains with many domain controllers at the same location it is not necessary to replicate DNS data to all the domain controllers. For example, take a large office building with four domain controllers. Two DNS servers are all that is required for fault tolerance—unless additional DNS servers are required at the location to handle the client load. Configuring only two of the four domain controllers as DNS servers would reduce the traffic needed to replicate the DomainDnsZones partition. It would also save hard drive space on the domain controllers that are not DNS servers (because they do not have to store a copy of the DomainDnsZones partition).

As one final note, in multiple-domain forests it is often necessary to locate the services provided by domain controllers in the forest root domain. If your DNS servers are running on Windows 2000 or non-Microsoft operating systems, it is also recommended that the forest root domain's _msdcs zone be replicated to all other DNS servers in the forest as a secondary zone. However, if your DNS servers are all running on Windows 2003 Server, then you can replicate the forest root zone to all domain controllers running DNS by using the ForestDnsZones application partition. In either configuration, making the forest root domain's _msdcs zone available on all DNS servers allows clients and servers to quickly access the zone's records.

As network designers gain experience and encounter more unique situations, they occasionally have good reason to deviate from the recommended configuration or best practice. However, doing something contrary to best practices should be a rare exception, not a rule, and the designer should always be able to justify the decision.

DESIGNING FORESTS

When designing Active Directory, start with forests and work down to domains. This logical approach of working from the big to the small ensures that you tackle the most important issues first and keeps you from letting small, operational decisions dictate the answers to large, enterprise-wide issues.

This section will begin by examining the characteristics of a forest and then discuss when multiple forests might be required within an organization. However, before continuing you will need to complete Activity 5-1, in which you will demote your domain controller.

Activity 5-1: Demoting a domain controller

Time Required: 20 minutes

Objective: Learn how a domain controller can be demoted back to a standalone server.

Description: In order to complete the activities in this chapter and future chapters, you need to first demote your domain controller. While promotion is the process of designating a server as a domain controller, demotion is the process of removing a server from performing the role of a domain controller.

1. If necessary, start your server and log on using the **AdminXX** account in the **CHILDXX** domain (where *XX* is the number of your server).

2. Click **Start** and then click **Run**.

3. In the Open combo box, type **DCPROMO** and then click **OK**.

4. Once the Welcome to the Active Directory Installation Wizard window appears, click **Next**.

5. In the Remove Active Directory dialog box, check the box next to **This server is the last domain controller in the domain**, as shown in Figure 5-4.

6. Click **Next**. The Application Directory Partitions dialog box opens as shown in Figure 5-5. If this is the last domain controller that holds a given application directory partition, it will be listed here.

7. Click **Next**. The Confirm Deletion dialog box opens.

8. Check the box next to **Delete all application directory partitions on this domain controller**, and click **Next**.

9. In the Network Credentials dialog box, enter a user account that has enterprise administrator privileges for the forest. In this case, enter **Administrator** for the User name, **Password01** as the Password, and confirm that **supercorp.net** is entered in the Domain text box.

10. Click **Next**.

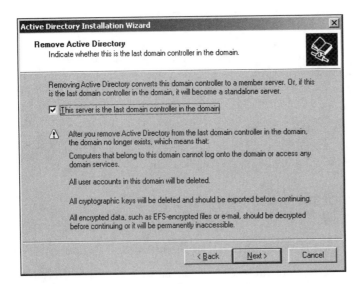

Figure 5-4   Remove Active Directory dialog box

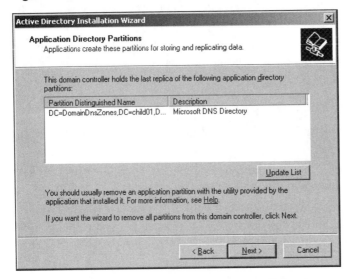

Figure 5-5   Application Directory Partitions dialog box

11. In the Administrator Password dialog box, you are prompted to assign a password to the server Administrator account. In the New Administrator Password and Confirm password text boxes, type **Password01** (note the capitalization), and then click **Next**. The Summary dialog box opens as shown in Figure 5-6.

NOTE

Because you are removing Active Directory from this server, it will once again have a local SAM database to store local users and groups after it is demoted. Think of this screen as just like being prompted for the local Administrator account when you install Windows. After demoting a domain controller, the server will have a fairly empty SAM database with only default users and groups.

5

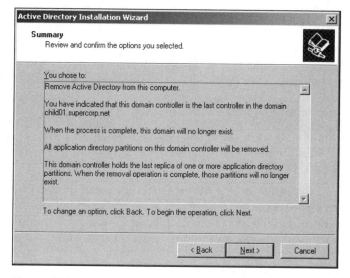

Figure 5-6   Active Directory Installation Wizard Summary dialog box

12. Review the information and then click **Next**. The demotion process begins. This may take several minutes.

13. Once the demotion process has completed, the Completing the Active Directory Installation Wizard dialog box opens. Click **Finish**.

14. A message box prompts you to restart now or not. Click **Restart Now**.

Characteristics of a Forest

A forest has some fundamental characteristics. First, it is the implementation of Active Directory. That is, one single forest really represents one single Active Directory installation. Each and every time you have an Active Directory structure, you have a forest. If you have two forests, you have two separate Active Directory structures. If you have multiple configurations of Active Directory, you have multiple forests.

As well as being an "instance" of Active Directory, a forest can also be viewed as a collection of domains, and a domain can be considered a section or division of a forest.

Keep in mind that the data for each domain is stored in a domain partition. All domain partitions, combined with the configuration partition, the schema partition, and any defined application partitions, make up the forest. Even though partitions are stored on separate domain controllers in a multiple-domain forest, the forest is not complete without its domains, and a domain cannot stand alone without its forest.

A forest is also a security and administrative boundary. Security information is not propagated between forests. Within the boundary of a forest, some information is common. All domains in a forest share these items:

- A centrally controlled schema, stored in a schema partition that is replicated to all domain controllers in the forest.

- A common configuration, stored in the configuration partition that is replicated to all domain controllers in the forest. This configuration information includes infrastructure and topology elements such as domains, sites, and site links. Sites and site links are discussed in Chapter 6.

- A single global catalog, stored on designated Global Catalog servers to allow for quick searches for any object in the forest. (Global Catalog servers have copies of the domain partition for their own domain, plus partial copies of the domain partitions from any other domains in the forest.)

- Complete trust relationships, in that Active Directory automatically creates transitive two-way trusts between all domains in a forest. Trusts are discussed more fully later in this chapter, but within a forest, any user from any domain in the forest can be granted access to any resource in any domain in the forest.

How Many Forests?

There is not usually a need to create more than one forest for an organization—even in a very large organization. A single forest can contain millions of objects and provide excellent performance. It is necessary to create multiple forests only when one of the items shared within a forest cannot be shared without violating a business objective. Here are some examples of situations that justify multiple forests:

- If two parts of an organization must have different schemas, then they must have different forests. For example, a division might require that Active Directory be populated with objects from new classes, or a subsidiary that runs custom software requiring a schema incompatible with the rest of the organization.

- If two parts of an organization must have complete separation of administration, they must have different forests. This is most commonly seen in multinational organizations, where specific national laws impose restrictions on where data is kept and how it is managed.

■ If one part of a company cannot participate in a complete trust model, then separate forests are justified. One example of this situation includes high-security areas, such as military or classified projects. Another situation where a second forest is justified is to support a large Web farm or Internet presence. If the computers serving the public need maximum isolation from the corporate network, but still require the services of Active Directory, it may be a good idea to have a second forest.

So when the business requirements dictate a high degree of separation between entities, creating separate forests may be necessary. Keep in mind, though, that making more forests adds work for administrators, and forfeits the benefit of a single global catalog. Additional costs are incurred for hardware, software, and labor.

Creating a new forest means creating a new implementation of Active Directory, and each forest must also have a clearly defined service owner. Create more than one forest only when it is necessary to meet a defined business requirement.

ACTIVITY

Activity 5-2: Promoting the First Domain Controller in a New Forest

Time Required: 30 minutes

Objective: Learn how to promote the first domain controller in a new Active Directory forest.

Only the student in a student group who has the lower server number should complete Activity 5-2. The second member of the student group should not perform these steps on their server.

NOTE

Description: In this activity, you will promote the first domain controller in a new Active Directory forest. The *supercorp.net* subdomain will be used as the company's Internet presence and will have a subdomain called child*XX*.supercorp.net delegated (which you have already configured in Chapter 2) to an internal DNS server for Active Directory. In the first part of this activity, you will create a new DNS zone for Active Directory. You will then promote the first domain controller for the new Active Directory forest. Finally, you will modify the DNS zone to store the zone in Active Directory and only allow secure dynamic updates.

NOTE

While in previous chapters your server was a domain controller in a child domain called childXX.supercorp.net, your server will now be a domain controller in a forest root domain called childXX.supercorp.net. While the DNS names are exactly the same, the Active Directory domain structure is different. That is, childXX.supercorp.net is now the forest root domain in a new forest. For example, Figure 5-7 illustrates the classroom setup prior to Chapter 5 for student servers 1 through 4. In contrast, Figure 5-8 illustrates the classroom setup for student servers 1 through 4 once Activity 5-3 is completed. Notice that each group of two students will have their own forest after Activity 5-3 is completed.

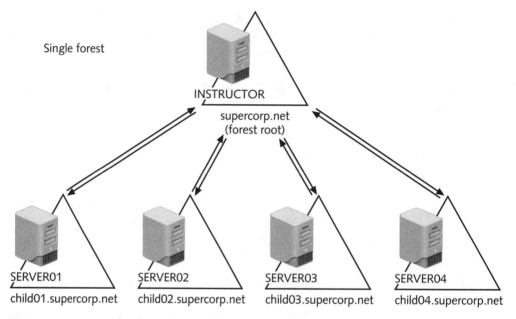

Figure 5-7   Example classroom setup prior to starting Activity 5-1

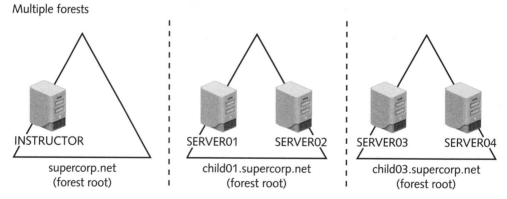

Figure 5-8   Example classroom setup after completing Activity 5-3

1. Log on locally to your server using the **Administrator** user account and the password **Password01**.

2. Check the **Don't display this page at logon** check box on the Manage Your Server window and close the Manage Your Server window.

3. If necessary, click **Start**, select **Administrative tools**, and then click **DNS**.

4. If necessary, expand **SERVERXX** (where *XX* is the number of your server) in the left tree pane.

NOTE

Although in this activity you are manually configuring the DNS zone for Active Directory before promoting the first domain controller, you could also allow DCPROMO to automatically create this zone for you during the promotion process. In most situations, you can configure your server's DNS settings (that is, under the TCP/IP Properties of the server's network connection) to use the correct DNS server and then allow DCPROMO to create the new zone—as you did in Chapter 1. However, in some situations, you may need to manually create the zone if DCPROMO is unable to.

5. In the left tree pane, right-click **Forward Lookup Zones**, and then click **New Zone**.

6. In the Welcome to the New Zone Wizard dialog box, click **Next**.

7. In the Zone Type dialog box, ensure that the **Primary zone** option button is selected, and click **Next**.

8. In the Zone Name dialog box, enter **childXX.supercorp.net** (where *XX* is the number of your server) in the Zone name text box.

9. Click **Next**.

10. In the Zone File dialog box, leave the default option to create a new file, and click **Next**.

11. In the Dynamic Update dialog box, select the **Allow both nonsecure and secure dynamic updates** option button, and click **Next**. The Completing the New Zone Wizard dialog box opens as shown in Figure 5-9.

12. Click **Finish**.

13. Close the DNS console.

NOTE

Keep in mind that your server has already been configured to use itself for DNS name resolution.

14. Click **Start** and then click **Run**.

15. In the Open combo box, type **DCPROMO**, and then click **OK**.

16. Once the Active Directory Installation Wizard welcome screen appears, click **Next**.

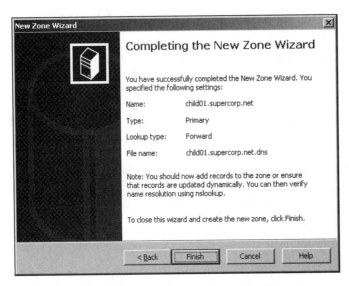

Figure 5-9   Creating a new zone for Active Directory

17. In the Operating System Compatibility dialog box, click **Next**.

18. In the Domain Controller Type dialog box, ensure that the **Domain controller for a new domain** option button is selected, and click **Next**.

19. In the Create New Domain dialog box, ensure that the **Domain in a new forest option** button is selected as shown in Figure 5–10.

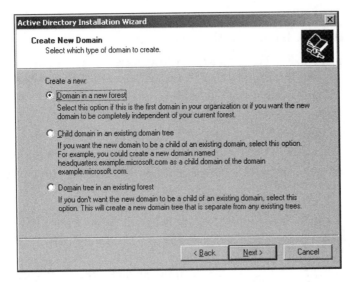

Figure 5-10   Create New Domain dialog box

20. Click **Next**.

21. In the New Domain Name dialog box, enter **childXX.supercorp.net** (where *XX* is the number of your server) in the Full DNS name for new domain text box, and then click **Next**.

22. In the NetBIOS Domain Name dialog box, leave the default NetBIOS name CHILD*XX*, and click **Next**.

23. In the Database and Log Folders dialog box, leave the default locations, and click **Next**. These options specify the location of the Active Directory store and the Active Directory log files, respectively.

24. In the Shared System Volume dialog box, leave the default location, and click **Next**. The DNS Registration Diagnostics dialog box opens as shown in Figure 5-11.

25. Click **Next**.

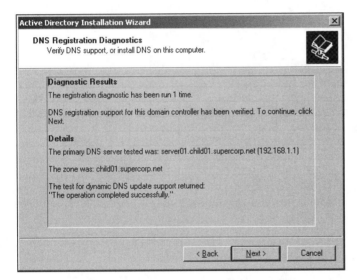

Figure 5-11   DNS Registration Diagnostics dialog box

26. In the Permissions dialog box, ensure that the default option button, **Permissions compatible only with Windows 2000 or Windows Server 2003 operating systems**, is selected and click **Next**.

27. In the Directory Services Restore Mode Administrator Password dialog box, enter **Password01** in the Restore Mode Password and Confirm password text boxes.

NOTE Some operations, such as restoring the Active Directory database from backup, require that the Active Directory store be off-line. In Chapter 13, you will learn how to start a domain controller in Directory Services Restore Mode (which requires the use of the Directory Services Restore Mode administrator password).

28. Click **Next**. The Summary dialog box opens as shown in Figure 5-12.

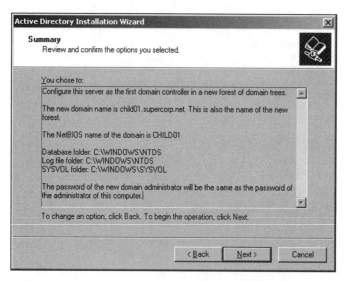

Figure 5-12   Active Directory Installation Wizard Summary dialog box

29. Click **Next**. The domain controller promotion process begins. This could take several minutes.

30. Once the promotion process completes, the Completing the Active Directory Installation Wizard dialog box opens. Click **Finish**.

31. A message box prompts you to restart now or not. Click **Restart Now**.

32. After your server restarts, log on using the **Administrator** account in the **CHILDXX** (where *XX* is the number of your server) domain using the password **Password01**.

33. Click **Start**, select **Administrative Tools**, and then click **DNS**.

34. If necessary, expand **SERVERXX** (where *XX* is the number of your server) and then expand **Forward Lookup Zones** in the left tree pane.

35. Right-click **childXX.supercorp.net** (where *XX* is the number of your server) in the left tree pane, and then click **Properties**.

36. On the General tab, click the **Change** button.

37. Check the box next to **Store the zone in Active Directory**, and then click **OK**.

38. A message box prompts you if you want the zone to become Active Directory integrated. Click **Yes**.

39. In the Dynamic updates list box, select **Secure only**.

40. Click **OK** in the zone's properties window.

41. Close the DNS console.

42. Log off your server if you do not intend to immediately continue to the next project. Otherwise, stay logged on.

5

Designing Domains

An important part of planning an Active Directory deployment is determining the number of domains that are needed. There are a few reasons for creating more than one domain. Some are organizational or administrative, and some are technical. In the sections that follow, you will first review the major functions of a domain, in particular the special role of the forest root domain. The sections then discuss the limitations of considering a domain as a security boundary. Next, you will look at the advantages of a single domain and the advantages of using multiple domains, and end with a discussion of Microsoft's recommendation of a dedicated forest root domain.

Functions of a Domain

A domain is a partition—or division—of a forest. The most important characteristic of a domain is that it's a **replication boundary**. As discussed in Chapter 4, every domain controller in a domain has a complete copy of that domain's partition in its Active Directory database. This means that the objects in a domain are replicated fully to all replicas in the domain, and except for the specific attributes replicated to Global Catalog servers, the domain data is not replicated at all outside the domain.

Limiting the replication of Active Directory data allows an Active Directory forest to be scaled out to a very wide area network, even over slow or heavily congested networks. A domain also provides some important and useful functions for a Windows network. The main functions of a domain include:

- Authentication—A domain stores objects representing users, groups, and computers—known as security principals—that can be granted or denied access to resources anywhere in the forest. However, the actual authentication involves a domain controller located in the same domain as the security principal object—not the domain that contains the resource.

- Policy-based administration—Group policy is easily applied at the domain level.

■ Setting account policies for user accounts in the domain—Account policies, such as password length, age, and complexity requirements, affect the entire domain. It is not possible to set multiple account policies for different users in the same domain—all users in a single domain share common account policies.

■ A directory for publishing shared resources—Objects in the domain represent printers, file shares, and other resources, making them easier to find.

A domain also functions as an administrative boundary. Each domain can be administered separately and have both service owners and data owners that are separate and distinct from those of other domains. Administrative rights assigned in one domain do not propagate to others. For example, if a forest has a domain called *northamerica.supercorp.net* and a child domain called *chicago.northamerica.supercorp.net*, the Domain Admins group in northamerica is not a member of the Domain Admins group in chicago. There is a common misconception that permissions and rights assigned in a parent domain are inherited to child domains in the tree, which is not the case.

NOTE   Administrators of the forest root domain are, by default, given special privileges throughout the forest. During installation, the administrator of the forest root domain is placed in the Enterprise Admins group as well as in the Domain Admins group (in the forest root domain). Additionally, the Enterprise Admins group is by default added to the Administrators group in every domain of the forest. This allows members of Enterprise Admins to manage any domain in the forest.

Is It a Security Boundary?

A great deal of discussion has taken place since the release of Windows 2000 about whether a domain can be considered a security boundary. On the one hand, a user is authenticated only by his or her own domain; group policy is often applied at the domain level, and account policies for domain users can only be set at the domain level. On the other hand, a domain is only part of a forest, sharing several partitions and sending information about security principals and other objects outside the domain. It is best, therefore, not to depend on a domain as a security boundary. If you need complete and secure isolation of a part of your directory, you should consider making it into a separate forest.

Which Works Better: Single or Multiple Domains?

Prior to the release of Active Directory, many large companies required multiple domains because of limitations in the Windows NT domain structure, primarily because an NT domain cannot practically scale beyond 40,000 objects, give or take. Active Directory has removed those limitations, and can support millions of objects in a single domain.

There are advantages to working with only a single domain and advantages to working with multiple domains.

Advantages of a Single Domain

A single domain is easier to manage. It is easier to delegate authority and apply group policies on organizational units, rather than across domains. It requires fewer hardware resources, such as domain controllers, and requires fewer domain administrators and less work for the current staff.

Advantages of Multiple Domains

By creating multiple domains, each can have a distinct set of administrators, policies, and data owners. This can provide tighter administrative control or support a decentralized administrative structure. For example, if two departments require different domain user account password policies, they can either come to some mutually acceptable agreement on policy, or two domains must be created. Another cause for multiple domains is the need to integrate external partner agencies into your directory, but keep them at a bit of a distance.

There may be organizational reasons to have separate domains. For example, if two divisions of an organization both have strong cases to be service owners and data owners of their own directory service, and neither is willing to "submit" to the administration of the other, then perhaps the easiest solution is to create two domains. To determine whether multiple domains are justified for organizational (or political) reasons, the designer must look at the vision and the business goals developed earlier in the process.

The most compelling technical reasons for multiple domains are to control replication and to support multiple account policies. For example, a multinational company may not wish to replicate the full database of all objects across slow and expensive wide area links between continents. Additionally, the company may require that staff in the Research Department change their passwords every 30 days, whereas other departments only need to change their passwords every 60 days.

Using a Dedicated Forest Root

The first domain created in an Active Directory forest is called the forest root domain. This domain has a few special characteristics not shared by other domains:

- It is the domain that holds the groups that can manage the forest, such as the Enterprise Admins group and the Schema Admins group.

- It is a central point for trust relationships. Each tree in the forest will have a trust relationship with the forest root domain.

- It is difficult to rename the forest root domain, and it cannot be deleted without deleting the entire Active Directory structure or using a complicated migration tool.

Microsoft recommends that the forest root domain be completely dedicated to managing the infrastructure of the forest. That is, no regular users or even regular domain administrators should be created in the forest root domain. Rather, a single child domain is created under the forest root to handle all user and resource objects. Microsoft has found that dedicating a forest root domain allows the greatest flexibility for the future and minimizes the chance of a complete Active Directory redeployment to support growth or change. Microsoft also states that in this structure, fewer administrators are allowed to make forest-wide changes, the forest root domain is easily replicated for redundancy, it never becomes obsolete, and it can have its ownership transferred fairly easily.

Beyond this dedicated forest root, Microsoft recommends that an organization use one domain, unless business needs dictate otherwise. If multiple domains are required, Microsoft's general recommendation is to create domains based on geography, since geography is stable (unlike politics or organizational charts). For example, a company may have a dedicated root domain, a domain for Europe, another for the Americas, and another for Africa, the Middle East, and Asia.

This is one of a series of recommendations, sometimes called "best practices," made by Microsoft. A best practice represents the opinion of consultants and developers in the industry, and is usually based on the real-life operations at companies using the product or technology in production.

Bear in mind, however, that Microsoft tends to view Active Directory, and Active Directory best practices in particular, from the point of view of large corporations. The dedicated forest root is an excellent idea for global corporations such as Microsoft and its largest clients. It is not a practical recommendation for small businesses to set up a dedicated root domain, even though small businesses use Active Directory.

Activity 5-3: Promoting an Additional Domain Controller in an Existing Domain

ACTIVITY

Time Required: 20 minutes

Objective: Learn how to promote an additional domain controller in an existing Active Directory domain.

Only the student in a student group who has the higher server number should complete Activity 5-3 . The first member of the student group should not perform these steps on their domain controller.

NOTE

Description: While it is possible to have an Active Directory domain with only a single domain controller, it is not recommended. Having multiple domain controllers has two primary benefits: redundancy and performance. (You will learn more about domain controller placement and requirements in the next chapter.) In this activity, you will promote your server as an additional domain controller in the domain that your partner created in Activity 5-2.

CAUTION
You must wait for your partner to complete Activity 5-2 before beginning this project.

1. Log on locally to your server using the **Administrator** user account and the password **Password01**.

NOTE
In order to add an additional domain controller to an existing domain, the new server must be able to locate the SRV records in DNS for the existing domain. To accomplish this, you will configure your server to use the DNS server located on your partner's server for DNS name resolution.

5

2. Click Start, select Control Panel, select Network Connections, right-click Local Area Connection, and then click Properties.

3. In the Local Area Connection Properties dialog box, select Internet Protocol (TCP/IP) from the This connection uses the following items list box.

4. Click Properties.

5. In the Preferred DNS server, replace the existing DNS server with 192.168.1.*XX* (where *XX* is the IP address of your partner's server, without any leading zeros), as shown in Figure 5-13.

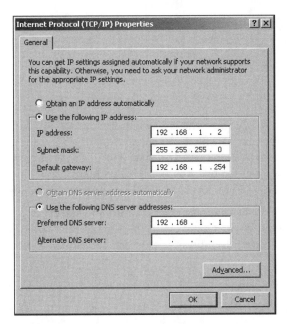

Figure 5-13   Configuring DNS settings on a second domain controller

6. Click **OK**.

7. Click **Close** to close the Local Area Connection Properties dialog box.

8. Click **Start** and then click **Run**.

9. In the Open combo box, type **DCPROMO**, and then click **OK**.

10. Once the Active Directory Installation Wizard welcome screen appears, click **Next**.

11. In the Operating System Compatibility dialog box, click **Next**.

12. In the Domain Controller Type dialog box, select the **Additional domain controller for an existing domain** option button, as shown in Figure 5-14.

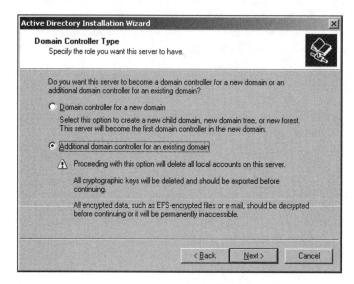

Figure 5-14   Domain Controller Type dialog box

13. Click **Next**.

14. In the Network Credentials dialog box, enter the credentials for an account that has administrative privileges in the domain to which you are attempting to add the additional domain controller. In this scenario, enter **Administrator** in the User name combo box, **Password01** in the Password text box, and **child*XX*.supercorp.net** (where *XX* is the number of your partner's server) in the Domain text box. Click **Next**.

15. In the Additional Domain Controller dialog box, type **child*XX*.supercorp.net** (where *XX* is the number of your partner's server) in the Domain name text box. This is the domain to which you are attempting to add the additional domain controller. Click **Next**.

16. In the Database and Log Folders dialog box, leave the default locations and click **Next**.

17. In the Shared System Volume dialog box, leave the default location and click **Next**.

18. In the Directory Services Restore Mode Administrator Password dialog box, enter **Password01** in the Restore Mode Password and Confirm password text boxes, and then click **Next**. The Summary dialog box opens.

19. Review the information and then click **Next**. The domain controller promotion process begins. This could take several minutes.

20. Once the promotion process completes, the Completing the Active Directory Installation Wizard dialog box opens. Click **Finish**.

21. A message box prompts you to restart now or not. Click **Restart Now**.

UNDERSTANDING AND IMPLEMENTING TRUST RELATIONSHIPS

A **trust relationship** is what gives a user in one domain the ability to access a resource in another without needing separate credentials for each domain. Recall that joining a domain lets a user access resources on more than one server in the domain without needing to reauthenticate to each server's local SAM database. In a similar way, trust relationships extend that ability across multiple domains, and possibly across multiple forests.

To help with terminology, remember that the *trusting domain* trusts the *trusted domain* to authenticate a user. The user exists in the trusted domain; the resource is in the trusting domain. Think of the *trusting domain* as trusting the *trusted domain* to vouch for one of the *trusted domain's* users. In Figure 5-15, the arrow points from the trusting domain to the trusted domain.

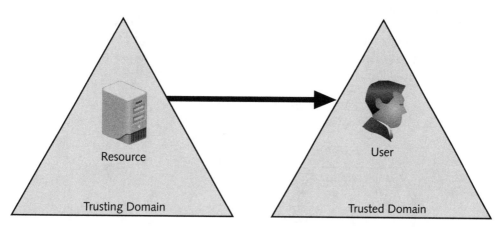

Figure 5-15   Example trust diagram

Transitive Trusts

Trust transitivity is used to determine if the trust extends outside the two domains in which the trust is formed. When a trust is transitive, it means that if A trusts B, and B trusts C, then A also trusts C. This is shown in Figure 5-16 where a user account is located in Domain C and a resource is located in Domain A. In the figure, Domain A trusts Domain B and Domain B trusts Domain C. Because the trusts are transitive in this example, Domain A also trusts Domain C because Domain B trusts Domain C.

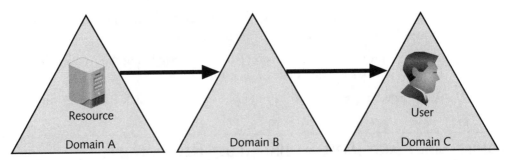

Figure 5-16   Example transitivity diagram

Two-Way, Transitive Trusts

As domains are added to an Active Directory forest, a **two-way, transitive trust** is created between the new domain and an existing domain of the forest. The term "two-way" means that domain A trusts domain B, and domain B trusts domain A. These default two-way, transitive trusts cannot be manually removed (unless the entire domain is removed).

In an Active Directory forest, trusts are established on a domain-to-domain level. Even though all domains in a single forest automatically participate in a complete trust model, the complete trust is built on a series of individual two-way, transitive trusts between particular domains in the forest. Take, for example, the forest pictured in Figure 5-17. There are six domains in this large forest. The domain named supercorp.net was the first domain created and is the forest root domain. Two other domains form part of its tree, while a second tree beginning with fastitstaff.com, is also part of the forest.

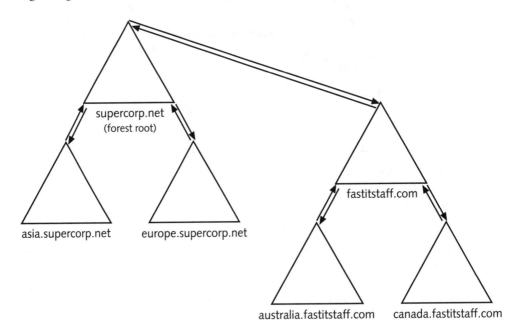

Figure 5-17   Trust relationships automatically created in a forest

If a domain is a child domain of another domain in a tree, there is a trust relationship formed between the parent domain and the child domain. If the domain is at the top of a tree, but is not the forest root domain, a trust is formed between it and the forest root domain. Each is a two-way, transitive trust.

Shortcut Trusts

The effect of two-way, transitive trusts within a forest is that a trust path can always be found from one domain to any other in the forest. This is sometimes called "walking the tree," as several domains may have to be traversed along the way. For example, take the domains shown in Figure 5-17. A user in europe.supercorp.net can be given permissions to resources in australia.fastitstaff.com, but in order to be authenticated, the domain controllers in australia.fastitstaff.com, fastitstaff.com, supercorp.net, and europe.supercorp.net all need to be involved in the process. Although the trusts are transitive, authentication must follow a trust path.

To cut down on the number of steps involved, administrators can define one-way or two-way, **shortcut trusts** that allow quicker authentication of security credentials by pointing one domain directly to another, without intervening steps. In this example, australia can trust europe directly. Shortcut trusts reduce the number of domain controllers that must be involved in a cross-domain authentication, thereby increasing efficiency and reducing the number of possible points of failure. If users in the europe.supercorp.net domain frequently access resources in the australia.fastitstaff.com domain, adding a shortcut trust is a good idea. The addition of a shortcut trust is shown in Figure 5-18.

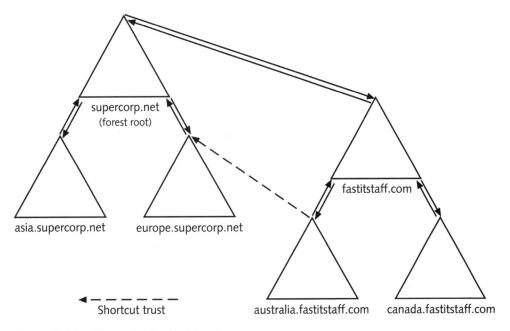

Figure 5-18   Example shortcut trust

Forest Trusts

Forest trusts allow a trust relationship to be established between two forests. A forest trust can be one-way or two-way, and is transitive. These trusts are particularly useful when two organizations merge and need to combine two existing Active Directory forests.

Forest trusts are transitive only between domains located in the two forests explicitly selected. For example, examine Figure 5-19. Forest 1 trusts forest 2, and forest 1 also trusts forest 3. This does not mean that forest 2 automatically trusts forest 3—it does not. By saying that forest trusts are transitive, it means that all domains in forest 1 trust all domains in forest 2. Thus, a user from domainh.forest3.net could access a resource in domainb.forest1.net, domainc.forest1.net, or domaina.forest1.net. However, that same user could not automatically access a resource in domaind.forest2.net.

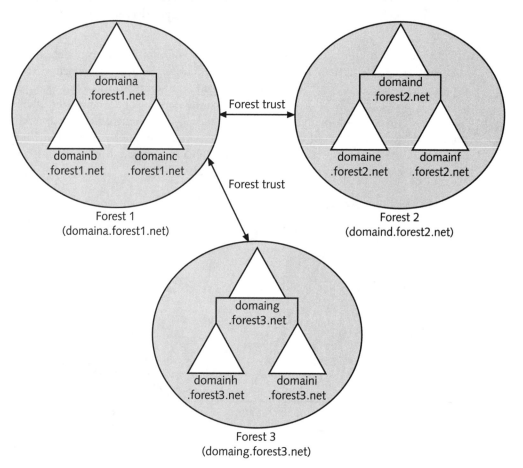

Figure 5-19   Example forest trust

NOTE   Forest trusts are only available in the Windows Server 2003 forest functional level, as discussed later in this chapter.

Realm Trusts

Realm trusts are used to create a trust relationship between a non–Windows Kerberos realm and a Windows domain. Realm trusts can be transitive or nontransitive and one-way or two-way. They allow for interoperability with other cross-platform security services that use Kerberos version 5 such as UNIX.

Nontransitive Trusts

In a **nontransitive trust**, a trust between two domains does not extend outside the two domains the trust is directly between. What this means is that if A trusts B and B trusts C, A does not automatically trust C when using nontransitive trusts. In order for A to trust C, an additional trust has to be explicitly created between the two domains.

External Trusts

An external trust is used between a Windows Server 2003 domain and a Windows NT domain. External trusts can also be used between two Windows 2000 Server or Windows Server 2003 domains located in different forests. An example of an external trust is shown in Figure 5-20. By default, external trusts are **one-way trusts**—which means that if A trusts B, B does not automatically trust A. However, two one-way, nontransitive trusts can be used to create an external two-way, nontransitive trust.

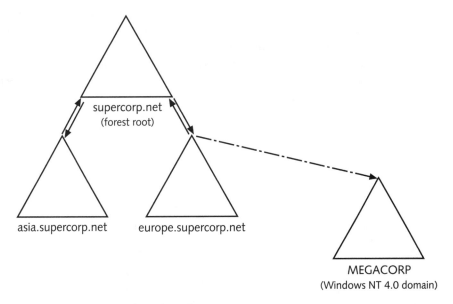

Figure 5-20   Example external trust

Realm Trusts

As already stated, realm trusts are used to create a trust relationship between a non-Windows Kerberos realm and a Windows domain. Realm trusts can be transitive or nontransitive and one-way or two-way. They allow for interoperability with other cross-platform security services that use Kerberos version 5, such as UNIX.

DESIGNING ORGANIZATIONAL UNITS

An organizational unit (OU) is used to group objects within a domain into a hierarchical structure. Having a hierarchical structure of organizational units allows objects to be grouped for categorization, as well as for management.

Although an organizational unit is not an administrative or replication boundary—like a domain—it is a division within the directory structure that allows for delegation of administration and controls the scope of policy application. Take, as an example, a mid-sized organization with about 1000 employees. A competent IT Department is the service owner for all of Active Directory. The HR Department is the data owner for user objects, creating and managing users in the directory as people join and leave the company. The research division is the data owner for a number of resources in a highly dynamic environment, and administration, sales, and marketing all depend on stable access to fixed resources. These other divisions have staff with fewer technical skills than those in IT or research. Prior to the release of Active Directory, designers may have been tempted to create multiple Windows NT domains to meet the needs of different user groups, and to allow various data owners to have control over objects without giving them more authority than necessary.

However, with Active Directory, this scenario fits easily within one domain with several organizational units. The IT Department delegates control over an organizational unit containing user objects to the HR Department. Separating the resources used by research into their own organizational unit allows different policies than those used by the rest of the company to be applied to those resources. One possible organizational unit structure for this situation is shown in Figure 5-21.

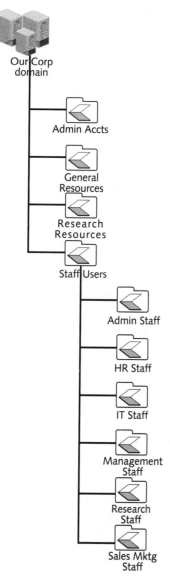

5

Figure 5-21   Example organizational unit structure

Best Practices for Designing Organizational Units

Although it is always a good idea to plan out your full structure before deploying Active Directory, the good news is that organizational units are comparatively easy to restructure. They can be created, deleted, or renamed with little difficulty, and objects such as users can be easily moved between organizational units. Using organizational units to organize one (or a few) domains is much more flexible than creating multiple domains.

Organizational units are a better choice than a separate domain when a division, department, or organization within the enterprise wants ownership of its directory data. There is no need to create separate domains when delegation of control can allow that business unit to be a data owner without being a service owner. Because true autonomy can only be achieved with a new forest (not just a new domain), there is little value in needlessly creating domains. Instead, use organizational units to organize and delegate a separate forest for those rare occasions when complete isolation is required.

Every organizational unit that you create should serve a purpose. It is not necessary for every box on a company's organizational chart to have a corresponding organizational unit in the directory. Unless a purpose is served (easier location, separate policies, separate administrative delegations, and so forth), there is no reason to make extra organizational units, as it results in an expenditure of time and resources without any return benefit. Also keep in mind, no matter how you come up with your organizational unit design, you should choose structures that remain relatively static.

Organizational units can be nested within one another. Technologically, there is no practical limit to how many levels of nesting Active Directory can support, but Microsoft recommends that nesting not be more than 10 levels deep. Nesting organizational units more than 10 levels deep introduces more complexity and confusion for administration, and could start to slow down the processing of **Group Policy objects (GPOs)** at logon.

While there are hundreds of ways an organizational unit hierarchy could be created, the following sections cover the three most common models. When choosing an organizational unit design, keep in mind how resources can be organized so that administrative tasks can be delegated to the appropriate authority.

Activity 5-4: Creating Organizational Units

Time Required: 10 minutes

Objective: Learn how to create new organizational units and nested organizational units.

Description: In this activity, you will create a new organizational unit in your domain. This is a very common job-related task for Active Directory administrators, and you can easily become proficient at it. Because organizational units are the most common and important way to organize objects in the directory, you will use the organizational units you create now to hold objects in later activities.

1. If necessary, start your server and log on using the **Administrator** account in the **CHILDXX** (where *XX* is the number of the forest root domain your server is a domain controller for) domain using the password **Password01**.

2. Click **Start**, select **Administrative Tools**, and then click **Active Directory Users and Computers**.

3. In the left tree pane, expand **childXX.supercorp.net** (where *XX* is the number of the forest root domain for which your server is a domain controller).

4. Right-click **childXX.supercorp.net** (where *XX* is the number of the forest root domain your server is a domain controller for), select **New**, and then click **Organizational Unit**.

5. In the New Object – Organizational Unit dialog box, enter **North America XX** (where *XX* is the number of your server) in the Name text box as shown in Figure 5-22.

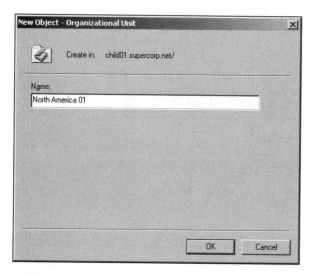

Figure 5-22   Creating a new organizational unit

6. Click **OK**.

7. In the left tree pane, right-click North America *XX* (where *XX* is the number of your server), select **New**, and then click **Organizational Unit**.

8. Enter **Atlanta** in the Name text box, and then click **OK**. The new organizational units appear, as shown in Figure 5-23.

9. Close Active Directory Users and Computers.

10. Log off your server if you do not intend to immediately continue to the next project. Otherwise, stay logged on.

Organizing Organizational Units by Location

In an organizational unit hierarchy based on location, each organizational unit represents an office or campus location or a general region. Determining if the company is statewide, nationwide, or worldwide determines how many levels are required. For example, Figure 5-24 shows an example organizational unit hierarchy based on location.

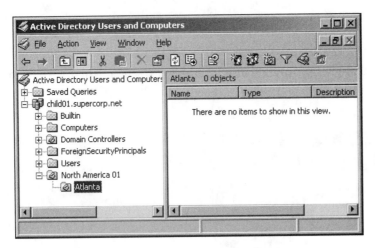

Figure 5-23   Newly created organizational units

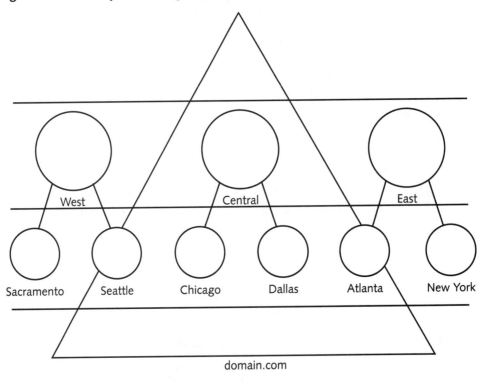

domain.com

Figure 5-24   Location-based organizational unit hierarchy

An organizational unit hierarchy based on location works best when administrative authority is different between locations. An example of this would be a company that has a central office and three branch offices, each with a single administrator. While the administrator at the central office may retain control over the entire domain, an organizational unit could be created for each of the three branch offices. The administrator at each office could then be delegated control over the organizational unit that represents their respective branch office. This would then allow each branch office administrator to manage the resources located in their organizational unit (and in turn their branch office).

Organizing Organizational Units by Function

In an organizational unit hierarchy based on function, each organizational unit represents a division, practice, or business unit. For example, in Figure 5-25 the first level of organizational units is based on how the company functionally operates. The second layer of the hierarchy represents subpractices in each of the company's functional divisions.

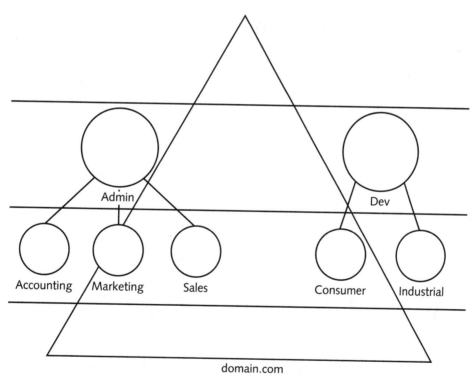

domain.com

Figure 5-25   Function-based organizational unit hierarchy

An organizational unit hierarchy based on function works best when each department or division of the company has its own administrative control—even when spread across multiple physical locations. It can also make the location of resources easier for users when the resources they need are located in many different physical locations.

Organizing Organizational Units by Location and Function

In a hybrid organizational unit hierarchy based on location and function, resources are grouped by location and then function, as shown in Figure 5-26.

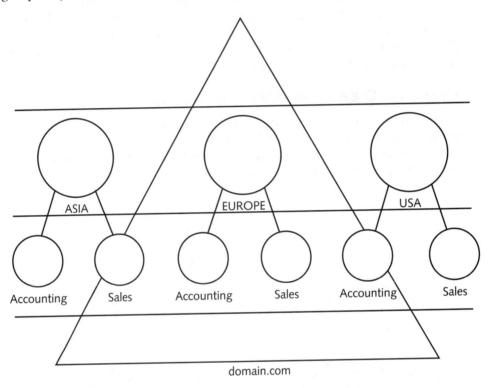

domain.com

Figure 5-26   Hybrid organizational unit hierarchy

This organizational unit design allows for the benefits of the location-based and function-based hierarchies. Administrative control for resources at a physical location can be delegated to staff for that location while still allowing for further delegation of each department or division. This makes the location of resources much easier for users when the resources they need are located within a single physical location.

UPGRADING WINDOWS NT OR WINDOWS 2000 DOMAINS

Before you introduce Windows Server 2003 into an existing network, there are a few things you should consider. For example, not all applications will run the same way on a new operating system. The default security settings in Windows Server 2003 are more restrictive than in previous versions. Also, the Web server (Internet Information Services, or IIS) is a new version that behaves a bit differently. Changing or upgrading the operating system on your network is not a task that should be taken lightly—you must be aware of the consequences.

There are a number of different methods for integrating Windows Server 2003 into an existing network, and you should understand each in order to choose the best method for a given situation.

Active Directory Functional Levels

5

Because new features have been introduced with each new version of Active Directory, its functionality varies depending on the version of Windows used on the domain controllers. Some functionality requires that all domain controllers in the domain use the same version, while other functionality requires that all domain controllers in the entire forest are able to support the new features.

To handle the different functions provided by different versions, and to allow the administrator to manage how domains and forests behave, Microsoft introduced the concept of functional levels. In the version of Active Directory introduced with Windows 2000, there were two domain functional levels—mixed mode and native mode. In the version of Active Directory included with Windows Server 2003, there are four domain functional levels:

- Windows 2000 mixed
- Windows 2000 native
- Windows Server 2003 interim
- Windows Server 2003

In addition to new domain functionality levels, Windows Server 2003 also introduces a new concept—the forest functional level. While the domain functional level affects domain-wide functions and features, the forest functional level affects forest-wide functions and features. There are three forest functional levels in Windows Server 2003:

- Windows 2000
- Windows Server 2003 interim
- Windows Server 2003

Activity 5-5: Raising the Domain Functional Level

Time Required: 10 minutes

Objective: Learn how to raise the domain functional level.

Only the student in a student group who has the lower server number should complete Activity 5-5. The second member of the student group should not perform these steps on their domain controller.

Description: In this activity, you will learn how to raise the domain functional level to Windows Server 2003. You will work with a partner because the conversion can only be completed once.

1. If necessary, start your server and log on using the **Administrator** account in the **CHILDXX** (where *XX* is the number of the forest root domain for which your server is a domain controller) domain using the password **Password01**.

2. Click **Start**, select **Administrative Tools**, and then click **Active Directory Domains and Trusts**.

3. Right-click **childXX.supercorp.net** (where *XX* is the number of the forest root domain for which your server is a domain controller) in the left tree pane, and then click **Raise Domain Functional Level**.

4. In the Select an available domain functional level list box, choose **Windows Server 2003** as shown in Figure 5-27.

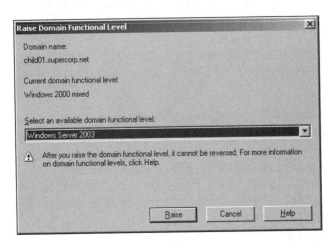

Figure 5-27   Raising the domain functional level

5. Click **Raise**. A message box opens informing you that this change affects the entire domain and is not reversible.

6. Click **OK**. Another message box informs you about the success of raising the domain functional level as shown in Figure 5-28.

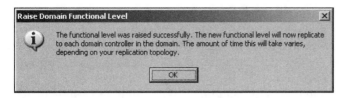

Figure 5-28   Confirmation of raising the domain functional level

7. Click **OK**.

8. Close Active Directory Domains and Trusts.

9. Log off your server if you do not intend to immediately continue to the next project. Otherwise, stay logged on.

Windows 2000 Mixed Domains

All domains are mixed-mode domains when they are first created (that is, they have a domain functional level of Windows 2000 mixed). A mixed-mode domain can contain a combination of domain controllers running Windows NT Server 4.0, Windows 2000 Server, and Windows Server 2003.

A Windows 2000 mixed-mode domain has the most limited functionality of the functional levels. However, Windows Server 2003 running Active Directory in Windows 2000 mixed mode can still do a few things that Windows 2000 Server in mixed mode cannot. The Active Directory enhancements available when Windows Server 2003 is introduced are:

- Install from media
- Global Catalog not required for all logons
- Application directory partitions

Installing from Media   When a Windows Server 2003 server is promoted to a domain controller, you have the option to install the directory information using media instead of copying it across the network. Installing from media can save a significant amount of time, especially if it is a large directory being copied across slow WAN links. The most commonly used media are backup tapes or CD-Rs. Before promoting a server in a remote location, a CD-R or CD-RW containing a replica of the Active Directory information can be shipped to the new site by overnight courier. During the Active Directory installation process, all required Active Directory information can be read from the CD. Normal replication will still update Active Directory, including any changes that occurred between the time the CD was created and the time Active Directory was installed on the new domain controller. See Chapter 14 for more details.

Global Catalogs Not Required for All Logons   Domain controllers require access to a Global Catalog server to provide universal group membership for logons in multi-domain forests (more specifically, when the user account is located in a domain at the Windows 2000 native or Windows Server 2003 functional level). If a Global Catalog server is not available, then non-administrative users cannot log on, even with a correct username and password. Windows 2003 can be configured to cache Universal Group membership, allowing logons even if a Global Catalog server cannot be contacted. Global Catalog servers are covered in more detail in the next chapter.

Application Directory Partitions   Application directory partitions can be part of Active Directory at this domain functional level. However, only Windows Server 2003 domain controllers can contain the application partition replicas. Note that the domain naming master must be running Windows Server 2003 in order for application partitions to be created in the forest. See Chapter 8 for more details on the domain naming master and Chapter 13 for more details on application partitions.

Windows 2000 Native Domains

When all domain controllers in a domain are Windows 2000 or newer, the domain can be switched to Windows 2000 native mode. This mode is never enabled by default, and therefore must be configured by an administrator.

Several useful features are enabled when a domain is switched to Windows 2000 native mode. These include:

- Nesting groups
- Universal Groups
- Remote access policies for dial-up and VPN servers
- SIDhistory for domain migration

Nesting Groups and Universal Groups   Nesting groups allows you to make a global group in one domain a member of another global group in the same domain. It also allows you to make a domain local group in a domain a member of a domain local group in the same domain.

Universal Groups and their membership are stored on Global Catalog servers. Universal Groups are used to aggregate the membership of global groups from different domains. Universal Groups are not available in the Windows 2000 mixed functionality level. Universal Groups and the nesting of groups are covered in Chapter 10.

Remote Access Policies   Remote access policies allow you to control VPN and dial-up access based on criteria such as time of day, group membership, caller ID, and many others. Without remote access policies, you have only limited ability to control how and when users can dial in or connect via a VPN.

SID History   The SIDhistory attribute is used in the migration of users from one domain to another. The SIDhistory attribute of the user in the new domain contains the SID used in the previous domain. In Chapter 9 you will learn more about SIDs.

Windows Server 2003 Interim Domains

Windows Server 2003 interim domains can contain only Windows NT Server 4.0 and Windows Server 2003 domain controllers. It is meant as a replacement for mixed mode when Windows 2000 domain controllers are not required.

Within the domain, the functionality at this level is the same as in Windows 2000 mixed mode. However, it does allow for increased functionality at the forest level. The option to enable this level is only available during the upgrade of the Windows NT Server 4.0 PDC.

5

Windows Server 2003 Domains

When all domain controllers in a domain have been upgraded to Windows Server 2003, the domain can be raised to the Windows Server 2003 functional level. This mode is never enabled by default, and must be enabled by an administrator using the Active Directory Domains and Trusts console.

Many Active Directory enhancements are enabled with the Windows Server 2003 functional level, in addition to the features that were available in Windows 2000 native mode. These Windows Server 2003 functional level features include:

- Replicating a logon timestamp
- User password on inetOrgPerson object
- DC rename

Logon Timestamp   A new attribute for user objects, named **lastLogonTimestamp**, is only used when the domain is in Windows Server 2003 native mode. This attribute is replicated between domain controllers and allows administrators to view the last time a user or computer account logged on to the domain. Conversely, the lastLogon attribute (included in all versions of Active Directory) is not replicated between domain controllers, so it only shows the last time a particular domain controller authenticated a user.

Passwords for inetOrgPerson Objects   Aside from Microsoft products, most directories that use Lightweight Directory Access Protocol (LDAP) use the **inetOrgPerson** object class to identify users that are security principals. Active Directory uses an object class named User to identify network users. In Windows Server 2003, you can create inetOrgPerson objects and assign passwords to them, allowing them to be used as security principals. Note that security principals are covered in more detail in Chapter 9.

DC Rename   Renaming domain controllers is only possible in the Windows Server 2003 native mode using the **NETDOM.EXE** utility. NETDOM.EXE ensures that DNS and Active Directory are updated with the new name, and can also be used to manage domains and trust relationships.

 NETDOM.EXE is not installed by default. It is located on the Windows Server 2003 CD-ROM in \SUPPORT\TOOLS\SUPPORT.CAB. You can install the tools in this file by running SUPPORT.MSI, which is located in the same folder.

NOTE

 Choosing to rename a domain controller is a decision that should not be taken lightly. Although Windows Server 2003 supports renaming domain controllers, it is possible that not all applications will be able to handle the renaming process. You should only rename domain controllers if it is absolutely necessary and the change has been tested in a lab environment with the applications you use.

CAUTION

Changing the name of a domain controller is a three-step process from a command prompt:

1. **NETDOM** *computername originalDCname /add newDCname*

   This command adds the new name of the domain controller to DNS and Active Directory. These changes must be fully replicated before performing Step 2. If the changes are not fully replicated, then users may be unable to access this domain controller.

2. **NETDOM** *computername originalDCname /makeprimary newDCname*

   This command marks the new name as the primary name to use when referring to this domain controller. However, both can be used at this point.

3. **NETDOM** *computername newDCname /remove originalDCname*

   This command removes references to the original name of the domain controller from DNS and Active Directory.

 ## Activity 5-6: Raising the Forest Functional Level

ACTIVITY

Time Required: 10 minutes

Objective: Learn how to raise the forest functional level.

 Only the student in a student group who has the higher server number should complete Activity 5-6 . The first member of the student group should not perform these steps on their domain controller.

NOTE

Description: In this activity, you will learn how to raise the forest functional level to Windows Server 2003. You will work with a partner because the conversion can only be completed once.

1. If necessary, start your server and log on using the **Administrator** account in the **CHILDXX** (where *XX* is the number of the forest root domain your server is a domain controller for) domain using the password **Password01**.

2. Click Start, select **Administrative Tools**, and then click **Active Directory Domains and Trusts**.

3. Right-click the **Active Directory Domains and Trusts** node in the left tree pane, and then click **Raise Forest Functional Level**.

4. In the Select an available forest functional level list box, confirm that **Windows Server 2003** is selected, as shown in Figure 5-29.

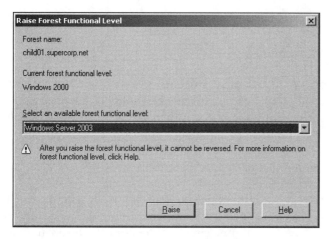

Figure 5-29   Raising the forest functional level

5. Click **Raise**. A message box opens informing you that this change affects the entire forest and is not reversible.

6. Click **OK**. Another message box informs you about the success of raising the forest functional level as shown in Figure 5-30.

7. Click **OK**.

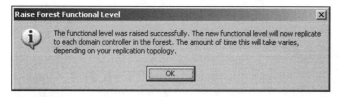

Figure 5-30   Confirmation of raising the forest functional level

8. Close Active Directory Domains and Trusts.

9. Log off your server if you do not intend to immediately continue to the next project. Otherwise, stay logged on.

Windows 2000 Forests

Windows 2000 is the default level of forest functionality. It can accommodate a mix of Windows 2000 Server, Windows NT Server 4.0, and Windows Server 2003 domain controllers. This is the standard level of forest functionality introduced with Windows 2000.

Windows Server 2003 Interim Forests

A Windows Server 2003 interim forest has been enhanced over a Windows 2000 forest. Only Windows NT Server 4.0 and Windows Server 2003 are supported as domain controllers in this forest functional level.

Enhancements include:

- Linked value replication
- Improved ISTG algorithms

Linked Value Replication   A linked value attribute is sometimes called a multivalued attribute. The most common example of a multivalued attribute is the *membership* attribute of a group, which can contain many members. When raised to this functionality level, Windows Server 2003 domain controllers implement improved replication of multivalued attributes. The improved replication allows only updates to group membership to be replicated, rather than the entire membership of the group.

Improved ISTG Algorithm   Using an improved replication algorithm, the Inter-Site Topology Generator (ISTG) can make better decisions regarding the replication of Active Directory information between sites. In some circumstances (usually involving lots and lots of small sites), it could take the ISTG (in Windows 2000) so long to calculate the best replication topology that it couldn't complete the calculation before it had to start calculating it again for the next cycle! In a small, single-domain forest, you would probably never know the difference, but this feature has been in demand by Microsoft's larger clients for some time.

NOTE   In Chapter 6, sites are covered in more detail. Additionally, Chapter 7 covers replication and the Inter-Site Topology Generator.

Windows Server 2003 Forests

When all domains have been upgraded to the Windows Server 2003 domain functional level, the forest can be raised to the Windows Server 2003 functional level. This enables many new features, in addition to the features available in Windows 2000 and Windows 2003 interim mode. These enhancements include:

- Forest trusts
- Domain renaming

- Deactivation and modification of schema attributes and classes
- Conversion of user objects to inetOrgPerson objects and vice versa
- Dynamic auxiliary classes

Forest Trusts As discussed earlier, forest trusts allow a trust relationship to be established between two forests. A forest trust can be one-way or two-way, and is transitive.

5

NOTE The supercorp.net domain/forest should be raised to the Windows Server 2003 domain functional level and the Windows Server 2003 forest functional level before students start Activity 5-7.

Activity 5-7: Creating a Forest Trust

ACTIVITY

Time Required: 10 minutes

Objective: Learn how to create a two-way, transitive trust with another forest root domain.

NOTE Only one student in a student group should complete Activity 5-7. The second student should not perform these steps on their domain controller.

Description: In this activity, you will create a forest trust between your domain and the supercorp.net domain (which is used to support the company's internet presence). You will work with a partner because only one forest trust between the same two domains can exist at a time.

1. Choose one computer (yours or your partner's) on which to perform the following steps.

2. If necessary, start your server and log on using the **Administrator** account in the **CHILDXX** (where *XX* is the number of the forest root domain your server is a domain controller for) domain using the password **Password01**.

3. Click Start, select **Administrative Tools**, and then click **Active Directory Domains and Trusts**.

4. In the left tree pane, right-click **childXX.supercorp.net** (where *XX* is the number of the forest root domain your server is a domain controller for) and then click **Properties**.

5. Click the **Trusts** tab.

6. On the Trusts tab, click **New Trust**.

7. In the New Trust Wizard welcome screen, click **Next**.

8. In the Trust Name dialog box, enter **supercorp.net** in the Name text box, as shown in Figure 5-31.

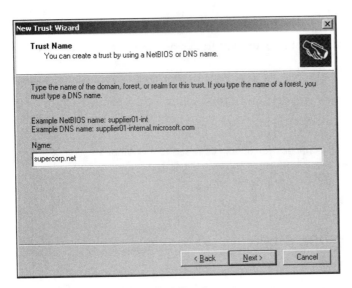

Figure 5-31   Trust Name dialog box

9. Click **Next**.

10. In the Trust Type dialog box, select the **Forest trust** option button, and then click **Next**.

11. In the Direction of Trust dialog box, ensure that the **Two-way** option button is selected, and then click **Next**.

12. In the Sides of Trust dialog box, select the **Both this domain and the specified domain** option button, as shown in Figure 5-32.

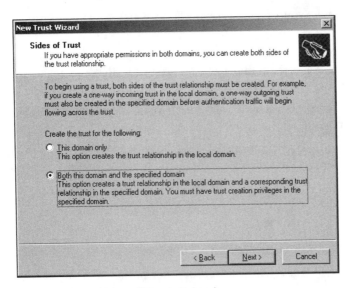

Figure 5-32   Sides of Trust dialog box

13. Click **Next**.

14. In the User Name and Password dialog box, enter **Administrator** in the User name list box and **Password01** in the Password text box. This is a user account that exists in the supercorp.net domain and has administrative privileges in that domain. Click **Next**.

CAUTION   If you receive an error that the specified forest is not at the necessary forest functional level, ask your instructor to raise the domain and functional levels of supercorp.net as noted before this project.

15. In the Outgoing Trust Authentication Level–Local Forest dialog box, ensure that the **Forest-wide authentication** option button is selected. This option is preferred when both forests are part of the same organization. Click **Next**.

16. In the Outgoing Trust Authentication Level–Specified Forest dialog box, ensure that the **Forest-wide authentication** option button is selected, and click **Next**. The Trust Selections Complete dialog box opens.

17. Review the information and then click **Next**. The Trust Creation Complete dialog box opens.

18. Review the information and then click **Next**.

19. In the Confirm Outgoing Trust dialog box, select the **Yes, confirm the outgoing trust** option button, and then click **Next**.

20. In the Confirm Incoming Trust dialog box, select the **Yes, confirm the incoming trust** option button, and then click **Next**. The Completing the New Trust Wizard dialog box displays the status of the changes.

21. Review the information and then click **Finish**. The new trust now appears on the Trusts tab of the domain's properties window, as shown in Figure 5-33.

22. Click **OK** to close the domain's properties.

23. Close Active Directory Domains and Trusts.

24. Log off your server.

Domain Renaming   In previous versions of Windows and Active Directory, the only way to rename a domain was to remove and recreate it. Now, domains can be renamed and relocated within the forest, allowing organizations to modify an existing Active Directory structure without migrating users between domains when a name change is required (due to reorganization, poor planning, or some other reason). See *www.microsoft.com/ windowsserver2003/downloads/domainrename.mspx* for more information and to obtain the tools necessary to rename a domain.

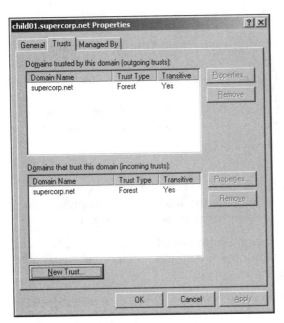

Figure 5-33   Newly created trust in the Trusts tab of the domain's properties

CAUTION   Do not let this feature be a substitute for good planning and design! Microsoft describes a domain rename as "a multistep process that requires detailed understanding." It is a resource-intensive operation that affects every domain controller in the forest, including those in the domains that aren't being renamed. You cannot rename a domain in a forest where Exchange 2000 or 2003 is in use (Microsoft hopes to have support for renaming domains in Exchange 2003 Service Pack 1). Additionally, the forest root domain can be renamed, but you cannot change which domain is the forest root domain. All clients and servers need to be restarted, causing some service disruption. It is possible, but not trivial, to rename a domain.

Deactivation and Modification of Attributes and Classes   When object classes and attributes were added to previous versions of Active Directory, they could be deactivated if no longer required. However, they could not be redefined if they were incorrectly created. Now, classes and attributes can be redefined. This is particularly useful for developers in test environments. It also removes some of the risk associated with schema upgrades because changes are no longer permanent.

Conversions between User and inetOrgPerson Objects   As described earlier, many LDAP-enabled directory applications use inetOrgPerson objects to represent users. Active Directory uses User objects to represent users. The ability to convert Users to inetOrgPerson objects and vice versa allows for an easier transfer of user information between Active Directory and other directories.

Dynamic Auxiliary Classes Auxiliary class objects are associated with other object classes to extend the attributes that are part of the class. In earlier versions of Active Directory, these could be statically linked. When associated with a class of object, statically linked auxiliary class objects are applied to all objects of that class. Now, auxiliary class objects can be linked to a single instance of an object rather than all instances of a class. This is known as **dynamic linking of auxiliary classes**.

Upgrading Windows NT Domains

5

Windows NT domains are not organized in a tree structure like Active Directory domains. Windows NT domains are independent of one another. For users in one domain to be granted access to resources in another domain, a trust relationship must be established.

Windows NT trust relationships are one-way, nontransitive trusts. For two domains to trust each other, two one-way trusts must be created in opposite directions. The creation of trusts is never automatic in Windows NT.

Because trusts are not transitive in NT 4.0, many trusts must be created for interoperability between domains. In a network with four Windows NT domains, 12 trusts must be established for full interoperability. As the number of domains increases, the number of required trusts continues to grow.

To calculate the number of trusts required, use the formula: n(n-1) (where n is the number of domains).

Domain Structure

Active Directory uses sites to control replication within a domain and between domains. Conversely, Windows NT does not perform replication between domains, and replication within a domain is automatic. Windows NT networks were designed to use domain boundaries as replication boundaries, often with each physical location its own domain.

When migrating to Active Directory from Windows NT domains, you must decide whether the existing domain structure is adequate for your needs. If not, you should create a new design and migrate existing information from the Windows NT domains to the new Active Directory forest.

Active Directory does not require NetBIOS to function, but Windows NT domains do. Ensure that your Active Directory domain controllers are configured to use WINS when pre-Windows 2000 clients and servers (such as Windows NT or Windows 95/98) are still in use.

Keeping the Existing Domain Structure

If you choose to keep your existing domain structure, then the upgrade process is relatively simple. The first domain upgraded becomes the forest root domain. Plan this very carefully, as it cannot be changed.

The first domain controller upgraded must be the PDC in the Windows NT 4.0 domain. This new Windows Server 2003 domain controller takes on the role of the PDC emulator for the domain. As the PDC emulator, it continues to provide directory updates to Windows BDCs.

When BDCs are upgraded to Windows Server 2003, the operating system upgrade is performed first. After the upgrade is complete, the server reboots. During the boot process, the server automatically logs on using the local administrator account that was created during the operating system upgrade, and presents you with the option to keep the server as a member server or promote it to a domain controller. After choosing one of these options, the system no longer automatically logs on using the administrator account.

As you upgrade each domain after the forest root, you choose to join the newly created forest. As each domain is upgraded, the two-way, transitive trusts are automatically made between the newly upgraded domain and its parent in the forest.

During an upgrade that involves many NT domains, you should raise the forest functionality level to Windows 2003 interim after completing the forest root domain (as long as you never intend to add domain controllers running Windows 2000). This gives you some of the advantages of the Windows 2003 functional level until the migration to Windows Server 2003 is complete.

Creating a New Domain Structure

Sometimes the existing Windows NT domain structure is not ideal. If you want a new domain structure, the easiest way to implement it is with entirely new hardware. Chances are good that if you are upgrading from Windows NT Server 4.0, it is time to upgrade the computers acting as domain controllers as well. This way, the new domain structure can be created without the logistical hassle of decommissioning your existing servers.

After the new servers are installed and the new domain structure is created, you can choose to either recreate all of the users and resources or migrate them to the new domains. For smaller organizations, recreating users and resources may be less complex than learning how to migrate the resources properly. For larger organizations, the benefits of a smooth migration are worth the time to learn, plan, and test.

The Active Directory Migration Tool (ADMT) migrates users, groups, and computer accounts from one domain to another. The objects can be migrated from Windows NT domains to Active Directory domains or between Active Directory domains.

The original version of ADMT was a graphical utility with wizards, trust migration, and testing options. The version that ships with Windows Server 2003 has been enhanced and includes:

- Password migration

- A scripting interface for use with VB Scripts

- An attribute exclusion list that allows you to define attributes not to migrate to the new domain

- A command-line migration utility

NOTE   To install ADMT, run ADMIGRATION.MSI located in the \I386\ADMT folder of your Windows Server 2003 CD-ROM.

The ADMT moves security principals from one domain to another. The source domain contains the original objects to be migrated. The target domain is where the new objects will be created. The target domain functional level must be a minimum of Windows 2000 native mode in order to proceed with the migration.

Other requirements for the migration include:

- Account auditing must be enabled in the source and target domain.

- A local group *sourcedomainname*$$$ (where sourcedomainname is the NetBIOS name of the source domain) must be created in the source domain.

- The local group *sourcedomainname*$$$ is used as part of the migration process and must have no members.

- The user performing the move must be a member of the Domain Administrators Group in both domains.

- The source domain controller must be the PDC if migrating from Windows NT.

- Administrative shares must exist on the domain controllers.

- The source domain must trust the target domain. Optionally, the target domain may be configured to trust the source domain in order to make configuration easier.

NOTE   Objects with well-known SIDs such as the Administrator account are not migrated. SIDs are covered in more detail in Chapter 9.

Migrating objects from a Windows NT domain is referred to as an inter-forest migration. A Windows NT domain can never be part of a forest. Inter-forest migration also refers to migrating objects from one Active Directory forest to another.

During an inter-forest migration, user accounts are cloned from the source domain and copied to the target domain. You can configure ADMT to disable the original user account or to leave it untouched, allowing the administrator performing the migration to prepare the new Active Directory forest while the existing system is still in use. Once the new Active Directory forest is ready, the old system can be decommissioned.

NOTE   A whitepaper entitled Migrating Windows NT Server 4.0 Domains to Windows Server 2003 Active Directory is available at www.microsoft.com/ windowsserver2003/evaluation/whyupgrade/nt4/nt4domtoad.mspx or by searching the Microsoft Web site if the URL has changed.

Upgrading Windows 2000 Domains

A forest with Windows 2000 domains will be at the Windows 2000 functionality level, with domains that are at Windows 2000 mixed or Windows 2000 native mode. Upgrading this type of forest is easy, because Active Directory has already been designed and implemented. There is no need to move user accounts, groups, or computer accounts.

NOTE   Before any Windows Server 2003 domain controllers are added to an existing Windows 2000 forest, the schema of the forest must be updated. On the schema master for the forest, run *ADPREP.EXE /forestprep*. In each domain to be upgraded, run *ADPREP.EXE /domainprep* on the infrastructure operations master for that domain. You can find this utility in the \I386 folder on the Windows Server 2003 CD-ROM. To run ADPREP.EXE /forestprep successfully, you must be a member of the Schema Admins and Enterprise Admins groups. To run ADPREP.EXE /domainprep successfully, you must be a member of the Domain Admins group (in the domain where you are running the command) or Enterprise Admins group. (Note that operations masters are covered in Chapter 8.)

Adding Windows Server 2003 Domain Controllers

When Windows Server 2003 domain controllers are added to the domain, you can upgrade an existing domain controller to Windows Server 2003, or install Windows Server 2003 as a member server and then promote it to a domain controller.

If a domain controller is to be upgraded, you must be sure that the server meets the upgrade requirements for Windows Server 2003. To find out if your hardware and software are capable of running Windows Server 2003, run **WINNT32.EXE /checkupgradeonly**. You can find this executable in the \I386 folder on the Windows Server 2003 CD-ROM.

Restructuring Existing Domains

When upgrading your domain controllers from Windows 2000 to Windows Server 2003, you may also decide to restructure your existing domains. Some Windows 2000 implementations are just simple upgrades of Windows NT domains, and are not structured for optimal use of Active Directory.

You can use the ADMT to migrate users, groups, and computer accounts from one domain to another within an Active Directory forest. This is referred to as **intra-forest migration**.

The requirements for using the ADMT for intra-forest migration are the same as those for inter-forest migration, with the following exceptions:

- A local group named *sourcedomainname$$$* is not required.
- You can run ADMT on a domain controller in the source or target domain, or on a Windows XP Professional client.
- Administrative shares must exist on the domain controllers.

NOTE
Accounts and groups that are moved during an intra-forest migration are not copied. This prevents two security principals in the same forest from having the same SID. Otherwise, a SID would exist on the original account and in the SIDhistory attribute of the new account. SIDs are covered in more detail in Chapter 9.

When a user account is migrated in an intra-forest migration, all groups of which that user is a member must also be migrated. When a group is migrated, all user accounts that are members of that group must also be migrated. This is referred to as **closed sets**, and is done to ensure that existing permissions are retained for all migrated security principals.

Planning your intra-forest migration is critical if you do not intend to migrate all users and groups within a domain. Users may need to be added to or removed from groups in order to move objects in closed sets.

CHAPTER SUMMARY

- ❑ DNS defines the namespace used by Active Directory, and you should carefully choose the best DNS name for your Active Directory domains and forests early in the planning process.

- ❑ A DNS name should be meaningful and represent your entire operation. It should be able to represent the organization across divisions and through expected growth.

- ❑ Most companies have two different uses for a DNS name: defining a public Internet presence for the company, and defining a namespace for Active Directory.

- ❑ The SRV resource records and other related records in DNS describe your network's internal operations; therefore, most organizations treat them as confidential information.

❑ When choosing DNS names for both an Internet presence and the Active Directory domain, there are three common choices: using the same DNS name for both, using completely different names altogether, or using a subdomain delegated from your Internet domain for your Active Directory domain.

❑ Using the same DNS name for both Internet presence and Active Directory requires complex administration to prevent the release of confidential information to the public networks. Therefore, it is not recommended.

❑ A forest is an "instance" of Active Directory; if you have multiple forests, you have multiple Active Directory installations.

❑ A domain is a replication and administrative boundary. A domain is not a true security boundary, although some security administration is managed at the domain level.

❑ Domains provide authentication and a directory in which to publish shared resources. They provide the basis for policy-based administration and setting domain user account policies.

❑ The first domain created in a forest is the forest root domain. The forest root domain is a central point for trust relationships. It cannot be deleted without deleting the entire Active Directory structure.

❑ Managing a multiple-domain forest is more complex and requires more resources than a single-domain forest, but it provides the ability to better support a decentralized structure with tighter administrative controls.

❑ Microsoft recommends creating a forest root domain dedicated to infrastructure functions (managing the forest).

❑ Besides the dedicated forest root domain, Microsoft recommends using only one domain for all directory objects, unless a business goal or defined requirement necessitates additional domains.

❑ If additional domains are required, Microsoft recommends using geographical, rather than organizational boundaries.

❑ Trusts automatically established between domains in a forest are only created between a child domain and its parent (or the root domain of a tree and the root domain of the forest), but they are two-way and transitive, so they can be followed up and down tree structures in the forest.

❑ A shortcut trust allows a direct route for authentication between one domain and another domain, within the same forest, to which it is not directly connected by an automatic trust. Shortcut trusts are transitive and can be either one or two-way.

❑ Forest trusts allow a trust relationship to be established between two forests. A forest trust can be one-way or two-way, and is transitive between the domains in the two forests the trust is between.

- An external trust is used between a Windows Server 2003 domain and a Windows NT domain. External trusts can also be used between two Windows 2000 Server or Windows Server 2003 domains located in different forests.

- Realm trusts are used to create a trust relationship between a non-Windows Kerberos realm (usually found in UNIX environments) and a Windows domain. Realm trusts can be one-way or two-way and can be transitive or nontransitive.

- Organizational units are used to group objects within a domain into a hierarchical structure for categorization and delegation of control to data owners.

- Organizational units can be nested without any practical limit; however, more than 10 levels of nesting is not recommended.

- Organizational units are comparatively easy to restructure, while domains and forests are more difficult to restructure. In many cases, a forest cannot be renamed or significantly restructured without extensive disruption to the network.

- Active Directory is capable of different functionality levels at the domain and forest levels.

- The Windows Server 2003 interim domain functional level can have only Windows NT Server 4.0 and Windows Server 2003 domain controllers. The domain functionality is the same as Windows 2000 mixed mode, but allows enhancements at the forest level.

- In the Windows Server 2003 domain functional level, domains can only contain Windows Server 2003 domain controllers to gain additional functionality beyond Windows 2000 native mode.

- Windows 2000 is the default forest functional level for Active Directory.

- Forests using the Windows 2003 interim functional level can contain only Windows NT Server 4.0 and Windows Server 2003 domain controllers. Forests using the Windows Server 2003 functional level can contain only Windows Server 2003 domain controllers.

- The first domain controller to be upgraded in a Windows NT domain must be the PDC. It becomes the PDC emulator in the domain.

- ADMT migrates user accounts, groups, and computer accounts from one domain to another.

- In an existing forest, ADPREP.EXE must be used to prepare Active Directory before the first Windows Server 2003 domain controller is added.

- When ADMT is used for intra-forest migration, closed sets are used to maintain proper assignment of permissions. In addition, users and groups are moved rather than copied.

KEY TERMS

Active Directory Migration Tool (ADMT) — A tool that migrates user accounts, groups, and computer accounts from one domain to another.

ADPREP.EXE /domainprep — A command run on the infrastructure master of the domain to prepare Active Directory before installing the first Windows Server 2003 domain controller in the domain.

ADPREP.EXE /forestprep — A command run on the schema master of the forest to prepare Active Directory before installing the first Windows Server 2003 domain controller in the forest.

child domain — A domain that is connected to another domain (its parent) in an Active Directory tree. The child domain uses a subdomain of the parent domain's DNS name in a contiguous DNS namespace. Child.parent.company.com is a child domain of parent. company.com. Parent and child domains are connected with a two-way, transitive trust.

closed sets — When intra-forest migration is performed, all groups of which a user is a member must be migrated when the user is migrated. In addition, when a group is migrated, all users that are members of that group must be migrated.

dynamic linking of auxiliary classes — Objects that can be linked to a single instance of an object to add attributes, rather than all instances of a class.

Group Policy objects (GPOs) — A set of specific group policy settings applied in Active Directory.

inetOrgPerson — An object used by most LDAP applications to represent users.

inter-forest migration — The migration of objects between two domains in different forests. Migration from a Windows NT domain is also inter-forest migration.

Internet presence — In the context of DNS, the Internet presence refers to the DNS subdomain name used by the public to reach an organization's e-mail or Web servers. The term can also be used generically, as in "our company needs an Internet presence."

intra-forest migration — The migration of objects from one domain to another domain in the same forest. Users and groups are moved in closed sets.

lastLogonTimestamp — A user attribute used to track the last time a user logged on to the network. It is replicated to all domain controllers in the domain and is only available if the domain is at the Windows Server 2003 functional level.

NETDOM.EXE — A command-line utility used to rename domain controllers, create trusts, and join computers to a domain.

nontransitive trust — A trust between two domains, realms, or forests where trust does not extend outside of the two domains/forests between which the trust exists.

one-way trust — A trust relationship where security principals in the trusted domain can use resources in the trusting domain, but not vice versa. Two one-way trusts in opposite directions are equivalent to a two-way trust.

replication boundary — A set of data that is replicated to only specific replicas, or a barrier (physical or logical) that prevents replication. In the case of Active Directory, it is used to describe the fact that domain information is not replicated to other domains (except for attributes sent to the global catalog).

shortcut trusts — A manually created trust that improves the efficiency of inter-domain authentications within a forest.

trust relationship — A link between two domains that allows security principals from one domain to be recognized by the other.

two-way, transitive trust — A trust relationship between two domains that can also be used by any other domains trusted by either of the domains. For example if A trusts B, and B trusts C, then A also trusts C.

WINNT32.EXE /checkupgradeonly — A command run on an existing Windows server to determine upgrade compatibility.

5

REVIEW QUESTIONS

1. In the context of Active Directory, the surest way to achieve complete separation, autonomy, and security control for a business unit is to place it in its own _____ .

2. A domain is a partition, or division, of a _____ .

3. Which option does Microsoft recommend as a best practice?

   a. using a delegated zone for a dedicated subdomain of your Internet name for your Active Directory DNS name

   b. using the same DNS name for your Internet presence as for your Active Directory implementation

   c. using a private or fictitious DNS name for your Active Directory domains

   d. ensuring that SRV records are replicated to your ISP's domain name servers

4. Which of the following are common across an entire forest, in all cases? (Choose all that apply.)

   a. configuration partition

   b. schema partition

   c. domain partition

   d. global catalog

5. A(n) _____ trust is manually created and used within a forest.

6. A(n) _____ is the ultimate security boundary.

7. A(n) _____ is a replication boundary.

8. Business units that require a different or unique schema from other business units must be placed in a different _____ .

9. Business units that require a unique account policy (such as password length or complexity settings) for domain users' accounts must be placed in separate _____ .

10. Should every department or division shown on the organizational chart have its own OU in Active Directory?

    a. always

    b. never

    c. when warranted by data ownership roles

    d. only if they are a service owner

11. When business units require that a different team of people create and manage user objects, which is the smallest or least divisive structure that allows control to be delegated to a data owner?

    a. forest

    b. domain

    c. OU

    d. site

12. Which of the following statements about the forest root domain is most accurate?

    a. The forest root domain can be created or deleted at any time.

    b. The forest root domain can be easily renamed.

    c. The forest root domain must have the same DNS suffix as all other domains.

    d. The forest root domain contains the groups that can manage the entire forest by default.

13. Which of the following statements best describes Microsoft's recommended best practice?

    a. Create a dedicated forest root domain for managing the forest infrastructure, and create one additional domain for all other directory objects.

    b. Create a dedicated forest root domain, and use it for all directory objects.

    c. Create a dedicated forest root domain and additional domains for each office location in your enterprise.

    d. Do not create a forest root domain unless you have more than three other domains to manage.

14. How many different functional levels are there for domains?

    a. one

    b. two

    c. three

    d. four

    e. five

15. Which is the lowest domain functional level that supports the installation of Active Directory from backup media such as a CD-R when using Windows Server 2003?

    a. Windows 2000 mixed

    b. Windows 2000 native

    c. Windows Server 2003 interim

    d. Windows Server 2003

16. Which domain controllers can hold an application partition? (Choose all that apply.)

    a. Windows NT Server 4.0

    b. Windows 2000 Server

    c. Windows Server 2003 in a Windows 2000 native domain

    d. Windows Server 2003 in a Windows Server 2003 interim domain

    e. Windows Server 2003 in a Windows Server 2003 domain

17. Which utility is used to rename domain controllers?

    a. Active Directory Users and Computers

    b. ADPREP.EXE

    c. Active Directory Domains and Trusts

    d. NETDOM.EXE

18. Which type of object is commonly used by LDAP applications to represent users?

    a. Alias

    b. inetOrgPerson

    c. User

    d. NetworkUser

19. Which domain functionality level allows the renaming of domain controllers?

    a. Windows 2000 mixed

    b. Windows 2000 native

    c. Windows Server 2003 interim

    d. Windows Server 2003

20. When a Windows NT domain is upgraded, which is the first domain controller upgraded?

    a. a member server

    b. a BDC

    c. the PDC

    d. Install Windows Server 2003 on a new server and promote it to a domain controller.

CASE PROJECTS

Super Corp has decided to proceed with an Active Directory implementation. Management considered delaying the project until details of the proposed merger and expansion were known, but decided that it was in the best interest of the organization to proceed immediately. They feel that a solid infrastructure and well-designed network will bring benefits in the short term, and would also reduce confusion during any future reorganization. However, you should keep in mind as you design their network directory services that some change is to be expected, so avoid decisions that would needlessly narrow their options.

CASE PROJECTS

Case Project 5-1: Choosing a DNS Name

As one of the first steps in planning the new Active Directory structure, your team will recommend a DNS name. In the first meetings with the technical staff, the following information has been gathered:

Up until now, Super Corp has only used stand-alone file servers with no domain structure. All DNS operations have been managed by their ISP, and it is not known which DNS servers each client computer is configured to use.

The CIO would prefer not to have to change the configuration on each client computer, because he feels this would involve visiting each computer in the system and manually effecting the required changes.

As part of its Internet connection package, the ISP used by Super Corp hosts a Web page containing basic contact information for the company. The address used is *www.supercorp.net*. The CEO likes this name and wishes to continue using it.

Super Corp does not want to deal with additional name registrations with ICANN and the .com registrars.

The following suggestions have been made for a DNS name for the forest root domain:

supercorp.net

ad.supercorp.net

supercorp.com

supercorp.local

Discuss the following issues in a small group or with your partner. Present your instructor with a summary of your answers.

1. Which of the choices do you recommend and why?

2. Where would you place DNS servers for zones hosting the Active Directory subdomain?

3. How does your solution avoid having to configure individual workstations?

4. Would your recommendation change if the company did not have an existing Web page?

5. In the future, Super Corp hopes to allow its clients and employees to retrieve information and submit forms for processing online. Will changes to your recommendations be required to support this?

Case Project 5-2: Establishing a Trust Relationship

Super Corp uses the services of Ad Magic, Ltd., a company that provides promotional and advertising services to various companies. To streamline the process of updating promotional materials, the CIO would like the staff at Ad Magic to save completed documents (in Microsoft Word format) directly to a designated share on one of the file servers. One of the ways to accomplish this is to build a trust relationship with the Windows NT domain at Ad Magic, called ADMAGDOM, and allow any member of the global group ADMAGDOM\Designers appropriate permissions for the share.

What type of trust would need to be created (internal, external, one-way, two-way)? Who would be responsible for deciding whether a specific individual can access the files? What concerns do you think this would raise?

Case Project 5-3: Domain and Forest Functional Levels

One of the network administrators at Super Corp has never worked with Windows 2000 or Windows Server 2003 before. Write a short description of each domain and forest functional level that can be given to the network administrator. Include the features that are enabled at each level, as well as the types of domain controllers that can exist at each level.

Case Project 5-4: Migration Planning

Super Development has three Windows NT domains. The research domain has three Windows NT domain controllers, five Windows NT member servers, and 65 client computers. The development domain has two Windows NT domain controllers, two Windows NT member servers, and 180 client computers. The general domain has three Windows NT domain controllers, four Windows NT member servers, four Windows 2000 member servers, and 625 client computers. The research domain, the development domain, and the general domain all have different password length and age requirements. Super Development does not have a WAN—all computers on the network are connected with a high-speed 100 Mbps Ethernet network. The management at Super Development has informed you that uptime is critical—they cannot afford to have any servers offline.

New servers will be ordered as part of the upgrade project. How do you propose to migrate to Active Directory?

6

ACTIVE DIRECTORY PHYSICAL DESIGN

After reading this chapter, you will be able to:

♦ Describe the objects and components of Active Directory that relate to the physical structure

♦ Understand how to plan the physical structure of Active Directory and consider how the topology of your network will affect your design

In Chapter 4, you learned about the underlying architecture of Active Directory—including the Active Directory store, schema, and naming contexts. Chapter 5 covered the logical structure of Active Directory—logical objects such as forests, domains, and organizational units. In this chapter, you will learn about the physical objects that represent the structure or physical topology of your network in Active Directory. A site is the most important object that Active Directory uses to represent your physical network.

A site is made up of one or more Internet Protocol (IP) subnets that are well connected. Sites allow you to control the timing of replication of information within Active Directory, and provide a method to ensure that users access certain resources in the most efficient and effective way. (This is discussed in more detail later in this chapter, as well as in Chapter 7.)

This chapter will start out by looking at the objects that represent your physical network: sites, site links, and domain controllers. After you are familiar with these physical objects and how they are created using Active Directory Sites and Services, you will then learn how to plan and design the physical structure of Active Directory. As with all other parts of an Active Directory network, you will learn that planning your design before implementation is crucial to success.

ACTIVE DIRECTORY PHYSICAL OBJECTS

To understand the role of sites in Active Directory, you must first understand how several components of Active Directory interact. The logical objects, such as forests and domains, which you learned about in the last chapter, represent logical structures. That is, while a domain is a logical grouping of computers, there is no physical object in the real world that you can point to and call a "domain." It is possible to point to a computer or a group of computers and say those computers are members of a domain, but the domain itself is strictly a software concept at its core. Similarly, a trust is a logical connection between two domains or forests. While the network connection between two domains located on different LANs is a physical object, a trust between two domains is a software configuration that has no equivalent cable or device in the real world.

Unlike logical objects, **physical objects** in Active Directory have, for the most part, an equivalent physical structure or component in the real world. For example, as you just learned, a site is one or more IP subnets that are well connected. This means that a site represents a single physical area of the enterprise network. This could be one building, one campus, one city, or even one region, depending on how well connected the network subnets are. Each one of these physical sites would have a site object in Active Directory to represent the site.

Keep in mind the "physical objects" that are used to represent the physical network are still just objects in Active Directory. They are called "physical objects" not because they are stored or exist differently in Active Directory, but because they have an equivalent physical object in the real world (which "logical objects" don't).

One important concept to understand is that the logical structure and physical structure of Active Directory are independent from one another. For example, a domain may be made up of computers located in three or more sites. Or, a single site could contain two, three, or even more domains. It is even possible that three domains could be spread across many different sites—with some sites containing domain members from all three domains, some sites containing domain members from two of the three domains, and some sites containing domain members from only one of the three domains. Some examples of these configurations are shown in Figure 6-1. Because the physical structure of Active Directory is independent of how domains are logically structured, information about physical objects is stored at the forest-wide level in the configuration naming context.

Remember that the configuration naming context is common across all domains in a forest and each forest has its own configuration naming context. If you have a network that consists of multiple forests, you need to recreate the physical structure of your network for each Active Directory forest. This is because the configuration naming context is unique for each forest.

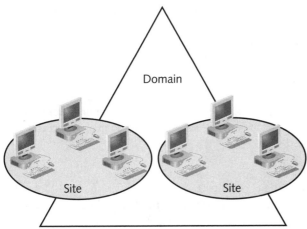

Multiple sites in a single domain

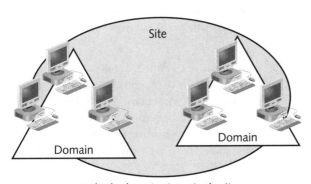

Multiple domains in a single site

Figure 6-1   Example site and domain configurations

In this section, you will learn more about the physical objects (sites, site links, and domain controllers) in Active Directory and what they represent in the real world. In addition to these physical objects, subnet objects are also covered. While subnet objects are not technically physical objects, they do define a site and are therefore closely related.

Site Objects

As stated in the first part of the chapter, a site in Active Directory is a region of your network infrastructure made up of one or more well-connected IP subnets. The term "well connected" is commonly understood to refer to a local area network (LAN) environment, as opposed to a wide area network (WAN). LANs are usually connected at high speeds (typically considered to be 10 Mbps or faster) using unshielded twisted pair or fiber-optic cabling, and offer a continuous connection. In contrast, a WAN has slower connections such as T1 lines, frame-relay circuits, or may rely on demand-dial telephone connections.

As an example, consider a small office building that contains five IP subnets that are connected through a 10/100 layer 3 Ethernet switch. Because these five subnets are considered to have "good" connectivity (or to be well connected), this building and the five subnets could constitute a site. In Activity 6-1, you will learn about, and perform, the steps necessary to create a site.

NOTE   Although uncommon, a well-connected physical network can be divided into multiple sites to control replication or the way in which resources are accessed. Doing so is an advanced skill.

When you promote the first domain controller in a forest, a site named Default-First-Site-Name is created in Active Directory. The **Default-First-Site-Name** site can, and often is, renamed and used as the first site in Active Directory. Alternatively, the Default-First-Site-Name site can be left alone and used to identify when servers cannot determine their site. Any domain controller that cannot identify which site it is located in is automatically placed in the Default-First-Site-Name site (or whatever the site is called if it is renamed). Note that the way clients and domain controllers determine what site they are located in is discussed later in this chapter.

Site objects are used in Active Directory to allow all Active Directory clients belonging to the same physical network area to access services from the servers in close proximity, rather than from servers located far away—across slow, expensive WAN links. Some of these services are domain controllers, global catalog servers, and the **distributed file system (DFS)**, among others. These services that can use the site information located in Active Directory to locate the closest server are referred to as **site-aware**. In addition to site-aware services, domain controllers also use site objects to select replication partners (the exact process is covered in the next chapter). As an example of the functional usage of Active Directory sites, take a look at Figure 6-2, which illustrates a simple site diagram.

TIP   DFS in Windows 2000 was not fully sight-aware. In Windows 2000, DFS would attempt to direct the client to a server in the client's site. However, if there was no server in the client's site, DFS would arbitrarily direct the client to a server in another site. In Windows Server 2003, DFS is now fully sight aware. Now, instead of arbitrarily directing the client to a server in another site, Windows Server 2003 directs the client to a server in the closest possible site.

As you examine the site diagram, notice that the clients within the site have access to various servers, such as a domain controller, without being required to cross the site boundary and communicate across a slow WAN link. Should the client be unable to contact a server within their own site or require services that do not exist within the site, then the client would cross the site boundary and use the WAN to obtain those services. The Active Directory site serves to localize client traffic within a defined part of your network. Sites also serve as a way to control replication traffic as discussed later in this chapter and in Chapter 7.

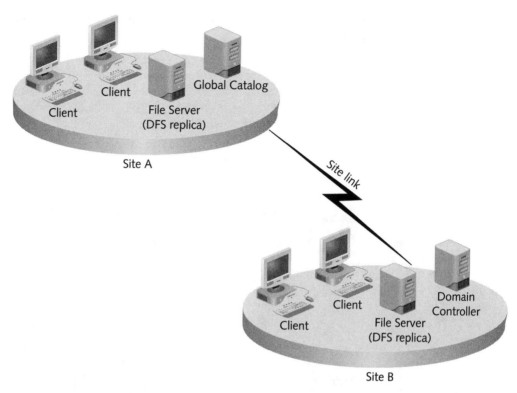

Figure 6-2   Simple site diagram

NOTE

Sites generally map the physical structure of your network, but it is up to the administrator to define sites in a manual process (you might use a program or script to help create the site objects in a large network, but it is not automatic). You need to plan carefully, as all other sites are created according to your implementation plan, with the exception of the initial Default-First-Site-Name site.

ACTIVITY

Activity 6-1: Creating Sites

Time Required: 5 minutes

Objective: This exercise is designed to familiarize you with the process of creating sites using Active Directory Sites and Services.

Description: When administering Active Directory, you need to create sites that enable connectivity in your Active Directory infrastructure. Sites form the basis of many different services in Active Directory. Over the next few activities, you and your partner will be implementing the site diagram shown in Figure 6-3 (where *XX* is your server number and the objects you create, and *ZZ* is your partner's server number and the objects your partner creates). Because sites affect all domains in the forest, you need to use an account that is a member of the Enterprise Admins group.

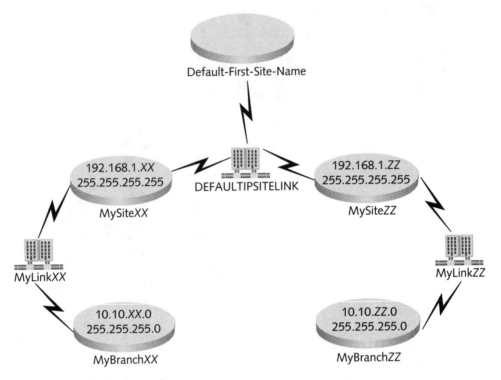

Figure 6-3   Student site diagram

1. If necessary, start your server and log on using the **Administrator** account in the **CHILDXX** domain (where *XX* is the number of the forest root domain for which your server is a domain controller) using the password **Password01**.

2. Click Start, select Administrative Tools, and then click Active Directory Sites and Services.

3. In the left tree pane, right-click the **Sites** object and then click **New Site**.

4. In the New Object – Site dialog box, type **MySiteXX** (where *XX* is the number of your server) as the name for the new site, and then choose the **DEFAULTIPSITELINK** as the Site Link object, as shown in Figure 6-4.

5. Click **OK** to continue. You will see a message box that lists other steps related to creating a site, and that suggests additional procedures. This message only appears once each time you run Active Directory Sites and Services. Click **OK**.

6. Close Active Directory Sites and Services.

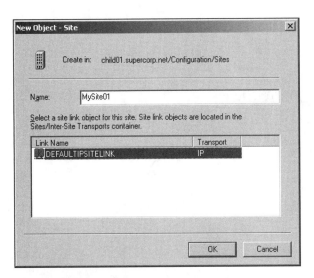

6

Figure 6-4   Creating a new site

7. Log off from your server if you do not intend to immediately continue to the next project. Otherwise, stay logged on.

Subnet Objects

Because a site is a group of one or more well-connected IP subnets, Active Directory uses **subnet objects** to identify the subnets on your network. Once subnet objects have been created, they can then be associated with sites. In Activity 6-2, you will learn how to create subnets and associate them with sites.

Subnet objects allow a client computer to determine in which site it is located by comparing its IP address and subnet mask to the subnets in Active Directory. The client computer can then locate with which site the subnet is associated and in turn in which site it (the client computer) is located. For example, take a look at Figure 6-5 which is similar to Figure 6-2, but also lists the subnets that make up each site.

Each time a client computer starts, it goes through the process of determining which site it is a member of. Because clients determine their site each time they start, physically moving a client from one site to another site is not a big deal—the client will automatically determine that it's in a new site (this assumes that its IP address has changed, of course). Note, however, that domain controllers don't determine their site each time they startup—only during promotion. The way domain controllers determine their site is discussed shortly.

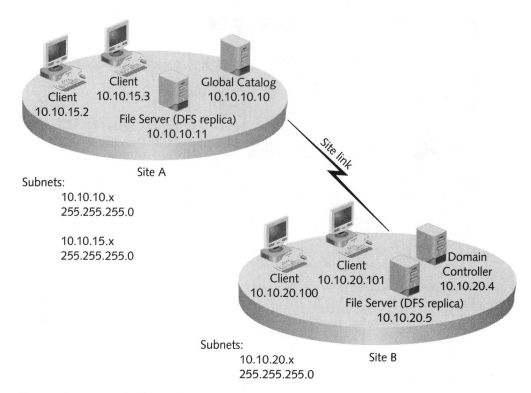

Figure 6-5   List of subnets that make up each site

Activity 6-2: Creating Subnets

Time Required: 5 minutes

Objective: Understand the process used to manually create a subnet object in Active Directory.

Description: After creating a site, you need to create one or more subnet objects using Active Directory Sites and Services. Because subnets affect all domains in the forest, you need to use an account that is a member of the Enterprise Admins group.

1. If necessary, start your server and log on using the **Administrator** account in the **CHILDXX** domain (where *XX* is the number of the forest root domain for which your server is a domain controller) using the password **Password01**.

2. Click Start, select Administrative Tools, and then click Active Directory Sites and Services.

3. If necessary, in the left tree pane, expand the **Sites** folder.

4. In the left tree pane, right-click **Subnets** and then click **New Subnet**.

5. In the Address text box, enter **192.168.1.XX** (where *XX* is the number of your server, without any leading zeros).

6. In the Mask text box, enter **255.255.255.255**.

NOTE

While in this project you are creating a subnet that is only for one IP address (because the subnet mask is 255.255.255.255), in a production environment you would normally enter a subnet mask that allows for a range of IP addresses (as shown in Figure 6-5), not just one address.

7. Select the **MySiteXX** site (where *XX* is the number of your server) from the list of available sites, as shown in Figure 6-6.

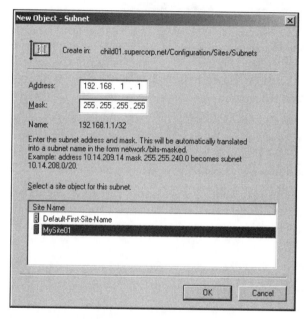

Figure 6-6   Creating a new subnet

8. Click **OK** to create the subnet and associate it with the selected site. The new subnet should appear under the Subnets folder as shown in Figure 6-7.

9. Close Active Directory Sites and Services.

10. Log off from your server if you do not intend to immediately continue to the next project. Otherwise, stay logged on.

Site Link Objects

As you create your site topology and assemble your subnets into sites, you will probably find that you have a collection of disjointed objects, defined by sites that are not well connected. When you reach this point, you are ready to begin assembling your site using site links. Note that a site link called **DEFAULTIPSITELINK** is automatically created when you promote

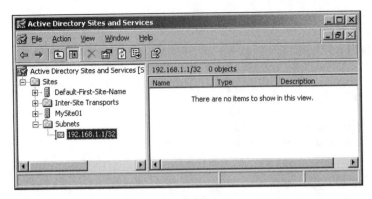

Figure 6-7   Newly created subnet

the first domain controller in the forest. In Activity 6-3, you will learn how to create site links and add sites to a site link.

Site links represent the fact that a physical connection exists between two or more sites. However, a site link does not represent a specific connection, just the fact that one or more connections exist. For example, take Figure 6-8. While multiple connections exist between sites A and B, only one site link object between the two sites is necessary in Active Directory.

Site links have several parameters that control replication and how clients and servers determine the closest site. Some of these parameters, such as cost and transport protocol, are discussed later in this chapter. The additional site link parameters are covered in the next chapter.

ACTIVITY

Activity 6-3: Creating Site Links

Time Required: 10 minutes

Objective: This exercise is designed to familiarize you with the process of creating site links using Active Directory Sites and Services.

Description: Once you have created sites and defined the subnets that make up each site, you must create site links to represent the connections between the sites. Because site links affect all domains in the forest, you need to use an account that is a member of the Enterprise Admins group.

1. If necessary, start your server and log on using the **Administrator** account in the **CHILDXX** domain (where *XX* is the number of the forest root domain for which your server is a domain controller) using the password **Password01**.

2. Click Start, select Administrative Tools, and then click Active Directory Sites and Services.

3. If necessary, in the left tree pane, expand the **Sites** folder. Before creating the new site link, you will add your second site as shown in the site diagram (Figure 6-3).

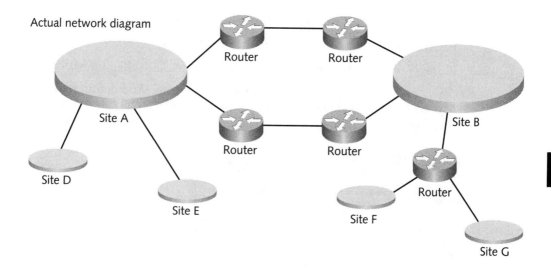

Actual network diagram

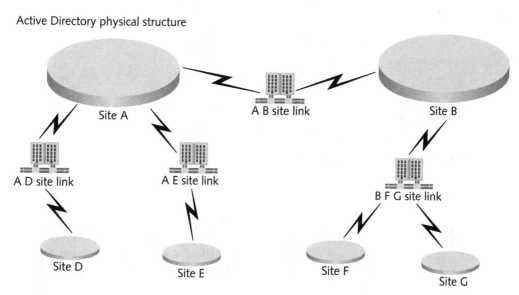

Active Directory physical structure

Figure 6-8   Example comparison of network connections to site links

4. Create a new site called **MyBranchXX** (where *XX* is the number of your server) and select **DEFAULTIPSITELINK** as the site link that connects the new site to the other sites. Note that adding the site to the DEFAULTIPSITELINK is only temporary—you will remove the site from this link once the new site is created.

5. Create a new subnet using the Address **10.10.XX.0** (where *XX* is the number of your server with no leading zeroes) and a mask of **255.255.255.0**. Associate the new subnet with the **MyBranchXX** (where *XX* is the number of your server) site.

6. In the left tree pane, expand the **Inter–Site Transports** folder.

7. Right-click the **IP** folder and select **New Site Link**.

8. In the **Name** text box, enter **MyLinkXX** (where *XX* is the number of your server).

9. A site link must have a minimum of two sites. Use the Add button to add the **MySiteXX** and **MyBranchXX** sites (where *XX* is the number of your server) to the Sites in this site link list box. Your screen should look similar to Figure 6-9.

Figure 6-9   Creating a new site link

10. Click **OK** to create the new site link.

NOTE
Remember that when you create a site, you must select a site link. Because you did not have any other site links when you created the MyBranchXX site, you had to choose the DEFAULTIPSITELINK. Now that you have a new site link created, you can go ahead and remove the site from the DEFAULTIP-SITELINK link.

11. With the new link created, you can now remove the MyBranchXX site from the DEFAULTIPSITELINK. In the left tree pane, click the **IP** folder under the Inter-Site Transports folder to show a list of site links in the right details pane.

12. In the right details pane, right-click **DEFAULTIPSITELINK** and then click **Properties**.

13. In the Sites in this site link list box, select **MyBranchXX** (where *XX* is the number of your server) and then click the **Remove** button. Your screen should look similar to Figure 6-10.

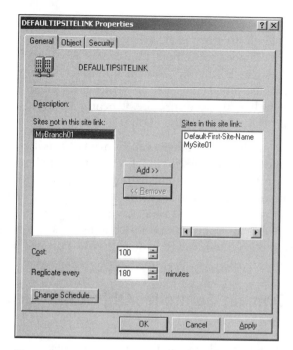

Figure 6-10   Removing a site from a site link

14. Click **OK**.

15. In the right details pane, right-click **MyLinkXX** (where *XX* is the number of your server) and then click **Properties**. Note the sites that are part of the link. Click **Cancel** to discard any accidental changes.

16. Close Active Directory Sites and Services.

17. Log off from your server if you do not intend to immediately continue to the next project. Otherwise, stay logged on.

Domain Controllers

At this point in the course, you should understand the concept and purpose of a domain controller in an Active Directory environment. As defined earlier, a domain controller is a Windows server computer that maintains a copy of the domain database. Users and computers use domain controllers for authentication, which allows access to domain resources and information. The domain controllers also contain information about the Active Directory environment in the form of the naming contexts. These naming contexts are replicated between domain controllers, and the replication process is affected by how sites are defined.

As domain controllers join Active Directory domains, the Active Directory Installation Wizard (DCPROMO) examines the IP address being used by the domain controller and places the domain controller into the appropriate site. This process occurs without intervention from the Active Directory administrator, and ensures that domain controllers enter the Active Directory sites they were intended to support. However, if the Active Directory Installation Wizard can't determine which site the domain controller belongs to, it is automatically placed in the Default-First-Site-Name site (or whatever the site is called if it is renamed). After the domain controller is placed in a site, it begins receiving replicated information for its own domain, as well as information about the forest.

There is one key difference between client computers and domain controllers that you should notice. While a client computer determines in which site it is located each time it starts, domain controllers only determine their site membership during promotion. Once a domain controller is promoted, you must manually move its domain controller server object in Active Directory if the server is physically moved to a new site. Otherwise, site-aware services continue to assume that the domain controller is located in its old site, even though it may have been moved to a new site 2000 miles away. In Activity 6-4, you will learn how to move a domain controller to another site.

ACTIVITY

Activity 6-4: Moving a Domain Controller Object Between Sites

Time Required: 5 minutes

Objective: Understand the process of manually moving a domain controller between sites.

Description: In Activity 6-2, you added a subnet object to the site you created in Activity 6-1. Although the subnet object you created is correctly associated with the new site, you still must manually move your domain controller's server object to the new site. In this activity, you will move your domain controller's server object to the site you created.

1. If necessary, start your server and log on using the **Administrator** account in the **CHILD**XX domain (where XX is the number of the forest root domain for which your server is a domain controller) using the password **Password01**.

2. Click Start, select Administrative Tools, and then click Active Directory Sites and Services.

3. If necessary, in the left tree pane, expand the **Sites** folder.

4. In the left tree pane, expand the **Default-First-Site-Name** site.

5. In the left tree pane, expand the **Servers** folder under the Default-First-Site-Name site and locate your server, as shown in Figure 6-11.

6. Right-click **SERVER**XX (where XX is the number of your server) and then click **Move**.

7. On the Move Server window, select the site to which you would like to move the domain controller. For this project, click **MySite**XX (where XX is the number of your server) and then click **OK**.

8. In the left tree pane, expand **MySite**XX (where XX is the number of your server).

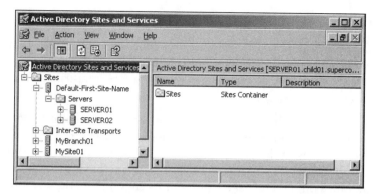

Figure 6-11   Servers located in the Default-First-Site-Name site

9. In the left tree pane, expand the **Servers** folder under the MySite*XX* site and locate your server, as shown in Figure 6-12.

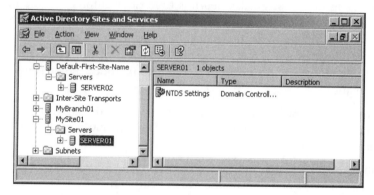

Figure 6-12   The site to which the domain controller has been moved

10. Close Active Directory Sites and Services.

11. Log off from your server if you do not intend to immediately continue to the next project. Otherwise, stay logged on.

PLANNING AND DESIGNING THE PHYSICAL STRUCTURE

Planning and designing your Active Directory physical implementation is an important task that you must complete prior to implementing the physical objects themselves. As with all other features of the Active Directory environment, failure to plan your physical structure carefully and understand the overall goals of the implementation can complicate the implementation and could ultimately lead to the failure of your Active Directory infrastructure.

Physical Network

All networks require one basic physical component to function. This is true regardless of whether your network is a basic, peer-to-peer network comprised of only two nodes, or it is the latest Windows Server 2003 Active Directory enterprise infrastructure supporting thousands of users and computers.

The physical network represents the actual physical objects that deliver a message from one place to another. From the simplest object, such as a child's toy made from a piece of string stretched between two tin cans, to the most complex, such as an optical network supporting terabytes of information transfer, all physical networks have three things in common: a point of transmission, a transmission medium, and a point of reception. (Of course, most modern computer networks have many points of transmission and many points of reception.) All other features and functionalities build upon these three basic concepts.

Begin planning your Active Directory sites by creating a diagram of your physical network infrastructure. There are several ways to determine the exact nature of your physical infrastructure, ranging from the original blueprints to various automated solutions. One particular automated solution is Microsoft Visio 2002 Enterprise, which is not the easiest tool to configure, but has the ability to dynamically scan your network infrastructure and create a diagram that illustrates the details of the physical network. This diagram can serve as an excellent starting point as you plan your implementation. Your diagram should include the following information:

- Cable types—Including unshielded twisted pair, thinnet, thicknet, fiber, ISDN, and digital and analog communication lines, and the lengths and cable grades associated with these items

- Approximate paths of cable routing, including unshielded twisted pair, thinnet, thicknet, fiber, ISDN, and digital and analog communication lines

- Server maps with detailed information about each server, including its role, IP address, name, domain membership (if any), and the owner's name and contact information

- Peripheral devices, such as print devices, infrastructure devices (hubs, switches, routers, and so forth), proxy servers, firewall servers, modems, and wireless access points (WAPs)

- WAN connections, including details such as the type of connection, available bandwidth for each connection, information about responsible parties, and contact information for the ISP providing the service

- The number of users and computers located at each physical location

- Any nonstandard implementations

You should also thoroughly document all firmware versions being used in your infrastructure, as well as the DHCP and static IP settings of all network-enabled hosts. Pay attention to name resolution services, such as WINS or DNS, and document the configuration of those servers, as well as any responsible parties or owners of these servers. Document any routing and remote access services or other dial-in servers or modem pools to include in your site implementation plans. After thoroughly documenting your physical network, you are ready to begin documenting your site topology.

TIP

The person who pays the phone bill is a great resource when trying to find out where leased network connections exist.

Site Topology

6

With a newly created physical network map in hand, you are now ready to begin designing your site topology. Remember that the site topology is a collection of objects in Active Directory that represent your physical network and does not necessarily map one to one to the actual physical topology. The arrangement of subnets (specifically the well-connected ones) within your physical network is a key factor that will allow you to define your site topology. You should consider one or more well-connected subnets to form a site in your Active Directory design.

NOTE

As you assemble these subnets into sites, be sure that all sites can reach each other (in network terms, this is called having a fully routed network). If this is not possible, you will have to plan more advanced site links and site link bridges, which will be discussed later in this section.

NOTE

Even if there are portions of your network into which you do not plan to place domain controllers, you still need to define sites for those areas. One reason for this is not only must domain controllers be able to determine in which site they are located, but client computers must be able to as well. When a client is locating a domain controller or a particular site-aware service, the client must know where it (that is, itself) is located in order to locate the closest server. This can be seen in Figure 6-13, where there is no domain controller in site C, but there is a client computer. If no site C were defined in Figure 6-13, the client would be unable to determine which site it was in and in turn which domain controller is closest.

Site Links

Microsoft's documentation describes site links in this way:

Site links are used to model the amount of available bandwidth between two sites. As a general rule, any two networks connected by a link that is slower than LAN speed is considered to be connected by a site link. A fast link that is near capacity has a low effective bandwidth, and can also be considered a site link.

While Microsoft and other experts have published some guidelines, each situation is different. The amount of traffic that crosses the network and the available resources will also affect your decisions. For example, assume that there are two buildings with 100-BaseT Ethernet internally, but they only have a 10-BaseT Ethernet connection between them that is already near full capacity. In this situation, it would be a good idea to make each building its own site and define the link between the buildings as a site link.

Cost

Several parameters are associated with site links. The first is the cost of the site link, which is a purely arbitrary value—meaning it is made up, not an actual dollar figure—that is assigned by the administrator. When deciding which of several possible servers to use, site-aware clients and services choose to connect to the server that has the lowest cost path. Figure 6-13 illustrates this concept.

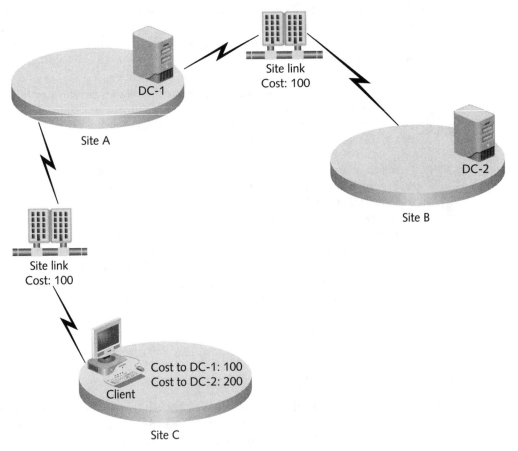

Figure 6-13   Example of choosing the closest server based on cost

In addition to clients using the cost to locate the closest server, domain controllers also use the site link cost to locate the closest replication partners. For example, examine Figure 6-14, which is slightly more complex than Figure 6-13.

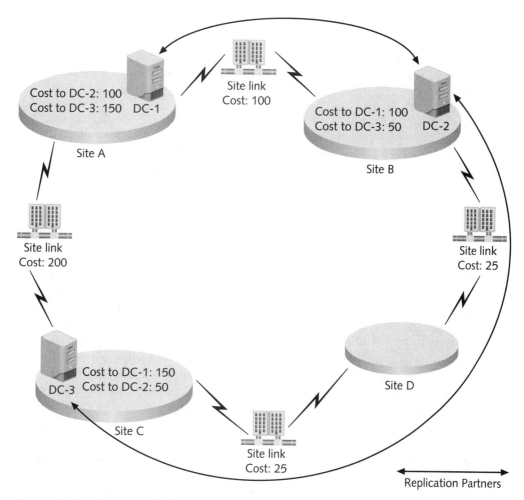

Figure 6-14   Example of choosing the closest replication partner based on cost

In Figure 6-14, there are several things you should notice. First, there are actually two paths available for domain controllers to communicate with one another—one clockwise and one counterclockwise. However, although multiple paths exist, only the lowest cost path between any two servers needs to be considered. Using DC-1 to DC-3 as an example, going clockwise the total cost from DC-1 to DC-3 is 150 (100 + 25 + 25), whereas going counterclockwise the cost from DC-1 to DC-3 is 200. 150 is less than 200, so the connection going clockwise is all you need to be concerned with.

Another thing you should notice is that domain controllers—or clients and servers for that matter—don't have to be in adjacent sites in order to communicate with one another (assuming the network is fully routed, but that is discussed shortly). For example, DC-2 and DC-3 are not in adjacent sites, but because the cost for DC-3 to replicate with DC-2 is less than replicating with DC-1, DC-3 chooses to replicate with DC-2.

NOTE   Do not be concerned with exactly how a domain controller chooses its replication partners right now—that is covered in much more detail in the next chapter.

While this may seem simple, there is also another layer you must consider. The lowest-cost path between DC-3 and DC-2 is C to D to B (total cost of 50)—and that is exactly the cost a domain controller uses when calculating with which other domain controller to replicate. However, can you identify—with absolute certainty—which path the *actual network traffic* between DC-3 and DC-2 will take on the network? The answer is actually no—it depends if the site link cost in Active Directory matches the underlying network configuration. That may be more than a little confusing, but just remember that sites and site links represent your physical network, but do not necessarily map one to one to the actual physical topology.

Continuing with the example, what if the router in site C were configured to route traffic destined for site B through site A? Although the domain controllers based the replication path cost on going from C to D to B, the router at site C would actually send the network traffic through site A—which would then send it on to site B. In such a situation, the site link costs in Figure 6-14 should be updated so that they match the actual network routing topology and so the domain controllers can select the closest replication partner(s). The important point to remember here is that clients and domain controllers use the site and site link information in Active Directory to determine the server or replication partner that has the lowest cost. However, once the lowest-cost server is selected, it is 100% up to the underlying network structure to determine how exactly the data gets from point A to point B.

NOTE   The above is just an example and in most cases you will configure the site link cost to match how your network is routed. That way you will not need to worry about the site information in Active Directory matching the network topology on a one-to-one basis or not. However, in a multi-site, multi-server configuration, it is possible to set up site link costs that purposely don't match the underlying network configuration to gain finer control over traffic. Doing so is an advanced skill.

As a final example, review Figure 6-15. Which domain controller do you think the client in site B will attempt to communicate with first? If you said DC-2—you're right. Although the path from the client to DC-2 passes through two extra sites (and probably two extra WAN connections), the cost to DC-2 is lower than the cost to DC-1—even though DC-1 is in an adjacent site. You can't rely just on how many sites away a server is; you have to factor in the site link cost.

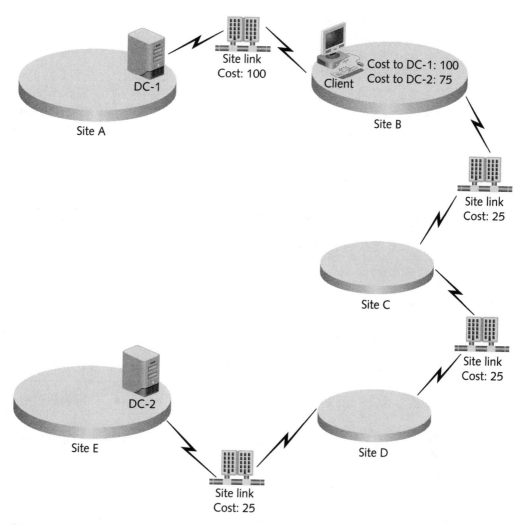

Figure 6-15   Number of hops versus site cost

When configuring site link cost, it is strongly suggested that you not use a value of 1 for a preferred link. The reason for this is simple. If you assign a site link cost of 1 to a preferred link, what will happen if, at some point in the future, you install a faster connection technology for this site? If you have already given the existing site link a cost of 1, how can you designate the new link as the preferred link with a lower numeric value than 1 (cost must be a whole number from 1 to 32767)? Note that in Activity 6-5 you will learn how to modify a site link's cost.

The Active Directory Sites and Services console lets you enter a value from 1 to 99999 for a site link cost; however, be aware that the actual maximum value supported is 32767. If you enter a cost over 32767, it is automatically set to the highest cost of 32767.

TIP

Many designers choose a value such as 100 or 500 to represent the default value, allowing them to add higher or lower cost links in the future. Others choose to use a formula such as the one used to derive Table 6-1. In Table 6-1, the cost of each connection is derived by dividing 1024 by the log (available on the scientific view of the Windows Calculator) of the available bandwidth of the connection in Kbps.

Table 6-1 Site link cost based on formula

Available Bandwidth (Kbps)	Cost
9.6	1024
19.2	798
38.4	644
56	586
64	567
128	486
256	425
512	378
1024	340
2048	309
4096	283

When determining the cost of a site link, speed should not be your only criteria. You should also take into consideration the quality of the link. If a link will be intermittently unavailable, you should assign it a higher cost so the link is avoided.

NOTE

Activity 6-5: Modifying the Cost of a Site Link

ACTIVITY

Time Required: 5 minutes

Objective: This exercise is designed to familiarize you with the process of modifying the cost of a site link.

Description: Once you have created sites and defined the site links, you can modify the cost of the site links. Modifying the cost of site links allows you to control how clients decide which server in remote sites to contact. Site cost is also used when determining the replication topology, as you will learn about in the next chapter.

1. If necessary, start your server and log on using the **Administrator** account in the **CHILDXX** domain (where *XX* is the number of the forest root domain for which your server is a domain controller) using the password **Password01**.

2. Click Start, select Administrative Tools, and then click Active Directory Sites and Services.

3. If necessary, in the left tree pane, expand the **Sites** folder.

4. In the left tree pane, expand the **Inter-Site Transports** folder.

5. In the left tree pane, click the **IP** folder to display a list of RPC over TCP/IP site links in the right details pane.

6. In the right details pane, right-click **MyLinkXX** (where *XX* is the number of your server) and select **Properties**.

7. In the Cost text box, enter **200** as shown in Figure 6-16.

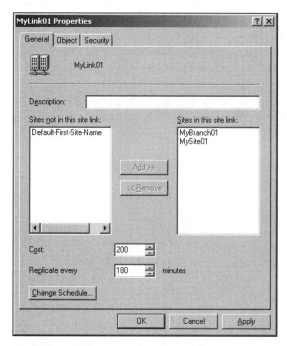

Figure 6-16   Modifying the cost of a site link

8. Click **OK**. Update the diagram you created in Activity 6-3 to include the cost of each site link.

9. Close Active Directory Sites and Services.

10. Log off from your server if you do not intend to immediately continue to the next project. Otherwise, stay logged on.

Replication Schedule/Interval

Another parameter associated with site links and site topology is the replication schedule. The replication schedule configuration will be covered in more detail in Chapter 7, but briefly stated, it defines the hours during the day when the site link is available for replication between domain controllers located in different sites. The replication schedule is manually configured and requires some consideration when determining the appropriate settings.

In addition to the replication schedule is the replication interval, which will also be discussed in more detail in Chapter 7. The replication interval controls the polling interval used by the replication process to contact a domain controller at the other end of the site link to determine if any changes to Active Directory need to be replicated.

Transport Protocol

The final parameter associated with the site link is the transport protocol used for Active Directory replication between sites. The choice of a replication transport protocol is very important, as the wrong choice can have far-reaching consequences. The two available protocols are RPC (Remote Procedure Call) over TCP/IP and SMTP. Each protocol is intended for specific circumstances that may exist when configuring the site links, and each has specific characteristics when used for Active Directory replication between sites. When you examine the site link container object in Active Directory for the site link being considered, you notice two child objects below the site link. These child objects are the IP container object and the SMTP container object. Each contains settings and parameters specific to the named protocol.

Replication within a site always uses RPC over TCP/IP, as you will learn more about in the next chapter.

NOTE

The decision of when to use a specific transport protocol should be based on the quality of network connectivity between the two sites in question. The speed of the link is not necessarily an indication of connection quality, although it may be a deciding factor in the selection. The availability of a connection should be the primary criterion used to determine the replication transport protocol. If you have reliable connectivity between the sites—for example, a 128 Kbps demand-dial link that is reliable—then your transport protocol should be RPC over TCP/IP. If the two sites have only intermittent or extremely unreliable connectivity, then you should implement SMTP as a transport protocol. SMTP is also used when a connection using RPC over TCP/IP cannot be established due to issues such as firewalls that block RPC connections.

Another factor that you must keep in mind when deciding to use RPC over TCP/IP or SMTP is that SMTP can only be used to replicate the schema, the configuration, and any application partitions. You cannot use the SMTP transport protocol to replicate domain partitions. This means that if the only site link available between two sites uses the SMTP transport protocol, you can only add domain controllers for a given domain to one of the sites—you cannot have domain controllers for the same domain in both sites. In most cases, a new domain would be created to support a site that is intermittently connected to the rest of the network.

Site Link Bridges

Another issue that may arise when configuring site links occurs when sites do not have a **fully routed IP environment** available to them for connectivity. In a fully routed IP environment, all devices on your network are able to exchange packets with other devices on your network. In other words, IP connectivity can be established between sites using the normal IP connectivity process—following paths through network routers and other hardware. For example, in a fully routed IP environment, if site A is connected to site B and site B is connected to site C, site A can connect to site C via site B (and vise versa).

If you are able to use the ping command to send packets from a computer in one Active Directory site to a computer in another Active Directory site that is not directly connected, then you have normal connectivity, and you do not need any special site implementations. However, if you cannot ping from one site to another site that is not directly connected, then you need to design and plan the site connections using additional objects called site link bridges. A **site link bridge** is composed of a minimum of two site links. For example, examine Figure 6-17.

There are six Active Directory sites in Figure 6-17: one in Los Angles (LAX), one in Denver (DEN), one in Boston (BOS), one in Detroit (DTW), one in Birmingham (BHM), and one in Dallas (DFW). While the LAX, BOS, DTW, and BHM networks are configured to route traffic between sites, the DEN and DFW networks are configured to not route traffic. For simplicity, the network is shown with only three domain controllers that are all part of the same domain: DC-L located at the LAX site, DC-B located at the BOS site, and DC-D located at the DFW site. DC-L can communicate with DC-D, and DC-B can communicate with DC-D. However, DC-L cannot communicate with DC-B.

By default, Active Directory assumes that all site links are transitive connections with the Bridge all site links setting enabled. This means that a fully routed IP infrastructure is assumed and each site can communicate with every other site. Because Active Directory attempts to replicate with the domain controller that has the lowest cost with which to communicate, DC-L would attempt to replicate with DC-B because its cost is only 100. (It would cost 200 for DC-L to replicate with DC-D.) A problem exists though; the way the physical network is configured, DC-L cannot communicate with DC-B.

To overcome the problem, you can disable the Bridge all site links option. By doing so, Active Directory no longer assumes that a fully routed IP infrastructure is in place. Instead, Active Directory assumes that only sites that have a site link directly between them can communicate. With the Bridge all site links option disabled, DC-L will replicate with DC-D because it is the only domain controller with which it can communicate. However, a new problem arises; there is no domain controller in the DEN or DTW site with which DC-B can replicate. Active Directory is assuming that only sites directly connected can communicate—and therefore DC-B has no other domain controller with which it can replicate.

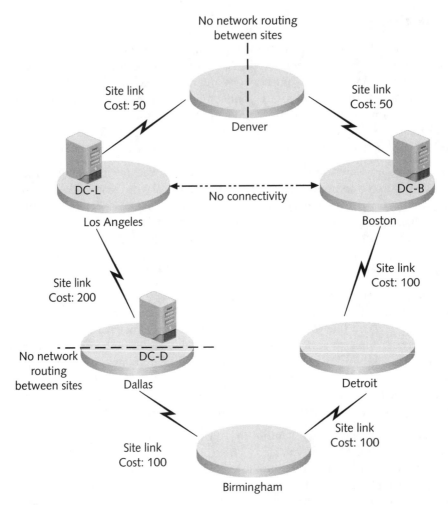

Figure 6-17   Example network that is not fully routed

NOTE   The Bridge all site links option exists for both the RPC over TCP/IP and SMTP transport protocols. That is, there is one Bridge all site links option for RPC over TCP/IP site links and another Bridge all site links option for SMTP site links. To locate these options, right-click the folder for the appropriate transport protocol in Active Directory Sites and Services and then click Properties.

With the Bridge all site links option disabled, site link bridges can be added so that Active Directory knows which sites can communicate with each other. Figure 6-18 illustrates the addition of two site link bridges. The first site link bridge DFW-LAX-DEN is made up of the DFW-LAX site link and the LAX-DEN site link. With the DFW-LAX-DEN site link bridge, Active Directory now knows that the DFW, LAX, and DEN sites can all communicate with each other.

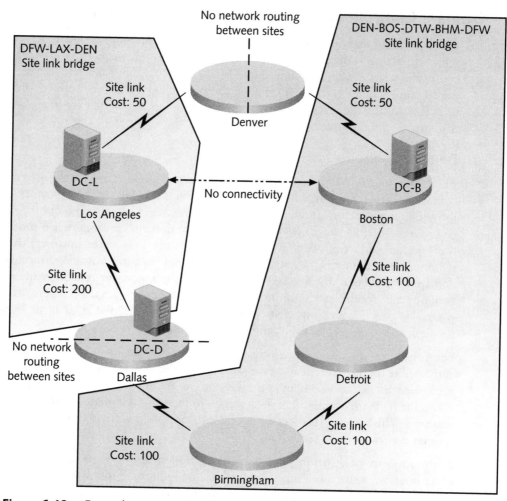

Figure 6-18   Example network that is not fully routed with site link bridges

Similarly, the DEN-BOS-DTW-BHM-DFW site link bridge is made up of the DEN-BOS site link, BOS-DTW site link, DTW-BHM site link, and BHM-DFW site link. The DEN-BOS-DTW-BHM-DFW site link indicates to Active Directory that the DEN, BOS, DTW, BHM, and DFW sites can all communicate with each other. Because Active Directory now knows that DFW can communicate with BOS using the DEN-BOS-DTW-BHM-DFW site link bridge, DC-B now has another domain controller with which it can replicate—DC-D.

The most important point to remember about site links and site link bridges is that if your infrastructure is fully routed, you do not need to use site link bridges. A normal fully routed IP network with the Bridge all site links option enables connections between sites.

Domain Controller and Global Catalog Placement

When deciding on where to locate domain controllers and global catalog servers, there are a few rules that you can use to help make decisions. However, just like deciding what constitutes a site, deciding where domain controllers and global catalog servers should be placed is dependent on the environment. Factors such as the number of sites, the number of users at each site, and if services such as Microsoft Exchange Server are in use are all factors that you need to consider.

Domain Controllers

At a minimum, every domain in the forest should have at least two domain controllers—even for domains with a very small number of users. This provides redundancy for authentication and other directory-related services in the event one of the domain controllers fails. In a small network with only two domain controllers, it is most likely that the two domain controllers will be located in the same site; however, this is not a requirement. If the network has two or more smaller sites, it is possible to locate one of the domain controllers at one site and the second domain controller at another site to fulfill the two domain controller minimum per domain. Choosing exactly where each domain controller goes depends on what type of redundancy is needed at each site, what type of network connection is available, and how many users are at each site.

For large sites, such as a main office, where there are many users that must be able to authenticate to the network and have fast access to the directory at all times, the best solution is to place at least two domain controllers at the site. In the event one of the two domain controllers fails, users will still have fast access to the second domain controller located in the same site. This means that users do not have to cross a slow WAN link for directory-related queries even when one server fails.

In the majority of situations, two domain controllers at a site can handle several thousand users, but how many more than two that may be required is highly variable and dependent on the environment and hardware. For example, it is assumed that most users will log on to the network in the morning over a period of time. That is, all users are not pressing OK on the logon screen at exactly 8:00 a.m.—which would require additional resources to log all the users on simultaneously instead of over a half-hour period or more. It may be necessary to collect performance statistics, as covered in Chapter 13, in order to determine how many domain controllers are needed at a site.

The goal at a large site should be to have $n+1$ domain controllers, where n represents the number of domain controllers required to handle the load and an additional domain controller in the event one of the n domain controllers is unavailable. While having two domain controllers at a single site is good for redundancy, if they are both almost at capacity and one goes offline, the remaining domain controller would not be able to handle the load. This would result in sluggish network performance and unhappy users. That is why it is important to have enough capacity to handle the load plus additional capacity to cover for any one server going offline.

While larger sites often have two domain controllers, smaller branch offices (with say 25 to 50 users) may only have one domain controller. When one domain controller is present at a site, the loss of a WAN connection does not impact user's access to the directory. Users can still access the directory from the domain controller located in the same site. In the event the domain controller at the local site fails, users then need to cross a slow WAN connection to a domain controller located in another site for authentication and directory-related queries. If both the WAN and the local domain controller are unavailable (unlikely), users will have no access to a domain controller.

NOTE If you have a main site that is designed to handle the load in the event a single domain controller at a smaller branch office fails, ensure that the main site has the capacity needed to handle the additional load.

CAUTION It is important that you keep domain controllers physically secure. It is not a good idea to place a domain controller in a branch office that does not have a secure area in which to store the server.

By placing a domain controller in a smaller branch office, users can have fast access to the directory from a local domain controller. While users requests are handled much faster because they do not have to cross a WAN connection, it is important to keep in mind that additional WAN bandwidth is required for replication. For very small branch offices, with say two or five users, it may not make sense to place a domain controller at that site. By not placing a domain controller at an extremely small site, no WAN bandwidth for that site is needed for replication. However, keep in mind that if the WAN connection fails, users will not be able to access the directory or authenticate to the network. Figure 6-19 shows what a site diagram may look like with domain controllers located at both large and small sites.

NOTE While the above recommendations are made from the perspective of a single domain, they are also applicable to multiple domains. If your forest has multiple domains, use the above recommendations for each domain. For example, a large office with 500 users in domain A and 800 users in domain B requires four domain controllers at the site—two for domain A and two for domain B.

Global Catalog Servers

As stated in Chapter 1, a global catalog is an index and partial replica of the objects and attributes most frequently used throughout the entire Active Directory structure (if necessary, review the information provided in Chapter 1). To understand the importance of a global catalog, imagine a forest of 10 domains, each with 10,000 users. If you wanted to search for Mary Smith in Active Directory but were not sure in which domain her user account was located, it would be necessary to search every domain in the forest. Instead of having to contact a domain controller for each domain in the forest across slow WAN links, Active Directory can contact a global catalog server in order to perform the lookup. In most

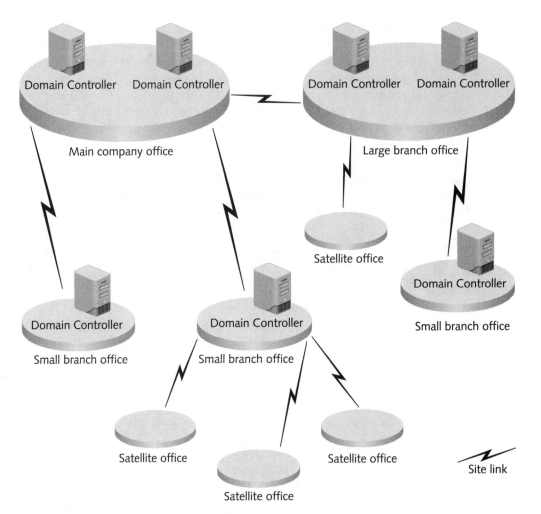

Figure 6-19   Example placement of domain controllers

cases, the global catalog server is in the same site as the client or in a site directly connected. Once Mary's account is located, you can retrieve any additional information that is not included in the global catalog directly from a domain controller from Mary's domain.

Microsoft recommends that one domain controller per site be designated as a global catalog server. This is a good recommendation, although the exact network environment will once again play a role. For large sites, it is a good idea to have at least two domain controllers designated as global catalog servers. In the event one global catalog server is unavailable, the second can fulfill the requests. Additionally, if the forest consists of only one domain, designate all domain controllers in all sites as global catalogs. In a single domain forest, all domain controllers already contain all objects in the forest. This means that no additional network bandwidth is required for replication when domain controllers are designated as global catalog servers. In Activity 6-6, you will check if your server is a global catalog server, and if not, designate it as one.

TIP

Microsoft recommends that you have a dedicated global catalog server for each Exchange 2000/2003 server. The global catalog server and Exchange server should be located in the same site.

For smaller branch offices, the decision to place a global catalog server at the site or not is a little more complicated. In Windows 2000 Server, if a global catalog server were unavailable (and the domain containing the user account was in native mode), authentication would fail and the user would not be allowed to log on (with the exception of the Administrator account). This is no longer true with Windows Server 2003's Universal Group caching. Universal Group caching allows the domain controllers within a particular site to query a global catalog server in another location for a user's Universal Group membership information, and then cache that information locally for use in subsequent logons. Branch offices that have a domain controller but do not have a global catalog server can now authenticate users to the domain even when the WAN is unavailable.

NOTE

Universal Group caching is set at the site level in the site's NTDS Site Settings object. By default, Universal Group caching is not enabled. To enable Universal Group caching for a site, select the site in the left tree pane of the Active Directory Sites and Services console and then double-click the site's NTDS Site Settings object in the right details pane. Check the box next to Enable Universal Group Membership Caching to enable Universal Group caching. The Refresh cache from the drop-down list can be used to specify the site that contains a global catalog server to cache from. The Default option will automatically select the closest site that contains a global catalog server. When enabling Universal Group caching for a site, be sure the site contains at least one Windows Server 2003 domain controller. Otherwise, even if caching is enabled for the site, there will be no server to actually cache the data at the site.

When deciding to place a global catalog server at a branch office, you must consider the need for additional WAN bandwidth to increase the speed when searching the directory. Because the global catalog is a partial replica of all objects in the forest, and not just the objects from a single domain, additional bandwidth is required for replication. However, placing a global catalog server in the same site as the user does speed up forest-wide queries. It is generally a good idea to place a global catalog server at each site—unless there are very few users at the site or the WAN connection is already near capacity.

6

NOTE

When you are deciding where to place domain controllers, you make decisions on a domain by domain basis. In contrast, when deciding where to place global catalog servers, decisions are made for the entire forest. For example, a large office with two domains A and B that have a total of four domain controllers would only require that two of the four domain controllers be marked as global catalog servers. It does not matter which domain the global catalog servers are members of (both from A, both from B, or one from each domain) because the global catalog is common across every domain in the forest.

ACTIVITY

Activity 6-6: Designating a Domain Controller as a Global Catalog Server

Time Required: 5 minutes

Objective: This exercise is designed to familiarize you with the process of designating a domain controller as a global catalog.

Description: By default, the first domain controller created in a forest is designated as a global catalog server. As you add additional domain controllers to the forest, you must manually designate them as global catalog servers.

1. If necessary, start your server and log on using the **Administrator** account in the **CHILDXX** domain (where *XX* is the number of the forest root domain for which your server is a domain controller) using the password **Password01**.

2. Click Start, select Administrative Tools, and then click Active Directory Sites and Services.

3. If necessary, in the left tree pane, expand the **Sites** folder.

4. In the left tree pane, expand the **MySiteXX** site (where *XX* is the number of your server).

5. In the left tree pane, expand the **Servers** folder located under the MySite*XX* site.

6. In the left tree pane, expand **SERVERXX** (where *XX* is the number of your server).

7. In the left tree pane, right-click **NTDS Settings** under SERVER*XX*, and then click **Properties**.

8. Check the box next to **Global Catalog** if it is not already checked. Your screen should look similar to Figure 6-20.

9. Click **OK**.

10. Close Active Directory Sites and Services.

11. Log off from your server.

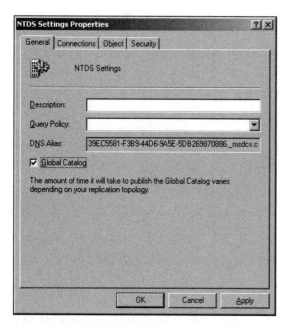

Figure 6-20   Designating a global catalog server

CHAPTER SUMMARY

□ Active Directory sites are composed of one or more well-connected subnets, where the term "well connected" is generally accepted to mean a LAN. Two or more sites are connected by a WAN.

□ Subnet objects are used to represent the network subnets that define a site. Client computers and domain controllers can compare their IP addresses to the available subnet objects to determine in which site they are located.

□ The object connecting two or more sites is called a site link. The site link is an object in Active Directory and has parameters attached to it. The parameters include site link cost, replication interval, replication schedule, and transport protocol.

□ The site link cost is an arbitrary value set by the administrator that is used when locating the closest server. When multiple site links must be crossed in order to connect to a server, the cost of all links is added together to get the total cost.

□ A site link can either use the RPC over TCP/IP or SMTP transport protocol. RPC over TCP/IP is used for reliable WAN connections, whereas SMTP is used for unreliable WAN connections.

□ Domain controllers are placed into the appropriate site based on their IP address during promotion and can be manually moved later by an administrator. In contrast, client computers are placed into sites based on their IP addresses each time they start.

❏ If a fully routed IP network does not exist between sites, then the administrator can construct another type of object in Active Directory called a site link bridge, which defines a set of site links that can be reached via one or more connecting sites that route IP traffic.

❏ The placement of domain controllers is determined by the client load and the availability required. All domains should have at least two domain controllers for redundancy.

❏ Global catalog servers provide a fast way to search for objects located throughout the forest. Normally, at least one global catalog server is placed at every site, unless the site is small. If you only have one domain in the forest, all servers should be designated as global catalog servers.

KEY TERMS

Default-First-Site-Name — The site that is automatically created when you promote the first domain controller in the forest.

DEFAULTIPSITELINK — The site link that is automatically created when you promote the first domain controller in the forest.

distributed file system (DFS) — A distributed service that integrates file shares located on multiple servers into a single logical namespace.

fully routed IP environment — A network where computers from one site can communicate with all other sites on the network.

physical objects — Active Directory objects that have an equivalent physical structure or component in the real world. Physical objects include sites, site links, and domain controllers.

site-aware — A service that can use site information in Active Directory to locate the closest server based on the cost of site links.

site link bridge — An object that exists in Active Directory to define which site links can communicate with one another on an IP network that is not fully routed.

subnet objects — An Active Directory object that is used to define an IP subnet. Subnet objects are associated with sites and in turn allow computers to determine in which site they are located.

REVIEW QUESTIONS

1. When configuring connectivity between sites in a nonrouted IP environment, which of the following should you disable first?

   a. all bridgehead servers

   b. all site link replication intervals

   c. automatic site link bridging

   d. IP routing

2. When a new domain controller is added to an Active Directory domain, the administrator must manually select to which site to join it. True or False?

3. The global catalog is a _____ that fulfills a specific role in the Active Directory environment.

   a. member server from a domain

   b. modified DNS server

   c. secondary forest root domain controller

   d. domain controller

4. A site link is an object in Active Directory with parameters that include which of the following?

   a. site link transitivity, replication interval, replication schedule, and transport protocol

   b. site link cost, replication interval, replication schedule, and transport protocol

   c. site link bridge cost, SMTP replication compression setting, replication schedule, and transport schedule

   d. site link cost, replication interval, replication schedule, and RPC transport schedule

5. By default, all site links are transitive connections with the Active Directory setting of Bridge all site links enabled. True or False?

6. The process used to create a site link bridge is identical to the process used to create a site link, with the exception of which of the following?

   a. Site link bridges have no settings for site link cost or replication interval.

   b. Site link bridges require configuration of SMTP transport protocol settings.

   c. Site link bridges require configuration of RPC over TCP/IP transport protocol settings.

   d. Site link bridges can only be configured using GC servers as endpoints.

7. Default-First-Site-Name is created automatically when Active Directory is first installed, and except for this first site, all other sites are created by which of the following? (Choose all that apply.)

   a. Automatically as child domains are created and joined to the forest

   b. Automatically as remote global catalog servers are added to the forest

   c. As dictated by your site implementation plan

   d. Manually as your Active Directory implementation grows over the course of time

8. Sites in Active Directory allow the administrator to control the replication topology for Active Directory information. True or False?

6

9. Remember that the site topology is a logical representation of your physical network and does not necessarily map directly to the actual physical topology. The key factor that allows you to delineate your site topology is which of the following?

   a. the number of nonrouted IP subnetworks in your network infrastructure

   b. the arrangement of subnets within your physical network

   c. the classes of IP addresses used in your infrastructure

   d. the number of IP host nodes assigned per subnet

10. It is not possible to change the name of the Default-First-Site-Name site container. True or False?

11. When creating site links, the administrator must configure a cost for the site link. The range of values for the site link cost is which of the following?

    a. 0 to 32

    b. 1 to 327

    c. 1 to 32767

    d. 0 to 32767

12. Site link costs are cumulative. Therefore, if Site Link A–B has a cost of 50, Site Link B–C has a cost of 75, Site Link C–D has a cost of _____ , and Site Link D–E has a cost of 251, then the total cost to connect from site A to site E is 487.

    a. 110

    b. 111

    c. 112

    d. 115

13. When configuring a site link, you can choose the _____ over TCP/IP or SMTP protocol for the link.

14. The _____ Admins group has permission to add and modify sites in Active Directory.

15. In Active Directory, a domain controller must be located at every site. True or False?

16. Replication within a site uses which protocol?

    a. RPC over TCP/IP

    b. SMTP

    c. RPC over TCP/IP or SMTP depending on how the administrator configures the site

    d. Neither RPC over TCP/IP or SMTP

17. Services or client software that is/are _____ can use the site information in Active Directory to locate a server that is closest.

18. When you are deciding where to place domain controllers, you make decisions on a _____ by _____ basis.

19. When deciding where to place global catalog servers, decisions are made for the entire _____ .

20. In a _____ IP environment, all sites are capable of communicating with every other site on the network.

Case Projects

Now that the Super Corp Active Directory implementation is starting to take form, it is time to turn your attention to some of the physical aspects of the company's Active Directory implementation. Working with Davia, one of Super Corp's junior administrators, you have begun the process of implementing sites in Active Directory. Examine the map in Figure 6-21 to understand why multiple sites may be necessary for Super Corp.

CASE PROJECTS

Case Project 6-1: An Introduction to Sites

In Figure 6-21, notice the layout of the different buildings that compose Super Corp's Atlanta building complex. Note that the office, administration, and training buildings are the only buildings Super Corp owns—the other surrounding buildings are not part of Super Corp.

The training facility is approximately 5 km (3 miles) from the administration building. Using the map, work with Mary to make some basic design decisions for the Super Corp Active Directory site implementation concerning only the Atlanta location.

1. From your first examination of the map, how many sites do you think should be implemented in this particular site model?

2. Examine the details carefully. Would the fact that the training building, which is an older facility that Super Corp purchased, still uses a token ring network affect your site design?

3. The office building and the administration building are located across the street from one another, a distance of approximately 60 m (200 ft). Is this separation sufficient to require multiple sites, or can a single site be used for these two buildings?

CASE PROJECTS

Case Project 6-2: Benefits of Using Sites

Using the updated fully routed network map shown in Figure 6-22, consider if it is necessary to update your network design.

1. A decision has been made not to place a DC in the training building. However, a resource server (file/print and other network services) will be placed at this location. The administration building will contain a forest root DC, as well as at least one resource server. The office building will contain at least one DC, as well as one resource server. The IT manager would like to minimize the amount of traffic between the office and administration buildings, even though they have a high-speed

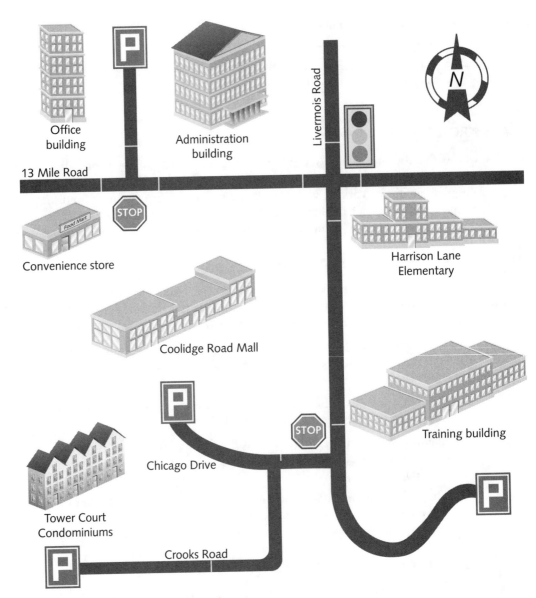

Figure 6-21   Super Corp Atlanta location map

network link between them. Does this information change the proposed site design you created in Case Project 6-1?

2. Will you need to implement any site links or site link bridges?

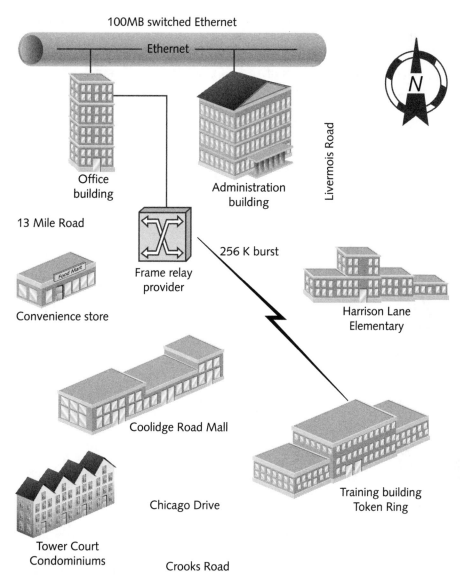

Figure 6-22   Super Corp Atlanta WAN

CASE
PROJECTS

Case Project 6-3: Creating and Using Sites

You and Mary may need to configure the cost, as well as other properties of site links.

1. Using Figure 6-22, determine the link cost you would use between the office site and the training site.

2. What would the effect on the network be if the direct link between the office site and the administration building were unavailable?

3. What would the effect on the network be if the direct link between the office site and the training site were unavailable?

4. You should plan for some redundancy in your network design. Using Figure 6-22 as a reference, is it necessary to place additional domain controllers or global catalog servers at any additional sites?

7

ACTIVE DIRECTORY REPLICATION

After reading this chapter, you will be able to:

♦ Describe how Active Directory identifies data that needs to be replicated

♦ Describe how the Active Directory replication topology is generated

♦ Describe and control when Active Directory replication occurs

♦ Monitor and troubleshoot Active Directory replication

♦ Describe SYSVOL and how its replication differs from Active Directory replication

In normal day-to-day administration, changes are made to objects in Active Directory. New users are added, passwords are changed, and objects are deleted. These changes need to be updated on all domain controllers in the network to ensure they have the most up-to-date information. This process of updating Active Directory changes to all domain controllers on the network is called **replication**.

In this chapter, you will learn how replication allows Windows Server 2003 to work with multiple copies of the Active Directory database and make changes at any **replica**.

Specifically, this chapter examines the inner workings of Active Directory replication, replication topology, how to manage and monitor replication, and some other issues that can arise. Finally, troubleshooting Active Directory replication is explored.

IDENTIFYING DATA TO REPLICATE

As mentioned in Chapter 1, Active Directory uses a multi-master model for replication. This means that you can make changes to Active Directory on any domain controller, and those changes are then replicated to other domain controllers. This is a significant enhancement over the replication in Windows NT 4.0, which has only one master (or writeable) copy. In a Windows NT 4.0 domain, only the Primary Domain Controller (PDC) can change the domain database. This means that if the PDC is not available, changes—such as adding users to the network or even changing a password—cannot occur.

When you make a change to Active Directory, such as adding a new user or changing a user's telephone number, the replication process begins. Replication is performed at the attribute level, not the object level. For example, if a user's fax number is changed, then only the new fax number of that user object is replicated. Other attributes of the user object that were not changed are not replicated, making the replication process in Windows Server 2003 very efficient.

Replication involves two types of updates—**originating updates** and **replicated updates**. An originating update is a change to Active Directory that was made on the local domain controller. For example, if a user's password is changed on DC1, then it is an originating update on DC1. A replicated update is a change that was made through replication. For example, if a user's password is changed on DC1, and the change is replicated to DC2, then it is a replicated update on DC2.

Because you can make changes to Active Directory on any domain controller, there must be a mechanism to track those changes and ensure that updates are replicated properly. In some other directory services, a timestamp is used to determine which directory updates need to be replicated. In these types of directory services, it is crucial that the time be synchronized, which can be challenging, if not impossible, to achieve. In some of these systems, if a network link fails and clocks start to drift, it is possible that data could be lost or the directory may be corrupted.

Fortunately, Active Directory does not rely on a time-based system to replicate directory changes—and therefore is not susceptible to the problems inherent with a replication system based on time. Instead, domain controllers track object changes using **Update Sequence Numbers (USNs)**. Each DC maintains its own unique USN count, which is independent from all other domain controllers. Every time the Active Directory database on a DC is modified, the USN is incremented by one and the updated object and attributes are stamped with the USN. The only downside to this system is that comparing USNs from different domain controllers is meaningless—but Active Directory's replication system was designed to work with this restriction, as you will see later in this section.

The use of a multi-master model does introduce an additional consideration: it is possible for two domain controllers in the same domain to show different information, even for the same object. This is caused by **latency**, which is the idea that the replication process takes some time. The latency could be only a few seconds or possibly a few minutes. In large, geographically dispersed networks, the latency could be hours. Once replication has finished and all domain controllers contain the same information for every object, the directory database is said to have reached **convergence** (or to have converged).

NOTE The membership attribute of a group object is treated differently by Windows Server 2003 than by Windows 2000. If the forest functionality level is set for Windows Server 2003, then only *changes* to group membership need to be synchronized. If it is set at a lower functionality level, then the *entire membership* must be replicated when new users are added or removed from the group. The way in which group membership changes are replicated is one of the most important differences between Windows Server 2003 and Windows 2000. The membership of a group is a single attribute—albeit a large one—which Windows 2000 must handle as a single unit.

Identifying Domain Controllers

Before identifying the data that needs to be replicated, the domain controllers themselves must first be identified. There are several identifiers for a domain controller: the domain controller's computer account, records registered in DNS, the NTDS Settings Server object, the server GUID, and the database GUID. The first two you do not need to be concerned with right now; however, the other three you do.

NTDS Settings Server Object

The NTDS Settings Server object is contained in the configuration partition and identifies the server as a domain controller. You can access the object by using Active Directory Sites and Services. It holds a link to the domain controller's computer account and cannot be deleted by an administrator on the local computer. Additionally, if the NTDS Settings Server object is deleted on another domain controller, it is automatically recreated by the domain controller for which the object exists.

Server GUID

The server **globally unique identifier (GUID)** is used to identify **replication partners**. Each domain controller registers a CNAME (alias) record in DNS that is used to locate the domain controller by using its GUID.

Database GUID

The database globally unique identifier, also called the Directory Service Agent (DSA) GUID, is used by domain controllers to identify other domain controllers during replication requests. That is, when storing and comparing vector information (discussed later), the database GUID is used. While the server GUID and the database GUID are initially the same, the database GUID changes if a domain controller is restored from backup in order to ensure that changes are replicated correctly.

Update Sequence Number

The update sequence number is a 64-bit number used to identify changes to data in Active Directory. Each object in Active Directory has two USNs—one set when the object is created (usnCreated) and one set every time the object is updated (usnChanged). In addition to the two USNs associated with each object, each attribute of an object has two USNs. The first USN associated with each attribute is the USN for the local domain controller, whereas the second USN is from the domain controller that performed the originating write operation. To better understand how USNs are set during the replication process, look at an example using two domain controllers and the creation of a new user account.

In Figure 7-1, a new user account is created on DC1. The first thing that happens is that DC1's USN counter is incremented by one to 8412. The object is created in the local domain controller's database with the usnCreated, usnChanged, attribute USNs, and originating write USNs all set to 8412. Because this is a new object, the version number of all attributes is set to 1. The originating timestamp contains the data and time the write operation was performed. Finally, the originating DSA GUID contains the GUID of the database on DC1—the domain controller where the write operation was originally performed on the directory.

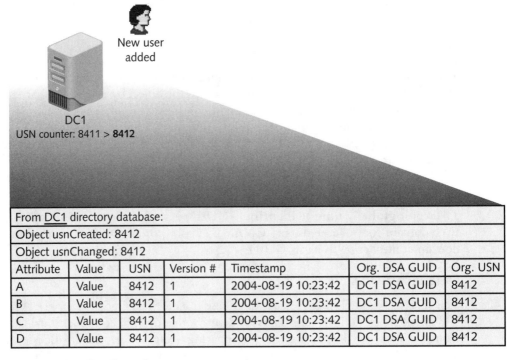

From DC1 directory database:						
Object usnCreated: 8412						
Object usnChanged: 8412						
Attribute	Value	USN	Version #	Timestamp	Org. DSA GUID	Org. USN
A	Value	8412	1	2004-08-19 10:23:42	DC1 DSA GUID	8412
B	Value	8412	1	2004-08-19 10:23:42	DC1 DSA GUID	8412
C	Value	8412	1	2004-08-19 10:23:42	DC1 DSA GUID	8412
D	Value	8412	1	2004-08-19 10:23:42	DC1 DSA GUID	8412

Figure 7-1   Creation of new user account

Once the user account is created on DC1, it is then replicated to DC2 as shown in Figure 7-2. DC2 increments its USN counter to 4653 and then creates the object in its local database, setting the usnCreated, usnChanged, and attribute USNs to 4653. Note however that the originating write USNs on the attributes are set to 8412—the USN from the domain controller (DC1) that performed the original write operation to Active Directory. Similarly, the version number, originating timestamp, and originating DSA GUID for all attributes are all copied from DC1.

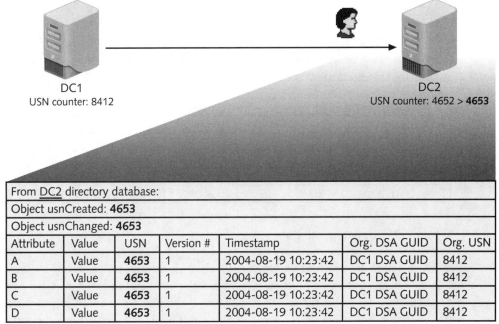

From <u>DC2</u> directory database:						
Object usnCreated: **4653**						
Object usnChanged: **4653**						
Attribute	Value	USN	Version #	Timestamp	Org. DSA GUID	Org. USN
A	Value	**4653**	1	2004-08-19 10:23:42	DC1 DSA GUID	8412
B	Value	**4653**	1	2004-08-19 10:23:42	DC1 DSA GUID	8412
C	Value	**4653**	1	2004-08-19 10:23:42	DC1 DSA GUID	8412
D	Value	**4653**	1	2004-08-19 10:23:42	DC1 DSA GUID	8412

Bold indicates a change from the previous figure

Figure 7-2   Replication of new user account

Now, assume that some time has passed, and the user account is updated with a new e-mail address (attributeC). Instead of making the update to the user account on DC1, the update is made on DC2, as shown in Figure 7-3. Again, the local USN counter on DC2 is incremented, this time to 5179. Notice that the usnChanged, USN of attributeC, and the originating write USN of attributeC are all updated to 5179. Additionally, the version number, timestamp, and originating DSA GUID are all updated to reflect the change made on DC2.

NOTE   The reason DC2's USN count jumped from 4653 all the way up to 5179 is because other changes have been made to the directory (between the time the user account was originally replicated and when the user's e-mail address was updated).

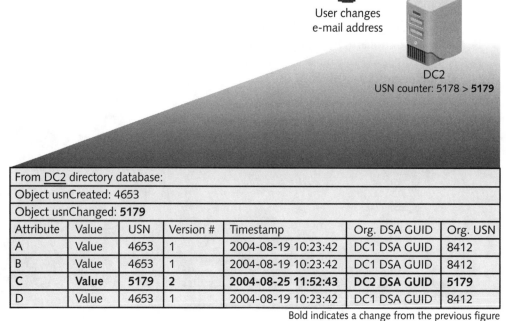

User changes
e-mail address

DC2
USN counter: 5178 > **5179**

From <u>DC2</u> directory database:						
Object usnCreated: 4653						
Object usnChanged: **5179**						
Attribute	Value	USN	Version #	Timestamp	Org. DSA GUID	Org. USN
A	Value	4653	1	2004-08-19 10:23:42	DC1 DSA GUID	8412
B	Value	4653	1	2004-08-19 10:23:42	DC1 DSA GUID	8412
C	**Value**	**5179**	**2**	**2004-08-25 11:52:43**	**DC2 DSA GUID**	**5179**
D	Value	4653	1	2004-08-19 10:23:42	DC1 DSA GUID	8412

Bold indicates a change from the previous figure

Figure 7-3   Updating attribute of user account

With the attribute updated on DC2, the data must now be replicated to DC1, as shown in Figure 7-4. DC1's USN counter is incremented to 9063 and then the usnChanged and USN of attributeC are set to the new USN. The originating write USN of attributeC is set to 5179—the USN from the domain controller (DC2) that performed the original write operation to Active Directory. Similarly, the version number, originating timestamp, and originating DSA GUID, are all copied from DC2 for attributeC.

If all this seems confusing, remember that in addition to the value of an attribute, the version number, originating timestamp, originating DSA GUID, and originating write USN are all copied from one domain controller to another during replication. The object's usnCreated value, usnChanged value, and the USN of each attribute are unique to each domain controller and are not replicated.

It is important to keep in mind that a USN only has meaning for a given replica. This means that comparing a USN from DC1 to a USN from DC2 gives no useful information. For example, if DC1 updated attributeA of an object with an originating write USN of 1000 and DC2 updated attributeB of the same object with an originating write USN of 5000, is it possible to tell which update was made first? The short answer is no. While attributeA updated by DC1 has a lower USN, it is possible that DC1 is a brand new domain controller just reaching 1000 today. DC2 could have been in service for quite some time and reached a USN of 5000 months ago. In this case, the update to attributeB would have been made

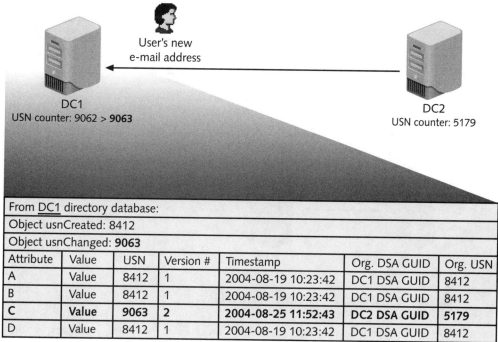

User's new
e-mail address

DC1
USN counter: 9062 > **9063**

DC2
USN counter: 5179

From DC1 directory database:						
Object usnCreated: 8412						
Object usnChanged: **9063**						
Attribute	Value	USN	Version #	Timestamp	Org. DSA GUID	Org. USN
A	Value	8412	1	2004-08-19 10:23:42	DC1 DSA GUID	8412
B	Value	8412	1	2004-08-19 10:23:42	DC1 DSA GUID	8412
C	**Value**	**9063**	**2**	**2004-08-25 11:52:43**	**DC2 DSA GUID**	**5179**
D	Value	8412	1	2004-08-19 10:23:42	DC1 DSA GUID	8412

Bold indicates a change from the previous figure

Figure 7-4   Replicating change of user account's attribute

before the update to attributeA, even though the originating write USN is higher. This is because each domain controller has its own USN counter that is independent of all other domain controllers.

While it is not possible to compare USNs from two different domain controllers, it is possible to compare USNs from the same domain controller. Continuing with the previous example, what if DC1 also updated attributeC with an originating write USN of 2000—is it possible to tell if attributeA or attributeC was updated first? Because the USNs are from the same domain controller, it is possible to compare the USNs and come to the conclusion that attributeA was updated first—it has a lower USN.

High-watermark Value

The high-watermark value is used to quickly identify which objects may need to be replicated from a specific replication partner for a specific naming context. Consisting of a table on each domain controller, the high-watermark value stores the highest USN from each of its replication partners for each naming context. An example of a high-watermark value table for a single naming context is shown in Figure 7-5. In the illustration, DC2 has DC1 and DC3 as its replication partners . Notice that DC4 is not contained in the high-watermark value table because it is not a replication partner with DC2.

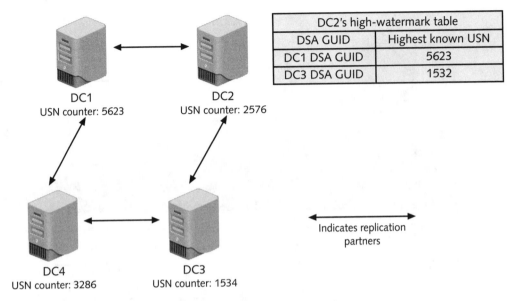

DC2's high-watermark table	
DSA GUID	Highest known USN
DC1 DSA GUID	5623
DC3 DSA GUID	1532

DC1
USN counter: 5623

DC2
USN counter: 2576

DC4
USN counter: 3286

DC3
USN counter: 1534

↔ Indicates replication
partners

Figure 7-5   Example high-watermark table

When a destination domain controller (DC2 in this example) contacts a source domain controller (either DC1 or DC3 in this example), the source domain controller sends updates starting with the object that has the lowest usnChanged value. Although the destination domain controller does not store the value of usnChanged from the source domain controller for every object, the destination domain controller does keep track of the highest usnChanged value it has successfully received from the source domain controller for a given naming context. This highest usnChanged value is known as the high-watermark value.

Using the USN count of each domain controller and DC2's list of high-watermark values in Figure 7-5, can you identify if either DC1 or DC3 has changes that have not necessarily been replicated to DC2?

NOTE

Each time a destination domain controller requests changes, it sends the high-watermark value to the source domain controller. The source domain controller can use the high-watermark value to reduce the number of objects that must be considered for replication. If an object's usnChanged value is less than or equal to the high-watermark value, the destination domain controller has already received any updates regarding that object. If an object's usnChanged value is greater than the high-watermark value, the object contains updates that the destination domain controller may not have received. This concept is shown in Figure 7-6 with four user accounts used as an example (note that DC2 also sends vector information, which is discussed shortly, but not shown in the figure).

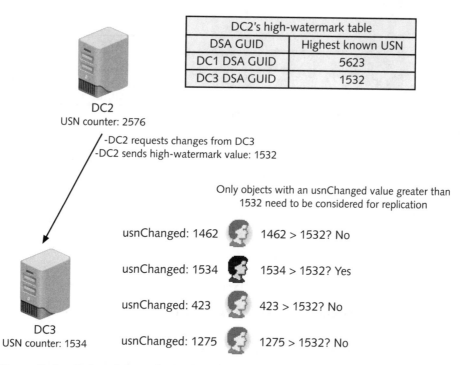

Figure 7-6   Determining which objects may need to be replicated

Up-to-dateness Vector

Whereas the high-watermark value is used to filter out *objects* that do not need to be replicated, the up-to-dateness vector helps the source domain controller to filter out *attributes* that do not need to be replicated (or entire objects if all the attributes are filtered out). Consisting of a table on each domain controller, the up-to-dateness vector stores the highest originating USN received from every source domain controller (typically every domain controller with a writable copy) for a given naming context. An example of an up-to-dateness vector table for a single naming context is shown in Figure 7-7. In the illustration, DC2 has DC1 and DC3 as its replication partners. Additionally, DC4 has DC1 and DC3 as its replication partners.

When a destination domain controller contacts a source domain controller, the destination domain controller sends its up-to-dateness vector. By using the up-to-dateness vector, the source domain controller can determine for which attributes the destination domain controller does and does not have updated values. The source domain controller does this by performing the following steps, as shown in Figure 7-8:

1. For the first attribute of the object that may need to be replicated, locate the originating DSA GUID.

2. In the up-to-dateness vector sent from the destination domain controller, locate the DSA GUID that corresponds to the originating DSA GUID of the attribute.

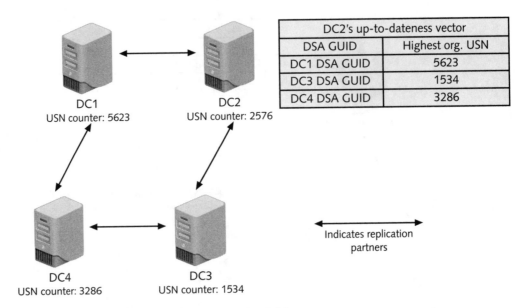

Figure 7-7 Example up-to-dateness vector table

3. If the originating write USN is less than or equal to the up-to-dateness vector for the given DSA GUID, the attribute does not need to be replicated. Otherwise, if the originating write USN is greater than the up-to-dateness vector for the given DSA GUID, the attribute needs to be replicated.

4. Repeat Steps 1 to 3 until all attributes have been checked.

Notice that while the high-watermark value works from the standpoint of a single source to a single destination, the up-to-dateness vector is based on all possible sources of original updates to a single destination. Also note that the high-watermark value only stores the highest USN for each direct replication partner, whereas the up-to-dateness vector stores the highest USN for every domain controller that has performed an originating write operation.

Propagation Dampening

It is possible that multiple paths can exist between two domain controllers, which is a good thing. By providing multiple paths for replication, fault tolerance and reduced latency are gained. However, if multiple paths exist, changes could propagate down each available path and could even end up in a never ending loop (A > B > C > A…). To prevent unnecessary replication caused by multiple paths, the up-to-dateness vector already described can be used

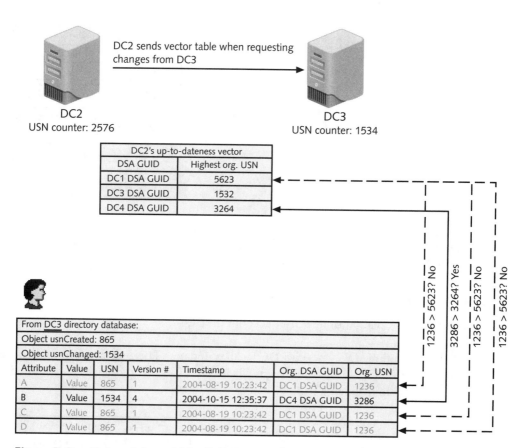

Figure 7-8   Determining which attributes need to be replicated

to provide **propagation dampening**. The following example demonstrates the replication process in a typical multiple path replication scenario. In Figure 7-9, the following domain controllers are replication partners (bidirectional):

- DC1 and DC2
- DC2 and DC3
- DC3 and DC4
- DC4 and DC1

Figure 7-9 illustrates the creation of a new user account on DC4. DC4's USN counter is incremented to 3287, which is the USN assigned to the new object. No changes are made to DC2.

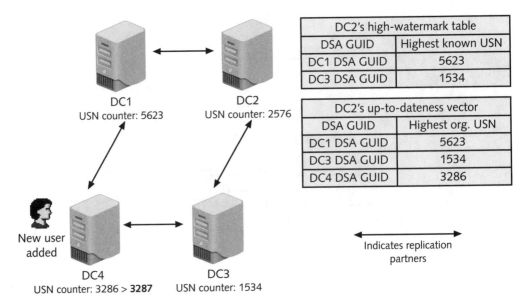

DC2's high-watermark table	
DSA GUID	Highest known USN
DC1 DSA GUID	5623
DC3 DSA GUID	1534

DC2's up-to-dateness vector	
DSA GUID	Highest org. USN
DC1 DSA GUID	5623
DC3 DSA GUID	1534
DC4 DSA GUID	3286

◄──────► Indicates replication partners

Figure 7-9   Creation of new user account on DC4

After a short time, DC4 notifies DC1 it has updates. The user account is then replicated from DC4 to DC1, as shown in Figure 7-10. DC1's USN counter is incremented to 5624. No changes are made to DC2.

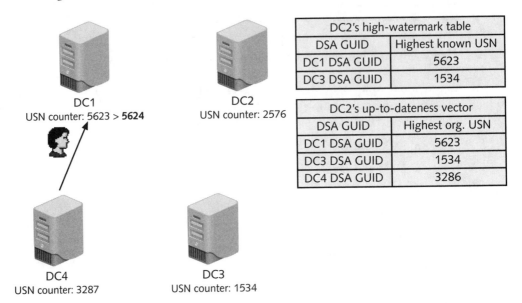

DC2's high-watermark table	
DSA GUID	Highest known USN
DC1 DSA GUID	5623
DC3 DSA GUID	1534

DC2's up-to-dateness vector	
DSA GUID	Highest org. USN
DC1 DSA GUID	5623
DC3 DSA GUID	1534
DC4 DSA GUID	3286

Figure 7-10   Replication of user account to DC4's first replication partner

After another short amount of time, DC1 informs DC2 that it has updates. As shown in Figure 7-11, DC2 then initiates replication with DC1 by sending DC1 the following information:

- The naming context updates are requested for
- The high-watermark value DC2 has for DC1 for the given naming context
- The maximum number of object update entries requested
- The maximum number of values requested
- DC2's up-to-dateness vector for the given naming context

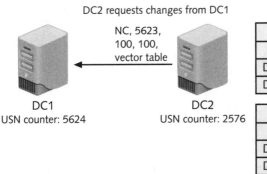

DC2 requests changes from DC1

NC, 5623,
100, 100,
vector table

DC1
USN counter: 5624

DC2
USN counter: 2576

DC2's high-watermark table	
DSA GUID	Highest known USN
DC1 DSA GUID	5623
DC3 DSA GUID	1534

DC2's up-to-dateness vector	
DSA GUID	Highest org. USN
DC1 DSA GUID	5623
DC3 DSA GUID	1534
DC4 DSA GUID	3286

DC4
USN counter: 3287

DC3
USN counter: 1534

Figure 7-11   DC2 requests updates from DC1

Once DC1 determines what information needs to be replicated, the data is sent (in this case, the new user account) to DC2, as shown in Figure 7-12. DC2's USN counter is incremented to 2577. Additionally, DC2 updates its high-watermark value for DC1 and its up-to-dateness vector for DC4.

DC1 responds with data (new user
account), new high-watermark value,
and updated vector data

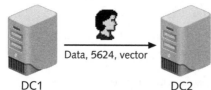

DC1
USN counter: 5624

Data, 5624, vector

DC2
USN counter: 2576 > **2577**

DC2's high-watermark table	
DSA GUID	Highest known USN
DC1 DSA GUID	**5624**
DC3 DSA GUID	1534

DC2's up-to-dateness vector	
DSA GUID	Highest org. USN
DC1 DSA GUID	5623
DC3 DSA GUID	1534
DC4 DSA GUID	**3287**

DC4
USN counter: 3287

DC3
USN counter: 1534

Figure 7-12   DC1 sends directory data, new high-watermark value, and vector data

NOTE

In Figure 7-12, notice that while DC2 updated DC1 in its high-watermark table, no changes were made to DC2's up-to-dateness vector for DC1. Remember that the high-watermark value is the highest known USN, whereas the up-to-dateness vector is the highest known *originating write* USN. Because DC1 was not the originating writer of any updates (it only had replicated updates), DC2's up-to-dateness vector for DC1 is unchanged.

Figure 7-13 illustrates the replication process of the user account from DC4 to DC3. DC3's USN counter is incremented to 1535. No changes are made to DC2.

After a short amount of time, DC3 informs DC2 that it has updates. As shown in Figure 7-14, DC2 then initiates replication with DC3 by sending it the necessary information.

DC2's high-watermark table	
DSA GUID	Highest known USN
DC1 DSA GUID	5624
DC3 DSA GUID	1534

DC2's up-to-dateness vector	
DSA GUID	Highest org. USN
DC1 DSA GUID	5623
DC3 DSA GUID	1534
DC4 DSA GUID	3287

DC1
USN counter: 5624

DC2
USN counter: 2577

DC4
USN counter: 3287

DC3
USN counter: 1534 > **1535**

Figure 7-13   Replication of user account to DC4's second replication partner

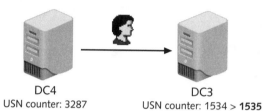

DC2 requests changes from DC3

DC2's high-watermark table	
DSA GUID	Highest known USN
DC1 DSA GUID	5624
DC3 DSA GUID	1534

DC2's up-to-dateness vector	
DSA GUID	Highest org. USN
DC1 DSA GUID	5623
DC3 DSA GUID	1534
DC4 DSA GUID	3287

DC1
USN counter: 5624

DC2
USN counter: 2577

NC, 1534,
100, 100,
vector table

DC4
USN counter: 3287

DC3
USN counter: 1535

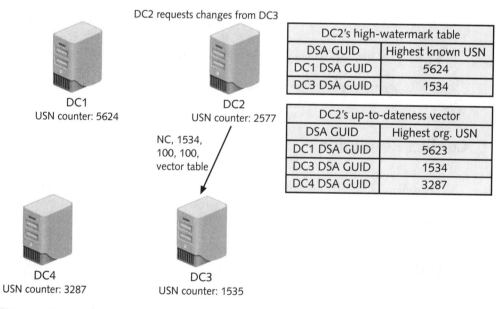

Figure 7-14   DC2 requests updates from DC3

Once DC3 determines that it has no updates for DC2, DC3 sends its high-watermark value and up-to-dateness vector, but does not send any data. Finally, DC2 then updates its high-watermark value for DC3 and up-to-dateness vector if necessary, as shown in Figure 7-15.

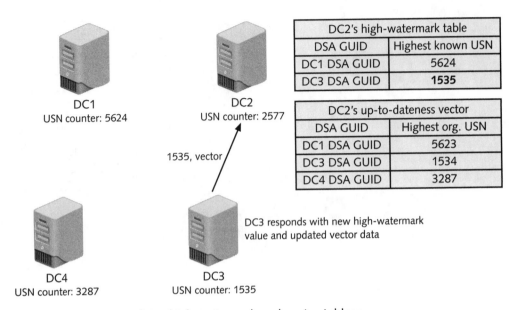

DC2's high-watermark table	
DSA GUID	Highest known USN
DC1 DSA GUID	5624
DC3 DSA GUID	**1535**

DC2's up-to-dateness vector	
DSA GUID	Highest org. USN
DC1 DSA GUID	5623
DC3 DSA GUID	1534
DC4 DSA GUID	3287

DC1
USN counter: 5624

DC2
USN counter: 2577

1535, vector

DC3 responds with new high-watermark value and updated vector data

DC4
USN counter: 3287

DC3
USN counter: 1535

Figure 7-15   DC2 updates high-watermark and vector tables

NOTE

In Figure 7-15, notice that while DC2 updated DC3 in its high-watermark table, no changes were made to DC2's up-to-dateness vector for DC3. Remember that the high-watermark value is the highest-known USN, whereas the up-to-dateness vector is the highest-known originating write USN. Because DC3 was not the originating writer of any updates (it only had replicated updates), DC2's up-to-dateness vector for DC3 is unchanged.

Conflict Resolution

As you've learned, a multi-master model allows changes to be made on any domain controller. These changes are then replicated to other domain controllers. This can cause problems when changes are made to the same object at the same time on different domain controllers. Fortunately, Active Directory has built-in safeguards to avoid or resolve these conflicts for you.

Attribute Update Conflict

First of all, replicating at the attribute level minimizes replication conflicts. In other words, only the changed attribute is replicated, not the entire object. A conflict only occurs if the same attribute is changed on the same object at the same time on two different domain controllers. If the department attribute of a user object is changed on DC1 and the fax number of the same user is changed on DC2, there isn't a conflict. This helps minimize the number of conflicts that occur in Active Directory.

If the same attribute is changed on two different domain controllers at the same time (before replication is complete), the version, timestamp, and originating DSA GUID are used to resolve the conflict. First, the version number is checked and the update with the higher version number is used. If the two updates have the same version number, the update with the most recent timestamp is written to the directory. In the event that both the version numbers and the timestamps are the same (highly unlikely), the update with the highest originating DSA GUID is used to break the tie in an arbitrary fashion.

NOTE Because GUIDs are, in part, random numbers, they are not generated in sequence. Therefore, using the GUID to resolve a conflict does not guarantee which change is the "better" choice. However, it does ensure that all domain controllers use the same data.

For example, say an Administrator updates a user's street address on DC1 while another administrator updates the same user's street address on DC2. When DC1and DC2 replicate, the version numbers of each attribute are checked by the destination domain controller, as shown in Figure 7-16. Normally, the version number of the updated attribute (which is being replicated) is higher than what a destination domain controller has in its local database—and the higher version number is used. However, when the same attribute is updated on two different domain controllers simultaneously, the version numbers can match (that is, both domain controllers increment the version number from x to $x+1$). When the destination domain controller encounters an instance where the version numbers match, it then looks at the time stamp of the attribute in its local database as well as the time stamp of the update—and uses the one with the more recent timestamp. In the event the timestamps match, the highest originating DSA GUID is used.

NOTE Notice in the figure that conflict resolution is done on the destination domain controller and is only used on the updated attributes (that is, changes that have not yet been replicated based on the high-watermark value and up-to-dateness vector).

Although the above example shows a conflict between two direct replication partners (both originating updates), it is also possible that conflict resolution needs to be used for replicated updates. For example, what if the update was made simultaneously on DC1 and DC3 instead of DC2 (where DC3 is a replication partner with DC2)? Exactly where the conflict is resolved depends on which domain controllers replicate first, as shown in Figure 7-17 (assume that the version number of DC1's and DC3's update are the same, but DC3's update has a higher timestamp than DC1's update):

- Scenario A—First, DC2 requests changes from DC3 and updates its local directory database with the user's new street address from DC3. DC1 then requests changes from DC2. When DC1 compares the version number of the user's street address (originally changed on DC3, but replicated from DC2) to its local directory database, it sees they are the same. DC1 then uses the timestamp and determines it should overwrite its local directory database with the street address from DC2 (originally from DC3). In this scenario, the conflict is resolved on DC1.

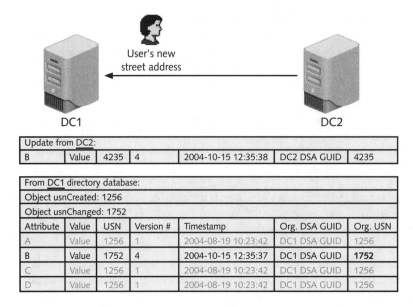

Update from DC2:						
B	Value	4235	4	2004-10-15 12:35:38	DC2 DSA GUID	4235

From DC1 directory database:						
Object usnCreated: 1256						
Object usnChanged: 1752						
Attribute	Value	USN	Version #	Timestamp	Org. DSA GUID	Org. USN
A	Value	1256	1	2004-08-19 10:23:42	DC1 DSA GUID	1256
B	Value	1752	4	2004-10-15 12:35:37	DC1 DSA GUID	**1752**
C	Value	1256	1	2004-08-19 10:23:42	DC1 DSA GUID	1256
D	Value	1256	1	2004-08-19 10:23:42	DC1 DSA GUID	1256

1. Which update has the higher version number? - They are the same, try timestamp.
2. Which update has the higher timestamp? - The update from DC2 has a higher timestamp.

Use the update from DC2, overwriting the update made locally.

Figure 7-16 Example conflict resolution

- Scenario B—First, DC2 requests changes from DC1 and updates its local directory database with the user's new street address. Next, DC3 requests changes from DC2. When DC3 compares the version number of the user's street address (originally changed on DC1, but replicated from DC2) to its local directory database, it sees they are the same. DC3 then uses the timestamp and determines it should use the version in its local directory database and discard the update. Next, DC2 requests changes from DC3. When DC2 compares the version number of the user's street address (originally from DC1) to its local directory database, it sees they are the same. DC2 then uses the timestamp and determines it should overwrite its local directory database with the street address from DC3. Finally, DC1 requests changes from DC2. When DC1 compares the version number of the user's street address (originally changed on DC3, but replicated from DC2) to its local directory database, it sees they are the same. DC1 then uses the timestamp and determines it should overwrite its local directory database with the street address from DC2 (originally from DC3). In this scenario, the conflict must be resolved on all three domain controllers.

- Scenario C—There are actually two ways this last scenario can happen (note that this is the most common scenario within a site):

  - First, DC2 requests changes from DC1 and updates its local directory database with the user's new street address. Next, DC2 requests changes from DC3.

When DC2 compares the version number of the user's street address (from DC3) to its local directory database, it sees they are the same. DC2 then uses the timestamp and determines it should overwrite its local directory database with the street address from DC3. Finally, DC1 requests changes from DC2. When DC1 compares the version number of the user's street address (originally changed on DC3, but replicated from DC2) to its local directory database, it sees they are the same. DC1 then uses the timestamp and determines it should overwrite its local directory database with the street address replicated from DC2 (originally from DC3). In this scenario, the conflict must be resolved by both DC1 and DC2.

- First, DC2 requests changes from DC3 and updates its local directory database with the user's new street address. Next, DC2 requests changes from DC1. When DC2 compares the version number of the user's street address (from DC1) to its local directory database, it sees they are the same. DC2 then uses the timestamp and determines it should use the version in its local directory database and discard the update. Finally, DC1 requests changes from DC2. When DC1 compares the version number of the user's street address (originally from DC3, but replicated from DC2) to its local directory database, it sees they are the same. DC1 then uses the timestamp and determines it should overwrite its local directory database with the street address replicated from DC2 (originally from DC3). In this scenario, the conflict must be resolved by both DC1 and DC2.

NOTE In Scenario C, there may be an additional replication request by DC3 for changes from DC2 because of the notify-pull replication (which is discussed later in the chapter) that occurs within a site. However, during these requests, the up-to-dateness vector filters out attributes for which the destination domain controller (DC3) already has current values, and in turn no data is actually sent (just an updated high-watermark value and updated up-to-dateness vector). Requests where the user's street address is not actually replicated are not shown in the figure.

Move Under Deleted Parent

Say an Administrator deleted an organizational unit on DC1. However, simultaneously another administrator created a new user account on DC2—in the same organizational unit that the first administrator has deleted. In this case, the object is automatically moved to the "lost and found" container when the domain controllers replicate. This container can be located in Active Directory Users and Computers by enabling the Advanced view. All objects that are created or moved under a deleted parent are automatically moved to this container.

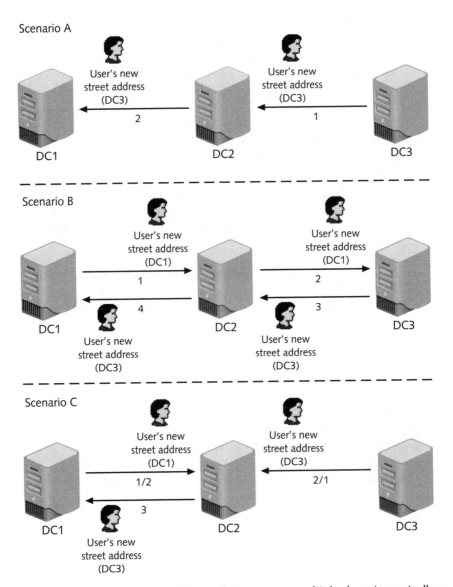

Figure 7-17   Example conflict resolution across multiple domain controllers

New Object Name Conflict

In the final type of conflict, two objects are created with the same relative distinguished name in the same container on different domain controllers. Because objects in the same container must have different relative distinguished names, one of the objects is renamed. The object with the higher timestamp keeps the original name. If the timestamps are identical, the higher originating DSA GUID is used to resolve which object keeps the name. The object that has the lower timestamp/GUID is automatically renamed to a system-wide unique value.

DETERMINING REPLICATION TOPOLOGY

A **replication topology** is the combination of paths used to replicate changes between domain controllers. Domain controllers do not communicate directly with every other domain controller when changes are made. However, given a sufficient amount of time, all updates propagate to every domain controller that hosts a given naming context.

Every naming context has its own replication topology. Some naming contexts such as the configuration and schema have identical replication topologies because they both exist on the same set of domain controllers. Other naming context's (such as the domain naming context) replication topology can differ from domain to domain. The naming context for an application partition could have even another replication topology—depending on which domain controllers hold a replica, or copy, of the partition. The important fact to remember here is that the replication topology is calculated for each naming context independently.

Each domain controller has one or more replication partners, each identified by a **connection object**. Connection objects are unidirectional (one-way), not bidirectional (two-way). Although the replication topology is calculated for each naming context independently, a connection object does not specify an individual naming context. It is possible for multiple naming contexts to be replicated across the same connection object.

Replication is either intra-site or inter-site. **Intra-site replication** is the process of updating domain controllers within the same site. **Inter-site replication** is the process of updating domain controllers between sites. (Sites were discussed in Chapter 6.)

Connection Objects

A connection object is a logical construct that exists in Active Directory to provide a representation of the connection between two or more domain controllers within a site, or in two different sites, for the purpose of Active Directory replication partners. Connection objects are created in one of two ways—either automatically by the **Knowledge Consistency Checker (KCC)** and **Inter-Site Topology Generator (ISTG)**, or manually by the Active Directory administrator.

Although connection objects created by the KCC are similar to the ones created by the Administrator, one key difference exists. The KCC does not optimize any connection objects created using a manual process. If you, as an Administrator, elect to create connection objects manually, then you are wholly responsible for maintaining them in the event of misconfiguration issues or unavailability. For this reason, unless you have a large number of sites (over 200 when at the Windows 2000 forest functional level or 5,000 when at the Windows Server 2003 interim/native forest functional level) or you need to troubleshoot replication issues, it is recommended that you do not manually create connection objects.

Activity 7-1: Manually Creating Connections

Time Required: 10 minutes

Objective: This exercise is designed to familiarize you with the process of manually creating replication connection objects.

Description: Normally, connection objects are created automatically by the KCC and ISTG. This exercise demonstrates the process of adding a connection object manually. You will add a one-way connection object that replicates updates from your partner's domain controller. Your partner will also add a connection object on their domain controller that replicates updates from your server. Once you and your partner add the connection objects, two-way replication will be configured between your domain controllers.

1. If necessary, start your server and log on using the **Administrator** account in the **CHILDXX** domain (where *XX* is the number of the forest root domain for which your server is a domain controller) using the password **Password01**.

2. Click **Start**, select **Administrative Tools**, and then click **Active Directory Sites and Services**.

3. If necessary, in the left tree pane, expand the **Sites** folder.

4. If necessary, in the left tree pane, expand the **MySiteXX** (where *XX* is the number of your server) site.

5. If necessary, in the left tree pane, expand the **Servers** folder located under the MySite*XX* site.

6. If necessary, in the left tree pane, expand **SERVERXX** (where *XX* is the number of your server).

7. In the left tree pane, click **NTDS Settings** under SERVER*XX* to show a list of connection objects (which represent inbound replication partners) for your domain controller.

If you are adding a manually created connection object to replace one that has already been created by the KCC, you do not need to remove the automatic connection created by the KCC (although you can if you wish). If the connection is redundant, the next time the KCC runs, the automatically generated connection will be removed by the KCC.

8. In the left tree pane, right-click **NTDS Settings**, and then click **New Active Directory Connection**.

9. In the Find Domain Controllers window, select **SERVERXX** (where *XX* is the number of your partner's server) as shown in Figure 7-18.

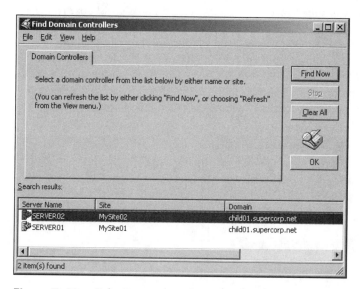

Figure 7-18   Selecting a domain controller from which to replicate

10. Click **OK**.

11. If an existing connection object already exists from the same source domain controller, you are prompted if you are sure you want to add the connection. Click **Yes**.

12. In the New Object – Connection window, accept the default name **SERVERXX** (where *XX* is the number of your partner's server). Click **OK**.

13. The new connection object should appear in the right details pane. If not, click the **Refresh** icon on the toolbar.

14. In the right details pane, right-click **SERVERXX** (where *XX* is the number of your partner's server) and then click **Properties**.

15. In the **Transport** drop-down list box, select **IP** as shown in Figure 7-19. Also notice the list of naming context(s) that replicate using this connection. Note that the naming context(s) you see may differ from those shown in Figure 7-19.

TIP

IP, RPC, or SMTP? While the SMTP transport listed in the Transports drop-down list box is obviously inter-site SMTP, the IP and RPC options are a little more ambiguous. As a review, remember that intra-site communications always use uncompressed RPC over TCP/IP. Additionally, inter-site communications have the option of using compressed RPC over TCP/IP (or SMTP). So what's the difference between the IP and RPC options in the drop-down list box? Nothing really: they both use RPC and they both use IP. The reason there are two options is to let you identify which connection objects are inter-site and which are intra-site. IP is used to denote an inter-site RPC over TCP/IP connection and RPC is used to denote an intra-site RPC over TCP/IP connection. Other than identifying the type of connection to the administrator, switching between IP and RPC has no apparent effect on how replication is performed.

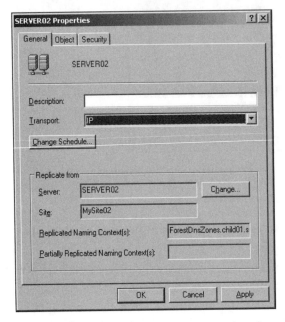

Figure 7-19   Selecting a transport protocol

16. Click **Change Schedule**.

TIP

If you attempt to change the replication schedule on an automatically created connection object, you are prompted to convert the connection to a manually created one. This is because you cannot set the schedule on automatically created connection objects. Automatically created connection objects use the site link's replication interval(s) if the connection is inter-site, or the replication schedule set on the site's NTDS Site Settings object if the connection is intra-site. Replication schedules are covered in more detail later in this chapter.

17. In the Schedule for SERVER*XX* window, select Sunday through Saturday from 1:00 a.m. to 3:00 a.m. Use the text indicating the selected date and time range at the bottom of the window to ensure you have the correct range selected.

18. Click the **Once per Hour** option, as shown in Figure 7-20. Using this schedule, your domain controller will pull directory updates from your partner's domain controller four times an hour—with the exception of 1:00 a.m. to 3:00 a.m. where only one replication request is scheduled.

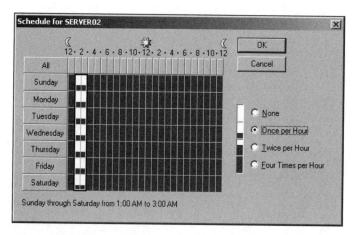

Figure 7-20   Setting when and how often to replicate

19. Click **OK** to close the schedule.

20. Click **OK** to close the connection object's properties.

21. Close Active Directory Sites and Services.

22. Log off your server if you do not intend to immediately continue to the next project. Otherwise, stay logged on.

Intra-site Replication

The KCC is responsible for the replication topology within a site. As a service that runs on all domain controllers, the KCC uses information in the configuration partition to identify replication partners and create connection objects on the local domain controller. By default, the KCC checks the replication topology every 15 minutes to ensure that the replication topology is up to date.

What the KCC attempts to do is create a replication topology made up of a bidirectional ring that provides fault tolerance and reliability. A bidirectional ring creates a minimum of two replication paths between domain controllers.

For example, imagine yourself as part of a group of people standing in a circle, holding hands. In this circle, every time your hand is squeezed, you would squeeze the hand of the person on the other side of you. So if the person on your left squeezes your hand, you would squeeze the hand of the person on your right, and so on. A hand squeeze would travel all around the circle until it got back to its originator. (This is one of the few network administration topics that can be turned into a party game.)

You could send a squeeze to the person on your left by simply squeezing your left hand. But what if you weren't able to keep your hands together with the person on your left and the ring was broken? You could send a squeeze to the person on your left by sending it around to your right—through all of the other people in the circle. This is the concept of a fault-tolerant ring. Messages can travel either way around the ring to bypass a break in one spot. An example of a simple bidirectional ring topology for two domains (four naming contexts in all) in the same site is shown in Figure 7-21.

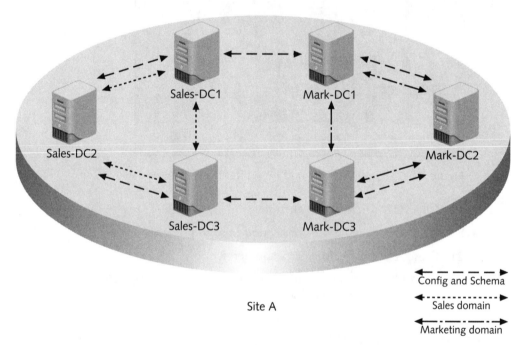

Figure 7-21   Example bidirectional ring replication topology

In addition to the bidirectional ring topology, the KCC adds additional connection objects to ensure that no more than three hops are required to replicate a change between all the domain controllers in a site. If no more than seven domain controllers are in a site, then a simple ring is sufficient. However, if more than seven domain controllers are present for a given naming context, the KCC adds additional connections between members of the ring to reduce the number of hops. An example of this is shown in Figure 7-22. By adding additional connections, the latency of propagating updates to all domain controllers is reduced.

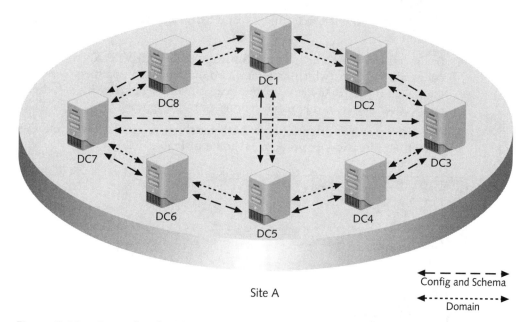

Site A

Config and Schema

Domain

Figure 7-22   Example of additional connections added to reduce latency in a large site

ACTIVITY

Activity 7-2: Manually Initiating the KCC

Time Required: 5 minutes

Objective: Learn how to manually initiate the KCC to check the replication topology.

Description: Although the KCC runs every 15 minutes by default, you may want to manually initiate a topology check after moving a domain controller to another site or adding new manual connections. Keep in mind that manually initiating a topology check only adds or removes connection objects as needed for the one domain controller. If you want multiple domain controllers to check the topology and update their automatic connections, you need to perform the following steps on each domain controller.

1. If necessary, start your server and log on using the **Administrator** account in the **CHILDXX** domain (where *XX* is the number of the forest root domain for which your server is a domain controller) using the password **Password01**.

2. Click **Start**, select **Administrative Tools**, and then click **Active Directory Sites and Services**.

3. If necessary, in the left tree pane, expand the **Sites** folder.

4. If necessary, in the left tree pane, expand the **MySiteXX** (where *XX* is the number of your server) site.

5. If necessary, in the left tree pane, expand the **Servers** folder located under the MySite*XX* site.

6. If necessary, in the left tree pane, expand **SERVERXX** (where *XX* is the number of your server).

7. In the left tree pane, click **NTDS Settings** under SERVER*XX* to show a list of connection objects (which represent inbound replication partners) for your domain controller. If the KCC has not run since you completed Activity 7-1, the automatic connection as well as the manual connection still appears.

8. In the left tree pane, right-click **NTDS Settings**, select **All Tasks**, and then click **Check Replication Topology**, as shown in Figure 7-23.

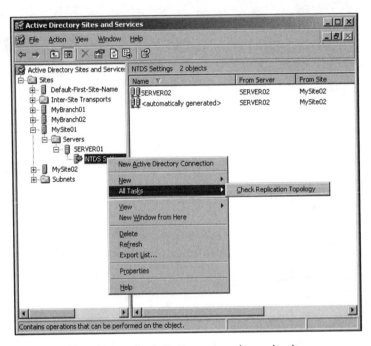

Figure 7-23   Manually initiating a topology check

9. A message box appears and informs you that the replication topology has been checked. Click **OK**.

10. On the toolbar, click the **Refresh** icon (it resembles a white piece of paper with two green arrows). The displayed list of connection objects is refreshed.

11. Close Active Directory Sites and Services.

12. Log off your server if you do not intend to immediately continue to the next project. Otherwise, stay logged on.

Global Catalog Replication

Before covering how the replication topology for global catalog servers is created, it is important to understand the difference between the two types of source replicas: master and read-only replicas. Each domain controller for a domain holds a master replica of the domain naming context for its own domain. During replication, a master replica can only be sourced from another domain controller that has a master replica. In contrast, a global catalog server holds a partial read-only replica of the domain naming context for each domain in the forest. A read-only replica can be sourced from either a master replica or another read-only replica. The important point to remember here is that a master replica cannot be sourced from a read-only replica.

The process of adding connection objects for global catalog replication is similar to the process used to calculate the replication topology of each domain naming context. First, the topology generated for replicating the domain's master replicas is used—this ensures that only additional connections are added. Connection objects are then added to connect the read-only replicas to the topology. A site replication topology for two domains including a global catalog server is shown in Figure 7-24 (note that in the figure, the one-way arrows point from the destination domain controller to the source domain controller).

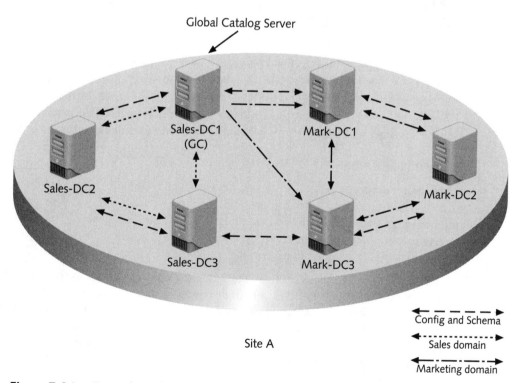

Figure 7-24   Example replication topology with a global catalog server

Unlike the intra-site replication topology for master replicas, the read-only replication topology for global catalog servers does not add extra connections to reduce latency.

NOTE

In Figure 7-24, Sales-DC1 is a global catalog server and holds a read-only replica of the Marketing domain naming context, in addition to the Sales, Configuration, and Schema naming contexts. Mark-DC1 and Mark-DC3 are the master replicas from which Sales-DC1 sources the Marketing domain naming context.

Inter-site Replication

In order to create the inter-site replication topology, one domain controller in each site is designated as the ISTG. The ISTG is the oldest server in a site by default and is responsible for creating connection objects with domain controllers located in other sites. The first DC retains the role of ISTG until it becomes unavailable for 60 minutes, at which point another DC in the site takes over the role.

You cannot control which DC is given the ISTG role, but you can verify which domain controller it is in Active Directory Sites and Services. Under a site, right-click the NTDS Site Settings object, then click Properties—the ISTG is listed on the Site Settings tab.

NOTE

Using the site information and site link costs, the ISTG attempts to create a minimum number of connections—while still ensuring that all naming contexts that need to be replicated between sites are connected. The ISTG is also responsible (by default) for choosing a bridgehead server, which is a domain controller in the local site that performs replication to and from other sites and then updates other domain controllers within its own site.

Bridgehead Server

A **bridgehead server** is used to designate a particular domain controller for replication purposes. Before getting into the specific operation of a bridgehead server, you must understand the basics of the replication process, as well as a little history. First, take a look at the replication process implemented in a Windows NT 4.0 domain so that you can then contrast that model against the new model implemented in Windows Server 2003.

Windows NT 4.0 domains follow the architectural model known as single master replication. (You may have heard of the single master domain model, but that is not the same thing.) Single master replication describes the situations in which one single master DC, called the primary domain controller (PDC), contains the read/write copy of the directory database. One or more other domain controllers, called backup domain controllers (BDCs), have read-only copies of the same database. All changes are made at the PDC and then sent (or replicated) to the BDCs.

By default, the PDC sends replicated domain information to 10 BDCs per replication session. A session begins when either a large number of changes have been made (by default, 2000) or when at least one change has been made and five minutes have gone by. Figure 7-25 shows a typical Windows NT 4.0 domain environment with the PDC and a number of BDCs.

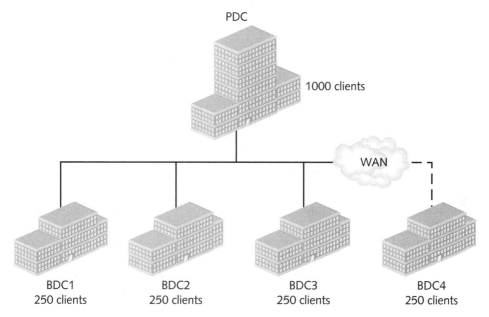

PDC

1000 clients

WAN

| BDC1 | BDC2 | BDC3 | BDC4 |
| 250 clients | 250 clients | 250 clients | 250 clients |

Figure 7-25   Typical Windows NT 4.0 domain environment

In Figure 7-25, the five domain controllers support 2000 users located in five separate physical locations, including an administration building. Three of the BDCs (BDC1, BDC2, and BDC3) enjoy good connectivity to each other and the PDC using a LAN. However, BDC4 is connected to the domain using an unreliable WAN connection (denoted by the dashed line).

In this example, the LAN network has a connection speed of 10 Mbps and the WAN connection has a speed of only 384 Kbps. It is obvious that BDC4 will experience difficulties maintaining up-to-date domain information, particularly if there are large or frequent changes to the directory database. In fact, this domain controller may never catch up! It could become locked in a perpetual state of replication with the PDC, never able to receive a complete domain update.

This situation with BDC4 can become even more critical if several additional domain controllers are added to the same location as BDC4. When more than one BDC exists at an NT 4.0 remote location, all BDCs receive domain updates over the WAN from the PDC, as shown in Figure 7-26, which builds upon Figure 7-25.

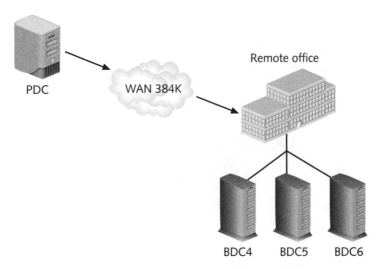

Figure 7-26   Additional BDCs at a remote location

In Figure 7-26, two additional domain controllers have been added to the remote location of BDC4. Now, instead of replicating the directory database to just one BDC across a WAN connection, the PDC replicates the directory database to three BDCs across the same WAN connection simultaneously, thereby degrading the performance of the WAN even further. If you add clients to this remote location who are also attempting to make use of the WAN for access to network resources located on the other side of the WAN, the situation becomes worse.

The preceding discussion illustrates the default behavior of the NT 4.0 directory replication mechanism. A method does exist to configure scheduled replication from the PDC to the BDCs; however, this needs to be configured at each BDC individually.

In many Windows NT 4.0 environments, the solution for this infrastructure design problem is to create the remote location as a separate Windows NT 4.0 domain with its own PDC. This eliminates replication issues across the WAN link. In exchange, though, it introduces issues related to the various trust relationships, and might still require the placement of a BDC from the primary domain in the remote location to support client logons.

To counter these problems in the Active Directory environment, the infrastructure makes use of designated domain controllers called bridgehead servers. The bridgehead server is a domain controller that has been either automatically selected by the ISTG, or has been selected by the Active Directory designers to be a bridgehead server. Once configured in a site, the bridgehead server functions as the single point of contact in that site for a given naming context. When communicating between sites, all replication traffic is between a bridgehead server at each site.

Note that an Active Directory site may contain several bridgehead servers. Some may belong to the same domain and serve a backup role in case the designated bridgehead server becomes unavailable. Others may belong to other domains in the forest and provide the same functionality for their domains.

The use of bridgehead servers eliminates the problem that was encountered in the Windows NT 4.0 environment when replicating to remote locations. Instead of providing replication information to all member domain controllers in a site, Active Directory replicates domain information to only the bridgehead server. Once the bridgehead server has replicated fully with its replication partner from the other site, the now updated bridgehead server replicates to its partners in the same site using LAN connectivity. Figure 7-27 illustrates this process.

7

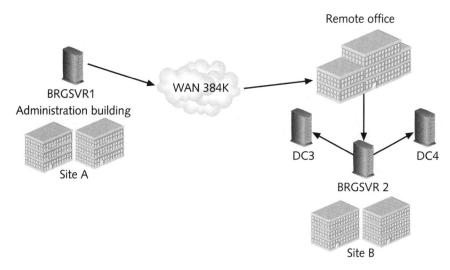

Figure 7-27   Bridgehead server functionality

In Figure 7-27, two Active Directory sites exist—Site A, which contains the administration building and the forest root, and Site B, which is a remote office and contains remote users. The network topology between these two sites is a single, 384 Kbps demand-dial link that, as a demand-dial connection, is only active when required. Site A contains a single bridgehead server named BRGSVR1, while Site B contains one bridgehead server and two other domain controllers, named BRGSVR2, DC3, and DC4, respectively. All four domain controllers belong to the same domain and, therefore, must all contain the naming context for the domain.

In operation, the bridgehead server in Site A, BRGSVR1, has directory changes that must be replicated from Site A to Site B. BRGSVR2 initiates communications using the demand-dial connection. Once the network establishes the connection, the primary bridgehead server in Site B, BRGSVR2, requests any changes that need to be replicated from BRGSVR1. When BRGSVR2 has replicated completely with its opposite in Site A, the

WAN connection is terminated because it is no longer required (assuming, of course, that there is no traffic for users or other services).

At this point in the replication process, BRGSVR2 replicates with its two partners in its own site, DC3 and DC4. Once these two domain controllers receive updated replication information from BRGSVR2, the process is complete. Instead of sending the same replication information to all domain controllers over the WAN, the replicated information is sent to only one domain controller, which then replicates this information (if necessary) to other domain controllers in that site.

If you contrast this process with the older methods used in Windows NT 4.0, you see that this way is much better. Active Directory has greatly reduced the need for multiple domains. The decision to create an additional domain is now more of a business decision than one based on technology or topology.

You must be aware that the selection of a bridgehead server can be either automatic or manual. Normally, the ISTG makes the selection; however, an administrator could override the automatic selection and choose a specific server. Servers selected in this way are called preferred bridgehead servers (PBSs).

You might choose to override this automatic selection if the DC selected by Active Directory is underpowered—that is to say, it may have limited system resources, such as RAM or CPU speed. For example, the ISTG may select a Pentium III computer with 512 MB of RAM as the bridgehead server; however, you may have acquired a new Pentium 4 with 2 GB of RAM that you wish to install in its place.

Another possible reason may be that the automatically selected server is leased, and you may want to designate a server that your company owns, even though it may be less powerful than the leased computer. There are negatives associated with a manual selection of the bridgehead server, and the details of that implementation are examined next.

The process used by the ISTG for the selection of a bridgehead server involves an examination of several parameters associated with both Active Directory and the individual domain controllers. However, the first step in the ISTG process determines whether any PBSs have been selected. The implementation of a PBS causes the ISTG to stop its bridgehead server selection process and use only the domain controller designated as the PBS by the Active Directory administrator. Although this manual configuration process may seem simple, and there may be perfectly valid reasons for using it in your environment, you must be aware of the failover process of each configuration. If the bridgehead server selected by the ISTG becomes unavailable or fails, the ISTG automatically performs a failover selection of a new bridgehead server without administrator intervention. If, on the other hand, you have elected to designate a single PBS, the ISTG will not manage the bridgehead server process, and there will be no automatic failover selection. Instead, you would need to examine the remaining domain controllers and manually select a server for the role.

NOTE

If you specify multiple PBSs and one becomes unavailable, the ISTG tries the next available PBS. However, once all PBSs have been tried, the ISTG does not attempt to select another bridgehead server. You will need to manually select a new bridgehead server.

ACTIVITY

Activity 7-3: Specifying a Preferred Bridgehead Server

Time Required: 5 minutes

Objective: Learn how to manually designate a domain controller as a preferred bridgehead server.

7

Description: In normal operation, the ISTG designates bridgehead servers in a Windows Server 2003 Active Directory domain environment. A significant advantage in allowing the ISTG to manage this process is that the ISTG automatically provides a failover if the ISTG-designated bridgehead server fails. However, you may have justifiable business reasons for manually selecting a designated bridgehead server in your environment. This exercise allows you to create such a server. Because sites and subnets affect all domains in the forest, you need to use an account that is a member of the Enterprise Admins group.

1. If necessary, start your server and log on using the **Administrator** account in the **CHILDXX** domain (where XX is the number of the forest root domain for which your server is a domain controller) using the password **Password01**.

2. Click **Start**, select **Administrative Tools**, and then click **Active Directory Sites and Services**.

3. If necessary, in the left tree pane, expand the **Sites** folder.

4. If necessary, in the left tree pane, expand the **MySiteXX** (where XX is the number of your server) site.

5. If necessary, in the left tree pane, expand the **Servers** folder located under the MySiteXX site.

6. If necessary, in the left tree pane, right-click **SERVERXX** (where XX is the number of your server) and then click **Properties**.

7. In the Transports available for inter-site data transfer list box, click **IP**.

8. Click the **Add** button. This specifies that your domain controller is a preferred bridgehead server for the IP transport protocol, as shown in Figure 7-28.

9. Click **OK**.

10. Close Active Directory Sites and Services.

11. Log off your server if you do not intend to immediately continue to the next project. Otherwise, stay logged on.

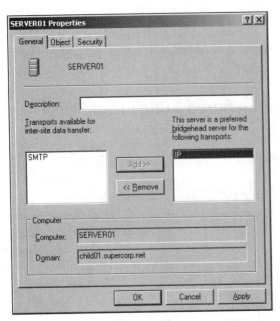

Figure 7-28   Designating a domain controller as a preferred bridgehead server

CONTROLLING REPLICATION FREQUENCY

Under different circumstances, data is replicated at different intervals. The two main factors that control the replication frequency are the location of the replication partners and the type of data being replicated. Some data, such as an update to an e-mail address, is not urgent and uses the normal replication schedule based on the location of the replication partners (intra-site or inter-site). Other updates, such as an account being locked out, are more urgent and require that the data be immediately replicated. The following sections describe how data is replicated in each of these scenarios. Additionally, how password changes are propagated is also covered.

Intra-site Replication Schedule

Intra-site replication is based on a notify-pull process. The process begins when an object is modified at a domain controller. The change could be made initially at the same domain controller (originating update), or could be received by replication from another domain controller (replicated update). By default, a Windows Server 2003 domain controller waits 15 seconds after the first change is made and then sends out a notification to its first replication partner that it has updates. If the domain controller has multiple replication partners, subsequent notifications are sent out at 3-second intervals until all replication partners have been notified of the updates. Once a replication partner has been notified of the updates, the replication partner then pulls the updates from the source domain controller by initiating replication.

NOTE While these values can be modified in the registry, it is not recommended they be modified. The longer it takes for a site to converge, the more likely there will be conflicts. Additionally, a long interval between propagating updates can lead to a very inconsistent view of Active Directory across domain controllers.

By waiting 15 seconds, many small changes made to Active Directory at almost the same time are collected into batches to enhance the efficiency of Active Directory replication. This makes sense because administrators often make many changes to several objects or one change that affects many attributes. This brief delay reduces the overhead otherwise involved in sending many small changes. Additionally, by delaying three seconds before informing the next replication partner, the source domain controller should not be over-whelmed by simultaneous update requests from its replication partners.

Because the KCC attempts to ensure that no two domain controllers are more than three hops away, the maximum time it should take an update to propagate within a site is approximately 45 seconds (depending on the number of replication partners). In addition to the notify-pull replication within a site, replication partners within a site also use a time-based replication schedule. By default, replication partners attempt to pull updates every hour regardless if they have been notified of updates or not. This allows domain controllers to confirm that their replication partners are still available.

NOTE These time delays have changed from Windows 2000. The default values in Windows 2000 are 5 minutes before notifying replication partners after an update and 30 seconds between notifying each replication partner. When working in a mixed 2000/2003 environment, you must take into account the longer default replication delay of Windows 2000. For example, an update from Windows Server 2003 (DC1) to Windows 2000 Server (DC2) to Windows Server 2003 (DC3) could take up to 5 minutes and 15 seconds to propagate from DC1 to DC3.

It is assumed that domain controllers within a site are well connected. Therefore, replication traffic between domain controllers in the same site is not compressed by default. Because compressing the replication traffic would require additional CPU time and bandwidth is not a concern, this trade-off makes sense.

Inter-site Replication Schedule

Unlike intra-site replication, where domain controllers can be notified of updates that they then pull, inter-site replication is only time-based—replicating changes at set intervals. The default replication interval between replication partners in different sites is every three hours. This is an important consideration for most organizations. You will need to fine-tune your inter-site replication, based on your WAN links, to meet the needs of your organization.

Another difference between intra-site replication and inter-site replication is that data for inter-site replication is compressed by default. While it takes additional CPU time to compress the data, the bandwidth saved over a slow WAN link could more than make up for the loss.

Site Link Replication Schedule and Interval

To better control when replication occurs between domain controllers in different sites, the replication schedule and replication interval can be set on a site link. The replication schedule controls when a site link is available for replication. By default, site links are always available. Additionally, the replication interval controls how often, by default, a domain controller should attempt to pull updates from a replication partner located in another site. The replication interval can be set in 15-minute increments from 15 minutes all the way up to 7 days.

NOTE   The ISTG sets the schedule of how often to replicate on automatically created connection objects (that is, connection objects the ISTG creates) based on the replication interval. However, if you manually create a connection object, you need to set the schedule for how often replication occurs on the connection object—the replication interval of a site link has no effect on it.

When setting the replication schedule and replication interval, you must keep in mind several issues. First, take a look at Figure 7-29, where DC1 is in Site A and DC2 is in Site C. Because there is no domain controller in Site B, there must be a window of time where both the A-B site link and B-C site link are available for replication. As shown in the figure, the A-B site link is available from 6:00 a.m. to 6:00 p.m. and the B-C site link is available from 3:00 p.m. to 9:00 p.m.. Replication between DC1 and DC2 only occurs from 3:00 p.m. to 6:00 p.m., because this is the only time all site links between the two domain controllers are available.

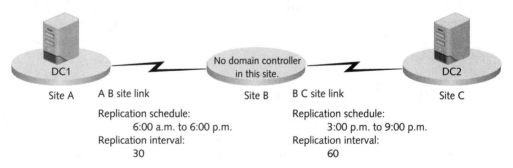

Figure 7-29   Example site link replication schedule and interval

When setting the replication interval, you must also be careful. The replication interval should be set to a value that is no more than the maximum amount of time the site link(s) between two domain controllers are available for replication. For example, if the replication schedule between two sites had a replication window that was six hours long, the replication interval should be set to six hours or less. This is to ensure that replication occurs at least once during the available replication window. If the replication interval was set to say 12 hours, there is no way to guarantee (unless you setup a manual connection object) that replication occurs during the 6 hours the site link is available. It is equally possible that replication would attempt to occur during the other six hours when the link would not be available.

Finally, when setting the replication interval, you must also take into account all the site links between the two domain controllers. If multiple site links must be traversed, the ISTG will use the replication interval from the site link with the highest replication interval. For example, look at Figure 7-29 again. The A–B site link has a replication interval of 30 minutes, whereas the B–C site link has a replication interval of 60 minutes. This means the ISTG will configure replication between DC1 and DC2 to occur every 60 minutes, because it is the highest replication interval.

ACTIVITY

Activity 7-4: Controlling Inter-Site Replication Using Site Link Settings

Time Required: 5 minutes

Objective: This exercise is designed to familiarize you with the process of setting the replication schedule and replication interval on a site link to control replication.

Description: In order to control when replication occurs between domain controllers in different sites, you can use the replication schedule and replication interval. You can use these settings to schedule replication to occur when the WAN is not being heavily used. In this activity, you reduce the amount of replication traffic during business hours by configuring a site link between two sites. You configure the site link so it is available only after business hours (5:00 p.m. to 9:00 a.m., Monday through Friday, and all day Saturday and Sunday) as well as during the lunch hour (noon to 1:00 p.m.) from Monday to Friday. You also set the replication interval to 60 minutes.

1. If necessary, start your server and log on using the **Administrator** account in the **CHILDXX** domain (where *XX* is the number of the forest root domain for which your server is a domain controller) using the password **Password01**.

2. Click **Start**, select **Administrative Tools**, and then click **Active Directory Sites and Services**.

3. If necessary, in the left tree pane, expand the **Sites** folder.

4. In the left tree pane, expand the **Inter-Site Transports** folder.

5. In the left tree pane, click the **IP** folder to display a list of RPC over TCP/IP site links in the right details pane.

6. In the right details pane, right-click **MyLinkXX** (where *XX* is the number of your server) and select **Properties**.

7. In the Replicate every text box, enter **60** to set the replication interval to 60 minutes, as shown in Figure 7-30.

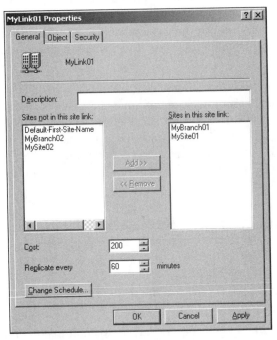

Figure 7-30   Setting replication interval

8. Click **Change Schedule**.

9. Configure the schedule as shown in Figure 7-31.

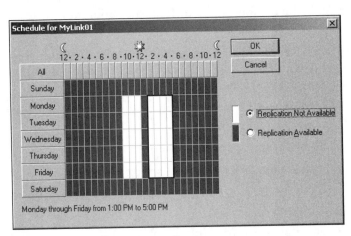

Figure 7-31   Configuring site link availability only during nonworking hours

10. Click **OK** to close the schedule.

11. Click **OK** to close the site link's properties.

12. Close Active Directory Sites and Services.

13. Log off your server if you do not intend to immediately continue to the next project. Otherwise, stay logged on.

Urgent Replication

Urgent replication occurs immediately within a site for certain important operations. No delay between updates within a site is observed. However, replication between sites will still observe normal replication intervals and restrictions—even if the replication is urgent. Events that trigger urgent replication in Windows Server 2003 are:

- An account lockout—If an account lockout policy is in place, accounts are locked after the defined number of log-on failures.

- Changing certain policies—Changing the domain password policy or account lockout policy triggers urgent replication.

- A Local Security Authority (LSA) secret change—LSA secrets store passwords used for establishing trust relationships and service accounts.

- The RID master role is assigned to a new server—The RID master is a single master operations role covered in the next chapter.

When considering these items, notice that they each represent something critically important, where all domain controllers must be in agreement immediately. If you think about it, there would be no point in locking out an account at one domain controller if the other domain controllers continue to act as if nothing is wrong.

NOTE You can configure change notification on site links to force urgent replication to occur between sites. However, this causes normal, nonurgent replication traffic between sites to increase. If change notification is configured on a site link, then the change notification that occurs within a site can also traverse the site link. For this reason, it is recommended that you manually initiate replication between sites as needed, rather than enable change notification between sites.

Password Replication

It is important for passwords to be synchronized between domain controllers more frequently than the default. Normally, you would have no control over which domain controller authenticates a particular user. If a user's password is changed on a particular domain controller, but the user's next logon didn't happen to be authenticated by the same domain controller, what would happen (assuming the change has not yet replicated)? The user would be refused access when he or she used the new password. Clearly, this is not acceptable. To avoid such situations, password changes are replicated a bit differently than urgent or nonurgent replication.

The most important part of password replication is the **PDC emulator**. Each domain has one domain controller that holds the role of PDC emulator. (Operations master roles are discussed in detail in the next chapter.) When the password of a user object is changed on a domain controller, the change is replicated immediately to the PDC emulator for the domain. This occurs whether the PDC emulator is in the same site or a different site. Normal replication of the password change also updates the other domain controllers.

 If the update to the PDC emulator fails, then only the normal, nonurgent replication process is used.

When a user attempts to log on using an incorrect password—such as a new password that has not yet been replicated—the domain controller being contacted (called the authenticating domain controller) does not immediately deny the logon. Instead, the authenticating domain controller forwards the authentication request to the PDC emulator. The PDC emulator then attempts to authenticate the user. If there is an updated password that the PDC emulator has received (that did not yet replicate to the original authenticating domain controller) that matches the password supplied by the user, then the user is allowed to log on.

MONITORING AND TROUBLESHOOTING REPLICATION

Active Directory replication occurs transparently over the network, making it difficult to verify that it is functioning. The symptoms of replication failure include log-on failure due to Active Directory updates not being replicated to other domain controllers, as well as other inconsistencies in Active Directory.

To monitor replication, Microsoft created **Active Directory Replication Monitor**, which is included in the Windows Server 2003 Support Tools. Replication Monitor can be used to:

- Monitor replication traffic between domain controllers
- Display a list of domain controllers in a domain
- Verify replication topology
- Manually force replication
- Check a domain controller's current USN and unreplicated objects
- Display bridgehead servers and trusts

In Activity 7-5, you use Replication Monitor (otherwise known as replmon) to verify replication.

Activity 7-5: Verifying Replication

Time Required: 10 minutes

Objective: Verify Active Directory replication between two domain controllers.

Description: Now that you have manually changed the replication topology, you verify that replication between two domain controllers in different sites is functioning.

1. If necessary, start your server and log on using the **Administrator** account in the **CHILDXX** domain (where *XX* is the number of the forest root domain for which your server is a domain controller) using the password **Password01**.

2. Click **Start** and then click **Run**.

3. In the Open drop-down list box, type **REPLMON**, and then click **OK**.

4. In the left tree pane, right-click **Monitored Servers** and then click **Add Monitored Server**.

5. Ensure that the **Add the server explicitly by name** option button is selected, and then click **Next**.

6. In the Enter the name of the server to monitor explicitly text box, enter **SERVERXX** (where *XX* is the number of your server), as shown in Figure 7-32.

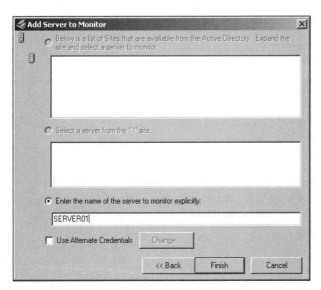

Figure 7-32   Specifying server to monitor

7. Click **Finish**.

8. In the left tree pane, right-click **SERVERXX** (where *XX* is the number of your server) and then click **Show Domain Controllers in Domain**. How many DCs do you see? Click **OK**.

9. Expand the domain naming context in the left tree pane. It is labeled DC=child*XX*,DC=supercorp,DC=net (where *XX* is the number of your forest root domain).

10. In the left tree pane, click your partner's server as shown in Figure 7-33. Using the log details in the right pane, note the last time your domain controller replicated from your partner's domain controller (you may need to scroll down).

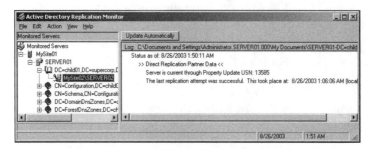

Figure 7-33   Reviewing replication log created by replmon

11. In the left tree pane, right-click your partner's server and then click **Synchronize with this Replication Partner**.

12. A message box informs you that synchronization has been successfully queued. Click **OK**.

13. On the View menu, click **Refresh**.

14. Verify in the log that the manual replication (that is, synchronization) you initiated was successful.

15. Close the Active Directory Replication Monitor.

16. Log off of your server.

TIP   You can use the Directory Service event log in Event Viewer in order to view information, warnings, and errors related to Active Directory on a domain controller. Event Viewer is accessible under Administrative Tools on the Start menu.

Most problems with Active Directory replication are caused by administrator error or network infrastructure glitches. A few of the most common problems are:

- Slow replication between sites—The most likely causes of slow replication between sites are slow WAN links and poorly configured site links. A slow WAN link limits the amount of changes that can be synchronized. The default time schedule for site links is every three hours. If faster replication is required between sites, you must configure the site links manually.

- DNS errors—Windows Server 2003, like Windows 2000, relies on DNS to locate domain controllers when replicating. If a domain controller has the wrong DNS server configured or the DNS entries are incorrect, replication to other domain controllers fails. Verify that all domain controllers can be resolved in DNS.

- Stopped replication between sites—The most likely cause of stopped replication between sites is failed WAN links. In addition, if no site link is configured, replication does not occur.

- Time differences between servers—This is an error that occurs when the time on two domain controllers is more than five minutes apart. Although time synchronization between domain controllers should be automatic, it occasionally fails. To fix it, reset the time properly. Ensure that UDP port 123 is not blocked between domain controllers.

- Excessive network traffic—If you use a relatively congested 10-Mbps LAN, then Active Directory synchronization traffic between servers may be excessive. Because replication traffic within a site cannot be compressed, you should upgrade to a faster network or build a dedicated segment between domain controllers for Active Directory traffic. If traffic is excessive across a WAN link, ensure that sites are properly configured and adjust the site links to control replication as required.

- Slow authentication when using new passwords—If a user does not log on quickly after a password is reset, then it is likely the domain controller he or she is authenticating to has not received the new password. In this case, the authenticating domain controller attempts to verify the password with the PDC emulator for the domain. If the PDC emulator is across a slow WAN link, then the logon is slow. To prevent this, change passwords using a DC that is local to the user, or move the PDC emulator to a location with faster network connectivity.

SYSVOL

While most data regarding the network is stored in Active Directory, there are some instances where storing a file (or files) is necessary. For example, you may have a logon script that maps network drives or that performs maintenance tasks. Additionally, the Group Policy feature, which you will learn more about in Chapter 11, stores part of its data as Active Directory objects and the rest as a set of files and folders.

In order to make these files available on all domain controllers in a domain, a folder called sysvol, which is shared as SYSVOL, is created during the promotion of a domain controller. The sysvol folder (which is the folder that is shared as SYSVOL) is stored in %SYSTEMROOT%\SYSVOL\ by default, although this path can be modified during promotion. The **File Replication Service (FRS)** is then used to replicate changes to files and folders in SYSVOL to all other domain controllers in the domain.

NOTE

Note that inside the sysvol folder another folder is created that matches the name of the domain—and this is where folders and files related to the domain are actually placed (that is, they are not placed directly in the sysvol folder—although there is nothing technically preventing you from doing so). For example, the default path to the supercorp.net domain folder would be %SYSTEMROOT%\SYSVOL\sysvol\supercorp.net.

NOTE

FRS replaces the LAN Manager Replication (LMRepl) service included with NT 4.0. Additionally, if you have ever worked on an NT 4.0 domain, you may be familiar with NETLOGON—which is similar in concept to SYSVOL. For backwards compatibility, each Windows Server 2003 domain controller also has a NETLOGON share (it is %SYSTEMROOT%\SYSVOL\sysvol*Domain*\scripts by default). Note, however, that if you have Windows NT 4.0 domain controllers, you must manually configure the NT 4.0 domain controllers LMRepl service to replicate NETLOGON from one of the Windows Server 2003 domain controllers—it is not automatic.

Although knowing the local path to SYSVOL is important, you need to know the network path. Each domain controller shares the sysvol folder as SYSVOL; therefore, you can access the sysvol folder on any domain controller by entering a path similar to *Domain_Controller*\SYSVOL. For example, to access the SYSVOL share on a domain controller named INSTRUCTOR in the supercorp.net domain, you would enter \\INSTRUCTOR.supercorp.net\SYSVOL (or just \\INSTRUCTOR\SYSVOL and let windows try to append DNS suffixes or use NetBIOS name resolution).

However, when referring to files in the SYSVOL folder, such as one script that starts another script, it is not a good idea to reference a single domain controller. Because the SYSVOL folder takes advantage of the distributed file system (DFS) by creating a domain-based DFS root, you can access the SYSVOL folder on the closest available domain controller by using a path similar to *Domain_Name*\SYSVOL. For example, the SYSVOL share for the supercorp.net domain could be accessed by entering \\supercorp.net\SYSVOL. Note that in addition to directing clients to the closest possible server, DFS also redirects clients to another server in the event a server becomes unavailable.

TIP

It is a good idea to only store network configuration and maintenance files (such as scripts) in SYSVOL. If you need to store large amounts of data, such as the installation files for an application or user data, it is a better idea to create a new DFS root and not store the data in SYSVOL.

The following sections look at how SYSVOL is replicated and how to troubleshoot SYSVOL replication.

SYSVOL Replication

The first thing to remember is that *SYSVOL replication is independent from Active Directory object replication* (that most of this chapter has focused on). SYSVOL uses the File Replication Service (FRS), which is a multi-threaded, multi-master replication engine to replicate changes. When the SYSVOL share on one domain controller is updated, such as the addition of a new file, FRS replicates the change to all other domain controllers that have a copy of SYSVOL for the domain. In the event of a conflict, FRS uses a last-writer wins algorithm—which means the changes from the last person to write to the file are retained and replicated.

While SYSVOL replication and Active Directory replication are independent, FRS uses some information from Active Directory replication in order to configure and control SYSVOL replication. First, FRS configures the replication topology of SYSVOL to match the connection objects of a domain controller. In other words, the FRS topology that is set up for SYSVOL will match the replication topology used to replicate the Active Directory domain database.

7

Second, while intra-site replication of SYSVOL does not follow a schedule (that is, replication is performed whenever a change is made), inter-site replication frequency of SYSVOL is controlled by the schedule on the replication partner's connection object. So for example, if a domain controller is configured to replicate Active Directory changes every three hours with one of its Active Directory replication partners, then FRS will also configure its schedule to replicate SYSVOL every three hours with that same partner.

NOTE   Just because FRS bases the topology/frequency of replicating SYSVOL on Active Directory connection objects, this does not mean the two mechanisms are connected. It is very important you remember Active Directory and SYSVOL replication are independent. FRS is a totally different mechanism than Active Directory replication. FRS is designed to replicate files, whereas Active Directory replication is designed to replicate changes to the Active Directory database.

Troubleshooting SYSVOL Replication

For the most part, replication of SYSVOL is transparent—the configuration is based on settings that should have already been configured. However, it is possible that replication of SYSVOL might fail and you will need to troubleshoot the issue. The following bullets provide some troubleshooting steps.

TIP   If you are experiencing Active Directory replication issues in addition to SYSVOL replication issues, try to resolve the Active Directory replication issues first—they may also solve the SYSVOL replication issues.

- Check the File Replication Service event log for any errors by using the Event Viewer located under Administrative Tools.

- Confirm that all domain controllers can resolve the fully qualified domain names (FQDNs) of their replication partners. Additionally, confirm that the FQDNs resolve to the correct IP addresses. Use the ping command to resolve a FQDN to an IP address and the ipconfig command to view a domain controller's IP address.

- Use the Services console located in Administrative Tools to confirm the File Replication Service is started. If the service is stopped, try starting the service. Set the service to start automatically if necessary. If the service is started, try restarting the service.

- Check that there is sufficient disk space on the drive where Windows is installed as well as the drive where the sysvol folder is located (if the drives are different).

- Check that the file(s) are not being filtered out by FRS. By default, FRS does not replicate files that are encrypted, start with a tilde (~), end in the .bak or .tmp extensions, or are on an NTFS junction.

CHAPTER SUMMARY

- Active Directory uses a multi-master model for replication, which means changes can be made on any domain controller and are replicated to other domain controllers.

- Replication of changes is performed at the attribute level, and not the object level. The exception is the membership attribute of group objects in the Windows Server 2003 forest functional level, where only the changes to the membership are replicated.

- Rather than using a time-based system for deciding which changes need to be replicated, Active Directory uses a system based on update sequence numbers that are unique for each domain controller.

- Intra-site replication occurs 15 seconds after a change is made to a domain controller via RPC and cannot be compressed. Inter-site replication is controlled with site links, and can be done via RPC or SMTP transports.

- Urgent replication, such as an account lockout, is performed immediately within a site, but is limited by site links between sites.

- Password changes are replicated immediately to the PDC emulator for a domain, regardless of site links. Standard intra-site and inter-site replication is used to synchronize password changes with other domain controllers.

- The replication topology for intra-site replication is created by the KCC—which is a process that runs on every domain controller in a site. One domain controller in each site is designated as the ISTG and is responsible for the inter-site replication topology for its own site.

- A bidirectional ring is used to create the intra-site replication topology. Inter-site replication topologies are based on the configuration of site links.

❏ Bridgehead servers are dedicated domain controllers that are used in the replication process and serve as a point of contact from one site to another. Directory updates travel between sites from one bridgehead server to another, and are then distributed to other domain controllers within each site.

❏ Replicating attribute-level changes minimizes replication conflicts. On the rare occasion that a conflict does occur, the version number, timestamp, and originating DSA GUID are used to choose the correct value.

❏ You can use Active Directory Replication Monitor to view both intra-site and inter-site replication information.

❏ SYSVOL is a share available on every domain controller in a domain and is used to store files such as logon scripts. SYSVOL is replicated between domain controllers in a domain using the File Replication Service (FRS). Active Directory replication and SYSVOL replication using FRS are independent from one another.

7

KEY TERMS

Active Directory Replication Monitor — A tool used to monitor, troubleshoot, and verify Active Directory replication.

bridgehead server — A domain controller that is configured to perform replication to and from other sites.

connection object — A connection between two domain controllers that is used for replication.

convergence — The state when all replicas of a database have the same version of the data. (In Active Directory, this means that all domain controllers have the same set of information.)

File Replication Service (FRS) — A multi-threaded, multi-master replication engine that replaces the LMREPL service in Microsoft Windows NT 4.0.

globally unique identifier (GUID) — A 16-byte value generated by an algorithm and should be different from every other GUID generated anywhere in the world. A GUID is used to uniquely identify a particular device, component, item, or object.

Inter-site replication — Replication occurring between sites.

Inter-Site Topology Generator (ISTG) — A process that runs on one domain controller in every site and is responsible for creating the replication topology between its site and other sites.

Intra-site replication — Replication occurring within a site.

Knowledge Consistency Checker (KCC) — A process that runs on each DC to create the replication topology within a site.

latency — The delay or "lag time" between a change made in one replica being recognized in another.

originating updates — A change to Active Directory made by an administrator on the local domain controller.

PDC emulator — An operations master for a domain that simulates a Windows NT 4 PDC for backward compatibility with older Windows clients and servers.

propagation dampening — The process of preventing a domain controller from replicating an update to another domain controller that already has the update.

replica — An instance of an Active Directory naming context stored on a domain controller.

replicated updates — Changes to Active Directory that were made through replication from another domain controller.

replication — The process of updating Active Directory on all domain controllers on the network.

replication partner — A domain controller that replicates with another domain controller.

replication topology — The set of connections used by domain controllers to replicate directory updates among domain controllers in both the same and different sites.

Update Sequence Number (USN) — A unique number assigned to every object and attribute in Active Directory to track changes. Each domain controller maintains its own set of USNs.

REVIEW QUESTIONS

1. By default, replication between sites in Active Directory occurs how often?

   a. every 5 minutes

   b. every 15 minutes

   c. every 60 minutes

   d. every 180 minutes

2. A DC in a site that sends and receives updates to and from other sites is known as what type of server?

   a. bridgehead server

   b. originating server

   c. replicated server

   d. global catalog server

3. Which of the following statements regarding intra-site replication is true?

   a. Replication occurs shortly after changes are made.

   b. Replication traffic is always compressed.

   c. Replication is determined only by a schedule.

   d. Replication occurs, by default, four times per hour.

4. Which changes in Active Directory are considered "urgent replication"?
   a. A new user is added.
   b. A user's password is changed.
   c. A user's group membership is changed.
   d. A user account is locked out.

5. Two administrators change the same user's department attribute in Active Directory on two different domain controllers at approximately the same time. Which change is replicated to all domain controllers if the attributes have the same version number?
   a. the update from the domain controller with the lowest DSA GUID
   b. the update with the earliest timestamp
   c. the update with the most recent timestamp
   d. Both updates are made to Active Directory.

6. Two administrators change the same user's properties in Active Directory on two different domain controllers at approximately the same time. One administrator changes the user's fax number attribute and the other administrator changes the user's city attribute. Which change is replicated to all domain controllers?
   a. the update from the domain controller with the lowest DSA GUID
   b. the update with the lower version number
   c. the update with the higher version number
   d. Both updates are made to Active Directory.

7. When all domain controllers have the same version of all naming contexts, the network is said to have what?
   a. consistency
   b. convergence
   c. replica
   d. state-based replication

8. By default, how often does the KCC run on each domain controller?
   a. every 15 minutes
   b. once an hour
   c. once every three hours
   d. once a day

9. You have created a new site link between two sites in Active Directory. What is the default replication interval?

   a. every 15 minutes

   b. twice an hour

   c. once an hour

   d. eight times a day

   e. once a day

10. The process of preventing a domain controller from receiving the same update from multiple domain controllers is called which of the following?

    a. loose consistency

    b. propagation dampening

    c. replication latency

    d. convergence

11. The KCC creates additional connection objects in a bidirectional replication ring so that an originating update does not go through more than how many hops?

    a. one

    b. two

    c. three

    d. ten

    e. There is no limit.

12. A change to an object in Active Directory made by an administrator on the local domain controller is called a(n)?

    a. originating update

    b. replicated update

    c. replica

    d. replication partner

13. Which of the following statements about USNs are true? (Choose all that apply.)

    a. USN numbers are the same on all domain controllers.

    b. Each DC maintains its own USNs.

    c. When a change is made, the object's USN is incremented by 10.

    d. USNs are used to determine if changes have been made to an object.

14. In intra-site replication, how long does a Windows Server 2003 domain controller wait before it starts notifying its replication partners(s) that it has updates?

    a. 5 seconds

    b. 15 seconds

    c. 5 minutes

    d. 15 minutes

15. Which of the following is used during replication by a source domain controller to determine which *objects* may need to be replicated?

    a. high-watermark value

    b. up-to-dateness vector

    c. the destination domain controller's server GUID

    d. the source domain controller's server GUID

16. Which of the following is used during replication by a source domain controller to determine which *attributes* need to be replicated?

    a. high-watermark value

    b. up-to-dateness vector

    c. The destination domain controller's server GUID

    d. The source domain controller's server GUID

17. A _____ is a 64-bit number used to identify changes to data in Active Directory.

18. In order for domain controllers to replicate changes to group memberships rather then replicate the entire group list, what level must the forest functional level be set to?

    a. Windows 2000

    b. Windows Server 2003 interim

    c. Windows Server 2003 mixed

    d. Windows Server 2003

19. In Active Directory, replication is performed at the _____ level, not the _____ level.

20. Password changes are first replicated to which of the following servers?

    a. the PDC emulator for the domain

    b. the PDC emulator for the forest

    c. the RID master for the domain

    d. the RID master for the forest

7

CASE PROJECTS

With your new familiarity with Active Directory replication, your boss has asked you to help on a project for a local hospital for which Super Corp is consulting. The hospital currently has 25 domain controllers located in 9 departments around the hospital. All domain controllers are connected through the LAN. Three departments are using older, 10-Mbps hubs, while the other departments are using 10/100-Mbps switches. Between the hours of 8:00 a.m. and 6:00 p.m., the network bandwidth utilization averages 95%. A research team just leased office space in a building located across town to house 20 researchers. The new office currently has a 56-Kbps ISDN connection to the hospital that needs to be upgraded to a T1 within the next six months.

Case Project 7-1: Designing Sites for Replication

CASE PROJECTS

The hospital's IT manager is concerned that there is too much Active Directory replication occurring during the day, consuming the bulk of the available bandwidth in the hospital. You just found out that the researchers will be using Active Directory to store research subject data that will be constantly updated and modified. Senior researchers at the hospital will review this data. You are concerned this will cause network slowdowns at the hospital. How should you design the hospital's replication topology to minimize the amount and frequency of replication during the day?

Case Project 7-2: Replication Conflicts

CASE PROJECTS

The head of the new research facility is concerned that crucial subject records will be deleted when two researchers are editing different fields in the same record in Active Directory. What can you tell him about Active Directory that will address his concerns?

Case Project 7-3: Troubleshooting Inter-site Replication

CASE PROJECTS

You received a call from a researcher in the new facility informing you that changes made by network administrative staff located at the hospital do not seem to take effect at the new facility. Similarly, research subject data is not being replicated from the new facility to the hospital. What tool(s) could you use to troubleshoot the issue? What are some possible causes of, and solutions to, this problem?

CHAPTER

8

ACTIVE DIRECTORY OPERATIONS MASTERS

After reading this chapter, you will be able to:

♦ Describe the forest-wide operations master roles and where they should be placed

♦ Describe the domain-wide operations master roles and where they should be placed

♦ Describe the process of transferring and seizing roles from operations masters

In the last chapter, you learned about the multi-master replication process Active Directory uses to replicate data. While the majority of Active Directory operations are multi-master—meaning multiple domain controllers can perform them—there are some operations that necessitate a single point of control. Some of these operations cannot tolerate the risk of inconsistency created by the multi-master replication process, while other operations do not lend themselves to a multi-master design—such as operations that must include backwards compatibility.

To support operations that must have a single point of control, certain domain controllers within a forest or domain are designated as **operations masters**—sometimes called Flexible Single Master Operation (FSMO) role holders. Each domain controller is designated as an operations master by being assigned one or more of the FSMO roles for either the forest or the domain—depending on the type of role. In this chapter, you will learn about the forest-wide and domain-wide roles, what operations each role holder is responsible for performing, and what impact the loss of an operations master has on the forest or domain. The chapter will conclude by covering how roles can be moved between domain controllers.

FOREST-WIDE ROLES

In an Active Directory forest, there are certain operations that can only be performed by a single domain controller in the entire forest. Known as forest-wide FSMO roles, the schema master and domain naming master are the two roles that only one domain controller (per role) in the entire forest can hold at any given point in time. This means that no matter how many domains exist in a forest, only one schema master and only one domain naming master exists. While the schema master and domain naming master can be located on different domain controllers, they are most often located on the same domain controller for easier management. The following sections cover the forest-wide FSMO roles in more detail.

Schema Master

Because modifying the schema is a process that can't deal with possible conflicts introduced by multi-master replication, it is important that only one domain controller be allowed to make modifications to the Active Directory schema. The **schema master** is the only domain controller that has a writable copy of the schema naming context for the entire forest. Only the schema master can add and modify the objects that make up the schema—no other domain controllers can make updates.

Once the schema master makes an originating update to the schema naming context, the changes are then replicated to all other domain controllers using standard non-urgent replication.

Placement

By default, the schema master FSMO role is assigned to the first domain controller in the forest. Because the schema is infrequently updated, the additional load placed on a domain controller designated as the schema master is negligible. The schema master role is often left on the first domain controller in the forest without any issues. However, it may be necessary to move the schema master role to another domain controller in the forest root domain if the server currently holding the role is frequently unavailable. In Activity 8-1, you learn how to use the Active Directory Schema snap-in to locate the schema master of a forest.

NOTE

It is possible to move the schema master FSMO role to a domain controller that is not located in the forest root domain—but it is not recommended. If you remember back to Chapter 5, Microsoft recommends that the forest root domain be dedicated to managing the infrastructure of the forest. Because the schema has an impact on all domains in the forest, the schema master should be located in the infrastructure domain—which should be the forest root domain.

Impact if Unavailable

In the event that the schema master becomes unavailable, users do not notice any impact on Active Directory. Additionally, network administrators most likely do not notice the loss unless they are attempting to modify the schema. Until the schema master is back online, or another domain controller seizes the role (described later in this chapter), you cannot make additions or modifications to the schema.

Activity 8-1: Identifying the Schema Master of a Forest

Time Required: 10 minutes

Objective: Learn how to use the Active Directory Schema snap-in to identify the schema master of a forest.

Description: As part of Super Management Corporation's Active Directory deployment, you have been asked to decide where the schema master should be located. As a first step, you decide to use the Active Directory Schema snap-in to identify the current schema master.

1. If necessary, start your server and log on using the **Administrator** account in the **CHILDXX** domain (where *XX* is the number of the forest root domain for which your server is a domain controller) using the password **Password01**.

2. Click **Start** and then click **Run**.

3. Type **MMC** and then click **OK**.

4. On the File menu, click **Add/Remove Snap-in**.

5. On the Add/Remove Snap-in screen, click **Add**.

6. On the Add Standalone Snap-in screen, select **Active Directory Schema** and then click **Add**.

7. Click **Close** to close the Add Standalone Snap-in screen.

8. Click **OK** to close the Add/Remove Snap-in screen.

9. In the left tree pane, click the **Active Directory Schema** node. As shown in Figure 8-1, notice how the name of the node and the title of the console change to indicate the domain controller to which the snap-in is connected. You may need to resize the Active Directory Schema console in order to see the full text. Later in this chapter, you will see why this is important to note when you learn to transfer operations masters.

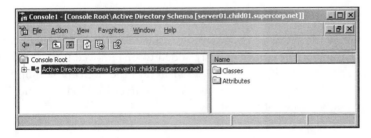

Figure 8-1   Identifying the server to which the Active Directory Schema Snap-in is connected

10. In the left tree pane, right-click the **Active Directory Schema** node and then click **Operations Master**. The schema master for the forest is displayed, as shown in Figure 8-2.

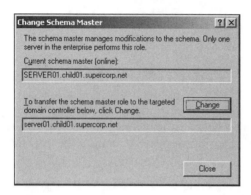

Figure 8-2   Identifying the schema master of the forest

11. Note the current schema master and its online status.

12. Click **Close**.

13. Close the Microsoft Management Console. Do not save any changes when prompted.

14. Log off your server if you do not intend to immediately continue to the next activity. Otherwise, stay logged on.

Domain Naming Master

In an Active Directory forest, every domain must have a unique name. As new domains are added to the forest, it is the job of the **domain naming master** to add the domain to the forest and ensure its name is unique. Additionally, the domain naming master is also responsible for removing domains from the forest. Because you can only designate one domain controller in the entire forest as the domain naming master FSMO role holder, the integrity of the Active Directory forest structure is ensured.

Placement

By default, the domain naming master FSMO role is assigned to the first domain controller in the forest. Because domains are not frequently added to or removed from the forest, the additional load placed on a domain controller designated as the domain naming master is negligible. In Activity 8-2, you learn how to use Active Directory Domains and Trusts to locate the domain naming master of a forest.

If the forest is set to a functional level of Windows 2000, you can only place the domain naming master on a global catalog server. However, if the forest functional level is set to Windows Server 2003, it is not necessary that the domain naming master reside on a global catalog server.

In order to support application partitions, the domain naming master must be placed on a domain controller running Windows Server 2003. If you add Windows Server 2003 domain controllers to an existing Windows 2000 forest, you should upgrade the domain naming master to Windows Server 2003 or move the domain naming master role to a Windows Server 2003 domain controller. Applications and services, such as the Windows Server 2003 DNS server, will be unable to create new application partitions until the domain naming master is moved to a server running Windows Server 2003.

While not technically required, the domain naming master FSMO role is often placed on the same domain controller as the schema master FSMO role. Because neither the domain naming master nor schema master role require many additional resources, placing all the forest-wide roles on the same domain controller can make management a little simpler.

8

Impact if Unavailable

Similar to the schema master, if the domain naming master becomes unavailable, users do not notice any impact on Active Directory. Additionally, network administrators most likely do not notice the loss unless they are attempting to add or remove a domain from the forest. Until the domain naming master is back online or the role is seized by another domain controller, you cannot add domains to or remove them from the forest.

ACTIVITY

Activity 8-2: Identifying the Domain Naming Master of a Forest

Time Required: 5 minutes

Objective: Learn how to use the Active Directory Domains and Trusts console to identify the domain naming master of a forest.

Description: In addition to the schema master, you have also been asked to decide where the domain naming master should be placed in Super Corp's Active Directory forest. Once again, as a first step, you decide to locate the current domain naming master of the forest. To accomplish the task, you decide to use the Active Directory Domains and Trusts console.

1. If necessary, start your server and log on using the **Administrator** account in the **CHILDXX** domain (where *XX* is the number of the forest root domain for which your server is a domain controller) using the password **Password01**.

2. Click **Start**, select **Administrative Tools**, and then click **Active Directory Domains and Trusts**.

3. In the left tree pane, right-click the **Active Directory Domains and Trusts** node and then click **Operations Master**, as shown in Figure 8-3.

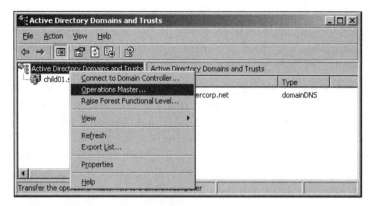

Figure 8-3   How to locate the domain naming master

4. The forest's domain naming master is then displayed, as shown in Figure 8-4. Note the current domain naming master, and then click **Close**.

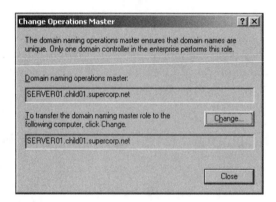

Figure 8-4   Identifying the domain naming master of the forest

5. Close Active Directory Domains and Trusts.

6. Log off your server if you do not intend to immediately continue to the next activity. Otherwise, stay logged on.

DOMAIN-WIDE ROLES

In an Active Directory domain, there are certain operations that can only be performed by a single domain controller in a domain. Known as domain-wide FSMO roles, the PDC emulator, RID master, and infrastructure master are the three roles that only one domain controller (per role) in the domain can hold at any given point in time. This means that every domain in a forest can have one PDC emulator, one RID master, and one infrastructure master. The following sections cover the domain-wide FSMO roles in more detail.

Note that it is possible that all three domain-wide roles reside on one domain controller, all three roles reside on different domain controllers, or that any combination of two of the roles are on one domain controller with the third role on its own domain controller. In other words, there can be any combination of domain-wide roles on a domain controller. Additionally, a domain controller may even hold domain-wide roles and forest-wide roles. The point here is that all the FSMO roles are independent from one another, but you can place two or more roles on the same domain controller if it makes sense for the Active Directory design.

PDC Emulator

The **PDC emulator** performs several different operations for an Active Directory domain. First, the PDC emulator acts as if it is a Windows NT 4.0 PDC for the domain. If a domain is at the Windows 2000 Mixed or Windows Server 2003 interim functional level and an update is made to Active Directory, it is the job of the PDC emulator to replicate the appropriate change(s) to any Windows NT 4.0 BDCs in the domain. Additionally, the PDC emulator is responsible for performing certain operations for client workstations running older operating systems such as Windows NT 4.0 Workstation or Windows 98. For example, password changes from computers running Windows NT and Windows 98 must be written directly to the PDC. In an Active Directory domain, the PDC emulator would be responsible for handling password updates from these older clients.

Windows NT 4.0 domain controllers can only be part of an Active Directory domain if the domain functional level is set to Windows 2000 Mixed or Windows Server 2003 interim. However, Windows NT 4.0 workstations and member servers can be domain members at any domain functional level.

A client computer running Windows 2000 or Windows XP can make a password update on any domain controller in the domain. Additionally, Active Directory client software is available for Windows NT and Windows 98 that can be installed separately—allowing these operating systems to make password changes on any domain controller.

In addition to acting as the PDC for backwards compatibility, the PDC emulator is also used for synchronizing the system clock (that is, the time) of computers in the domain. Because the Kerberos authentication protocol—which is covered in the next chapter—requires that the client computer and the domain controller's clocks are within five minutes (by default) of each other in order for authentication to occur, it is important that clocks be synchronized.

In an Active Directory domain, all domain controllers synchronize their clocks based on the date and time of the PDC emulator's clock. Additionally, client computers and member servers synchronize their clocks with the domain controller that authenticates the user during logon. While this process of synchronizing time from PDC emulator, to domain controllers, to clients synchronizes the clocks of all computers in the domain, the PDC emulator is also used to synchronize time across the entire forest.

In an Active Directory forest, the PDC emulator of a child domain synchronizes its clock with the PDC emulator of its parent domain. The PDC emulator in the forest root domain is therefore the clock by which all other computers in the forest synchronize their time. To ensure the time is accurate, you can configure the PDC emulator in the forest root domain to synchronize its clock with an outside source such as the United States Naval Observatory.

NOTE For more information on synchronizing time with an outside time source, see knowledge base article 216734 at *support.microsoft.com*. The article is written for Windows 2000, but the information is still applicable to Windows Server 2003.

The last operation that the PDC emulator performs has to do with password replication. As you learned in the last chapter, password updates are preferentially replicated to the PDC emulator for the domain. This reduces the latency of password updates, because any authentication attempt that fails on a domain controller is forwarded to the PDC emulator, which in most cases has the most up-to-date password.

Placement

By default, the PDC emulator FSMO role is assigned to the first domain controller in every new domain. Because the PDC emulator is frequently contacted by other domain controllers for such tasks as: password updates, forwarding failed authentication requests, time synchronization, and providing backwards compatibility support for Windows NT 4.0 BDCs and Windows NT/98 clients, place the PDC emulator role on a domain controller that is highly available. Additionally, choose a domain controller that has additional processing power for the PDC emulator in a large domain. If all domain controllers have equal processing power, try to place the PDC emulator on a domain controller that is not also a global catalog server.

In addition to choosing a domain controller that has the required processing power, you must also consider the physical location of the server. Because the PDC emulator must communicate with servers and workstations located throughout the network, place the PDC emulator role on a domain controller that is centrally located on the network. In Activity 8-3, you learn how to use Active Directory Users and Computers to locate a domain's PDC emulator.

Impact if Unavailable

If the PDC emulator becomes unavailable, users may notice an impact on Active Directory. Older Windows NT/98 clients not running the Active Directory client software will be unable to change passwords. Plus the latency in propagating password updates will increase and validation of user passwords may randomly pass or fail because the password update may have not replicated to all domain controllers and there is no longer a single server to which failed authentication requests can be forwarded. In addition, replication of updates to any Windows NT 4.0 BDCs will not occur.

RID Master

In Active Directory, objects that can be assigned permissions to resources, such as users, groups, and computer accounts, are referred to as security principles. While security principles are covered in more detail in the next chapter, for now understand that each security principle has its own unique security identifier (SID). When a user or group is given permission to a resource, the user or group's SID is used to identify the user/group. By using a SID rather than the name of, say, a user account, the user account can be renamed while still keeping the user account's access to resources.

A security principle's SID is made up of the SID of the domain (domain SID) and a **relative identifier (RID)**. While all objects created in the same domain have the same domain SID, the RID is unique for every security principle in a domain. In order to ensure that all RIDs are unique, it is the responsibility of the **RID master** to allocate blocks of RIDs to domain controllers. When a domain controller creates a new security principle, it then uses a RID from its allocated block.

While the RID master is responsible for allocating blocks of RIDs, it is also responsible for moving objects between domains to prevent object duplication. Object duplication could occur because in a multi-master environment it is possible that the same object could be moved to a different domain on two different domain controllers at the same time—before the domain controllers have a chance to replicate. By having a single point for move operations between domains, the RID master can move the object to the new domain and then delete it from the old domain. With the object deleted on the RID master, there is no way the object could be moved again—it has been deleted and the RID master knows about the deletion.

NOTE

Chapter 10 covers moving objects between domains in more detail.

Placement

By default, the RID master FSMO role is assigned to the first domain controller in every new domain. Because RIDs are assigned in blocks containing 500 RIDs, domain controllers do not (typically) need to request new blocks of RIDs very frequently. Additionally, most object move operations occur within the same domain, rather than between domains. For these two reasons, the additional load placed on a domain controller designated as the RID master is negligible.

Because all new security principles require a RID as part of their SID, choose a domain controller that is highly available as the RID master—ensuring that RIDs are always available to domain controllers. Additionally, locate the RID master in a site where most new security principles are created—a common scenario when all the network administrators are located at the same site. By placing the RID master where most new security principles are created, the loss of a WAN link does not impact the creation of new security principles at that site.

Alternatively, if no one site creates most of the security principles, locate the RID master centrally. In this scenario, the RID master is often placed on the same domain controller as the PDC emulator to simplify management. You learn how to use Active Directory Users and Computers to locate a domain's RID master in Activity 8-3.

Impact if Unavailable

If the RID master becomes unavailable, users do not notice any impact on Active Directory. Additionally, network administrators most likely do not notice the loss unless they are attempting to create many security principles and a domain controller runs out of RIDs. Network administrators may also notice the loss of the RID master if they are attempting to move objects between domains. Until the RID master is back online or the role is seized by another domain controller, no domain controller can get a new RID block nor can objects be moved between domains.

Infrastructure Master

The role of the **infrastructure master** in Active Directory is to update object references in its domain that point to objects located in another domain. Object references contain the GUID of the object, the distinguished name of the object, and possibly the SID of the object if it is a security principle. The infrastructure master periodically checks these references and updates the distinguished name and SID if the object moves within or between domains. The infrastructure master also updates the reference if the object is renamed or removes the reference if the object is deleted.

 Every object in Active Directory has a GUID in addition to a distinguished name. Because an object's GUID is never changed, the infrastructure master can use an object's GUID to identify changes even if the object is renamed or moved.

NOTE

To make this a little clearer, look at an example. Assume that a domain called ad.company. com contains a user named Paul in the Marketing OU. The distinguished name for Paul's user account would be DN=Paul,OU=Marketing,DC=ad,DC=company,DC=com. Additionally, say that Paul is a member of the Supervisors group in the dev.ad.company.com domain in the same forest. The Supervisors group object holds a reference to Paul's user account, because Paul is a member of the group.

Now, what if Paul's user account was moved from the Marketing OU to the Sales OU? Simple, the distinguished name for Paul's account would change to DN=Paul,OU=Sales,

DC=ad,DC=company,DC=com. However, the reference to Paul's account by the Supervisors group object would still point to the old distinguished name of Paul's account. To update the reference, the infrastructure master for the domain holding the reference makes the update. Because in this example the Supervisors group object holds the reference, the infrastructure master for the dev.ad.company.com domain updates the reference.

The infrastructure master identifies references that need to be checked by locating references to objects that are not contained in its local directory database. In other words, if an object reference is to an object that exists in the infrastructure master's local directory database, the infrastructure master assumes the reference is to an object in its own domain (meaning it does not need to be checked). However, if the infrastructure master finds an object reference to an object that is not located in its local directory database, the infrastructure master assumes the reference is to an object in a different domain and checks the reference by querying a global catalog server.

NOTE

If the forest consists of a single domain, the infrastructure master does nothing because there are no references to objects in other domains.

Placement

The most important thing to remember is *to not* place *the infrastructure master FSMO role on a global catalog server* in a forest with multiple domains. Because a global catalog server has a copy of every object in the entire forest, when the infrastructure master (running on a global catalog server) looks for object references to which an object does not exist in its local directory database, it would never find any. In other words, the infrastructure master would never update any references because as far as it is concerned, all objects exist in its local directory database. However, note that if the forest consists of only a single domain, you may place the infrastructure master on a server that is also a global catalog server because there are no cross domain references.

By default, the infrastructure master FSMO role is assigned to the first domain controller in every new domain. While the operation of updating references to objects in other domains may sound resource intensive, it does not actually place that much additional load on a domain controller. Additionally, because the loss of the infrastructure master does not result in the possible loss of any data, it does not have to be placed on a server that is highly available.

While you should never place the infrastructure master role on a domain controller that is a global catalog server (in a multi-domain forest), you should locate the infrastructure master role in a site that contains a global catalog server. Because the infrastructure master queries a global catalog server to update cross-domain references, it is important that only a short path exist between the infrastructure master and global catalog server. This speeds up the infrastructure master as well as reduces possible WAN activity from querying a global catalog server in another site. In Activity 8-3, you learn how to use Active Directory Users and Computers to locate a domain's infrastructure master.

Impact if Unavailable

If the infrastructure master becomes unavailable, users typically do not notice any impact on Active Directory. However, network administrators may notice that group membership does not appear to be updated in the user interface when group membership is updated. Additionally, user accounts may appear with incorrect names in a group's membership list. Until the infrastructure master is back online or the role is seized by another domain controller, no references to objects located in other domains are updated.

ACTIVITY

Activity 8-3: Identifying the Domain-wide FSMO Role Holders

Time Required: 5 minutes

Objective: Learn how to use the Active Directory Users and Computers console to identify the PDC emulator, RID master, and infrastructure master of a domain.

Description: After having located the forest-wide FSMO role owners for Super Corp's network, you decide to turn your attention to the domain-wide FSMO roles. In order to locate the current PDC emulator, RID master, and infrastructure master, you decide to use Active Directory Users and Computers.

1. If necessary, start your server and log on using the **Administrator** account in the **CHILD**XX domain (where XX is the number of the forest root domain for which your server is a domain controller) using the password **Password01**.

2. Click **Start**, select **Administrative Tools**, and then click **Active Directory Users and Computers**.

3. In the left tree pane, right-click the **child**XX**.supercorp.net** (where XX is the number of the forest root domain for which your server is a domain controller) node, and then click **Operations Masters**. The Operations Masters window opens, as shown in Figure 8-5 with a tab for each of the domain-wide roles. Note the RID master, PDC emulator, and infrastructure master for the domain by selecting the appropriate tab.

4. Click **Close** to close the Operations Masters window.

5. Close Active Directory Users and Computers.

6. Log off your server if you do not intend to immediately continue to the next activity. Otherwise, stay logged on.

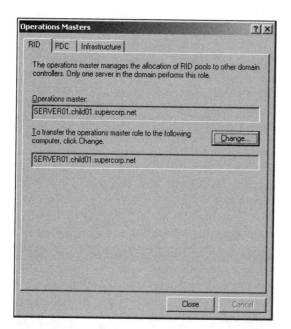

Figure 8-5   Domain-wide operations masters

TRANSFERRING AND SEIZING ROLES

When initially configuring a forest or domain, it may be necessary to transfer the FSMO roles from their default servers to other servers located in the domain or forest. Also, as time progresses, old servers are retired and may contain one or more roles that need to be moved to other domain controllers. It may even be necessary to transfer a role to a new, more powerful server if the load on the network increases.

While moving a role from one server to another as the network evolves is an orderly process, there may be situations where the original role holder is permanently unavailable. In such situations, the role will most likely need to be seized by another domain controller in the forest or domain—depending on the role. The following sections describe the processes of both transferring and seizing roles in more detail.

Transfer Roles

When a role must be moved to a different domain controller either for initial configuration of the forest/domain or a forest/domain restructuring, the preferred method is to perform a transfer operation. In a transfer operation between domain controllers, the domain controller that currently holds the role must be available (in addition to the domain controller where the role is being moved). Because both servers are available in a transfer operation, the current role holder can replicate any recent changes to the new role holder—ensuring that no data loss occurs. In Activity 8-4, you and your partner team up to transfer the infrastructure master of your domain to another domain controller.

NOTE

When a domain controller is demoted, any operations master roles it holds are arbitrarily moved to other domain controllers. If you want control over the domain controller to which a role is moved, transfer the role before demoting the domain controller.

In order to move roles from one server to another, you need to be a member of a certain group, depending on the role that you want to move. Table 8-1 lists the different FSMO roles and the group that can move the role by default. Note that this table is also applicable when seizing roles, not just transferring them.

Table 8-1 Groups authorized to move FSMO roles between domain controllers

FSMO Role	Authorized Group
Schema master	Schema Admins
Domain naming master	Enterprise Admins
PDC emulator	Domain Admins
RID master	Domain Admins
Infrastructure master	Domain Admins

ACTIVITY

Activity 8-4: Transferring Domain-wide FSMO Roles

Time Required: 10 minutes

Objective: Learn how to transfer the infrastructure master role to another domain controller.

Description: After assessing the current location of all FSMO roles in Super Corp's forest and domain, you have decided to relocate some of the role holders. To get a feel for the process, you have decided to start by moving the infrastructure master for one of Super Corp's domains.

CAUTION

Because there is only one infrastructure master for a domain, only the student with the higher server number should perform the following steps. However, the student who has the higher server number needs to log on to his or her partner's server (that is, the server with the lower server number) in order to complete the following steps.

1. If necessary, start your partner's server (the server with the lower server number) and log on using the **Administrator** account in the **CHILDXX** domain (where *XX* is the number of the forest root domain for which your partner's server is a domain controller) using the password **Password01**.

2. Click **Start**, select **Administrative Tools**, and then click **Active Directory Users and Computers**.

NOTE In order to move a FSMO role, you must first target the console so it connects to the domain controller that is to become the new role holder. By default, Active Directory Users and Computers connects to the domain controller to which you are logged on. This is why you are logged on to your partner's server and not your own—you would not have to perform the following three steps because Active Directory Users and Computers would have already connected you to the domain controller you are about to select.

3. In the left tree pane, right-click the **Active Directory Users and Computers** node, and then click **Connect to Domain Controller**.

4. In the list of available domain controllers, select **SERVERXX.childZZ.supercorp.net** (where *XX* is the server with the higher server number and *ZZ* is the number of the forest root domain), as shown in Figure 8-6. This is the server to which you will be moving the infrastructure master role.

8

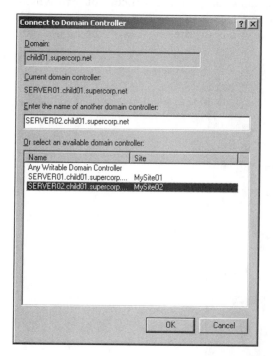

Figure 8-6   Selecting another server to which to connect the console

5. Click **OK**. Notice that the console is updated to indicate that it is now connected to SERVER*XX* (where *XX* is the server that you just selected), as shown in Figure 8-7. You may need to resize the Active Directory Users and Computers console in order to see the full text.

6. In the left tree pane, right-click the **childXX.supercorp.net** (where *XX* is the number of the forest root domain) **node**, and then click **Operations Masters**.

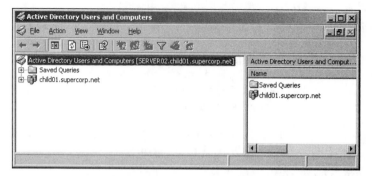

Figure 8-7   Console now shows connection to a different server

7. Click the **Infrastructure** tab. The current operations master should be the server with the lower server number. Additionally, the domain controller to which the operations master role is to be transferred is the same as the domain controller to which the console is connected (in this case, the server with the higher number). This is shown in Figure 8-8.

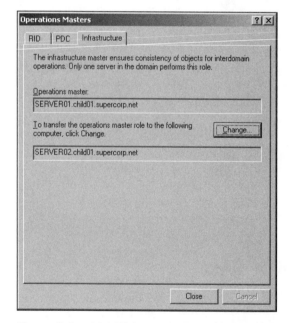

Figure 8-8   Identifying current and new infrastructure master

8. Click **Change**. You are prompted if you are sure that you want to transfer the role. Because your forest only has one domain, moving the infrastructure master to a global catalog server is not an issue.

9. Click **Yes**. A message box appears informing you that the role was successfully moved.

10. Click **OK**. Notice that the Operations Master window is updated to display the change of infrastructure master.

11. Click **Close**.

12. Close Active Directory Users and Computers.

13. Log off the server if you do not intend to immediately continue to the next activity. Otherwise, stay logged on.

NOTE

While Activity 8-4 only shows moving the infrastructure master, you can use the same exact steps to move the PDC emulator or RID master roles. Also, the steps of connecting the console to another domain controller (that you want to be the new operations master for the role) work the same way when moving the schema master or domain naming master. The only difference is that you use the Active Directory Schema snap-in and Active Directory Domains and Trusts console, respectively, to transfer the roles. If you like, try connecting to your partner's domain controller using the Active Directory Domains and Trusts console, but do not move the domain naming master.

Seizing Roles

In some instances, it may become necessary to move a FSMO role from one domain controller to another even if the original role holder is unavailable. This process of forcibly moving a role is called seizing the role and should only be done as a last step. In a role seizure, any recent changes that were performed on the original role holder cannot be replicated to the new role holder and may be lost. Additionally, the original role holder cannot be informed that it no longer holds the role.

CAUTION

Seizing a role is not something that you should take lightly. Only seize a role if the original domain controller that held the role cannot be restored. Before seizing a role, disconnect the domain controller that originally held the role from the network. In most cases, you should never place the server back on the network unless it is formatted and Windows is reinstalled.

CAUTION

In order to reduce possible data loss, it is a good idea to seize the schema, domain naming master, and RID master roles to one of the old role holder's direct replication partners—preferably a domain controller located in the same site, if at all possible. This reduces the chance of lost data, because the old role holder's direct replication partner(s) would have been the first to receive any updates made before the server failed.

NOTE
When designing your Active Directory infrastructure, it is a good idea to explicitly designate a domain controller as a "backup" operations master (that is, where the role can manually be seized by an administrator) for the schema master, domain naming master, and RID master. Again, the "backup" operations master should be a direct replication partner with, and in the same site as, the "normal" operations master to ensure it has the most recent updates. Although the role(s) must still manually be seized by an administrator in the event of a failure, having a plan in place when something does go wrong can make things run a little smoother.

When a role holder comes back online, it automatically waits until it replicates with its partners before resuming the role. This allows the domain controller to see if another domain controller has seized the role. If a new domain controller has taken over the role, the old role holder can then remove the roles from its configuration. While this process sounds simple, there are situations where the change of the new role holder may have not completely replicated by the time the old role holder comes back online. This can lead to two operations masters attempting to perform the same role—which is a big mess and can require that an entire domain or even forest be rebuilt. Table 8-2 describes the possible consequences of bringing a domain controller back online after it has had a FSMO role seized.

Table 8-2   Consequences of bringing a domain controller back online after FSMO role seizure

FSMO Role	Consequences
Schema master	Can lead to a corrupted forest and the need to rebuild the entire forest. A schema master should never be brought back online after seizure.
Domain naming master	Can require that one or more domains would need to be rebuilt. A domain naming master should never be brought back online after seizure.
PDC emulator	User authentication may be temporarily erratic, but no damage to the directory will occur. You can bring a PDC emulator back online after seizure if necessary.
RID master	Can require that the entire domain would need to be rebuilt. Never bring a RID master back online after seizure.
Infrastructure master	No adverse effects or damage to the directory will occur. You can bring an infrastructure master back online after seizure if necessary.

There are actually two methods for seizing an operations master role. Because seizing the PDC emulator or infrastructure master roles has no dangerous consequences, you can use Active Directory Users and Computers to seize these two domain-wide roles in the same way they are normally transferred. Alternatively, you can use a command-line utility called NTDSUTIL to seize any of the five operations master roles. While you can seize the PDC emulator or infrastructure master roles by either method, you can only seize the schema master, domain naming master, and RID master using NTDSUTIL. In Activity 8-5, you and your partner team up to seize the infrastructure master role.

Activity 8-5: Using NTDSUTIL to Seize a FSMO Role

Time Required: 10 minutes

Objective: Learn how to seize the infrastructure master role using NTDSUTIL.

Description: Shortly after you moved the infrastructure master in one of Super Corp's domains, the server became permanently unavailable. Until a replacement domain controller is purchased and reconfigured, you decide to seize the infrastructure master role and move it back to the domain controller that originally held the role.

Because there is only one infrastructure master for a domain, only the student with the lower server number on his or her own server should perform the following steps. Additionally, you should shut down the domain controller with the higher server number (that is, the current infrastructure master for the domain).

8

1. Shut down the server with the higher server number. This should be the server that is currently the infrastructure master for the domain. Wait for the server to shut down before continuing.

2. If necessary, start the server with the lower server number and log on using the **Administrator** account in the **CHILDXX** domain (where *XX* is the number of the forest root domain for which your server is a domain controller) using the password **Password01**.

3. Click **Start** and then click **Command Prompt**.

4. Type **NTDSUTIL** and then press **Enter**.

5. Type **roles** and then press **Enter**. The prompt should change to "fsmo maintenance."

6. Type **connections** and then press **Enter**. The prompt should change to "server connections."

7. Type **connect to server SERVERXX.childZZ.supercorp.net** (where *XX* is the number of your server and *ZZ* is the number of the forest root domain) and then press **Enter**. This is the server that you want to seize the operations master role(s) to.

8. Type **quit** and then press **Enter**. The prompt should change back to "fsmo maintenance" as shown in Figure 8-9.

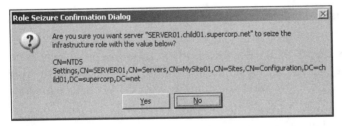

Figure 8-9   Seizing a FSMO role using NTDSUTIL

NOTE
Your command prompt is most likely not going to be C:\> by default (as shown in Figure 8-9), but rather C:\Documents and Settings\Administrator. SERVERXX> (where XX is the number of your server). It could even be something else, depending on your server's configuration. The command prompt has been changed in the rest of this text's figures to keep commands from wrapping to the next line as much as possible. Unless noted otherwise, the prompt at which you execute the commands does not matter. If you would like to change your Start menu's Command Prompt shortcut to start the prompt at C:\>, you can do so by clicking Start, right-clicking Command Prompt, and then clicking Properties. Change the Start in textbox to C:\, or any path you like, and then click OK. The next time you click the Command Prompt shortcut, the prompt will start in the directory you specify.

9. Type **seize infrastructure master** and then press **Enter**. A message box appears asking if you are sure you want to seize the infrastructure master role, as shown in Figure 8-10.

Figure 8-10   Message box prompting to confirm seizure

TIP
You can type a question mark (?) at any of the NTDSUTIL prompts to see a list of available commands for the current prompt. Typing a question mark (?) at the "fsmo maintenance" prompt lists the commands to seize the other four FSMO roles as well as other available commands.

10. Click **Yes**. The NTDSUTIL utility first attempts a normal transfer operation. You may see several error messages because the current infrastructure master is unavailable. If the normal transfer operation fails, the NTDSUTIL utility then forcibly seizes the role.

11. Once the "fsmo maintenance" prompt reappears, type **quit** and then press **Enter**.

12. Type **quit** and then press **Enter** to exit the NTDSUTIL utility.

13. Type **exit** and press **Enter** to close the Command Prompt window.

14. Referring back to Activity 8-3 if necessary, use Active Directory Users and Computers to confirm the infrastructure master role has been moved.

15. Log off your server.

8

CHAPTER SUMMARY

- ❑ There are two forest-wide operations master roles: the schema master and the domain naming master. No matter how many domains exist in a forest, there is only one schema master and one domain naming master.

- ❑ The schema master is the only domain controller in the entire forest that has a writable copy of the schema.

- ❑ The domain naming master is the only domain controller that can add or remove domains to the forest.

- ❑ There are three domain-wide operations master roles: the PDC emulator, the RID master, and the infrastructure master. Each domain in an active directory forest has its own PDC emulator, RID master, and infrastructure master.

- ❑ The PDC emulator is responsible for replicating changes to any Windows NT 4.0 BDCs and performing certain functions for older clients running operating systems such as Windows NT 4.0 and Windows 98. The PDC emulator is also used as a source by other domain controllers for synchronizing their system clocks. Finally, the PDC emulator receives preferential replication of password updates to shorten password replication latency.

- ❑ The RID master is responsible for distributing blocks of RIDs to other domain controllers for use when creating new security principles. The RID master is also responsible for moving objects between two domains.

- ❑ The infrastructure master is responsible for updating object references in its own domain that reference objects located in other domains. If a forest contains multiple domains, do not place the infrastructure master on a global catalog server.

- ❑ When the operations master that currently holds a role is online, the role can be transferred to another domain controller. When a role is transferred, the old and new operations masters replicate with each other to ensure no data is lost. Additionally, the old operations master that held the role can gracefully give up the role.

❑ If an operations master becomes permanently unavailable, another domain controller can forcibly seize any roles it performed. Do not take seizing a role lightly. In most cases, you should never bring the original operations master back online.

KEY TERMS

domain naming master — The forest-wide operations master that controls the addition and removal of domains in the forest.

infrastructure master — The operations master for a domain that updates references to objects in other domains.

operations masters — Domain controllers that manage specific changes to Active Directory that would be impractical to manage using a multi-master replication model. (Also called Flexible Single Master Operations roles, or FSMO.)

PDC emulator — An operations master for a domain that simulates a Windows NT 4.0 PDC for backward compatibility with older Windows clients and servers. It also is used for time synchronization, and it receives preferential replication of password changes.

relative identifier (RID) — Combined with the domain SID to create the SID for a security principle such as a user, group, or computer account.

RID master — The operations master for a domain that allocates blocks of RIDs to domain controllers for use when creating security principles such as users, groups, and computer accounts.

schema master — The forest-wide operations master that controls changes to the Active Directory schema.

REVIEW QUESTIONS

1. Which of the following are forest-wide flexible single master operation roles? (Choose all that apply.)

   a. PDC emulator

   b. infrastructure master

   c. schema master

   d. domain naming master

   e. RID master

2. Which of the following are domain-wide Flexible Single Master Operation roles? (Choose all that apply.)

   a. PDC emulator

   b. infrastructure master

   c. schema master

   d. domain naming master

   e. RID master

3. The _____ is the only domain controller with a writable copy of the schema.

4. The _____ is responsible for updating object references to other domains.

5. The _____ is the only domain controller that moves objects between domains to ensure duplicates are not created.

6. Which of the following tools can you use to identify which server holds the RID master FSMO role?

   a. Active Directory Users and Computers

   b. Active Directory Domains and Trusts

   c. Active Directory Sites and Services

   d. Active Directory Schema

7. The _____ is a domain controller in the forest root domain with which all computers in the forest synchronize their clocks (either directly or indirectly).

8. The _____ is responsible for adding and removing domains to and from the forest.

9. The _____ is responsible for replicating changes to Windows NT 4.0 BDCs.

10. An Active Directory Forest with six domains, two trees, and 10 sites has how many domain naming masters?

   a. one for the entire forest

   b. one for each domain tree

   c. one for each domain

   d. one for each site

11. An Active Directory Forest with six domains, two trees, and 10 sites has how many infrastructure masters?

   a. one for the entire forest

   b. one for each domain tree

   c. one for each domain

   d. one for each site

12. Which of the following domain controllers would be the best place to locate the infrastructure master—assuming a multi-site forest?

   a. as close as possible to a domain naming master

   b. on any available global catalog server

   c. on a global catalog server that is a domain controller for the domain

   d. on a domain controller for the domain with a global catalog server located in the same site

8

13. Which of the following physical locations would be the best place to locate the PDC emulator?

    a. in a central point on the network

    b. in the same site as the schema master

    c. in the same site where most new security principles are created

    d. physical placement of the PDC emulator is not a concern

14. When you need to move a FSMO role to another domain controller and the original server holding the role is available, you should do which of the following?

    a. Transfer the role.

    b. Reclaim the role.

    c. Seize the role.

    d. Take ownership of the role.

15. Which of the following tools can you use to identify which server holds the PDC emulator FSMO role?

    a. Active Directory Users and Computers

    b. Active Directory Domains and Trusts

    c. Active Directory Sites and Services

    d. Active Directory Schema

16. You can use the _____ command-line utility to seize any of the five FSMO roles.

17. By default, you must be a member of the _____ group in order to move the domain naming master FSMO role between domain controllers.

18. Which of the following tools can you use to identify which server holds the domain naming master FSMO role?

    a. Active Directory Users and Computers

    b. Active Directory Domains and Trusts

    c. Active Directory Sites and Services

    d. Active Directory Schema

19. By default, you must be a member of the _____ group in order to move the RID master FSMO role between domain controllers.

20. As a best practice, you should place the schema master and domain naming master FSMO roles on which of the following domain controllers?

    a. a domain controller in the first site

    b. a domain controller in the forest root domain

    c. a domain controller in the domain with the most objects

    d. a domain controller in the root of any domain tree

CASE PROJECTS

Case Project 8-1: Describing Operations Masters

So the junior network administrators can have a better idea of what the different operations masters are responsible for, Super Corp's IT manager has asked you to write a short description of operations masters. He would like you to only include the different types of roles and some examples of the operations each perform. Because he does not want to overwhelm the junior network admins, he has told you that including information related to placing the roles is not necessary.

Case Project 8-2: Identifying Operations Masters

As part of Super Corp's Active Directory proposal, you have decided to include diagrams relating to placement of operations masters. The first diagram you must create should expand on Figure 8-11 by identifying which domains contain operations masters by default.

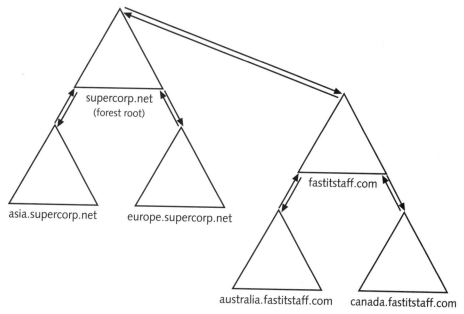

Figure 8-11   Identifying operations masters

CHAPTER

9

ACTIVE DIRECTORY
AUTHENTICATION AND SECURITY

After reading this chapter, you will be able to:

♦ Describe security principles and how they are identified

♦ Describe the user authentication process in an Active Directory domain using the NTLM and Kerberos authentication protocols

♦ Demonstrate the use of DACLs to control access to objects in Active Directory

♦ Demonstrate the use of SACLs to control auditing of objects in Active Directory

♦ Describe how network resources can be protected using security based on Active Directory

In the early chapters of this book, you learned a great deal about the structure of Active Directory and how to design an effective Active Directory forest. In this chapter, you will learn how to control access to objects in Active Directory; that is, you will learn how to protect your network by limiting access to Active Directory.

There are two important aspects to consider when implementing security (or access control) in a network. First, someone must decide who should have access to what. This is not a trivial decision, nor is it a decision that should be left only to the staff operating the network. It is a business decision. Just like airport security, the more secure things are, the less convenient it is for users. Deciding how much security is enough is a decision that should be made on a case-by-case basis. Secondly, after the roles and policies have been decided, the network administrators have to implement the proper access controls.

Accordingly, this chapter will open with a look at security principals, including a close examination of the role of SIDs. The chapter then examines how the authentication process works, including Kerberos authentication, NTLM authentication, PKI Certificate-based methods, and two-factor authentication. The chapter will then look at how to use DACLs to control access to objects. In addition, this chapter provides discussion and examples of how to use inheritance and the delegation of control, based on the granularity available in Active Directory permissions, to manage the protection of your network. The chapter also covers how to use SACLs to audit object access in the directory. The chapter concludes with a look at other network resources that can be protected using Active Directory.

Of course, there is nothing to stop you from operating a computer network in which every user has full access to all resources. However, in doing so, you are just waiting for trouble. Even in a small network at a small business, there is still confidential information, and there are still configurations that should not be changed. In any serious network, security must be in place and access must be controlled appropriately.

SECURITY PRINCIPLES

In Active Directory, every object has a relative distinguished name (RDN) and a globally unique identifier (GUID), both of which you can use to identify objects in the directory. As you have already learned, an object is given an RDN when it is created and is updated whenever the object is renamed. While a GUID is also automatically assigned to an object when the object is created, unlike an RDN, the GUID never changes—even if the object is moved or renamed. While all objects in the directory have both an RDN and a GUID, some objects also have a **Security Identifier (SID)**. Objects in Active Directory that have a SID are referred to as **security principals** and include the user object, inetOrgPerson object, computer object, and security group object.

You are probably familiar with the user, computer, and security group objects, but you may not have heard of the inetOrgPerson object. In the first version of Active Directory that shipped with Windows 2000, Microsoft called a user a user, plain and simple. Unfortunately, many other directories, including Novell's Novell Directory Services (NDS), use the inetOrgPerson object to represent a user. To allow greater interoperability between Active Directory and other directory services, Active Directory now supports the use of the inetOrgPerson class. Unless you are working in a multiplatform environment, you can consider an inetOrgPerson and a user to be functionally equivalent, once a domain is set to use the Windows Server 2003 functionality level.

SIDs are what the Windows security subsystem uses to identify security principals. For example, because a user has a SID, it can be given permissions to access resources. In the statement: "Bill is allowed to print to the color printer," Bill is the security principal, the color printer is the resource, and "allowed to print" is the permission. In slightly more technical terms, the user Bill is granted the print permission on the color printer. Because SIDs are the primary means of identifying security principals, the following section covers SIDs in more detail.

TIP
When you are talking with nontechnical people in business, they will use plain statements such as, "Bill is allowed to change that file," rather than talking about rights and permissions. Sometimes, you will have to translate between terms used by those well-versed in technology and those who aren't.

Security Identifiers

Microsoft defines the **objectSID** attribute as a binary value that specifies the SID of a user object. The SID is a unique value used to identify the user as a security principal.

There are a number of formats used to display the SID of an object. If you look at the value using ADSI Edit, the default is hexadecimal notation. More often than not, you see SIDs expressed in a format called **Security Descriptor Definition Language (SDDL)**. A SID expressed in SDDL looks something like this: S-1-5-21-606747145-436374069-1343024091-1166. You may have seen this format appear briefly in the Windows tools while the system is searching for the name that matches the SID. Table 9-1 shows SIDs from a test domain.

Table 9-1   Sample SIDs

Security Principal	Security Identifier
User1	S-1-5-21-1993962763-287218729-725345543-1628
User2	S-1-5-21-1993962763-287218729-725345543-2109
User3	S-1-5-21-1993962763-287218729-725345543-1638
User4	S-1-5-21-1993962763-287218729-725345543-1616
User5	S-1-5-21-1993962763-287218729-725345543-1629
Domain Admins	S-1-5-21-1993962763-287218729-725345543-512
BUILTIN\Administrators	S-1-5-32-544
Everyone	S-1-1-0
Group1	S-1-5-21-1993962763-287218729-725345543-1758

A SID in SDDL format begins with S to indicate it is a SID, and is followed by three to seven numbers, separated by hyphens that divide the SID into parts. The SIDs of normal users and groups contain all seven parts.

The first number is the revision level of the SDDL format, and hasn't changed since Windows NT was introduced, so it will probably always be 1. Notice the revision level for User1 highlighted in the following example: S-**1**-5-21-1993962763-287218729-725345543-1628.

The next portion of the SID is called the identifier authority, and identifies the security authority that issued the SID. The identifier authority for User1 is as follows: S-1-**5**-21-1993962763-287218729-725345543-1628. Most of the SIDs that you will be working with begin with S-1-5 and indicate the NT authority.

While most SIDs are uniquely generated, there are a group of SIDs called well-known SIDs that identify generic users or groups. The term "well-known" indicates that it is recognized by all Windows systems to mean the same thing. It also becomes well known in the sense that it is easily recognized by experienced administrators, but the term is technical and refers to the fact that it is known to the operating system. Among the well-known SIDs are: S-1-1-0, which is the Everyone group; S-1-3-0, which belongs to the special CREATOR OWNER group; and S-1-5-11, which belongs to the special Authenticated Users group.

NOTE   Groups with well-known SIDs are covered in more detail in the next chapter. Additionally, you may choose to review the list of well-known SIDs contained in the Microsoft Knowledge Base Article 243330 at *support.microsoft.com*.

The next section is called a subauthority identifier. For User1, the subauthority identifier is 21, highlighted in the following example: S-1-5-**21**-1993962763-287218729-725345543-1628. The value 21 indicates that this SID is for a security principal in a domain. Other values can also be used, such as 32, which indicates the BUILTIN groups. It is beyond the scope of this book to delve into the arcane and mysterious history of how and why subauthority identifiers came about. The value 21 is what you see most often, and SIDS with a 21 in this position have a domain identifier as well, which will be discussed in the next section.

Domain and Relative Identifiers

When a domain is first created, a set of three long integer numbers are calculated. When used together, these numbers are guaranteed to (a.k.a "should") be unique. Every object that belongs to this domain has the same three numbers. Each number is 32 bits long, for a total of 96 bits. These bits are called the domain security identifier (domain SID) or just the **domain identifier**. The domain identifier for User1 is highlighted in the following example: S-1-5-21-**1993962763-287218729-725345543**-1628. Notice that all of the other security principals in Table 9-1 are from the same domain and have the same number in this part of their SID.

It is not clear how many domains Microsoft was expecting its customers to create, but 2^{96} (2 to the 96th power) is a very large number—more than 79 octillion. (You can calculate this number by figuring out how many different values can be stored in 96 bits. For example, 8 bits can store 256 different values.)

Another 32 bits is used to uniquely identify the object within the domain, allowing for more than 4 billion individual SIDs within a domain. This number is called the **Relative Identifier (RID)** because it is relative to the domain. The RID for User1 is highlighted in the following example: S-1-5-21-1993962763-287218729-725345543-**1628**.

Each time an object with a SID is created, the domain assigns it a RID. Each domain controller has a pool of RIDs available for new objects, and requests more from the RID Master as needed. (The RID Master is one particular domain controller in a domain. The role of the RID Master was discussed in Chapter 8.) The domain controller combines the domain identifier and the RID to create the last four parts of the object's SID.

Access Tokens

As part of the authentication process, Windows builds an **access token** that contains several important pieces of information, including the user's SID. A number of additional SIDs will also be in the user's access token, including the SID for every group of which the user is a member. When the Windows security subsystem needs to check if a user has access to a resource, it can examine the user's access token and quickly determine if the user or one of the groups of which the user is a member has access to the resource. In Activity 9-1, you will examine the SIDs contained in your access token.

Exactly how the access token is generated depends on which authentication protocol is being used. An upcoming section covers the authentication process in more detail and how access tokens are generated.

ACTIVITY

Activity 9-1: Access Tokens

Time Required: 5 minutes

Objective: View the contents of an access token.

Description: In this activity, you will use the whoami utility to show the contents of your access token, including the SID for your account and any groups of which you are a member. Knowing how to use this utility is useful because it helps to troubleshoot resource access in a network environment.

1. If necessary, start your server and log on using the **Administrator** account in the **CHILDXX** domain (where *XX* is the number of the forest root domain for which your server is a domain controller) using the password **Password01**.

2. Click **Start** and then click **Command Prompt**.

3. At the command prompt, type **whoami /user**, and then press **Enter**. The username and SID of the user you are currently logged on as should be displayed, as shown in Figure 9-1.

Figure 9-1   Username and SID of the current user

4. Compare your SID to the SID shown in Figure 9-1. Identify the parts of the two SIDs that are the same and the parts that differ.

5. To view your group memberships, type **whoami /groups /fo list**, and then press **Enter**. A list of groups of which your user account is a member and the associated SIDs are displayed, as shown in Figure 9-2.

NOTE

The /fo parameter means to format output, in this case as a list. Other output options are *table* or *csv* to format the output as a table or comma-separated values.

```
Command Prompt                                                      _ □ ×

C:\>whoami /groups /fo list

GROUP INFORMATION
----------------

Group Name: Everyone
Type:       Well-known group
SID:        S-1-1-0
Attributes: Mandatory group, Enabled by default, Enabled group

Group Name: BUILTIN\Administrators
Type:       Alias
SID:        S-1-5-32-544
Attributes: Mandatory group, Enabled by default, Enabled group, Group owner

Group Name: BUILTIN\Users
Type:       Alias
SID:        S-1-5-32-545
Attributes: Mandatory group, Enabled by default, Enabled group

Group Name: BUILTIN\Pre-Windows 2000 Compatible Access
Type:       Alias
SID:        S-1-5-32-554
Attributes: Mandatory group, Enabled by default, Enabled group
```

Figure 9-2   Groups of which the current user is a member and their SIDs

6. Scroll, if necessary, to view all of the groups of which you are a member. Can you identify which groups have domain SIDs and which are well known?

7. Type **exit** and press **Enter**.

8. Log off your server if you do not intend to immediately continue to the next activity. Otherwise, stay logged on.

Permissions and Rights

Once a user is authenticated and an access token is generated, a user must then be authorized to perform specific actions. Permissions and rights, both of which are basically a list of SIDs, are used to control access on a system. Although the terms *permission* and *right* are often used interchangeably, they actually have two distinct meanings.

Permissions are rules associated with an object that define which users can gain access to the object and what actions they can perform on the object. Some examples of generic permissions would be read, write, and delete. Each object, such as an Active Directory object, file, or folder, has its own set of permissions. Later in this chapter you will learn how to use an object's **discretionary access control list (DACL)** to set permissions on Active Directory objects, files, and folders on NTFS volumes, the registry, and printers.

Rights, on the other hand, define what tasks or operations a user can perform on a computer system or domain (that is, they are not specific to one object). Rites are actually divided into two subcategories: logon rights and privileges. **Logon rights** define how a user can logon to a system. For example, the Access this computer from a network right defines which users are allowed to access a system over the network. **Privileges** are specific tasks a user can perform once they are logged on to a system. For example, the Change the system time right defines which users can change a system's clock. In Chapter 11, you will learn more about the different user rights and how they can be set using Group Policy.

You can use the whoami /PRIV command to view a list of privileges a user has.

TIP

If the difference between permissions and rights is confusing, the concept may become clearer after reading this chapter and Chapter 11. The important thing to remember is that permissions define access on a specific object whereas rights define access at a system or domain level.

9

ACTIVE DIRECTORY AUTHENTICATION

In this section, you will examine in greater depth exactly what happens when users log on to the network and are authenticated. To many administrators, the authentication process is like a black box—it either works or it doesn't. Many administrators operate their networks without a clear understanding of what is going on "under the hood." However, just like the driver of a car, the more you know about what happens under that hood, the easier it is to troubleshoot problems and deal with issues that might arise.

This section looks at the two authentication methods used in Windows Server 2003: **NT LAN Manager (NTLM)** and **Kerberos**. The section then discusses how to handle authentication from other down-level clients, and moves on to discuss two-factor authentication and the use of certificates and smart cards.

NTLM Authentication

NTLM authentication is actually the *second* option when authenticating a user in Windows Server 2003, and is supported mainly for backward compatibility with Windows NT 4.0 client computers, although it is occasionally used by newer clients as well. While NTLM authentication is not the primary means of authentication in Windows Server 2003, reviewing the older of the two models first allows you to more easily identify the benefits of

Kerberos—which is covered next. The NTLM authentication protocol is used in various scenarios, as follows:

- A Windows NT-based computer authenticates to a Windows 2000 Server or Windows Server 2003 domain controller.

- A Windows 2000/XP/2003 computer authenticates to a Windows NT-based server.

- A log-on request is sent to a Windows 2000 or 2003 stand-alone server (that is, one that is not a domain member).

- A security principal needs to be authenticated for access to a resource in a different forest when using an external trust relationship between two domains in different forests (or between a forest and a Windows NT domain). Note that this is not applicable to a cross-forest trust, but only an external trust.

- A security principal (such as a user) needs to be authenticated by a domain controller that is running as part of a Windows 2000 cluster server environment.

NTLM is based on an older, and less secure, authentication protocol called LAN Manager (LM). Still, the NTLM protocol is significantly less secure than Kerberos, and many password-cracking tools have been developed to capture and decrypt NTLM authentication traffic. With Windows NT 4.0 Service Pack 4, Microsoft introduced a new version called NTLM v2. This new version includes additional security, such as a unique session key for each time a new connection is established and an advanced key exchange to protect the session keys.

NOTE When a Windows 95/98 computer authenticates to a Windows 2000 Server or Windows Server 2003 domain controller, the older LM protocol is used by default. However, you can install the Active Directory Client Extensions for Windows 95/98 to allow Windows 95/98 computers to use NTLM v2 authentication.

Figure 9-3 illustrates the process of logging on to a domain and then accessing a domain resource using NTLM authentication. In the first step (1), a user logs on to a workstation by entering his or her username, password, and the domain where the user account is located. The workstation then computes a cryptographic hash of the user's password and discards the user's actual password. This prevents a password from easily being retrieved from the workstation in plaintext.

In the second step (2), the workstation sends the username to a domain controller, as illustrated in Figure 9-3. The domain controller then generates a 16-byte random number, which is called a challenge, and sends it to the workstation (3). The workstation then uses the hash of the user's password to encrypt the challenge sent by the domain controller, and then returns the result to the domain controller (4).

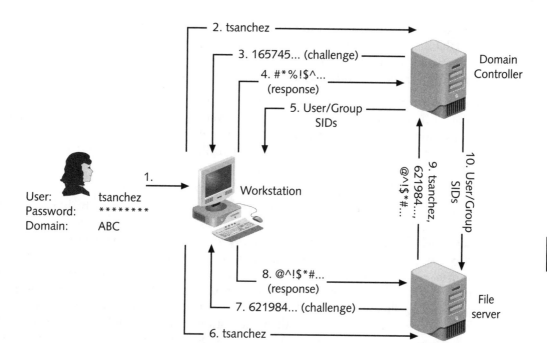

Figure 9-3   NTLM authentication example

NOTE

On a domain controller, the netlogon service is responsible for responding to domain authentication requests.

By using the username, the domain controller retrieves a hash of the user's password from Active Directory (or the SAM database if the domain controller is Windows NT Server 4.0). Note that Active Directory uses a special filter designed to support NTLM and allow the verification of the user's existence and correct password. The domain controller then uses the hash it retrieved from the directory to encrypt the challenge.

After the domain controller encrypts the challenge, it compares the results it computed to the results sent by the workstation in Step 4. If the two encrypted challenges match, then authentication is successful. The domain controller then responds with the user's SID and any SIDs of the group(s) of which the user is a member (5).

Once a domain controller authenticates the user, the workstation can then create an access token and complete the logon process. Note at this point that if the workstation has any local groups in its own security database of which the user (or one of the user's groups) is a member, the SIDs of the local groups are added to the user's access token by the workstation.

This whole process (Steps 1 through 5) is referred to as an interactive logon because a user is establishing an interactive session at the workstation. With the user logged on interactively to the workstation, the following steps describe the process that occurs when accessing a resource over the network—which is referred to as a network logon.

Referring back to Figure 9-3, when the workstation wants to access a resource on the file server, it must first authenticate to the file server. When using NTLM authentication, the workstation first sends the username of the user attempting to access the resource (6). The file server then generates a 16-byte random challenge and sends it to the workstation (7). The workstation then uses the saved hash of the user's password to encrypt the challenge sent by the server, and then returns the result to the server (8).

Because the server does not contain a copy of the user's password hash, it forwards the username, challenge, and the workstation's response to a domain controller (9). By using the username, the domain controller retrieves a hash of the user's password from Active Directory (or the SAM database if the domain controller is Windows NT Server 4.0). The domain controller then uses the hash it retrieved from the directory to encrypt the challenge. After the domain controller encrypts the challenge, it compares the results it computed to the results originally sent by the workstation to the file server in Step 8. If the two encrypted challenges match, then authentication is successful. The domain controller then responds with the user's SID and any SIDs of the group(s) of which the user is a member (10).

The file server then generates an access token and a connection with the client is established. Note at this point that if the file server has any local groups in its own security database of which the user (or one of the user's groups) is a member, the SIDs of the local groups are added to the user's access token by the file server. Additionally, keep in mind that the only process that has occurred is authentication. That is, the user's identity has been confirmed. The decision of whether the user has access to a particular resource has not yet been made. It is authorization—not authentication—that determines what exactly a user can and cannot do.

The difference between NTLM and NTLM v2 in the previous example is that communications are encrypted using a session key. Each time a new connection is established, a different session key is used.

NOTE

There are a few downsides to NTLM that you may have noticed after reviewing the previous example. First, each time a user wants to access a resource that requires establishing a new connection, the user must be reauthenticated by a domain controller (Steps 9 and 10 in the example). This means that the domain controller must find the users account in the directory, check the client's response to the challenge, and then locate all the groups of which the user is a member for every connection that is established on the network.

Second, NTLM only provides client authentication—the server does not have to prove its identity to the client. This means that it is possible for a client to think it is talking to the correct server, but it could just as easily be talking to a malicious system.

Finally, although the user's password is not sent over the network when using NTLM authentication, it is easier to capture the NTLM challenge and use hacking tools to discover the password than it is with NTLM v2 or Kerberos. With Kerberos, it is impossible to do so in any reasonable period of time. In Activity 9-2, you will configure the domain controller security policy to reject authentication requests that are using LM and NTLM (but not NTLM v2).

NOTE

LM authentication is even easier to crack than NTLM because the actual password hash is sent across the network and the method of creating hashes is much weaker. It is possible to crack an LM password in anywhere from a few seconds to a few minutes. Because of this, it is recommended that you disable at least LM, and preferably LM *and* NTLM, authentication on all domain controllers. Just be aware that this may impact older client operating systems that rely on these authentication protocols.

9

ACTIVITY

Activity 9-2: Preventing the Use of LM and NTLM

Time Required: 10 minutes

Objective: Prevent clients who are not using Kerberos or NTLMv2 from connecting. This activity requires you to work with a partner.

Description: Because of the security vulnerabilities in down-level clients, Super Corp has decided to require all clients to use Kerberos or NTLMv2. This requires Windows 95/98 clients to have the Active Directory extensions installed. In this activity, you will change the domain security policy to support this decision.

1. Because you are changing a security policy that affects all domain controllers, work with your partner and perform this activity from one of the two domain controllers of your domain.

2. If necessary, start your server and log on using the **Administrator** account in the **CHILDXX** domain (where *XX* is the number of the forest root domain for which your server is a domain controller) using the password **Password01**.

3. Click **Start**, select **Administrative Tools**, and then click **Domain Controller Security Policy**.

4. In the left tree pane, expand the following nodes: **Security Settings** and **Local Policies**.

5. Click the **Security Options** node in the left tree pane.

6. In the right details pane, locate and double-click **Network security: LAN Manager authentication level**, as shown in Figure 9-4.

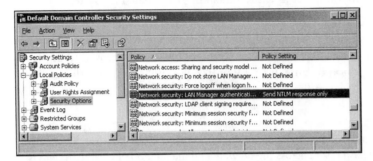

Figure 9-4   Locating the LAN Manager authentication-level security policy

7. Click the drop-down list and select **Send NTLMv2 response only\refuse LM & NTLM**, as shown in Figure 9-5.

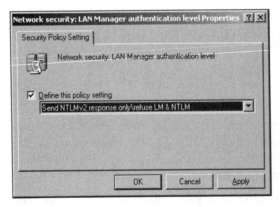

Figure 9-5   Setting domain controllers to only respond to NTLMv2 and Kerberos authentication requests

8. Click **OK**.

9. Close the domain controllers' security policy.

10. Log off your server if you do not intend to immediately continue to the next activity. Otherwise, stay logged on.

Kerberos Authentication

Kerberos v5 authentication is the default protocol for network authentication for all Windows Server 2003 computers. Windows XP Professional and Windows 2000 also use Kerberos for authentication by default. Kerberos v5 is based on Request for Comments (RFC) number 1510 (available from *www.ietf.org/rfc/rfc1510.txt* at the time of this writing).

Kerberos v5 can interoperate with other servers and clients that follow this RFC specification. Unfortunately, most implementations, including Microsoft's, vary slightly from the RFC specifications. This is because most vendors want to provide their product with additional functionality that might not be present in the standard protocol.

Kerberos is used for network authentication for access to network resources. The components involved in Kerberos include:

- The security principal who is requesting access
- The Key Distribution Center (KDC), which is an Active Directory domain controller
- The server holding the resource or the service that is being requested

In the Windows Server 2003 implementation of Kerberos, the **Key Distribution Center (KDC)** is a domain controller that stores the directory database containing all users and passwords. (In theory, a KDC could be some other server, but in Active Directory, it is a domain controller.) The KDC provides two main services for the security of the network:

- Authentication Service—Authenticates and issues ticket-granting tickets (TGTs) to users
- Ticket-granting Service—Issues session tickets for access to network resources

NOTE

In Active Directory, all domain controllers running Windows 2000 Server and Windows Server 2003 act as KDCs.

Authentication Service

The process of authenticating and granting access to resources requires two tickets from the KDC. The first ticket is the **ticket-granting ticket (TGT)** and is issued to the user when he or she is first authenticated during a successful logon. The TGT simply allows the user to request session tickets.

By default, a TGT is valid for 10 hours. This allows the user to request session tickets for the entire length of a normal business day, without needing to go back to the KDC for a new TGT. It also means that a TGT has to be occasionally refreshed, even if a user never logs off. You can adjust this default lifetime in the security policy of the domain. In Activity 9-3, you will modify the default maximum lifetime of TGTs for your domain.

Ticket-granting Service

Each time a user needs to access a resource, the TGT is submitted to the Ticket-granting Service on the KDC. The KDC sends two copies of a session ticket back to the user's machine. One copy is encrypted for the user's computer and is stored in the client computer's ticket cache system. The second copy is encrypted for the server that is hosting the desired resource.

Each time that the user needs to access the resource or service, the client presents the session ticket to the target resource. The session ticket has a default lifetime of 600 minutes (10 hours), which can also be adjusted in the security policy of the domain. The target resource unpacks its copy of the session ticket and examines the user's SID and any group SIDs contained in the session ticket in order to generate an access token.

Kerberos in Action

The process of Kerberos authentication involves many steps. RFC 1510, which details how Kerberos v5 works, is about 112 pages long. Figure 9-6 illustrates the process in a simpler manner.

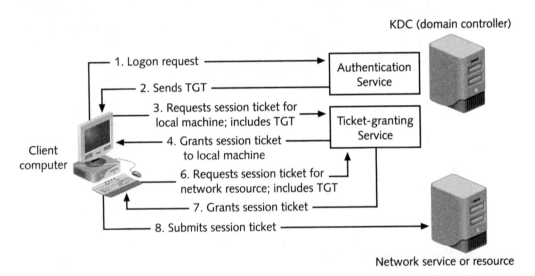

Figure 9-6   Kerberos authentication example

Step 1

In the first step, a user performs an interactive logon to a workstation by entering their username, password, and the domain where their user account is located. The workstation performs a one-way hashing function on the user's password and saves it in its secure credential cache. This one-way hash of the users password is known as the user's long-term key.

Logging on by typing a username and password prompts the workstation to send a packet to the KDC. (In technical literature, this request is called the Kerberos Authentication Service Request or KRB_AS_REQ packet.) The packet includes:

- The username
- A request for a TGT
- The username and timestamp, encrypted using the user's long-term key

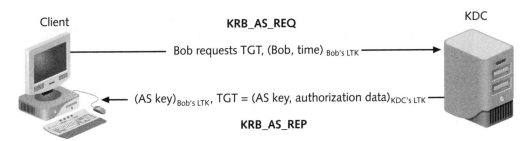

Figure 9-7   Authentication Service exchange

When the packet arrives at the server, the server looks at the username and then searches the directory database for the long-term key associated with the user's account. The server then decrypts the data in the packet using the user's long-term key and checks the timestamp. If the decryption is successful and the timestamp is within five minutes of the current time on the server, the user is authenticated.

If the timestamp cannot be decrypted correctly (that is, after decryption the data is not in a valid time/date format), then the password entered must be wrong, so the authentication fails. If the timestamp is not within five minutes of the KDC's time, or if the KDC cannot find the user, the authentication also fails.

The reason for requiring that the timestamp be fairly recent is to prevent an attacker from capturing and recording the authentication packets and then replaying them at a different time. You can configure the maximum allowable time difference in the domain's security policy.

Step 2

After the user is authenticated, the KDC generates a session key that is encrypted using the user's long-term key. This key is called the AS session key to avoid confusing it with other session keys. Next, the KDC creates a TGT that contains the following:

- A second copy of the AS session key
- Authorization data (the user's SID and any SIDs for groups of which the user is a member)

The TGT is encrypted using the KDC's long-term key (which the client does not know). Why two copies of the AS session key? Because the copy inside the TGT cannot be read or decrypted by the client computer. The AS session key and TGT are sent back to the client. (In technical literature, this request is called the Kerberos Authentication Service Reply or KRB_AS_REP packet.)

When the packet arrives at the client computer, the user's long-term key is used to decrypt the AS session key. The client stores both the decrypted AS session key and (still) encrypted TGT in its secure credentials cache. Both the AS session key and TGT remain in the cache for 10 hours by default. Bear in mind, however, that the user's computer now has a newly issued AS session key, but cannot read or change the contents of the TGT because it doesn't know the KDC's long-term key.

Steps 1 and 2 are the Authentication Service exchange.

Step 3 and 4

It may seem silly, but it's true—the user still hasn't logged on to the local computer. The user needs a session ticket valid for his or her own workstation in order to proceed.

This is the first Ticket-granting Service exchange, and it begins with the client building a Ticket-granting Service request, or KRB_TGS_REQ packet. This request packet is sent to the KDC and contains the TGT that the client received from the Kerberos Authentication Service. It also contains the name of the user, the name of the server or service for which access is desired (in this case, the local workstation), and a timestamp along with a second copy of the username. The timestamp and second copy of the user name are encrypted with the AS session key issued in Step 2.

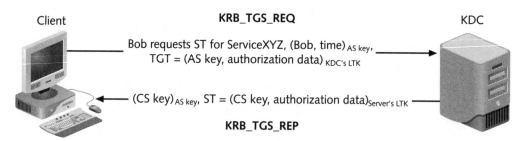

Figure 9-8 Ticket-granting Service exchange

The KDC needs to decrypt both the TGT and the timestamp. The KDC knows its own long-term key so it can decrypt the TGT. Inside the TGT is a copy of the AS session key, which the KDC can use to decrypt the timestamp. If the timestamp is decrypted correctly and within the five-minute window, the KDC knows the client has a copy of the AS session key—and therefore knows they must be who they say they are.

The KDC then creates a new session key that is used by the client and the server; it is referred to as the CS session key. A copy of the CS session key and the user's authorization data (from the TGT) are encrypted with the server's long-term key (which is known only to the computer hosting the resource and the KDC). The client does not know the server's long-term key. This encrypted block is called a **service ticket (ST)**.

NOTE

As you will learn about in the next chapter, computers running Windows 2000, Windows XP, and Windows Server 2003 all must have a computer account in the domain (Windows NT 4.0 systems must also have computer accounts, but they cannot use Kerberos so are not discussed here). A computer account is stored in Active Directory and contains a hashed password that only the computer knows. The computer's hashed password allows the computer to identify itself to the domain using the computer account. Additionally, the password hash is also used as a computer's long-term key, because it is known by only the computer and KDC (in a similar way that only the user and KDC know the user's long-term key). For more information on computer accounts, see the next chapter.

A second copy of the CS session key is encrypted using the AS session key. The service ticket and encrypted copy of the CS session key are then returned to the client in a KRB_TGS_REP packet. The client can use the AS session key to decrypt the new CS session key, but because the client does not know the server's long-term key, the client cannot decrypt the service ticket. Both the decrypted session key and service ticket are stored in the client's secure credential cache. By default, service tickets are cashed for 600 minutes (10 hours).

Steps 3 and 4 exemplify the Ticket-granting Service exchange.

9

Step 5

NOTE

This step is not shown in Figure 9-6.

The client can now contact the server. In this particular case, because the resource is on the same machine as the client, the logon process (running as the user) contacts the Local Security Authority (LSA). When contacting the server, the client sends the service ticket as well as a timestamp and username encrypted using the CS session key. This is known as the Kerberos Application Request (KRB_AP_REQ).

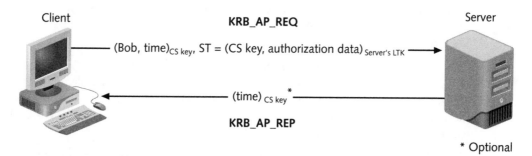

Figure 9-9 Application exchange

When the server (LSA on the local system in this case) receives the data, it decrypts the service ticket by using its own long-term key (that is, the server's long-term key). From the service ticket, the server extracts the CS session key and the authorization data. The server then uses the CS session key to decrypt the timestamp. If the timestamp is decrypted correctly and within the five-minute window, the server knows the client has a copy of the CS session key—and in turn must be who they say they are.

NOTE

It is also possible for the client to request mutual authentication. When the client requests mutual authentication, the server takes the unencrypted timestamp (which was originally sent encrypted by the client using the CS session key), re-encrypts just the timestamp (that is, without the username) using the CS session key, and sends the encrypted timestamp as a Kerberos Application Reply (KRB_AP_REP). The client can use the CS session key to decrypt the timestamp. Finally, the client can compare the timestamp sent by the server to the timestamp originally sent by itself. If the timestamps match, then the server is legitimate—you know it has a copy of the server's long-term key (which the client does not actually know) because it was able to get a copy of the CS session key. If the timestamps don't match, then the server is not legitimate.

The server (LSA on the local system in this case) then extracts the user's authorization data and creates an access token. The server also adds any local groups of which the user may be a member to the access token at this time. By definition, these machine local groups are not known outside of the local machine.

Step 5 exemplifies the Application exchange.

Step 6 and 7

When the client needs access to another network resource, such as a file on a file server, the request is sent to the KDC for another session ticket—just as in Step 3. The request includes the TGT and a timestamp that is encrypted with the AS session key.

The KDC decrypts and verifies the data in the packet. If the data is acceptable, the KDC issues the session ticket to the client using the same process followed in Step 4.

Steps 6 and 7 exemplify a Ticket-granting Service exchange, as do Steps 3 and 4.

Step 8

Step 8 represents the Application exchange, and is similar to Step 5. The client sends a service ticket to the server (KRB_AP_REQ). If the data is acceptable, the server uses its long-term key to extract the authorization data and create an access token. If requested by the client, the server also performs mutual authentication by sending a KRB_AP_REP packet back to the client (not shown in Figure 9-6).

If the client needs subsequent use of the resource or service, the session ticket is pulled up from the ticket cache and reissued to the target resource server. If the session ticket has expired, the client has to return to the KDC to obtain a new ticket. If the client needs access to a different server, Steps 6–8 are repeated to obtain a new service ticket for the server.

This process of obtaining a session ticket from the KDC before accessing a network resource is completely different than the process used in NTLM authentication. When trying to access a resource using NTLM authentication, the client would connect directly to the resource and request access. The server holding the resource would then perform pass-through authentication by contacting a domain controller to authenticate the user. With Kerberos, the client does not connect to the resource until it has received a session ticket from the KDC, but the server doesn't need to contact a domain controller for authorization.

In NTLM, each time a user wants access to a resource, a domain controller must authenticate the user. In Kerberos, a domain controller (or KDC) only needs to authenticate the user once when the TGT is created (and once every 10 hours thereafter, by default). Plus the fact that service tickets are also cached for 10 hours means that a client can disconnect from a server and then reconnect to that server hundreds of times, within a 10 hour period, without needing to go back to the KDC.

NOTE

Another important difference to remember is that Kerberos can provide mutual authentication of both client and server, whereas NTLM cannot.

ACTIVITY

Activity 9-3: Changing the Kerberos Ticket Lifetime

Time Required: 10 minutes

Objective: View and change Kerberos settings for the domain. This activity requires you to work with a partner.

Description: Because Super Corp's staff often work 12-hour shifts, it has been decided to increase the default TGT lifetime from 10 hours to 12 hours. In this activity, you will examine and change the account policy settings that control how Kerberos behaves in your domain. Note that you can only change these Kerberos settings at the domain level.

NOTE

Because you are changing a domain-wide policy, work with your partner and perform this activity from one of the two domain controllers of your domain.

1. If necessary, start your server and log on using the **Administrator** account in the **CHILDXX** domain (where *XX* is the number of the forest root domain for which your server is a domain controller) using the password **Password01**.

2. Click **Start**, select **Administrative Tools**, and then click **Domain Security Policy**.

3. In the left tree pane, expand the following nodes: **Security Settings** and **Account Policies**.

4. Click the **Kerberos Policy** node in the left tree pane.

5. In the right details pane, note the Kerberos settings that you can change and their defaults as shown in Figure 9-10.

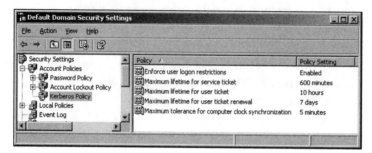

Figure 9-10 Default Kerberos settings

6. In the right details pane, double-click **Maximum lifetime for user ticket**.

7. Change the value from 10 to **12**, as shown in Figure 9-11.

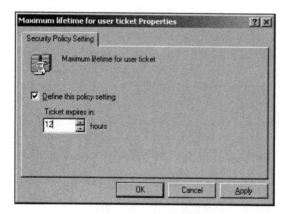

Figure 9-11 Modifying the maximum lifetime for user ticket Kerberos security policy

8. Click **OK**.

9. Close the domain's security policy.

10. Log off your server if you do not intend to immediately continue to the next activity. Otherwise, stay logged on.

Down-level Client Authentication

Almost all large corporate networks have a mixture of client operating systems, including Windows 95, Windows 98, Windows NT 4.0, Windows 2000, and Windows XP. The older clients (pre-Windows 2000) are referred to as **down-level clients**. These down-level clients (Windows 95/98 and NT) create a security concern when implemented within a Windows 2000/2003 network. In particular, Windows 95/98 clients are the most vulnerable because they use LM authentication, which is one of the weakest authentication protocols available. Windows NT 4.0 uses NTLM, which you can update to version 2 in Service Pack 4.

To help remedy these security concerns, the Directory Services Client is available as an add-on component to Windows 95/98, enabling these clients to use NTLMv2 on the Windows 2000/2003 network. The Directory Services Client, which is also available for Windows NT 4.0, implements additional features such as Active Directory site awareness, search capabilities in Active Directory, and the ability to connect to any domain controller to change passwords rather than having to connect to the PDC emulator.

There are certain features that the Directory Services Client does not provide, such as Kerberos or Group Policy support, IPSec support, dynamic DNS support, and user principal name authentication capabilities. To use these features, upgrade to Windows 2000 Professional or Windows XP Professional.

The Active Directory Client Extensions for Windows 95/98 are included on the *Windows 2000 Server* CD. You can find them in the *X*:\clients\win9*x* folder (where *X* is the letter of your CD-ROM drive). The Windows NT 4.0 Directory Services Client can be downloaded from the Microsoft Web site, and requires Service Pack 6a and Internet Explorer 4.01 or higher.

Two-factor Authentication

Traditionally, security experts have described three possible factors that help identify you for authentication:

- Something you know—a password, a PIN, or a secret phrase
- Something you have—a key to your house or a bankcard
- Something you are—an indelible characteristic that can't be imitated, your fingerprint, your signature, or your DNA

In general, the more of these factors you use in security, the more secure your resource is. For example, you can't access a bank account at an automated teller without both a card (something you have) and a PIN (something you know). It would be too easy to have cash stolen if all you needed was the card, and most agree that it would also be too easy to find out the PIN.

Traditional name and password combinations rely on only one factor—something that you know. A number of systems are available to increase the security of a network or computer system by introducing a second factor. This is called **two-factor authentication**. By way of example, RSA Security Corporation markets a product line, SecurID, which requires a user to have a small portable device (the size of a key). This device displays a changing number that must also be entered as part of the logon process. The device by itself is not sufficient—the user still needs a password.

Several companies market biometric devices that scan hands, fingerprints, or retinas. The cost of these devices is gradually decreasing, but user acceptance remains an issue, except in the most secure environments. Some manufacturers are starting to integrate facial recognition software into computer programs for use with low-cost Web cams. Though facial recognition may not be ready for mainstream use, new products are released every week.

Unlike certificates and smart cards (discussed in the next section), these types of products require additional hardware or software, and are not directly supported by Active Directory or Windows. Though they add cost and complexity to your network, they do make it more secure.

Public Key Infrastructure for Authentication with Smart Cards

Active Directory does support the use of smart cards and certificates to enhance the security of the logon process. Smart cards and certificates are part of a **Public Key Infrastructure (PKI)**. To understand PKI, you need to delve a little bit into the science of cryptography.

Most encryption is done with **symmetric keys**. In symmetric key cryptography, the same secret key can be used to encode and decode a message. The effectiveness of the encryption is based, in part, on the length of the key and, in part, on the quality of the algorithm used to generate the encrypted text. However, the biggest problem has always been how to keep the key secret, while at the same time getting it to the people who need it. In this kind of encryption, you have to be absolutely sure that no one is eavesdropping when you tell someone the key that you're using to encrypt a document.

Recently, public key cryptography has come to the forefront as a solution to this problem. In public key cryptography, two different keys—which are numbers that have a very special mathematical relationship—are used. If you use one key to encrypt something, the other key, and only the other key, can decrypt it. These related numbers, called a key pair or a **private/public key pair**, are usually very large.

One of the keys is called the private key, and is held privately by its owner. It is never sent with a message or disclosed to another party. On the other hand, the public key can, and should, be widely distributed. It can be painted on billboards, published in the newspaper, or stored in an electronic directory for anyone to find. If you wish to send me an encrypted message, you can find my public key anywhere you like and then use it to encrypt your message, knowing that only I can read it.

TIP

In practice, public key encryption is comparatively slow, so it is often used to encrypt a symmetric key sent with a message. The receiver decrypts the symmetric key and then uses it to quickly decrypt the message.

One possible hiccup remains. If Joe gives you a public key and says, "Here's Bill's public key," how would you know whether it was really Bill's public key? If someone has replaced Bill's key with their own, they could read messages you intended for only Bill. Certificates help address this issue.

In PKI, the term "certificate" usually refers to an **X.509 digital certificate**, which contains information about the person or entity it represents (called the subject of the certificate). It also contains the public key and a digital signature of the person who issued the certificate. (Digital signing is another feature of public key cryptography.)

There is a Star Trek episode where the android Data has to give the computer his complex password. Because the Star Trek computer is voice activated, he lists off a long string of numbers, spoken very quickly. As an android, he can repeat this sequence flawlessly. In the real world, however, even professional actors would have a hard time remembering private or public keys, which are often several hundred or even thousands of bytes long.

You can use Active Directory as a repository for X.509 certificates, so you can easily find someone's public key. You can store private keys on a hard drive, but most organizations that invest in a PKI system are not comfortable with the possibility that someone in possession of the hard drive and the user's password could compromise the key. Private keys are, therefore, usually stored on removable media, or better still, on a smart card.

Smart cards are much more common in Europe and Asia than in North America. In the United States and Canada, many of our bankcards have a magnetic stripe that can store information, such as an account number. In theory, a private key could be written to a magnetic stripe and read when necessary; however, that would mean that as the key is passed from card reader to computer, it could be intercepted or recorded.

A smart card is different. It provides nonvolatile memory that stores the owner's certificate and private key, as well as a small amount of computing power to perform the encryption and decryption requiring the private key on the card itself. The smart card is called smart because it contains a small CPU. The private key is never read off the card. For more details about the internal workings of smart cards, visit the Web sites of some of its major manufacturers, such as Datakey (*www.datakey.com*) or the Smart Card Alliance (*www. smartcardalliance.org*).

You can use smart cards and certificates to increase the security of the Windows-authentication process. Windows Server 2003 supports extensions to Kerberos that allow the authentication session to be changed slightly. Rather than employing the user's password (or any derivative of it) to encrypt the timestamp, the system uses the user's private key. The KDC then employs the public key of the user (stored with the user's certificate in the Active Directory database) to decrypt it.

9

However, because the user's private key is stored on the smart card, decryption can only occur if the card is present. Smart cards also require the user to enter a PIN to access the private key functions.

You can configure your domain to require smart cards for logons, you can make them optional, or require them for some users, but not others. Recently, Microsoft Corporation began requiring smart cards for logons for remote connections to its corporate network, a decision that affected thousands of employees. Implementing smart cards in a domain adds complexity and cost to your network, but increases security substantially.

NOTE   For more information on implementing smart cards, search for *smart cards* in Windows Server 2003 help and support.

ACTIVE DIRECTORY AUTHORIZATION

Once a user has been authenticated, the process of authorization is used to determine what actions a user can or cannot do. A discretionary access control list (DACL) is defined as "an access control list that is controlled by the owner of an object and that specifies the access that particular users or groups can have to the object." For a better understanding of how DACLs are used, the following sections cover DACLs and their behavior in more detail.

Discretionary Access Control List (DACL)

Most resources that can be secured have a **discretionary access control list (DACL)** associated with them. In the case of an Active Directory object, the DACL, along with the SACL and ownership information, is stored in a **security descriptor** attribute called ntSecurityDescriptor.

A DACL is a list of **access control entries (ACEs)** each of which specifies a "who" and a permission. For example, in the statement: "Human Resources staff can modify this object," an ACE grants access to the Human Resources staff (the "who") and specifies the appropriate permission ("modify") to change the object. The Human Resources group would be listed in the ACE not by name, but by SID.

When a member of the Human Resources staff tries to modify the object, Active Directory compares each SID in the user's access token to each ACE until a match is found. In this case, a match would be found on the ACE that gives permission to the group, and the user would be allowed to make the change.

If a user who is not a member of the Human Resources group tries to make the change, what would happen? First of all, assume that the user is not an administrator and has not been granted any special rights. His access token would contain a SID for himself, one for the Everyone group, and probably one for the domain Users group. A few other well-known SIDs would also be present, such as the authenticated users SID, and either the interactive or network SID. None of those special groups, however, have been given permissions to change this object. The end result? The system would compare each SID in the user's access token to each ACE and find no matches. Therefore, the user would be denied permission to make the change and would receive an error.

Each ACE can be very specific. An ACE can specify that a security principal is able to read but not change an object. Depending on the class of the object being protected by the DACL, there are various options for what can be included in an ACE. This is a very powerful feature of Windows Server 2003, as it allows control not only of who has access, but of the specific level of access for each user.

ACEs that Allow or Deny

When you edit a DACL, you notice that you can create ACEs that allow or deny access. It is very important to understand the effects of each type of ACE.

The first thing to remember is that if no match is found between an access token and a DACL, access is not permitted. This is sometimes called an "implicit deny," because the system automatically denies access, unless it has been explicitly told to allow access. Imagine a doorman at a fancy ball—if someone is not on his list, he or she isn't getting in.

Normally, most access control entries allow access. If you want to allow the Queen of England to come to your party, then you would add her name to the doorman's list. In technical terms, if you had a resource named "party" and the Queen tried to access that resource, the system would match a SID in her access token with the SID in the ACE, allowing her access.

You can also use ACEs to deny access to a resource. For example, if Billy is not welcome at the party, adding his name to the doorman's list with a big warning not to let him in would ensure he was kept out. The system would match Billy's SID (in his access token) with a SID in the ACE; however, this time, the match would say to deny his access to the resource.

You may wonder why this would be necessary. After all, if no ACE match is found, access is denied. The biggest reason that deny ACEs are used is to change the effect of permissions that a user would otherwise have as a member of a group.

The ability to deny access to a resource can save the administrator a great deal of time. For example, it is easier to grant access to groups of users than to grant it individually. (Remember that group SIDs are also included in the access token.) For example, our doorman's list might say, "admit all reigning monarchs," as opposed to listing them all individually. As a member of that group, the Queen of England's access token would have a SID to match the SID in the ACE, and she would be admitted. However, there may be a member of this group that you don't want to allow in, such as the Queen of Broken Hearts. By employing a deny ACE, her access token would also contain a SID that matches an ACE, but it would deny access instead of granting it.

Remember, a deny permission overrides all other permissions. Most users are members of several groups and match SIDs on several ACEs, allowing them the combined permissions of all their groups. If a user were a member of both group A and group B, he or she would receive the permissions given to both groups (that is, the superset), with two exceptions—deny overrides allow and owners can own. The following section looks at these exceptions more closely.

As an example of the deny overrides allow exception, suppose you were a member of both group A and group B. What would happen if group A is allowed access and group B is denied? Our doorman would know what to do—the deny always applies first.

 It is very important that you keep in mind that deny overrides everything else. For this reason, use denies sparingly.

CAUTION

As an example of the owners can own exception, consider what would happen if you removed all of the ACEs from an object's DACL, or you entered an ACE that denied access to the Everyone group. Is it possible to lock out everyone, including the administrators of Active Directory? Thankfully, no. Every object in the directory has an owner, as shown in Figure 9-12. The owner of an object can always gain access to that object by resetting its permissions. By default, the owner of most Active Directory objects is the Domain Admins Group. An administrator on a domain controller can also use the take ownership command to become the owner of an object in Active Directory. The owner of an object is always able to access and reset the object's permissions.

In Windows Server 2000 ownership was a one-way process—you could take ownership but never assign ownership. That is, any user who has the Take Ownership permission (which is included in the Full Control permission) on an object could make themselves the owner of the object. However, no other user—not even an administrator—could set the ownership of an object to a user other than themselves.

In Windows Server 2003 ownership has changed a little. A user can still take ownership of an object, as long as they have the Take Ownership permission on the object. New to Windows Server 2003, the owner of an object (and any users with the Take Ownership permission on the object) can now assign ownership of the object to a group of which they are a member. This means if a user named Bob is a member of the Sales and Marketing groups, Bob can assign ownership of objects he owns to the Sales or Marketing *group*. Note, however, that this does not mean he can assign ownership to another *member* of the Sales or Marketing group—just the group itself.

In addition to allowing any user to assign ownership to a group of which they are a member, users that have the Restore files and directories right (which include members of the Administrators, Backup Operators, and Server Operators groups by default) in Windows Server 2003 can assign ownership to any user or group (regardless if they are a member of the group).

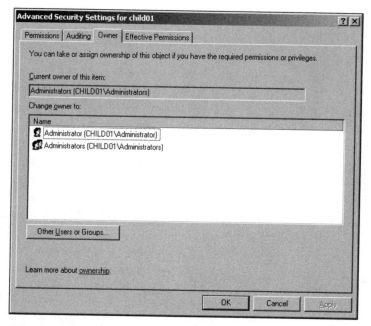

Figure 9-12   Owner of an object

Inheritance

Permissions can be applied directly to an object in the directory, or they can be inherited. If a directory contains thousands or millions of entries, it would be tedious and time consuming to apply permissions to each individual object. Instead, permissions can be inherited from parent objects, such as organizational units; this is referred to as **inheritance**.

In Active Directory, each ACE is marked to indicate whether it is directly applied or inherited. If a change is made to permissions on an organizational unit, all objects in that organizational unit are updated with the inherited permissions. You do have control over which permissions are inherited, allowing you to exempt child objects from being assigned the same permissions as their parents. To help administrators see which permissions apply, the Active Directory Users and Computers console includes a tab to display the effective permissions on a given object. In Activity 9-5, you will learn how to view effective permissions on a given object.

Groups in Security

A Windows Server 2003 security group is a container object that is used to organize a collection of users, computers, or other groups into a single security principal. You would use a group object to simplify administration by assigning rights and permissions to a group rather than to individual users. Groups sound similar to organizational units in that both organize other objects into logical containers. The main differences between an organizational unit and a group are as follows:

- Organizational units are not security principals and as such cannot be used to define permissions on resources or be assigned rights. Active Directory security groups are security principals that can be assigned both permissions and rights.

- Organizational units can only contain objects from their own domain. Some groups can contain objects from any domain within the forest.

There is no good reason to grant rights and permissions explicitly to individual users. In a large domain, it is nearly impossible to manage, and in a small domain, it is a bad habit that usually indicates poor planning in the control of access to resources. In addition to saving administrators from unmanageable headaches, remember that all permissions need an ACE. A DACL consisting of 500 individually granted permissions would be much larger, and take much longer to process. In the next chapter, you will look at groups and how to create a group strategy in more detail.

Delegation of Control

Delegation of control is all about giving data owners the ability to manage their own objects. As discussed in Chapter 3, a service owner is responsible for the operation of the directory service, but a data owner is responsible for its content. Giving data owners the ability to modify only certain objects, or only certain attributes, is called delegation of control.

An administrator can delegate control manually, but the easiest, most effective way involves two steps:

- First, organize the directory so that all objects in an organizational unit have the same data owner.

- Second, use the Delegation of Control Wizard to create the appropriate ACEs in the DACL on the organizational unit, and then allow them to be inherited to the objects in the organizational unit. In Activity 9-4, you will learn how to use the Delegation of Control Wizard.

There is no way to automatically undo the effects of the Delegation of Control Wizard, so document any changes you make. To undo changes made by the wizard, an administrator must manually edit security settings. You can manually edit security settings without the wizard, as described in the next section.

Activity 9-4: Using the Delegation of Control Wizard

Time Required: 5 minutes

Objective: Set the permissions on an organizational unit using the Delegation of Control Wizard.

Description: By default, Active Directory allows non-administrators to only see a limited subset of a user's account properties. When troubleshooting security settings, several of Super Corp's server operators have expressed frustration that they cannot view the groups of which a user is a member. To remedy this issue, you have been asked to use the Delegation of Control Wizard and grant members of the Server Operators group the necessary access to view all user account properties.

1. If necessary, start your server and log on using the **Administrator** account in the **CHILD*XX*** domain (where *XX* is the number of the forest root domain for which your server is a domain controller) using the password **Password01**.

2. Click **Start**, select **Administrative Tools**, and then click **Active Directory Users and Computers**.

3. If necessary, in the left tree pane, expand the **child*XX*.supercorp.net** node (where *XX* is the number of the forest root domain for which your server is a domain controller).

4. In the left tree pane, right-click the **North America *XX*** organizational unit (where *XX* is the number of your server), and then click **Delegate Control**.

5. When the Welcome dialog box appears, click **Next**.

6. Click **Add** on the Users or Groups dialog box.

7. If you know the name of the user or group to which you want to delegate control, you can simply type the names in the text box provided and click OK. However, because you do not know the exact name, click the **Advanced** button to search for the user or group.

8. In the Name text box type **Server** and then ensure the **Starts with** option is selected.

9

9. Click **Find Now**. A list of users and groups matching your search criteria will be displayed, as shown in Figure 9-13.

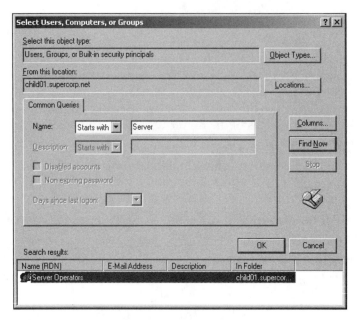

Figure 9-13   Searching for a user or group

 TIP   If you want to see all the users and groups, you can simply click the Find Now button while leaving all the search criteria (such as Name) blank. Note that you can also use the Locations button to search for users or groups from another trusted domain. You can also use the Locations button to specify a specific organizational unit within a domain, rather then searching the entire domain.

10. In the Search results list box, select **Server Operators** and then click **OK**.

11. Click **OK** again to add the user or group.

12. Click **Next**.

13. On the Tasks to Delegate dialog box, check the box next to **Read all user information**, as shown in Figure 9-14.

 NOTE   Notice that you can also use the Delegation of Control Wizard to delegate custom tasks—not just the ones that are predefined. Using custom tasks is similar (in terminology) to assigning permissions directly to an object's DACL from the security tab, which you will learn about in Activity 9-6.

14. Click **Next**.

15. Click **Finish**.

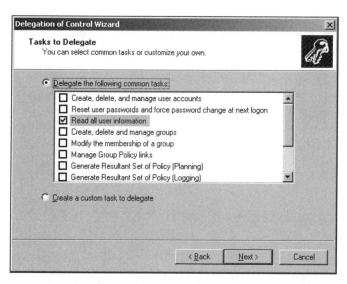

Figure 9-14   Selecting tasks to delegate

16. Log off your server if you do not intend to immediately continue to the next activity. Otherwise, stay logged on.

Granular Control

Way back when dinosaurs roamed the earth and Windows NT was new, delegation was largely an all-or-nothing proposition. You either were a Domain Admin or you weren't. Administrators were all-powerful and everyone else wasn't. It was nearly impossible to separate data ownership from service ownership in the directory without spending a lot of time or money on custom software or third-party solutions.

With Active Directory however, you can delegate control with precision. Normally, a data owner is given fairly broad permissions over objects contained in an organizational unit. Although, it is possible to be more exact when the situation warrants. Each ACE created on an Active Directory object offers choices for how it is applied:

- Should it apply to all objects or just certain types of objects?

- Should it apply to this container, objects in this container, objects in child containers below this container, or some combination of these?

- Should it apply to all attributes, or just certain attributes?

- To whom are you giving, or from whom are you denying, the permission?

Whenever you change permissions, either manually or by using the Delegation of Control Wizard, you should carefully record or document the changes and the reasons for them.

TIP

This ability to granularly control exactly who can do what is an important part of the flexibility of Active Directory. The Advanced Security Settings dialog box in the Active Directory Users and Computers console features a tab to display effective permissions for any user or group, as shown in Figure 9-16, as well as a command button to reset the DACL to its default state on the Permissions tab. In Activity 9-5, you will use the Effective Permissions tab to view the permissions granted to users on an Active Directory Object.

Activity 9-5: Viewing Effective Permissions on an Active Directory Object

ACTIVITY

Time Required: 5 minutes

Objective: View the effective permissions on an object in the directory.

Description: Because of the complex combinations of group memberships, inheritance, and standard and special permissions, it can be difficult to calculate what the effective permissions on an object are for a given user. In this activity, you will use the Active Directory Users and Computers console to display effective permissions.

1. If necessary, start your server and log on using the **Administrator** account in the **CHILDXX** domain (where *XX* is the number of the forest root domain for which your server is a domain controller) using the password **Password01**.

2. Click **Start**, select **Administrative Tools**, and then click **Active Directory Users and Computers**.

3. On the View menu, enable **Advanced Features** if necessary. Note that a check mark appears next to the Advanced Features menu item if advanced features are enabled.

4. If necessary, in the left tree pane, expand the **childXX.supercorp.net** node (where *XX* is the number of the forest root domain for which your server is a domain controller).

5. In the left tree pane, right-click the **North America XX** organizational unit (where *XX* is the number of your server), and then click **Properties**.

6. Click the **Security** tab.

7. Click **Advanced**.

8. Click the **Effective Permissions** tab.

9. Click **Select**.

10. Type **Administrator**, as shown in Figure 9-15. Note that you can enter multiple users and/or groups at once by separating each user or group with a semicolon (;).

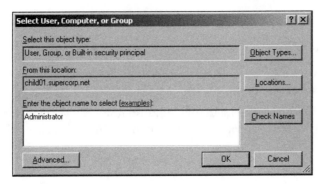

Figure 9-15   Selecting a user or group

11. Click **OK**. If prompted that multiple names were found, select **Administrator**, and then click **OK**.

12. The Effective Permissions tab is updated to show the permissions the Administrator user has on the North America *XX* organizational unit, as shown in Figure 9-16.

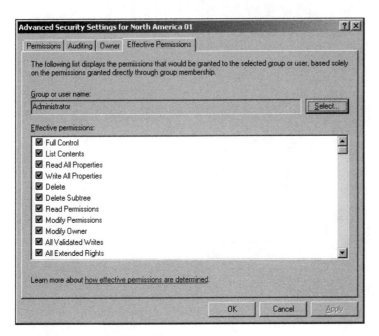

Figure 9-16   Viewing effective permissions on an object

13. Repeat Steps 9 and 10, except this time use the Authenticated Users group instead of the Administrator user account.

14. Click **OK**.

15. Click **OK**.

16. Close Active Directory Users and Computers.

17. Log off your server if you do not intend to immediately continue to the next activity. Otherwise, stay logged on.

To make management of permissions easier for administrators, Active Directory offers standard and special permissions. In Activity 9-6, you will use standard and special permissions to grant access to an organizational unit.

Standard Permissions

Standard permissions are those permissions that are used for everyday tasks, and are found on the main Security tab of an object, as shown in Figure 9-17. For example, you'd use the full control permission to grant or deny all possible permissions on an object.

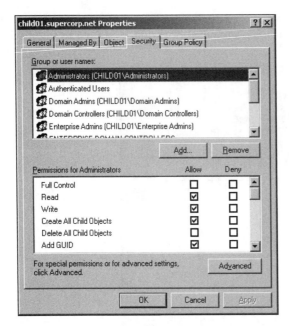

Figure 9-17   Standard permissions

Special Permissions

Special permissions represent the exact and granular permissions available, and can be very specific. To access them, click the Advanced button on the Security tab to open the Advanced Security Settings dialog box. This dialog box is shown in Figure 9-18. Most tasks require only the standard permissions; use special permissions for advanced granular control or special situations.

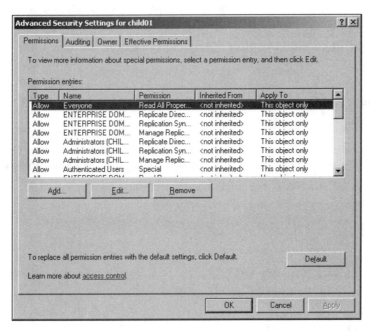

Figure 9-18   Special permissions

Activity 9-6: Modifying an Active Directory Object's DACL

Time Required: 10 minutes

Objective: Change the DACL protecting an Active Directory object.

Description: Super Corp has decided to allow its more advanced users to add contacts to a designated organizational unit using a custom application. Additionally, the creator of an object should be able to update and delete their objects as needed. Using special permissions you will allow all domain users to create contact objects. You will then use standard permissions to allow the creator owner of an object to modify their own objects—including contacts.

Contact objects are used to store information about a person in Active Directory who does not need security access to the network. While a user account has a SID, contact objects do not have SIDs and therefore cannot be granted access to resources on the network.

1. If necessary, start your server and log on using the **Administrator** account in the **CHILDXX** domain (where *XX* is the number of the forest root domain for which your server is a domain controller) using the password **Password01**.

2. Click **Start**, select **Administrative Tools**, and then click **Active Directory Users and Computers**.

3. If necessary, in the left tree pane, expand the **childXX.supercorp.net** node (where *XX* is the number of the forest root domain for which your server is a domain controller).

4. In the left tree pane, expand the **North America XX** organizational unit (where *XX* is the number of your server).

5. Under North America *XX* (where *XX* is the number of your server), right-click the **Atlanta** organizational unit, select **New**, and then click **Organizational Unit**.

6. In the Name text box, enter **Contacts**, and then click **OK**.

7. In the left tree pane, expand the **Atlanta** organizational unit if necessary. Right-click the **Contacts** organizational unit you have just created, and then click **Properties**.

8. Click the **Security** tab. Note that if the Security tab does not appear, you need to enable the Advanced Features on the View menu.

9. Click **Advanced**.

10. On the Permissions tab, click **Add**.

11. Enter **Domain Users** and click **OK**. All users of a domain are automatically added to the Domain user group when they are created.

12. In the Permissions list box, locate Create Contact Objects and add a check mark in the Allow column, as shown in Figure 9-19.

 Both an Object and a Properties tab are available. This allows you to not only set permissions at the object level, but also at the property (a.k.a. attribute) level.

NOTE

13. Ensure that the Apply onto drop-down list box is set to **This object and all child objects**, and then click **OK**.

14. Click **OK** to close the advanced security settings.

15. On the Security tab, click **Add**.

16. Enter **CREATOR OWNER** and then click **OK**. CREATOR OWNER is a special well-known SID that represents the creator or current owner of the object or resource.

17. With **CREATOR OWNER** selected in the Group or user names list box, place a check mark next to Write and Delete All Child Objects (Read should also be selected by default), as shown in Figure 9-20. This allows the owner of the object to write attributes on the objects he or she creates as well as delete any objects they create.

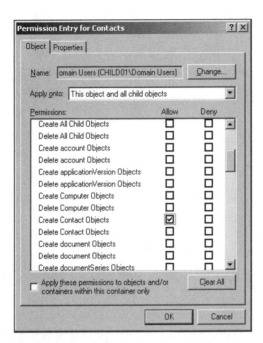

Figure 9-19   Setting special permissions

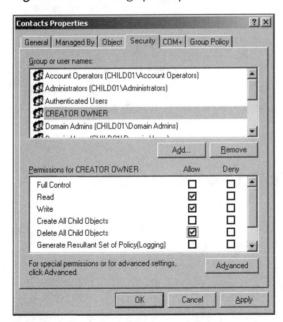

Figure 9-20   Setting standard permissions

18. Click **OK**.

19. Close Active Directory Users and Computers.

20. Log off your server if you do not intend to immediately continue to the next activity. Otherwise, stay logged on.

ACTIVE DIRECTORY AUDITING

In addition to a DACL, all objects in active directory also have a system access control list (SACL), which is used for auditing object access. A SACL is defined as "an access control list that controls the generation of audit messages for attempts to access a securable object." Because the way SACLs behave is very similar to DACLs, the following section gives a brief description of SACLs and then jumps right into an example. The section then looks at the different types of auditing event categories that can be enabled for a system.

System Access Control List (SACL)

A **system access control list (SACL)** has the same basic structure as a DACL and they are both very similar. However, instead of determining whether the SID is granted access to the resource, a SACL determines if the access is audited. Because all users have the Everyone SID in their access token, including it in an ACE for a SACL allows an administrator to turn on auditing for everyone accessing the object or resource in question. By carefully choosing your SACL entries, you can control the level of auditing in your environment. In Activity 9-7, you will set up auditing on the organizational unit you just created.

 NOTE Auditing slows down a computer because the system must record events that occur. You must be careful to not set up unnecessary auditing that only slows the system down.

 ACTIVITY

Activity 9-7: Auditing Object Access

Time Required: 10 minutes

Objective: Create a SACL on an Active Directory object so that access to the object can be monitored. Part of this activity requires you to work with a partner.

Description: In this activity, you will create a SACL on the organizational unit you just created that will instruct the operating system to record all types of access to the organizational unit or its child objects to monitor who is accessing it. This is a useful skill, because as a network administrator, you will need to activate auditing on your servers to monitor access and watch for intrusion attempts.

NOTE Because you are changing a security policy that affects all domain controllers, work with your partner and perform the first part of this activity from one of the two domain controllers of your domain.

1. If necessary, start your server and log on using the **Administrator** account in the **CHILDXX** domain (where *XX* is the number of the forest root domain for which your server is a domain controller) using the password **Password01**.

2. In order for SACLs you set on individual Active Directory objects to take effect, you must ensure directory service access auditing is enabled. To check the status of directory service access auditing for just the domain controllers, start by clicking **Start**, select **Administrative Tools**, and then click **Domain Controller Security Policy**.

TIP By default in Windows Server 2003, auditing is enabled for successful directory service access events. However, directory service access events that fail are not logged by default. Even if you set up SACLs, if the appropriate auditing event category is not enabled, the events are not logged.

3. In the left tree pane, expand the following nodes: **Security Settings** and **Local Policies**.

4. In the left tree pane, click **Audit Policy**.

5. In the right details pane, double-click **Audit directory service access**.

6. If necessary, add a check mark next to **Success** in order to audit successful use of permissions, as shown in Figure 9-21.

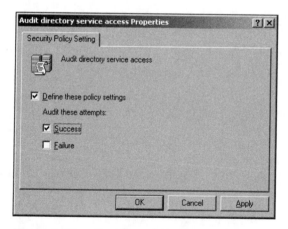

Figure 9-21   Enabling object access for successful events

7. Click **OK**.

8. Close the domain controllers' security policy. You have now enabled directory service access auditing on domain controllers (note that the domain controllers security policy actually applies to the Domain Controllers organizational unit). Both partners may now complete the rest of the steps in this activity individually.

NOTE

It may take several minutes for the domain controller's security policy to replicate to the second domain controller and then refresh. You can manually initiate replication using Active Directory Sites and Services if you wish. After replication has completed, run the GPUPDATE command from a command prompt to manually refresh your domain controller's security policy.

9. Click **Start**, select **Administrative Tools**, and then click **Active Directory Users and Computers**.

10. If necessary, in the left tree pane, expand the **childXX.supercorp.net** node (where *XX* is the number of the forest root domain for which your server is a domain controller).

11. In the left tree pane, expand the **North America XX** organizational unit (where *XX* is the number of your server) and then expand **Atlanta**.

12. Right-click the **Contacts** organizational unit and then click **Properties**.

13. Click the **Security** Tab.

14. Click **Advanced**.

15. Click the **Auditing** tab.

16. Click **Add**.

17. Type **Everyone** and then click **OK**.

18. In the Access list box, check **Full Control** in the Successful column. This checks all other successful events, as shown in Figure 9-22.

NOTE

Note that both an Object and a Properties tab are available. This allows you to not only audit events on an object, but events on individual properties (a.k.a. attributes).

19. Ensure that the Apply onto drop-down list box is set to **This object and all child objects**, and then click **OK**.

20. Click **OK** to close the advanced security settings.

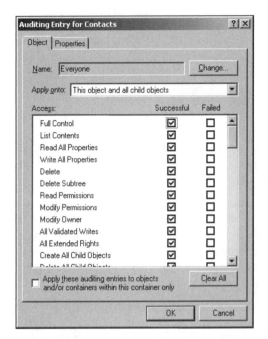

Figure 9-22   Selecting specific operations to audit on an organizational unit

21. Click **OK** to close the Contacts organizational unit's properties. You have now enabled auditing on the Contacts organizational unit. All successful operations to the Contacts organizational unit or its children are logged in the Security log. You can access the Security log by using the Event Viewer, which is available under Administrative Tools on the Start menu.

22. Close Active Directory Users and Computers.

23. Log off your server.

Auditing Event Categories

In addition to auditing directory service access, there are also a number of events that occur on a system that can be audited. The following is a list of different auditing event categories and their descriptions:

- Audit account logon events—Logon events are generated when a user logs on to a computer and this computer (the computer where auditing is enabled) performs the authentication. For example, when a user logs on to a domain workstation using a domain account, an account logon event is generated in the domain controller's security log. The event is logged at the domain controller that performed the authentication and not at the workstation, because the workstation did not actually perform the authentication.

- Audit account management—Account management events are generated when account or group modifications are made on a system. Examples of modifications that are logged include:
  - Creating, changing, or deleting user accounts or groups
  - Renaming, disabling, or enabling user accounts
  - Changing or resetting account passwords
- Audit directory service access—Determines if events that occur when users access objects in Active Directory should be logged. The exact events that are recorded are based on the SACL set on the Active Directory objects.
- Audit logon events—Logon events are generated when a user logs on to the computer. For example, when a user logs on to a workstation using a local account, a logon event is recorded. When a user logs on to a workstation using a domain account, a logon event is recorded. Note that if a user logs on to a domain controller, both an account logon and a logon event are recorded. Also note that logon events include both interactive logons and network logons.
- Audit object access—Determines if events that occur when users access objects (such as files and folders on NTFS drives, printers, or registry keys) should be logged. The exact events that are recorded are based on the SACL set on the objects.
- Audit policy change—Determines if changes to the user rights assignment policies, audit policies, or trust policies should be logged.
- Audit privilege use—Determines if use of a user right should be logged.
- Audit process tracking—Determines if events such as program activation, process exit, handle duplication, and indirect object access should be logged. These events are often used by programmers when debugging complex applications.
- Audit system events—Determines if events relating to the system should be logged. System events include when the system is restarted or shut down, when the security log settings are modified, or events that affect the system's security.

TIP

For more details on the different audit policies, search for Audit policy in Windows Server 2003 Help and Support. Chapter 11 also covers how to set audit policies using Group Policy in more detail.

Each of these auditing event categories can be used to log both Success and Failure events. Success events are recorded when the event completed successfully—when a user was authenticated correctly, for example. Failure events are recorded when the event did not complete successfully—when a user was denied permission to log on due to a bad password, for example. A common use of success events is to determine if someone has access to something they *should not* have. Success events can also be used for capacity planning. In contrast, failure events can be used to determine if someone is attempting to gain access to something to which they *do not* have access. For example, you can audit failed account logon events to determine if someone is trying to guess a password over and over. If you notice thousands of failed account logon events related to the same user account, that's a good sign someone is using a password generator to try passwords one after another automatically.

PROTECTING NETWORK RESOURCES

Protecting objects in Active Directory is essential. However, there are a number of other resources on the network that also rely on Active Directory for security. Most protected resources use a DACL that is similar in format to the one found on Active Directory objects. In the next few sections, you will look at NTFS, printers, shares, and registry keys. Some other related applications will be discussed, such as SQL Server, which use their own ACL systems for authorization but use Active Directory for authentication.

9

TIP

Most components of the operating system use the same security descriptor and DACL structure. This means that by learning one interface, you can use the same technique with files, shares, printers, and Active Directory objects.

NT File System (NTFS)

Windows Server 2003 servers support the **NT File System (NTFS)**. While it is possible to use disks formatted with the **simpler File Allocation Table (FAT)** format, it is not recommended. NTFS is much more robust than FAT, because it uses a journaling or logging system to keep track of changes to a file, so fewer problems occur if the system crashes or loses power during an update. NTFS also assigns a security descriptor to each object, in a similar way that Active Directory has security descriptors for Active Directory objects. The structure of the security descriptors on files and folders is the same as those found on Active Directory objects: Each object in the file system has an owner, a DACL, and a SACL. The DACL and SACL are both composed of a series of ACEs containing SIDs and permissions. The Security tab that is present on all Active Directory objects is also present on files and folders on an NTFS partition. This is an important point because if you format your file system with FAT, you cannot use DACLs and SACLs to control access or audit these resources.

TIP

You must enable object access auditing in order to log events using NTFS SACLs.

The difference between an NTFS DACL and an Active Directory DACL is in the types of permissions that you can grant or deny. Rather than permissions that relate to attributes, the NTFS DACL permissions relate to what the users can do with the files and folders. There are also fewer permissions for files, folders, shares, and printers than there are for Active Directory objects. The standard permissions for a file are shown in Figure 9-23, and consist of full control, modify (the ability to change the file or its properties), read and execute, read, and write. In addition to those previously listed for files, a folder also has the standard permission called list folder contents. The standard folder permissions are shown in Figure 9-24.

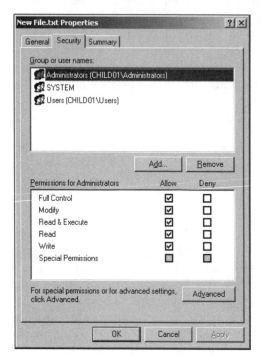

Figure 9-23   Standard file permissions

NTFS also supports a number of special permissions, as shown in Figure 9-25.

The authentication process is where Active Directory plays its biggest role in NTFS security. At logon, the access token is populated to include the user's SID and SIDs from the user's group memberships. When the user accesses a file, the SIDs in the file's DACL are compared to the SIDs in the user's access token in search of a match, just like accessing an Active Directory object. The same rules for allowing and denying access apply.

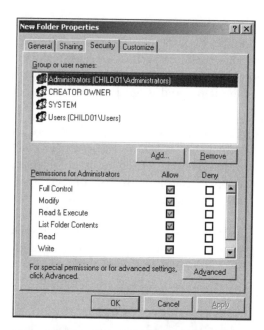

Figure 9-24 Standard folder permissions

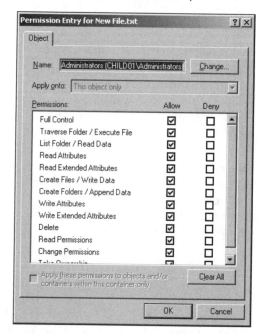

Figure 9-25 NTFS special permissions

NTFS permissions can also be inherited. For instance, folders and files inside a folder usually inherit the permissions set on the parent folder. For example, if C:\Folder1 has a DACL that includes read permissions for the Users group, then that permission is normally inherited to C:\Folder1\Folder2. You can add additional permissions to just Folder2 (by adding ACEs to the Folder2 DACL), and/or prevent the inheritance and assign a new DACL to Folder2 that does not contain the inherited ACEs.

Note that the default NTFS permissions set on the root of a hard drive have changed in Windows Server 2003. In Windows 2000, the Everyone group was given full control to the root of each drive. Additionally, the permissions were inherited by all subfolders and files by default. In Windows Server 2003, the default permissions on the root of each drive are much more secure. The Everyone group now only has read and execute access to the root of each drive—but this is not inherited by files or subfolders by default. This means that the Everyone group can see the drive, but they cannot see any files or inside any subfolders on the drive. Instead of giving the Everyone group access, the Users group has been given access instead. By default, the Users group has read and execute access to files and folders on the root of a drive, the ability to create folders on the root of a drive, and the ability to create files in subfolders. The CREATOR OWNER group is given full control on any files or subfolders they create. Finally, the Administrators group and SYSTEM are given full control. Note that in the next chapter the different default groups are covered in much more detail.

Printers

In Windows Server 2003, a printer also has a security descriptor with an owner, a DACL, and a SACL. The standard permissions allow you to choose who can print to a printer, who can change printer settings, and who can manage documents. These standard printer permissions are shown in Figure 9-26. Note the use of the special well-known security principal CREATOR OWNER, which allows users to manage their own documents without being able to manage other user's documents.

 NOTE Do not confuse the DACL on the printer with the DACL on the Active Directory printer object that may exist for a shared printer. The DACL on the printer controls who can print, while the DACL on the Active Directory object controls who can search for the printer in Active Directory, and who can change the Active Directory printer object. You will learn how to create Active Directory printer objects in the next chapter.

File Shares

When accessing files from a network share, the user must first be allowed access to the share, and then access to the file (if it is on an NTFS formatted volume). Share permissions control access via the network. To access the share permissions, click Permissions on the Sharing tab of the folder's property sheet, as shown in Figure 9-27.

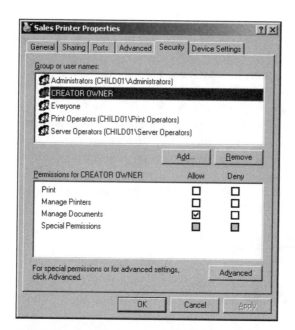

Figure 9-26   Standard permissions for a printer

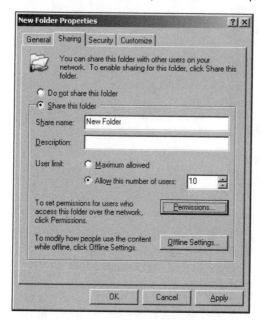

Figure 9-27   Accessing share permissions

Share permissions have very few choices; they are not as granular as either Active Directory permissions or NTFS permissions. With standard permissions, you can allow or deny full control, change, or read access, as shown in Figure 9-28. There are no special permissions for file shares. In situations where more flexibility is needed, ensure that the actual folder is on a hard disk partition formatted with NTFS, and then use NTFS permissions to further restrict access to the folder. Remember, both the NTFS DACL and the share DACL are combined to control access for users who are connecting via the share. This means that if one of the permissions is more restrictive than the other, then the more restrictive permission is in effect. For example, if a user has NTFS write permissions and only read share permissions, the user is only allowed read access when accessing the share. Conversely, if a user has write share permissions and only read NTFS permissions, the user is still only allowed read access when accessing the share.

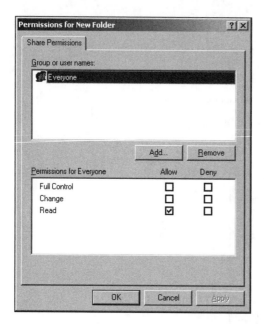

Figure 9-28   Share permissions

As with printers, do not confuse the DACL on the share with the DACL on the Active Directory shared folder object that may exist for a shared folder. The DACL on the share itself controls who can access files through that share. The DACL on the Active Directory object controls who can search for the shared folder in Active Directory and who can manage the Active Directory object. You will learn how to create Active Directory shared folder objects in the next chapter.

NOTE   The default share permissions have changed in Windows Server 2003. While in Windows 2000, the Everyone group was given the full control share permission by default, the Everyone group is only given read permission in Windows Server 2003.

Registry Keys

To store configuration settings about the computer, Windows operating systems use a hierarchical database called the registry. The registry is divided into **registry hives**, each of which store a particular group of settings. The two most important hives are HKEY_LOCAL_MACHINE (or HKLM) for system-wide configuration settings, and HKEY_CURRENT_USER (or HKCU) for user-specific settings. Many applications also store settings in the registry.

Within each hive, there is a set of **registry keys**. A registry key can contain more registry keys, values, or both. The logical layout of a registry key is similar to the nesting structure of organizational units and folders. As an example, Figure 9-29 shows the registry keys that keep track of a user's printer settings. The tool you use to edit the registry is called Registry Editor (regedit.exe) and has been updated to include security-related functionality. In older versions of regedit, you could not make security changes and had to use another program called regedt32.exe. In Windows Server 2003, running either regedit.exe or regedt32.exe now starts the same application.

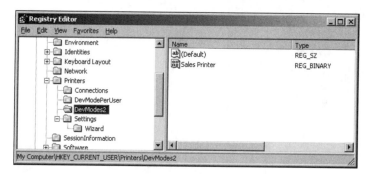

Figure 9-29   Registry Editor, showing key related to printer settings

Values stored in the registry control how the computer system operates. Registry values can enable or disable functionality. There may be times when you won't want users or programs to be able to change certain values in the registry. For example, nonadministrative users can change fewer settings than users who are administrators.

To allow for the control of access to the registry, each registry key has the typical Windows 2003 security descriptor with a SACL, a DACL, and a specified owner. Figure 9-30 shows the standard permissions that you can set on a registry key. Figure 9-31 shows the special permissions.

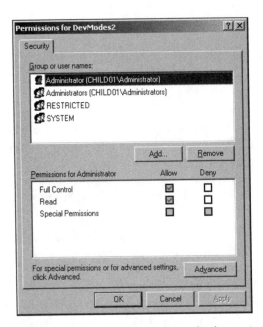

Figure 9-30 Registry key standard permissions

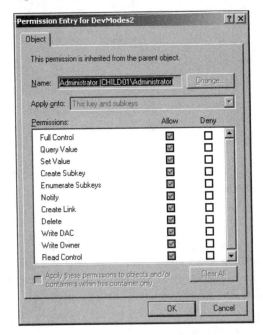

Figure 9-31 Registry key special permissions

Setting registry key permissions incorrectly or changing registry values can render your computer inoperable.

Other Applications

In Chapter 1, you learned that applications are becoming more Active Directory-aware and are starting to use Active Directory to control access to the application. There are several approaches in use, ranging from a tightly integrated application such as Exchange Server 2000/2003 that stores data in Active Directory, to loosely integrated applications that use just NTFS security. Which approach is used usually depends on whether the application is using Active Directory for authentication, authorization, both, or neither.

As described in Chapter 1 and this chapter, authentication is the process of identifying and proving who you are. This is usually performed with a username and password. Authorization occurs when the system determines whether you are allowed access to a specific resource—you don't have to authenticate again; the system already knows who you are. The system does, however, need to verify your access permissions to the resource.

Many applications do not perform any authentication or authorization. For example, anyone can run Notepad. Notepad has no security awareness. However, even within this category, most applications can be given a certain amount of access control by setting NTFS permissions on their executable files or directory. If you were to create a DACL on the notepad.exe file that only permitted administrators to read it, you would, in effect, prevent nonadministrators from using Notepad.

It is still possible to run another copy of the notepad.exe application if another copy of the program is accessible from a different location. Restricting access to an application's executable file only stops access to that particular executable copy—not all copies.

Some applications perform authentication and authorization internally. You can recognize these applications when they prompt you for a username and password after you have already logged on to the domain. These applications can also gain added protection using NTFS permissions.

More sophisticated applications often use Active Directory for authentication, but provide their own authorization. Microsoft SQL Server is a good example. When connecting to a SQL Server, a user provides his or her access token, just like accessing a shared folder over a trusted connection. SQL Server is aware that the user has been authenticated, and can see who the user is by examining his or her name and SID.

Microsoft SQL Server maintains its own access control lists internally, which are different in format from a security descriptor used by most other Windows components. SQL Server provides its own authorization mechanisms, but can rely on the operating system and Active Directory for authentication.

Microsoft Exchange Server 2000/2003 is a complex and full-featured e-mail and group collaboration server. Unlike earlier versions of Exchange, Exchange 2000/2003 relies on Active Directory to be the directory for e-mail. Exchange 2000/2003 extends the Active Directory schema, adding several new classes and attributes. By setting DACLs on the objects it uses (including users that have mailboxes), Exchange 2000/2003 uses Active Directory not only for authenticating users, but also for authorizing access to mailboxes and other Exchange resources.

CHAPTER SUMMARY

- ❏ Security principals are special because they have a SID. SIDs work with ACEs in DACLs to control access to resources or objects and with ACEs in SACLs to control auditing of resource use.

- ❏ Permissions are rules associated with an object that define which users can gain access to the object and what actions they can perform on the object. Rights, on the other hand, define what tasks or operations a user can perform on a computer system or domain (that is, they are not specific to one object).

- ❏ Security principals can be granted specific permissions to access resources or objects. There are standard permissions for common applications and special permissions for advanced purposes.

- ❏ DACLs are a list of ACEs used to define permission. Each ACE specifies a SID and the type of permission being granted or denied. The system compares each SID in a user's access token to the SID in each ACE. If a match is found, the defined action (allow or deny) is taken. If no match is found, the user is denied access.

- ❏ SACLs are a list of ACEs used to define auditing. Each ACE specifies a SID and the type of permission being audited.

- ❏ Delegation of control refers to assigning permissions on Active Directory objects so that data owners can manage their own objects. The Delegation of Control Wizard assists with setting permissions for common tasks.

- ❏ Permissions in Active Directory can be inherited from a parent level to a child level for simpler administration.

- ❏ The two primary user authentication methods in a Windows Server 2003 network are NTLM and Kerberos. Two-factor and biometric authentication is available, but they add complexity and cost to your network. Most two-factor or biometric solutions are third-party add-ons for Active Directory and Windows.

❑ Active Directory supports smart cards and X.509 certificates with extensions to the Kerberos protocol, enabling asymmetric encryption during the exchange.

❑ Other applications may use Active Directory for authentication, authorization, both, or neither. Even applications that do not use Active Directory for authentication can still be made more secure by protecting their data files with NTFS permissions.

KEY TERMS

access control entry (ACE) — An entry in a DACL or SACL that lists a security principal (by SID), a type of action (such as read or write), and whether that SID is allowed or denied the action (or if it should be audited in the case of a SACL).

access token — A binary structure that lists the identity, rights, and group membership of a user on the network. An access token contains, among other items, the user's SID and the SID of each group to which the user belongs.

delegation of control — Refers to assigning permissions on Active Directory objects so that data owners can manage their own objects. The Delegation of Control Wizard assists with setting permissions for common tasks.

discretionary access control list (DACL) — A list of ACEs used to control access to an object or resource.

domain identifier — Three 32-bit numbers that are statistically unique and identify a particular domain.

down-level clients — A computer running an operating system that is not Active Directory-aware or Kerberos-capable, such as Windows 3.*x*, Windows 95/98, Windows ME, or Windows NT.

File Allocation Table (FAT) — An older file format used by down-level clients and DOS. FAT disks do not support file-based permissions, auditing, or journaling.

inheritance — The concept that a security setting on one object can be inherited by objects lower (that is, deeper) in the hierarchy. Examples include folders inheriting settings from parent folders, or OUs inheriting settings from parent OUs.

Kerberos — An authentication protocol first developed at MIT to allow for a wide-area, distributed method of securely authenticating users before they are allowed to access network resources.

Key Distribution Center (KDC) — A network service that is made up of an Authentication Service and Ticket-granting Service. The Authentication Service authenticates users and issues TGTs. The Ticket-granting Service issues session tickets for access to network resources. All domain controllers in Active Directory are KDCs by default.

NT File System (NTFS) — Known almost exclusively by its initials, NTFS is the robust file system used by Windows NT, Windows 2000, Windows XP, and Windows Server 2003. NTFS supports the ability to control and audit access, and uses a journaling system to minimize corruption.

9

NT LAN Manager (NTLM) — More commonly known by its initials, NTLM is the older network authentication protocol used by all Windows systems prior to Windows 2000. It is still used with Windows 2000, Windows XP, and Windows Server 2003 in certain circumstances.

objectSID — The Active Directory attribute that stores a security principal's security identifier (SID).

private/public key pair — A set of two mathematically related keys used in public key cryptography (or asymmetric encryption). If a message is encrypted with one key, it can only be decrypted with the other. The public key is widely distributed; the private key is closely guarded.

Public Key Infrastructure (PKI) — An organized system that issues and manages certificates and key pairs to support the use of public key cryptography in an organization.

registry hives — Major sections of the Windows registry that contain a set of related registry keys.

registry keys — One or more related settings stored in the Windows registry. A key is similar to a folder in the file system; it can contain other keys or values.

Relative Identifier (RID) — A 32-bit number, unique within the domain, that makes up part of a security principal's SID.

security descriptor — A package of binary information associated with an object or a resource, which contains the DACL, SACL, object owner, and related security information. For Active Directory objects, the security descriptor is an attribute of all objects and is called ntSecurityDescriptor.

Security Descriptor Definition Language (SDDL) — A format that efficiently describes SIDs. SDDL is both reasonably compact and easily read by humans.

Security Identifier (SID) — A binary number that uniquely represents a security principal. For most security principals, the two key components are a domain identifier and a RID that are unique within the domain.

security principals — An object in the directory to which resource permissions can be granted. In Active Directory, security principals are user objects (including inetOrgPerson objects), computer objects, and security group objects.

service ticket (ST) — A Kerberos ticket presented to a resource server allowing it to authenticate the user.

special permissions — A specific, granular permission available from the Advanced dialog box when setting permissions.

standard permissions — Permissions shown on the main Security tab in an object's properties that represent the most common permissions granted to users. A standard permission represents several related special permissions.

system access control list (SACL) — A list of ACEs used to determine which actions are audited or logged for a particular object or resource.

symmetric keys — Encryption keys that can be used to encrypt or decrypt a message. The same key is used for both encryption and decryption.

ticket-granting ticket (TGT) — A Kerberos ticket used to request service tickets from a KDC.

two-factor authentication — Authentication systems that require possession of a physical object (or present a biometric identification) and a password or PIN.

X.509 digital certificate — A specially structured electronic document that describes the identity of a person or service. The certificate is digitally signed by its issuer.

REVIEW QUESTIONS

1. All objects in Active Directory have an objectSID attribute to control who can modify that object. True or False?

2. A _____ access control list controls auditing of an object.

3. The share \\SERVER\Download is a security principal. True or false?

4. Access to a resource is granted by which of the following?

    a. comparing the user's SID to the SAM database on the DC

    b. comparing the user's SID to the DACL on the resource

    c. comparing the user's password against the resource password

    d. comparing the user's access token to the SACL

5. A SACL controls which of the following?

    a. auditing on a resource

    b. system account passwords

    c. services configured to run as a user

    d. access to a resource

6. Every time a user requires access to a resource, the user's computer must send a request to the KDC. True or False?

7. When a user first logs on, his or her workstation sends which of the following to the KDC?

    a. A timestamp

    b. A service ticket

    c. A password

    d. A private key

8. You can recognize a security principal in Active Directory because it has the _____ attribute.

9. SIDs are usually displayed to humans in the _____ format.

9

10. All security administrators should recognize the SID S-1-1-0 because it represents which of the following?

    a. Domain Admins

    b. Everyone

    c. Nobody (that is, no matching user could be found)

    d. BUILTIN\Administrators

11. Assume that a user with the username mydomain\jsmith has a SID of S-1-5-21-1993962763-287218729-725645543-1642. The _____ part of the SID represents his or her domain, and the _____ part of the SID represents his or her RID. (*Hint:* Answer by using the numbers from the SID.)

12. Which information contained in a user's access token is used to allow servers to decide if the user should be authorized access to a resource? (Give a short 1- or 2-line answer.)

13. Who can always reset the permissions of an object to allow himself or herself access to the object?

    a. the administrator of an object

    b. the delegate of an object

    c. the owner of an object

    d. the master of an object

14. It is preferable to assign permissions directly to users, not groups. True or False?

15. All classes of objects have the same special permissions available. True or False?

16. Which of the following is a security principal? (Choose all that apply.)

    a. organizational units

    b. users

    c. contacts

    d. computers

17. Order the following authentication protocols from most to least secure:

    a. NTLM v2

    b. NTLM

    c. LM

    d. Kerberos

    e. Kerberos with smart cards

18. A smart card has a magnetic stripe that stores the user's private key, which is read back by swiping the card through a reader. True or False?

19. For each of the following applications, indicate whether they use Active Directory for authentication, authorization, neither, or both.

   a. Notepad

   b. SQL Server

   c. Exchange 2000

20. On which file system can you control access to files and folders with the most detail?

   a. Compact Disc File System (CDFS)

   b. File Allocation Table (FAT)

   c. 32-bit File Allocation Table (FAT32)

   d. NT File System (NTFS)

9

CASE PROJECTS

Now that Super Corp's Active Directory is beginning to come together, some meetings have been taking place with the key staff involved in shaping the network and its infrastructure. In one of these meetings, the staff began the process of formulating the security model for Active Directory. The following personnel were present: Matt Butler, Carolyn Commander, Pat Horton, and Chris Snyder. (You can refer to the organization chart introduced in Chapter 3 (Figure 3-1) for more details on the participants.) The meeting centered on the basic concepts of security in the Super Corp Active Directory.

Pat has been fighting to maintain an initially simple, clean security implementation and phase in additional security protection over the course of a year. These are Pat's arguments:

   a. Let's get everyone used to Active Directory before turning on the bells and whistles.

   b. Jenn and I simply don't have the time available on a day-to-day basis to run all over fixing problems for people who aren't yet ready for this. Let's keep things simple and reasonably secure initially, and then lock it down as we go along. Also, Jenn and I don't yet fully understand what we're turning on, and if you're not going to allow us to receive training, we need to learn this on the job. Even if we get a class scheduled, who is going to manage the network while we are in class?

Matt had different concerns and objectives. Because he is responsible for network security, he would like to see all of the bells and whistles turned on—yesterday. He also feels that as the responsible party for physical security, he should also be responsible for infrastructure security—not necessarily in terms of implementation, but of the requirements and design of the company's security policy. Because of his extensive security experience, Pat didn't express any concerns over Matt's ability to design or define security, but she still maintains the concerns she voiced earlier regarding the effects of his security initiative on both staff and employees. Some of Matt's concerns were:

a. There are a lot of bad guys out there. I don't think we should just blindly commit all of our confidential and business information to a system without locking everything down first.

b. I want smart cards for everyone who draws a paycheck, before they're allowed to access the system.

c. I want strict local settings on the computers. I don't want users to be able to use their floppy drives or CD drives for anything. I want the desktop and list of applications standardized and the Web sites controlled...*everything*.

Chris is concerned that users will only be given access to the resources needed to perform their jobs. He feels that strict access controls should be balanced against any perceived infringement of personal freedoms. Though recent case law has sided with corporations that restrict user access and use of corporate computer networks, such cases are expensive to litigate and win. Chris wants to avoid any such possibilities for the time being. His arguments include:

a. I want to make sure that we don't do something that will invite a lawsuit. We don't have the budget right now to handle a major incident.

b. Can't we just roll out this Active Directory thing and keep the security we have now? Why do we need to switch anything at all?

c. I still don't understand everything that's being discussed, and I think that the Legal Department needs to exercise more control and have more input into the process.

Carolyn is concerned that the office staff will be impacted by new training on the computer systems, and that vital, need-to-know information won't be available to her staff. However, she is generally in favor of Pat's concept of slowly rolling out the additional security features after everyone has gotten used to dealing with Active Directory on a daily basis. Some of her comments include:

a. I like Pat's idea of slowly rolling out additional features for the company. I don't think we should hit everyone with everything at the same time. Give everyone a chance to get used to what is happening.

b. One concern is that my staff wouldn't be able to access vital information when needed, and I'd like to meet offline with Pat to go over possible solutions to eliminate this potential problem. I'm also interested in finding out what this new technology can do to help our clients...can we use this new system to improve our customer relations?

c. Can we add additional functionality for my staff using this tool? I'd like to reduce the amount of paperwork that my people need to deal with on a daily basis. I'd also like to explore some new technologies that will help the managers get the information they need to manage client project's more effectively.

There are a lot of issues being brought to the table in terms of securing and protecting the Super Corp Active Directory network infrastructure, and many differing views from each of the primary stakeholders. You should now begin the process of planning this implementation.

Note that network design is frequently an exercise in compromise. You need to design something that satisfies the largest number of stakeholders and addresses their issues while still providing an implementation that is usable and secure. You may need to refer to the Super Corp organization chart and network diagram (Figures 3-1 and 3-2) to complete these exercises.

Case Project 9-1: Delegating Control in Active Directory

You have looked at who the possible data owners are, as well as who the key security stakeholders are. Who should have permissions over objects in Active Directory? Who should be Domain Administrators? Should any one person or group have complete control to access every object in Active Directory? Should particular data owners manage some organizational units?

Case Project 9-2: Planning to Upgrade and Deploy Resources

With some basic permissions now configured for Active Directory, you need to configure security settings for your network resources. Matt Butler was recently able to purchase two network file servers—NAS1 and NAS2, respectively—and some resources are stored on these servers. However, many file shares are still located on departmental servers and have not yet been migrated to the new servers.

Permissions on the departmental file servers are so confusing that Matt has decided to simply decommission those machines and completely rebuild them after their file shares have been moved to the new servers. To do so, any shared printers located on the departmental servers will be redeployed to a neighboring department's server as an interim measure. After the specific department server has been rebuilt, the department's shared printer will be returned to the original host server and reconfigured.

Using the resources available to you, design the deployment document for this process. Create a document for each department. Determine which department should be moved first, where its printer should be positioned, and if possible, a time frame for the process. You also need to move all remaining file shares from the departmental servers to the NAS servers. The two NAS servers are both using Windows Server 2003 Enterprise Edition and are both member servers in the Super Corp North America Active Directory domain.

This activity can be completed individually, with your partner, in a small group, or as a class discussion, as decided by your instructor.

Case Project 9-3: Weighing User Authentication Options

In an effort to ease Matt Butler's concerns regarding Active Directory security, Dan DiNicolo has decided to implement either certificate-based smart cards for authentication or another two-factor authentication scheme for user logons.

Dan would prefer to delay this implementation as long as possible, for several reasons, not the least of which is the cost of hardware such as card readers. Also, he hasn't been able to obtain the buy-in of Phyllis Green for the added expense. He has asked Matt and Mike to justify the need in a document that will be delivered to Phyllis.

Prepare a "decision paper" (not to exceed one page in length) for Phyllis to consider, which either recommends or discourages the use of smart card-based certificates. Do your best to estimate the cost by acquiring current information from the Internet or your instructor. Create a short, cost-benefit analysis in which you compare the cost to the perceived benefits.

In preparing your recommendation, use all available resources, such as the online material at *http://msdn.microsoft.com*, *www.reskit.com*, or TechNet, which is also available at *www.microsoft.com/technet*. Case studies are also published at other manufacturer's Web sites, such as *www.rsasecurity.com*, *www.datakey.com*, and *www.smartcardalliance.org*.

This activity can be completed individually, with your partner, in a small group, or as a class discussion, as decided by your instructor. Your instructor will advise you as to the final format of your report.

CHAPTER
10

MANAGING USERS, GROUPS, COMPUTERS, AND RESOURCES

After reading this chapter, you will be able to:

♦ Create user objects in Active Directory and set values for the attributes of a user object

♦ Create and manipulate groups in Active Directory, and understand the effects of different group scopes

♦ Create and manage computer accounts

♦ Create objects for other resources, such as shared folders and printers

♦ Organize objects in Active Directory by leveraging the use of organizational units

Although it is essential to understand the basics of Active Directory design and structure, most administrators don't spend much time redesigning or migrating their networks. Instead, they spend the majority of their time managing the network. Whether the network is a new Active Directory deployment or one that has existed since the time of the first release of Active Directory, there are many day-to-day tasks that need to be performed. This chapter looks at some of those tasks, including working with common objects.

PLANNING AND ADMINISTERING USER ACCOUNTS

Although an Active Directory design is fairly static, the contents of the directory can be very dynamic, and the most frequently changed objects are usually **user objects**, which are the objects in the directory that represent real people using your computer network.

Most changes made to the data in a network directory have to do with users. When a new employee is hired, someone creates a user object. When a user changes his or her password, changes are made to an attribute of a user object. When a user is assigned to a different security group, more changes are made to the directory. Although other types of objects are also modified, managing users and the objects that represent them is usually the most frequent task for network administrators.

User Classes, Properties, and Schema

Recall from Chapter 1 and Chapter 4 that the Active Directory schema defines the attributes that make up a class of objects. The user class defines a number of required and optional attributes that are used with a user object. Specifically, every user object must have some value assigned to each mandatory attribute. Active Directory automatically manages several of the user object attributes for you, while other attributes hold values assigned by you (the object's creator) at the time the object is created. The following are the mandatory attributes for a user object:

- cn—This attribute uniquely identifies the object in its container.

- instanceType, objectCategory, and objectClass—These attributes contain fixed values that are automatically assigned. Because these attributes represent the class of which an object is an instance, they are the same for all user objects, because all user objects are built from the same class definition (or blueprint).

- objectSID—This attribute holds the user's Security Identifier (SID), which is assigned automatically by the system, but is always unique.

- sAMAccountName—This attribute is a version of the username that can be used by older clients that don't expect to talk to Active Directory. For example, a Windows NT Workstation 4.0 user would have to use this version of the username to log on.

The default schema provides more than 200 optional attributes for a user object; however, administrators rarely have to deal with the majority of these attributes. An average user object is likely to have values assigned to around 40 or 50 of these attributes. It would be rare to find a company that populates all 200 attributes for every user, but it is possible, at least in theory.

The Names of a User

Each user has two different names they can use to log on to the domain. Names in Active Directory are stored in attributes called **sAMAccountName** and **userPrincipalName (UPN)**. However, the Active Directory Users and Computers console refers to the UPN as **user logon name** and the sAMAccountName as **user logon name (pre-Windows 2000)**. In Active Directory, only the sAMAccountName is a mandatory attribute, but the New Object - User dialog box requires both.

NOTE

You can use code or scripts to create a user that does not have a UPN, but this is not normally desirable.

Before creating user accounts, you should decide on a naming convention for your accounts. The most common convention is to use the user's first initial followed by the user's last name. Alternatively, using the user's last name followed by the user's first initial is another acceptable naming convention. For example, Bob Smith's username could be bsmith or smithb.

When choosing a naming convention, you must be careful to consider all possible names in the organization. A small company may be fine by using only the user's first initial and their last name, but a larger company may end up with multiple users with the same first initial/last name combination. In order to give every user a unique username, the naming convention should describe what to do if multiple users have similar—or even the same—names. For example, if the username bsmith is already taken and Barbra Smith joins the organization, the naming convention could specify that the first two letters (or more, if necessary) of the person's first name be used instead of just the first initial. Alternatively, the user's middle initial, nickname, or even a number could be used. However, the exact naming convention chosen is not the big issue. No matter what convention you choose, the most important thing is to follow it.

A user with a down-level client such as Windows 98, Windows 95, or Windows NT must use the older format of the user name—the sAMAccountName—to log on, manually specifying the name of the domain or choosing it from a drop-down list. This pre-Windows 2000 logon name is made up of two parts—the domain's NetBIOS name and the user's logon name, separated by a backslash; for example: MYDOMAIN\SomeUser. The domain's NetBIOS name is set when the domain is created, and is not that easy to change.

The preferred method of logging on to a domain using Windows 2000, Windows XP Professional, or Windows Server 2003 is to use the UPN. The UPN is also composed of two parts—the username and a UPN suffix, joined by an @ symbol, for example SomeUser@mydomain.com. This format resembles an e-mail address, and in some organizations a user's UPN is set to match his or her e-mail address, but this is not a necessity. Note that a UPN (that is, the user logon name including the suffix) must be unique within the entire forest.

10

By default, the UPN suffix is the DNS name of the user's domain, but you can choose a different suffix from the drop-down list when creating a user (or change it in the user's account properties at a later time). While the DNS domain names of all domains in the forest are available by default as UPN suffixes, you can also manually add UPN suffixes to the forest using Active Directory Domains and Trusts, as shown in Figure 10-1. For example, if your domain uses *supercorp.net* as its DNS name, but your users have e-mail addresses that end in *supercorp.com*, you can add the UPN suffix *supercorp.com* so users' logon names and e-mail addresses match. As another example, if a corporation has many domains, it can still choose to have all UPNs end with the same suffix. Instead of having some users with the UPN suffix *childdomain.mycompany.local* and others with the UPN suffix *mycompany.local*, the users in the *childdomain* domain can have their UPNs changed to *mycompany.local*. In Activity 10-1, you will create a new UPN for your forest.

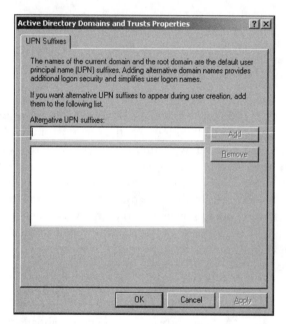

Figure 10-1   Window used to add alternative UPN suffixes to the forest

Name Suffix Routing

One new consideration with forest trusts in Windows Server 2003 is name suffix routing, which provides name resolution across forests. When you create a forest trust between two forests, name suffix routing is used to route authentication requests to the correct forest. For example, if a user with an account in forest A logged on to a computer in forest B, the authentication request would be routed to the correct forest. In this case, the user's account is from forest A so the authentication request is sent to forest A.

NOTE Do not confuse UPN suffixes with unique name suffixes. Unique name suffixes do include all UPN suffixes, but they also include **service principal name (SPN)** suffixes, DNS forest names, and domain names. Name suffix routing is used for all unique name suffixes, not just UPN suffixes.

This brings up an important point: in order for name suffix routing to work, a given unique name suffix can only exist in one forest. If the same suffix exists in two forests, name suffix routing is disabled for that suffix. The following are instances when a conflict can occur between two forests:

- The same Domain Name System (DNS) name is already in use.
- The same NetBIOS name is already in use.
- A domain Security ID (SID) conflicts with another name suffix SID.

For example, assume that both the *supercorp.net* forest and *dev.supercorp.net* forest (note that these are separate forests and not just separate domains) had the UPN suffix *supercorp.com*. If a user logged on to the network using a UPN ending in the *supercorp.com* suffix, Active Directory would not know if the user was part of the local forest or another forest.

Because name suffix routing is disabled when a conflict occurs, what essentially happens is the authentication request stays within the local forest. If a user with an account in the *supercorp.net* forest logged on to a workstation in the supercorp.net forest using a UPN with the suffix *supercorp.com*, the user would be authenticated by a domain controller with their account (because the user's account is in the forest). However, if that same user tried to log on to a workstation in the *dev.supercorp.net* forest, the authentication request would stay in the local forest and go to a *dev.supercorp.net* domain controller. Most likely, the same username/ password combination would not exist in the *dev.supercorp.net* forest and authentication would fail.

NOTE Technically, the user could have a matching account in both forests. However, this defeats the whole point of forest trusts. Forest trusts allow for a single user account to be used across more than one forest for authorization and authentication.

While most conflicts probably occur because the same UPN suffix was created in two domains, keep in mind it's not the only situation where a conflict can occur. As another conflict example, consider a situation where a forest called *supercorp.net* and another forest called *fastitstaff.com* each contain a domain called dev.local (that is, four domains in all, two per forest). If a forest trust is created between the *supercorp.net* forest and *fastitstaff.com* forest, there would be a conflict for the DNS name *dev.local* between the two forests.

There are two important points to notice here. First, name suffix routing between the *fastitstaff.com* domain and the supercorp.net domain would work without issue because there is no conflict between those names. Second, users within a forest could still access the *dev.local* domain in their local forest without issue. However, they could not access resources in the *dev.local* domain located in the other forest. In other words, users in the *fastitstaff.com* domain could access the *dev.local* domain located in the *fastitstaff.com* forest. Users in the *fastitstaff.com* domain could not, however, access the *dev.local* domain located in the *supercorp.net* forest. Similarly, users in the *supercorp.net* domain could access the *dev.local* domain located in the *supercorp.net* forest. Users in the *supercorp.net* domain could not, however, access the *dev.local* domain located in the *fastitstaff.com* forest.

When you create a forest trust, by default, name suffix routing is automatically enabled for all existing suffixes. If you add a child suffix of an existing suffix, the child inherits the routing setting of its parent (that is, either disabled or enabled). For example, assume you have a forest trust with routing enabled for the domain *supercorp.net*. If you added the domain *sales.supercorp.net* as a child domain of *supercorp.net*, routing would automatically be enabled for the *sales.supercorp.net* domain. In contrast, if you create a new domain tree, or a new UPN suffix that does not have an existing parent for that matter, after the forest trust is established, routing is disabled by default. You must manually enable name suffix routing for these suffixes. In Activity 10-1, you will enable name suffix routing once you create a new UPN suffix.

Activity 10-1: Adding a UPN Suffix and Configuring Name Suffix Routing

Time Required: 10 minutes

Objective: Add a UPN suffix and then configure name suffix routing on an existing forest trust.

Description: Super Corp's IT manager would like users to be able to log on to the network using the same name as their e-mail address. All Super Corp employees have an e-mail address in the format *username@supercorp.com*. In addition, the IT manager would like you to configure the existing forest trust so that users can log on in either forest using their new UPN.

1. If necessary, start your server and log on using the **Administrator** account in the **CHILDXX** domain (where *XX* is the number of the forest root domain for which your server is a domain controller) using the password **Password01**.

2. Click **Start**, select **Administrative Tools**, and then click **Active Directory Domains and Trusts**.

3. In the left tree pane, right-click **Active Directory Domains and Trusts**, and then click **Properties**.

4. In the Alternative UPN suffix text box, enter **supercorpXX.com** (where *XX* is the number of your server), and then click **Add**. Your new UPN should now be added, as shown in Figure 10-2.

5. Click **OK**. You now configure name suffix routing for the UPN you just created. Because rooting is performed by the remote forest (not the local forest in which the UPN was created), you must connect to the remote forest to enable routing.

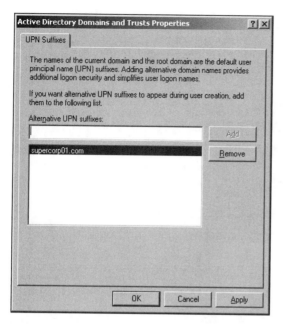

Figure 10-2   Adding an UPN suffix

NOTE

You could also physically log on to a domain controller for the remote domain instead of establishing a remote connection from your domain controller.

6. In the left tree pane, right-click **Active Directory Domains and Trusts**, and then click **Connect to Domain Controller**.

7. In the Domain text box, enter **supercorp.net** (this is the remote forest with which your domain has a forest trust already established), and then press **Enter**.

8. A message box prompts you if you want to administer the forest rooted at domain supercorp.net by using any writable domain controller. Click **Yes**.

9. In the left tree pane, right-click **supercorp.net** and then click **Properties**.

10. Click the **Trusts** tab.

11. In the Domains trusted by this domain list box, select **childXX.supercorp.net** (where *XX* is the number of the forest root domain for which your server is a domain controller), and then click **Properties**.

12. Click the **Name Suffix Routing** tab.

13. A dialog box prompts you for credentials to ensure that you have permission to modify the trust. In the User name drop-down list box, enter **supercorp.net\Administrator**. In the Password text box, enter **Password01**, and then click **OK**.

14. In the Name suffixes in the child*XX*.supercorp.net forest list box, select
    *.supercorpXX.com (where *XX* is the number of your server), and then click
    Enable. Routing for the UPN suffix you created should now be enabled, as shown
    in Figure 10-3.

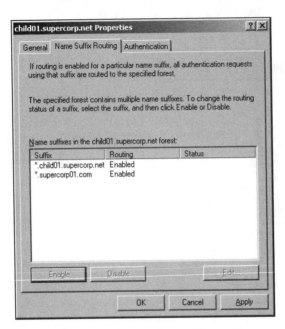

Figure 10-3   Enabling name suffix routing

15. Click **OK**.

16. Click **OK** on the supercorp.net Properties window, and then close Active Directory
    Domains and Trusts.

17. Log off your server if you do not intend to immediately continue to the next
    activity. Otherwise, stay logged on.

Creating Users with Active Directory Users and Computers

To create a user with the Active Directory Users and Computers console, you must be
working at a domain controller or have the administrative tools installed at your workstation.
To start the console, click Start, select Administrative Tools, and then click Active Directory
Users and Computers.

Before creating the object, choose the correct container that will hold the object. In most
cases, this will be an organizational unit, but you can create a user directly under the domain
object or in one of the container objects (such as Users).

The New Object - User dialog box

To create a new user, start by expanding the nodes in the tree pane on the left side of the Active Directory Users and Computers console until the desired organizational unit is visible. Right-click the name of the object in the left tree pane, then select New, and then click User. The New Object - User dialog box appears, as shown in Figure 10-4.

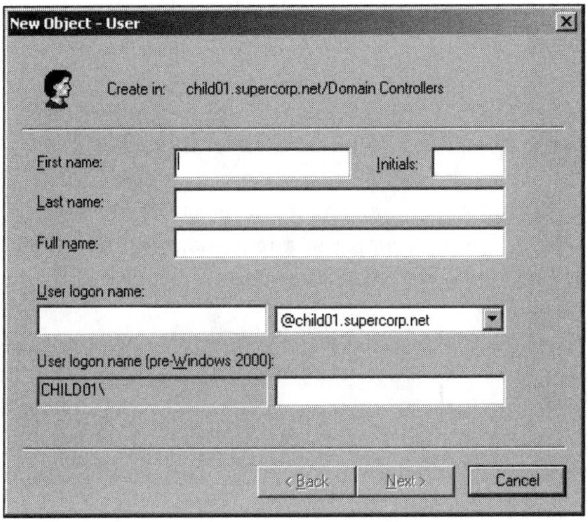

Figure 10-4 The New Object - User dialog box for a user object

TIP
Just because you can do something, doesn't mean you should. This is an important maxim for administration in networks, servers, and Active Directory installations. You can create users in the domain without using organizational units. You can create users in the Domain Controllers organizational unit. But that doesn't mean you should.

By looking at this dialog box, you see that creating a new user object isn't very intimidating. Instead of being presented with hundreds of attributes, there are only a few text boxes to fill in. The top portion of the dialog box allows the administrator to specify the name attributes of the new object. As you type text in the First name, Initials, or Last name text boxes, the console automatically builds the full name for you, even adding a period after the initials. The specific components of the name are available for the basis of searches (such as finding all the users with a first name of John), but the Full name is displayed in most cases. If your organization requires names in a unique format, or if the user account is for a service, not a person, then you might want to override the automatically generated Full name, and type it in directly.

The Active Directory Users and Computers console automatically fills in the same information from the User logon name text box to the User logon name (pre-Windows 2000) text box, as normally the username part of both is the same. However, if you have a need to do so, you can make them different. You could have a user known as both *SOMEDOMAIN*\Bob and *Bill@somedomain.com*. However, this can be very confusing, so you should avoid making the username parts of the UPN and sAMAccountName different.

When a user logs on using a UPN, the domain controller issues a query to the closest global catalog to determine which domain can authenticate the user. Thus, the DNS system and the global catalog must be operational for this to function properly. If the domain controller handling the initial authentication request is unable to locate a global catalog, the domain logon fails.

NOTE   There are actually specific cases in which this query to the global catalog is skipped. A global catalog is required for resolving a UPN when, in a multi-domain forest, the domain where the user is logging on has no direct knowledge of the user. A global catalog is not needed for resolving a UPN when there is only a single domain in the forest, or when, in a multi-domain forest, the domain where the user is logging on has direct knowledge of the user.

After supplying the logon name and information, click Next. Before creating the new user object, Windows issues a query to the global catalog to verify that the UPN is unique within the forest. If a global catalog cannot be located, an error occurs. You can still create the user object, but the account is not active until it has been checked against a global catalog.

Initial Security Settings

The next page of the wizard, as shown in Figure 10-5, is where you can set essential security attributes.

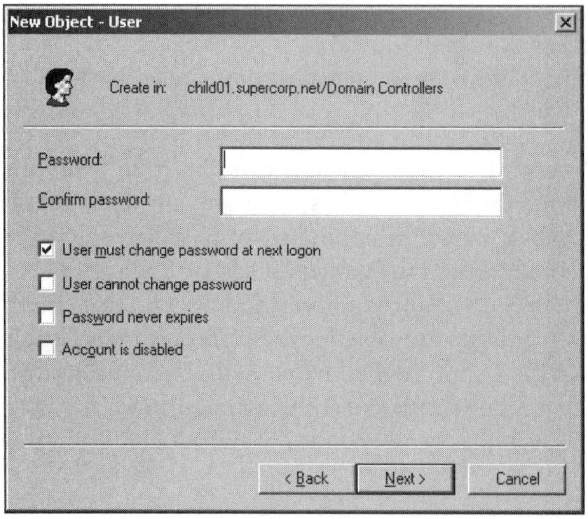

Figure 10-5   Password and security attributes

Two text boxes are supplied to enter and confirm a password. Active Directory does not require a password—that is, it is not a mandatory attribute of the User class. However, the default account policy in place with Windows Server 2003 requires that all passwords be at least seven characters in length and be complex. You can locate the domain's account policies related to passwords by clicking Start, selecting Administrative Tools, and then clicking Domain Security Policy. Expanding the Account Policies node in the left tree pane and then clicking Password Policy displays the domain's password policies, as shown in Figure 10-6. In the next chapter, you will learn how to set account policies.

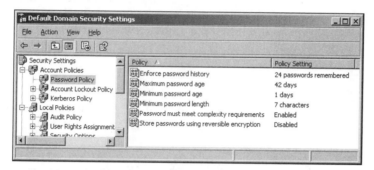

Figure 10-6   Domain Password Policy

 Account policies only have effect on domain accounts when they are set at the domain level.

NOTE

The User must change password at next logon check box is provided so that a new user is forced to immediately change his or her password, as even an administrator should not know the user's password in most cases. In some organizations, however, passwords are centrally controlled, so clicking the User cannot change password check box prevents this user from changing his or her password. This check box is useful for service accounts or accounts used, say, at a kiosk-type workstation. Clicking the Password never expires check box overrides the password expiration policy set on the domain, and clicking the Account is disabled check box prevents the account from being used.

You need to decide whether you control the password for each user or whether users are allowed to maintain their own passwords. A password policy that requires a password at least seven characters long, containing a variety of alphanumeric characters, and that has a password expiration setting is considered a best practice by many organizations.

After supplying a password, choosing the desired options, and clicking Next, the summary page appears. Review the summary to avoid errors, and then click Finish, which actually creates the user object in Active Directory. In Activity 10-2, you will create a new user object.

Activity 10-2: Creating a New User Object

Time Required: 10 minutes

Objective: Practice creating new user objects.

Description: In this activity, you will create three user objects. These users will be used throughout the chapter. Knowing how to create user objects is an essential skill because it is one of the fundamental tasks required to operate or administer a computer network.

1. If necessary, start your server and log on using the **Administrator** account in the **CHILD***XX* domain (where *XX* is the number of the forest root domain for which your server is a domain controller) using the password **Password01**.

2. Click **Start**, select **Administrative Tools**, and then click **Active Directory Users and Computers**.

3. Expand the nodes in the left tree pane until the Atlanta organizational unit under the North America *XX* organizational unit is visible (where *XX* is the number of your server).

4. Right-click the **Atlanta** organizational unit, select **New**, and then click **User**.

5. In the First name text box, type **User***XX***A** (where *XX* is the number of your server). The Full name text box will automatically be filled in.

6. In the User logon name text box, type **User***XX***A** (where *XX* is the number of your server). The User logon name (pre-Windows 2000) text box will automatically be filled in.

7. In the drop-down list box next to User logon name, select **@supercorp***XX***.com** (where *XX* is the number of your server). Your screen should look similar to Figure 10-7.

8. Click **Next**.

9. In the Password and Confirm password text boxes, type **Password01**.

10. Uncheck the box next to **User must change password at next logon**.

11. Check the box next to **Password never expires**, as shown in Figure 10-8.

12. Click **Next**.

13. Click **Finish**.

14. Repeat Steps 4 through 12 to create a user named **User***XX***B** (where *XX* is the number of your server), using the same password and options.

15. Repeat Steps 4 through 12 to create a user named **User***XX***C** (where *XX* is the number of your server), using the same password and options.

16. Confirm that the Atlanta organizational unit contains the three users you just created.

17. Close Active Directory Users and Computers.

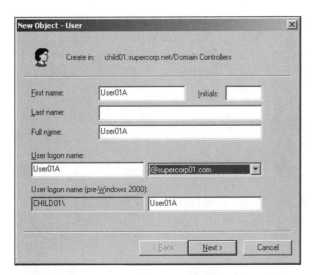

Figure 10-7   Setting the names of a new user account

10

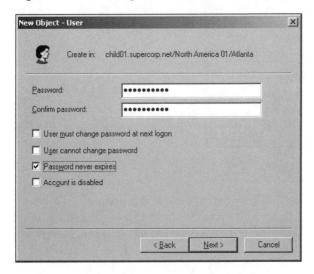

Figure 10-8   Configuring a password and account settings

18. Log off your server if you do not intend to immediately continue to the next activity. Otherwise, stay logged on.

Setting Additional Attributes

There remain dozens—potentially hundreds—of other attributes that you can set for each user. Some of these attributes are only used internally. Others can only be managed programmatically with code, script, or a tool like ADSI Edit. However, many of the attributes are exposed through property pages in the Active Directory Users and Computers console. To open the property pages for a user object, simply right-click the object in Active Directory Users and Computers and choose Properties. The window shown in Figure 10-9 appears. Note that you can open the same window by double-clicking the user object or choosing Properties from the Action menu.

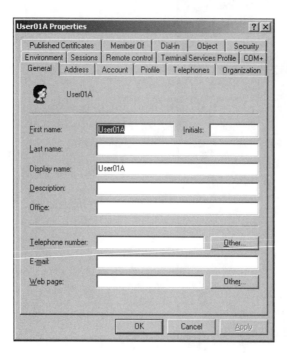

Figure 10-9   User object properties

The number of tabs and the tab headings that appear in this chapter may differ from what you see on your system. Because Active Directory is extensible (that is, the schema can be extended with new attributes and new classes), Active Directory-aware applications may add tabs to the property pages of the Active Directory objects. A good example of this is Exchange 2000, which adds three new tabs to the user property page.

TIP   When describing a value stored in the Active Directory database, or describing a class or object defined in the schema, the term "attribute" is usually used. The term "property" is generally used when describing the same piece of information exposed in a graphical user interface. You can consider these words to be synonyms, although "attribute" is a more precise and technical term, and a property may be used to create or manipulate more than one attribute.

The properties for each object are shown on several tabs in the Properties dialog box, and they can be categorized as follows:

- General and business information—General, Address, Telephones, and Organiza-tion tabs

- Account and profile settings—Account, Member Of, Profile, and COM+ tabs

- Terminal Services settings—Environment, Sessions, Remote control, and Terminal Services Profile tabs

- Dial-in settings—Dial-in tab

- Advanced properties—Object, Published Certificates, and Security tabs (shown only if View Advanced features is turned on)

TIP

In Windows 2000 Server, there were very few operations that could be per-formed when multiple users were selected in Active Directory Users and Com-puters at one time. In Windows Server 2003, this has changed. You can now select multiple users in Active Directory Users and Computers and then change certain properties simultaneously on all selected accounts. For example, in Windows 2000, to change the Logon hours property for more than one user you would either have to change them one by one or write a custom script (that is, outside of Active Directory Users and Computers) to make the change. In Windows Server 2003, to change properties on multiple accounts, select the first account in Active Directory Users and Computers' right details pane, hold down the shift key, then select the last user account you want the change to affect (note that you can hold down the Ctrl key instead to select accounts one at a time), right-click the selection(s), and then click Properties. You can now make changes to all the selected accounts' Logon hours properties simultaneously. If you would like, use the accounts you created in Activity 10-1 to try selecting multiple users. Note the subset of properties that you can change when multiple users are selected.

General and Business Information

The General, Address, Telephones, and Organization tabs show properties that relate to general attributes of the user and the user's role in the enterprise. The General tab (see Figure 10-9) contains the same name information as the New Object - User dialog box, along with a general description. The office attribute is used to hold a room number or other location information. You can also specify an e-mail address, telephone number, and Web page URL on this tab. The telephone number and Web page attributes each have an Other button to allow for entering more numbers.

The information contained in the telephoneNumber attribute of the General tab is not as useful as you might expect. You can enter any string, and issues with formatting always arise, such as how to handle international numbers or whether to include area codes. More importantly, though, there is no consistent way to discern between different types of telephone numbers, such as home, office, and mobile.

The Telephones tab, shown in Figure 10-10, allows for some classification and general notes. However, it is important to realize that the telephone number(s) entered on the General tab do not appear on the Telephones tab. The first telephone number on the General tab is stored in the telephoneNumber attribute. Those entered by clicking Other are stored in the otherTelephone attribute, which is a multivalued attribute. The numbers from the Telephones tab are stored in specific attributes, such as the homePhone and otherHomePhone attributes, or the mobile and otherMobile attributes.

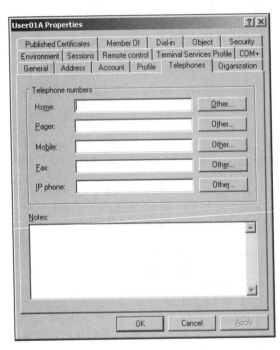

Figure 10-10 The Telephones tab

If an organization is going to use the attributes to store this sort of information (which would be very useful), its design should specify which locations will be used, or a process should be in place to ensure that the relevant data is stored in both locations. Otherwise, the ability to retrieve the expected data or perform expected searches will be compromised.

Figure 10-11 shows the Address tab, which provides a way to record mailing address information. Active Directory is somewhat limited for this purpose, because there is no way to record multiple mailing addresses (such as home, work, summer, alternate) or to link many users to one address. (In database terms, Active Directory is not "well normalized.") For this reason, many organizations do not make full use of Active Directory's address attributes, or choose to populate them automatically from other databases.

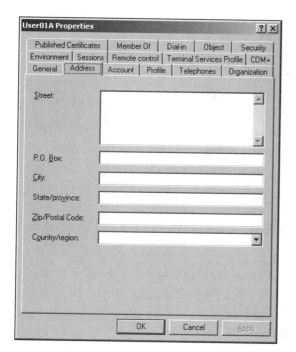

Figure 10-11   The Address tab

The Organization tab, as shown in Figure 10-12, is used to capture or display information about a user's role in the organization. The Title, Department, and Company attributes are used to describe the user's job. The Manager and Direct reports sections can be used to show how a user relates to other users in the company. The names shown in these areas are also objects in Active Directory. To create a list of Direct reports, set the Manager value on the user objects of those subordinate employees.

Account and Profile Settings

The Account tab, shown in Figure 10-13, is used to control most security-related account settings. The User logon name and User logon name (pre-Windows 2000) were described previously. Click the Logon Hours button to open a schedule, which controls the times and days this user account can be accessed. In Activity 10-3, you will set up logon hour restrictions. Click the Log On To button to restrict this user account to certain computers. (This is an excellent idea for service accounts, such as those used by SQL or Exchange. However, be aware that it relies on NetBIOS name resolution.)

10

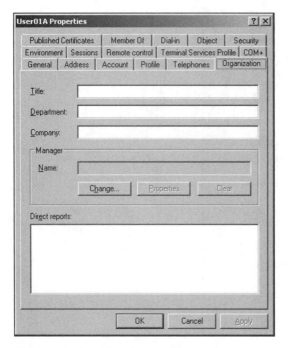

Figure 10-12 The Organization tab

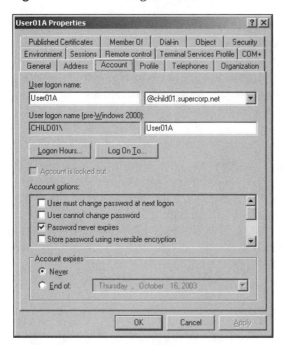

Figure 10-13 The Account tab

ACTIVITY

Activity 10-3: Adding Account Restrictions

Time Required: 5 minutes

Objective: Practice adding account restrictions to Active Directory user objects.

Description: Your User*XX*C is a junior employee working with sensitive information. To reduce the risk of a confidentiality breech, company policy states that all such employees are restricted from logging on after hours. You will now add account information that prohibits the user from logging on outside of an 8 a.m. to 6 p.m. time frame.

1. If necessary, start your server and log on using the **Administrator** account in the **CHILD*XX*** domain (where *XX* is the number of the forest root domain for which your server is a domain controller) using the password **Password01**.

2. Click **Start**, select **Administrative Tools**, and then click **Active Directory Users and Computers**.

3. Expand the nodes in the left tree pane until the Atlanta organizational unit under the North America *XX* organizational unit is visible (where *XX* is the number of your server).

4. Select the **Atlanta** organizational unit to show the users and other objects it contains in the right details pane.

5. In the right details pane, right-click **User*XX*C** (where *XX* is the number of your server), and then click **Properties**.

6. Click the **Account** tab.

7. Click the **Logon Hours** button.

8. Use the schedule grid to select all hours outside of the 8 a.m. to 6 p.m., Monday to Friday range, and then click **Logon Denied** to exclude them. (You may do this in several steps. If you accidentally select too many sections of the schedule, use the Logon Permitted button to reactivate them. You can also select an entire column or row with the buttons at the top and left of the schedule grid.) Your screen should look similar to Figure 10-14.

9. Click **OK**.

10. Click **OK** again to close the user's account properties.

11. Close Active Directory Users and Computers.

12. Log off your server if you do not intend to immediately continue to the next activity. Otherwise, stay logged on.

You can also set a number of options, including the use of smart cards, how Kerberos is used with the account, and an expiration date. Be aware, however, that some of these settings can be overridden by the application of Group Policies.

10

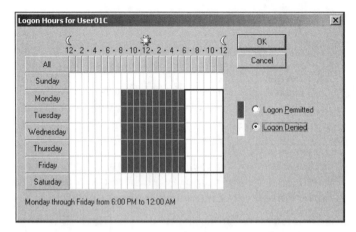

Figure 10-14   Schedule of when a user can log on

Accounts can also be **disabled** or **locked out**. The effect of these two states is similar—an account cannot be used when disabled or locked out—but the implementation of each differs slightly. Enabling and disabling an account is an action usually performed by an administrator, although it can be automated. Disabling an account sets an option described as "Account is disabled." An account can be disabled from its property pages, or by right-clicking a user account in Active Directory Users and Computers and selecting **Disable Account**.

On the other hand, an account cannot be locked out manually. Only the system can lock out accounts after too many consecutive bad password attempts. If this occurs, the Account is locked out check box will be checked on this property page. An administrator can reset the locked-out status by clearing this check box, or you can configure the system to automatically reset the lockout after a specified period of time. You can locate the domain's account policies related to account lockout by clicking Start, selecting Administrative Tools, and then clicking Domain Security Policy. Expanding the Account Policies node in the left tree pane and then clicking Account Lockout Policy displays the domain's account lockout policies, as shown in Figure 10-15.

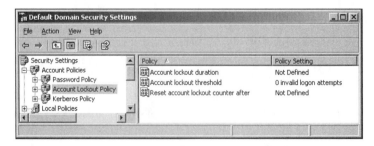

Figure 10-15   Domain Account Lockout Policy

The Profile tab, shown in Figure 10-16, controls some of the user's experience as he or she logs on to a Windows workstation. The profile path allows the user's settings (such as the desktop, menus, and favorites) to be stored centrally, rather than on the local workstation. This setting also allows administrators to set a mandatory profile that cannot be changed by the individual user. The logon script name specifies a batch file or script that runs every time the user logs on. The home folder settings allow you to specify a particular path to a local or network drive that is available to the user. (Note that Group Policies can also set logon scripts and control the elements found in the profile.)

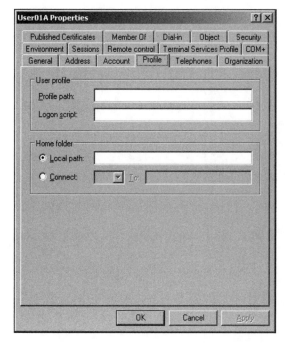

Figure 10-16   The Profile tab

The Member Of tab, shown in Figure 10-17, lists the groups to which the user belongs. Groups are used to manage permissions in the network for multiple users, rather than for each user individually. They are discussed in detail later in this chapter. A user can be added to or removed from groups using this property page, or from the property pages of the group object.

The COM+ tab, shown in Figure 10-18, configures how a user interacts with COM+ partition sets. A new feature of COM+ is the ability to concurrently load multiple versions of COM+ objects on one computer. In such an instance, COM+ partitions are used to manage which versions of which objects are used when. This tab allows the matching of users to particular COM+ partitions. (COM+ partitions are not related to Active Directory partitions or naming contexts.) This feature is used mostly with service accounts, which are accounts being used only to run server applications.

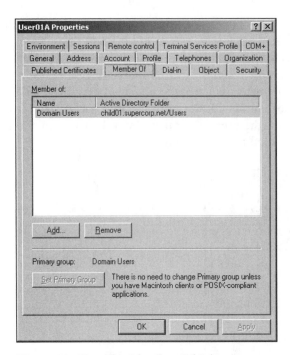

Figure 10-17   The Member Of tab

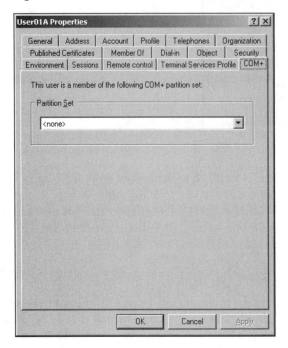

Figure 10-18   The COM+ tab

Terminal Services Settings

Beginning with the release of Windows 2000, Microsoft has promoted the use of Terminal Services (TS). Using TS, users connect to a server using thin clients, such as the Remote Desktop client that is included with Windows XP Professional. The programs that the user needs actually run on the server, and only keystrokes, mouse movements, and screen updates travel across the network (or dial-up connection). Several of the user attributes in Active Directory are designed to support the use of TS. The Environment tab, shown in Figure 10-19, allows administrators to override the default behavior of TS for a user and have TS automatically start a particular application. The properties on this tab also control the connection of client disk drives and printers.

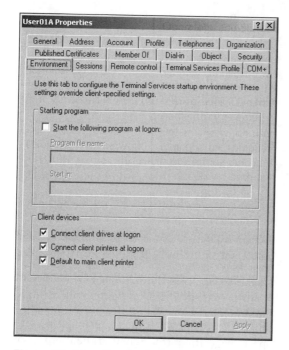

10

Figure 10-19   The Environment tab

The properties in the Sessions tab, shown in Figure 10-20, control how the server manages idle and disconnected TS sessions. A session is active when a client is connected and activity is occurring. It is idle if it remains connected but no activity occurs, and it is disconnected if a client is not connected. In the disconnected state, a user can still be logged on, and programs can still be executing. By configuring the settings on this tab, an administrator can choose whether to allow idle or disconnected sessions to consume resources on the server, or to end those sessions, freeing server resources.

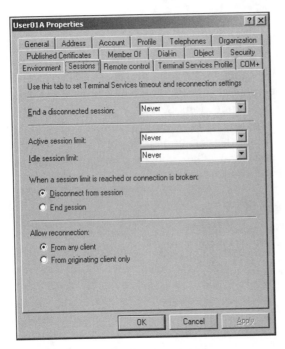

Figure 10-20   The Sessions tab

The Remote control tab, shown in Figure 10-21, controls whether a user's TS sessions can be remotely controlled by another TS client, such as an administrator or help desk support technician. These remote control settings apply only to TS sessions, not to interactive logons made at a workstation. Also, they do not govern remote assistance for Windows XP clients.

The properties on the Terminal Services Profile tab, shown in Figure 10-22, override the same properties shown on the Profile tab when the user is connected to a TS session. This allows you to have separate profiles for TS sessions and workstation sessions. One of the most important properties—the check box labeled Allow logon to terminal server—is barely noticeable at the bottom of this property page. It controls whether the user is allowed to log on to any TS server that is a member of the domain. (Note that clearing this check box does not prevent administrators from accessing servers running TS in administrative mode.)

Dial-in Settings

The Dial-in tab, shown in Figure 10-23, is used to control whether a user can access the dial-in services of servers running Routing and Remote Access Services (RRAS) in the forest. Several of these options are only available if the domain is operating at the Windows 2000 native or Windows Server 2003 functional level.

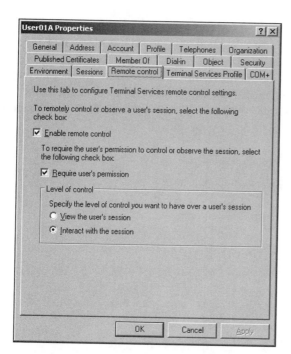

Figure 10-21   The Remote control tab

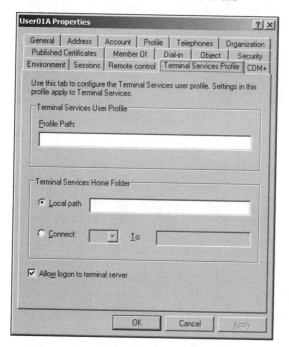

Figure 10-22   The Terminal Services Profile tab

At the Windows 2000 native or Windows Server 2003 functional level, you can require a user to dial in from one specific number (verified by caller-ID services), and assign static IP addressing and routing information. You can also use remote access policy to control dial-in access on a granular level, using group memberships, time of day, and other parameters. For more information about Remote Access Policies, see *MCSE Guide to Managing a Microsoft Windows Server 2003 Network* (ISBN: 0-619-12029-0). In a domain at the Windows 2000 mixed functional level, the unavailable options are grayed out.

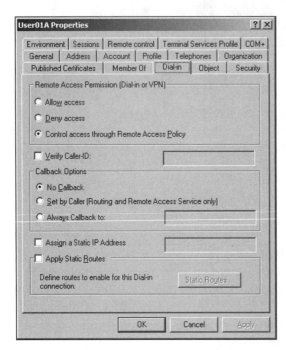

Figure 10-23   The Dial-in tab

Advanced Properties Tabs

Three tabs are visible only if you have activated the viewing of advanced features. The Security tab, shown in Figure 10-24, allows you to control access to the user object in Active Directory. Although it is recommended that you apply security settings to organizational units or containers, it is possible to apply them on an object-by-object basis. Security settings in Active Directory were covered in Chapter 9.

The Object tab, shown in Figure 10-25, contains information that may be of interest if you are troubleshooting an Active Directory problem, or require specific detail about the object itself. It is not used for daily operations.

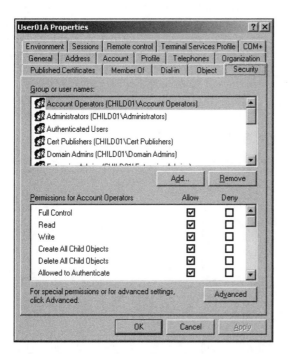

Figure 10-24   The Security tab

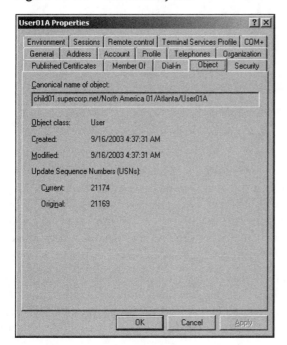

Figure 10-25   The Object tab

The Published Certificates tab, shown in Figure 10-26, displays information about Public Key Infrastructure (PKI) certificates that are stored and published in Active Directory. The full details of a PKI implementation are beyond the scope of this book, but some general PKI information was discussed in Chapter 9. If your enterprise uses PKI and stores certificates in Active Directory, this tab allows you to see which certificates are published for a particular user, as well as add additional certificates.

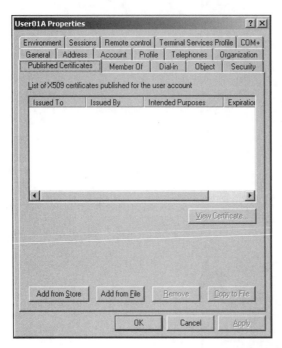

Figure 10-26   The Published Certificates tab

Resetting Passwords

When creating a new user, you are prompted for a password for that user; however, that password does not appear anywhere in the property pages. The user's password is stored in an encrypted form, which the operating system can access to validate a user. The original or plaintext version of the password cannot normally be recreated from the encrypted version, although there are hacking tools that use brute force to try millions of possible combinations, if the hacker has administrative access to the computer.

If a user forgets his or her password, an administrator cannot retrieve it for them. Instead, the password must be reset (see Activity 10-4). Right-clicking on the name of the user in the Users and Computers console and clicking Reset Password (see Figure 10-27), brings up the simple dialog box shown in Figure 10-28. (Note that you can access the same command from the Action menu.)

Only reset a user's password in this way if no other options are available. When a password is reset in this way, access to encrypted files may be lost, as the system does not allow access to parts of the user's private certificate store after a password reset.

Activity 10-4: Reset a Password

Time Required: 5 minutes

Objective: Practice resetting a user's password.

Description: UserXXA has just returned from a six-week vacation and has forgotten his password. In this activity, you will reset it to a known value. Such resetting is a common task for network administrators.

1. If necessary, start your server and log on using the **Administrator** account in the **CHILDXX** domain (where *XX* is the number of the forest root domain for which your server is a domain controller) using the password **Password01**.

2. Click **Start**, select **Administrative Tools**, and then click **Active Directory Users and Computers**.

3. Expand the nodes in the left tree pane until the Atlanta organizational unit under the North America *XX* organizational unit is visible (where *XX* is the number of your server).

4. In the left tree pane, select the **Atlanta** organizational unit to show the users and other objects it contains in the right details pane.

5. In the right details pane, right-click **UserXXA** (where *XX* is the number of your server), and then click **Reset Password**, as shown in Figure 10-27.

10

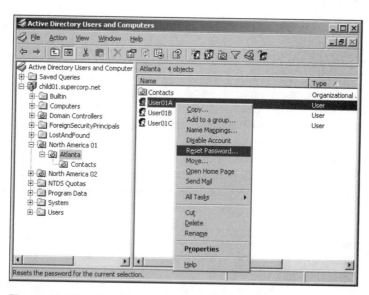

Figure 10-27   Locating reset password command

6. In the New password and Confirm password text boxes, enter **Password01** as shown in Figure 10-28.

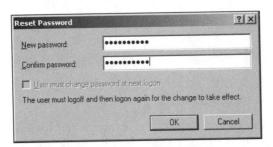

Figure 10-28   Resetting a password

NOTE   Because the UserXXA account has the Password never expires option selected, it is not possible to have the user change their password at the next logon and thus the option is grayed out.

7. Click **OK**.

8. A message box informs you that the password has been reset. Click **OK**.

9. Close Active Directory Users and Computers.

10. Log off your server if you do not intend to immediately continue to the next activity. Otherwise, stay logged on.

User Account Templates

In order to reduce the time and administrative burden associated with creating new user accounts, many administrators choose to create new user objects by copying a predefined template. A **user account template** is simply a preconfigured user account that already has the common attributes associated with a particular type of user configured. For example, when creating new user accounts for users in the Marketing Department, a large number of attributes are likely to be similar for these users. Because of this, an administrator could create a new user account called Marketing Template, and then populate this account with the common attributes required by all marketing users, such as group membership, user profile, and organizational information. Then, when a new user account for a user in the Marketing Department needs to be created, an administrator can simply copy this account, providing new username and password information specific to the user. Copying a user account is a simple process that can be initiated by right-clicking a user account and selecting Copy.

NOTE   Only the most common attributes are copied to a new user account by default. You can control the attributes that are copied when a new user account is created from a template by modifying the Attribute is copied when duplicating user check box in the Active Directory schema.

Command-line Utilities

While Active Directory Users and Computers is the primary tool used to create and manage domain user accounts, Windows Server 2003 includes a variety of new utilities that allow you to create and manage user accounts from the command line. These utilities are aimed at administrators who prefer to work from the command line, or those looking to create or manage user accounts automatically, in a more flexible manner. The command-line utilities included with Windows Server 2003 for managing users include:

- DSADD—Used to add objects such as users
- DSMOD—Used to modify object attributes and settings
- DSQUERY—Used to query for objects
- DSGET—Used to display attributes of an object
- DSMOVE—Used to move objects to different locations within a domain
- DSRM—Used to delete objects from the directory

10

NOTE

For a complete list of the various switches and options available for these commands, search for the command in Windows Server 2003 Help and Support or type *COMMAND /?* (where *COMMAND* is the command you want help with) at a command prompt. You can also find more information in Chapters 3 and 4 of *MCSE Guide to Managing a Microsoft Windows Server 2003 Environment* (ISBN: 0-619-12035-5).

Bulk Import and Export

In large environments, companies may be in the process of transitioning from one directory service to another, or have reams of user data stored in various databases. Rather than manually create hundreds or thousands of user accounts and related objects from scratch, many companies look for utilities that allow them to import existing stores of data.

Along the same lines, a directory service such as Active Directory contains a wealth of useful information that is properly maintained and kept up to date. Companies might be interested in exporting this information for the purpose of populating secondary databases, such as an application used by human resources staff.

To provide administrators with the flexibility to import and export data to or from Active Directory, Windows Server 2003 includes two main utilities, known as **CSVDE** and **LDIFDE**. You will learn more about each of these utilities in the following sections.

CSVDE

CSVDE is a command-line tool that supports the bulk export and import of Active Directory data to and from comma-separated value (CSV) files. One of the benefits of the CSV file format is that its structure allows these files to be easily created or opened in a traditional text editor, database program, or spreadsheet application such as Microsoft Excel. When data is exported from Active Directory using CSVDE, the first line of the file contains the name of each attribute being exported, separated by commas. Each subsequent line represents a specific object stored in the directory, with attribute values ordered according to that first line.

NOTE   You can only use CSVDE to create new objects or export a list of objects. You cannot use CSVDE to modify existing objects.

For example, you can use CSVDE to export information about all current objects stored in Active Directory to a text file. In the following example, information about objects stored in Active Directory would be exported to a text file named output.csv:

```
CSVDE -f output.csv
```

Opening the resulting file in a text editor such as Notepad would display the exported information in CSV format, as illustrated in Figure 10-29.

Figure 10-29   Example CSV file

The output of the CSVDE command can also be filtered. For example, the following would output only user objects:

```
CSVDE -f output.csv -r "(objectClass=user)"
```

To further refine the output, the following would output only user objects in the users container of the child01.supercorp.net domain (note that the command should all be on one line):

```
CSVDE -f output.csv -r "(objectClass=user)" -d
"cn=users,dc=child01,dc=supercorp,dc=net"
```

Ultimately, an administrator might choose to import the information stored in the CSVDE file to a different directory or application. In a similar manner, data stored in an existing CSV file, perhaps exported from another LDAP directory, can also be imported into Active Directory to create new objects (such as user accounts) using a bulk process. When importing a file for the purpose of creating new user objects, the key consideration is that the format of the CSV file is correct. For best results, use the first line of an exported CSV file to determine the correct syntax required for such a file to be imported.

NOTE

For more information about the CSVDE command, see the CSVDE topic in Windows Server 2003 Help and Support Center, or type CSVDE /? at the command line.

LDIFDE

In a manner similar to CSVDE, the LDIFDE utility is a command-line tool that you can use to import and export data from Active Directory. Unlike CSVDE, which works with CSV files, LDIFDE uses a file format known as LDAP Interchange Format (LDIF). LDIF is an industry standard method for formatting information to be imported into or exported from LDAP directories.

Some common uses of LDIFDE, and the LDIF file format, include extending the Active Directory schema; adding, modifying, and deleting user and group objects; and importing bulk data from an existing directory to populate the Active Directory database. Unlike CSVDE, you can use LDIFDE to modify existing objects as well as create new objects. In Activity 10-5, you will use LDIFDE to modify an existing user account.

Unlike a CSV file, where a comma separates every attribute, LDIF files place each attribute and its associated value on a separate line, with a blank line separating individual objects.

The file format associated with LDIFDE is LDF, but these files can be read in any text editor in a manner similar to files created with CSVDE.

ACTIVITY

Activity 10-5: Using LDIFDE to Modify User Accounts

Time Required: 10 minutes

Objective: Use LDIFDE to modify an existing user account.

Description: Like User*XX*C, User*XX*B is also a junior employee working with sensitive information. To reduce the risk of a confidentiality breech, company policy states that all such employees are restricted from logging on after hours. Rather than manually editing User*XX*B's account properties using Active Directory Users and Computers, you decide to use LDIFDE to copy the logonHours attribute from User*XX*C to User*XX*B.

1. If necessary, start your server and log on using the **Administrator** account in the **CHILD*XX*** domain (where *XX* is the number of the forest root domain for which your server is a domain controller) using the password **Password01**.

2. Click **Start** and then click **Command Prompt**.

3. Type **LDIFDE –f D:\ldfout.ldf –d "OU=Atlanta,OU=North America**
   XX,DC=child YY,DC=supercorp,DC=net" –r "(cn=UserXXC)" –l
   "logonHours" (where *XX* is the number of your server and *YY* is the number of
   the forest root domain for which your server is a domain controller) and then press
   Enter, as shown in Figure 10-30. Note that if you do not have a hard drive labeled
   D:, substitute the "D:" in "D:\ldfout.ldf" for another hard drive. If you use a hard
   drive that is labeled something other than D:, you will also need to substitute D: in
   steps 5, 12, 13, and 14 for the correct hard drive.

NOTE   The -r parameter of the LDIFDE and CSVDE utility is very flexible because it
allows the use of an LDAP search filter. For more information about LDAP
search filters see RFC 2254 at *www.ietf.org/rfc/rfc2254.txt*. You can also find
more information at *msdn.microsoft.com/library/en-us/adsi/adsi/search_*
filter_syntax.asp.

Figure 10-30   Exporting data using LDIFDE

NOTE   The -d parameter specifies the container to be searched. Additionally, the -l
parameter specifies which attributes of the object(s) should be returned. If you
want to output more than one attribute, separate each attribute by a comma (,)
such as: "attribute1,attribute2,attribute3". If the -l parameter is not specified,
all attributes will be returned.

4. Click **Start** and then click **My Computer**.

5. Navigate to the **D:** drive.

6. Double-click the file **ldfout.ldf** to open it.

7. On the dn: line, change CN=User*XX*C to **CN=UserXXB** (where XX is the number of your server).

8. On the changetype line, change add to **modify**.

NOTE The first line of this file specifies the Distinguished Name (DN) of the object to be added or modified. The next line of the file, *changetype*, specifies the type of operation to be performed on the object. Other valid values for *changetype* include *add*, to create a new object with the specified DN; and *delete*, to delete an object with the specified DN.

9. Between the changetype line and logonHours line, add a new line as follows: **replace: logonHours**

10. On the last line of the file, add a hyphen (**-**).

 NOTE When you specify modify as the changetype, you can specify one or more operations to be performed on the object's attributes. Valid operations include add, to add a new value to an attribute; replace, to replace an existing value; and delete, to remove an existing value. You must separate each operation by a hyphen (-).

11. On the File menu, click **Save As**.

12. Save the file to the D: drive and name the file **ldfin.ldf**. Your file should now look similar to Figure 10-31.

 CAUTION When saving the file, be sure you set the Save as type to All Files. Otherwise, when you save the file, it will be named ldfin.ldf.txt.

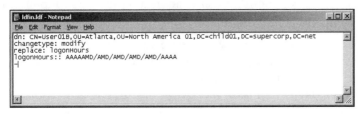

Figure 10-31 Modifying an LDIF file

13. Close Notepad and the Windows Explorer window currently displaying the D: drive.

14. At the command prompt window you already have open, type **LDIFDE -i -f D:\ldfin.ldf** and then press **Enter**. You should receive a message that one entry was modified successfully. If you receive an error, ensure your ldfin.ldf file is formatted correctly and then try again.

15. Close the command prompt.

16. Use Active Directory Users and Computers to confirm the logon hours have changed for User*XX*B to match User*XX*C (where *XX* is the number of your server).

17. Log off your server if you do not intend to immediately continue to the next activity. Otherwise, stay logged on.

NOTE   For more information about the LDIFDE command, see the LDIFDE topic in Windows Server 2003 Help and Support Center, or type LDIFDE /? at the command line. You can also find more information on LDIFDE in Microsoft Knowledge Base Article 237667 at *support.microsoft.com*. For information on the LDIF file format see RFC 2849 at *www.ietf.org/rfc/rfc2849.txt* (note that the LDIFDE utility does not support the "control:" keyword from RFC 2849).

Creating and Modifying User Accounts Programmatically

Because Active Directory supports a number of open standards and interfaces, there are many ways to create a user, besides the Users and Computers console. You can create users by scripts or programs, or automatically by a variety of tools. It is fairly common to create users from a script, program, or enterprise-wide tool such as Microsoft Metadirectory Services (MMS). (MMS is a product allowing Active Directory to participate with other directory services and databases, such as Novell NDS or SQL server, by synchronizing data between them. MMS can also synchronize information between separate forests.)

One scripting interface you can use to create users is the Active Directory Service Interface (ADSI). ADSI provides a single abstract set of directory service interfaces for the management of a network. Because ADSI abstracts the underlying directory service, administrators can use the same interface to manage directories that use LDAP, Novell NetWare Directory Services (NDS), Windows NT Server 4.0 directory, and more. ADSI makes it simple for administrators to automate common tasks such as creating users and groups, modifying group membership, and setting permissions.

ADSI can be accessed in many different ways. While a programmer can use ADSI from a Visual Basic, C#, or VC++ application, most network administrators choose to use the Windows Scripting Host (WSH) and VBScript (or another scripting language that WSH supports). The following is an example of a VBScript that uses ADSI to add a new user:

```
Set objCN = GetObject("LDAP://cn=users,dc=child01,dc=supercorp,
dc=net")

Set objUser = objCN.Create("User", "cn=James Horner")
objUser.Put "sAMAccountName", "jhorner"
objUser.SetInfo

objUser.ChangePassword "", "Password01"
objUser.AccountDisabled = FALSE
objUser.SetInfo
```

To start, you must open a program in which to create the script. A script is nothing more than a simple text file with a different extension (such as .vbs), so Notepad works well to create scripts. The first step the script must perform is to connect, or bind, to a directory object. This can be done by using the GetObject method and specifying an LDAP path. The following code connects to the user's container in the child01.supercorp.net domain.

```
Set objCN = GetObject("LDAP://cn=users,dc=child01,dc=supercorp,
dc=net")
```

What this code does is create a connection and then assign the connection to a variable that you can use. In other words, the variable objCN now holds a reference (or points to) the connection to the container that GetObject returned.

NOTE Note that objCN is just a variable name and can be just about anything (except reserve keywords used by the scripting language). Instead of using the name objCN, myConnection, myCon, or ABCD would all work (although the latter is not very descriptive). Also note that the Set keyword is required in this instance because GetObject returns a reference to an object.

With a connection to the container object, the script must now create the new user. The following creates a new user account for James Horner in memory:

```
Set objUser = objCN.Create("User", "cn=James Horner")
```

Using the connection to the container referenced by objCN (that GetObject originally returned), the Create method is called. The Create method takes two parameters: the type of object you want to create and the name of the object. The Create method then returns a reference to the newly created object. Note, however, that this new object is only created in memory and has not actually been written to the directory. A variable named objUser is used to store the reference to the new object. With a new object, the script can now set some of the user's attributes. The following sets the user's sAMAccountName:

```
objUser.Put "sAMAccountName", "jhorner"
```

Using the objUser variable (which holds a reference to the new user account), the Put method is used to set an attribute. The Put method takes the name of the attribute you want to set and the value. With the required attribute(s) set, the new user can now be written to the Active Directory database:

```
objUser.SetInfo
```

The SetInfo method writes the new object, and any attribute changes, to the directory. If the SetInfo method were not called, the new user would never actually be written to the directory. It is important to note, however, that not all attributes can be set until after a new object is written to the directory. For example, you cannot set a user's password or disable the account until after the user is created. Continuing with the script, the following code could be added at the end to set the user's password and then write the password change to the directory:

```
objUser.ChangePassword "", "Password01"
objUser.AccountDisabled = FALSE
objUser.SetInfo
```

The ChangePassword method is used to change a user's password and takes two parameters: the user's old password and the new password. The AccountDisabled property determines if the account is disabled or not. Set the AccountDisabled property to TRUE to disable the account and to FALSE to enable the account.

10

Once you have the script written in Notepad, you can then save the file with a .vbs (when writing VBScripts) extension such as NewUser.vbs. There is one trick you should note: when you save the file with the .vbs extension in Notepad, be sure to select the All Files in the Save as type drop-down list. Otherwise, Notepad saves the file as Filename.vbs.txt, which does not execute (it just opens the script back up in the text editor). With the script created and saved, you can then double-click the script in Windows Explorer to execute it.

NOTE   Don't worry if you don't totally follow the above scripts—scripting is an entire topic (or book) on its own. The important thing you understand for the 70-294 exam is the flow of the script and the general idea of what each line is doing. That is, establish a connection, create a new user, set attributes, and write the changes to the directory. You should be able to identify what each of the above code lines does and place them in the correct order.

TIP   The World Wide Web is a terrific resource for scripts. If you would like to script something and you're not sure how to get started, an example has probably already been made. By using a search engine, you can find scripts that perform all but the most unusual tasks. Additionally, Alan Finn has written a nice introduction to scripting for administrators at *www.2000trainers.com* (currently located in the Windows 2000 section). You can also visit *www.15seconds.com/focus/ADSI.htm* to find another terrific resource to learn about ADSI.

PLANNING AND ADMINISTERING GROUPS

Administrators may be responsible for thousands of user accounts and hundreds of resources. Trying to manage each individual account is not very efficient. If you had 5 printers, 10 file shares, 2 SQL database servers, and 150 users in your company, that would be more than 2500 sets of permissions to manage—at a minimum. On the other hand, if those 150 users all required the same level of access, then assigning permissions to a group—which could encompass all of those users with the same access needs—would take only a few minutes.

In the following sections, you will learn more about the different group types and scopes available in a Windows Server 2003 Active Directory environment, as well as the various membership rules that apply to those groups.

Group Types

A group's type is used to define how that group can be used within an Active Directory domain or forest. There are two different **group types** in Active Directory: **distribution groups** and **security groups**. The distinction between each type of group is important, because each is created for a different purpose and has different characteristics. The following sections look at both security and distribution groups in more detail.

Security Groups

Security groups are typically the most popular type of group in an Active Directory environment. In a manner similar to a user account, security groups are defined by a Security Identifier (SID) that allows them to be assigned both permissions for resources in discretionary access control lists (DACLs), as well as rights to perform different tasks. When trying to determine whether to create a **security group** or a distribution group, an administrator first needs to consider how that group will be used. Any group that will ultimately be assigned permissions or rights must be a security group, because permissions and rights cannot be assigned to distribution groups.

Although the assignment of permissions and rights is the primary function of security groups, these groups can also be used as e-mail entities. Sending an e-mail message to an Active Directory security group (such as when Microsoft Exchange 2000/2003 is installed) sends the message to all of the members of that group.

Distribution Groups

Distribution groups are the second type of group in an Active Directory environment. Unlike security groups, distribution groups do not have an associated SID and therefore cannot be used to assign permissions or rights to members. The primary purpose of a **distribution group** is for use with e-mail applications such as Microsoft Exchange 2000/2003, where sending an e-mail message to the distribution group sends the message to all members of that group. For example, you might use an "all employees" distribution group to send important e-mail announcements to everyone in the company, even though everyone in the company does not have the same security privileges on the network.

10

While distribution groups may not seem useful in light of the fact that e-mail messages can also be sent to security groups, they differentiate themselves in an important way. Because distribution groups do not have a SID associated with them, they do not impact the user authentication process unnecessarily with excess information not required for security purposes. For this reason, if a group will never be used for security purposes, its type should be configured as a distribution group rather than a security group.

Changing a Group's Type

If you discover that you have created a security group that you don't need for permissions, but would like to use as a distribution group, you can change its type if the domain is at the Windows 2000 native or Windows Server 2003 functional level. You can also change a distribution group (such as an e-mail list) into a security group, if you wish to include it in DACLs for permissions. Again, this conversion can only be made if the domain is at the Windows 2000 native or Windows Server 2003 functional level. To change the group type in Active Directory Users and Computers, access the properties of the group and then on the General tab select the appropriate group type that is needed.

NOTE If the domain is at the Windows 2000 mixed or Windows Server 2003 Interim functional level, a group's type cannot be changed.

Group Scopes

The **group scope** determines where that group can be used in the forest and which objects it can contain. In other words, the scope determines when a group can be nested in other groups, and when it can be referenced in DACLs and SACLs. In Windows Server 2003 and Active Directory, there are four possible scopes that a group can have:

- Local scope
- Domain local scope
- Global scope
- Universal scope

Technically speaking, a group is described as "a group with global scope." However, most people simply call it a global group. Likewise, the terms universal group and domain local group are also commonly used.

Local Scope

A **local group** (or, a group with local scope) is a group that is used only within the context of a specific machine. For this reason, they are often called machine local groups to make clear the distinction between machine local groups and domain local groups. Because the scope of a machine local group is the one machine only, you can only make reference to that machine local group on that local machine. For example, you could create a machine local group called Color Printer Users on a print server named PrintSrv01 that is running Windows Server 2003. You could assign permissions controlling the access to a printer called FastColor served by PrintSrv01—allowing the Color Printer Users group to use the printer. However, the machine FileSrv01 would know nothing about this group (because it is local to PrintSrv01), and thus you could not assign permissions to access resources on FileSrv01 using the Color Printer Users group. This concept is illustrated in Figure 10-32.

NOTE It would be perfectly valid to have a second local group called Color Printer Users on FileSrv01. However, a group named Color Printer Users on PrintSrv01 would have a different SID from a group named Color Printer Users on FileSrv01. This means that although the names are the same, they are in reality two different groups—each only being visible on the respective local computer.

In addition to machines that are part of a workgroup, machines that are members of the domain (that is, member servers and workstations) can also have machine local groups. Machine local groups are not stored in Active Directory, but in the local SAM database on

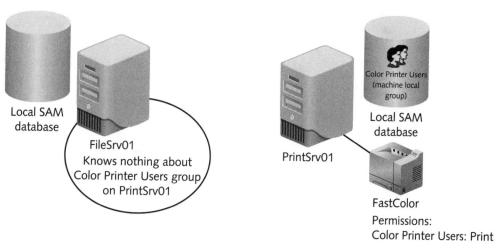

Figure 10-32   Example of machine local groups

10

each local machine. This means that you cannot create machine local groups on a Windows Server 2003 computer that is configured as a domain controller.

 Starting with Windows 2000 and continued in Windows Server 2003, Microsoft recommends that domain local groups be used rather than machine local groups.

NOTE

Although a machine local group can only be assigned access to resources on the machine on which it exists, a machine local group can contain users from its local security database, any users, global groups, or universal groups in the forest, and any domain local groups in its own domain. In addition, any user or groups from a trusted domain can also be a member of a machine local group. Figure 10-33 illustrates some (but not all) of these possibilities.

Domain Local Scope

A **domain local group** is created on a domain controller and can only be assigned permissions to a resource available in the local domain in which it is created. However, group membership can come from any domain within the forest. A domain local group can contain user or global groups from any domain. Domain local groups are mainly used to assign access permissions to a resource. For example, you may want to add users, global groups, or universal groups to a domain local group and then assign the domain local group the actual permissions to a resource within the domain. This technique allows you to assign permissions once rather than many times for individuals or multiple groups.

The difference between a machine local group and a domain local group is where it can be used. A machine local group can only be used to assign permission on one machine, but a domain local group can be used on any machine in the domain. Figure 10-34 illustrates some (but not all) of the possible group memberships for a domain local group.

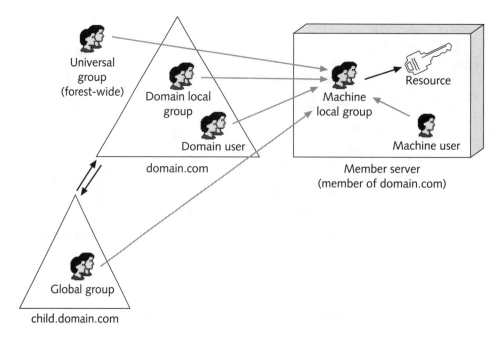

Figure 10-33 Machine local group membership and resource access

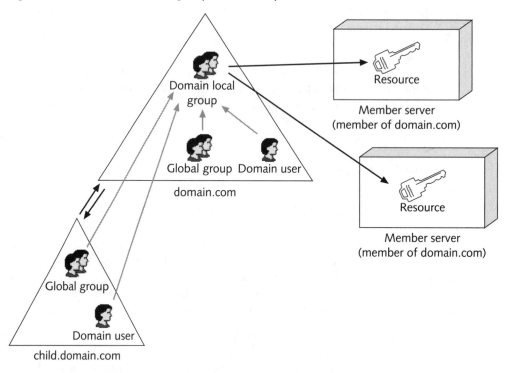

Figure 10-34 Domain local group membership and resource access

NOTE

Although all the figures in this section show the group membership going from *child.domain.com* to *domain.com* (that is, from child domain to parent domain), it is also perfectly acceptable to have users/groups in a parent domain be members of a group in a child domain. For example, take Figure 10-34. If a domain local group was created in the *child.domain.com* domain, global groups and domain users from *domain.com* could be members of the *child.domain. com* domain local group (in addition to global groups and domain users from *child.domain.com*).

The functional level of a domain impacts the membership rules of domain local groups. When an Active Directory domain is configured to the Windows 2000 mixed domain functional level, the following rules apply to domain local groups within an Active Directory forest:

- Can contain user accounts from any domain in the forest or any trusted domain
- Can contain global groups from any domain in the forest or any trusted domain

When a domain is configured to the Windows 2000 native or Windows Server 2003 domain functional levels, the following rules apply to domain local groups:

- Can contain user accounts from any domain in the forest or any trusted domain
- Can contain global groups from any domain in the forest or any trusted domain
- Can contain universal groups
- Can contain other domain local groups from the same domain

Global Scope

A **global group** can be assigned permissions to any resource in any domain within the forest (or any other *trusting* domain that trusts the domain where the global group exists). The main limitation of a global group is that it can only contain users from the same domain in which it is created. Global groups are mainly used to organize user objects into logical groupings according to function. For example, if sales managers from *child.domain.com* need access to a shared file stored in *domain.com*, you can create a global group in *child.domain.com* called sales managers, place all individual sales manager user accounts from *child.domain.com* A into this group, and then add the global group to a domain local group that has permission to access the

10

resource located in *domain.com*. (Note that you could also give the sales managers group direct access to the resource in *domain.com*—but this is not recommended.) Figure 10-35 illustrates some (but not all) of the possible group memberships for a global group.

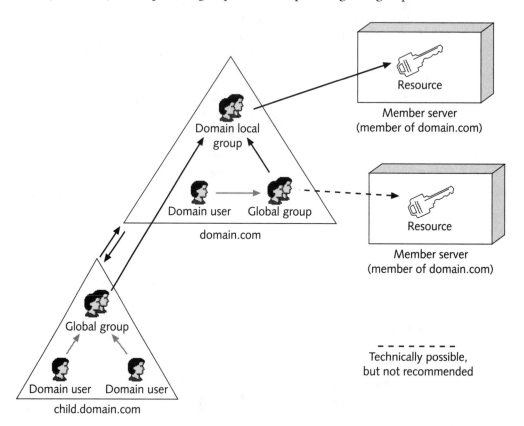

Figure 10-35   Global group membership and resource access

In much the same way that the functional level of a domain impacts the membership rules for domain local groups, the same is true of global groups. When a domain is configured to the Windows 2000 mixed domain functional level, the following rules apply to global groups within an Active Directory forest:

- Can contain user accounts from the same domain
- Cannot be added to universal groups in the forest, because universal groups do not exist at the Windows 2000 mixed domain functional level
- Can be added to machine local groups or domain local groups in any domain

When a domain is configured to the Windows 2000 native or Windows Server 2003 domain functional levels, the following rules apply to global groups within an Active Directory forest:

- Can contain user accounts or other global groups from the same domain

- Can be added to universal groups

- Can be added to machine local groups or domain local groups in any domain

NOTE   It is perfectly acceptable—and not that uncommon—to have multiple global groups *in different domains* with the same name. While each group will have its own SID and therefore is a different group, you still need a way of distinguishing groups from different domains that have the same name. To explicitly specify the domain where the group exists, you use: *domain_name\group_name* (where *domain_name* is the name of the domain that contains the group and *group_name* is the name of the group). For example, assume you had two global groups called Sales Staff—one existing in the *domain.com* domain and one existing in the *child.domain.com* domain. To refer explicitly to the Sales Staff group in *domain.com*, you would use: *domain.com\Sales Staff*. To refer explicitly to the Sales Staff group in *child.domain.com*, you would use: *child. domain.com\Sales Staff*. Also keep in mind that if you do not specify any domain, the local domain is assumed.

Universal Scope

Universal groups are typically created for the purpose of aggregating groups in different domains throughout an Active Directory forest. A universal group can be assigned permissions to any resource in any domain within the forest. This seems very similar to a global group, but it actually has two main differences. First of all, a universal group can consist of user objects from any domain in the forest; global groups can only consist of user objects from the same domain. Second, universal groups are only available when a domain is configured at the Windows 2000 native or Windows Server 2003 functional level. If your domain is at the default Windows 2000 mixed functional level, this group scope is disabled.

For example, a universal group named Enterprise Marketing might be configured in a large organization with multiple domains. Then, the Marketing Users global groups from various domains (which contain individual marketing user accounts) could be added to the Enterprise Marketing universal group, forming a single group that encompasses all of the marketing users within an organization across domain boundaries. Then, when rights or permissions need to be assigned to all marketing users in the forest, they could be assigned once to the Enterprise Marketing universal group, rather than individual Marketing Users groups from each domain. Figure 10-36 illustrates some (but not all) of the possible group memberships for a universal group.

10

Incoming arrows! Don't worry if you have to stare at Figure 10-36 for several minutes—it's complicated. To make the figure easier to understand, start by following the domain users from each domain until you reach the universal group. Once you have located all the members of the universal group, follow the arrows leaving the universal group to see what resources the universal group has permissions for.

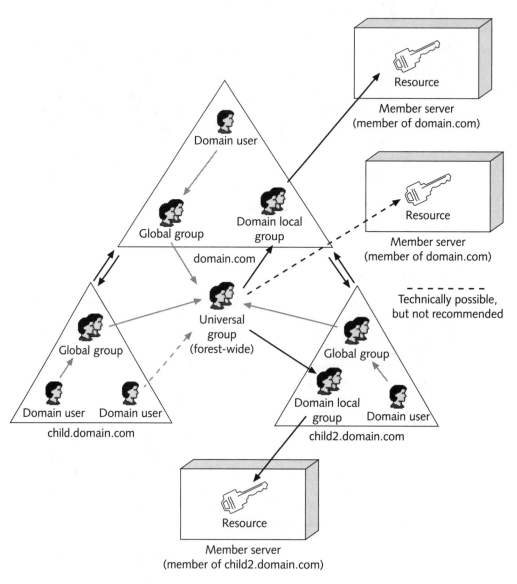

Figure 10-36   Universal group membership and resource access

Many new administrators wonder why they should even bother with domain local or global groups; why not just use universal groups exclusively? It is impractical in large forests to use universal groups exclusively because of one key feature of universal groups: all universal groups, including the details of their membership, are recorded in the global catalog. Groups that are large in size, if created as universal groups, generate large amounts of data to be stored in the global catalog. Even more crucially than that, however, is that changes to the membership of a universal group must be replicated to all global catalog servers in the forest, as well as to all domain controllers in its own domain. Although Windows Server 2003 adds new features so only the changes to group memberships need to be replicated (instead of the entire group list), the replication traffic could still be extensive.

NOTE

Because universal groups are stored on global catalog servers, a global catalog server may be required to retrieve a user's universal group membership during the logon process. A global catalog server is required for retrieving universal group membership during logon when, in a multi-domain forest, the domain containing the user account is at the Windows 2000 native or Windows Server 2003 domain functional level. A global catalog is *not* required for retrieving universal group membership during logon when there is only a single domain in the forest (regardless of what functional level the domain is at), or when, in a multi-domain forest, the domain containing the user account is at the Windows 2000 mixed or Windows Server 2003 Interim level. The Administrator account (RID 500) can still log on even if a global catalog server is unavailable.

NOTE

In Windows 2000, Microsoft recommended that a group hold no more than 5,000 members because of the way groups were replicated in addition to manageability. To overcome this limitation, users should be placed in multiple global groups that are then placed into a single universal group (or another global group if you are using group nesting). If the forest is at the Windows Server 2003 functional level, the 5,000-user recommendation is not as much of a concern—it's only an issue of manageability. However, you should still always avoid adding users directly to universal groups.

The following rules apply to universal groups:

- Can contain user accounts from any trusted domain
- Can contain global group accounts from any trusted domain
- Can contain other universal groups

Table 10-1 provides a summary of each group type, its use, and its membership options within an Active Directory forest. The process of creating different groups will be looked at in more detail later in this chapter.

10

Table 10-1 Windows Server 2003 group summary

Group Type	General Use	Windows 2000 Mixed or Windows Server 2003 Interim Membership Options	Windows 2000 Native or Windows Server 2003 Membership Options
Local	Assigned permissions to resources on a local computer	User accounts and global groups from any domain; domain local groups from the domain of which the machine is a member	User accounts, global, and universal groups from any domain; domain local groups from the domain of which the machine is a member
Domain local	Assigned permissions to resources within local domain	User accounts, and global groups from any domain	User accounts, global, and universal groups from any domain; other domain local groups from the same domain
Global	Used to organize individual objects such as user accounts into administrative units	User accounts from only the domain in which the group exists	User accounts and other global groups from only the domain in which the group exists
Universal	Used to organize various objects into administrative units	Not available	User accounts, global, domain local, and universal groups from any domain

Changing a Group's Scope

If an administrator decides that a group should have a different scope, it may be possible (in certain circumstances) to change the scope if the domain is at the Windows 2000 native or Windows Server 2003 functional level. To change the group scope in Active Directory Users and Computers, access the properties of the group and then on the General tab select the appropriate group scope that is needed. The following types of conversions are allowed:

- Global to universal—allowed as long as the group is not a member of another global group itself.

- Domain local to universal—allowed as long as the group does not contain another domain local group as one of its members.

- Universal to global—allowed as long as the group does not contain another universal group as one of its members.

- Universal to domain local—always allowed regardless of members or membership.

NOTE

If the domain is at the Windows 2000 mixed or Window Server 2003 Interim functional level, a group's scope cannot be changed.

Managing Security Groups

As you start to implement the use of security groups, a general strategy is to use the acronym **A G U DL P**. This refers to the following:

1. Create user **A**ccounts, and organize them within **G**lobal groups. Often users are grouped in global groups based on departments in the organization.

2. Optional: Create **U**niversal groups and place global groups from any domain within the universal groups.

3. Create **D**omain **L**ocal groups that represent the resources in which you want to control access, and add the global or universal groups to the domain local groups.

4. Assign **P**ermissions to the domain local groups.

NOTE The use of universal groups is optional. If you only have a single domain, it does not make sense to use universal groups. Universal groups should be used when you have *multiple* global groups in different domains that require access to the same resources throughout the forest.

TIP Another, shorter, way of remembering the acronym **A G U DL P** is: **A**ccounts go in **G**lobal groups, which in turn go into **U**niversal groups, which in turn go in **D**omain **L**ocal groups, which are assigned **P**ermissions.

For example, Super Corp has a shared folder called SalesReports. All users in all domains that work in the Marketing Department must have read access to the SalesReports share. Following the steps previously discussed, this is how you could organize access:

1. In each domain, create a global group called Marketing Users, and add any appropriate user accounts to the group.

2. Optional: Create a universal group called Super Marketing, and add all global groups created in Step 1 from all domains to the universal group.

3. Create a domain local group called SalesReports Readers, and add the Super Marketing universal group to the local group. (If you skipped Step 2, you can add the Marketing Users global group(s) instead.)

4. Assign the SalesReports Readers local group to the access control list of the actual share on the network, and specify the appropriate permissions.

TIP This is one of the best practices that Microsoft loves to test on. You should remember the acronym A G U DL P and be able to apply it.

TIP If you have a multi-domain forest with domains at the Windows Server 2000 native or Windows Server 2003 domain functional level, but you do not want to use universal groups, you can disable the requirement that universal group membership be retrieved from a global catalog server using the

10

IgnoreGCFailures registry entry. Although universal group caching has reduced the need to use this registry entry, there may be instances where it is useful. For example, even if you do not use universal groups, universal group caching requires that the user log on at least once at the site before the fact that the user is not a member of any universal groups is cached. If you do decide to use this registry entry on remote sites without a global catalog server, it is very important that you do not use universal groups, because a user may be denied some permission or right by being a member of a universal group. In such a situation, if universal groups were not added to the user's token, the user may be able to access resources they would not normally have access to. For more information, see Microsoft Knowledge Base Article 241789 at *support.microsoft.com*. The article is written for Windows 2000 Server but is still applicable to Windows Server 2003.

Figure 10-37 illustrates the implementation of the previous steps without using a universal group. In contrast, Figure 10-38 illustrates the implementation of the previous steps using a universal group.

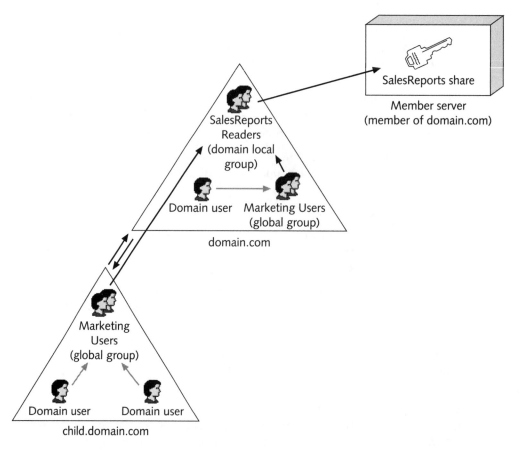

Figure 10-37   Example of A G DL P group strategy

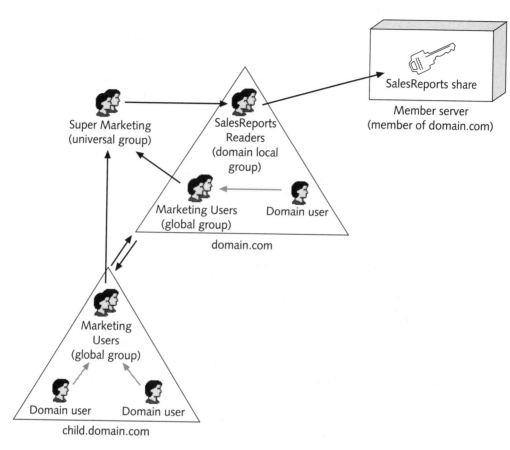

Figure 10-38   Example of A G U DL P group strategy

Again, many new administrators wonder why they should even bother with creating so many groups. Why not just put the users in a single group and then give the group the necessary permissions? In a small domain, using a single group may work, but in a larger domain, it's a management nightmare. The A G U DL P group strategy has the following benefits:

- Reduced need to set permissions—once domain local groups are created for a resource (such as SalesReports Readers, SalesReports Writers, SalesReports Full Control), administrators can give users the necessary permissions from Active Directory Users and Computers (by adding the user/group to the appropriate domain local group).

- Ability to divide authority—by using multiple group layers, administration can be divided. Server administrators can create domain local groups and assign the necessary permissions to the domain local groups. Domain administrators can create global groups and add the necessary users to the global groups. Enterprise administrators can create universal groups and add the necessary global groups to the universal groups.

- Reduce replication traffic—adding or removing users from a group does not require the change be replicated across the entire forest. For example, if a user was directly a member of a universal group and then was removed, the change would have to be replicated throughout the forest. In contrast, if the user was a member of a global group that was in turn a member of the same universal group, the change would only have to replicate throughout the global group's domain when the user is removed. The only time a change would have to replicate throughout the forest is when an entire global group is added to or removed from a universal group.

Group Nesting

If your domain is running at the Windows 2000 native or the Windows Server 2003 functional level, you can use the option of nesting groups to simplify administrative tasks. For example, Super Corp may have three global groups called Help Desk, IT Managers, and Network Support. Together, these three groups of users may represent the Information Technology Department of Super Corp. You could create the Information Technology global group and put the Help Desk, IT Managers, and Network Support groups into this one group, thus simplifying the assignment of permissions for resources to which all three groups should have access. You do not need to add individuals to the Information Technology group. When you are assigning permissions to resources, assign the permissions to domain local groups.

Note that if you are working in a single domain forest, you can use global group nesting or universal groups interchangeably. Choose one of these options to group your users, and then add these groups to the local domain groups.

Understanding the Built-in Groups

When Windows Server 2003 Active Directory is installed, a number of built-in local security groups with various preassigned rights are created, which you may want to use to allow users to perform certain network tasks. Whenever possible, you should use one of the built-in local groups to assign rights because this eases the implementation of delegation and security rights throughout the network. For example, rather than creating a special group with rights to back up and restore servers, you can use the built-in backup operators group.

The built-in groups created automatically when Active Directory is installed are stored in two different locations, namely the Builtin container and the Users container. The following sections outline the built-in groups found in each location.

The Builtin Container

The Builtin container, shown in Figure 10-39, contains a number of domain local group accounts that are allocated different user rights based on common administrative or network-related tasks. Table 10-2 outlines the name of each of the built-in domain local groups found in this container, as well as a description of the purpose or capabilities of members of the group.

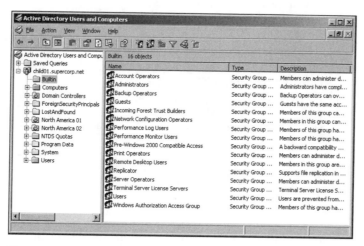

Figure 10-39   Builtin container

Table 10-2   Domain local groups found in the Builtin container

Built-in Group	Description
Account Operators	Able to create, delete, and modify user accounts and groups within the domain; they cannot place themselves or anyone else in the Administrators group
Administrators	Assigned complete unrestricted access to the local computer and possibly the domain
Backup Operators	Able to override security restrictions for the purpose of backing up or restoring files
Incoming Forest Trust Builders	Able to create one-way incoming trusts to the forest
Network Configuration Operators	Able to change TCP/IP settings on domain controllers within the domain
Performance Log Users	Able to remotely access servers to schedule logging of performance counters
Performance Monitor Users	Able to remotely access servers to monitor performance
Guests	Have no default permissions or rights (Note: The guests group is a member of the special group Everyone. This means that any access permissions to the Everyone group gives permission to the Guests group.)

10

Table 10-2   Domain local groups found in the Builtin container (continued)

Built-in Group	Description
Pre-Windows 2000 Compatible Access	This group is created to support applications that work with Windows NT 4.0, but may have problems with Windows Server 2003 security. This group has read access on all users and groups within the domain. This is used primarily for Windows NT RAS servers that require access to Active Directory.
Print Operators	Have all print administration rights
Remote Desktop Users	Able to log on to domain controllers within the domain remotely
Replicator	Used by the File Replication Service
Server Operators	Able to share disk resources, back-up and restore files, and shut down or restart the server
Terminal Server License Servers	Contains computer accounts for all servers configured as Terminal Server License Servers
Users	Have no default permissions, except for permissions assigned by the administrator
Windows Authorization Access Group	Allows members to query user accounts for the group membership information of a user

The Users Container

The Users container, shown in Figure 10-40, contains a number of different domain local and global group accounts. Table 10-3 outlines the name of each of the domain local and global groups found in this container, as well as a description of the purpose or capabilities of members of the group. Note that some of the groups listed are only found in the root domain of an Active Directory forest rather than each individual domain.

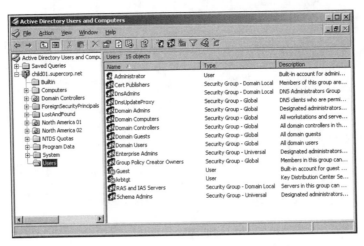

Figure 10-40   Additional groups available

Table 10-3 Domain local and global groups found in the Users container

Group Name	Group Scope	Description
Cert Publishers	Domain local	Able to publish certificates in Active Directory
DnsAdmins	Domain local	Able to administer DNS server settings and configuration
DnsUpdateProxy	Global	Able to perform DNS dynamic updates on behalf of other clients
Domain Admins	Global	Able to perform domain administration tasks
Domain Computers	Global	Contains all workstations and server computer accounts in the domain
Domain Controllers	Global	Contains all domain controller computer accounts in the domain
Domain Guests	Global	Guest accounts in the domain should be added to this group.
Domain Users	Global	All domain user accounts are added to this group
Enterprise Admins	Global	Able to perform administrative tasks throughout an Active Directory forest; this group only exists in the forest root domain
Group Policy Creator Owners	Global	Able to modify group policy objects and settings in the domain
RAS and IAS Servers	Global	Servers in this group can access the remote access properties of a user account
Schema Admins	Global	Able to perform administrative tasks related to the Active Directory schema; this group only exists in the forest root domain
WINS Users	Domain local	Allows read-only access to WINS server settings

10

Understanding Special Identities

In addition to the built-in groups, there are several special identity groups of which you should be aware. What makes these groups special is that the operating system—not the administrator—controls membership of these groups. You cannot add or remove a user, nor can you view a list of members in the group. The operating system dynamically determines in which special identity groups a user should be a member. These groups can, however, be assigned rights and permissions to resources.

NOTE

Special identity groups have well known SIDs. Additionally, special identity groups are not affected by group scope.

Table 10-4 lists some of the special identity groups available in Active Directory and which users are automatically members.

Table 10-4   Special identity groups and their membership

Special Identity	Members
Anonymous Logon	Any user that is not authenticated; for example, a user or service has not supplied a username, password, or domain name
Authenticated Users	Any user that is authenticated using a valid user account; the Authenticated Users group does not include guests
Creator Owner	The user who creates or takes ownership of a resource
Dialup	Any user that is connected using a dial-up connection
Everyone	Any user that is authenticated using a valid user account or is a guest (Note: In Windows 2000, the Everyone group included Anonymous Logons. However, in Windows Server 2003, the Everyone group no longer includes Anonymous Logons by default.)
Interactive	Any user that is logged on locally to a machine either physically or using a Terminal Services connection
Network	Any user that is accessing a resource over the network (as opposed to users that are logged on directly to the computer hosting the resource)

Creating Groups

Like many processes in Active Directory, planning the correct use of groups can be complicated, especially in a large network. However, actually creating a group is very straightforward. Simply right-click the container or organizational unit that will hold the group and click New, then choose Group.

Figure 10-41 shows the single dialog box that is used to actually create the group (which you will do in Activity 10-6). Like a user, a group has a CN attribute that is its name in Active Directory, as well as a NetBIOS-style name for use with older clients. This dialog box also allows you to specify the group type and scope. By clicking OK, the group is created and listed with other objects in Active Directory.

Activity 10-6: Creating Groups

Time Required: 10 minutes

Objective: Practice creating a domain local and global group.

Description: In this activity, you will create a domain local group that you can use to assign permissions to resources within your own domain. It is common, especially in large forests, to use domain local groups to control access to resources. You will then create a global group that you can use to assign permissions to resources anywhere in the forest. Finally, you will add the global group to the domain local group you created. You will need to know how

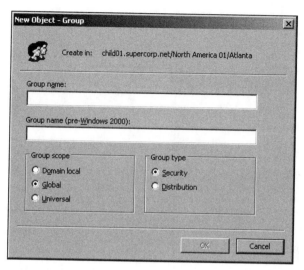

Figure 10-41   New Object dialog box for a group object

10

to create these two types of groups and add groups to other groups in order to effectively manage access to resources.

1. If necessary, start your server and log on using the **Administrator** account in the **CHILDXX** domain (where *XX* is the number of the forest root domain for which your server is a domain controller) using the password **Password01**.

2. Click **Start**, select **Administrative Tools**, and then click **Active Directory Users and Computers**.

3. Expand the nodes in the left tree pane until the Atlanta organizational unit under the North America *XX* organizational unit is visible (where *XX* is the number of your server).

4. In the left tree pane, right-click the **Atlanta** organizational unit, select **New**, and then click **Group**.

5. In the Group name text box, enter **Marketing Users XX** (where *XX* is the number of your server).

6. In the Group scope area, ensure that the **Global** option button is selected. Your screen should look similar to Figure 10-42.

7. Click **OK**.

8. In the left tree pane, right-click the **Atlanta** organizational unit, select **New**, and then click **Group**.

9. In the Group name text box, enter **SalesReports Readers XX** (where *XX* is the number of your server).

10. In the Group scope area, select the **Domain local** option button.

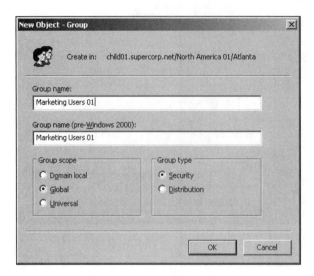

Figure 10-42 Creating a new global group

11. Click **OK**.

12. In the left tree pane, select the **Atlanta** organizational unit to show the users, groups, and other objects it contains in the right details pane.

13. In the right details pane, right-click **SalesReports Readers XX** (where *XX* is the number of your server), and then click **Properties**. Note the information on the General tab.

14. Click the **Members** tab.

15. Click **Add**.

16. Type **Marketing Users XX** (where *XX* is the number of your server), and then click **OK**. The Marketing Users *XX* group is added to the SalesReports Readers *XX* group as shown in Figure 10-43.

17. Click **OK**.

18. Close Active Directory Users and Computers.

19. Log off your server if you do not intend to immediately continue to the next activity. Otherwise, stay logged on.

The command-line utilities, bulk import utilities, and scripting techniques shown earlier to create user accounts can also be used to create and work with groups.

TIP

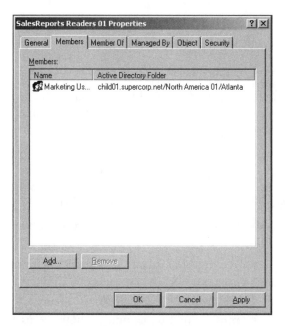

Figure 10-43   Adding a global group to a domain local group

Changing Group Membership

For a group to be of much use, it has to have members. There are two common ways to add members, such as users, to a group. Deciding which method is easier depends on whether you are working with a group or with an individual account. You will add users to the group you created in Activity 10-6.

To work with the group as a whole, view members, add members, or remove members, open the group's properties by double-clicking the group or right-clicking it and choosing Properties. A tabbed dialog box opens, similar to the one shown in Figure 10-43. Select the Members tab, and use the Add and Remove buttons as necessary to change the membership of the group.

Most objects in Active Directory also have a tab in their property sheets called Member Of. This tab allows you to work with the individual objects and put them into groups, rather than work from the group perspective. Both methods have the same effect—as soon as you add a user to a group using the group's Member tab, that group appears in the user's Member Of tab. This is shown in Figure 10-45.

NOTE

The Member Of tab displays a group of which the object is a member only if the group is in the object's local domain. This is not a design flaw—it would take a large amount of resources to retrieve the groups to which the user is a member in all trusting domains. Use the group's Members tab to view, add, or remove members when the group and member are not in the same domain.

Activity 10-7: Adding Members to a Group

Time Required: 5 minutes

Objective: Practice managing group memberships.

Description: In this activity, you will make your three users members of the global group you created in Activity 10-6. You will add the first two users using the group's properties and then the third user by using the user's properties. All Active Directory network administrators need to know how to manage the memberships of groups.

1. If necessary, start your server and log on using the **Administrator** account in the **CHILDXX** domain (where *XX* is the number of the forest root domain for which your server is a domain controller) using the password **Password01**.

2. Click **Start**, select **Administrative Tools**, and then click **Active Directory Users and Computers**.

3. Expand the nodes in the left tree pane until the Atlanta organizational unit under the North America *XX* organizational unit is visible (where *XX* is the number of your server).

4. In the left tree pane, select the **Atlanta** organizational unit to show the users, groups, and other objects it contains in the right details pane.

5. In the right details pane, right-click **Marketing Users XX** (where *XX* is the number of your server), and then click **Properties**.

6. Click the **Members** tab.

7. Click **Add**.

8. Type **UserXXA; UserXXB** (where *XX* is the number of your server), as shown in Figure 10-44, and then click **OK**. (Note the semicolon used to separate multiple names). The two users are added to the Marketing Users *XX* group.

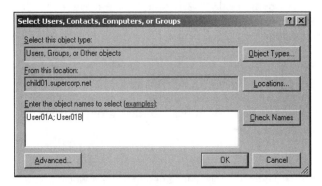

Figure 10-44   Entering the usernames of multiple users simultaneously

9. Click **OK**.

10. In the right details pane, right-click **UserXXC** (where *XX* is the number of your server), and then click **Properties**.

11. Click the **Member Of** tab.

12. Click **Add**.

13. Type **Marketing Users XX** (where *XX* is the number of your server), and then click **OK**. The User is added as a member of the Marketing Users *XX* group, as shown in Figure 10-45.

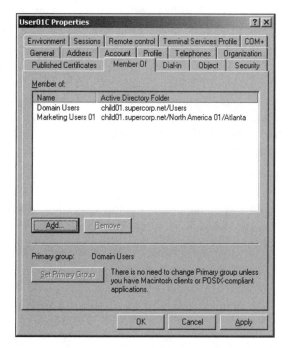

Figure 10-45   Adding a user to a group using the user's properties

14. Click **OK**.

15. Close Active Directory Users and Computers.

16. Log off your server if you do not intend to immediately continue to the next activity. Otherwise, stay logged on.

Determining Group Membership

One of the most important jobs of any Windows Server 2003 network administrator is to ensure that users are members of the correct groups. If not managed effectively, membership (or a lack thereof) of incorrect groups can lead to problems with user access to required resources, or worse still, the ability to access resources they should not be able to access.

The easiest method to determine the groups of which a user is a member is via the Member Of tab in the properties of their user account. As you learned earlier in this chapter, this tab lists all of the global, domain local, and universal groups in which a user's account is a member (assuming the group and user exist in the same domain). Unfortunately, the Member Of tab only displays those groups in which a user has been directly added. For example, if a user account is made a member of a global group named Marketing Users, they appear as a member of this group. However, if the same user account is a member of the Marketing Users global group, and the Marketing Users global group is in turn a member of the Marketing Resources domain local group, the Member Of tab displays membership in the Marketing Users group only. This is not a design flaw—instead, the Member Of tab is designed to strictly list the groups in which the user account is directly a member. To dig deeper, an administrator could use the Member Of tab for the Marketing Users global group to gather additional information.

One additional tool that provides an exceptionally easy method of determining a user's group membership from the command line is DSGET. The DSGET command allows you to display the results of a query on the screen, in a manner similar to DSQUERY, but with different switches supported. For example, the DSGET GROUP command could be used to gather information about all the members of the Marketing Users group in the Users container of the child01.supercorp.net domain if the following command were issued:

```
DSGET GROUP "CN=Marketing Users,CN=users,DC=child01,DC=supercorp,DC=net"
– members
```

Similarly, the DSGET GROUP command could also be used to view all of the groups of which the Marketing Users group is a member:

```
DSGET GROUP "CN=Marketing Users,CN=users,DC=child01,DC=supercorp,DC=net"
– memberof
```

The DSGET USER command can also be used to determine the groups of which a specific user is a member. For example, to view all of the groups of which the user Allan Jones in the Users container of the child01.supercorp.net domain is a member, the following command is issued:

```
DSGET GROUP "CN=Allan Jones,CN=users,DC=child01,DC=supercorp,DC=net"
– memberof
```

By default, the output of the DSGET command is displayed on the screen. In some situations, however, it might be better for the output of this command to be saved to a text file, perhaps to ultimately be imported to a spreadsheet or database application. This is easily accomplished by using a standard redirect at the command line. For example, issuing the following command sends a listing of all members of the Marketing Users group to a text file named mktgusers.txt:

```
DSGET GROUP "CN=Marketing Users,CN=users,DC=child01,DC=supercorp,DC=net"
– members >> mktgusers.txt
```

For a complete list of the various switches and options available with the DSGET command, see the DSGET topic in Windows Server 2003 Help and Support, or type DSGET /? at the command line.

NOTE

CREATING AND MANAGING COMPUTER ACCOUNTS

In much the same way that users on a network require user accounts, computers running Windows NT 4.0, Windows 2000, Windows XP, and Windows Server 2003 require computer accounts to be members of an Active Directory domain. While computer accounts can be created in a domain during the operating system installation processes, they can also be added manually after the fact. While the primary tool used to create and manage computer accounts is the familiar Active Directory Users and Computers, computer accounts can also be created from the System applet in Control Panel from the workstation being added to the domain, as long as the user doing so has been granted appropriate privileges in Active Directory. Alternatively, an administrator can create a computer account in the domain and then assign permission for another user or group to actually join the computer to the domain—using the computer object the administrator created.

Computers running Windows 95 and Windows 98 do not support advanced security features and as such are not assigned computer accounts in a domain.

NOTE

By default, Active Directory allows all authenticated users to add up to 10 computers to a domain. While the default number is 10, you can change the maximum by using ADSI edit. To do so, start by opening the domain partition in ADSI Edit. Then right-click the domain object (for example, dc=child01,dc=supercorp,dc=net) and select Properties. Scroll down and locate the **ms-DS-MachineAccountQuota** attribute and then change the attribute to the number of computers you would like an authenticated user to be able to add. If you set the value to zero, then domain users cannot add computers to the domain unless they have explicitly been given permission.

If you do not want to allow authenticated users to add computers to the domain, a better solution is to remove the Authenticated Users group's Add workstations to domain right. To do so, open the Default Domain Controller Security Policy, expand Local Policies, and then click User Rights Assignment. You can then double-click the Add workstations to domain and remove the Authenticated Users group. By removing the Authenticated Users group rather then editing the **ms-DS-MachineAccountQuota** attribute, you could still allow a particular group of users to join a limited number of computers to the domain. For example, giving a group called Supervisors the Add workstations to domain right (but not the Authenticated Users group) would allow only supervisors to join up to 10 computers to the domain by default.

TIP

10

While most users don't need the ability to join many computers to the domain, there is probably a small group of users that do. For example, you may have a group of workstation technicians that add many computers to the domain. By granting the workstation technicians the Create Computer Objects special permission on the container or organizational unit where you keep computer objects, the technicians can create as many computer objects as necessary. This works because the Add workstations to domain right acts like a security bypass and is only used if needed. For example, assume a user does not have permission to create computer objects in the Computers container and they add a computer to the domain. Because the user does not have permission in the Computers container to create computer accounts, the Add workstations to domain right is used instead—which allows the user to "bypass" security (up to the number of times specified in the ms-DS-MachineAccountQuota attribute) and create a computer account. In contrast, assume a second user has permission to create computer accounts in the Computers container. When the second user attempts to add a computer to the domain, they already have the necessary permissions to create the computer account. Therefore, the computer account is created without having to use (or even consider) the Add workstations to domain right. Because the Add workstations to domain right is not used by the second user, there is no limitation to the number of computers he or she can add to the Computers container.

TIP

It is also a good idea to give the Delete Computer Objects permission and Full Control permission (only on Computer objects!)—as well as the Create permission—to the user or group that manages computer accounts. This allows the user or group permission to manage all computer accounts even ones that they did not create.

Note that when using the System applet in Control Panel to join computers to a domain, computer accounts are created in the Computers container. If the technicians in this example had to use the System applet, they would need permission to create computer objects in the Computers container. Alternatively, instead of using the System applet, the NETDOM command-line utility (2000/2003/XP version only—not NT 4.0) can be used to join a computer to a domain while specifying where the computer account should be created. For example, to join a computer to a domain, you issue the following command at the command line:

```
NETDOM JOIN computername /domain: domainname /ou:
distinguishedname
```

In this example, *computername* is the name of the workstation to be joined, *domainname* is the domain to which the computer is being joined, and *distinguishedname* is the distinguished name of the organizational unit where the computer account should be created.

Although only allowing a small group of users to create computer accounts may be sufficient most of the time, there could also be a situation where you need to create a computer account but actually let a user join the computer to the domain. When you create a Computer Account in Active Directory Users and Computers, one option available is to set which user or group will be joining the computer to the domain. This allows an administrator to have control over what computer accounts get created while still letting a user perform the actual process of joining computers. In Activity 10-8, you will learn how to create computer accounts using Active Directory Users and Computers.

Activity 10-8: Creating Computer Accounts

Time Required: 5 Minutes

Objective: Use Active Directory Users and Computers to create and manage computer accounts.

Description: The IT manager at Super Corp has asked you to document the process for creating new computer accounts in Active Directory Users and Computers. In this activity, you will create and configure the properties of a new computer account.

1. If necessary, start your server and log on using the **Administrator** account in the **CHILDXX** domain (where *XX* is the number of the forest root domain for which your server is a domain controller) using the password **Password01**.

2. Click **Start**, select **Administrative Tools**, and then click **Active Directory Users and Computers**.

3. Expand the nodes in the left tree pane until the Atlanta organizational unit under the North America *XX* organizational unit is visible (where *XX* is the number of your server).

4. In the left tree pane, select the **Atlanta** organizational unit to show the users, groups, and other objects it contains in the right details pane.

5. In the left tree pane, right-click the **Atlanta** organizational unit, select **New**, and then click **Computer**.

6. In the Computer name text box, type **MyWSXX** (where *XX* is the number of your server). The Computer name (pre-Windows 2000) text box should automatically be filled.

7. Click the **Change** button.

8. In the Enter the object name to select text box, type **Marketing Users XX** (where *XX* is the number of your server) and then click **OK**. This will allow users of the Marketing Users *XX* group to add this computer to the domain. Your New Object - Computer dialog box should now look similar to Figure 10-46.

9. Click **Next**.

10. At the Managed screen, click **Next**. By setting up a managed computer, you can take advantage of the Windows Server 2003 Remote Installation Service (RIS).

11. Click **Finish**. The new computer account will appear in the Atlanta organizational unit.

12. In the right details pane, right-click on **MyWSXX** and click **Properties**.

10

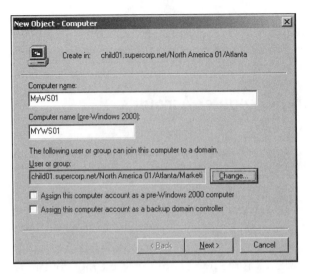

Figure 10-46   New Object - Computer dialog box

13. Review the settings on the General tab, as shown in Figure 10-47.

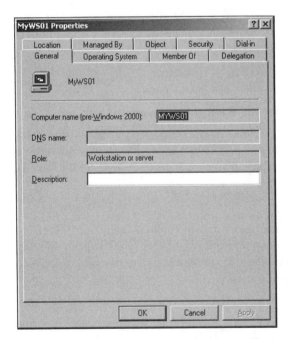

Figure 10-47   Computer account properties

14. Click the **Operating System** tab. Notice that no information is available on the Operating System tab. This information would be generated automatically if a computer named MyWS*XX* actually existed on (and was added to) the domain.

15. Click the **Member Of** tab. Notice that My WS*XX* is a member of the Domain Computers group by default.

16. Click **Cancel** to discard any accidental changes and then close Active Directory Users and Computers.

17. Log off your server.

In the same way that user and group accounts can be created and managed using the various directory service command-line tools mentioned earlier in this chapter, so too can computer accounts. For example, the DSADD COMPUTER command can be used to create new computer accounts from the command line, while DSMOD COMPUTER can be used to change the settings of existing computer accounts. For more information on creating and modifying computer accounts from the command line, see the appropriate command in Windows Server 2003 Help and Support.

Resetting Computer Accounts

10

Computers that are members of a domain use a secure communication channel known as a secure channel to communicate with a domain controller. A password is associated with this secure channel that is changed every 30 days by default and is synchronized automatically between the domain and the workstation. In rare cases, such as if a particular computer has not been connected to the network (or turned off) for longer than this or the channel is somehow disrupted, a user logging on to that workstation may not be able to authenticate due to synchronization issues. The error messages associated with this problem are typically listed in Event Viewer as Event IDs 3210 and 5722.

When synchronization problems of this manner occur, an administrator must reset the computer account associated with the workstation. The two primary ways to accomplish this include:

- Using Active Directory Users and Computers
- Using the NETDOM utility from the Windows Support Tools

To reset a computer account using Active Directory Users and Computers, simply right-click on the computer account object and choose the Reset Account option. Once this step is confirmed, the workstation must be rejoined to the domain from the System applet in Control Panel.

To reset a computer account using NETDOM, the following command should be issued from the command line:

```
NETDOM RESET computername /domain:domainname
```

In this example, *computername* is the name of the workstation to be reset, and *domainname* is the domain in which the computer account resides.

For more information on computer accounts, see the Computer Management
topic in Windows Server 2003 Help and Support.

NOTE

PUBLISHING RESOURCES

Recall that Active Directory, in addition to organizing security principals (such as users), also
organizes resources on your network. An object in the directory represents a resource. Each
object is created the same way, by choosing New (either from the context menu presented
when a container is right-clicked, or from the Action menu), then choosing the correct
object.

Don't be confused, however, between creating the directory object to represent the resource,
and creating the resource itself. For example, creating a shared folder object in Active
Directory does not create the file share on the file server; that must be done separately. The
shared folder object in Active Directory is only a listing that informs clients of an available
shared folder on the network.

Shared Folder

Creating an object to represent a file share simply involves completing the dialog box shown
in Figure 10-48. A **shared folder object** provides only a representation of the actual share
in order to help network users locate resources. Active Directory does not even check to see
if the server or the share exists.

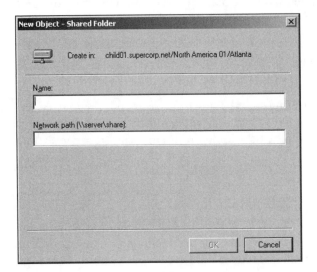

Figure 10-48   Creating a shared folder object

NOTE   To get to the dialog box shown in Figure 10-48, open Active Directory Users and Computers, right-click the container or organizational unit where you would like the Shared Folder object to be created, select New, and then click Shared Folder.

Printers

The process for creating a **printer object** in the directory is more robust than for shared folders. The dialog box requests the network path to the printer, as shown in Figure 10-49. Unlike objects representing shared folders, Active Directory does check for the existence of a printer at the path specified. In addition to manually publishing printers, when a printer is set up on a print server in Windows 2000 or Windows Server 2003, an option is presented to automatically publish the printer in Active Directory.

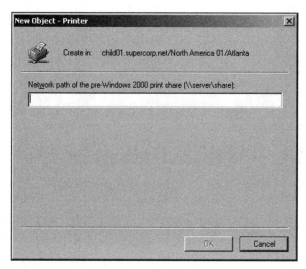

10

Figure 10-49   Creating a printer object

NOTE   To get to the dialog box shown in Figure 10-49, open Active Directory Users and Computers, right-click the container or organizational unit where you would like the Printer object to be created, select New, and then click Printer.

Other Resources

As more Active Directory-aware and Active Directory-enabled applications are released, administrators will have the ability to locate more and more information in the Active Directory database. Some of these applications will use existing classes, although others will need to extend the schema.

By way of example, Microsoft included objects in the default Active Directory schema to work with its flagship database product, SQL Server 2000. One role of SQL Server is publishing database information for replication to other databases. SQL Servers and their publications can be represented by objects in Active Directory, allowing them to be more easily located by those needing to connect to the services offered.

You may have noticed the option to create a MSMQ queue alias. MSMQ is the Microsoft Message Queuing architecture used to facilitate interprocess communications with distributed applications. Active Directory provides a way to publish names for these queues, making it easier to set up the distributed applications. Each type of application or resource has its own requirements; however, the specifics are beyond the scope of this book.

ORGANIZING OBJECTS IN THE DIRECTORY

Many network administrators, especially when starting out, work with networks that are fairly small, like the networks featured in most training courses and lab exercises. If a network has only a dozen users, there isn't much need for organization; finding an object such as a user or a network resource is straightforward and the lists are short. A large network, though, must be well organized. Before Active Directory, the Windows domain model was flat—it had no organization or structure. One of the major advantages of Active Directory is that information can be organized in a logical way.

Organizing and Controlling with Organizational Units

You can organize an Active Directory structure by using organizational units. Chapters 3 and 5 looked at some design criteria for organizational units within a forest and a domain. This chapter will look specifically at how to create and use organizational units for separating data ownership, facilitating directory browsing, and supporting the application of Group Policy. (Group Policy is discussed in detail in Chapter 11.)

Using Organizational Units to Separate Service Ownership and Data Ownership

Chapter 3 introduced the concept of data ownership and service ownership in a directory service. The service owner is responsible for the operation of the directory as a whole and for maintaining the infrastructure and ensuring that the directory is available when it is needed. A data owner is responsible for the actual contents of the directory—that is, for the actual values stored in each object. In practical terms, a data owner creates or deletes objects, grants or denies access to resources, and modifies object attributes as the information that it represents changes. An organization may have many data owners, each responsible for a different part of the directory.

Organizational units provide a way to separate the objects belonging to one data owner from another. Each data owner can have their own organizational unit or group of organizational units. The Active Directory Users and Computers console provides a Delegation of Control

Wizard that allows the service owner to easily assign the correct permissions that enable each data owner to manage the objects in their own organizational unit, without giving more permissions than are necessary.

To launch the Delegation of Control Wizard, simply click the organizational unit to be controlled, and then click Delegate Control on the Action menu (or from the shortcut menu that appears when you right-click the organizational unit). In the wizard, specify which users should be given control over the organizational unit, and what permissions they are to have.

The wizard doesn't do anything magical—it only sets permissions on the organizational unit by making entries in the DACL, but it does make it easy to implement.

TIP There is no "undelegate" wizard. To undo the effects of the Delegation of Control Wizard, you must manually change the permissions on the organizational unit. Therefore, it is always good to plan your delegations before using the wizard and to clearly document what permissions are delegated. You may also want to delegate permissions to a group and then add the users to the group. If users no longer need delegated permissions, they can simply be removed from the group.

10

Using Organizational Units to Facilitate Browsing the Directory

Sometimes you know exactly what you are looking for when you search a directory. For example, if you are looking for a person and you know his or her last name, that is a specific piece of information and is a good basis from which to begin a search. However, there may be times when you don't have a specific piece of information to use, or you may simply want to browse the network.

Imagine a mobile user with a laptop who is attending a meeting in another office of his company. A large company could have hundreds or even thousands of printers. He connects his laptop to the network—perhaps wirelessly, or at a "hot desk" network jack—and logs on without trouble. He needs to print a document and doesn't want to retrieve it at his own desk, which is at his office across town. Which would be easier to find, a nearby printer from a list of hundreds of printers, or a nearby printer from a structure similar to the one shown in Figure 10-50?

Of course, it is possible to get carried away. In addition to the recommended maximum of 10 levels of organizational unit nesting, it is also possible to create too many organizational units. In the fictitious example, notice an organizational unit created for the YellowHat Printer. Is it reasonable to have an organizational unit for just one resource? In most cases, it isn't.

TIP Active Directory also includes a built-in feature designed explicitly to help users locate printers (which can be used regardless of the organizational unit structure). The feature is called printer location tracking and has several requirements in order to function. For more information see the topic "Enabling printer location tracking" in Windows Server 2003 Help and Support Center.

Figure 10-50   One possible browsing structure

Using Organizational Units to Support the Application of Group Policy

Group Policy, which is discussed in Chapter 11 and 12, is used to apply security settings, scripts, administrative registry settings, and to install software to client computers. One of the easiest places to apply Group Policy is at the organizational unit level. Therefore, it makes sense to group objects (mostly users and computers) that will have the same settings in the same organizational unit.

Imagine a company that offers classroom training and seminars. It has a staff that uses computers to accomplish its work. It also has an Internet café set up at each site, allowing its customers a place to browse the Internet or check their e-mail during breaks. This company uses Group Policy to control how these computers are configured. For them, a structure like the one shown in Figure 10-51 might make good sense.

Figure 10-51   Possible organizational unit structure to support Group Policy

Moving Objects between Organizational Units

It may seem complicated to find the right balance between supporting data ownership, browsing, and applying Group Policy. It can be difficult to determine how much organization is needed without overorganizing, which can be just as hard to manage. Thankfully, it is fairly simple to move objects from one organizational unit to another, so an error in your organizational unit structure is rarely fatal.

When you move an object between organizational units (that is, within the same domain), the only thing that changes is the object's distinguished name. The object's GUID and SID (if it has one) do not change when the object is moved to different organizational units within the same domain.

Moving objects between organizational units is extremely easy. Simply select the object you wish to move and choose Move from the Action menu, or right-click the object and select Move from the shortcut menu that appears.

TIP

In Windows Server 2003, you can now drag and drop objects between organizational units.

Moving Objects between Domains

10

Moving objects between domains is not nearly as simple as moving between organizational units. A security principal's SID is made up, in part, of an identifier from its domain. Because it is changing domains, this part of the SID must also change. But the system also needs to keep track and recognize the security principal as the same object. To accomplish this, the **SIDhistory** attribute is used in the migration of users from one domain to another.

The SIDhistory attribute of the user in the new domain contains the SID used in the previous domain. Recall from Chapter 9 that access to resources is controlled by adding SIDs to a DACL on a resource. When a user is migrated from one domain to another, the user receives a new SID. Without the use of SIDhistory, all of the DACLs would need to be updated. Instead, the system uses the SIDhistory to include the old SID in the user's access token, in addition to the new SID. This allows the user to retain access to resources where the DACL contains the old SID.

NOTE

SIDhistory is only available when a domain is at the Windows 2000 native or Windows Server 2003 functional level. Only the domain where the object is being moved to needs to support SIDhistory—so the functional level of the domain from which the object was moved does not matter.

NOTE

Although the object's SID and distinguished name both change when an object is moved between domains, remember that an object's GUID never changes.

There are two tools that are used to move objects (such as users), between domains. Both of these tools can use the SIDhistory attribute in order to retain a user's old SID.

Movetree

Movetree is a utility supplied with Windows Server 2003. It is one of the Windows support tools included on the CD. (It's a good idea to install the support tools along with the operating system.) Movetree also helps an administrator move an object or an entire OU from one domain to another. While Movetree can be used to move many types of objects, ADMT is the preferred tool to use. Movetree should only be used to move objects, such as contacts, which ADMT can't currently move. You can find the details of the Movetree syntax by clicking Start and then clicking Help and Support and searching for the term "Movetree."

ADMT

If you only have a need to move one object, or even a few objects, it might be simpler to manually create the new object(s) and delete the old ones. However, if you are faced with moving a large number of objects and want to retain their identities, then ADMT or a third-party tool may be useful. To install ADMT, run ADMIGRATION.MSI, located in the \I386\ADMT folder of your Windows Server 2003 CD-ROM. After the installation is completed, you can start ADMT by clicking Active Directory Migration Tool under the Administrative Tools menu. For more help on ADMT, open ADMT and then click Help Topics on the Help menu. ADMT's wizard-based interface makes moving objects simple, but it's important that you read about all the details before beginning.

CHAPTER SUMMARY

- ☐ Although an Active Directory design is fairly static, there are usually frequent changes to the objects contained in the directory, especially user objects.

- ☐ The primary tool used to create and manage user accounts in a Windows Server 2003 Active Directory environment is Active Directory Users and Computers. You can also use this tool to configure user templates that can then be copied as a means of simplifying the user account creation process.

- ☐ To create a user object in Active Directory Users and Computers, you must supply a display name, a UPN, and a sAMAccountName. After the user object is created, you can manage properties in Active Directory Users and Computers on multiple property pages.

- ☐ Windows Server 2003 introduces a number of tools to allow user accounts to be created and managed from the command line, including DSADD, DSMOD, DSQUERY, DSMOVE, and DSRM. Additionally, you can also use the bulk import/export utilities CSVDE and LDIFDE as well as ADSI to work with users.

- ☐ The primary purpose of groups in a network environment is to ease the administrative burden associated with assigning rights and permissions with individual user accounts.

❏ Windows Server 2003 supports two group types, known as security groups and distribution groups. Security groups have an associated SID and can be assigned rights and permissions. Distribution groups are primarily used as e-mail entities and do not include a SID.

❏ There are four possible scopes of groups: local (or machine local), domain local, global, and universal. The scope of a group impacts how it can be used in an Active Directory environment. The configured functional level of a domain also impacts the scopes of groups that can be created and associated membership rules. The most scalable method of managing security groups to assign rights and permissions is A G U DL P. The method provides administrators with maximum flexibility and minimizes the need to assign rights and permissions more often than necessary.

❏ Windows Server 2003 Active Directory includes a number of built-in global and domain local groups in both the Users and Builtin containers. Many of these groups have pre-assigned rights and permissions to perform common administration-related functions.

❏ In addition to the built-in groups, Windows Server 2003 includes several special identity groups. What makes these groups special is that the operating system—not the administrator—controls membership of these groups. You cannot add or remove a user, nor can you view a list of members in the group.

❏ The primary tool used to create and manage group accounts in a Windows Server 2003 Active Directory environment is Active Directory Users and Computers. You can also use the directory service command-line tools to manage group accounts, such as DSADD, DSMOD, DSQUERY, DSMOVE, and DSRM. Additionally, you can use the bulk import/export utilities CSVDE and LDIFDE as well as ADSI to work with groups.

❏ The primary tools used to gather group membership information are the Member Of and Members tabs in the properties of objects, and the DSGET command-line utility.

❏ Workstations running Windows NT 4.0, Windows 2000, Windows XP, and Windows Server 2003 require computer accounts in Active Directory. Computer accounts are typically created and managed using Active Directory Users and Computers, but can also be created and managed from the command-line using such tools as DSADD and DSMOD.

❏ Resources can be published in Active Directory so users can quickly locate them.

❏ As objects are created, they should be organized in a logical way by the proper use of organizational units. Objects can be easily moved between organizational units.

❏ Objects can be moved between domains, but it is more complicated. Movetree is a utility that can move objects between domains in the same forest. ADMT is used to move objects within or between forests, including migrating objects from older domains.

KEY TERMS

CSVDE — A command-line utility that can be used to import and export data to and from Active Directory in a comma-separated file format.

disabled — An account is disabled or enabled by an administrator. Disabled accounts cannot be used. See also locked out.

distribution groups — Groups that can be used for tasks such as sending e-mail to a list of users and contacts. It cannot be used to control security.

domain local group — Can only be assigned permissions to a resource available in the domain in which it is created. However, group membership can come from any domain within the forest. Created on domain controllers within the domain.

DSADD — A command-line utility used to add objects to Active Directory.

DSMOD — A command-line utility used to modify Active Directory objects.

DSMOVE — A command-line utility used to move or rename Active Directory objects.

DSQUERY — A command-line utility used to query for Active Directory objects.

DSRM — A command-line utility used to delete Active Directory objects.

global group — A group that is mainly used for organizing other objects into administrative units. A global group can be assigned permissions to any resource in any domain within the forest. The main limitation of a global group is that it can only contain members of the same domain in which it is created.

group — A container object that is used to organize a collection of users, computers, contacts, or other groups into a single object reference.

group scope — Groups can have the following scopes: local (also called machine local), domain local, global, or universal. A group's scope determines who can be a member of the group and where the group can be assigned permissions.

group types — Groups can be either security groups or distribution groups. Distribution groups cannot be included in SACLs or DACLs.

LDIFDE — A command-line utility that can be used to import and export data to and from Active Directory using the LDAP Interchange Format.

local group — Can only be assigned permissions to a resource available on the local machine in which it is created.

locked out — An account can be locked out automatically by the system after too many failed log-on attempts. A locked-out account cannot be used. See also disabled.

Movetree — A tool to move objects from one domain to another within the same forest.

printer object — An object in Active Directory that represents a print queue (which in Windows NT, 2000, and 2003 is also referred to as a "printer").

sAMAccountName — A unique attribute of a user object that specifies the username used to log on to the domain. Active Directory domains can use the sAMAccountName or the userPrincipalName.

security groups — A group that can be used as a distribution group and can also be included in SACLs and DACLs to control access and auditing.

service principal name (SPN) — The name by which a client uniquely identifies an instance of a service on the network.

shared folder object — An object in Active Directory that represents a shared folder (a share folder) on the network.

SIDhistory — A user attribute that is enabled only in domains at the Windows 2000 native or Windows Server 2003 functional level. It is used to track the previous SIDs of migrated users and groups.

universal group — Can be assigned permissions to any resource in any domain within the forest. Universal groups can consist of any user or group object except for local groups.

user account template — A user account configured with attributes that can be copied in order to simplify the creation of user accounts with common attributes.

user logon name — The Active Directory Users and Computers property that maps to the userPrincipalName attribute.

user logon name (pre–Windows 2000) — The Active Directory Users and Computers property that maps to the sAMAccountName attribute.

user objects — Objects in Active Directory that represent users in your domain. A user is a security principal and may be a person or a network service.

userPrincipalName (UPN) — A unique attribute of a user object that specifies the username that can be used to log on to the domain from clients that support Active Directory.

10

REVIEW QUESTIONS

1. A user object must have a CN attribute, which is also known as the Full Name property. True or False?

2. You must set all available user properties before the user can log on to the system. True or False?

3. Which of the following tools do you use to reset a user's password in an Active Directory domain at the Windows Server 2003 functional level?

   a. User Manager for Domains

   b. Active Directory Migration Tool

   c. Active Directory Users and Computers

   d. Active Directory Sites and Services

4. Which is the best choice for a location to create a new user object?

   a. in an organizational unit called employees

   b. in the Domain Controllers organizational unit

   c. in the root container of the domain

   d. anywhere except in the Users container

5. Which statement is the most accurate?

   a. Users running Windows NT Workstation 4.0 normally use the userPrincipalName to log on to an Active Directory domain.

   b. Users running Windows XP can use the userPrincipalName or the sAMAccountName to log on to an Active Directory domain.

   c. You cannot use the userPrincipalName to log on to a domain that is at the Windows 2000 native functional level.

   d. You cannot use the userPrincipalName unless the domain is at the Windows 2000 native or Windows Server 2003 functional level.

6. When creating a new user object, Active Directory Users and Computers issues a query to a _____ to make sure the userPrincipalName is unique in the forest.

7. Under what circumstance is a user account locked out?

   a. when it is first created, but has not yet been used

   b. when it is locked out by an administrator, perhaps because an employee is fired

   c. when Active Directory detects too many failed logon attempts

   d. when the password is not complex enough to meet the domain security policy

8. In addition to the Member tab of a group object's properties, where else can you see information about group memberships in Active Directory Users and Computers? (Give a short one-sentence answer.)

9. A user has forgotten her password. What should you do?

   a. Delete the user object for her account and create a new object with the same name.

   b. Use the Active Directory Users and Computers console to reset her password.

   c. Use the Active Directory Users and Computers console to display her password.

   d. Log on to her workstation as an administrator and run the newpass command.

10. Which of the following group types require that the domain functional level be set to Windows 2000 native or Windows Server 2003 before they can be created?

    a. machine local groups

    b. domain local groups

    c. global groups

    d. universal groups

11. You can use a(n) _____ group to send e-mails to multiple recipients, but you cannot assign it permissions.

12. You can change a group's type or scope in a domain at the Windows 2000 native or Windows Server 2003 functional level. True or False?

13. You can change a group's type or scope in a domain at the Windows 2000 mixed functional level. True or False?

14. You can easily move objects between _____ using Active Directory Users and Computers.

15. Which type of security group has its entire membership stored in the global catalog?

    a. machine local groups

    b. domain local groups

    c. global groups

    d. universal groups

    e. all of the above

16. An administrator attempts to create a universal group, but the option is grayed out. What could be the problem?

    a. He must create a global group first and then convert it to a universal group.

    b. Universal groups can only be created on the first domain controller in the forest.

    c. The domain needs to be converted to the Windows 2000 native or Windows Server 2003 domain functional level.

    d. The domain needs to be converted to the Windows 2000 mixed functional level.

17. A good OU structure supports which of the following?

    a. a logical browsing structure

    b. delegation of control and permissions

    c. logical application of Group Policy

    d. all of the above

18. You try to modify permissions to various objects using Active Directory Users and Computers, but you notice that the Security tab is missing. You are an administrator of the domain. What is the problem?

    a. You cannot modify Active Directory object permissions using Active Directory Users and Computers.

    b. Advanced features is not selected in the View menu of the console.

    c. Active Directory only allows changes on one domain controller at a time.

    d. none of the above

19. You want to give the help desk personnel the right to reset passwords for all user accounts in your office except for the user accounts for the executives and managers. Which of the following is the easiest way to do this?

    a. Give the help desk personnel the right to reset user accounts at the domain level.

    b. Put all the help desk personnel into an organizational unit, and assign the organizational unit the right to reset passwords.

10

    c. Put the executive and manager accounts into an organizational unit, and assign the help desk personnel the reset password permission at the domain level.

    d. Put all the nonexecutive and nonmanager user accounts into an organizational unit, and give the help desk personnel the right to reset passwords for the organizational unit.

20. You can only convert a global group to a universal group if it is not a member of any other global groups. True or False?

CASE PROJECTS

Your basic design of Active Directory is complete and you've created an empty, pristine Active Directory environment. You now need to begin populating your forest with everyone and everything that Super Corp needs to place in its Active Directory structure. In the following projects, you will create the users, contacts, groups, and resources that Active Directory was designed to encompass.

Case Project 10-1: Creating Us

CAUTION

In this case project, you need to append all user names with your server number, so that your accounts do not conflict with your partner's accounts. For example, if you are creating an account called bsmith, you should instead create an account called bsmith*XX* (where *XX* is your server number).

Using the Super Corp organization chart from Chapter 3, you can create your user accounts in Active Directory. Create user objects for P. Green, C. Commander, D. Bloemer, C. Snyder, and D. DiNicolo in a new organizational unit called Executives under your Atlanta organizational unit. Set their passwords to "Password01", but set their accounts so the password must be changed at their next logon.

Create five additional organizational units under the Atlanta organizational unit with the following names: Business, Accounting, Legal, IT, and Assistance. Choose at least three more users and create objects for them as well. Place the users in the appropriate organizational units. You may create user accounts for other users shown on the chart.

Case Project 10-2: Managing Users

After creating the Super Corp users, you need to manage them by configuring additional settings in Active Directory. Use Table 10-5 to enter job title, department, and telephone information for the users in the table. Use the organizational chart to enter job title and department information for the other users you created. You may enter sample telephone numbers for them as well.

Table 10-5 Super Corp user information

Name	Title	Department	Telephone
Phyllis Green	Chief Executive Officer	Administration	x5551
Carolyn Commander	Chief Administration Officer	Business Office	x5552
Dan Bloemer	Chief Financial Officer	Accounting	x5553
Chris Snyder	Chief Legal Officer	Legal	x5554
Dan DiNicolo	Chief Information Officer	IT	x5555

CASE
PROJECTS

Case Project 10-3: Working with Groups

Users and contacts need to be in groups to ease the management of your domain. Create a
security group for each department. Populate each group with the user objects created from
that department. (Remember to append your student number at the end of group names to
keep each group's name unique in the domain.)

10

11

GROUP POLICY FOR CORPORATE POLICY

After reading this chapter, you will be able to:

♦ Understand and describe the purpose of Group Policy

♦ Describe how Group Policy is applied

♦ Manage desktop computers using Group Policy

♦ Analyze and configure security settings using Group Policy

♦ Install and use the Group Policy Management Console

♦ Troubleshoot Group Policy

Group Policy is used to configure workstations and servers that are part of an Active Directory forest. It can be used to manage the configuration of computers, control the settings and options available to users, manage or enforce security policies, and distribute software across the network.

Group Policy is nothing short of amazing. It can be used in the smallest organization or the largest enterprise to bring consistency and enforce the wishes of the organization's management. This chapter will help you understand how Group Policy is configured and managed, as well as how Group Policy Objects (GPOs) integrate with Active Directory. You will learn to manage users' desktops with Group Policy. This chapter will also cover the analysis and configuration of security settings, as well as how to troubleshoot Group Policy settings. Note that using Group Policy to distribute software is covered in the next chapter.

GROUP POLICY

To understand Group Policy in Active Directory, it helps to have some background. The ability to use policies to manage Windows desktop computers was first introduced with Windows 95 and Windows NT. These older operating systems used a feature called **system policies** to change a number of registry entries that controlled desktop settings. A system policy file created on a domain controller would either enable or disable a particular setting on the client computer.

System policies are stored in a policy file that must be placed in the **netlogon share**, a share found on every domain controller in a domain. More specifically, Windows NT-based systems use a file named ntconfig.pol and Windows 95/98-based systems use a file called config.pol. Client computers using system policies then download the appropriate policy file from the domain controller during the authentication process.

Once policies are applied to these client computers, the registry entries in the policies are permanently set on these computers. Therefore, with Windows 95, Windows 98, and Windows NT 4.0, these settings still apply unless they were deliberately removed. For example, if Bob logs on with a policy that restricts access to the display properties, and his computer is disconnected from the network or the policy file is merely deleted from the netlogon share, he would still be restricted from accessing the display properties. In order for Bob to have access to display properties again, the registry needs to be manually edited (using Registry Editor or the old System Policy Editor tool) or a new policy file needs to be created in the netlogon share.

TIP

This effect of permanently changing the registry is known as **tattooing the registry**.

Windows XP, Windows 2000, or Windows 2003 clients that participate in a Windows NT domain can still use system policies. When authenticating to an Active Directory domain controller, though, these newer clients use Group Policy instead of system policies.

TIP

If you have both Windows NT 4.0 and Active Directory domain controllers in your domain, the Windows 2000 and newer clients will use only the Active Directory domain controllers once they are discovered. Once the client starts using Group Policy, it does not go back to system policies.

Group Policy, introduced in Windows 2000 and enhanced in both Windows XP and Windows Server 2003, is still largely a collection of registry entries. However, management of the policies has been significantly enhanced. These enhancements include:

- Transient policy settings—The registry entries applied by Group Policy are automatically removed when the policy no longer applies.

- Expanded capabilities—The system policies in older operating systems allowed basic user interface controls. New client-side extensions allow control of security settings, IPSec settings, software distribution, and more.

Administrative Templates

Most policies are based on **administrative templates**, which are files with an .adm extension. These administrative templates describe registry settings that can be configured in a policy or Group Policy.

Several administrative templates are included with Windows Server 2003, but you can also create your own. Creating your own administrative templates allows you to create customized registry settings to configure the operating system and applications on your network, ensuring that all of your systems are configured to a corporate standard. You can control any setting in the registry with a custom administrative template; however, some settings can only be managed in custom templates by tattooing the registry, in the same way that system policies do.

NOTE

For more information on creating your own administrative templates, visit *msdn.microsoft.com/library/en-us/policy/policy/administrative_template_file_format.asp*. (The Microsoft Web site is frequently reorganized as content is updated. If the file is not found at this URL, then search the Microsoft site using the term "group policy administrative templates.")

The administrative templates included with Windows Server 2003 are:

- System.adm—This administrative template contains a variety of system settings that restrict the operation of the operating system. It includes security settings and desktop restrictions.

- Inetres.adm—This administrative template controls settings for Internet Explorer. It includes the ability to set and restrict access to settings such as menu items and proxy servers.

- Wmplayer.adm—This administrative template includes settings for Windows Media Player. It is not applicable to 64-bit versions of Windows XP or Windows Server 2003.

- Conf.adm—This administrative template has settings for Microsoft NetMeeting. It is not applicable to 64-bit versions of Windows XP or Windows Server 2003.

- Wuau.adm—This administrative template controls settings for Windows Update. It allows administrators to control where and when client computers receive operating system updates.

Client-side Extensions

In addition to the use of administrative templates to control a number of registry settings, Group Policy also includes a number of client-side extensions that allow for more advanced control and configuration. These extensions run on the client, but typically also include a server-side user interface (implemented as an MMC extension to the Group Policy Object Editor snap-in) that allows an administrator to configure the policy. Alternatively, the client-side extension can use registry settings defined in an administrative template to control its behavior. The client-side extensions included with Windows Server 2003 and Windows XP include:

- EFS (encrypting file system) recovery
- Folder redirection
- Internet Explorer maintenance
- IP security
- Microsoft Disk Quota
- QoS Packet Scheduler
- Scripts
- Security
- Software installation
- Wireless

NOTE   Some of these client-side extensions are new to Windows Server 2003 and Windows XP. Older Windows 2000 clients do not have some of these client-side extensions (QoS Packet Scheduler and Wireless) and are therefore unable to apply the related policies.

Group Policy Storage

Policy objects are stored on domain controllers and on local computers. Every computer capable of using Group Policy (Windows 2000, Windows Server 2003, and Windows XP) holds a local policy object in a hidden folder called %systemroot%\system32\GroupPolicy. This local GPO, referred to as a **local computer policy**, applies only to the local computer. Figure 11-1 shows an example of the storage of a local computer policy.

Local computer policies are great for a workgroup environment because they still allow you to configure policies that apply to each computer. However, they must be configured on each system individually.

When talking about Group Policy, though, one is almost always referring to Group Policy managed in a domain or forest, where GPOs are stored on domain controllers as part of Active Directory. Group policies are centrally managed, and a single GPO typically affects many users and computers.

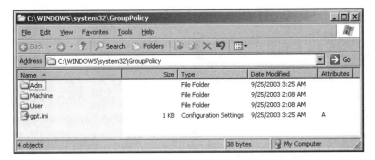

Figure 11-1   Storage location of local computer policy

TIP

Some people are confused by the term Group Policy Object (GPO), because it isn't really an object and it isn't directly linked to groups—although it can apply to groups of people or computers. Think of a GPO as a group of policy settings.

Group Policy in a forest is managed in sets of GPOs. These GPOs are stored on domain controllers, and are virtual objects—meaning that what you see and manipulate as one object or policy is really made up of several components. A GPO is not a single object in the directory the way a user or contact is.

One part of a GPO is stored in the Active Directory database, while the other is stored in the SYSVOL share. (SYSVOL is automatically replicated between all domain controllers.) The Active Directory portion of a group policy is called the **group policy container (GPC)**. The GPC contains information regarding the version of individual GPOs as well as software installation information. The GPC exists in the domain partition (CN=Policies,CN=System, *DC=domainname...*) of the domain where the GPO is created and is used to track the status of the GPO.

Clients, however, do not read the GPO entirely from the Active Directory database. The portion of the GPO stored on the SYSVOL share is referred to as a **group policy template (GPT)**. A GPT is a collection of subfolders stored in %systemroot%\SYSVOL\ sysvol*domain_dns_name*\Policies. Each GPT is stored in a separate subfolder named with the GUID of the GPO. An example of the full path to a GPT would be %systemroot%\SYSVOL\sysvol\supercorp.net\Policies\{6AC1786C-016F-11D2-945F-00C04fB984F9}, as shown in Figure 11-2.

Figure 11-2   GPT stored on a domain controller

The subfolders that may be present within a GPT folder include:

- Adm—Contains all of the custom administrative templates (.adm files) used to create the GPO.

- USER—Contains a registry.pol file that holds registry settings that are applied to users; the registry entries are applied to the HKEY_CURRENT_USER hive.

- USER\applications—A subfolder in the USER folder, it contains application advertisement scripts (.aas) used to distribute and install applications through Group Policy. These are for applications associated with users.

- MACHINE—Contains a registry.pol file that holds registry settings that are applied to computers; the registry entries are applied to the HKEY_LOCAL_ MACHINE hive.

- MACHINE\applications—A subfolder in the MACHINE folder, it contains application advertisement scripts (.aas) used to distribute and install applications through Group Policy. These are for applications associated with computers.

Do not confuse a GPT with an administrative template used for Group Policy.

TIP

Creating a Group Policy Object

You can create a GPO in two different ways: use the Group Policy standalone Microsoft Management Console (MMC) snap-in (as shown in Activity 11-1), or use the Group Policy extension in Active Directory Users and Computers (Activity 11-2).

Activity 11-1: Creating a Group Policy Object Using the MMC

ACTIVITY

Time Required: 10 minutes

Objective: Use the Group Policy Object Editor MMC snap-in to create GPOs.

Description: The IT manager at Super Corp has decided that the company will use GPOs for the purpose of configuring a standard user desktop environment. You have been asked to explore some of the different ways in which GPOs can be created from a Windows Server 2003 system. In this activity, you will create a new GPO using the Group Policy Object Editor MMC snap-in.

1. If necessary, start your server and log on using the **Administrator** account in the **CHILDXX** domain (where *XX* is the number of the forest root domain for which your server is a domain controller) using the password **Password01**.

2. Click **Start**, and then click **Run**. In the Open drop-down list box, type **mmc** and click **OK**.

3. Click **File** on the menu bar, and then click **Add/Remove Snap-in**.

4. Click **Add**. In the Add Standalone Snap-in dialog box, select **Group Policy Object Editor**, as shown in Figure 11-3, and then click **Add**.

Figure 11-3   Adding a standalone snap-in

5. In the Select Group Policy Object dialog box, click **Browse**.

6. In the Browse for a Group Policy Object dialog box, click the **All** tab to display a list of all GPOs that currently exist.

7. In the All Group Policy Objects stored in this domain section, right-click a blank area and click **New**.

8. Rename the new GPO using the name **Test Policy XX** (where XX is the number of your server) and press **Enter**. Click **OK**, and then click **Finish**.

9. Click **Close** on the Add Standalone Snap-in window, and click **OK** on the Add/ Remove Snap-in window. You can now edit the GPO using the console.

10. Close the MMC window without saving your changes.

11. Log off your server if you do not intend to immediately continue to the next activity. Otherwise, stay logged on.

Activity 11-2: Creating a Group Policy Object and Browsing Settings Using Active Directory Users and Computers

Time Required: 20 minutes

Objective: Use Active Directory Users and Computers to create GPOs.

Description: While the Group Policy Object Editor MMC snap-in provides one method to create new GPOs or edit existing GPOs, you have learned that another alternative is to create and edit these objects from within the Active Directory Users and Computers tool. Because this tool is the primary administrative application in use at Super Corp, you have decided to explore its integrated GPO management features. In this activity, you will create a new GPO and explore some of the settings that can be configured using Group Policy.

1. If necessary, start your server and log on using the **Administrator** account in the **CHILDXX** domain (where *XX* is the number of the forest root domain for which your server is a domain controller) using the password **Password01**.

2. Click **Start**, select **Administrative Tools**, and then click **Active Directory Users and Computers**.

3. If necessary, expand the **childXX.supercorp.net** domain (where *XX* is the number of the forest root domain for which your server is a domain controller) in the left tree pane.

4. Right-click the **North America XX** organizational unit (where *XX* is the number of your server) and then click **Properties**.

5. Click the **Group Policy** tab.

6. Click **Add**. The Add a Group Policy Object Link window opens. Click the **All** tab.

7. In the All Group Policy Objects stored in this domain section, click **Test Policy XX** (where *XX* is the number of your server) and then click **OK**. Notice that the GPO named Test Policy now appears in the list of Current Group Policy Object Links for your North America organizational unit.

8. Click the **New** button to create a new GPO named **Desktop Security Policy XX** (where *XX* is the number of your server) and then press **Enter**. This new GPO is now linked to your North America organizational unit.

9. Ensure that **Desktop Security Policy XX** is selected and click **Edit**. The Group Policy Object Editor opens to allow the configuration settings of the Desktop Security Policy to be viewed and configured, as shown in Figure 11-4.

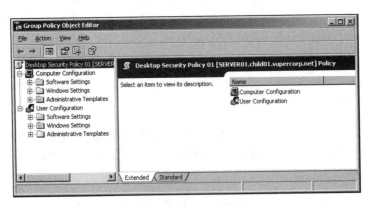

Figure 11-4   Creating a Group Policy Object

10. In the left tree pane under the User Configuration node, click the **+** (plus symbol) next to **Administrative Templates** to expand its contents, and then click the **Start Menu and Taskbar** container.

> To specify additional administrative templates, simply right-click one of the Administrative Templates folders and then click Add/Remove Templates. Use the dialog box to add or remove templates as necessary.
>
> **TIP**

11. Double-click **Remove Run menu from Start Menu** in the right details pane. Notice that the configuration settings include Not Configured, Enabled, and Disabled, as shown in Figure 11-5. Do not change any configuration settings at this point.

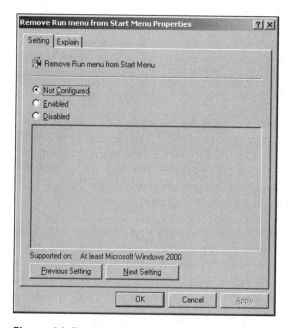

Figure 11-5   Viewing settings on an individual policy

12. Click the **Explain** tab, and read the purpose and notes associated with this setting. Click **OK** to close the window.

13. As time permits, browse through additional Group Policy settings in both the User Configuration and Computer Configuration sections. Do not configure any settings during this exercise.

14. Close the Group Policy Object Editor window when you are finished.

15. Click **Close** in the Properties dialog box for your North America organizational unit.

16. Close Active Directory Users and Computers.

17. Log off your server if you do not intend to immediately continue to the next activity. Otherwise, stay logged on.

GROUP POLICY PROCESSING

Group Policy Objects are composed of user configuration settings and computer configuration settings. The user configuration settings apply only to users, and the computer configuration settings apply only to computers. User and computer settings are applied according to where the user or computer objects are located in Active Directory and how the GPOs are linked to the containers in Active Directory.

GPOs stored on domain controllers are linked to sites, domains, and organizational units using **GPO links**. A GPO applies to the user and computer objects that exist in the container (and child containers) to which they are linked. For example, when a GPO is linked to a domain, it applies to all computers and users in the domain. If it were linked to an organizational unit, then it would apply to all computers and users in that organizational unit and in child organizational units.

NOTE

It is very important to understand the difference between a GPO and a GPO link. The GPO contains all the policy settings and is made up of the GPC and GPT. A site, domain, or organizational unit has a GPO link attribute that specifies one or more GPOs that should apply. The GPO link attribute holds a reference to the GPO. The GPO is independently stored from the site(s), domain(s), or organizational unit(s) to which it is linked.

Linking a GPO to a site is a little different than linking it to a domain or organizational unit. When a GPO is linked to a site, it applies to computers assigned to that site (by IP number and subnet, as discussed in Chapter 6), and to users who log on to computers in that site, regardless of their domains or organizational units. Linking a GPO to a site is usually done because there is a particular setting that needs to apply in only one specific geographic location—internet proxy server settings, for example.

A single GPO can be linked with multiple organizational units, sites, or even domains. However, GPOs are only stored on domain controllers in the domain where they are created. You should avoid linking GPOs between domains, as it makes user logons less efficient. Most networks are designed to allow users to authenticate to a local domain controller for their domain; however, retrieving the GPO from another domain will involve a second domain controller and might cross a WAN link.

For example, a GPO created in supercorp.net is replicated to all domain controllers for that domain. You can also link this GPO to the dev.supercorp.net domain, and it is applied to users and computers in that domain. However, because the GPO is not replicated to domain controllers in dev.supercorp.net, when a user in that domain logs on, the GPO must be retrieved from a domain controller in supercorp.net—even though the rest of the logon is processed at a domain controller in dev.supercorp.net.

If a domain controller for supercorp.net is not in the same site, then the GPO would be retrieved across slower WAN links, which is normally something that should be avoided.

Activity 11-3: Deleting Group Policy Objects

ACTIVITY

Time Required: 5 minutes

Objective: Use Active Directory Users and Computers to permanently delete a GPO.

Description: Having learned how to create new GPOs, you are interested in learning about what happens if you attempt to delete one of these objects when it has been linked to one or more containers. In this activity, you will attempt to delete a linked GPO to learn more about the options presented to you.

1. If necessary, start your server and log on using the **Administrator** account in the **CHILDXX** domain (where *XX* is the number of the forest root domain for which your server is a domain controller) using the password **Password01**.

2. Click **Start**, select **Administrative Tools**, and then click **Active Directory Users and Computers**.

3. If necessary, expand the **childXX.supercorp.net** domain (where *XX* is the number of the forest root domain for which your server is a domain controller) in the left tree pane.

4. Right-click the **North America XX** organizational unit (where *XX* is the number of your server) and then click **Properties**.

5. Click the **Group Policy** tab.

6. From the list of GPOs select **Test Policy XX** (where *XX* is the number of your server) and then click **Delete**.

7. In the Delete dialog box, click the **Remove the link and delete the Group Policy Object permanently** option, as shown in Figure 11-6, and then click **OK**. This will remove both the link and the GPO itself.

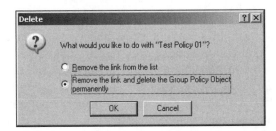

Figure 11-6   Selecting to delete the link to a GPO or the GPO itself

8. When the Delete Group Policy Object dialog box opens, click **Yes**. Notice that the Test Policy GPO is removed from the list.

9. Click **Add** and click the **All** tab to confirm that the Test Policy *XX* GPO has been deleted. Then click **Cancel**.

10. Click **Close** in the Properties dialog box for your North America organizational unit.

11. Close Active Directory Users and Computers.

12. Log off your server if you do not intend to immediately continue to the next activity. Otherwise, stay logged on.

Group Policy Priority

GPOs are applied and processed in a specific order. This first section discusses the order in which GPOs are applied, then why the processing order is important.

1. The first policy to be applied is the local computer policy. These policies only affect the one computer, and are always overridden if other GPOs exist at the site, domain, or organizational unit level.

2. Second, any GPOs linked to the site are applied.

3. Third, any GPOs linked to the domain are applied. GPOs for the domain set options for the entire domain.

4. Fourth, GPOs linked to organizational units are applied by working down from the domain to the organizational unit that holds the computer object or user account object.

This process is followed twice—once for the Computer Configuration portion of Group Policy (when the computer starts up) and once for the User Configuration portion of Group Policy (when the user logs on). The default processing sequence is illustrated in Figure 11-7. There are settings that can override this default sequence. You will learn more about them later in this chapter.

You may see the acronym LSDOU in reference to GPOs. It stands for local, site, domain, and organizational units, and was created to help you remember the order in which they apply.

TIP

As shown in Figure 11-7, when the computer starts, the first policy to be applied is the computer's local policy (1). Next, the computer applies any policies linked to the site at which it is located (2). Then, the computer applies any policies linked to the domain for which the computer is a member (3). Finally, the computer follows the organizational unit hierarchy by applying any policies linked to the All Computers organizational unit (4) and then any policies linked to the Desktop Computers organizational unit (5) until it reaches the computer's account. Note that only the Computer Configuration portion of Group Policy has been processed.

With the computer started and the Computer Configuration portion of Group Policy processed, a user can now log on. Again referring back to Figure 11-7, when the user logs on to a workstation, the first policy to be applied is the computer's local policy (A). Next,

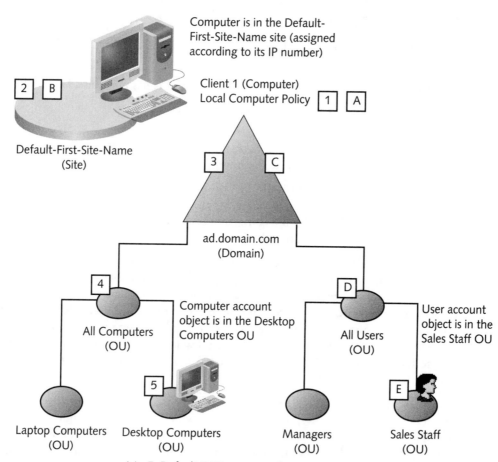

Computer is in the Default-First-Site-Name site (assigned according to its IP number)

Client 1 (Computer)
Local Computer Policy

Default-First-Site-Name (Site)

ad.domain.com (Domain)

Computer account object is in the Desktop Computers OU

User account object is in the Sales Staff OU

All Computers (OU)

All Users (OU)

Laptop Computers (OU)   Desktop Computers (OU)   Managers (OU)   Sales Staff (OU)

1 to 5: Default GPO sequence for computer settings
A to E: Default GPO sequence for user settings

Figure 11-7   Default GPO processing order

any policies linked to the site at which the computer is located are applied (B). Then, any policies linked to the domain for which the user is a member are applied (C). Finally, the organizational unit hierarchy is followed by applying any policies linked to the All Users organizational unit (D) and then any policies linked to the Sales Staff organizational unit (E) until the user's account is reached. Keep in mind that these steps (A to E) refer only to the User Configuration portion of Group Policy.

CAUTION   Be careful about the number of GPOs that are to be applied. Computer startup and logon performance may be affected if a large number of GPOs need to be applied to the user or workstation.

Dealing with Conflict

There are three options available for most policy settings: Enabled, Disabled, and Not Configured.

- Enabled—Put the policy into effect, even if it has been disabled at a higher level.

- Disabled—Do not put the policy into effect, even if it has been enabled at a higher level.

- Not Configured—I do not care if the policy is enabled or disabled, use whatever is set at a higher level (if anything).

Different policy settings from multiple GPOs can be combined, as long as they do not conflict. For example, if a GPO linked to the domain removes the Run command from the Start menu, and another GPO linked to an organizational unit adds the My Computer icon to the Windows XP desktop, then both settings are applied.

However, if there is a conflict between GPOs linked at different levels that configure the same policy, then the last GPO to be applied wins the conflict and configures the policy (unless you change this behavior). Local computer policy objects always have the lowest priority, and therefore always lose. For example, if a policy is enabled that removes the Run command from the Start menu in a local policy, and the same policy is disabled in a GPO linked to the domain, then the Run command will be present on the Start menu. You can also consider it this way: GPOs that are "closer" to the user or computer object have higher priority.

If multiple GPOs are linked to a single site, domain, or organizational unit, as shown in Figure 11-8, the administrator has to choose which one has the highest priority. When multiple GPOs are linked at the same level, they are processed from bottom to top. This means the GPO at the top of the list has the highest priority. You can change the order of GPOs by highlighting a GPO and clicking the Up and Down buttons.

Modifying Group Policy Priority

In most situations, the standard priority in applying Group Policy meets the needs of network administrators. However, you can modify the priority by configuring No Override, Block Policy Inheritance, and Loopback Processing Mode.

No Override

When **No Override** is enabled on a GPO link, it always has the highest priority. This is useful when enforcing organizational or departmental settings. For example, take a GPO linked to the domain that disables a common peer-to-peer file-sharing application. You might be concerned that an administrator who has control over some organizational units will configure a GPO for his or her organizational unit that allows a program to run. By configuring No Override on the GPO at the domain level, you ensure that GPOs linked to child organizational units cannot override your GPO. The No Override option is accessible

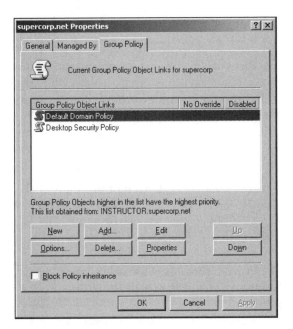

Figure 11-8   Multiple GPOs linked to an organizational unit

by selecting a GPO link on the Group Policy tab and then clicking Options (which is visible in Figure 11-8). Figure 11-9 shows No Override enabled on a group policy object link.

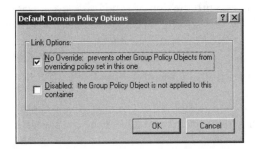

Figure 11-9   No Override enabled on a GPO link

No Override is set on the individual GPO links and not the GPO itself. The No Override option is available for links to sites, domains, and organizational units.

NOTE

If two GPOs are linked at *different* levels (such as one GPO linked at the site level and another linked at the domain level—or even just different organizational units) with No Override and there is a conflict, then the first policy object processed will be in effect. This means that a site-linked GPO with No Override has priority over a domain-linked GPO with No

Override. Similarly, a domain-linked GPO with No Override has priority over an organizational unit-linked GPO with No Override.

However, if multiple GPOs linked to the *same* site, domain, or organizational unit have No Override turned on, and they try to configure the same setting, which GPO wins? The one higher in the list of linked GPOs. This may not be intuitive, but it does make sense from a feature standpoint. When using No Override, always test your GPOs carefully to be sure that you understand the effect.

Block Policy Inheritance

When **Block Policy Inheritance** is configured on a domain or organizational unit, GPOs higher in the tree do not apply (unless No Override is set). This allows for exemptions from corporate policy for a particular organizational unit (or department). The Block Policy inheritance option is accessible on the Group Policy tab and can be seen in Figure 11-8.

CAUTION
Using Block Policy Inheritance can make managing and troubleshooting Group Policy more difficult. For this reason, it is recommended that Block Policy Inheritance be used sparingly.

For example, say you've created a GPO that contains settings that lock down user desktops. You've linked them to the domain, but don't want the restrictions to apply to users in the IT Department. Rather than create an additional GPO that removes all of these settings, you could configure Block Policy Inheritance on the organizational unit containing the IT staff. This would ensure that the GPOs associated with the domain and other organizational units do not affect the IT staff, allowing them unrestricted access to repair the organization's computers. However, all settings (without No Override) are blocked, including those that distribute software or configure settings that are beneficial. A better solution would be to use permissions to control the application of Group Policy, as discussed shortly.

TIP
Block Policy Inheritance cannot be used to stop a No Override. This means administrators with control higher in the domain's object hierarchy can always force a policy to apply.

Loopback Processing Mode

Loopback Processing Mode controls how user-based Group Policy settings are applied. It is a computer configuration setting and can be used to replace or modify the standard method of applying Group Policy.

Remember that Group Policy applies to computers and to users. In each GPO, there are settings for both computers and for users. Look back to Figure 11-7 and consider what would happen to user settings in a GPO that is linked to the Desktop Computers organizational unit. What would happen to computer settings in a GPO that is linked to the

Sales Staff organizational unit? Normally, computer settings apply at startup, when processing Group Policy for the computer, and user settings apply at logon, when processing Group Policy for the user.

Loopback Processing Mode lets you modify that behavior by applying user settings based on the location of the computer's object in Active Directory. In Activity 11-4, you will learn how to enable Loopback Processing.

TIP

Loopback Processing Mode is commonly used on computers in a public area or kiosk. No matter who logs on to that computer, specific user settings apply, even if a user account has other settings assigned.

Loopback Processing Mode has two settings—replace and merge. When Loopback Processing is enabled and set in replace mode, the user settings are taken from the GPOs that apply to the computer, not the user. The group policy engine does not even bother to look up the GPOs that apply to the user's account.

When Loopback Processing is enabled and set in merge mode, the user configuration settings from the computer are added to the user configuration settings that apply to the user. The user settings that apply to the computer are applied last, and have a higher priority than the user settings that apply to the user.

For example, in Figure 11-7, the object for the user Bob is located in the Sales organizational unit. Normally, when Bob logs on to a computer, his user configuration comes from GPOs linked to the domain, Users organizational unit, and Sales. But, if Bob logs on at Client1 (which has Loopback Processing enabled in replace mode), then the normal process for applying user configuration settings is not used. Instead, the user configuration settings for Bob are read from GPOs linked to the domain, All Computers organizational unit, and Desktop Computers organizational unit.

ACTIVITY

Activity 11-4: Configuring Loopback Processing

Time Required: 15 minutes

Objective: Change the default process that Group Policy uses to apply GPOs.

Description: Super Corp has been experiencing problems with users reconfiguring workstations located in meeting rooms. To tighten security on these workstations, you have decided to create a new GPO that enables Loopback Processing.

1. If necessary, start your server and log on using the **Administrator** account in the **CHILDXX** domain (where *XX* is the number of the forest root domain for which your server is a domain controller) using the password **Password01**.

2. Click **Start**, select **Administrative Tools**, and then click **Active Directory Users and Computers**.

3. If necessary, expand the **childXX.supercorp.net** domain (where *XX* is the number of the forest root domain for which your server is a domain controller) in the left tree pane.

4. If necessary, expand the **North America XX** organizational unit (where *XX* is the number of your server) in the left tree pane.

5. In the left tree pane, right-click the **Atlanta** organizational unit (under your North America *XX* organizational unit), select **New**, and then click **Organizational Unit**.

6. In the name text box, enter **Meeting Rooms** and then click **OK**.

7. In the left tree pane, expand the **Atlanta** organizational unit.

8. Right-click the **Meeting Rooms** organizational unit and then click **Properties**.

9. Click the **Group Policy** tab.

10. Click the **New** button and name the new GPO **Meeting Workstations XX** (where *XX* is the number of your server), and then press **Enter**.

11. Select the **Meeting Workstations XX** GPO link and then click **Edit**.

12. In the left tree pane, under Computer Configuration, expand **Administrative Templates**, **System**, and then click **Group Policy**.

13. In the right details pane, double-click **User Group Policy loopback processing mode**.

14. Select the **Enabled** option.

15. In the Mode drop-down list box, select **Merge**, as shown in Figure 11-10.

16. Click **OK**. Loopback Processing has now been enabled. Next, you configure the policy to remove the Run command from the Start menu.

17. Collapse the Computer Configuration section of the GPO by clicking the − (minus symbol) next to Computer Configuration.

18. Under User Configuration, expand **Administrative Templates** and then click **Start Menu and Taskbar**.

19. In the right details pane, double-click **Remove Run menu from Start Menu**.

20. Select the **Enabled** option and then click **OK**. Any user that logs on to a workstation with a computer account in the Meeting Rooms organizational unit now has the Run command removed from the Start menu.

21. Close the Group Policy Object Editor window when you are finished.

22. Click **Close** in the Properties dialog box for your North America organizational unit.

23. Close Active Directory Users and Computers.

24. Log off your server if you do not intend to immediately continue to the next activity. Otherwise, stay logged on.

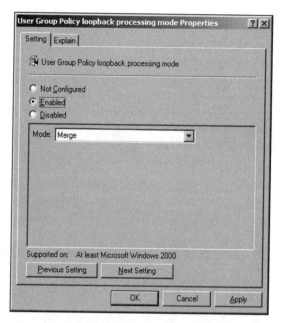

Figure 11-10   Enabling Loopback Processing

Controlling Group Policy Application with Permissions

GPOs cannot be linked to groups. To control the way Group Policy is applied to different users, those users must be placed in different organizational units, unless you change the default permissions.

The application of Group Policy for users and groups can be controlled through permissions. The standard permissions available to a GPO are Full Control, Read, Write, Create All Child Objects, Delete All Child Objects, and Apply Group Policy.

A user or computer must have the Read and Apply Group Policy permissions on a GPO in order for the policy to apply to that user or computer. By default, the Authenticated Users group, which includes all computers and all users (except the Guest account), has these permissions. To configure a GPO that only applies to a specific user or group of users, you can assign the read and apply permissions to the user or group. You then need to remove the Authenticated Users group from the list of groups with permission. Alternatively, if only a small number of users should not apply the policy, you can specify the users and groups that should be exempted from the policy by denying them these permissions.

To use the same example as earlier, say you've created a GPO that contains settings that lock down user desktops (linked at the domain level), but you don't want it to apply to IT staff. While this policy applies to all authenticated users by default, it is possible to deny the IT Staff group the Apply Group Policy permission. By denying the IT Staff group the ability to apply the policy, the desktop restrictions do not take effect.

TIP This is one instance where deny is beneficial. However, be careful not to deny the IT staff Read permission to the GPO, only deny the Apply Group Policy permission. If the Read permission is denied, members of the IT Staff group would be unable to read or edit the GPO.

As another example, you might create a GPO that applies to all department managers, that installs a specific piece of software (which is discussed in the next chapter). However, the user objects for the managers are located in multiple organizational units, making it harder to apply the policy at the organizational unit level.

To configure a GPO that applies only to the managers, you link it to the domain and remove the default ACE that assigns Read and Apply Group Policy permissions to the Authenticated Users group. You then add a new ACE granting the Managers group the Read and Apply Group Policy permissions.

Activity 11-5: Filtering Group Policy Objects Using Security Permissions

ACTIVITY

Time Required: 10 minutes

Objective: Use security permissions to filter and control the application of policy settings.

Description: Although the organizational unit structure in place in the ChildXX. supercorp.net domain was designed with network administration issues in mind, the IT manager is concerned, because in some cases he does not want policy settings to groups to apply to all users. For example, he would rather not restrict the desktop settings of the Administrators group. In this activity, you will use security permissions to configure how policy settings are applied.

1. If necessary, start your server and log on using the **Administrator** account in the **CHILDXX** domain (where *XX* is the number of the forest root domain for which your server is a domain controller) using the password **Password01**.

2. Click **Start**, select **Administrative Tools**, and then click **Active Directory Users and Computers**.

3. If necessary, expand the **childXX.supercorp.net** domain (where *XX* is the number of the forest root domain for which your server is a domain controller) in the left tree pane.

4. Right-click the **North America XX** organizational unit (where *XX* is the number of your server) and then click **Properties**.

5. Click the **Group Policy** tab.

6. From the list of GPOs, select **Desktop Security Policy XX** (where *XX* is the number of your server) and then click **Properties**.

NOTE

The properties you are looking at are the GPO's properties, not the GPO link's properties.

7. Click the **Security** tab, and review the permissions associated with the Authenticated Users group as shown. Note that this group has both the Read and Apply Group Policy permissions set to allow.

8. Click **Add**. In the Enter the object names to select text box, type **Administrators** and then click **OK**.

9. Ensure that the Administrators group is selected and then note the permissions associated with the group. Check the **Deny** check box for the Apply Group Policy permission, as shown in Figure 11-11. This stops settings in the Marketing Policy GPO from applying to the Administrators group.

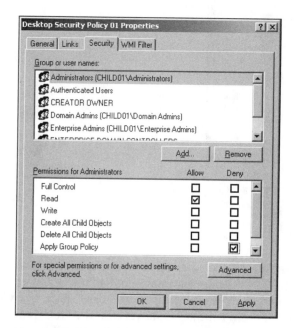

Figure 11-11   Setting GPO permissions

10. Click **OK**. Click **Yes** in the Security dialog box.

11. Click **OK** in the Properties dialog box for your North America organizational unit.

12. Close Active Directory Users and Computers.

13. Log off your server if you do not intend to immediately continue to the next activity. Otherwise, stay logged on.

Windows Management Instrumentation Filters

Windows Management Instrumentation (WMI) filters can be used to restrict the application of GPOs. There is a WMI filter tab in the Properties dialog box of each GPO (refer back to steps 1 through 6 of Activity 11-5 if you do not remember how to access a GPO's properties). Figure 11-12 shows the Properties dialog box that allows you to specify a WMI filter. In the next chapter, you will learn how to create a WMI filter to control the distribution of software.

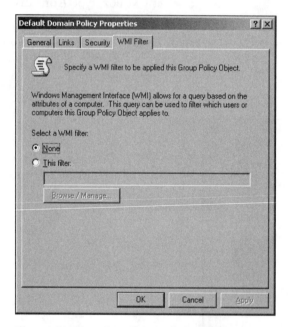

Figure 11-12 Specifying a WMI filter

WMI filters control GPO application based on computer configuration. For example, GPO application can be controlled based on a hardware configuration, file existence or attributes, applications being installed, or the amount of free hard drive space. If a WMI filter evaluates true, the GPO is applied. If the WMI filter evaluates false, the GPO is not applied. A GPO can only be linked to one WMI filter. However, a single WMI filter can be linked to multiple GPOs.

WMI filters are written in WMI Query Language (WQL). For more information on creating WMI filters, read the WMI solution developer kit at *msdn.microsoft.com/library/ en-us/wmisdk/wmi/wmi_start_page.asp* and *msdn.microsoft.com/library/en-us/wmisdk/wmi/ querying_with_wql.asp*

Note that only Windows XP Professional and Windows Server 2003 evaluate WMI filters. Windows 2000 does not understand WMI filters on GPOs, and therefore applies the GPO regardless of the filter. However, if you need a GPO to apply to Windows XP workstations but not Windows 2000 workstations, you can work around this limitation. Start by creating one GPO with settings for Windows 2000 workstations and a second GPO with settings for Windows XP workstations. Link both GPOs at the same level, placing the Windows 2000 GPO link higher in the list of linked GPOs. Finally, add the following WMI filter to the Windows 2000 GPO (you will learn how to add WMI filters in Activity 12-2 of the next chapter):

```
Select * from Win32_OperatingSystem where Caption = "Microsoft
Windows 2000 Professional"
```

When processing GPOs, a Windows XP system will first start with the Windows XP GPO and will apply the GPO. Next, a Windows XP system will look at the Windows 2000 GPO but will not apply the GPO—because of the WMI filter that specifies that it should only apply to Windows 2000. As for a Windows 2000 system, it will first start with the Windows XP GPO and will apply the GPO. Next, the Windows 2000 system will look at the Windows 2000 GPO and apply it—regardless of the WMI filter. This means that any conflicting settings in the Windows XP GPO will be overwritten by the Windows 2000 GPO.

In contrast, if you only need a GPO to apply to Windows 2000 but not Windows XP (that is, the reverse of the previous example) you can simply use the above WMI filter on the GPO—there is no need to create two GPOs. When a Windows XP system evaluates the WMI filter, it will return false and the GPO will not be applied. However, because Windows 2000 systems don't understand WMI filters, they will ignore the filter and apply the GPO.

Slow Link Detection

When connecting over a slow link, such as a dialup or VPN connection, it may be undesirable to apply parts of Group Policy. For example, installing software, redirecting folders, or running scripts can be extremely slow and you may not want these portions of Group Policy to apply to remote users and machines. To solve the problem of slow links, Group Policy provides slow link detection—which can be used to disable portions of Group Policy.

To determine link speed, the client pings the domain controller several times. If the first ping takes less than 10 milliseconds, the link is considered to be fast. Otherwise, an algorithm is used to determine the average transfer rate based on additional ping requests. If the calculated value is less than 500 Kbps (by default) the link is considered to be slow. However, the exact speed used to determine what is and is not a slow link can be set by the administrator. Table 11-1 describes the default behavior of Group Policy when a slow link is detected.

Table 11-1   Default slow link behavior

Settings	Default
Administrative Templates	Enabled (cannot be disabled)
EFS recovery	Enabled
Folder redirection	Disabled
Internet Explorer maintenance	Enabled
IP security	Enabled
Scripts	Disabled
Security	Enabled (cannot be disabled)
Software installation	Disabled
Wireless	Enabled

NOTE

To change the way Group Policy decides what is a slow link and how it deals with slow links, the settings found under Computer Configuration\ Administrative Templates\System\Group Policy and the settings found under User Configuration\Administrative Templates\System\Group Policy can be used to control slow link behavior for computer-related policies and user-related policies, respectively. You can change these GPO settings by using the Group Policy Object Editor.

DESKTOP MANAGEMENT WITH GROUP POLICY

Desktop management is one of the primary goals that can be accomplished with Group Policy. Using Group Policy settings, you can restrict access to or change Windows settings, reduce user errors, redirect folders to a central location, and define scripts to create standardized environments for users.

Restricting Windows

Many Windows functions are restricted based on group membership. For example, you must be a member of the Administrators local group or Power Users local group to add printers to a workstation. However, there are many Windows features that are available to all users, such as desktop wallpaper settings, the Run command on the Start menu, and applets in Control Panel.

Restricting access to Windows features can protect users from their own mistakes. For example, a user that accidentally changes the proxy setting in Internet Explorer cannot access the Internet. Restricting the ability to change the proxy setting in Internet Explorer ensures that this never happens.

Or, you may simply wish to have a consistent and professional image throughout your operations. More than one company has restricted users from changing desktop wallpaper after complaints about too many swimsuit models (or worse!).

Activity 11-6: Configuring Group Policy Object User Desktop Settings

Time Required: 10 minutes

Objective: Configure and test the application of Group Policy settings.

Description: The IT manager at Super Corp has asked you to test the use of GPO settings for the purpose of controlling the user desktop environment. The settings he has given you are not restrictions, but rather configuration settings that he would like applied to all users—even administrators. In order to accomplish this, you will create a new GPO used for setting a standard desktop environment.

1. If necessary, start your server and log on using the **Administrator** account in the **CHILDXX** domain (where *XX* is the number of the forest root domain for which your server is a domain controller) using the password **Password01**.

2. Click **Start**, select **Administrative Tools**, and then click **Active Directory Users and Computers**.

3. If necessary, expand the **childXX.supercorp.net** domain (where *XX* is the number of the forest root domain for which your server is a domain controller) in the left tree pane.

4. Right-click the **North America XX** organizational unit (where *XX* is the number of your server) and then click **Properties**.

5. Click the **Group Policy** tab.

6. Click **New** and name the new GPO **Desktop Preferences XX** (where *XX* is the number of your server), and then press **Enter**.

7. Select the **Desktop Preferences XX** GPO link and click **Edit**.

8. In the left tree pane under the User Configuration node, click the **+** (plus symbol) next to Administrative Templates to expand its contents, and then click the **Start Menu and Taskbar** container.

9. Double-click **Remove user name from Start Menu** in the right details pane.

10. Select the **Enabled** option and then click **OK**. Notice that the Policy is now listed as Enabled, as shown in Figure 11-13.

11. Close the Group Policy Object Editor window when you are finished.

12. Click **Close** in the Properties dialog box for your North America organizational unit.

13. Close Active Directory Users and Computers.

14. Log off your server if you do not intend to immediately continue to the next activity. Otherwise, stay logged on.

11

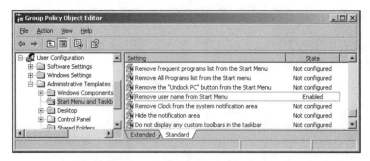

Figure 11-13   Newly enabled policy setting

Folder Redirection

Folder redirection allows you to change the location of default Windows folders. Centralizing the contents of these folders on a server allows users to access this information from any computer on the network. The redirected folders can be backed up as part of the daily backup of the server and protects the user's data from the loss or failure of an individual computer.

Network administrators can instruct users to save their files on the server, but users don't always remember or want to comply. Many applications save documents to the My Documents folder by default, storing files on the local hard drive. Rather than relying on the users, Group Policy can be used to redirect the folder.

The folders that can be redirected are:

- Application data—Holds user-specific files for various applications; Microsoft Office stores document and spreadsheet templates here.

- Desktop—Contains the files, folders, and shortcuts placed on the user desktop.

- My Documents—Contains files created by users and the My Pictures folder; many applications use My Documents as the default location for saving data.

- Start menu—Contains the folders and shortcuts that make up the user-specific portion of the Start menu.

How and Where to Redirect

To redirect a folder, expand the User configuration, Windows Settings, and Folder Redirection nodes in the left tree pane of the GPO. Next, right-click the folder you would like to redirect in the left tree pane and then select Properties.

There are two ways that folders can be redirected. Basic redirection directs all users affected by the GPO to the same location. Advanced redirection allows the administrator to specify different locations for different security groups.

When folders are redirected using basic or advanced redirection, there are four options that specify where the folder is redirected, as shown in Figure 11-14.

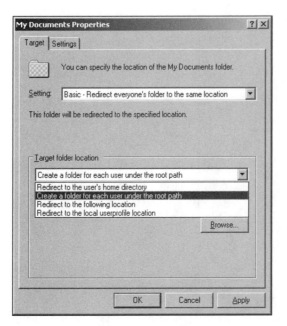

Figure 11-14   Options for folder redirection

The options are:

- Redirect to the user's home directory—Places the folder in the home directory specified in the Active Directory user object on the Profile tab; this option is only available for the My Documents folder.

- Create a folder for each user under the root path—Allows the administrator to specify a location where subdirectories are created for each user's redirected folder; when the folder is created, the NTFS permissions are automatically set to allow only that user to access the folder. This option is not available for the Start menu.

- Redirect to the following location—Allows the administrator to set a single location to be shared by all users; this is useful when you want all users to share the same Start menu, store all files in the same location, or share application files. The administrator can also use variables such as *%USERNAME%* to create a folder that is specific to each user.

- Redirect to the local user profile location—Redirects the folder back to the user's profile.

Other Folder Redirection Settings

There are a number of other folder redirection settings regarding security, folder contents, and the behavior that should occur when the policy is removed. Figure 11-15 shows these settings for the My Documents folder.

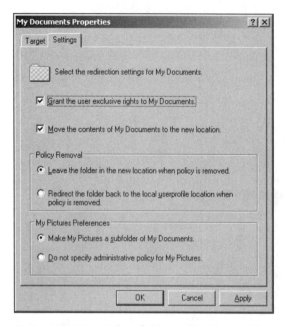

Figure 11-15   Other folder redirection settings

When the Grant the user exclusive rights to *Folder_Name* option (where Folder_Name is the name of the redirected folder, such as My Documents) is selected, only the local system and the user have rights to this folder. Not even the administrator is able to access the folder. This is enforced by setting NTFS permissions when the group policy engine creates the folder. (If the folder already exists, and permissions are incompatible with this setting, an error is logged in the event log and the folder is not redirected.)

If the Move the contents of *Folder_Name* to the new location option (where Folder_Name is the name of the redirected folder, such as My Documents) is selected, then the contents of the existing folder are copied to the new location. This is useful when the folder is redirected to a private storage area for each user on the server. However, do not use this option when redirecting to a single folder shared by multiple users, as their files will become disorganized and may be overwritten as multiple files with the same name are copied from various computers.

For policy removal, you can choose the Leave the folder in the new location when policy is removed option, which allows the redirection to continue even after the policy is removed. To stop the redirection and force the folder back to the default location on the local machine, you must configure a new GPO. If the Redirect the folder back to the local userprofile location when policy is removed option is selected, then the redirected folder is automatically returned to its default location when the policy is removed.

The settings for My Pictures are only available when redirecting My Documents. It is recommended that you keep My Pictures as a subfolder in My Documents so that they can be stored in a central location. Because My Pictures always appears as a subfolder in My Documents, users can become very confused if they are told that My Documents is stored on the server and backed up, but My Pictures is not.

Scripts

GPOs can contain **logon, logoff, startup**, and **shutdown scripts**, which can be written in languages such as **VBScript (.vbs)**, or **JScript (.js)**. Windows Script Host processes both types on the computer that is connecting to the network or logging on. For example, if a user is logging on to the domain at a Windows XP client, then the logon script is processed on the Windows XP client, not the domain controllers. You can also use batch files (.bat) and executable files (.exe).

To specify a startup or shutdown script, expand the Computer configuration and Windows Settings nodes in the left tree pane of the GPO. Next, select the Scripts (Startup/Shutdown) node in the left tree pane. Finally, right-click either Startup or Shutdown in the right details pane and then select Properties. You can then add one or more scripts using the dialog box shown in Figure 11-16.

11

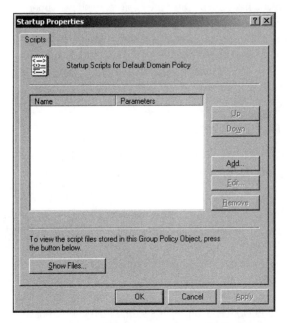

Figure 11-16   Startup Properties dialog box

Similarly, to configure logon or logoff scripts, expand the User configuration and Windows Settings nodes in the left tree pane of the GPO. Next, select the Scripts (Logon/Logoff) node in the left tree pane. Finally, right-click either Logon or Logoff in the right details pane and then select Properties. You can then use a dialog box similar to the one shown in Figure 11-16 to configure one or more scripts.

You must store scripts in a location that is accessible to the users running them. The netlogon share on a domain controller or the GPT are the most common locations for storing scripts. Startup and shutdown scripts are run when the client computer starts up and shuts down, respectively. They run under the system account because they are processed before a user logs on. These scripts are assigned to computers.

Logon and logoff scripts are run when the user logs on or logs off the network. They run with the security privileges of the user that is logging on or off. These scripts configure the environment for users by performing various tasks, such as mapping drive letters to network shares. Logon and logoff scripts are assigned to users.

TIP   To store a script in the GPT, the Show Files button (visible in Figure 11-16) on the dialog box used to add scripts is extremely useful. When clicked, a Windows Explorer window is opened to the correct location for storing scripts. Note that each script type (startup/shutdown/logon/logoff) has its own folder inside of the GPT for storing scripts. The Show Files button will open the folder corresponding to the script dialog you have open. Once the Explorer window is open, you can either drag and drop or copy and paste your scripts into the folder. However, note that you will still need to use the Add button and specify the script in order for the script to be run—scripts are not automatically run just because they are in one of the GPT's scripts folders.

Security Management with Group Policy

GPOs have a variety of security-related settings. This collection of settings is known as a **security policy**. These settings are located in all GPOs, whether they are on a local machine or stored on domain controllers.

The security policy settings that apply to users are found in the User Configuration section of a GPO, under Windows Settings, Security Settings. Only public key policies and software restriction policies exist here. Use public key policies to control the way users receive certificates used for authentication and encryption. Software restriction policies restrict the ability to run and install software.

TIP   The Domain Security Policy and Domain Controller Security Policy, which have shortcuts on the Administrative Tools menu of a domain controller, are actually part of the Default Domain Policy GPO object (which is linked to the domain) and the Default Domain Controllers Policy GPO object (which is linked to the Domain Controllers organizational unit), respectively.

The majority of security policy settings apply to computers. In a GPO, the security settings that apply to computers are found in the Computer Configuration section, under Windows Settings, Security Settings. The categories of security settings that exist for computers are shown in Figure 11-17. The next few sections examine some of the more important issues surrounding these settings.

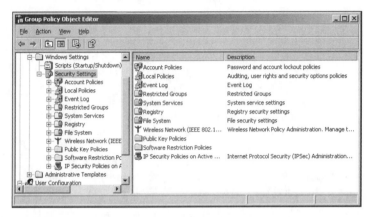

Figure 11-17   Computer security policy categories

Account Policies

One security category that deserves special attention is the **Account Policies** node. This node includes configuration settings that may be the initial step to securing the computer network. Account policies must be configured in a GPO linked to the domain in order to affect domain accounts. If these settings are configured at any other level, they will affect only local accounts on member servers and workstations. The Account Policies node can be found under the Computer Configuration section of a GPO and includes three subcategories: Password Policy, Account Lockout Policy, and Kerberos Policy.

TIP

Remember that domain controllers do not have local accounts. In practice, account policy settings are almost always managed in the Default Domain Policy GPO.

Password Policy

The Password Policy node contains configuration settings that refer to the password's history, length, and complexity. Table 11-2 describes each setting.

Table 11-2 Password policies

Configuration Setting	Description
Enforce password history	Defines the number of passwords that have to be unique before a user can reuse an old password. The default setting for Windows Server 2003 domains is 24.
Maximum password age	Defines the number of days that a password can be used before the user is required to change it; if you never want the passwords to expire, set the number of days to 0. The default setting for Windows Server 2003 domains is 42.
Minimum password age	Defines the number of days that a password must be used before a user is allowed to change it again. The default setting for Windows Server 2003 domains is 1.
Minimum password length	Defines the least number of characters required in a password (values can be from 1 to 14 characters); if no password is required, set the value to 0. The default setting for Windows Server 2003 domains is 7.
Password must meet complexity requirements	Increases password complexity by enforcing rules that passwords must follow (see the list of complexity requirements after this table). Windows Server 2003 domains require complex passwords by default.
Store passwords using reversible encryption	This setting is the same as storing passwords in, essentially, plaintext; this policy provides support for applications using protocols that need the passwords in plaintext for authentication of users in the domain. You should not enable this setting unless it is absolutely required—it is a potential security risk.

If you enable the Passwords must meet complexity requirements setting, passwords must meet the following requirements:

- They cannot contain any part of the user's account name.
- They must be at least six characters in length.
- They must contain characters from three of the four categories below:
  - English uppercase letters
  - English lowercase letters
  - Numbers
  - Nonalphanumeric (for example, !, $, #)

Activity 11-7: Configuring Password Policy Settings in the Default Domain Policy

Time Required: 15 minutes

Objective: Use policy settings at the domain level to configure password policies.

Description: In the past, Super Corp has not enforced any password requirements on domain users because previous attempts to do so have resulted in increased calls to the help desk owing to users forgetting their passwords. As a result, many users have configured very simple passwords, and in some cases even use blank passwords. Concerned about the potential security risk that this represents, the IT manager at Super Corp has asked you to evaluate the use of password policies to control elements such as minimum password length, the number of passwords remembered by the system, and so forth. In this activity, you will configure and test a new password policy for the ChildXX.supercorp.net domain. Because these settings can only be set at the domain level, you and your partner should work as a team, performing these steps on only one of your servers.

1. If necessary, start your server and log on using the **Administrator** account in the **CHILDXX** domain (where *XX* is the number of the forest root domain for which your server is a domain controller) using the password **Password01**.

2. Click **Start**, select **Administrative Tools**, and then click **Active Directory Users and Computers**.

3. In the left tree pane, right-click **ChildXX.supercorp.net** (where *XX* is the number of the forest root domain for which your server is a domain controller) and then click **Properties**.

4. Click the **Group Policy** tab, ensure that the **Default Domain Policy** is selected, and then click **Edit**.

5. In the left tree pane under the Computer Configuration section, click the **+** (plus symbols) next to Windows Settings, Security Settings, and Account Policies to expand them.

6. Click **Password Policy** to view its contents in the right details pane.

7. Double-click **Enforce password history** to view the default number of passwords that are remembered, as shown in Figure 11-18.

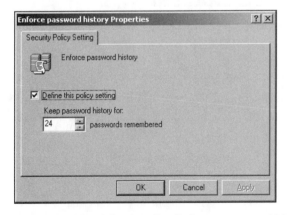

Figure 11-18   Viewing the Enforce password history Properties

8. Click the **passwords remembered** up arrow to change the number of passwords remembered to **8**, and then click **OK**.

9. Double-click **Minimum password length** to view its properties. Click the Characters up arrow to change the required password length to **5** characters, and then click **OK**.

10. Double-click **Password must meet complexity requirements** to view its properties. Select the **Disabled** option, and then click **OK**.

11. Close the Group Policy Object Editor window.

12. Click **OK** in the Properties dialog box for your domain.

13. In the left tree pane, double-click the **North America XX** organizational unit (where *XX* is the number of your server) to expand it.

14. Click the **Atlanta** organizational unit under North America *XX* to show its contents in the right details pane.

15. Right-click the **UserXXA** user account (where *XX* is the number of your server) and then click **Reset Password**.

16. In the Reset Password dialog box, type **art** as the password in both the New password and Confirm password text boxes, and click **OK**.

17. Read the message that appears as a result of attempting to change the password length to one that does not meet the password policy requirements, as illustrated in Figure 11–19. Click **OK**.

Figure 11-19   Attempting to change the password length without meeting the requirements

18. Close Active Directory Users and Computers.

19. Log off your server if you do not intend to immediately continue to the next activity. Otherwise, stay logged on.

Account Lockout Policy

The Account Lockout Policy node contains configuration settings that refer to the password lockout threshold and duration, as well as reset options. Table 11-3 describes each setting.

Table 11-3   Account lockout policies

Configuration Setting	Description
Account lockout threshold	Determines the number of failed logon attempts that results in the user account being locked out.
Account lockout duration	Determines the number of minutes that a locked account remains locked; after the specified number of minutes, the account automatically becomes unlocked. You can specify that an administrator must manually unlock the account by setting the value to 0. To manually unlock an account, uncheck the Account is locked out check box in the account's properties.
Reset account lockout counter after	Determines the number of minutes that must elapse after a single failed logon attempt before the bad logon counter is reset to 0.

Kerberos Policy

The Kerberos Policy node contains configuration settings that refer to the Kerberos ticket-granting ticket (TGT), session ticket lifetimes, and time stamp settings. Table 11-4 describes each setting. Recall that in Activity 9-3 you learned how to set the Kerberos ticket lifetime for your domain.

Table 11-4   Kerberos policies

Configuration Setting	Description
Enforce user logon restrictions	Requires the Key Distribution Center (KDC), a service of Kerberos V5, to validate every request for a session ticket against the user rights policy of the target computer; if enforced, there may be performance degradation on network access.
Maximum lifetime for service ticket	Determines the maximum amount of time, in minutes, that a service ticket is valid to access a resource; the default is 600 minutes (10 hours).
Maximum lifetime for user ticket	Determines the maximum amount of time, in hours, that a TGT may be used; the default is 10 hours.
Maximum lifetime for user ticket renewal	Determines the amount of time, in days, that a user's TGT may be renewed; the default is seven days.
Maximum tolerance for computer clock synchronization	Determines the amount of time difference, in minutes, between the client machine's clock and the time on the server's clock that Kerberos tolerates; the default is five minutes (used to prevent replay attacks).

11

Remember, to configure an account policy for the domain, the GPO must be linked at the domain level of Active Directory. Account policy configurations applied at an organizational unit level only affect the local SAM database of the computers within the organizational unit and do not affect domain logons.

NOTE

Local Policies

Local policies contain a wide variety of settings and are very flexible in how they can be applied. For example, say you have two first-level organizational units: Systems and Secure Systems. You may decide to create a GPO that disables all auditing (although that would not be recommended in a production environment) and link it to the Systems organizational unit. At the same time you could also create a second GPO that requires every type of auditing be enabled and link it to the Secure Systems organizational unit. Any computers with accounts in the Systems organizational unit would not log audit events. In contrast, any computers with accounts in the Secure Systems organizational unit would audit everything.

The categories of local policies include:

- Audit policy—Establishes the auditing configuration for all computers for which it applies; this includes tracking of file access, user logons, and use of rights. Refer back to Chapter 9 for a list of the different audit policies that you can enable.

- User rights assignment—Configures a user's rights to modify some system configuration options when logging on to a computer; each user right has a list of security principals that is able to perform a specified task. Two important user rights that you can configure are the Allow log on locally option and the Deny log on locally option. In the Default Domain Controllers Policy, these are configured to allow only administrators to log on locally. This means that average users on the network cannot log on to a domain controller at the keyboard or via Terminal Services. Table 11-5 lists available logon rights and Table 11-6 lists *some* of the available privileges. For the difference between logon rites and privileges, refer back to Chapter 9. Also, for more details on specific privileges not listed, search for the privilege in Windows Server 2003 Help and Support.

- Security options—Contain a large number of operating system security features that you can enable or disable; these are not dependent on the user that logs on. Options include cryptography settings, disabling the guest account, and disabling operating system features. Recall that in Activity 9-2 you learned how to set the Network security: LAN Manager authentication level security option. For more details on specific security options, search for the security option in Windows Server 2003 Help and Support.

Table 11-5 and 11-6 list the default rights on Windows XP and Windows Server 2003 systems. On Windows 2000 systems, the default users and groups may be different. For more details, please see Windows Server 2003 Help and Support as well as the documentation provided with Windows 2000.

NOTE

Table 11-5 Logon rights

Right	Description
Access this computer from a network	Determines which users and groups can access the computer via the network (network logon). By default, on workstations and servers, the Administrators, Backup Operators, Power Users, Users, and Everyone groups have this right. On domain controllers, the Administrators, Authenticated Users, and Everyone groups have this right by default.
Allow log on locally	Determines which users and groups can log on locally to the computer (interactive logon). By default, on workstations and servers, the Administrators, Backup Operators, Power Users groups, and Guest have this right. On domain controllers, the Account Operators, Administrators, Backup Operators, Print Operators, and Server Operators groups have this right by default.
Allow log on through Terminal Services	Determines which users and groups can establish a Terminal Services connection with the computer. By default, on workstations and servers, the Administrators and Remote Desktop Users groups have this right. On domain controllers, only the Administrators group has this right by default.
Deny access to this computer from network	Determines which users and groups are explicitly not allowed to access the computer via the network (network logon). This policy setting overrides the Access this computer from a network policy if both policies apply to a user. By default, no users or groups are assigned this policy.
Deny log on as a batch job	Determines which users and groups are explicitly not allowed to log on as a batch job. This policy setting overrides the Log on as a batch job policy if both policies apply to a user. By default, no users or groups are assigned this policy.
Deny log on as a service	Determines which users and groups are explicitly not allowed to start a process as a service. This policy setting overrides the Log on as a service policy if both policies apply to a user. By default, no users or groups are assigned this policy. Note that this policy does not apply to the System, Local Service, or Network Service accounts.
Deny log on locally	Determines which users and groups are explicitly not allowed to log on locally to the computer (interactive logon). This policy setting overrides the Allow log on locally policy if both policies apply to a user. By default, no users or groups are assigned this policy.
Deny log on through Terminal Services	Determines which users and groups are explicitly not allowed to establish a Terminal Services connection with the computer. This policy setting overrides the Allow log on through Terminal Services policy if both policies apply to a user. By default, no users or groups are assigned this policy.

11

Table 11-5 Logon rights (continued)

Right	Description
Log on as a batch job	Determines which users and groups can log on as a batch job. For example, if a user creates a scheduled task, Task Scheduler will log on using the configured user account as a batch logon—rather than an interactive logon. By default, only the Local System is assigned this right. However, on Windows 2000 or newer systems, Task Scheduler automatically grants this right as needed.
Log on as a service	Determines which users and groups can start a process as a service. By default, no users or groups are assigned this right.

Table 11-6 Privileges

Right	Description
Add workstations to a domain	As you learned in the last chapter, this right determines which users and groups can "bypass" security checks and add a computer to a domain. Only domain controllers use this policy setting. By default the Authenticated Users group has this right on domain controllers. For more information, refer to Chapter 10.
Back up files and directories	Determines which users and groups can bypass the permissions set on file and directory, registry keys, and other objects in order to back them up. By default, the Administrators and Backup Operators groups have this right.
Manage auditing and security log	Determines which users and groups can modify SACLs on objects such as Active Directory objects, files, and registry keys. This right also allows a user or group to view and clear the security log. Note, however, this does not give the user or group the permissions to enable or disable the Audit object access setting. By default, only the Administrators group has this right.
Restore files and directories	Determines which users and groups can bypass the permissions set on file and directory, registry keys, and other objects in order to restore them from backup. This right also allows the user or group to assign ownership of an object to any valid security principal (refer back to Chapter 9, if necessary). By default, on workstations and servers, the Administrators and Backup Operators groups have this right. On domain controllers, the Administrators, Backup Operators, and Server Operators groups have this right by default.

Table 11-6 Privileges (continued)

Right	Description
Shut down the system	Determines which users and groups that are logged on locally can shutdown the computer. By default, on workstations, the Administrators, Backup Operators, Power Users, and Users groups have this right. By default, on servers, the Administrators, Backup Operators, and Power Users groups have this right. On domain controllers, the Account Operators, Administrators, Backup Operators, Server Operators, and Print Operators groups have this right by default.
Take ownership of files or other objects	Determines which users and groups can take ownership of objects such as Active Directory objects, files, and registry keys—even if the user does not have the Take Ownership permission on the object. This right acts like a "bypass" for the Take Ownership permission. By default, only the Administrators group has this right.

TIP

When assigning rights, consider assigning the right(s) to a group as a "best practice." Once the right(s) are assigned to a group, you can then add users or other groups to the group as needed.

11

Restricted Groups

Restricted groups define the users that are allowed membership to specific groups. When Group Policy is applied or refreshed, any member of a restricted group that is not listed in the restricted group's member list is removed. This prevents administrators from accidentally adding users to sensitive groups, such as Domain Admins, Enterprise Admins, Schema Administrators, or Administrators. Additionally, any user or group that is on the restricted group's member list but is not a member of the group is added to the group.

TIP

Restricted groups cannot be used to remove the Administrator account from the Administrators group. In other words, even if you make Administrators a restricted group and you do not add Administrator to the member list, the Administrator account is not automatically removed from the Administrators group.

In addition to controlling the members of a group, you can also use restricted groups to add the group as a member of another group. Unlike the members list, the member of list is used to add the group to other groups. If the group is not a member of one of the groups on its member of list, the restricted group is added to the group(s). Note, however, that unlike the members list, the member of list only adds the group to other groups—it does not remove the restricted group from any groups of which the restricted group is already a member.

For more information on configuring restricted groups, search for "Restricted Groups" in Windows Server 2003 Help and Support.

NOTE

System Services

System services define which services are started, stopped, or disabled on computers. You can also configure security for services, which allows you to define which users can start and stop them. This is an effective way to disable unnecessary services on client computers and servers to increase security.

To configure a particular service, select the System Services node in the left tree pane. Next, in the right details pane, right-click the service you would like to configure and then click Properties. You must check the Define this policy setting check box, as shown in Figure 11-20, in order to configure the service's startup parameters. The Edit Security button is used to define which security principals can start/stop/pause the service, modify the service's settings, and so forth.

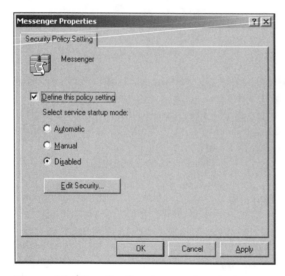

Figure 11-20 Configuring service startup parameters

Registry Settings

Registry settings define security permissions for registry entries. These permissions are then applied to all computers affected by the GPO and you can use them to change permissions if you wish to restrict access to some registry settings that are part of a new application. Registry settings are usually applied by using a security template, which are covered later in this chapter.

This section of a GPO controls access to the registry or parts of it. Do not confuse it with administrative template settings, which change the values stored in the Windows registry.

File System

File system defines the NTFS permissions that are applied to the local hard drives of computers affected by the GPO. You can use this section to enhance security by removing permissions to files and folders. File permissions are usually applied by using a security template, which are covered later in this chapter.

Wireless Network Policies

Wireless network (IEEE 802.11) policies define settings for wireless network connectivity. They allow you to configure which wireless networks' workstations can connect to and automatically configure Wireless Encryption Protocol (WEP). Only Windows XP Professional and Windows Server 2003 apply this policy setting. To start the Wireless Network Policy Wizard, simply right-click the Wireless network node in the left tree pane and then click Create Wireless Network Policy.

Public Key Policies

Public Key Policies define configuration settings relating to the use of different public key-based applications such as the encrypting file system (EFS), automatic certificate enrolment settings, and Certificate Authority (CA) trusts. This node is available under both the Computer configuration and User configuration sections.

The Encrypting File System node under the Public Key Policies node is used to specify data recovery agents for EFS. To specify a new data recovery agent, in the left tree pane under Computer configuration, expand the Public Key Policies node. Next, right-click the Encrypting File System node and then select Add Data Recovery Agent. Use the Add Recovery Agent Wizard to import the certificate of the new recovery agent. You can also select the Encrypting File System node in the left tree pane to view a list of current recovery agents in the right details pane.

If you want to prevent computers from allowing users to encrypt files altogether, you can right-click the Encrypting File System node in the left tree pane and then select Properties. In the properties window, uncheck Allow users to encrypt files using Encrypting File System (EFS). Any systems affected by the GPO will not allow files to be encrypted on their local drives.

The Automatic Certificate Request Settings node under the Public Key Policies node is used to configure client workstations to automatically request certificates. Only a limited number of certificate types are supported. However, this feature only requires Windows 2000 clients and Windows 2000 CAs, at a minimum. To configure automatic requests, right-click the Automatic Certificate Request Settings node in the left tree pane, select New, and then click Automatic Certificate Request. Then use the Automatic Certificate Request Setup Wizard to configure clients to automatically request certificates.

The Trusted Root Certificate Authorities node and Enterprise Trust node (which is available under both the Computer and User configuration sections) are used to specify trusted CAs. If you are using one or more Windows 2000 or newer CAs on your Active Directory network, you do not have to be concerned with publishing their certificates—it is done automatically. However, if you are using non-Microsoft CAs, you can use the Trusted Root Certificate Authorities node to import the CAs' certificates. If you do not have any CAs but rather depend on outside CAs, you can use the Enterprise Trust node to create a certificate trust list to set up trust of external CAs. To configure either Trusted Root Certificate Authorities or Enterprise Trust, simply right-click the node and then select Import to start the appropriate wizard. Additional certificate trust settings can be found by right-clicking the Trusted Root Certificate Authorities node and then selecting properties.

Autoenrollment is a new feature of Windows Server 2003 and Windows XP. Autoenrollment allows not only computers, but also users, to request version 2 certificate templates automatically. While autoenrollment is much more flexible than the Automatic Certificate Request Settings node, autoenrollment does have the following requirements:

- The forest's schema must be upgraded to Windows Server 2003

- Domain controllers must be at least Windows Server 2000 running Service Pack 3 or later

- Windows XP Professional or Windows Server 2003 clients

- A Windows Server 2003 Enterprise or Datacenter Edition Enterprise CA

To configure autoenrollment settings, select the Public Key Policies node in the left tree pane under the Computer configuration or User configuration (depending on whether you want to configure autoenrollment settings for users or computers) section of a GPO. In the right details pane, right-click Autoenrollment Settings and then click Properties. The dialog box shown in Figure 11-21 will then appear.

From the dialog box shown in Figure 11-21, you can enable or disable automatic certificate enrollment. In order to take full advantage of autoenrollment, you will need to select the Renew expired certificates, update pending certificates, and remove revoked certificates and Update certificates that use certificate templates options.

NOTE   For more details on certificates or setting up a CA, please see Chapter 9 of MCSE Guide to Planning a Microsoft Windows Server 2003 Network (ISBN: 0-619-12025-8). An excellent article on autoenrollment policies is also available at: *www.microsoft.com/technet/prodtechnol/windowsserver2003/plan/autoenro.asp*.

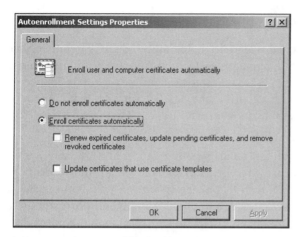

Figure 11-21   Autoenrollment settings

Software Restriction Policies

Software restriction policies define security settings related to what programs are allowed to run on a system. An administrator can choose to allow no applications to run by default and then make explicit exceptions for applications that can run. Alternatively, an administrator can allow all applications to run except those applications explicitly disallowed.

Individual rules can be based on a file's hash (which is like a fingerprint of the executable), a digital certificate that was used to sign the executable, the file's path, or the Internet zone. Software restriction policies also allow you to control what programs are considered executable. One limitation to software restriction policies, however, is they only work on Windows XP Professional and Windows Server 2003 systems.

The software restrictions node is available both under Computer configuration and User configuration—and each provides the same functionality for their respective objects. A computer security setting overrides the same setting for a user, if both are defined.

NOTE

For more information on software restriction policies, search for "software restriction policies" in Windows Server 2003 Help and Support. An excellent article on software restriction policies is also available at: *www.microsoft.com/technet/prodtechnol/winxppro/maintain/rstrplcy.asp*.

IP Security Policies

IP security policies in Active Directory define IPSec settings, such as IP traffic encryption. By enabling these policies, you can enable IPSec for an entire network with very little effort. For more information on IPSec, please see Chapter 10 of MCSE Guide to Planning a Microsoft Windows Server 2003 Network (ISBN: 0-619-12025-8).

Security Templates

An administrator uses a **security template** to define, edit, and save baseline security settings to be applied to computers with common security requirements to meet organizational security standards. Templates help ensure that a consistent setting can be applied to multiple machines and be easily maintained. Security templates are .inf files that contain options for some or all of the computer settings in a security policy. They can be applied to a local computer or imported into a GPO.

Using a security template, you can test security configuration in a test lab environment and then easily apply the tested security template to the production network. For example, suppose you want to restrict access to the local file system on workstations. You decide to create a security template that restricts access to the file system. This first attempt causes the test workstation to crash because the permissions are too limited for the local system account. After several modifications, the template works properly. You can then copy the security template onto a floppy disk, log on to your workstation, and import the security settings into a GPO that applies to all user workstations. In Activity 11-8, you will import a security template into an existing GPO.

The Default Template

When Windows Server 2003 is installed, the default security settings applied to the computer are stored in a template called Setup Security.inf. The contents of this template are different depending upon the original configuration of the computer, such as whether the operating system was freshly installed or upgraded from a previous version of Windows. The purpose of this template is to provide a single file in which all of the original computer security settings are stored. If the security settings of a computer are ever changed and an administrator wishes to easily return the system to its original settings, you can simply reapply the Setup Security.inf template.

CAUTION   You should never apply the Setup Security.inf template using Group Policy because it contains a large number of settings that can seriously degrade Group Policy processing performance. Instead, you should deploy the settings using the Security Configuration and Analysis snap-in.

Incremental Templates

If the basic security settings do not meet your security needs, you can apply various additional security configurations using incremental templates. These templates modify security settings incrementally. However, you should only apply these templates to machines already running the default security settings because they do not include any of the initial configurations that the template created during the initial installation.

- Compatws.inf—You can apply this template to workstations or servers. Windows Server 2003 has increased the default security considerably over previous versions, such as Windows NT 4.0. In some cases, this increased security brings application compatibility problems, especially for noncertified applications that require user access to the registry. One way to run these applications is to make users members of the Power Users group, which has a higher level of rights and permissions than a normal user. Another option is for the administrator to increase the security permissions for the Users group. The compatws.inf template provides a third alternative by weakening the default security to allow legacy applications to run under Windows Server 2003.

- Securews.inf and securedc.inf—These templates provide increased security for areas such as account policy, auditing, and registry permissions. The securews template is for any workstation or server, whereas the securedc template should only be applied to domain controllers.

- Hisecws.inf and hisecdc.inf—You can apply these templates incrementally after you have applied the secure templates. Security is increased in the areas that affect network communication protocols through the use of such features as packet signing. You should only apply these templates to client computers running Windows 2000 or higher, and all domain controllers must be running Windows 2000 or Windows Server 2003. You should apply these templates to all machines to ensure proper connectivity. The hisecws template is for workstations or servers, whereas the hisecdc template should only be applied to domain controllers.

- DC security.inf—This template is applied automatically whenever a Windows 2000 or Windows Server 2003 member server is promoted to a domain controller. This is available to give the administrator the option to reapply the initial domain controller security settings if the need arises.

- Rootsec.inf—This template specifies the original permissions assigned to the root of the system drive. The main purpose of this template is for use in reapplying security permissions to resources on the system drive that have been changed, whether on purpose or by accident.

The security templates included in Windows Server 2003 provide the administrator with acceptable security configurations for a variety of situations. If there is a unique situation where a preconfigured template is not suitable, you can also create custom templates to meet your needs. You can use the **Security Templates snap-in** to create custom templates.

NOTE

You can view the detailed settings in the default security templates using the Security Templates snap-in.

ACTIVITY

Activity 11-8: Importing a Security Template into a GPO

Time Required: 10 minutes

Objective: Import a security template into a GPO so it can be applied to the computers in an organizational unit.

Description: After upgrading all of Super Corp's workstations to Windows XP, some of the older applications are not able to run. In your test lab, you found that applying the compatws.inf security template allowed these applications to run. To apply this template to many computers at once, you will import it into a GPO.

1. If necessary, start your server and log on using the **Administrator** account in the **CHILDXX** domain (where *XX* is the number of the forest root domain for which your server is a domain controller) using the password **Password01**.

2. Click **Start**, select **Administrative Tools**, and then click **Active Directory Users and Computers**.

3. If necessary, expand the **childXX.supercorp.net** domain (where *XX* is the number of the forest root domain for which your server is a domain controller) in the left tree pane.

4. Right-click the **North America XX** organizational unit (where *XX* is the number of your server) and then click **Properties**.

5. Click the **Group Policy** tab.

6. Select the **Desktop Security Policy XX** GPO link and then click **Edit**.

7. In the left tree pane under the Computer Configuration node, click the **+** (plus symbol) next to Windows Settings to expand its contents.

8. In the left tree pane, right-click **Security Settings** and then click **Import Policy**, as shown in Figure 11-22.

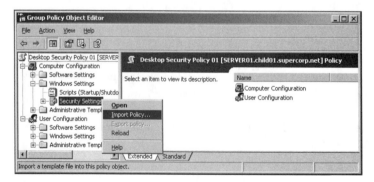

Figure 11-22   Importing a security template

9. Double-click **compatws.inf**. The settings from compatws.inf have now been imported into this GPO. These settings will be automatically distributed to all workstations in the North America *XX* organizational unit within approximately 90 minutes, although some settings may not take effect until the computer(s) is/are restarted.

10. Close the Group Policy Object Editor window when you are finished.

11. Click **OK** in the Properties dialog box for your North America organizational unit.

12. Close Active Directory Users and Computers.

13. Log off your server if you do not intend to immediately continue to the next activity. Otherwise, stay logged on.

Analyzing Security

The Security Configuration and Analysis utility, illustrated in Figure 11-23, allows administrators to compare current system settings to a previously configured security template. The comparison identifies any changes to the original security configurations and any possible security weaknesses that may be evident when compared to a stronger security baseline template.

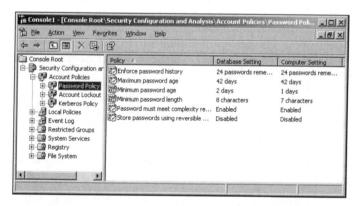

Figure 11-23   Security Configuration and Analysis snap-in

The Security Configuration and Analysis tool uses a container, also referred to as a database, to store the imported templates that are compared to the current system. The administrator imports a template into the database and then compares the template settings to the actual computer settings. If desired, the administrator can import more than one template to compare the effects of combining templates on the current settings. Once you have created a combined template, you can save and export it for future analysis, or you can use it to configure working computer systems.

After the analysis process is complete, the security categories appear. As each node is expanded, you can see the comparison between the database (imported templates) and the computer's current configuration. A green check mark indicates that the two settings match; a red *x* indicates a mismatch. You can make changes by double-clicking any configuration entry and selecting the desired configuration.

Activity 11-9: Using the Security Configuration and Analysis tool

Time Required: 10 minutes

Objective: Compare the security configuration on your domain controller with the hisecdc.inf security template.

Description: The standard security configuration for domain controllers at Super Corp is the default security settings. You are considering upgrading your security level by applying the hisecdc.inf security template to all domain controllers. However, before you do this, you want to see what changes will be made.

1. If necessary, start your server and log on using the **Administrator** account in the **CHILDXX** domain (where *XX* is the number of the forest root domain for which your server is a domain controller) using the password **Password01**.

2. Click **Start**, and then click **Run**. In the Open drop-down list box, type **mmc** and press **Enter**.

3. Click **File** on the menu bar, and then click **Add/Remove Snap-in**.

4. Click **Add**. In the Add Standalone Snap-in dialog box, select **Security Configuration and Analysis** and then click **Add**.

5. Click **Close** and then click **OK** to close the Add/Remove Snap-in dialog box.

6. In the left tree pane, click **Security Configuration and Analysis**. This displays the instructions for using the snap-in.

7. In the left tree pane, right-click **Security Configuration and Analysis** and then click **Open Database**.

8. By default, no databases exist. You can enter any valid filename for the database. Type **DCsec** in the File name drop-down list box and then click **Open**. The database is used to hold the configuration of security settings. By using a database rather than the security settings actually applied to the local computer, you can create, view, and modify security templates without affecting the local computer.

9. Select **hisecdc.inf**, then click **Open**. This is the security template that is compared to the configuration of the local computer. Note that you can add multiple security templates to the same database by right-clicking Security Configuration and Analysis in the left tree pane and selecting Import template.

10. In the left tree pane, right-click **Security Configuration and Analysis** and then click **Analyze Computer Now**.

NOTE If you want to apply the security settings to a single computer or server, you can use the Configure Computer Now option. Using the Configure Computer Now option modifies the local computer's security settings.

11. Click **OK** to accept the default error log path.

12. After the analysis is complete, double-click **Local Policies** and then double-click **Audit Policy** in the right details pane. As shown in Figure 11-24, most of the audit settings are not configured as strongly as the security template. An icon with a red *x* indicates a setting that is weaker than the security template. An icon with a green check mark indicates a setting that is equal to or stronger than the security template. A question mark icon indicates a setting that is configured on the system but not the analysis database. An exclamation point icon indicates a setting that is configured in the analysis database but not on the system.

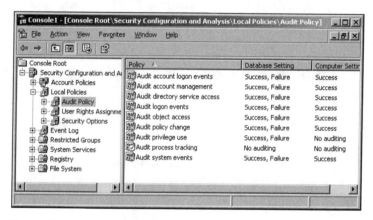

Figure 11-24   Comparing computer and database security settings

13. Double-click **Audit policy change** in the right details pane.

14. Uncheck the box next to **Failure** and then click **OK**. This modifies the current analysis database (that is, DCsec).

15. If you wish, in the left tree pane, right-click **Security Configuration and Analysis** and then click **Export template**. Type **DCcust** as the filename and then click **Save**. This creates a custom security template based on the analysis database's security settings. The custom template can then be imported into a GPO and deployed to all domain controllers in the domain.

16. Browse through any other settings that interest you.

17. Close the MMC window without saving your changes.

18. Log off your server if you do not intend to immediately continue to the next activity. Otherwise, stay logged on.

TIP

The Secedit command-line utility can also be used to analyze security settings and work with security templates. For more information on Secedit, search for "Secedit" in Windows Server 2003 Help and Support.

Using the Group Policy Management Console

Microsoft has developed a new tool called the Group Policy Management Console (GPMC). Although GPMC isn't included on the Windows Server 2003 CD, it is available as a free download for Windows Server 2003 customers. GPMC brings together tools and options that have been accessible from a number of different tools, including Active Directory Sites and Services, Active Directory Users and Computers, and the Resultant Set of Policy (RSoP) snap-in, and lets you access them from one console. GPMC also adds new functionality—such as the ability to back up or restore a GPO separately from the system state data (backups are covered in Chapter 14). This tool is highly recommended, as it makes working with Group Policy in a large environment much easier.

ACTIVITY

Activity 11-10: Installing the Group Policy Management Console

Time Required: 20 minutes

Objective: Install and explore the Group Policy Management Console.

Description: Super Corp's IT staff has been able to save a substantial amount of time by using Group Policy to configure corporate workstations. However, the IT staff is now spending a lot of time juggling between multiple consoles to manage Group Policy. To simplify administration, you decide to install the GPMC on one of the company's domain controllers.

1. If necessary, start your server and log on using the **Administrator** account in the **CHILDXX** domain (where XX is the number of the forest root domain for which your server is a domain controller) using the password **Password01**.

2. Click **Start**, select **All Programs**, and then click **Internet Explorer**.

3. In the Address toolbar, enter **www.microsoft.com/windowsserver2003/gpmc** and then click **Go**.

4. Scroll down to the Download the GPMC with Service Pack 1 (SP1) section and then click the **Group Policy Management Console with SP1** link (note that the section and/or link may be called something slightly different when you visit Microsoft's Web site).

5. Click the **Download** link.

6. When prompted to open or save the file, click **Open**. Alternatively, your instructor may have already downloaded the file and made it available to you on the network. If so, follow your instructor's directions to run the file.

7. Once the download is completed, the GPMC Setup Wizard starts. Click **Next**.

8. Select the **I Agree** option and then click **Next**.

9. Once the installation is completed, click **Finish**.

10. Close Internet Explorer.

> **NOTE**
>
> After installing the GPMC, the Group Policy tab in Active Directory Users and Computers as well as Active Directory Sites and Services is modified. Instead of displaying a list of GPO links you saw in previous activities, the Group Policy tab now only displays a single Open button that opens the GPMC. You are now unable to create, link, or modify GPOs directly from Active Directory Users and Computers or Active Directory Sites and Services.

11. Click **Start**, select **Administrative Tools**, and then click **Group Policy Management**. The GPMC opens.

12. In the left tree pane, expand **Forest: childXX.supercorp.net** (where *XX* is the number of the forest root domain for which your server is a domain controller), expand **Domains**, and then expand **childXX.supercorp.net**.

13. In the left tree pane, click **Domain Controllers** to list the GPO(s) that are linked to the Domain Controllers organizational unit, as shown in Figure 11-25. Note that you can link additional GPOs by right-clicking the site, domain, or organizational unit in the left tree pane and then clicking Link an Existing GPO. You can also create a new GPO at the same time when linking a GPO to a domain or organizational unit.

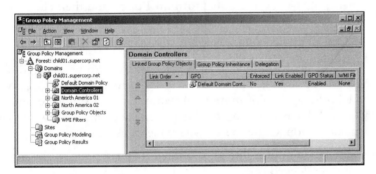

Figure 11-25   Group Policy Management Console

14. In the left tree pane, click **Group Policy Objects**. All of the GPOs that are stored in the childXX.supercorp.net domain are listed. You can create new GPOs that are not initially linked to a site, domain, or organizational unit by right-clicking Group Policy Objects and then selecting New.

If you want to link a new GPO to a site using the GPMC, you must first create the GPO in one of the forest's domains. For the best performance, create the new GPO in a domain that has domain controllers located at the site to which the GPO applies. By doing so, clients do not have to cross the WAN to retrieve GPO data.

NOTE

If you want to link a GPO to a site but do not see the site in the left tree pane, you can right-click the Sites folder in the left tree pane and then click Show Sites. Additionally, in a multiple domain forest, if you do not see the domain you want to manage in the left tree pane, you can right-click the Domains folder in the left tree pane and then click Show Domains.

TIP

15. In the right details pane, double-click **Default Domain Policy**. Note the location(s) to which the GPO is linked. Also note the users and/or groups that can apply the GPO.

16. In the list of sites, domains, and OUs to which the GPO is linked, right-click one of the links. Note the options available. Press the **Escape** key on your keyboard to close the menu without making a selection.

The Enforce option is the same as the No Override option.

NOTE

17. In the left tree pane, right-click **Default Domain Policy** and then click **Edit**. You can now edit the GPO as you normally would.

18. Close the Group Policy Object Editor window when you are finished.

19. Explore the GPMC as desired. Notice that RSoP data can also be accessed directly from the GPMC instead of using the RSoP snap-in. In Activity 11-11, you will learn how to use the RSoP snap-in. For more information on performing common tasks with the GPMC, click Help Topics on the Help menu and then review the Group Policy Management section. Close the GPMC when finished.

20. Log off your server if you do not intend to immediately continue to the next activity. Otherwise, stay logged on.

If you decide you don't like the GPMC, you can always remove it by using Add or Remove Programs in Control Panel.

NOTE

TROUBLESHOOTING GROUP POLICY

The most important thing to be aware of when implementing Group Policy is how the links to containers, priority ordering by administrators, No Override, Block Inheritance, ACL permissions, Loopback Processing Mode, and WMI filters all interact to determine how and when a GPO applies. It can be complicated, but you must gain an understanding of them to be successful with Group Policy.

TIP

It is also important to ensure that your clients have DNS configured correctly. Group Policy cannot work properly if the client is unable to properly locate a Windows 2000 Server or Windows Server 2003 domain controller.

Most Group Policy issues occur when GPOs do not apply in the priority they should. If this happens, look for the following situations:

- Do any of the Group Policy Object links have No Override enabled? If so, then this GPO may apply regardless of the settings on any other GPOs.

- Is Block Policy Inheritance enabled on an organizational unit? If so, then GPOs from other locations may not apply.

- Is Loopback Processing enabled for Group Policy? If so, then the user settings are taken from the GPOs that apply to the computer and possibly the user (depending on the mode).

- Is the GPO newly created or linked? If so, workstations and member servers only refresh Group Policy information every 90 minutes (with a 0 to 30 minute random offset) by default. Domain controllers refresh Group Policy information every five minutes. (A few settings, including software installation and startup/logon scripts, do not apply until a restart or new logon.) To force the refresh of Group Policy information, you can restart the computer or use the Gpupdate.exe utility on Windows Server 2003 and Windows XP. Note that the Gpupdate.exe utility replaces the secedit.exe /refreshpolicy machine_policy and secedit.exe /refreshpolicy user_policy commands used in Windows 2000.

- Is Group Policy applied over a slow link? A slow link is calculated based on the ping time between the client and domain controllers. Some parts of Group Policy may not be applied if a client is connected by a slow link. However, security settings and settings based on administrative templates are always applied over slow links. You can control which parts of your policies are applied over slow links.

11

Troubleshooting Tools

There are several tools to help you troubleshoot group policy configuration:

- **Resultant Set of Policy (RSoP)**—This is an MMC snap-in. When used in logging mode, it allows you to see the policy settings that apply to a particular user when logged on to a particular computer. It also tells you from which GPO the setting originated. When used in planning mode, RSoP can show you how policies would vary in different "what-if" scenarios, such as for users in different containers in different security groups, if slow links are in effect, and for other configured variables. Some RSoP functions are also available from menus within Active Directory Users and Computers when working with GPOs.

- **Gpresult**—This is a command-line utility that performs the same task as RSoP in logging mode. It is useful when documenting settings for many users or computers through logon scripts.

- **Gpupdate**—This is a command-line utility that you can use to force the update of Group Policy information on the local workstation. It saves time when testing new GPOs. Without this utility, workstations need to be restarted to ensure that Group Policy information is refreshed.

- **Dcgpofix**—This is a command-line utility that resets the Default Domain Controller Policy and the Default Domain Policy back to their default configuration. This is useful if one of these policies has been accidentally deleted or misconfigured. All previous changes to these GPOs are lost.

Activity 11-11: Using the RSoP snap-in

Time Required: 10 minutes

Objective: Use the RSoP snap-in to see from where the policy settings applied to your domain controller originate.

Description: After making several policy changes that did not correctly apply to your server, you decide to use the RSoP snap-in to see what GPOs are affecting your server.

1. If necessary, start your server and log on using the **Administrator** account in the **CHILDXX** domain (where *XX* is the number of the forest root domain for which your server is a domain controller) using the password **Password01**.

2. Click **Start**, and then click **Run**. In the Open drop-down list box, type **mmc** and press **Enter**.

3. Click **File** on the menu bar, and then click **Add/Remove Snap-in**.

4. Click **Add**. In the Add Standalone Snap-in dialog box, select **Resultant Set of Policy** and then click **Add**.

5. Click **Close** and then click **OK** to close the Add/Remove Snap-in dialog box.

6. In the left tree pane, right-click **Resultant Set of Policy** and then click **Generate RSoP Data**.

7. Click **Next** to start the Resultant Set of Policy Wizard.

8. Confirm that the **Logging mode** option is selected, then click **Next**.

9. Confirm that the **This computer** option is selected, then click **Next**.

10. Click **Do not display user policy settings in the results (display computer policy settings only)** option, as shown in Figure 11-26, and then click **Next**.

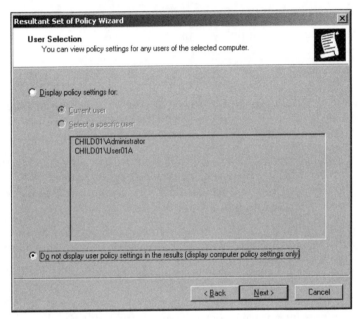

Figure 11-26   Selecting user on which to base RSoP data

11. View the selection summary, then click **Next**.

12. Click **Finish**.

13. In the right details pane, double-click **Computer Configuration**, double-click **Windows Settings**, double-click **Security Settings**, double-click **Local Policies**, then double-click **Audit Policy**. You see that all of the audit policy settings are configured in the Default Domain Controllers Policy, as shown in Figure 11-27. Note that you may need to scroll to the right to see the Source GPO column.

14. Browse any other settings that interest you.

15. Close the MMC window without saving your changes.

16. Log off your server.

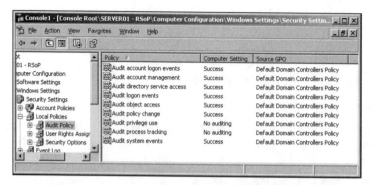

Figure 11-27   Determining source of policy settings

Chapter Summary

◻ Group Policy is a way to apply a group of settings to users and computers in a site, domain, or organizational unit. You can also set it in a local GPO that exists on each workstation and server. Only Windows 2000 and newer systems support Group Policy.

◻ The local computer policy (sometimes called a local GPO) is stored on the computer's local hard drive. Nonlocal GPOs are stored in two parts: the Group Policy Container (GPC) is stored in Active Directory and the Group Policy Template (GPT) is stored in the SYSVOL share on domain controllers.

◻ The order of application for GPOs is local, site, domain, organizational unit. The last GPO applied has the highest priority. You can modify the default priority settings for GPOs by using No Override, Block Policy Inheritance, Loopback Processing, security permissions, and WMI filters.

◻ When No Override is enabled on a GPO link, it always has the highest priority. This is useful when enforcing organizational or departmental settings. If two GPOs are linked at different levels with No Override and there is a conflict, then the first policy object processed will be in effect. If two GPOs are linked at the same level with No Override and there is a conflict, then the policy higher in the list of linked GPOs will be in effect.

◻ When Block Policy Inheritance is configured on a domain or organizational unit, GPOs higher in the tree do not apply (unless No Override is set). This allows for exemptions from corporate policy for a particular organizational unit (or department). The Block Policy Inheritance setting is not available on sites.

◻ A user or computer must have the Read and Apply Group Policy permissions on a GPO in order for the policy to apply to that user or computer. To configure a GPO that only applies to a specific user or group of users, you can remove the Authenticated Users group's permissions and then assign the Read and Apply Group Policy permissions to the desired user or group. Alternatively, if only a small number of users should not apply the policy, you can specify the users and groups that should be exempted from the policy by denying them the Apply Group Policy permission.

◘ WMI filters control GPO application based on computer configuration. For example, GPO application can be controlled based on a hardware configuration, file existence or attributes, applications being installed, or the amount of free hard drive space. Only Windows XP Professional and Windows Server 2003 understand WMI filters. Windows 2000 systems will ignore WMI filters and apply the GPO regardless.

◘ Loopback Processing is typically used for computers in a public area or kiosk. When Loopback Processing is enabled and set in merge mode, the user configuration settings from the computer are added to the user configuration settings that apply to the user. When Loopback Processing is enabled and set in replace mode, the user settings are taken from the GPOs that apply to the computer, not the user.

◘ Slow link detection provides a mechanism for disabling portions of Group Policy when a slow dialup or VPN connection is used to connect to the network. By default, a slow link is defined as 500 Kbps or slower. Folder redirection, software installation, and scripts are all disabled by default when a slow link is detected.

◘ To affect domain accounts, account policies must be set at the domain level. If set at the organizational unit level, account policies will only affect local accounts on member servers and workstations.

◘ When using Group Policy for desktop management, you can restrict Windows functions, redirect folders, and define scripts for logon, logoff, startup, and shutdown.

◘ Security management using Group Policy is accomplished with security templates. Security templates are .inf files with security settings configured and can be imported into a GPO. You can also use security templates as a baseline to examine security settings using the Security Configuration and Analysis snap-in.

◘ The main tools used to troubleshoot Group Policy are the RSoP snap-in, Gpresult, Gpupdate, and Dcgpofix.

KEY TERMS

account policies — Configuration settings for passwords, account lockouts, and Kerberos. They must be linked to the domain to affect settings for the domain.

administrative templates — Files containing settings used by the GPO Editor to define the registry key that should be changed, the options, and a description of the effects.

Block Policy Inheritance — A setting in the Group Policy configuration for a domain or organizational unit that prevents settings from GPOs higher in the tree from being inherited.

Dcgpofix — A command-line utility that recreates the Default Domain Policy and the Default Domain Controllers Policy.

Folder redirection — A user configuration setting that redirects folders from the local user profile to the server. Basic redirection redirects all users' folders to the same path (although you can use variables such as %USERNAME%). Advanced redirection allows completely different paths based on security group memberships.

GPO link — GPOs are assigned to a site, domain, or OU by linking them. You can link a single GPO to multiple locations.

Gpresult — A command-line utility that is equivalent to RSoP.

Gpupdate — A command-line utility that forces the update of Group Policy on a workstation or server. It replaces the portion of the secedit command that was used to refresh Group Policy in Windows 2000.

group policy container (GPC) — The collection of objects in Active Directory that holds GPOs and their settings.

group policy template (GPT) — A set of files and folders in the SYSVOL folder that holds settings and files for a GPO.

IP security policies — Security policy settings relating to IPSec configuration.

JScript (.js) — A scripting language that you can use to write logon, logoff, startup, and shutdown scripts. It is similar to JavaScript.

local computer policy — A GPO that is stored on the local computer, and is only available on the local computer. It is sometimes called the local GPO.

local policies — A wide variety of settings for auditing, user rights, and security options.

logoff script — A script that runs when a user logs off.

logon script — A script that runs when a user logs on.

Loopback Processing Mode — A computer configuration setting that changes the processing of user configuration settings. When in effect, a user's settings from the GPOs that apply to the computer is used rather than the GPOs that apply to the user.

netlogon share — A default share that is available on all NT 4.0 domain controllers. It is commonly used to hold logon scripts and system policies.

No Override — A link setting that prevents policies linked at a lower level from having priority over the settings in the GPO.

Restricted groups — A security policy setting that defines group membership.

Resultant Set of Policy (RSoP) — A tool used to show how settings are applied, and which GPO supplied a particular setting.

security policy — The collection of user configuration and computer configuration settings located in Windows Settings, Security Settings. You can update these using security templates.

security template — An .inf file that contains settings for some or all of the computer settings in a security policy.

Security Templates snap-in — An MMC snap-in that edits existing security templates or creates new ones.

shutdown script — A script that runs when a computer is shut down.

startup script — A script that runs when a computer starts up.

system policies — Collections of registry entries that are used to control Windows 9x and Windows NT workstations.

tattooing the registry — The normally undesired effect of leaving permanent changes in the Windows registry, even after the policy no longer applies.

VBScript (.vbs) — A scripting language that you can use to write logon, logoff, startup, and shutdown scripts. It is based on Visual Basic and is sometimes called Visual Basic Scripting Edition.

Windows Management Instrumentation (WMI) — The Windows implementation of Web-Based Enterprise Management (WBEM) that uses a common set of interfaces to present information about a computer system in a consistent way across a variety of tools and platforms.

Wireless network (IEEE 802.11) policies — Security policy settings that configure settings for wireless access.

REVIEW QUESTIONS

1. Which of the following describe Group Policy? (Choose all that apply.)
   a. Policy files must be manually copied to each domain controller.
   b. Replication is automatic between domain controllers.
   c. Registry entries are permanently applied to workstations.
   d. Group Policy can be used to distribute applications.
   e. Group Policy can only be used with Windows Server 2003.

2. When a GPO is stored on a domain controller, it has a unique name in the SYS-VOL folder. On what is the name based?
   a. the name of the GPO
   b. the GUID of the GPO
   c. the SID of the GPO
   d. the GUID of the user that created the GPO
   e. the domain SID and the SID of the GPO

3. Which folders on SYSVOL may contain a file named registry.pol, which contains registry settings? (Choose all that apply.)
   a. Adm
   b. Scripts
   c. User
   d. Machine
   e. Applications

4. In what order are GPOs applied?
   a. site, local, domain, OU
   b. local, OU, domain, site
   c. site, domain, OU, local
   d. local, site, domain, OU

11

5. A single GPO can only apply to computers in a single domain. True or False?

6. A Group Policy Object linked at what level has the lowest priority?

   a. local

   b. site

   c. domain

   d. OU

7. Which of the following settings is applied to a Group Policy Object link in order to control Group Policy application?

   a. No Override

   b. Block Policy Inheritance

   c. Loopback Processing

   d. security permissions

8. Which of the following settings is applied to a domain or organizational unit in order to control Group Policy application?

   a. No Override

   b. Block Policy Inheritance

   c. Loopback Processing

   d. security permissions

9. Which of the following settings is used to force the user configuration settings from the policies that affect the computer account?

   a. No Override

   b. Block Policy Inheritance

   c. Loopback Processing

   d. security permissions

10. For Group Policy settings to apply to a user, that user must have, or be a member of a group that has, both the read and apply group policy permissions set to allow. True or False?

11. Which Group Policy feature can you use to point the My Documents folder to a location on the server rather than the local hard drive?

    a. folder redirection

    b. Windows restrictions

    c. security settings

    d. administrative templates

12. You have created a GPO that removes the Run command and have linked it to the domain level. At the organizational unit level, you have created a GPO to enable the Run command. Which GPO takes effect?

    a. the organizational unit level

    b. the domain level

    c. The GPO settings cancel each other out and have no effect.

    d. Because there is a conflict, local policy is used to decide the effect.

13. Which languages can you use to write logon, logoff, startup, and shutdown scripts? (Choose all that apply.)

    a. Visual Basic .NET

    b. VBScript

    c. JScript

    d. C++

14. You need to redirect the My Documents folder to a server location based upon security group memberships. Which setting do you choose?

    a. basic

    b. advanced

    c. either of the above

    d. none of the above

15. Which policies must be linked to the domain to have an affect?

    a. account policies

    b. local policies

    c. system services

    d. restricted groups

16. Which security template is not designed to be applied to domain controllers?

    a. hisecws.inf

    b. rootsec.inf

    c. securedc.inf

    d. hisecdc.inf

17. Which utility can use security templates as a baseline to compare security settings?

    a. Gpresult

    b. Gpupdate

    c. RSoP snap-in

    d. Security Configuration and Analysis snap-in

    e. Dcgpofix

18. Which utility can you use to recreate the Default Domain Policy and the Default Domain Controllers Policy?

   a. Gpresult

   b. Gpupdate

   c. RSoP snap-in

   d. Security Configuration and Analysis snap-in

   e. Dcgpofix

19. You can use both the Gpresult and Resultant Set of Policy tools to view the aggregated policy settings that apply to a user. True or False?

20. A security template named Setup Security.inf is automatically applied when you promote a Windows Server 2003 to act as a domain controller. True or False?

CASE PROJECTS

Like any other large organization, Super Management Corporation has problems with misconfigured desktop computers and security settings. As she is learning more about Active Directory, Pat Horton asks you if Group Policy can help her and Jenn reduce the amount of time they spend managing these issues.

CASE PROJECTS

Case Project 11-1: Windows Restrictions

At Super Corp, users who have attempted to fix their own computers have misconfigured some workstations. Most of these computers are located in offices; however, some are located in meeting rooms that are shared by many users. It is helpful to have a consistent interface on these computers that is free of unauthorized software—no matter who is logged on.

Describe some of the policy settings that might be appropriate for the computers located in meeting rooms. If some of these settings are user configuration settings, how can you ensure that they apply regardless of who logs on?

CASE PROJECTS

Case Project 11-2: Security Baselining

Matt Butler calls you. He is a bit frustrated because neither he nor Pat Horton can be sure whether the current configuration of Super Corp's servers matches the company's written security policy. You invite Matt and Pat to a meeting to help them determine how to proceed. Explain how you can use security templates to generate reports that indicate compliance with company policy.

Case Project 11-3: Equal Rights

Like many organizations, Super Corp assigns administrative tasks to different staff members. You have been asked to examine the rights that should be given to the following job roles:

- Web server backup and restoration administrator—responsible for backing up (and restoring, if necessary) a limited number of Web servers located in an organizational unit called Web Servers.

- Active Directory security administrator—responsible for archiving and monitoring security logs on only domain controllers.

The company's security policy states that administrators should only be given permissions and rights they need to complete their jobs. What rights do each of the above job roles need to be assigned? Are there any existing GPOs to which you could make the change? If a new GPO needs to be created, where should it be linked? Are there any other "best practices" you would employ when configuring user rights? Note: assume that the administrators already have the necessary logon rights—you only need to be concerned with privileges.

11

CHAPTER
12
DEPLOYING AND MANAGING
SOFTWARE WITH GROUP POLICY

After reading this chapter, you will be able to:

♦ Prepare software for distribution using Group Policy

♦ Deploy software using Group Policy

♦ Manage software deployed with Group Policy

♦ Remove software deployed with Group Policy

♦ Troubleshoot software deployment

In addition to managing user desktops, maintaining security, applying scripts, and redirecting folders, which you learned about in Chapter 11, Group Policy can also help you deploy and maintain software installations throughout the domain. There are a variety of applications that can be deployed using Group Policy, including business applications such as Microsoft Office, utilities such as antivirus software, and software updates such as service packs.

When a company rolls out a new software application, there are four main phases: preparation, deployment, maintenance, and removal. In this chapter, you will learn how to use Group Policy to address each of these four phases.

PREPARING SOFTWARE DEPLOYMENT

The first phase in rolling out a new software application is preparation. In the preparation phase, the main tasks include preparing the software for deployment, setting up distribution points on the network, and identifying which users or computers require what software.

Preparing the Software

Software installation using Group Policy takes advantage of a service called the **Windows Installer**. The Windows Installer service runs on all Windows 2000, Windows XP, and Windows Server 2003 computers and can fully automate the software installation and configuration process. In addition, the Windows Installer service can repair installed applications—ensuring that all the necessary files and registry entries exist on a computer. To provide these features, the Windows Installer service requires a Windows Installer package for each application. The following are benefits of using Windows Installer:

- Installation customization—Optional parts of an application such as drawing features, charting features, or clip art can be available in an application, but not actually installed until their first use. This saves disk space and speeds up the initial installation time because rarely used features do not have to be installed.

- Application resilience—If a file that is critical to the operation of an application is missing or becomes corrupted, Windows Installer automatically retrieves a copy of the file from the installation source and replaces the corrupted or missing file.

- Privilege elevation—In order to install correctly, many applications require access to the registry or file system that an end user does not normally have write access to. When an application is assigned or published by an Administrator using Group Policy, Windows Installer uses the security context of the local system to perform the installation. This allows software to be installed even when the user does not have all the necessary permissions.

NOTE

By default, Windows Installer only uses the security context of the local system when installing applications assigned or published using Group Policy. When a user manually initiates a Windows Installer package, Windows Installer uses the security context of the user who started the installation. Although you can configure Group Policy to instruct Windows Installer to use the local system's privileges when a user manually initiates an installation, it is not recommended. Allowing the user to initiate the installation of unapproved Windows Installer packages is a security risk. It is possible that a malicious user could permanently take control of the system by creating a Windows Installer package of their own.

- Clean removal—Windows Installer logs all files copied to the hard drive and modifications made to the registry. When an application is removed, Windows Installer uses the installation logs to ensure all files and registry entries related to the application are removed. Because of this, there is no chance of orphaned files or registry entries after an application is removed. Additionally, shared files (that is, files used by more than one application) are not removed until the last application using the file is removed; thus, uninstalling one application does not break another application.

- Installation rollback—In the event an installation fails part way through, the installation logs are used to roll back the installation. This can be done because any files that the Windows Installer intends to delete or overwrite are moved to a temporary backup location until the installation is successfully completed. Once this occurs, the temporary backups are deleted.

NOTE

A version of Windows Installer is also available for Windows NT 4.0 and Windows 95/98. However, Windows NT 4.0 and Windows 95/98 cannot take advantage of Group Policy. Therefore, you cannot use Group Policy to distribute or maintain software on these platforms.

A **Windows Installer package (.msi) file** contains the information necessary to install and remove an application using the Windows Installer service. The Windows Installer package consists of two parts: the .msi file that describes the installation and, optionally, any external files required to install or remove the application. The .msi file contains a list of all required files, their correct locations, registry entries, as well as summary information about the application, such as its version number. You can initiate the installation of an application using a Windows Installer package manually, by double-clicking the .msi file from an application's CD-ROM or by using Group Policy.

Many software vendors are starting to include preconfigured Windows Installer packages with their applications to enable administrators to take advantage of the features provided by Windows Server 2003 Group Policy. For older applications, you can create your own Windows Installer package using third-party utilities, such as a program called WinINSTALL from VERITAS.

If a Windows Installer package is not available for an application, and you cannot repackage the application using an application like WinINSTALL, you have an option to use another file type called a **ZAP (.zap) file**. A ZAP file is a text file that can be used by Group Policy to deploy an application. However, the following limitations apply to applications deployed using a ZAP file:

- Can only be published and not assigned
- Are not resilient and do not repair themselves automatically
- Always use the permissions of the currently logged on user

To create a ZAP file, use a text editor such as Notepad and save the file with a .zap extension. The following is an example of a simple ZAP file:

```
[Application]
FriendlyName = "My Custom Application"
SetupCommand = "\\FileServer\Software\MyApp.exe"
```

For more information on creating a ZAP file, consult Knowledge Base article 231747 at *support.microsoft.com*.

Preparing the Distribution Point

Once you have obtained the necessary installation files, you must make the files available on the network. While you can create a **distribution point** by simply creating a shared folder on a file server, keep the following in mind:

- Consider using DFS to create multiple distribution points that contain the same software. When a client requests the installation files, DFS automatically redirects the client to the closest server. This is very important when you have a single GPO that applies to users in multiple sites.

- Try to use a single distribution point (or one distribution point using DFS on multiple servers) in order to simplify distribution and troubleshooting. Additionally, create a folder for the different categories of software (discussed later in the chapter) in the distribution point. Then create a folder in the appropriate category for each application. This makes it easier to locate applications when creating policies.

- For security reasons, only administrators should have write/modify permission on a distribution point. The appropriate users and computers should be given read access to the distribution point. Also consider using a hidden share such as SWdist$ (where the $ at the end indicates that the share should not appear when browsing the network) in order to reduce the chance of a user manually installing applications. Finally, auditing should be set up on the .msi files of any sensitive applications.

ACTIVITY

Activity 12-1: Creating a Software Distribution Point

Time Required: 10 minutes

Objective: Create a shared folder to use as a distribution point.

Description: The IT manager at Super Corp has asked you to configure a shared folder on one of the servers to act as a temporary software distribution point. This shared folder will be used to test the software distribution feature available with Group Policy. In this activity, you will create a shared folder and then copy the Windows Support Tools into the shared folder.

1. If necessary, start your server and log on using the **Administrator** account in the **CHILDXX** domain (where *XX* is the number of the forest root domain for which your server is a domain controller) using the password **Password01**.

2. Click **Start** and then click **My Computer**.

3. Double-click the **D:** drive. Alternatively, your instructor may specify you use a different drive. If so, use the drive specified by your instructor.

4. On the File menu, select **New** and then **Folder**. Name the new folder **Software** and then press **Enter**.

5. Right-click the **Software** folder and then click **Sharing and Security**.

6. Click the **Share this folder** option. Use the default Share name of Software.

7. Click **Permissions**.

8. Click **Add**, type **Administrators** and then click **OK**.

9. Grant the Administrators group the allow Full Control, Change, and Read share permissions.

10. Once you have given the Administrators group the correct permissions, click **OK**.

11. Click **OK** to close the Software Properties dialog box.

12. Double-click the **Source** folder. Alternatively, your instructor may provide you with another location to locate the Windows Server 2003 files. If so, use the path specified by your instructor.

13. Double-click the **SUPPORT** folder.

14. Double-click the **TOOLS** folder.

15. Select both the **SUPPORT.CAB** and **SUPTOOLS.MSI** files. You can do this by holding down the Ctrl key and clicking each of the files. Let go of the Ctrl key once you have selected both of the files.

16. On the Edit menu, click **Copy**.

17. Navigate back to the root of the D: drive. You can do this by clicking the **Back** button multiple times.

18. Right-click the **Software** folder you have already created and then click **Paste**.

19. Double-click the **Software** folder. The two files you copied should now appear in the folder, similar to Figure 12-1.

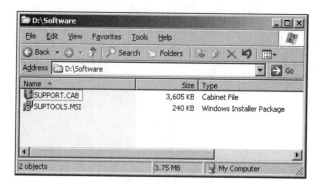

Figure 12-1   Creating a distribution point

20. Close the Windows Explorer window.

21. Log off your server if you do not intend to immediately continue to the next activity. Otherwise, stay logged on.

Determining Installation Scope

Once you have made the software available on your network, you must decide which users and/or computers will have what software installed. Because software distribution is part of Group Policy, the methods you learned in the last chapter for controlling the application of policies also apply to controlling software installation. For example, you can set up a GPO object that installs antivirus software on all computers in a domain and set the No Override option on the GPO link. This ensures that administrators of individual organizational units in the domain do not intentionally or unintentionally block the installation of the antivirus software.

During this step, you must also take into consideration how software will be configured and managed. For example, you may have a Sales organizational unit and Quality Assurance organizational unit. Both the Sales and Quality Assurance departments require Microsoft Office. However, the Sales Department needs Word, Excel, PowerPoint, and Outlook, but the Quality Assurance Department only needs Word, Excel, and Outlook. In this situation, it is necessary to set up two GPOs (or use two existing GPOs that apply to the correct organizational units) instead of using a single GPO at the domain level (or a higher organizational unit in the tree). By using two GPOs, you can configure what Office applications are installed for the two departments.

As another example, say there is a small group of users in the IT Department that are the first to receive new software updates before they are deployed to the rest of the company (that is, they are the guinea pigs). Although the same application is deployed both to the selected IT employees and other employees in the company, in order to manage the application separately for the two different groups of users, you must use two different GPOs. Setting up one GPO that deploys the application to the selected IT employees and another GPO for the other employees allows you to deploy software patches to only the selected IT employees.

There are several other options you must consider when deploying software. In the next few sections, you will see how software is deployed using Group Policy and the options available. It is a good idea to review the following sections before determining the installation scope for your applications. With a better understanding of how software is deployed and managed after deployment, you can define an application's scope much easier.

CONFIGURING SOFTWARE DEPLOYMENT

Group Policy can be used to deliver applications to users and computers. When an application is delivered to a user, it is available on every computer used by that user (providing, of course, that the computer is able to process Group Policy and is joined to a domain in the forest). When software is delivered to a computer, the application remains on that computer and is available to all users of that computer. Using Windows Server 2003 Group Policy, you can deploy applications in one of two ways:

- Assigning applications
- Publishing applications

Assigning Applications

Applications can be **assigned** to computers or users. When an application is assigned in the computer section of Group Policy, any computer to which the policy applies has the application automatically installed the next time that the computer is started. Applications assigned to computers are visible (for example, the application's Start menu icons) to all users of the computer.

When an application is assigned in the user section of Group Policy, any user to which the policy applies has the application's shortcut(s) advertised on the Start menu. However, by default, the application is not actually installed. Instead, any necessary registry keys are added and the shortcuts on the Start menu are configured to start the installation of the application. The application is not actually installed until the user clicks the application's shortcut for the first time. Alternatively, the user can also open a document type (for example, .doc or .xls) that is associated with an assigned application. When the user attempts to open the document, the application is then installed. This is called **document invocation**.

Applications assigned to users will "follow" the user around when they log on to different computers. For example, say Lori has PowerPoint assigned through Group Policy, which she usually uses from the computer at her desk. Lori is preparing for a meeting in one of the conference rooms. Although the computer in the conference room does not have Power-Point assigned or installed, PowerPoint is assigned to her. Therefore, when Lori logs on, the icon for PowerPoint is available on her Start menu, which installs PowerPoint when clicked. Alternatively, she could open one of her PowerPoint presentations directly, which would also install PowerPoint.

Continuing with the example, Lori is finished with her meeting and she logs off. Ted then logs on to the same computer Lori was using, but he does not have PowerPoint assigned to him. Although PowerPoint was installed on the computer when Lori used it, the icons for PowerPoint do not appear for every user of that computer—just the users who have it assigned. Because Ted is not assigned PowerPoint and neither is the computer, the Power-Point Start menu icons do not appear to him.

12

CAUTION Just because a user has not been granted access to a distribution point, or does not have the application assigned or published to them using Group Policy, does not mean that they are prevented from accessing an application after it is installed on a system. For example, if User A has application XYZ assigned using Group Policy, there is nothing preventing User B from logging on to User A's computer and running the application. While the application's Start menu icons do not appear on User B's Start menu, User B can still access the application's executable by navigating to the executable using Windows Explorer. If you have a sensitive application that only particular users should be allowed to run, consider using Group Policy to set the NTFS permissions on the installed application. Additionally, it is a good idea to assign sensitive applications to computers, rather than users, to ensure the application is only installed on the appropriate machines.

This example brings up two important points. First, applications are only advertised by default when assigned to a user, because when the user roams between computers it would not be practical to have them wait 15 minutes for software to install. If Lori had to wait for Word, Excel, Outlook, PowerPoint, Access, FrontPage, and a half dozen other custom applications to install, it could take quite a long time for her to log on. Instead, she only needed PowerPoint and that is all that was installed. Because applications only need to be advertised and not installed, it not only speeds up the logon process, but also saves disk space.

Second, if an application is divided into multiple components or features—such as Microsoft Office being divided into Word, Excel, and so forth and then further subdivided into features—only the features (of an assigned application to a user) that the user actually uses are installed by default. For example, if a user has Office's thesaurus assigned to them but the user never actually uses the thesaurus, it is never installed. Again, this reduces the time the user must wait for an application to be installed and also reduces the hard drive space required for features that are never used.

NOTE In Windows 2000 Server, this was the default—and only—behavior available when assigning applications to users. However, in Windows Server 2003, the option to fully install an application when a user logs on is now available. The new feature is called the Install this application at logon option and is discussed later in this section.

Publishing Applications

While you can assign an application to a user or computer, you can only **publish** applications to users. When an application is published to a user, the user can install the application by accessing Add or Remove Programs in Control Panel. Alternatively, the user can use document invocation by opening a document type associated with the application. Note however that the application's Start menu icons are not advertised like they are when an application is assigned.

One difference to note between published and assigned applications (to either a user or computer) is that assigned applications are resilient to uninstallation. Note that this "resilient" is not the same "resilient" discussed earlier in the chapter. Earlier in the chapter, "resilient" was used to define Windows Installer's ability to repair an installation if a file is missing or becomes corrupted. Both published and assigned applications take advantage of this feature provided by Windows Installer. If a published or assigned application has a missing or corrupt file, Windows Installer attempts to repair the installation. In this meaning, both published and assigned applications are resilient.

The other "resilient" is used to describe the user's ability to uninstall an application. If an application is published and a user uninstalls the application (after it has been installed, of course) the application is not reinstalled—although the option to reinstall the application is still available in Add or Remove Programs. In contrast, if an application is assigned to a user or computer and a user uninstalls the application, the application is automatically reinstalled the next time the computer starts, or the application is readvertised the next time the user logs on. In this meaning, assigned applications are resilient but published applications are not.

Activity 12-2: Publishing Software Using Group Policy

Time Required: 10 minutes

Objective: Publish an application to users using Group Policy.

Description: Super Corp has traditionally used Microsoft Systems Management Server to deploy software packages and updates to domain users. Although the system is effective, the IT manager at Super Corp has found it both difficult and expensive to train system administrators in the use of this product. Understanding that Windows Server 2003 Group Policy includes features associated with software deployment, the IT manager has asked you to evaluate the ability to make software available for installation by users without administrative privileges. In this activity, you will publish an application to users in the North America organizational unit. You will then configure a WMI filter to only apply the GPO to users with more than 25 megabits of free disk space.

1. If necessary, start your server and log on using the **Administrator** account in the **CHILDXX** domain (where *XX* is the number of the forest root domain for which your server is a domain controller) using the password **Password01**.

2. Click **Start**, select **Administrative Tools**, and then click **Active Directory Users and Computers**.

3. If necessary, expand **childXX.supercorp.net** (where *XX* is the number of the forest root domain for which your server is a domain controller) in the left tree pane.

4. Right-click the **North America XX** organizational unit (where *XX* is the number of your server) and then click **Properties**.

5. Click the **Group Policy** tab.

6. If you do not have the GPMC installed, click **New** to create a new GPO and name

12

it **Software Installation XX** (where *XX* is the number of your server) and then press **Enter**. Alternatively, if you have installed the GPMC, click **Open** to open the GPMC. Once the GPMC is opened, right-click the **North America XX** organizational unit (where *XX* is the number of your server) and then click **Create and Link a GPO Here**. Name the new GPO **Software Installation XX** (where *XX* is the number of your server) and then click **OK**.

7. Right-click the **Software Installation XX** GPO link and then click **Edit** to open the Group Policy Object Editor.

8. In the left tree pane, expand the **Software Settings** folder under User Configuration.

9. Right-click **Software installation**, select **New**, and then click **Package**.

10. In the File name drop-down list box, enter **\\SERVERXX\Software** (where *XX* is the number of your server) and then press **Enter**.

11. Select the **SUPTOOLS.MSI** file and then click **Open**.

12. In the Deploy Software window, ensure that Published is selected, as shown in Figure 12-2.

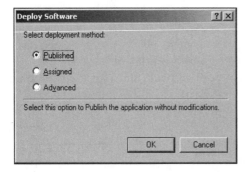

Figure 12-2   Selecting how software should be deployed

13. Click **OK**.

14. In the left tree pane, click **Software installation**. The application you just deployed should appear in the right details pane, as shown in Figure 12-3.

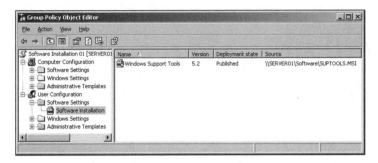

Figure 12-3   Newly deployed application

15. You must next configure a WMI filter that requires the client to have at least 25 megabits of free disk space on its C: drive. If a client does not have at least 25 megabits free, then the GPO will not apply and in turn the software will not be installed. To add the WMI filter, in the left tree pane, right-click the **Software Installation XX** node and then click **Properties**.

16. Click the **WMI Filter** tab.

17. Select the **This filter** option.

18. Click the **Browse/Manage** button.

19. Click the **Advanced** button. Additional options appear.

20. Click **New**.

21. Type **25 Mb Free** in the Name text box and **25 Mb free space on fixed disk C:** in the Description text box.

22. In the Queries text box, type the following query:

```
SELECT * FROM Win32_LogicalDisk WHERE Name = "C:" AND
DriveType = 3 AND FreeSpace > 26214400
```

DriveType = 3 in the query specifies that the C: drive must be a local fixed disk (that is, a hard drive).

NOTE

23. Click **Save**. Your screen should look similar to Figure 12-4.

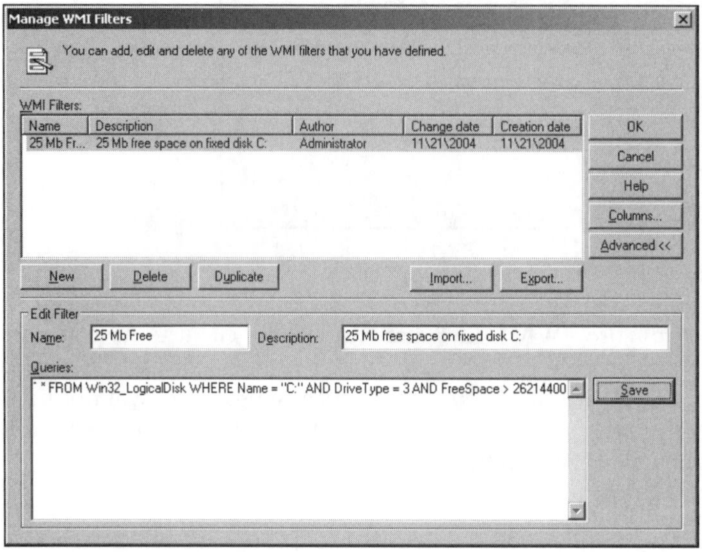

Figure 12-4   Adding a WMI filter to a GPO

24. With the 25 Mb Free filter already selected in the WMI Filters list box, click **OK**.

25. Click **OK** to close the Software Installation *XX* GPO Properties dialog box.

26. Close all windows and log off your server if you do not intend to immediately continue to the next activity. Otherwise, leave the Group Policy Object Editor open and stay logged on.

Configuring the Deployment

Configuring the deployment of the software package involves creating or editing a GPO and then specifying application deployment options. For example, an administrator might choose to assign a certain application to all computers at the domain level, which would automatically install the application the next time individual computers were started. Similarly, a different application might be published to members of the Marketing organizational unit only, allowing users to whom this policy applies to install the application, if necessary, at their own discretion.

In addition to configuring whether applications are published or assigned, there are also various other options you can set when deploying applications. The default installation options of a Windows Installer package can be modified by using a transform file. Additionally, the priority of different applications installed through document invocation can be controlled. Applications can be grouped into one or more categories to help users find the correct software in Add or Remove Programs. Finally, additional behavior options can be specified depending if the software is deployed to a user or computer and whether the software is published or assigned. The following sections look at these options in more detail.

Software Modification

Applications such as Microsoft Office have many different features and components that can be installed. While it is possible to use just the default installation options, most organizations choose to install different sets of features and components to match their needs. Additionally, the selected features and components are typically modified from department to department.

In order to modify the default options of a Windows Installer package, you can use a **Windows Installer transform (.mst) file**. The transform file allows an administrator to customize the options when an application is installed. Applications, such as Microsoft Office, have a setup wizard that you can use to create one or more transform files. The transform file(s) can then be specified when deploying the application. Transform files allow multiple departments to use the same Windows Installer package—even if the departments have different requirements.

To specify one or more transform files when you are deploying an application, choose the Advanced option (which is visible in Figure 12-2) and then click the Modifications tab. As shown in Figure 12-5, you can then specify one or more transform files by clicking the Add button. If multiple transform files are specified, they are applied starting at the bottom. Therefore, transform files higher in the list override transform files lower in the list. Be careful not to click OK until you are sure the correct transform files are added and they are in the correct order. Once the package is deployed, the transform files and their order cannot be modified.

You can only set transform file settings when you are first deploying the software package. Once you deploy a package, you cannot modify the transform files used or the order in which multiple transform files are applied.

For more information on creating transform files, please see the documentation provided with your application.

Software Association

As you have already learned, assigned and published applications can be installed using document invocation. Document invocation allows users to open a file and have the appropriate application installed automatically based on the file's extension. Once the application is installed, it is then used each time the user opens a document type associated with the application.

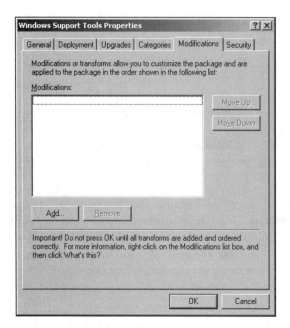

Figure 12-5   Modifications tab when deploying a new software package

However, there may be instances where multiple applications deployed using Group Policy use the same file extension. For example, an organization may require the use of both Word 2000 and Word 2002, which are assigned at the domain level. The Support Department may prefer to use Word 2002, whereas the Sales Department may prefer Word 2000. By creating a new GPO for the Support organizational unit and another GPO for the Sales organizational unit, the application precedence feature of software installation can be used to control which version of Word is used during document invocation.

When you publish or assign an application, the extension(s) used by the application are registered in Active Directory. Application precedence allows an administrator to control which software package is used when multiple packages share the same file extension(s). While you cannot add additional extensions (all extensions must be added through a software package), you can control the priority of registered extensions. When two or more applications share the same extension, the application highest in the application precedence list (that applies to the user or computer) is used.

Figure 12-6 shows the File Extensions tab, which is used to set application precedence. To access this tab, right-click Software installation in the left tree pane of a GPO and then click Properties. If you have installed applications that register extensions, the available extensions are listed in the Select file extension drop-down list box. The application(s) that has/have registered the selected extension then appear in the Application precedence list box. If multiple applications have registered the same extension, you can use the Up and Down buttons to set their precedence.

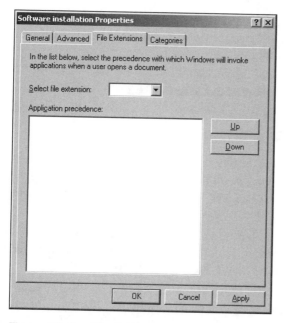

Figure 12-6   File Extensions tab used to set application precedence

Software Categories

Software categories allow deployed software to be organized into meaningful groups in Add or Remove Programs. Users can select from the various software groups the Administrator has defined in order to locate the needed software. For example, creating a Graphics category would allow members of the Graphics Department to quickly locate the applications they use most. Figure 12-7 shows an example of how a user could select from a list of available software categories.

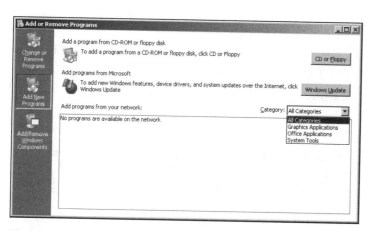

Figure 12-7   Example software categories in Add or Remove Programs

One important thing to note about software categories is that software categories created in one GPO are available to all other GPOs in the domain. You only need to define a software category once in order to use it throughout the domain.

Activity 12-3: Creating Software Categories

Time Required: 10 minutes

Objective: Create a software category and add an application to the new category.

Description: Having now seen the results of publishing applications to users, the IT manager at Super Corp has asked you if it is possible to organize published applications in Add or Remove Programs. In this activity, you will configure a new software category and then add the application you published in Activity 12-2 to the category.

1. If necessary, start your server and log on using the **Administrator** account in the **CHILDXX** domain (where *XX* is the number of the forest root domain for which your server is a domain controller) using the password **Password01**.

2. Open the Software Installation *XX* GPO (where *XX* is the number of your server) in the Group Policy Object Editor. Refer back to Activity 12-2 if you need to locate where you created this GPO.

3. If necessary, in the left tree pane, expand the **Software Settings** folder under the User Configuration section of the GPO.

4. In the left tree pane, right-click **Software installation** and then click **Properties**.

5. Click the **Categories** tab.

6. Click **Add**.

7. In the Category text box, enter **Software Tools *XX*** (where *XX* is the number of your server) and then click **OK**. The new category is added, as shown in Figure 12-8.

8. Click **OK**. The new software category has been created.

9. If necessary, in the left tree pane, click **Software installation** to display a list of applications deployed to users in the right details pane.

10. In the right details pane, right-click **Windows Support Tools** and then click **Properties**.

11. Click the **Categories** tab.

12. In the Available categories list box, select **Software Tools *XX*** (where *XX* is the number of your server) and then click **Select**. The Software Tools *XX* category is now one of the Windows Support Tools' selected categories, as shown in Figure 12-9.

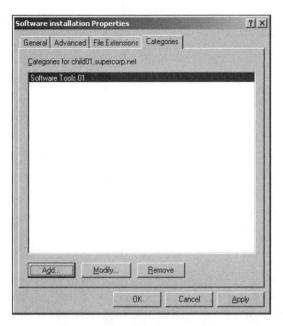

Figure 12-8   Creating a new software category

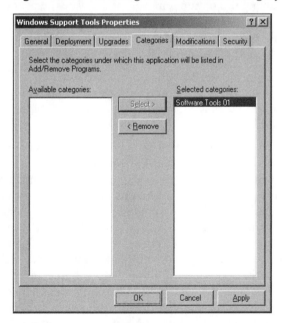

Figure 12-9   Adding a software package to a category

13. Click **OK**. The Windows Support Tools will now appear under the Software Tools *XX* category in Add or Remove Programs for any user to which this policy applies.

14. Close all windows and log off your server if you do not intend to immediately continue to the next activity. Otherwise, leave the Group Policy Object Editor open and stay logged on.

Deployment Options

In addition to software modifications, associations, and categories, there are several other deployment options available.

- Auto-install this application by file extension activation—Specifies if document invocation should be used or not when an application is published to a user. By default, this option is enabled. This option is not available when an application is assigned to a user or computer.

- Uninstall this application when it falls out of the scope of management—It is possible that a computer or user object can be moved so that software deployed using Group Policy no longer applies to that user or computer. Additionally, a GPO or GPO link may be deleted that deployed software to users or computers. In either event, this option specifies whether software installed through Group Policy should be removed if it no longer applies to a user or computer. By default this option is disabled. Enabling this option removes the software the next time the user logs on or the next time the computer starts if the software no longer applies. This option is not available when using ZAP files—applications installed using ZAP files cannot be removed using Group Policy.

- Do not display this package in the Add/Remove Programs control panel—Specifies that the package should not appear in Add or Remove Programs in Control Panel. This option is available only when assigning or publishing applications to users and is disabled by default.

- Install this application at logon—Specifies that an application and its components should be installed when the user logs on. This option modifies the default behavior of advertising an application to users, rather than installing the application. When enabled, assigned applications are installed during the logon process. This option is only available when assigning applications to users. As an example, this option is useful when users have laptops and are not always connected to the network. A laptop user may be connected to the network during the day and have a new application advertised on their Start menu. However, the user may not decide to first use the application until they are at home and no longer connected to the network. Because the user does not have network connectivity at home (more specifically, access to the software distribution point), the installation fails when the user tries to run the new application for the first time. The Install this application at logon option solves this problem by actually installing the application—not just advertising it—when the user is connected to the network.

- Installation user interface options—Most Windows Installer packages have a Basic and Maximum user interface option when installing the application. The Basic interface typically uses all the default options and only prompts the user for required information, if any. Using the Basic interface and a transform file, the Administrator can specify any required information, such as a CD Key, that the application needs in order to provide a fully automated installation. In contrast, the Maximum user interface typically provides the user with all available options during the installation. This option is available only when assigning or publishing applications to users and is set to Maximum by default. Note that this option is not available when using ZAP files.

NOTE

Additional advanced deployment options are available by clicking the Advanced button on a software package's Deployment tab.

ACTIVITY

Activity 12-4: Modifying Deployment Options

Time Required: 10 minutes

Objective: Modify the deployment options of an existing application as well as the deployment defaults.

12

Description: The IT manager at Super Corp likes that users can easily install the applications they need. However, he would like to make some modification in the way software is deployed. He would also like to change the default options set when a new software package is deployed. In this activity, you will modify the deployment options on the software package you deployed in Activity 12-2. You will then modify the default deployment options for software deployed to users.

1. If necessary, start your server and log on using the **Administrator** account in the **CHILDXX** domain (where *XX* is the number of the forest root domain for which your server is a domain controller) using the password **Password01**.

2. Open the Software Installation *XX* GPO (where *XX* is the number of your server) in the Group Policy Object Editor. Refer back to Activity 12-2 if you need to locate where you created this GPO.

3. If necessary, in the left tree pane, expand the **Software Settings** folder under the User Configuration section of the GPO.

4. If necessary, in the left tree pane, click **Software installation** to display a list of applications deployed to users in the right details pane.

5. In the right details pane, right-click **Windows Support Tools** and then click **Properties**.

6. Click the **Deployment** tab.

7. Click the **Uninstall this application when it falls out of the scope of management** check box.

8. In the Installation user interface options section, select the **Basic** option. Your screen should look similar to Figure 12-10.

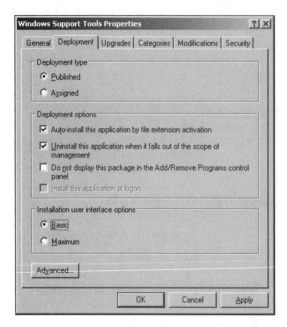

Figure 12-10   Modifying the options of a deployed software package

9. Click **OK**. You have now modified the deployment options on a previously deployed package. However, you now want to modify the default options so all new software packages deployed to users use the same settings.

10. In the left tree pane, right-click **Software installation** and then click **Properties**.

11. On the General tab, in the Installation user interface options section, select the **Basic** option.

12. Click the **Advanced** tab.

13. Click the **Uninstall the applications when they fall out of the scope of management** check box, as shown in Figure 12-11.

14. Click **OK**.

NOTE

You have only modified the defaults when deploying software to users. If you want to also modify the defaults when deploying software to computers, you must also perform Steps 10 through 14 on the Software installation node located under the Computer Configuration section of Group Policy.

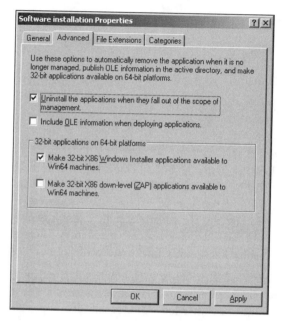

Figure 12-11   Modifying the default deployment options

15. Log off your server if you do not intend to immediately continue to the next activity. Otherwise, stay logged on.

MAINTAINING DEPLOYED SOFTWARE

After an application has been deployed, there are various types of maintenance tasks that usually need to be performed. Most vendors provide periodic updates and service patches to fix reported problems with their applications. You have the task of keeping the deployed software updated with the latest service releases. If vendors release new versions of the software, your users may want to transition slowly to the new version. You may want to allow the users to use both the old and new versions of the software simultaneously.

NOTE

To upgrade or redeploy software using Group Policy, the application must have been originally installed using a Windows Installer package. Applications deployed using a ZAP file cannot be automatically updated using Group Policy.

CAUTION

When dealing with upgrades and redeployments, it is wise to fully test your plans in a test environment. It wouldn't look good to accidentally force a large application like Microsoft Office to reinstall on a thousand desktops when everyone comes in on Monday morning.

When deploying application patches or upgrades, you have three choices for how the deployment is performed:

- A mandatory upgrade
- An optional upgrade
- Redeploying an application

Mandatory Upgrade

A **mandatory upgrade** is used when a new major version (such as going from version 1.0 to 2.0) of a software package is available and you want all users to upgrade to the new version. In a mandatory upgrade, the old package is removed and the new package is installed. If a user or computer did not have the old version installed, only the new package is installed—the old package is not installed. For these reasons, mandatory upgrades are not suitable for deploying service packs or hotfixes—only full versions of the new software.

Figure 12-12 shows the Upgrades tab, which is used to specify which existing software packages this new package upgrades. To perform a mandatory upgrade, the Required upgrade for existing packages option must be checked. Additionally, if any packages in the GPO upgrade the current package (that is, the package for which you are viewing the properties), they are displayed at the bottom of the Upgrades tab.

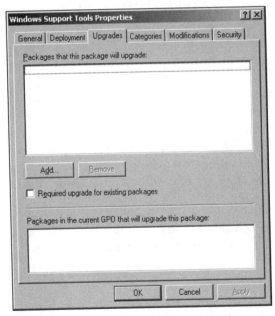

Figure 12-12   Upgrades tab used for upgrading existing packages

If the original package and the updated package are both native Windows Installer files, the update automatically knows that it is to replace the original package; you just have to configure the mandatory selection box.

NOTE

Optional Upgrade

An **optional upgrade** is also used when a new major version (such as going from version 1.0 to 2.0) of a software package is available. However, unlike a mandatory upgrade, optional upgrades are, well, optional. When using an optional upgrade, if the user has already installed the older software package, all shortcuts still open the older version of the software package. To install the upgrade, the user has to access Add or Remove Programs from Control Panel and choose to install the upgrade. However, if a user did not have the old version installed, only the new package is installed—the old version is not available. Again, for these reasons, optional upgrades are not suitable for deploying service packs or hotfixes—only full versions of the new software. To perform an optional upgrade, do not check the Required upgrade for existing packages option (refer back to Figure 12-12 if necessary).

When upgrading software deployed to computers, the only option is a mandatory upgrade. When upgrading software deployed to users, you can choose between a mandatory or an optional upgrade.

NOTE

12

Redeployment

Redeployment of a package means that you force an application to reinstall itself everywhere that it is already installed. You may have to do this if you need to deploy an application service pack or hotfix. The first step in deploying an application service pack or hotfix is to update the files in the distribution point. You should follow the steps provided by the software publisher in order to update the files. If a new .msi file is provided, in most cases it can be copied right over the old one. However, a **Windows Installer patch (.msp) file** can also be provided to update the existing .msi package (again, see the update's documentation for details).

Once the distribution point has been updated with the new files, the application can then be redeployed. To redeploy the application, open the original GPO that deployed the package, right-click the application, select All Tasks, and then click Redeploy application, as shown in Figure 12-13. If the application is assigned to a computer, the computer reinstalls the application the next time the computer starts. If the application is assigned or published to a user, the application is reinstalled the next time the user tries to run the application or at the next logon (depending on what the Install this application at logon option is set to).

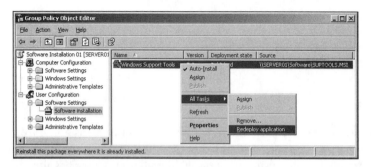

Figure 12-13 Redeploying a software package

NOTE Windows *operating system* service packs and hotfixes are not deployed in the same way *application* service packs and hotfixes are. (This section covered how to update applications, not operating systems.) The next section looks at how you can configure Group Policy to automatically update client and server operating systems. For more information on deploying operating system hotfixes and service packs, see the documentation included with the service pack or the support Web site at *support.microsoft.com*. Also be sure to check out Software Update Services at *www.microsoft.com/sus*.

Configuring Automatic Operating System Updates

In addition to updating applications, you can also configure Group Policy to automatically update Windows 2000, Windows XP Professional, and Windows Server 2003 systems running the automatic update client. The latest version of the automatic update client is included with Windows 2000 Service Pack 3 or newer, Windows XP Service pack 1 or newer, and comes by default with Windows Server 2003. If you do not want to upgrade to the latest service pack, you can also download the client by itself from *www.microsoft.com/sus*.

Using automatic updates, you can configure a computer to automatically download operating system updates from the Microsoft Windows Update Web site or a local Software Update Services (SUS) server. Once downloaded, the client computer can prompt the user to install the operating system updates. Alternatively, the installation can be scheduled to occur at a predetermined time by the administrator. In Activity 12-6, you will learn how to configure automatic updates by using Group Policy.

Having a SUS server allows an administrator to manage operating system updates for every client from a single location. On a scheduled basis, the SUS server automatically contacts the Windows Update Web site (or another SUS server) and downloads available operating system updates. You can configure the SUS server to automatically approve updates it downloads or wait for an administrator to approve new updates before deploying them to clients. By only deploying approved updates, the administrator can first test updates in a non-production environment. In Activity 12-5, you will learn how to install the SUS server.

Allowing the administrator to choose where clients and SUS servers download updates from makes the update infrastructure very flexible. For example, say you have a main office and two branch offices. Also assume that the main office is the only office with an Internet connection and the branch offices are connected by T1 lines to the main office. In this situation, a central SUS server could be placed at the main office and an additional SUS server could be placed at each branch office. The central SUS server at the main office could be configured to download updates from Windows Update and require that updates be approved by the administrator. The SUS servers at each branch office could be configured to download updates from the SUS server at the main office and synchronize their list of approved updates with the central SUS server. Finally, client computers could be configured to download updates from a SUS server at their local office. This configuration is shown in Figure 12-14.

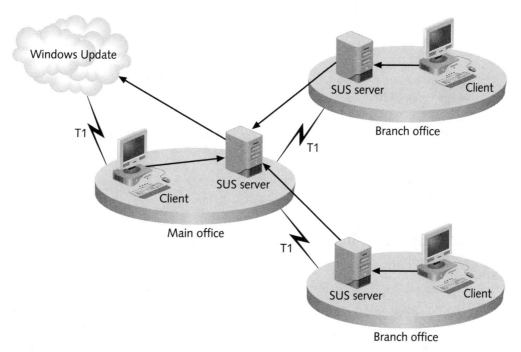

Figure 12-14   Example SUS infrastructure

This example has two important benefits. First, operating system updates only need to be sent across any given WAN connection once. This is because the only computer pulling updates from the Windows Update Web site is the central SUS server in the main office. Additionally, the only computer pulling updates across each branch office's T1 line is the branch office's local SUS server. The second important benefit is that the administrator has full control over what updates are approved—but only needs to specify this once for all three SUS servers. This is because the SUS servers at each branch office are configured to automatically synchronize their list of approved updates with the central SUS server.

NOTE

One limitation to SUS is that you can't approve updates for only a selected number of clients—either everyone gets it or no one does. If you have a small number of test clients on whom you would like to first test updates, you have two options. The first option is to have the selected clients locate and download updates directly from the Windows Update Web site. The other option is to set up a second SUS server for the selected test clients. The selected clients would then be configured to pull updates from the second server.

The SUS server software is not included with Windows Server 2003, but you can download it for free from *www.microsoft.com/sus*. To install SUS on a server, the server must meet the following requirements:

- Running Windows 2000 Server with Service Pack 2 or higher
- Internet Information Server 5 or higher must be installed
- Internet Explorer 5.5 or higher must be installed

TIP

The original release of SUS could not be installed on a domain controller. However, SUS server with Service Pack 1 can now be installed on a domain controller.

NOTE

Note to instructors: The SUS server installation file is over 30 MB. It is highly recommended that you download the SUS server installation file to a shared folder. Instruct students to use the downloaded file to start the SUS installation rather than download the file individually.

ACTIVITY

Activity 12-5: Installing SUS

Time Required: 25 minutes

Objective: To install SUS on a Windows Server 2003 System.

Description: Super Corp's IT manager has decided to use SUS for deploying operating system updates to network clients. He has asked you to install SUS on one of Super Corp's available servers. However, the server does not have IIS installed so you will need to install IIS first. You have been asked to configure SUS so that updates are downloaded from the Windows Update Web site. Additionally, SUS should be configured so updates must be approved before they are deployed to clients.

1. If necessary, start your server and log on using the **Administrator** account in the **CHILDXX** domain (where *XX* is the number of the forest root domain for which your server is a domain controller) using the password **Password01**.

2. Click **Start**, select **Administrative Tools**, and then click **Configure Your Server Wizard**.

3. Click **Next** on the Welcome dialog box and **Next** again on the Preliminary Steps dialog box.

4. When the Server Role dialog box appears, select **Application server (IIS, ASP.NET)** from the list of server roles and then click **Next**. Note that if this role has already been added, continuing with the wizard will remove the role.

5. Make sure the FrontPage Server Extensions and Enable ASP.NET check boxes are not checked and then click **Next**.

6. Click **Next** on the Summary dialog box. IIS will now be installed. If you are prompted for the Windows Server 2003 CD, enter the path D:\Source\i386 or whatever the location of your Windows installation files are if the files were not copied to the D: drive.

7. Once the installation has finished, click **Finish**.

8. Close the Manage Your Server window.

9. Click **Start** and then click **Internet Explorer**.

10. In the Address bar, enter **www.microsoft.com/sus** and then click **Go**.

11. Scroll down to the Downloads heading and then click the **Download SUS with Service Pack 1 (SP1)** link. The Microsoft Web site is frequently reorganized—the download link may have been renamed or relocated.

12. Click **Download** to start the download. When prompted if you would like to save or open the file, click **Open**. Alternatively, your instructor may have already downloaded this file for you. If so, follow your instructor's directions to locate the SUS installation file.

13. Click **Yes** on the Security Warning dialog box to run the installation program.

14. On the Welcome dialog box, click **Next**.

15. Select the **I accept the terms in the License Agreement** option and then click **Next**.

16. Click **Custom**.

17. Accept the default location in which to store files and then click **Next**.

18. On the Language Settings dialog box, select the **English only** option and then click **Next**.

19. Ensure the option to manually approve updates is selected and then click **Next**.

20. Note the URL that clients should be configured to download updates from and then click **Install**.

21. When the installation completes, note the Web site URL that can be used to manage the SUS server and then click **Finish**. Internet Explorer should then automatically open to the SUS server management Web site for the local SUS server.

12

22. In the left menu, click **Set options**. As shown in Figure 12-15, you can set the SUS server to use a proxy server for downloading updates from the Windows Update Web site. The option section also includes many other settings such as where to download updates from, if new versions of previous updates should be automatically approved or not, and more.

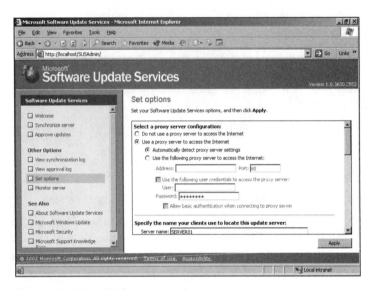

Figure 12-15   SUS server options

23. Click **Synchronize server** in the left menu.

24. Click **Synchronization Schedule**. As shown in Figure 12-16, you can configure the SUS server to automatically download updates daily or weekly and at a given time.

25. In a production environment, you would set up automatic synchronization and use the Synchronize Now button to manually start the first synchronization cycle. However, due to the large amount of bandwidth it would take to download the updates to each student server, you will not be synchronizing your SUS server. Click **Cancel**.

26. Click **Approve updates** in the left menu. From here you can see which updates have been downloaded to the SUS server as well as approve downloaded updates. Because your SUS server has not yet synchronized with Windows Update, no updates will be listed.

27. Close Internet Explorer.

28. Log off your server if you do not intend to immediately continue to the next activity. Otherwise, stay logged on.

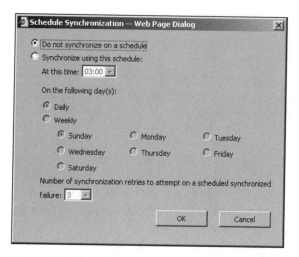

Figure 12-16   SUS server synchronization schedule

ACTIVITY

Activity 12-6: Configuring Automatic Client Updates

Time Required: 5 minutes

12

Objective: To configure clients to automatically download and install operating system updates.

Description: Continuing with Super Corp's plan to use SUS, you must now configure clients to automatically download and install updates from the SUS server you just configured.

1. If necessary, start your server and log on using the **Administrator** account in the **CHILDXX** domain (where *XX* is the number of the forest root domain for which your server is a domain controller) using the password **Password01**.

2. Open the Software Installation *XX* GPO (where *XX* is the number of your server) in the Group Policy Object Editor. Refer back to Activity 12-2 if you need to locate where you created this GPO.

3. In the left tree pane, expand the **Administrative Templates** and **Windows Components** folders under the Computer Configuration section of the GPO.

4. In the left tree pane, select **Windows Update**.

5. In the right details pane, double-click the **Specify intranet Microsoft update service location** policy.

6. Select the **Enabled** option.

7. In the Set internet update service for detecting updates and Set the internet statistics server text boxes enter **http://SERVERXX** (where *XX* is the number of your server), as shown in Figure 12-17.

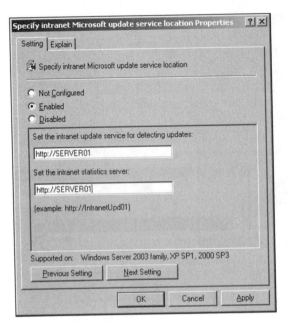

Figure 12-17 Location to determine updates from and to report statistics

8. Click **OK**.

9. In the right details pane, double-click the **Configure Automatic Updates** policy.

10. Select the **Enabled** option.

11. In the Configure automatic updating drop-down list box, select **4 – Auto download and schedule the install**.

12. In the Scheduled install time drop-down list box, select **05:00** as shown in Figure 12-18.

13. Click **OK**. Clients to which this GPO applies will now automatically install any available updates from your SUS server at the scheduled time.

If you just want clients to automatically download updates from the Windows Update Web site (that is, rather than a local SUS server), simply configure the Configure Automatic Updates policy and leave the Specify intranet Microsoft update service location policy Not Configured (or Disabled). Client computers will then contact the Windows Update Web site at the scheduled time to retrieve updates.

14. In the right details pane, double-click the **Reschedule Automatic Updates scheduled installations** policy.

15. Click the **Explain** tab. Read the policy's explanation and then click **Cancel**.

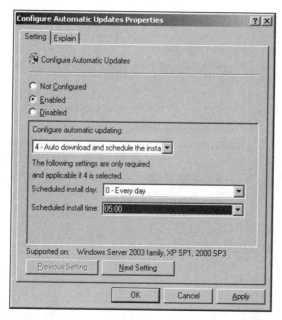

Figure 12-18 Automatic download and installation options

12

16. In the right details pane, double-click the **No auto-restart scheduled Automatic Updates installations** policy.

17. Click the **Explain** tab. Read the policy's explanation and then click **Cancel**.

18. Log off your server if you do not intend to immediately continue to the next activity. Otherwise, stay logged on.

REMOVING DEPLOYED SOFTWARE

The final phase of an application life cycle is the removal process. When you need to remove an application that you no longer want to deploy in the organization, Group Policy can save a great amount of time and money. Again, the only note is that the application must have been originally installed using a Windows Installer package. Applications deployed using a ZAP file cannot be automatically removed using Group Policy.

When you remove an application, you are given two choices about how the removal process takes place:

- A forced removal
- An optional removal

Forced Removal

A **forced removal** automatically uninstalls the application from all computers. The removal takes place either the next time the computer restarts (for computer-based policies) or when the user logs on (for user-based policies).

Optional Removal

An **optional removal** does not remove any of the installed copies of the software, but it does not perform any future installations either. Users or computers that still have the software installed can continue to use the application. Applications that were never installed will no longer appear in Add or Remove Programs. If users remove the application, they are not able to reinstall it.

ACTIVITY

Activity 12-7: Removing Installed Software

Time Required: 5 minutes

Objective: Remove an application that was distributed using Group Policy.

Description: Super Corp's IT manager has decided to only deploy the support tools to IT staff, instead of all users. To accomplish this goal, you must first remove the software from the GPO that deploys the software to all users. The IT manager has decided that any users who have already installed the support tools should be allowed to continue using the software. Therefore, you will perform an optional removal of the software package.

1. If necessary, start your server and log on using the **Administrator** account in the **CHILDXX** domain (where *XX* is the number of the forest root domain for which your server is a domain controller) using the password **Password01**.

2. Open the Software Installation *XX* GPO (where *XX* is the number of your server) in the Group Policy Object Editor. Refer back to Activity 12-2 if you need to locate where you created this GPO.

3. If necessary, in the left tree pane, expand the **Software Settings** folder under the User Configuration section of the GPO.

4. If necessary, in the left tree pane, click **Software installation** to display a list of applications deployed to users in the right details pane.

5. In the right details pane, right-click **Windows Support Tools**, select **All Tasks**, and then click **Remove**.

6. In the Remove Software window, select the **Allow users to continue to use the software, but prevent new installations** option, as shown in Figure 12-19.

7. Click **OK**.

8. Close all open windows.

9. Log off your server.

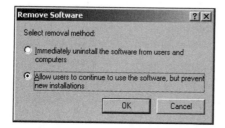

Figure 12-19   Removing deployed software

TROUBLESHOOTING SOFTWARE DEPLOYMENT

The first step in troubleshooting software deployment is to troubleshoot Group Policy. You can use the skills you learned in the last chapter to troubleshoot Group Policy application. Make sure that the No Override option, Block Inheritance option, ACL permissions, Loopback Processing Mode, and WMI filters are not the source of the problem. If all other aspects of Group Policy are working correctly, you can then use the following information to troubleshoot software deployment.

The following are some of the more common issues encountered when using software distribution, some causes of each, and possible solutions:

- Applications are not visible on the Start menu

  - The application was published rather than assigned to users. Reconfigure the GPO to assign the software to users.

  - The GPO containing the software may not have applied to the user or computer. Use the skills you learned in the last chapter to troubleshoot Group Policy application.

- Applications are not visible in Add or Remove Programs

  - The Do not display this package in the Add/Remove Programs control panel option has been enabled in Group Policy. Disable the option in order to show the application in Add or Remove Programs.

  - The GPO containing the software may not have been applied to the user. Use the skills you learned in the last chapter to troubleshoot Group Policy application.

- Applications are visible on the Start menu and/or in Add or Remove Programs, but fail to install correctly or at all

  - The distribution point may not be accessible. Make sure that a server hosting the distribution point is available. Also ensure that the user or computer attempting to install the software has the appropriate share and NTFS permissions.

- The installation files may have been moved within, or removed from, the distribution point. Make sure the software is available where clients expect to find it in the distribution point, or reconfigure the GPO to install the software from the new location.

- A previously installed application(s) that would not uninstall is preventing the installation of the new application. Use the MSIZap utility, described shortly, to clean up the previous installation(s).

- The application may not be compatible with the version of Windows or a previously installed application. Review the application's documentation to ensure all compatibility requirements have been met.

- The setup files may have been corrupted. Try replacing the files in the distribution point from the application's installation CD.

- If a custom Windows Installer package created with a tool such as WinINSTALL fails, try recreating the package on a brand new installation of Windows 2000, Windows XP, or Windows Server 2003 (depending on the target platform). Assigning the application to computers, rather than users, may also solve the issue.

 Windows Installer logs many events in the Windows Application event log. If you are experiencing problems with software installation, look for events with a source of Application Management, MsiInstaller, and Software Installation.

Troubleshooting Tools

In addition to the tools you learned about in the last chapter, such as RSoP, there are a couple of other tools to help you troubleshoot software installation:

- Msiexec—This command-line utility provides access to Windows Installer from the command line. For example, you can use the msiexec /I \\server\share\app.msi command to install a Windows installer package where \\server\share\app.msi is the name of the package you want to install. You can specify additional parameters—such as the /l command used for logging. For more information on msiexec command-line parameters, search for msiexec in Windows Server 2003 Help and Support or view Knowledge Base articles 227091 and 314881 at *http://support.microsoft.com*.

- MSIZap—This command-line utility is used to remove all information associated with a particular package or even all packages installed on a computer.

CHAPTER SUMMARY

- There are four phases to the software life cycle: preparation, deployment, maintenance, and removal.

- The Windows Installer service is used to fully automate the software installation and configuration process. The Windows Installer service requires a Windows Installer package for each application.

- A Windows Installer package contains all the files necessary to install and remove an application using the Windows Installer service. The Windows Installer package consists of two parts: an .msi file that describes the installation and, optionally, any external files required to install or remove the application.

- Many vendors include Windows Installer packages with their applications. You can use third-party utilities such as WinINSTALL to create custom Windows Installer packages when a package is not available from the software vendor.

- A ZAP file is a text file that can be used by Group Policy to deploy an application when a Windows Installer package cannot be created. However, ZAP files cannot take advantage of most maintenance and removal features provided by Group Policy.

- When deploying software, a distribution point needs to be created on the network. A distribution point can be a simple file share on one server; however, the use of DFS to make the distribution point available at multiple locations is recommended. Only administrators should be given write access to the distribution point—all other users who require access should only be given read access.

- Applications can be assigned to either computers or users. When an application is assigned to a computer, the application is automatically installed the next time the computer starts. When an application is assigned to a user, the application is advertised on the Start menu, but the application is not actually installed by default. A new feature in Windows Server 2003 allows the modification of this behavior so that an application is fully installed when the user logs on, not just advertised. Document invocation can also be used to install assigned applications.

- Applications can only be published to users, not computers. When an application is published, a user can use the Add or Remove applet in Control Panel to install the application. Document invocation can also be used to install published applications.

- When a new version of software is available, Group Policy can be used to deploy the new version. In a mandatory upgrade, the old package is removed and the new package is installed. All users are forced to use the new version and any future installations will use the new version. In an optional upgrade, the old package is left in place until the user manually upgrades the package using Add or Remove Programs. Users who already have the software installed can continue to use the old version. Any new installations, however, must use the new version.

12

❑ A package can be redeployed in order to distribute a new service pack or hotfix. When an application is redeployed, the application is automatically reinstalled anywhere it is currently installed.

❑ You can use Group Policy to configure clients to automatically download and install operating system updates. You can configure clients to retrieve a list of updates from the Windows Update Web site or a local Software Update Services (SUS) server.

❑ When an application is no longer needed, Group Policy can be used to remove the application. In a forced removal, the application is removed the next time the computer starts or the user logs on. In an optional removal, any existing installations of the application are not removed; however, no new installations are performed. The user must manually remove the software using Add or Remove Programs.

Key Terms

assigned — Applications can be assigned to either computers or users. When assigned to computers, applications are installed when the computer starts. When assigned to users, applications are installed the first time the user runs the application by default.

distribution point — A file share on the network that provides the files necessary to install an application.

document invocation — Allows users to open a file and have the appropriate application installed automatically based on the file's extension.

forced removal — A removal where all existing installations of the software are removed and no new installations are performed.

mandatory upgrade — An upgrade that is performed automatically the next time a computer starts or the user runs the application (by default). All existing installations are upgraded to the new version and no new installations of the old version are performed.

optional removal — A removal where existing installations are not removed, but no new installations are performed.

optional upgrade — An upgrade that users can run manually at their discretion. Existing installations of the old version are not removed; however, no new installations of the old version are performed.

publish — A published application appears in Add or Remove Programs and must be installed manually by the user or through document invocation. Applications cannot be published to computers.

redeployment — Forces an application to be reinstalled the next time the computer starts or a user runs the application (by default).

Windows Installer transform (.mst) file — Customized settings for a Windows Installer package that are applied during installation.

Windows Installer package (.msi) file — A file that contains all of the information needed to install an application using the Windows Installer service.

Windows Installer patch (.msp) file — An update to a Windows Installer package that usually contains bug fixes or new functionality.

Windows Installer service — A service that can be used to fully automate the software installation and configuration process.

ZAP (.zap) file — A text file that is used by Group Policy to deploy applications for which a Windows Installer package cannot be created.

REVIEW QUESTIONS

1. An application can be published to which of the following?

    a. only users

    b. only computers

    c. both users and computers

    d. both users and computers, but only if a ZAP file is used

2. Which methods can be used to install a published application? (Choose all that apply.)

    a. Click a desktop shortcut.

    b. Click a Start menu item.

    c. Add or Remove Programs

    d. document invocation

3. Assigned applications are only added to Add or Remove Programs, allowing them to be manually installed by a user if necessary. True or False?

4. Which type of file modifies the default installation options of a Windows Installer package?

    a. .msi

    b. .mst

    c. .msp

    d. .zap

5. When would you redeploy an application?

    a. when a new version of the application is available and you want to allow users to upgrade when they are ready

    b. when an application has been patched using a hotfix

    c. when you would like to reconfigure the installation options on existing installations by adding an additional transform file

    d. when you would like to upgrade to a new version of an application deployed using a ZAP file

6. A ZAP file can be used by a GPO to publish an application for which an MSI file is not available. True or False?

12

7. If an application has been assigned to a computer using Group Policy, when is the application installed?

   a. when a user logs on

   b. the next time the computer is started

   c. the next time the computer is shut down

   d. when a user logs off

8. A user has accidentally deleted a required file on his local machine for an application that you had previously assigned to the domain using an MSI file and Group Policy. What must you do to make sure that the application continues to function?

   a. Redeploy the application using the original GPO and MSI file.

   b. Do nothing; the application automatically fixes itself.

   c. Publish the application to the domain.

   d. Reinstall the application locally on the user's machine using a CD-ROM or the distribution point.

9. Which removal option allows users to continue to work with an installed application but prevents any new installations?

   a. forced removal

   b. optional removal

   c. installation removal

   d. none of the above

10. Published applications are resilient in that they reinstall automatically if they are uninstalled. True or False?

11. Which upgrade option allows users to continue to work with the old version of an application but requires new installations to use the new version?

    a. mandatory upgrade

    b. optional upgrade

    c. redeployment upgrade

    d. none of the above

12. When a Windows Installer package is assigned to a user through Group Policy, the Windows Installer service uses which of the following security contexts?

    a. the user

    b. the local system

    c. the local Windows Installer account

    d. the domain Windows Installer account

13. Which of the following deployment options support document invocation?

    a. assigned applications

    b. published applications

    c. both assigned and published applications

    d. neither assigned nor published applications

14. Operating system service packs and hotfixes are deployed in the same exact way application service packs and hotfixes are. True or False?

15. Software categories are used to organize software in which of the following ways?

    a. on the Start menu

    b. in Add or Remove Programs

    c. in the Configure Your Server Wizard

    d. none of the above

16. Which of the following is true about registering application extensions with Active Directory?

    a. An administrator can manually add an extension to an application.

    b. An administrator can set the priority of multiple applications that use the same extension.

    c. No two applications installed using Group Policy can use the same extension.

    d. none of the above

17. Which type of file directly modifies an existing Windows Installer package and is typically used to fix software bugs?

    a. .msi

    b. .mst

    c. .msp

    d. .zap

18. When software categories are created, they have which of the following scopes?

    a. They are only available in the GPO in which they are created.

    b. They are available in the GPO in which they are created and any child GPOs.

    c. They are only available in the domain in which they are created.

    d. They are available in any domain in the entire forest.

19. Which removal option automatically removes an application the next time the computer starts or the user logs on?

    a. forced removal

    b. optional removal

    c. installation removal

    d. none of the above

20. After installing the Windows Installer service on a Windows 98 computer, it can then install software assigned through Group Policy. True or False?

CASE PROJECTS

CASE
PROJECTS

Case Project 12-1: Application Distribution

The IT manager at Super Corp needs to request new software for the next few years. Some software publishers are advertising that their software works with Active Directory and is shipped as Windows Installer packages. Others state that they do not support Active Directory, and some make no mention one way or the other. He is considering the recommendation that all new software installed on client computers support management by Group Policy.

Would you support this recommendation? If so, help him by describing some of the advantages of using Group Policy for software distribution. Include information about how applications can be upgraded and patched. If you would not support this recommendation, explain why.

CASE
PROJECTS

Case Project 12-2: Distribution Options

Super Corp has decided to implement the software distribution feature of Group Policy for users and computers within IT-related organizational units. All members of the Server Support organizational unit should have the Windows Support Tools fully installed on any computer to which they log on—not just advertised. Users in the Workstation Support organizational unit should have the ability to install the Windows Support Tools only if necessary. Finally, any user that logs on to a computer located in the Help Desk organizational unit should have the Windows Support Tools available. The Server Support, Workstation Support, and Help Desk organizational units are all child organizational units of the IT organizational unit. Given these requirements, what GPOs would you create and what options would you set when deploying the support tools?

Case Project 12-3: Patch, Patch, and Re-patch

Super Corp has decided to implement automatic updates using a central SUS server. However, Matt is concerned that not all client computers will be turned on during the scheduled patch time of 05:00. Also, Matt wants to know if SUS server will allow him to test patches in the IT department before they are deployed to other departments. In addition to Matt's concerns, Pat is also concerned that client computers will spontaneously reboot after being patched. She is afraid that users may lose their work and would like to know what can be done to keep systems from automatically restarting.

What would you tell Matt and Pat about SUS, automatic updates, and Group Policy in order to alleviate their concerns?

12

13

MONITORING AND OPTIMIZING ACTIVE DIRECTORY

After reading this chapter, you will be able to:

◆ Use performance counters to monitor Active Directory performance

◆ Maintain the Active Directory store

◆ Optimize the location of Active Directory files

◆ Work with application directory partitions

O verall, the best way to optimize the performance of Active Directory is to use a carefully thought-out logical and physical design. The placement of domain controllers, global catalog servers, domains, trusts, sites, and site links all impact how Active Directory operates. When designing, it is important to take the time to analyze the situation carefully and follow best practices. Doing so ensures that you end up with an Active Directory implementation that runs smoothly.

While previous chapters have covered the details necessary to optimize your Active Directory design, this chapter looks at how to monitor and optimize Active Directory once it is deployed. In this chapter, you will learn about performance counters that you can use to monitor Active Directory performance on a domain controller. You will then learn how Active Directory deletes objects and how defragmentation is performed. You will also learn how to move the Active Directory files on a domain controller to optimize performance. Finally, the chapter concludes with an overview of working with application directory partitions.

USING PERFORMANCE COUNTERS TO MONITOR ACTIVE DIRECTORY

Maintaining a server is similar to maintaining an automobile. When you purchase a new automobile, it must be serviced on a regular basis to ensure its performance over time. Many of the new cars and trucks today also come with tools that can alert you to problems when they occur. Server maintenance is similar. Often, administrators configure servers for network use, while not realizing that over time, server performance can deteriorate for a number of reasons.

One of the more important reasons for monitoring the health of your server is that it can help alert you to problems before they occur or become more serious. Over time, networks change; the demands placed on a server can vary or increase. Monitoring server performance can help you determine what normal behavior is for your server under the current demands and alert you to any performance issues that may be occurring if the normal behavior changes. This normal behavior is known as **baseline** performance.

Performance Console

Windows Server 2003 includes an administrative tool known as the Performance console, which allows detailed information to be gathered using various methods. The **Performance console** consists of two different tools—System Monitor, and Performance Logs and Alerts. System Monitor allows an administrator to view data gathered from a wide variety of counter objects in real time, usually by viewing a graphical representation of collected data. Performance Logs and Alerts allows an administrator to gather similar information, but it periodically logs samples to a data file to be imported into other applications (such as Microsoft Excel or SQL Server), or to generate alerts when certain configured thresholds are met. The Performance console is displayed in Figure 13-1.

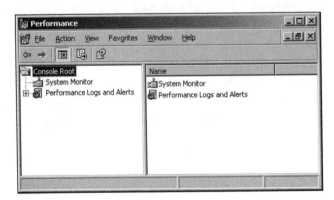

Figure 13-1   The Performance console

System Monitor

System Monitor is one of the most useful tools for collecting data on real-time server performance. As part of the Windows Server 2003 Performance MMC, this tool allows you to track how system resources are being used and how they are behaving under the current workload. System Monitor collects data that you can use for the following tasks:

- Server performance—If you use System Monitor on a regular basis, it can help you understand how the server performs under the current workload.

- Problem diagnosis—You can use the data that is collected to diagnose server components that may not be performing optimally, causing a bottleneck within the server.

- Capacity planning—You can use the information to see how server usage is changing over time and plan ahead for future upgrades.

- Testing—If configuration changes are made, you can use the data to observe the impact that the changes have on the server.

Using System Monitor, you can define the components you want to monitor and the type of data you want to collect. You choose the performance objects you want to monitor, such as memory, and the specific type of performance counters or data associated with the object for which you want to gather data. You can further customize the data you want to capture by specifying the source or computer you want to monitor. You can use System Monitor to gather data from the local computer or from a network computer for which you have appropriate permissions. Although the System Monitor tool includes a number of performance objects and associated counters to monitor by default, additional objects and counters are added when various services and applications are added to a server, such as DNS or Microsoft SQL Server.

Using System Monitor

When you first open the Performance console, System Monitor automatically begins displaying performance data. By default, the tool displays data related to the memory, processor, and physical disk objects for the local computer, as displayed in Figure 13-2.

The information that System Monitor captures can be displayed in one of three views:

- Graph—Displays counter information as a continuous graph updated in real time

- Histogram—Displays counter information as a histogram, with information updated in real time

- Report—Displays a text-based report view of counters, with information updated in real time

The System Monitor interface provides a number of options for viewing performance data, including the ability to add additional performance counters as required, switch between display views, highlight a selected counter, copy and paste selected information, and freeze the display for analysis purposes. The System Monitor toolbar, found at the top of the details

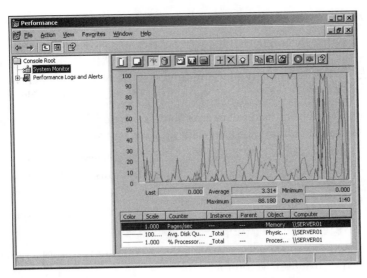

Figure 13-2   The default display of System Monitor

pane in System Monitor, allows you to easily control these functions. In Activity 13-1, you will explore the various settings of the System Monitor tool.

ACTIVITY

Activity 13-1: Exploring System Monitor Settings

Time Required: 10 minutes

Objective: Explore Windows Server 2003 System Monitor settings.

Description: The IT manager at Super Corp has informed you that all corporate servers will eventually be monitored for performance purposes using the Windows Server 2003 System Monitor utility. He has asked you to become familiar with the tool and explore its various features because all networking-related staff will eventually need to be trained on this tool. In this activity, you will explore the various features of System Monitor.

1. If necessary, start your server and log on using the **Administrator** account in the **CHILDXX** domain (where *XX* is the number of the forest root domain for which your server is a domain controller) using the password **Password01**.

2. Click **Start**, select **Administrative Tools**, and click **Performance**. The Performance console opens and System Monitor begins running automatically using the three default counters.

3. Click the **View Histogram** button on the toolbar at the top of the System Monitor details pane, as shown in Figure 13-3. This illustrates the same counter information but in the form of a histogram.

4. Click the **View Report** button on the System Monitor toolbar. This shows the same counter information in the form of a report.

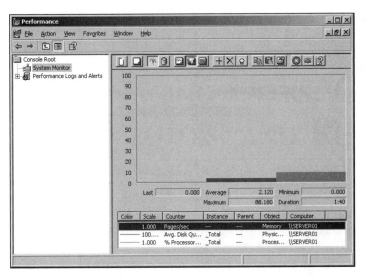

Figure 13-3   Viewing System Monitor data as a histogram

5. Click the **View Graph** button to return to the original graph view.

6. Click the **% Processor Time** counter at the bottom in the list box of counters, and then click the **Highlight** toolbar button (looks like a light bulb). Notice that the % Processor Time counter in the graph now appears as a thick white line to make it easier to distinguish from the other counters. Click the **Highlight** button again to remove highlighting from the counter.

7. Right-click on any area within the counter list box at the bottom of the right details pane and click **Properties**.

8. In the System Monitor Properties dialog box, click **\Processor(_Total)\% Processor Time** if necessary, and then select the largest line thickness in the Width counter list box, as shown in Figure 13-4. Click **OK**. The % Processor Time counter now appears as a thick red line on the graph.

9. Click the **Freeze Display** button (looks like a white X in a red circle) on the System Monitor toolbar. This pauses the System Monitor view until the button is pressed again.

10. Click the **Update Data** button (looks like a camera) four or five times to allow the graph to move forward. This button allows you to update the on-screen data manually.

11. Click the **Freeze Display** button again to allow data to be gathered.

12. Click the **Clear Display** button on the System Monitor toolbar to clear and restart all on-screen counters.

13. Close the Performance console and log off your server if you do not intend to immediately continue to the next activity. Otherwise, leave the Performance console window open.

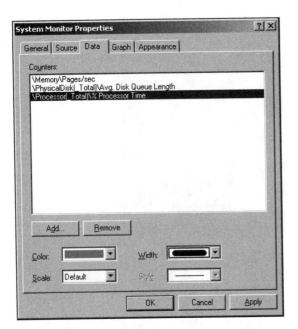

Figure 13-4   Configuring counter properties

Performance Objects and Counters

Monitoring performance on your server should be a regular maintenance task. The information you gather can help to establish a baseline of server performance and identify what is considered normal server performance under typical operating conditions. As you continue to monitor your server over time, you can compare the data against the baseline to identify how performance is changing as the network changes and workloads increase. Doing so allows you to pinpoint bottlenecks, such as components that may be hindering server performance, before they become a serious problem.

TIP
Any time you upgrade or add a component to a system, whether it is a hardware or software component, you should run System Monitor to determine the effect the change has on server performance.

When monitoring performance of any server, there are a few performance objects that should be included, as well as specific performance counters associated with each one:

- % Processor Time—This processor counter measures the percentage of time that the processor is executing a nonidle thread. If the value is consistently at or over 80%, a CPU upgrade may be required.

- % Interrupt Time—This processor counter measures hardware interrupts. If you experience a combination of % Processor Time exceeding 90% and % Interrupt Time exceeding 15%, check for malfunctioning hardware or device drivers.

- Pages/second—This memory counter measures the number of pages read in or out to disk to resolve hard page faults. If this number exceeds 20 or more page faults per second, add more RAM to the computer.

- Page Faults/second—This memory counter measures the number of hard and soft page faults per second. A hard page fault refers to a request that required hard disk access, whereas a soft page fault refers to a request found in another part of memory.

- % Disk Time—This physical and logical disk counter measures the percentage of elapsed time that the selected disk drive is busy. If above 90%, try moving the page file to another physical drive or upgrade the hard drive.

- Average Disk Queue Length—This physical and logical disk counter measures the average number of requests currently outstanding for a volume or partition. If averaging over two, then drive access may be a bottleneck. You may want to upgrade the drive or hard drive controller. Implementing a stripe set with multiple drives may also fix this problem.

NOTE In Windows NT, all disk counters are turned off by default. In Windows 2000, the physical disk object is turned on by default and the logical disk object is turned off by default. In Windows Server 2003, all disk counters are enabled automatically and only when required.

13

When monitoring a domain controller, there are a few performance objects that should be included, as well as specific performance counters associated with each one. Unlike the previous set of performance counters, the following counters do not have a specific threshold. Baseline data should be collected in order to determine if one of the following counters is out of its normal range:

- DRA Inbound Bytes Compressed (Between Sites, After Compression)/sec—This NTDS counter measures the amount of replication traffic per second received by the domain controller from domain controllers in other sites.

- DRA Outbound Bytes Compressed (Between Sites, After Compression)/sec—This NTDS counter measures the amount of replication traffic per second sent by the domain controller to domain controllers in other sites.

- DRA Inbound Bytes Not Compressed (Within Site)/sec—This NTDS counter measures the amount of replication traffic per second received by the domain controller from domain controllers in the same site.

- DRA Outbound Bytes Not Compressed (Within Site)/sec—This NTDS counter measures the amount of replication traffic per second sent by the domain controller to domain controllers in the same site.

- DRA Inbound Bytes Total/sec—This NTDS counter measures the amount of replication traffic per second received by the domain controller from domain controllers in the same or different sites.

- DRA Outbound Bytes Total/sec—This NTDS counter measures the amount of replication traffic sent by the domain controller to domain controllers in the same or different sites, per second.

- DS Search Suboperations/sec—This NTDS counter measures, approximately, the number of objects a search query must consider per second. When a search is performed, Active Directory must check one or more objects to see if they match the search criteria. This counter indicates the number of objects Active Directory considers (checks) each second.

- LDAP Searches/sec—This NTDS counter measures the number of LDAP searches performed each second.

- LDAP Client Sessions—This NTDS counter measures the number of LDAP clients that have connections open to the server.

- NTLM Authentications/sec—This NTDS counter measures the number of NTLM authentications per second the domain controller is processing.

- KDC AS Requests—This NTDS counter measures the number of AS requests per second the domain controller is processing. AS requests are used by a client to obtain a ticket-granting ticket.

- KDC TGS Requests—This NTDS counter measures the number of TGS requests per second the domain controller is processing. TGS requests are used by a client to obtain a ticket to a resource.

- % Processor Time LSASS—This process counter measures the percentage of time that the processor is executing a thread from the Local Security Authority Subsystem (LSASS) process.

- Private Byte LSASS—This process counter measures the amount of memory, in bytes, allocated by the LSASS process, that cannot be shared with other applications.

- Handle Count LSASS—This process counter measures the number of handles opened by the LSASS process.

Activity 13-2: Adding Counters to System Monitor

Time Required: 10 minutes

Objective: Add object counters to the System Monitor.

Description: After exploring the various features of the System Monitor interface, you decide to add various counters to the tool to get a better sense of server performance and the purpose of the various counters. In this activity, you will add counters to the System Monitor interface, explore the Explain feature for counter objects, and view the counter results using the graph, histogram, and report views.

1. If necessary, start your server and log on using the **Administrator** account in the **CHILDXX** domain (where *XX* is the number of the forest root domain for which your server is a domain controller) using the password **Password01**.

2. If necessary, open the Performance console.

3. In the Performance console, click the **New Counter Set** button on the System Monitor toolbar. Notice that all counters are removed from the System Monitor details pane.

4. Click the **Add** button on the System Monitor toolbar. The Add Counters dialog box opens, as shown in Figure 13-5.

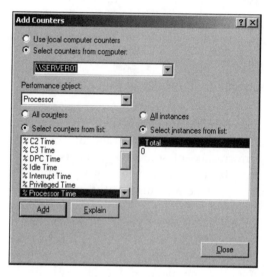

Figure 13-5   The Add Counters dialog box

5. In the Performance object list box, select **NTDS**.

6. In the Select counters from list list box, select **DRA Inbound Bytes Total/sec** and then click **Add**.

7. In the Performance object list box, click **Process**.

8. In the Select counters from list list box, click **% Processor Time**. In the Select instances from list list box, click **lsass**.

9. Click the **Explain** button. This opens a window that explains the purpose of the selected counter, as shown in Figure 13-6.

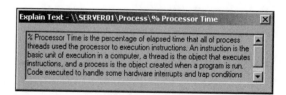

Figure 13-6   Using the Explain button to view the purpose of a selected counter

10. Close the Explain Text window.

11. Click the **Add** button to add the counter to System Monitor.

12. In the Performance object list box, click **Network Interface**.

13. Click the **All counters** option button, and then click **Add**. This adds all of the performance counters for the Network Interface object to the graph.

14. Click **Close**.

15. Notice that the number of counters now available on the graph has increased dramatically. Click the **View Histogram** button to view the counter data using that method, and then click the **View Report** button.

16. Click the **New Counter Set** button to clear all counters from System Monitor.

17. Close the Performance console window.

18. Log off your server if you do not intend to immediately continue to the next activity. Otherwise, stay logged on.

Gathering data with a tool such as System Monitor is the easy part. The more difficult part is interpreting the information to determine what component is affecting performance. The difficulty lies in the fact that the performance of some components can affect other components. It may appear from the data that one component is performing poorly when this can be the result of another component performing poorly, or even too well. For example, if you determine that your processor is running over 80%, your first instinct may tell you to upgrade the processor or install multiple processors if the motherboard supports it. Through further analysis, however, you may find a lack of memory is the bottleneck that is causing excess paging. You would have discovered this by monitoring the Pages/second memory counter. Thus, monitoring multiple components on a regular basis should give you an idea of how they perform together and make troubleshooting server performance that much easier.

For more information on monitoring server performance, please see Chapter 11, "Monitoring Server Performance," in *MCSE Guide to Managing a Microsoft Windows Server 2003 Environment* (ISBN: 0-619-12035-5).

NOTE

MAINTAINING THE ACTIVE DIRECTORY DATABASE

For the most part, Active Directory maintains itself. However, you must be aware of these maintenance processes and what they affect. One of the most important processes to be aware of is the method in which old data is deleted from the directory. Simply deleting an object does not work—it just ends up being replicated back from another domain controller. Instead, Active Directory uses tombstones to ensure objects are removed from all domain controllers.

Over time, Active Directory becomes fragmented as new objects are added and deleted. Fragmentation of a database, similar to fragmentation of hard drive files, means that related information is spread out in little pieces everywhere instead of being neatly collected in order. As the database becomes more fragmented, it takes longer to find information. Just like a hard drive, the database needs to be defragmented to rearrange the data and optimize the data store. **Defragmentation** is done by physically grouping related information together inside of the file. There are two types of defragmentation—online and offline.

NOTE When reading this section, remember that each domain controller has its own directory database. Active Directory replicates changes between domain controllers, not the actual database file. For this reason, processes such as garbage collection and defragmentation—which are discussed in this section—occur on all domain controllers independently. This is why one domain controller's directory database could be 50 MB while another domain controller's directory database could be 25 MB—even if both domain controllers currently contain the same partitions.

Managing Deleted Objects

When an object is deleted from Active Directory, it is not immediately purged from the database. Instead, the object is tagged as being in the tombstone state. A **tombstone** allows all other domain controllers to delete the object from their directory databases.

To understand the importance of a tombstone, consider this example of the replication process: Imagine that you have two domain controllers, named DC1 and DC2, respectively. If you were to delete an object on DC1, completely removing it from the database so no trace remained, what would happen during the next replication cycle? Theoretically, without a tombstone, when the domain controllers replicated, DC2 would happily send a copy of the object back to DC1.

Tombstones are used to ensure that deleted objects are removed from all domain controllers. When an object is deleted, most of its attributes are deleted, the object is marked as tombstoned, and it is moved to the Deleted Objects container. The tombstone information is then replicated to all other domain controllers holding a copy (or partial copy in the case of a global catalog) of the object. The time a tombstoned object remains in the directory database is known as the **tombstone lifetime**. By default, the tombstone lifetime is 60 days, but an administrator can change the tombstone lifetime using ADSI Edit.

Every 12 hours, by default, a process called **garbage collection** is performed on domain controllers. If an object has been tombstoned for longer than the tombstone lifetime, garbage collection removes the tombstone from the domain controller's directory database. When comparing the time the object was tombstoned to the tombstone lifetime, all domain controllers use the date and time the object was originally tombstoned (or deleted) on the first domain controller. This means that tombstoned objects are collected as garbage by all domain controllers at about the same time (within 12 hours of each other).

While 60 days may seem like a long time to hold a tombstone in the directory, it's actually not. It is important that the tombstone lifetime be significantly higher than the total replication latency across the entire forest. In other words, the tombstone lifetime must be longer than the time it takes the tombstone to replicate to all domain controllers. For example, imagine that you have three domain controllers: DC1, DC2, and DC3. For this example, say the tombstone lifetime is set to five days. DC3 is taken offline for a week to perform upgrades to the hardware. The first day DC3 is offline, objects are deleted from the directory on DC1. DC1 tombstones the objects and replicates the tombstones to DC2. Five days later, the tombstones are older than the tombstone lifetime and both DC1 and DC2 remove the tombstones from their directory databases.

Now, what would happen if DC3 was placed back on the network seven days later? Because DC1 and DC2 have already removed the tombstones from their directory databases, DC3 would have no idea that some objects were deleted. This would introduce inconsistencies into the directory and could require extensive repairs or a total rebuild of the directory. Fortunately, Windows Server 2003 prevents this scenario from occurring. If a domain controller has not replicated with a replication partner within the tombstone lifetime, it refuses to replicate. In this example, DC3 would refuse to replicate with DC1 and DC2 because the last time DC3 replicated with either domain controller was seven days ago—which is longer than the five-day tombstone lifetime. DC3 would have to be forcibly demoted and then repromoted before it could replicate with other domain controllers again.

Windows 2000 domain controllers running Service Pack 3 or later also refuse to replicate if they have not replicated with a replication partner within the tombstone lifetime.

For more information on forcibly demoting a domain controller and cleaning up the server's metadata in the directory, see knowledge base articles 332199 and 216498 at *support.microsoft.com*.

In addition to the tombstone lifetime playing a role in how long a server can be offline, it also has an impact on backups. While backups are covered in much more detail in the next chapter, quickly put, you can't restore a backup of Active Directory that is older than the tombstone lifetime.

Activity 13-3: Modifying the Tombstone Lifetime

ACTIVITY

Time Required: 10 minutes

Objective: Modify the tombstone lifetime in an Active Directory forest.

Description: Super Corp needs to ship a domain controller to one of its new locations in Europe. Unfortunately, the new office does not yet have a connection to Super Corp's network and one will not be installed for at least 30 to 45 days. The IT manager wants to configure a domain controller and ship it to the Europe office; however, he is afraid the domain controller will not be able to replicate with another domain controller for at least 60 days. To allow a server to be configured at Super Corp's Atlanta office and then shipped to the new Europe office, you will increase the tombstone lifetime to 90 days.

Because the tombstone lifetime has scope across the entire forest, you need to work with your partner to complete this activity. Select only one server on which to perform the following steps.

CAUTION

1. If necessary, start your server and log on using the **Administrator** account in the **CHILDXX** domain (where *XX* is the number of the forest root domain for which your server is a domain controller) using the password **Password01**.
2. Click **Start** and then click **Run**.
3. Type **mmc** and then click **OK**.
4. On the File menu, click **Add/Remove Snap-in.**
5. Click **Add**.
6. Select **ADSI Edit** and then click **Add**.
7. Click **Close** and then click **OK**.
8. In the left tree pane, right-click **ADSI Edit** and then click **Connect to**.
9. In the Select a well known Naming Context drop-down list box, select **Configuration** as shown in Figure 13-7.
10. Click **OK**.
11. If necessary, in the left tree pane expand **ADSI Edit**.
12. In the left tree pane, expand **Configuration**, **CN=Configuration,DC=childXX,DC=supercorp,DC=net** (where *XX* is the number of the forest root domain for which your server is a domain controller), **CN=Services**, and **CN=Windows NT**.
13. In the left tree pane, right-click **CN=Directory Service** and then click **Properties**.
14. In the list of attributes, scroll down and then double-click the **tombstoneLifetime** attribute.

13

Figure 13-7 Selecting the Configuration naming context

15. On the Integer Attribute Editor dialog box in the Value text box, enter **2160** (this attribute is in hours, so you must multiply the number of days by 24 to get the number of hours). Click **OK**.

If the tombstoneLifetime attribute is not set, the 60-day default is assumed.

NOTE

16. The tombstoneLifetime attribute is now set to 2160 hours (90 days), as shown in Figure 13-8. Click **OK**.

17. Close the custom MMC console. Do not save changes when prompted.

18. Shut down your server for the next activity.

Online Defragmentation

Online defragmentation is performed on a domain controller every 12 hours by default as part of the garbage collection process. As the name suggests, online defragmentation is performed with the Active Directory Store (or database) online; meaning users can continue to read and write to the directory. During online defragmentation, space used by deleted objects is reclaimed (freed) for later use by new objects. Additionally, the data inside the database is reorganized to optimize performance.

The one process that online defragmentation does not do, however, is shrink the Active Directory database file (NTDS.DIT). While an online defragmentation can free space inside of the database for use by other objects, it cannot shrink the actual size of the file. To actually shrink the Active Directory database file, an **offline defragmentation** must be performed.

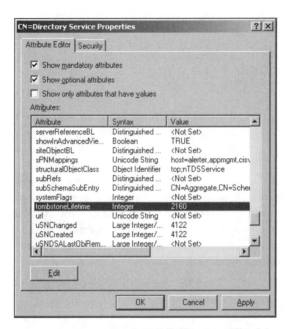

Figure 13-8   Editing the tombstoneLifetime

13

Offline Defragmentation

In normal day-to-day operations, old objects are deleted and new objects are created. Overall, in most situations, the number of new objects created exceeds the number of objects deleted. In other words, the directory database typically grows more than it shrinks. Because of this, online defragmentation is sufficient for most situations. When a small number of objects are deleted, online defragmentation frees the space in the file, thus making it available for other objects. If only a few objects are deleted, only a few new objects have to be created before the freed space is used, and the database file must be expanded.

There might be instances, however, where you delete several hundred or thousand objects from the directory. For example, you might delete an entire organizational unit that contains objects that are no longer part of the company. While online defragmentation does reclaim the space used by the deleted objects, it does not shrink the file. In this situation, an administrator can manually perform an offline defragmentation that does compact the database. The compacted database takes up less space because the free space in the database file is removed. In Activity 13-4, you will learn how to perform an offline defragmentation of the Active Directory database.

Activity 13-4: Defragmenting and Compacting the Active Directory Database

Time Required: 10 minutes

Objective: Defragment and compact the Active Directory database.

Description: In this activity, you will perform an offline defragmentation of the Active Directory database to compact the database files and free up disk space.

1. If your server is already started, shut down your server.

2. Press the power button on your server to start the server. As soon as your server's BIOS posts correctly (usually indicated by a single beep), start repeatedly pressing **F8** until the Windows Advanced Options Menu appears. If you are not quick and the Windows Server 2003 startup logo appears, you need to allow your server to start, then you must logon, and then shut down the server again. You can then try starting the server again, but this time start pressing F8 sooner.

3. Using the up and down arrow keys, select **Directory Services Restore Mode**, as shown in Figure 13-9, and then press **Enter**.

```
Windows Advanced Options Menu
Please select an option:

    Safe Mode
    Safe Mode with Networking
    Safe Mode with Command Prompt

    Enable Boot Logging
    Enable VGA Mode
    Last Known Good Configuration (your most recent settings that worked)
    Directory Services Restore Mode (Windows domain controllers only)
    Debugging Mode

    Start Windows Normally
    Reboot
    Return to OS Choices Menu

Use the up and down arrow keys to move the highlight to your choice.
```

Figure 13-9   Windows Advanced Options Menu

4. Select the installation of Windows you would like to start. There should only be one, so press **Enter**. The server now boots in Directory Services Restore Mode.

5. Log on to your server using the **Administrator** account and the Directory Services Restore Mode password. The Directory Services Restore Mode password was set when you promoted your domain controller using DCPROMO and should be **Password01**.

6. A message box appears informing you that Windows is running in safe mode. Click **OK**.

7. Click **Start** and then click **Command Prompt**.

8. In the command-prompt window, type **Ntdsutil** and then press **Enter**.

9. At the Ntdsutil prompt, type **Files** and then press **Enter**.

10. At the file maintenance prompt, type **Info** and then press **Enter**. This shows the current location of the Active Directory database as well as the size of the database and the log files.

11. Type **Compact to C:\Temp** and press **Enter**, as shown in Figure 13-10. Note the information displayed regarding this procedure. If the compaction was successful, you can now copy the compacted database over the uncompacted copy of the database and delete the old log files.

```
Command Prompt - NTDSUTIL
file maintenance: Compact to C:\Temp
Opening database [Current].
Creating dir: C:\Temp
Executing Command: C:\WINDOWS\system32\esentutl.exe /d"C:\WINDOWS\NTDS\ntds.dit"
/t"C:\Temp\ntds.dit" /p /o

Initiating DEFRAGMENTATION mode...
            Database: C:\WINDOWS\NTDS\ntds.dit
      Temp. Database: C:\Temp\ntds.dit

              Defragmentation Status (% complete)

         0    10   20   30   40   50   60   70   80   90  100
         |----|----|----|----|----|----|----|----|----|----|
         ...................................................

Note:
   It is recommended that you immediately perform a full backup
   of this database. If you restore a backup made before the
   defragmentation, the database will be rolled back to the state
   it was in at the time of that backup.

Operation completed successfully in 9.109 seconds.

Spawned Process Exit code 0x0(0)

If compaction was successful you need to:
   copy "C:\Temp\ntds.dit" "C:\WINDOWS\NTDS\ntds.dit"
and delete the old log files:
   del C:\WINDOWS\NTDS\*.log

file maintenance:
```

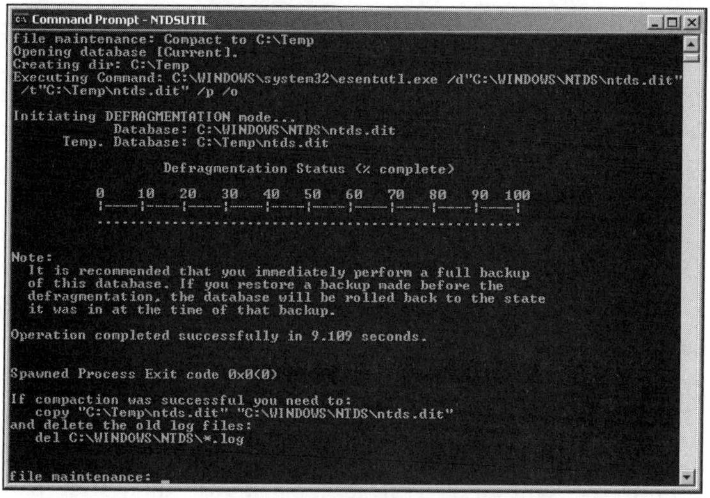

Figure 13-10   Compacting the Active Directory store

12. At the file maintenance prompt, type **Quit** and then press **Enter**.

13. At the Ntdsutil prompt, type **Quit** and then press **Enter**.

14. Type **copy C:\temp\ntds.dit C:\windows\ntds\ntds.dit** and then press **Enter**.

15. When asked if you'd like to overwrite C:\Windows\ntds\ntds.dit, type **Y**, and then press **Enter**.

16. Type **del C:\Windows\Ntds*.log** and then press **Enter**.

17. Type **Exit** and then press **Enter** to close the command-prompt window.

18. Shut down your server if you do not intend to immediately continue to the next activity. Otherwise, stay logged on. Note that you would usually restart your server in normal mode after compacting the database. The only reason you are staying logged on is because the next activity also requires you to be in Directory Services Restore Mode.

13

Manually deleting objects is not the only scenario where an offline defragmentation may be necessary. Remember that all partitions (or naming contexts) are stored in the same database file—NTDS.DIT. Obviously, if you remove a partition from a domain controller, all the objects in that partition are removed. While online defragmentation frees the space used by objects in the deleted partition, an offline defragmentation must be performed to shrink the database.

For example, take a global catalog server named GC1 in the domain *supercorp.net*. The forest consists of three domains: *supercorp.net*, *sales.supercorp.net*, and *dev.supercorp.net*. Each domain contains approximately 50,000 objects. GC1 contains a full copy of all objects in *supercorp.net* and a partial copy of all objects in the other two domains. It is decided that the *dev.supercorp.net* domain is going to be removed. All domain controllers for *dev.supercorp.net* and the domain itself are removed from the forest. Because *dev.supercorp.net* is no longer part of the forest, GC1 removes the *dev.supercorp.net* partition from its directory database. Fifty thousand objects lighter, GC1 now has a lot of free space in its directory database. An offline defragmentation should be performed to free the space previously used by the *dev.supercorp.net* partition.

Continuing with this example, what if GC1 was no longer required to function as a global catalog server (but still a domain controller)? If GC1 were no longer a global catalog server, all the partitions for other domains in the forest would be removed from GC1's directory database. In this scenario, the partition containing objects for the *sales.supercorp.net* domain would be removed. Fifty thousand objects lighter, GC1 once again has a lot of free space in its directory database. An offline defragmentation should be performed to free the space previously used by the *sales.supercorp.net* partition.

In addition to the removal of the partial domain partitions from global catalog servers, you must also pay attention to the removal of application partitions. Application partitions add a new scenario for when an offline defragmentation may be necessary. For example, say you have a Windows Server 2003 domain controller that is also running DNS (which stores data in the ForestDnsZones and DomainDnsZones application partitions). You then decide to remove the DNS server along with the ForestDnsZones and DomainDnsZones application partitions from the domain controller. Once again, while the space used by these two partitions is freed within the directory database, the file is not shrunk. An offline defragmentation should be performed to free the space previously used by the ForestDnsZones and DomainDnsZones application partitions.

OPTIMIZING THE LOCATION OF ACTIVE DIRECTORY FILES

In Chapter 4, you learned about the different files that make up Active Directory. However, the optimal placement of these files was not discussed. In this section, you will see how to optimize the placement of Active Directory files.

Optimizing File Location

The first step in optimizing the location of files is to understand how the different types of files are used. For Active Directory, this means understanding about the Active Directory store and the related log files. However, because Active Directory runs on Windows, you must also take into account the Windows system files and Windows page file.

The Active Directory store is accessed in a random fashion. That is, an object from the beginning of the file may be retrieved, followed by the retrieval of an object stored at the end of the file. In contrast, the Active Directory log files are accessed sequentially—writing one transaction to the log after another.

While the Active Directory store and Active Directory log files were covered in Chapter 4, the Windows system files and Windows page file were not. The Windows system files are simply the operating system files located in %SYSTEMROOT%. There are many executables (.exe), dynamic link libraries (.dll), and other file types that make up the Windows operating system. Although there are tools available to optimize the location of system files on the hard disk, system files are accessed in a random fashion. In other words, a file at the beginning of the disk may be used, followed by a file located in the middle of the disk.

Although it would be nice to have an unlimited amount of memory (RAM) available in a computer, unfortunately that's not the case (at least not today). Instead, the Windows page file is used as virtual memory. When more physical memory is needed, Windows takes a portion of physical memory (called a page) and stores it on the hard disk in the page file. The freed physical memory can then be used by another application. If the data that was placed in the page file is needed in the future, Windows can load the data from the page file back into memory. This process of moving data in and out of physical and virtual memory is called swapping or page swapping. That is why you sometimes hear the page file called the "swap file."

NOTE The above is just a brief overview of the Windows page file for anyone who is not familiar with it.

Using the description of the page file, can you tell if data is accessed sequentially or randomly in most cases? If you said randomly, you're correct. The Windows page file swaps pages in and out that are located throughout the page file.

Looking at these four categories of files, one thing becomes obvious—the Active Directory log files are the only category of file accessed sequentially. The other three categories are all accessed randomly. In a perfect world, the Active Directory store, log files, system files, and page file would all be stored on separate physical hard drives. However, in most cases, more than one—or all—of these categories have to share the same physical hard drives.

NOTE

Many servers run perfectly fine with everything located on one drive. Optimizing file locations is typically only necessary in large environments.

To optimize the location of files, the first step is to separate the randomly accessed files from the sequentially accessed files. Accomplishing this requires two physical redundant drives—one for the Active Directory store, system files, and page file, and another for the Active Directory log files.

CAUTION

Note the use of the term "redundant" in the above paragraph. In a production environment, it is very important that you use a Redundant Array of Independent (Inexpensive) Disks (RAID) level that is fault tolerant for each drive. For example, mirroring (RAID 1) uses two disks that each hold an exact copy of the data. In the event one disk fails, the other disk is still available with all the data. Although other RAID levels provide redundancy (such as RAID 5 and 10), a discussion on RAID is well outside the scope of this text and the 70-294 exam.

The good thing about separating out the Active Directory log files is that the log files don't take up much space and therefore don't require a large hard drive. By placing the Active Directory log on its own drive, the drive's read/write head is in place (or nearly in place) for the next read or write operation. This is because the log files are written to and read from sequentially.

After separating out the log files from the rest of the files, the next step to optimize performance is to place the Active Directory store and/or Windows page file on their own disk. In most cases, moving the page file to its own disk improves performance more than moving the Active Directory store to its own disk. By moving the page file to its own disk first, the entire operating system and other applications see improved performance—not just Active Directory. However, if you do have four separate disks available, moving the Active Directory store to its own drive also increases performance.

TIP

If your domain controller is also acting as a file server, try not to place user data file shares on the same drive as the Windows system files, Active Directory store, or Active Directory log files. When a domain controller is promoted, write-behind caching is disabled on the drive(s) containing the Active Directory store, Active Directory log files, and typically the Windows system files. Write-behind caching allows the operating system to cache write operations in memory to improve performance. However, if power is lost, the data stored in the write-behind cache could be lost. Therefore, to ensure Active Directory is not corrupted from lost data, write-behind caching is disabled for drives containing the Windows system files, Active Directory store, and Active Directory log files. To still take advantage of write-behind caching for user and department files, place the files on a separate physical hard drive (or use a RAID controller that has a battery backup).

Keep in mind that these are only guidelines. The exact hardware configuration and services the domain controller provides all have an effect on the design. The best solution is to use the skills you learned in the first section of this chapter to collect performance data each time you make a change. You can then compare the data from different configurations of your hardware and software to find which gives the best performance.

Moving Active Directory Files

After a domain controller is promoted, it may be necessary to move the Active Directory store or log files. Files may be moved to improve performance or simply be relocated to a drive with more free space. In Activity 13-5, you will learn how to move Active Directory files.

Activity 13-5: Moving Active Directory Log Files

Time Required: 10 minutes

Objective: Move the Active Directory log files to a second hard drive.

Description: Super Corp's IT manager has decided to place a set of mirrored drives in all domain controllers to hold the Active Directory log files. On domain controllers that have already been promoted, you must move the Active Directory log files.

1. If your server is already started in normal mode, shut down your server. If your server is already started in Directory Services Restore Mode, skip to Step 7.

2. Press the power button on your server to start the server. As soon as your server's BIOS posts correctly (usually indicated by a single beep), start repeatedly pressing **F8** until the Windows Advanced Options Menu appears. If you are not quick and the Windows Server 2003 startup logo appears, wait for your server to start, then logon, and then shut down the server again. You can then try starting the server again, but this time start pressing F8 sooner.

3. Using the up and down arrow keys, select **Directory Services Restore Mode** and then press **Enter**.

4. Select the installation of Windows you would like to start. There should only be one, so press **Enter**. The server now boots in Directory Services Restore Mode.

5. Log on to your server using the **Administrator** account and the Directory Services Restore Mode password. The Directory Services Restore Mode password was set when you promoted your domain controller using DCPROMO and should be **Password01**.

6. A message box appears informing you that Windows is running in safe mode. Click **OK**.

7. Click **Start** and then click **My Computer**.

13

8. Double click the **D:** drive. Alternatively, your instructor may provide you with an alternate path if D: is not a hard drive.

9. On the File menu, select **New** and then click **Folder**. Name the new folder **NTDS** and press **Enter**.

10. Close the D: Explorer window.

11. Click **Start** and then click **Command Prompt**.

12. In the command-prompt window, type **Ntdsutil** and then press **Enter**.

13. At the Ntdsutil prompt, type **Files** and then press **Enter**.

14. At the file maintenance prompt, type **Info** and then press **Enter**. Note the current location of the log directory.

15. At the file maintenance prompt, type **Set path logs D:\NTDS** and then press **Enter** to move the log files to the D: hard drive. Alternatively, if you did not create a folder on the D: drive named NTDS in Steps 8 and 9, use the path provided by your instructor instead. The status of the move operation is displayed as shown in Figure 13-11.

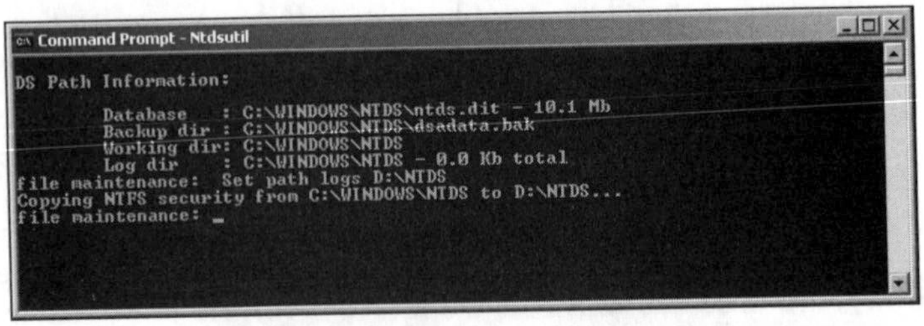

```
Command Prompt - Ntdsutil                                          _ □ ×

DS Path Information:

        Database    : C:\WINDOWS\NTDS\ntds.dit - 10.1 Mb
        Backup dir  : C:\WINDOWS\NTDS\dsadata.bak
        Working dir : C:\WINDOWS\NTDS
        Log dir     : C:\WINDOWS\NTDS - 0.0 Kb total
file maintenance: Set path logs D:\NTDS
Copying NTFS security from C:\WINDOWS\NTDS to D:\NTDS...
file maintenance: _
```

Figure 13-11   Moving Active Directory log files

TIP   Type a question mark (?) and then press Enter to see the syntax for moving the other Active Directory file locations.

16. At the file maintenance prompt, type **Info** and then press **Enter**. Note the new location of the log directory.

17. At the file maintenance prompt, type **Quit** and then press **Enter**.

18. At the Ntdsutil prompt, type **Quit** and then press **Enter**.

19. Type **Exit** and then press **Enter** to close the command-prompt Window.

20. Click **Start** and then click **Shutdown**.

21. In the What do you want the computer to do? drop-down list box, select **Restart**. With the Planned check box checked, select **Operating System: Reconfiguration (Planned)** from the Option drop-down list box. Click **OK**.

22. Once your server restarts, log on using the **Administrator** account in the **CHILD***XX* domain (where *XX* is the number of the forest root domain for which your server is a domain controller) using the password **Password01**.

23. Click **Start** and then click **My Computer**.

24. Navigate to the folder you created in Step 9. Confirm that the Active Directory log files are in the new location, which should look similar to Figure 13-12 (although your exact view of the files may vary).

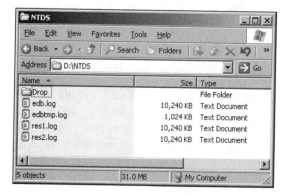

Figure 13-12   New location of Active Directory log files

25. Close the Explorer window.

26. Log off your server if you do not intend to immediately continue to the next activity; otherwise, stay logged on.

WORKING WITH APPLICATION DIRECTORY PARTITIONS

One new feature for optimizing the directory in Windows Server 2003 is application directory partitions (or just "application partitions"). Using application partitions, an administrator has fine-grain control over where data is replicated. By only replicating data to the domain controllers where the data is needed, replication traffic can be lowered. Additionally, hard drive space and other server resources can be saved on servers that don't need to hold a replica of the data in the application partition. In this section, you will learn how to create application partitions, add and remove application partition replicas, and also how to delete application partitions from the directory.

NOTE

Remember that in order to support application partitions, the domain naming master for the forest must be placed on a domain controller running Windows Server 2003. Additionally, only domain controllers running Windows Server 2003 can store replicas of application partitions. Finally, recall that any object can be stored in an application partition, except security principles.

Creating Application Directory Partitions

There are several ways an administrator can create a new application partition. If a third-party application comes with a utility to set up the necessary application partition(s), you should use the utility provided by the application vendor. By using the vender's utility, the new partition(s) can be configured exactly how the application needs them set up. For more information on using a provided utility, please see the vender's documentation.

Alternatively, if no utility is provided with a third-party application to create the required application partitions, you can use the Ntdsutil utility to create the necessary application partition(s). In Activity 13-6, you will use the Ntdsutil utility to create a new application partition.

Selecting a Name for an Application Directory Partition

Before creating a new application partition, you must first select a name for the partition. Like a domain partition, an application partition is part of the forest's namespace. This means application partitions follow the same DNS naming conventions as any other domain in the forest. A new application partition can have one of three possible locations in a forest's namespace:

- A child of an existing domain partition
- A child of an existing application partition
- The root of a new tree

As a first example, assume a forest consisted of one domain called *ad.supercorp.net*. Also assume that you want to add an application partition named testapp as a child of the *ad.supercorp.net* domain. In this case, the new application partition's DNS name would be *testapp.ad.supercorp.net*. Similarly, the new application partition's distinguished name would be DC=testapp,DC=ad,DC=supercorp,DC=net. This is an example of a child application partition with a domain partition as its parent.

Continuing with the same example, assume you wanted to add a second application partition named crm as a child application partition to the testapp application partition. The DNS name of the new application partition would be *crm.testapp.ad.supercorp.net* and the distinguished name would be DC=crm,DC=testapp,DC=ad,DC=supercorp,DC=net. This is an example of a child application partition with another application partition as its parent.

Finally, assume you wanted to create a new application partition named *contacts.internal* in an existing forest with only one domain called *ad.supercorp.net*. The application partition's DNS name would be *contacts.internal* and the distinguished name would be DC=contacts,DC=internal. This is an example of an application partition as the root of a new tree.

There is one very important fact to note about these examples—a domain partition cannot be the child of an application partition. This means that if you have an application partition named *testapp.ad.supercorp.net*, you cannot create a domain named *newdomain.testapp.ad.supercorp.net*. In other words, only an application partition can have another application partition as its parent.

Understanding Application Directory Partition Replication

For the most part, replication of an application partition works in the same way as for a domain partition (review Chapter 7, if necessary). However, there are two important differences between application partitions and domain partitions when it comes to the global catalog.

The first difference to be aware of is that application partitions are never replicated to global catalog servers as partial read-only replicas (as domain partitions are). This does not mean a global catalog server cannot hold a master replica of an application partition—it can. Any domain controller, including global catalog servers, in the forest can hold a master replica of an application partition.

The second difference has to do with how queries to the global catalog are processed by a global catalog server. If a global catalog query is sent to a global catalog server, the server can respond with objects from any domain partition in the forest. However, a global catalog server does not return any objects from an application partition when a global catalog query is submitted—even if the global catalog server also holds a master replica of the application partition. This is done so that the results returned by a global catalog query are consistent between global catalog servers that do and do not have a master replica of a given application partition. Do keep in mind that this only relates to global catalog queries—not queries directly to the application partition master replica that is on a global catalog server.

Selecting a Security Descriptor Reference Domain

As you learned in Chapter 9, every object in the directory has a security descriptor that controls access to the object. When an object is created, a security descriptor can be assigned by the application or service that created the object. Alternatively, if a security descriptor is not defined for the new object, a default security descriptor is used. Every object class has its own default security descriptor that is stored in the schema and can be edited using the Active Directory Schema snap-in.

There is one potential issue when using application partitions and default security descriptors—ambiguous references. For example, a default security descriptor may grant full control to the Domain Admins group; however, it does not explicitly define to what domain the group belongs. This is not a problem when creating an object in a domain partition—the domain where the object is being created is assumed. This means that if a new object was created in the *ad.supercorp.net* domain, the ad.supercorp.net\Domain Admins group would be used.

Application partitions, on the other hand, do not store any user or groups and therefore just substituting the same name as the application partition does not work (like it does for a domain partition). Additionally, if a forest consisted of three domains (*ad.supercorp.net*, *sales.ad.supercorp.net*, and *dev.ad.supercorp.net*) and an application partition name *crm.ad.supercorp.net*, which of the three domains should be assumed for objects created in the application partition if only Domain Admins is specified? The application partition may exist on domain controllers from all three domains, so just assuming the same domain as the domain controller where the object is created does not work (at least not without a lot of headaches).

To solve the issue of ambiguous references, each application partition has a default security descriptor reference domain set when the partition is created. The reference domain defines what domain is used when an object's security permissions are based on a default security descriptor. By default, the reference domain is set depending on where the application partition is in the forest:

- A child of an existing domain partition—The new application partition uses the parent domain as the default reference domain.

- A child of an existing application partition—The new application partition uses the parent application partition's reference domain as its own reference domain.

- The root of a new tree—The new application partition uses the forest root domain as the default reference domain.

NOTE

You can also manually specify the reference domain for an application partition using the Ntdsutil utility. For more information, search for "Application Directory Partitions" in Windows Server 2003's Help and Support Center.

ACTIVITY

Activity 13-6: Creating Application Directory Partitions Using Ntdsutil

Time Required: 10 minutes

Objective: Create a new application partition using the Ntdsutil utility.

Description: To reduce the replication traffic for data related to a custom application used by Super Corp, you have decided to explore application partitions. In order to test the effectiveness of the new configuration, you must first set up the application partition.

1. If necessary, start your server and log on using the **Administrator** account in the **CHILDXX** domain (where *XX* is the number of the forest root domain for which your server is a domain controller) using the password **Password01**.

2. Click **Start** and then click **Command Prompt**.

3. In the Command Prompt window, type **Ntdsutil** and then press **Enter**.

4. At the Ntdsutil prompt, type **Domain management** and then press **Enter**.

5. At the domain management prompt, type **Connections** and then press **Enter**.

6. At the server connections prompt, type **Connect to server SERVERXX** (where *XX* is the number of your server) and then press **Enter**.

7. At the server connections prompt, type **Quit** and then press **Enter**.

8. At the domain management prompt, type **Create NC DC=testappXX,DC=childZZ,DC=supercorp,DC=net NULL** (where *XX* is the number of your server and *ZZ* is the number of the forest root domain for which your server is a domain controller) and then press **Enter**. If the partition was successfully created, you should receive a message similar to Figure13-13.

```
Command Prompt - Ntdsutil                                          _ □ x
Microsoft Windows [Version 5.2.3790]
(C) Copyright 1985-2003 Microsoft Corp.

C:\>Ntdsutil
Ntdsutil: Domain management
domain management: Connections
server connections: Connect to server SERVER01
Binding to SERVER01 ...
Connected to SERVER01 using credentials of locally logged on user.
server connections: Quit
domain management: Create NC DC=testapp01,DC=child01,DC=supercorp,DC=net NULL
adding object DC=testapp01,DC=child01,DC=supercorp,DC=net
domain management: _
```

Figure 13-13   Creating a new application partition

NOTE   The NULL specifies to use the server to which you are currently connected. Alternatively, you can specify the DNS name of another domain controller on which to create the application partition.

9. At the domain management prompt, type **List NC Replicas DC=testappXX,DC=childZZ,DC=supercorp,DC=net** (where *XX* is the number of your server and *ZZ* is the number of the forest root domain for which your server is a domain controller) and then press **Enter**. A list of domain controllers that hold a replica of the new application partition is displayed, as shown in Figure 13-14.

10. If you do not intend to immediately continue to the next activity, at the domain management prompt, type **Quit** and then press **Enter**.

11. If you do not intend to immediately continue to the next activity, at the Ntdsutil prompt, type **Quit** and then press **Enter**.

12. If you do not intend to immediately continue to the next activity, type **Exit** and then press **Enter** to close the command prompt.

13. Log off your server if you do not intend to immediately continue to the next activity. Otherwise, stay logged on.

```
Command Prompt - Ntdsutil                                         _ □ ×
Microsoft Windows [Version 5.2.3790]
(C) Copyright 1985-2003 Microsoft Corp.

C:\>Ntdsutil
Ntdsutil: Domain management
domain management: Connections
server connections: Connect to server SERVER01
Binding to SERVER01 ...
Connected to SERVER01 using credentials of locally logged on user.
server connections: Quit
domain management: Create NC DC=testapp01,DC=child01,DC=supercorp,DC=net NULL
adding object DC=testapp01,DC=child01,DC=supercorp,DC=net
domain management: List NC Replicas DC=testapp01,DC=child01,DC=supercorp,DC=net
The application directory partition DC=testapp01,DC=child01,DC=supercorp,DC=net'
s Replicas are:
        CN=NTDS Settings,CN=SERVER01,CN=Servers,CN=MySite01,CN=Sites,CN=Configur
ation,DC=child01,DC=supercorp,DC=net
domain management:
```

Figure 13-14   List of replicas for a given naming context

NOTE

At this point, you would typically set up your custom application to use the application partition you just created. However, because you do not actually have an application to test this step (plus the fact that just about every application is configured differently), you will not actually be configuring an application to use the application partition in this activity.

Adding and Removing Application Directory Partition Replicas

Once an application partition is created, you can add or remove replicas of the partition from one or more domain controllers as needed. Again, there are several ways to add and remove replicas of application partitions. If a third-party application comes with a utility to add and remove replicas of an application partition, you should use the utility provided by the application vendor.

Alternatively, if no utility is provided with a third-party application to add or remove replicas, you can use the Ntdsutil utility to manage replicas. In Activity 13-7, you will use the Ntdsutil utility to add and remove an application directory partition replica.

ACTIVITY

Activity 13-7: Adding and Removing Application Directory Partition Replicas Using Ntdsutil

Time Required: 10 minutes

Objective: Add and remove application partition replicas using the Ntdsutil utility.

Description: With a new application partition created, you must now add and remove replicas of the partition on domain controllers to optimize performance. In this activity, you will add (and then remove) a replica on your partner's server of the application partition you created in the last activity.

1. If necessary, start your server and log on using the **Administrator** account in the **CHILD*XX*** domain (where *XX* is the number of the forest root domain for which your server is a domain controller) using the password **Password01**.

2. If you did not continue from the last activity, click **Start** and then click **Command Prompt**.

3. If you did not continue from the last activity, in the Command Prompt window, type **Ntdsutil** and then press **Enter**.

4. If you did not continue from the last activity, at the Ntdsutil prompt, type **Domain management** and then press **Enter**.

5. If you did not continue from the last activity, at the domain management prompt, type **Connections** and then press **Enter**.

6. If you did not continue from the last activity, at the server connections prompt, type **Connect to server SERVER*XX*** (where *XX* is the number of your server) and then press **Enter**.

7. If you did not continue from the last activity, at the server connections prompt, type **Quit** and then press **Enter**.

8. To create a new replica of an application partition, at the domain management prompt, type **Add NC Replica DC=testapp*XX*,DC=child*ZZ*,DC=supercorp,DC=net SERVER*YY*.child*ZZ*.supercorp.net** (where *XX* is the number of your server, *ZZ* is the number of the forest root domain for which your server is a domain controller, and *YY* is the number of your *partner's* server) and then press **Enter** to add the new replica.

9. At the domain management prompt, type **List NC Replicas DC=testapp*XX*,DC=child*ZZ*,DC=supercorp,DC=net** (where *XX* is the number of your server and *ZZ* is the number of the forest root domain for which your server is a domain controller) and then press **Enter**. Your partner's server should now appear as a replica of your application partition (in addition to your server), as shown in Figure 13-15.

Figure 13-15   Adding a new application partition replica

10. To remove a replica of an application partition, type **Remove NC Replica DC=testappXX,DC=childZZ,DC=supercorp,DC=net SERVERYY.childZZ.supercorp.net** (where *XX* is the number of your server, *ZZ* is the number of the forest root domain for which your server is a domain controller, and *YY* is the number of your partner's server) and then press **Enter** to remove the new replica.

If you remove the last replica of an application partition (that is, so there are no more replicas), all data stored in the partition will be lost.

CAUTION

11. At the domain management prompt, type **List NC Replicas DC=testappXX,DC=childZZ,DC=supercorp,DC=net** (where *XX* is the number of your server and *ZZ* is the number of the forest root domain for which your server is a domain controller) and then press **Enter**. Your partner's server should no longer appear as a replica of your application partition, as shown in Figure 13-16.

Rather than retyping the same commands over and over, you can use the up and down arrow keys on your keyboard to select previously typed commands.

TIP

Figure 13-16   Removing an application partition replica

12. If you do not intend to immediately continue to the next activity, at the domain management prompt, type **Quit** and then press **Enter**.

13. If you do not intend to immediately continue to the next activity, at the Ntdsutil prompt, type **Quit** and then press **Enter**.

14. If you do not intend to immediately continue to the next activity, type **Exit** and then press **Enter** to close the command prompt.

15. Log off your server if you do not intend to immediately continue to the next activity. Otherwise, stay logged on.

Deleting Application Directory Partitions

If an application partition is no longer needed, you can delete it from the directory. When you delete an application partition, any replicas of the partition are automatically removed from all domain controllers in the forest. Additionally, configuration data about the application partition is also removed from the directory.

Note that deleting an application partition is not the same as removing all the replicas (you learned how to remove replicas in Activity 13-7) of the partition. If you remove all replicas of a given application partition, the data stored in that partition is lost. However, even though there may be no replicas of a given application partition, there is still configuration data about the application partition in the directory (specifically, data in the configuration partition).

Just like the last two sections, there are several ways to delete application partitions. If a third-party application comes with a utility to delete the application partition(s) it created, you should use the utility provided by the application vendor. Alternatively, if no utility is provided with a third-party application to delete application partitions, you can use the Ntdsutil utility to delete the old application partition(s). In Activity 13-8, you will use the Ntdsutil utility to delete an application partition.

When deleting an application partition, it may take time for the deletion to replicate throughout the forest.

NOTE

13

ACTIVITY

Activity 13-8: Deleting Application Directory Partitions Using Ntdsutil

Time Required: 10 minutes

Objective: Delete an application partition using the Ntdsutil utility.

Description: After testing Super Corp's custom application using an application partition, you now want to remove the test application partition from the directory. By deleting the application partition, you will ensure that all replicas of the partition are removed from the forest.

1. If necessary, start your server and log on using the **Administrator** account in the **CHILDXX** domain (where *XX* is the number of the forest root domain for which your server is a domain controller) using the password **Password01**.

2. If you did not continue from the last activity, click **Start** and then click **Command Prompt**.

3. If you did not continue from the last activity, in the Command Prompt window, type **Ntdsutil** and then press **Enter**.

4. If you did not continue from the last activity, at the Ntdsutil prompt, type **Domain management** and then press **Enter**.

5. If you did not continue from the last activity, at the domain management prompt, type **Connections** and then press **Enter**.

6. If you did not continue from the last activity, at the server connections prompt, type **Connect to server SERVERXX** (where *XX* is the number of your server) and then press **Enter**.

7. If you did not continue from the last activity, at the server connections prompt, type **Quit** and then press **Enter**.

8. At the domain management prompt, type **Delete NC DC=testappXX,DC=childZZ,DC=supercorp,DC=net** (where *XX* is the number of your server and *ZZ* is the number of the forest root domain for which your server is a domain controller) and then press **Enter**. If the partition was successfully deleted, you should receive a message similar to Figure 13-17.

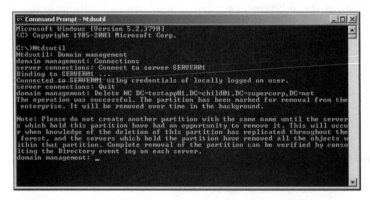

Figure 13-17   Deleting an application partition

9. At the domain management prompt, type **List** and then press **Enter** to view a list of naming contexts in the forest. Confirm that your application partition is not listed in the naming contexts displayed.

10. At the domain management prompt, type **Quit** and then press **Enter**.

11. At the Ntdsutil prompt, type **Quit** and then press **Enter**.

12. Type **Exit** and then press **Enter** to close the command prompt.

13. Log off your server.

CHAPTER SUMMARY

❑ The Performance console is the primary server-monitoring utility provided with Windows Server 2003. The NTDS performance object contains many counters that can be used to monitor Active Directory performance on a domain controller.

❑ Deleted objects are not removed from Active Directory immediately. Instead, they are marked as tombstone for 60 days, by default. When an object has been tombstoned for more than the tombstone lifetime, it is removed by the garbage collection process.

❑ If a domain controller does not replicate with one of its partners within the tombstone lifetime, the domain controller will refuse to replicate. Similarly, you cannot restore a backup that is older than the tombstone lifetime.

❑ Online defragmentation of the Active Directory store is automatically performed every 12 hours, by default. An online defragmentation can reclaim space used by deleted objects and reorganize data to optimize performance. However, online defragmentation cannot shrink the file size of the Active Directory store.

❑ Offline defragmentation of Active Directory must be performed manually in Directory Services Restore Mode. An offline defragmentation can do everything an online defragmentation can; an offline defragmentation can also shrink the file size of the Active Directory store.

❑ To optimize performance, the location of the Active Directory database and log files can be changed.

❑ Application partitions follow the same DNS naming structure as any other domain partition in the forest. An application partition can be created as any of the following: a child of an existing domain partition, a child of an existing application partition, or the root of a new tree. A domain partition cannot be created as a child of an application partition.

❑ You can use the Ntdsutil utility to create application partitions, add and remove application partition replicas, and delete application partitions from the directory.

13

KEY TERMS

baseline — A performance benchmark that is used to determine what is normal server performance under a specific workload.

defragmentation — The process of reorganizing the data inside of the Active Directory store in order to improve performance.

garbage collection — The process of purging deleted objects from Active Directory. By default, garbage collection occurs every 12 hours.

offline defragmentation — A defragmentation process that occurs with Active Directory offline. An offline defragmentation can do everything an online defragmentation can, plus an offline defragmentation can shrink the file size of the Active Directory store.

online defragmentation — A defragmentation process that occurs with Active Directory online. Online defragmentation can reclaim space used by deleted objects and reorganize data to optimize performance. However, online defragmentation cannot shrink the file size of the Active Directory store.

Performance console — A predefined MMC that includes both the System Monitor and Performance Logs and Alerts tools.

tombstone — A marker in the Active Directory database that indicates an object has been deleted.

tombstone lifetime — The time period after which deleted objects' tombstones are removed from Active Directory. The default is 60 days.

REVIEW QUESTIONS

1. The DRA Inbound Bytes Not Compressed/sec performance counter measures which of the following?

    a. intrasite replication traffic received by a domain controller

    b. intersite replication traffic received by a domain controller

    c. intrasite replication traffic sent by a domain controller

    d. intersite replication traffic sent by a domain controller

2. Which of the following counters are displayed by default in the System Monitor display when the Performance console is opened? (Choose all that apply.)

    a. Pages/sec

    b. Avg. Disk Queue Length

    c. % Memory Time

    d. % Processor Time

3. Which of the following are available views in the System Monitor tool? (Choose all that apply.)

    a. Report

    b. Histogram

    c. Graph

    d. Pie Chart

4. The DRA Outbound Bytes Compressed/sec performance counter measures which of the following?

    a. intrasite replication traffic received by a domain controller

    b. intersite replication traffic received by a domain controller

    c. intrasite replication traffic sent by a domain controller

    d. intersite replication traffic sent by a domain controller

5. Collecting performance data during normal operation is used to set which of the following?

a. a minimum

b. a maximum

c. a baseline

d. You do not have to collect performance data during normal operation.

6. Which of the following is the default tombstone lifetime?

a. 6 hours

b. 6 days

c. 60 days

d. 90 days

7. On a domain controller, garbage collection occurs how often by default?

a. every 3 hours

b. every 6 hours

c. every 12 hours

d. every 24 hours

8. You can use the _____ attribute of the Directory Service object to modify the default tombstone lifetime.

9. To ensure objects are deleted from all domain controllers, the tombstone lifetime must be greater than which of the following?

a. the replication latency across the slowest domain

b. the replication latency across the entire forest

c. the replication latency across the forest root domain

d. The replication latency should be set individually for each domain's latency.

10. You can restore a backup from tape, even if the backup is older than the tombstone lifetime. True or False?

11. Which of the following statements regarding an offline defragmentation are correct? (Choose all that apply.)

a. An offline defragmentation can free up hard disk space.

b. The Active Directory database cannot be in use during an offline defragmentation.

c. An offline defragmentation runs every 12 hours by default.

d. An offline defragmentation is performed during garbage collection.

13

12. Which of the following statements regarding an online defragmentation are correct? (Choose all that apply.)

    a. An online defragmentation can free up hard disk space.

    b. The Active Directory database cannot be in use during an online defragmentation.

    c. An online defragmentation runs every 12 hours by default.

    d. An online defragmentation is performed during garbage collection.

13. After which of the following events should you perform an offline defragmentation to free disk space? (Choose all that apply.)

    a. on all domain controllers in a domain after deleting an organizational unit containing 5000 user accounts.

    b. on all domain controllers in the forest after deleting an organizational unit containing 5000 user accounts.

    c. on all global catalog servers in the forest after deleting an organizational unit containing 5000 user accounts.

    d. You do not have to perform an offline defragmentation—an online defragmentation will release the free space back to the hard drive.

14. To perform an offline defragmentation, the server must be started in which of the following modes?

    a. safe mode

    b. normal mode

    c. Directory Services Restore Mode

    d. safe mode with networking

15. Although two domain controllers may contain the same exact partitions, their local directory database files may be different sizes. True or False?

16. If you have multiple domain controllers, you only need to perform an offline defragmentation on one domain controller in order to shrink the Active Directory database on all other domain controllers. True or False?

17. For best performance, it is a good idea to separate the files that are accessed _____ from those that are accessed _____ .

18. Which of the following is an example of file(s) that are randomly accessed? (Choose all that apply.)

    a. Active Directory store

    b. Active Directory log file

    c. Windows system files

    d. Windows page file

19. Which of the following is an example of file(s) that are sequentially accessed? (Choose all that apply.)

a. Active Directory store

b. Active Directory log file

c. Windows system files

d. Windows page file

20. To move the Active Directory log files, the server must be started in which of the following modes?

a. safe mode

b. normal mode

c. Directory Services Restore Mode

d. safe mode with networking

CASE PROJECTS

Case Project 13-1: Defragmentation

You have been asked to create a report that describes the different Active Directory defragmentation options available. This report will be given to junior network administrators at Super Corp so they will have a better understanding of when they need to defragment the Active Directory store on a domain controller. In your report, include the different types of defragmentation that can be performed, what benefits each provides, and when they are (or should be) performed.

13

Case Project 13-2: Optimizing File Locations

Super Corp has just received a new server that will become a domain controller. The new server has the following drives:

1. C: 36 GB—System files, page file

2. D: 36 GB—Unused

3. E: 72 GB—User documents

4. F: 4 GB—Unused

You have been asked where the Active Directory database and log files should go. Where would you place the Active Directory database? Where would you place the Active Directory log files? Would you move any other files? Explain the reasons for your answer.

Case Project 13-3: Using Application Partitions

Super Corp's IT manager has asked you about storing data generated by Super Corp's custom outsourcing staff management application in an application partition. Because the application stores objects that are derived from the Contact class (recall that the Contact class is not a security principal), he is unsure if the objects can be stored in an application partition. Additionally, he would also like to use an internal namespace for the new partition (crm.local) but he is unsure if that is valid or not. What can you tell Super Corp's IT manager about application partitions to alleviate his concerns?

14

DISASTER RECOVERY

After reading this chapter, you will be able to:

♦ Create backups of the Active Directory database

♦ Check the integrity of the Active Directory database

♦ Recover the Active Directory database in the event of failure

♦ Create a disaster recovery plan

The goal of every administrator is to protect data from hardware or software failure, including the failure of Active Directory. When implemented properly, Active Directory is very stable. It is based on a fault-tolerant, transactional database that is designed to maintain data integrity after any system failure. Employing best practices, such as using multiple domain controllers, helps minimize the risk and scope of such problems.

However, some unavoidable events, such as a complete server failure, a hard disk controller failure, or human error, may prevent Active Directory from running. If this happens, it may be necessary to manually restore parts of Active Directory, or completely restore Active Directory to another server. In this chapter, you will learn how to back up and restore the Active Directory database as well as how to create a disaster recovery plan.

BACKING UP ACTIVE DIRECTORY

One major benefit of Active Directory's design is that copies of a directory partition can exist on multiple domain controllers. This design provides fault tolerance, because if one server fails, a client can be redirected to another domain controller that also has a copy of the partition. Additionally, the chances of losing data when a domain controller fails are minimized, because the copies of a partition on different domain controllers are regularly updated thanks to Active Directory replication.

So you may be asking: if multiple copies of the directory exist, why bother backing up Active Directory at all? While having multiple copies of the directory on multiple domain controllers protects you against the loss of a single server, they cannot protect you against everything. For example, what if an administrator accidentally deletes a user account, or worse, an entire organizational unit containing thousands of objects? As soon as the command to delete the objects is issued, the local domain controller removes most of the object's attributes and tombstones the object. A few seconds later, the object's tombstone is replicated to other domain controllers in the site—and then to domain controllers in other sites as the replication schedule dictates. By the time the administrator realizes what has happened, the deletion has probably replicated throughout the site and maybe even to other sites.

TIP   To reduce the chance of human error, service owners and data owners should only be given permissions to the parts of the directory (or its data) that they manage—and only the minimum level of access they need to do their job. This not only prevents a malicious user from damaging the entire directory, but prevents users from accidentally modifying something they should not. While it may be more complex to set up in the first place, it can save time in the long run. Note that this concept of only giving users the level of access they need is commonly referred to as **least privilege**.

As another example, what if all your domain controllers are located at one facility that suffers a catastrophic fire, flood, or other major disaster? Although there are multiple copies of the directory, they could all easily be destroyed. Even if you do have multiple domain controllers at different sites, what if the directory becomes corrupted? While the odds of the directory becoming corrupted on its own are slim to none, some actions can corrupt the directory. For example, bringing an old domain naming master back online after seizing the role to another server could corrupt the directory and require it be rebuilt or restored from a backup.

To protect against these scenarios, it is important that you make regular backups of Active Directory. It just can't be overstated how important it is to back up Active Directory. When something goes wrong, it's the administrator's job to get things up and running as soon as possible. If the administrator is unable to get the network up and running in a short period of time, or worse, if data that cannot be easily recreated is lost, then the administrator's job is very likely on the line.

Having a good solid backup strategy in place can help things go smoother when something catastrophic does occur. In the rest of this section, you will learn how to perform backups of

Active Directory and its related components. Then, later in this chapter, you will learn how to create a backup plan.

Active Directory Backups

Active Directory is backed up as part of the System State. **System State**, shown in Figure 14-1, includes the following (not all items are shown in figure):

- Registry (always)
- COM+ Class Registration database (always)
- Boot files (always)
- Certificate Services database (if Certificate Services is installed)
- Active Directory (only on domain controllers)
- SYSVOL directory (only on domain controllers)
- Cluster service (if the server is part of a cluster)
- IIS Metadirectory (if IIS is installed)
- System files (always)

NOTE   The Backup Utility included with Windows Server 2003 cannot back up the System State of a remote server. However, System State information can be backed up remotely when you use third-party backup software, such as Veritas BackupExec or Computer Associates ArcServe. Make sure that the version you select is approved for Windows Server 2003.

If you have backed up file servers before, you are probably familiar with the different types of backups you can perform. While the Windows Server 2003 **Backup Utility** lets you make a **normal backup**, a **differential backup**, and an **incremental backup** of files and folders, the System State is always backed up using a normal backup—even if you select a different backup type. This means that all files and folders that make up the System State are backed up—even if they have not changed from the last backup that was taken. Additionally, you can perform a System State backup with the Active Directory database online and in use. In Activity 14-1, you will create a backup of Active Directory.

Activity 14-1: Creating a System State Backup

Time Required: 15 minutes

Objective: Make a backup of Active Directory by backing up the System State.

Description: Because your server is also a domain controller, the IT manager at Super Corp has asked you to explore the capabilities of the Backup Utility in terms of backing up System State data, including individual components. Ultimately, this will be an important consideration in whether the IT manager decides to rely on the Backup Utility or a third-party alternative. In this activity, you will back up the System State data for your server.

1. If necessary, start your server and log on using the **Administrator** account in the **CHILDXX** domain (where *XX* is the number of the forest root domain for which your server is a domain controller) using the password **Password01**.

2. Click **Start**, select **All Programs**, select **Accessories**, select **System Tools**, and then click **Backup**.

3. If the Backup or Restore Wizard appears, click the **Advanced Mode** link to open the Backup Utility window. Otherwise, continue with the next step.

4. In the Backup Utility window, click the **Backup** tab.

5. In the left tree, click the **System State** icon to view its contents in the right details list box. Notice that the individual check boxes are grayed out because individual System State components cannot be backed up individually by this utility.

6. Click the check box next to the **System State** icon in the left tree view.

7. In the Backup media or file name text box, type **D:\systemstate.bkf**, as shown in Figure 14-1. Note that your instructor may provide you with an alternate location if you do not have a hard drive labeled D:.

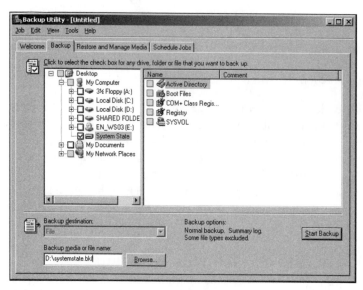

Figure 14-1   Backing up System State data

8. Click the **Start Backup** button.

9. In the Backup Job Information dialog box, click the **Start Backup** button.

10. After the backup process is complete the dialog box should look similar to Figure 14-2.

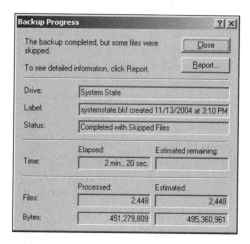

Figure 14-2 Backup Progress dialog box

TIP   If the Status text box in the Backup Progress dialog box shows a message of Completed with Skipped Files, you can click on the Report button to see a list of files or folders that were skipped during the backup. There is a known issue with the Backup Utility trying to back up the DO_NOT_REMOVE_NtFrs_PreInstall_ Directory directory as part of the System State backup (which it should not). However, this issue does not impact your ability to correctly restore the backup. For more information, see Microsoft Knowledge Base Article 822132 at *support.microsoft.com*.

11. Click the **Close** button on the Backup Progress dialog box.

12. Close the Backup Utility.

13. Click **Start**, and then click **My Computer**. Double-click on the **D:** drive to view its contents. Alternatively, select the drive that contains the Systemstate.bkf file if D: is not a hard drive.

14. Right-click on the file **Systemstate.bkf** and then click **Properties**. From the General tab, review the size of this file to get a better sense of how large a System State backup of your system is.

15. Close all open windows.

16. Log off your server if you do not intend to immediately continue to the next activity. Otherwise, stay logged on.

14

TIP

Earlier in this text, you learned about the new install from media feature of Windows Server 2003 that allows you to promote a domain controller using a copy of Active Directory from media such as CD or tape. To take advantage of this feature, start by making a System State backup of an existing domain controller, as shown in Activity 14-1. On the new server you want to promote, type DCPROMO /adv in the Run dialog box and click OK to start the Active Directory Installation Wizard. When running the wizard, an additional window appears, asking if you would like to copy domain information from a domain controller over the network or from restored backup files. To use the backup you made from the existing domain controller, restore the backup to an alternate location on the new domain controller and then select the From these restored backup files option in DCPROMO. (Restoring a backup to an alternate location is covered later in this chapter.) Be sure when using this feature that you use a fairly current backup of an existing domain controller. This is because the new domain controller still needs to replicate any changes that occurred between the time the backup was taken and the time the new domain controller is promoted.

TIP

Note that you can use the install from media feature to promote a domain controller and make the new domain controller a global catalog server simultaneously. To make the new server a global catalog server, simply back up a domain controller that is currently a global catalog server and follow the previous directions. An additional window appears, while running the Active Directory Installation Wizard, asking if you want to make the new domain controller a global catalog server or not.

Backups and the Tombstone Lifetime

In the last chapter, you learned that the tombstone lifetime controls how long tombstones remain in the directory. In addition to playing a role in how long a domain controller can go without replicating, the tombstone lifetime also controls the maximum age of a backup that can still be restored. A backup that is older than the tombstone lifetime cannot be restored.

The best way to describe why a backup older than the tombstone lifetime can't be restored is with an example. Assuming the default tombstone lifetime of 60 days, imagine that you have two domain controllers: DC1 and DC2. A backup is taken of DC1's System State data. After the backup is made, normal operations take place—more specifically, the deletion of objects from the directory. As objects are deleted, DC1 and DC2 replicate the tombstones, and then remove the tombstones once they are older than the tombstone lifetime. Now, 90 days later, DC1's directory database becomes corrupted and must be restored from backup. If DC1 was restored from backup, what would happen to objects that were deleted over 60 days ago?

Restoring DC1 from backup would be like taking the server back in time. Because DC1's directory database would be 90 days old, DC1 would have no clue what objects have been deleted, added, or modified in the last 90 days. While DC2 has a current copy of the directory database and can replicate all the objects that were added or modified in the last 90 days and deleted within the last 60 days, it knows nothing about objects that were deleted more than 60 days ago. This is because DC2 has removed the tombstones for objects that were deleted more than 60 days ago. Because DC2 does not know that these objects have already been deleted, DC1 will replicate the deleted objects more than 60 days old back to DC2.

Allowing this scenario to occur would introduce inconsistency into the network and could require the network to be rebuilt. Fortunately, Windows Server 2003 does not allow you to restore a backup that is older than the tombstone lifetime—preventing this scenario from occurring. This is why backups have a shelf life of 60 days by default and then are no longer useful.

NOTE

For more information on backups, please see Chapter 12, "Managing and Implementing Backups and Disaster Recovery," in MCSE Guide to Managing a Microsoft Windows Server 2003 Environment (ISBN: 0-619-12035-5).

IDENTIFYING ACTIVE DIRECTORY CORRUPTION

Some corruption problems with Active Directory are easy to identify. If a domain controller displays a message box at startup informing you of a problem with Active Directory, it's usually correct. However, it's possible that a problem can exist without it being obvious. To verify the integrity of Active Directory, you can run an integrity check and a semantic check. These checks are described in the following two sections.

Checking File Integrity

A file integrity check performs a low- (binary) level check of the Active Directory database file (NTDS.DIT). In other words, the check determines if the file is formatted correctly. An integrity check also checks the overall structures of the tables in the database, ensuring that they are accessible and have the correct columns. In Activity 14-2, you will perform an integrity check on your domain controller.

NOTE

You must be in Directory Services Restore Mode to perform an integrity check.

14

In a production environment, if the domain controller was shut down incorrectly—or if you are not absolutely sure if the domain controller was shut down correctly—you should perform recovery before performing an integrity check. Activity 14-4 describes how to manually initiate the recovery process.

Activity 14-2: Performing an Integrity Check

Time Required: 20 minutes

Objective: Perform an integrity check of the Active Directory database.

Description: One of Super Corp's domain controller's UPS and power supply was hit by lightning when a severe storm passed through the area. While the server's UPS and power supply have been replaced, the IT manager would like you to check the Active Directory database on the damaged domain controller for any possible corruption. To check the low-level structure of the database, you will perform an integrity check.

1. Restart your server in Directory Services Restore Mode. Refer back to Activity 13-4 if necessary.

2. Log on to your server using the **Administrator** account and the Directory Services Restore Mode password. The Directory Services Restore Mode password was set when you promoted your domain controller using DCPROMO and should be **Password01**.

3. A message box appears informing you that Windows is running in safe mode. Click **OK**.

4. Click **Start** and then click **Command Prompt**.

5. In the Command Prompt window, type **Ntdsutil** and then press **Enter**.

6. At the Ntdsutil prompt, type **Files** and then press **Enter**.

7. At the file maintenance prompt, type **Integrity** and then press **Enter**. If the integrity check is completed successfully, you should receive the message shown in Figure 14-3.

8. After the integrity check is completed, type **Quit** and then press **Enter**.

9. Type **Quit** again and then press **Enter**.

10. Close the Command Prompt window.

11. Shut down your server if you do not intend to immediately continue to the next activity. Otherwise, stay logged on.

```
Command Prompt - Ntdsutil                                          _ □ X
C:\>Ntdsutil
Ntdsutil: Files
file maintenance: Integrity
Opening database [Current].
Executing Command: C:\WINDOWS\system32\esentutl.exe /g"C:\WINDOWS\NTDS\ntds.dit"
 /o

Initiating INTEGRITY mode...
        Database: C:\WINDOWS\NTDS\ntds.dit
  Temp. Database: TEMPINTEG560.EDB

Checking database integrity.

                Scanning Status (% complete)

     0    10   20   30   40   50   60   70   80   90  100
     !----!----!----!----!----!----!----!----!----!----!
     ...................................................

Integrity check successful.

Operation completed successfully in 3.438 seconds.

Spawned Process Exit code 0x0(0)

If integrity was successful, it is recommended
 you run semantic database analysis to ensure
 semantic database consistency as well.

file maintenance:
```

Figure 14-3   Performing an integrity check

Checking Database Integrity

While an integrity check looks at the Active Directory database file at a low level, a semantic check verifies the Active Directory database at a higher level. For example, a semantic check determines if every object has a GUID, distinguished name, and valid security descriptor. A semantic check also checks metadata, up-to-dateness vectors, and more. In Activity 14-3, you will perform a semantic check on your domain controller.

14

You must be in Directory Services Restore Mode to perform a semantic check.

NOTE

ACTIVITY

Activity 14-3: Performing a Semantic Check

Time Required: 20 minutes

Objective: Perform a semantic check of the Active Directory database.

Description: One of Super Corp's domain controller's UPS and power supply was hit by lightning when a severe storm passed through the area. While the server's UPS and power supply have been replaced, the IT manager would like you to check the Active Directory database on the damaged domain controller for any possible corruption. After having checked the low-level structure of the database, you will now perform a semantic check.

NOTE

If you intend to fix errors found by the semantic check, it is recommended that you first back up the directory. You already did this in Activity 14-1, so performing another backup is not necessary.

1. If necessary, restart your server in Directory Services Restore Mode.

2. If necessary, log on to your server using the **Administrator** account and the Directory Services Restore Mode password. The Directory Services Restore Mode password was set when you promoted your domain controller using DCPROMO and should be **Password01**.

3. A message box appears informing you that Windows is running in safe mode. Click **OK**.

4. Click **Start** and then click **Command Prompt**.

5. In the Command Prompt window, type **Ntdsutil** and then press **Enter**.

6. At the Ntdsutil prompt, type **Semantic database analysis** and then press **Enter**.

7. At the semantic checker prompt, type **Go** and then press **Enter**. Wait for the integrity check to complete, as shown in Figure 14-4. Note that your screen may appear slightly different, depending on whether inconsistencies were found.

```
Command Prompt - Ntdsutil                                              _ □ ×
Microsoft Windows [Version 5.2.3790]
(C) Copyright 1985-2003 Microsoft Corp.

C:\>Ntdsutil
Ntdsutil: Semantic database analysis
semantic checker: Go
Fixup mode is turned off
Opening database [Current].......Done.

Getting record count...3229 records
Getting security descriptor count...111 security descriptors

Writing summary into log file dsdit.dmp.0
SDs scanned:          111
Records scanned:     3229
Processing records..
Error: Inconsistent refcounts detected.
Done.

semantic checker: _
```

Figure 14-4   Performing a semantic check

8. Note the log file name. In Figure 14-4, the log file is shown as dsdit.dmp.0.

9. To view the log, click **Start** and then click **Command Prompt**.

10. Type **type *dsdit.dmp.0*** (where *dsdit.dmp.0* is the name of the file you noted in Step 8) and then press **Enter**. This displays the contents of the output log as shown in Figure 14-5. Note that your screen may appear slightly different, depending on whether inconsistencies were found.

```
c:\ Command Prompt                                          _|□|×|
Microsoft Windows [Version 5.2.3790]
(C) Copyright 1985-2003 Microsoft Corp.

C:\>type dsdit.dmp.0
Property Metadata vector missing for 2($ROOT_OBJECT$)
Summary:
Active Objects      3113
Phantoms               2
Deleted              114
RefCount mismatch for DNI 1462 [RefCount    6 References    5] [Not Fixed]
RefCount mismatch for DNI 3346 [RefCount    6 References    5] [Not Fixed]
Security descriptor summary:
SD count:            111
Total SD size before single-instancing:        1075 Kb
Total SD size after single-instancing:           108 Kb

C:\>
```

Figure 14-5   Log file generated by semantic check

TIP   You can also use Notepad or another text editor to view the log file.

11. Type **Exit** and then press **Enter**.

12. If the semantic check indicated inconsistencies exist, type **Go fixup** at the semantic checker prompt and then press **Enter**. Do not run this command unless inconsistencies were found. The Go fixup command attempts to repair any inconsistencies found. If you wish, use the type command or Notepad to view the new log file.

13. Type **Quit** and then press **Enter**.

14. Type **Quit** again and then press **Enter**.

15. Close the Command Prompt window.

16. Shut down your server if you do not intend to immediately continue to the next activity. Otherwise, stay logged on.

14

RECOVERING ACTIVE DIRECTORY

As you learned in Chapter 4, Active Directory uses a transactional database to store its data. When a domain controller restarts after a system failure, or after any sort of improper shutdown, any transactions that exist in the log file but not in the database file are written to the Active Directory database automatically as part of the startup process. This is called soft recovery and is performed without user intervention. If a domain controller crashes, a restart is often all that is required to fix problems with the Active Directory files.

On rare occasions, Active Directory can become corrupted, in which case restarting the system may not help. The corruption may be due to hardware or software problems, such as a bad hard disk controller, a faulty memory chip, a serious virus, or a corrupted system file.

The corruption may also have been the result of user error. In those cases, there are four options for recovering Active Directory:

- Perform soft recovery of the Active Directory database.
- Restore Active Directory from a backup.
- Reinstall Active Directory.
- Perform a repair of the Active Directory database.

NOTE

Although they sound similar, restore and recover have different meanings when talking about databases such as Active Directory. To **restore** the database means to replace the current copy (or part of it) with a backup copy. To **recover** the database means to repair it—to return it to a consistent state or to fix some sort of corruption. If you have to restore your database, the system performs some recovery and integrity checks as part of the restore process. However, you can sometimes recover the database without restoring it.

Soft Recovery

Although soft recovery is performed automatically when a domain controller is shut down incorrectly, you can also initiate soft recovery manually. If you are having problems with the directory database on one domain controller, manually performing soft recovery is a first step you may want to try. Windows Server 2003 includes a utility called Esentutl.exe, which you can use to recover or repair a damaged directory database. (Although Esentutl is a separate program, it is also used by NTDSUTIL.) In Activity 14-4, you will manually perform soft recovery using NTDSUTIL.

NOTE

You must be in Directory Services Restore Mode to manually perform soft recovery.

ACTIVITY

Activity 14-4: Using NTDSUTIL to Perform Soft Recovery

Time Required: 15 minutes

Objective: Manually perform soft recovery on the Active Directory database.

Description: Super Corp's Atlanta facility has been experiencing an unusually high number of power outages. During the last outage, a junior network administrator noticed that one of the domain controllers was connected to a faulty UPS. Instead of being supplied backup power by the UPS, the UPS failed and in turn the domain controller abruptly shut down. After replacing the UPS and starting the server, you receive an error that the Active Directory service could not start. To troubleshoot the issue, you decide to first manually perform soft recovery.

1. If necessary, restart your server in Directory Services Restore Mode.

2. If necessary, log on to your server using the **Administrator** account and the Directory Services Restore Mode password. The Directory Services Restore Mode password was set when you promoted your domain controller using DCPROMO and should be **Password01**.

3. A message box appears informing you that Windows is running in safe mode. Click **OK**.

4. Click **Start** and then click **Command Prompt**.

5. In the Command Prompt window, type **Ntdsutil** and then press **Enter**.

6. At the Ntdsutil prompt, type **Files** and then press **Enter**.

7. At the file maintenance prompt, type **Recover** and then press **Enter**. If soft recovery completed successfully, you should receive the message shown in Figure 14-6.

Figure 14-6   Manually performing soft recovery

8. Once soft recovery is completed, type **Quit** and then press **Enter**.

9. Type **Quit** again and then press **Enter**.

10. Close the Command Prompt window.

11. Shut down your server if you do not intend to immediately continue to the next activity. Otherwise, restart your server in normal mode.

Restoring Active Directory

If you cannot successfully recover a domain controller's directory database, the next step is to restore it from a recent backup. Additionally, restoring from a recent backup can be used when an object is deleted from the directory. There are two types of restore processes that you can perform: a **non–authoritative restore** or an **authoritative restore**.

Remember that a System State backup consists of more than just Active Directory. If you restore a System State backup, you will also restore the registry, system files, and so forth. This means if you add new hardware, make configuration changes in the operating system, or install new software after the backup was taken, you will have to reinstall or reconfigure the changes you made.

Non-authoritative Restore

A non-authoritative restore is used to restore a damaged Active Directory database from a good System State backup made before the database was corrupted. The older copy of the database will be restored to the domain controller. Any changes made after the backup was taken are then replicated from other Windows 2000 Server or Windows Server 2003 domain controllers during the next replication cycle. A non-authoritative restore is usually performed when there are multiple domain controllers in the domain and a single domain controller becomes corrupted. In Activity 14-5, you will learn how to perform non-authoritative as well as authoritative restores.

If you have only one domain controller in the domain, you will lose any changes made after the backup was created. This is one of the main reasons that most Active Directory installations have at least two domain controllers.

You cannot use a non-authoritative restore to restore a deleted object to Active Directory. When the deleted object is restored from the backup, its USN at the time of the deletion is also restored. Other domain controllers will have a newer USN for the deleted object and will replicate the tombstone information to the restored Active Directory database. To restore a deleted object, you must perform an authoritative restore, as discussed in the next section.

Authoritative Restore

An authoritative restore is a special restore performed on an Active Directory domain controller to restore objects that were mistakenly deleted or modified. It does this by incrementing the object's USN by 100,000 for each day between the time the backup was taken and restored. This ensures that the restored object's USN is the highest and will then be replicated to other domain controllers in the domain. If the USN was not incremented, the restored object would just be overwritten at the next replication cycle.

You use an authoritative restore to undo changes or deletions, as it overwrites any changes to Active Directory that were performed after the backup was made, no matter which domain controller processed those changes. The database is reset to the state it was in when the backup was made. You can choose to authoritatively restore the entire Active Directory database (with the exception of the schema) during an authoritative restore, or a selected part of it, such as one organizational unit or even one object. In Activity 14-5, you will learn how to perform non-authoritative as well as authoritative restores.

NOTE

Allowing the schema to be restored from backup could cause serious data consistency issues. Therefore, the schema cannot be marked as authoritative during an authoritative restore. The only way to restore the schema is to take the domain controllers for which you have backups offline, restore those domain controllers from backup, demote all remaining domain controllers for which you do not have backups, place the restored domain controllers back on the network, and then promote any domain controllers that you demoted. Note however that any changes to the directory made after the backups were taken will be lost.

TIP

If possible, you should manually initiate replication before restoring Active Directory. This prevents any recent changes made on the domain controller from being lost. While this is less important now that Windows Server 2003's intra-site replication notification interval is only 15 seconds, it's still a good practice. After initiating replication, you should check the Directory Service event log for any replication errors.

CAUTION

Both trusts and computer accounts automatically change the passwords used for secure communication on a regular basis. Depending on how much of the directory you authoritatively restore, you may need to reset trusts and/or computer accounts (due to the fact you are restoring an old password). You can use the Active Directory Domains and Trusts console to reset trust relationships. Similarly, you can use Active Directory Users and Computers or the NETDOM utility to reset computer accounts.

14

ACTIVITY

Activity 14-5: Performing Non-authoritative and Authoritative Restores

Time Required: 30 minutes

Objective: Learn how to perform non–authoritative and authoritative restores.

Description: A new network administrator from one of Super Corp's remote offices is temporarily at the Atlanta location for training. The IT manager has asked you to show the new administrator how to perform authoritative and non–authoritative restores. For demonstration purposes, you will first delete an old organizational unit to illustrate an accidental deletion.

CAUTION

Only one student per group should perform Activity 14-5 at a time. Before the second student starts Activity 14-5, ensure that the first student has finished all steps in Activity 14-5. It is also important that both domain controllers have a chance to fully replicate after the first student completes Activity 14-5. To ensure replication has occurred, manually initiate replication on both domain controllers and then wait a few minutes. Alternatively, your instructor may choose to have you and your partner work as a team, performing Activity 14-5 on only one of your servers.

1. If necessary, start your server and log on using the **Administrator** account in the **CHILD*XX*** domain (where *XX* is the number of the forest root domain for which your server is a domain controller) using the password **Password01**.

2. To illustrate the restore process, you start by deleting some objects. These steps are not required as part of the restore process, but are strictly for illustration. Click **Start**, select **Administrative Tools**, and then click **Active Directory Users and Computers**.

3. In the left tree pane, right-click **North America *XX*** (where *XX* is the number of your server) and then click **Delete**.

4. When prompted if you are sure you want to delete this object, click **Yes**.

5. When you are warned that the object is a container and contains other objects, click **Yes**.

6. Close Active Directory Users and Computers. The steps you have just performed are a common example of someone accidentally deleting something they should not have. You will now restore the directory database from a backup in order to recover the deleted objects.

7. Use Active Directory Sites and Services to manually initiate replication with your partner's server. If your partner is also performing these steps, wait for them to complete replication before continuing.

8. Restart your server in Directory Services Restore Mode.

9. Log on to your server using the **Administrator** account and the Directory Services Restore Mode password. The Directory Services Restore Mode password was set when you promoted your domain controller using DCPROMO and should be **Password01**.

10. A message box appears informing you that Windows is running in safe mode. Click **OK**.

11. Click **Start** and then click **Run**.

12. In the Run dialog box, type **Ntbackup** and then click **OK**. Note that you can also access the Backup Utility directly from the Start menu.

13. If the Backup or Restore Wizard appears, click the **Advanced Mode** link to open the Backup Utility window. Otherwise, continue with the next step.

14. In the Backup Utility window, click the **Restore and Manage Media** tab.

15. In the left tree, expand **File** and then expand **systemstate.bkf created *date at time*** (where *date at time* is the date and time you made the backup you want to restore).

TIP

If the backup you made is not listed, you can use the Catalog a backup file command on the Tools menu to catalog the backup.

16. In the left tree, click **System State** to show its contents in the right details pain.

17. In the left tree, check **System State**, as shown in Figure 14-7.

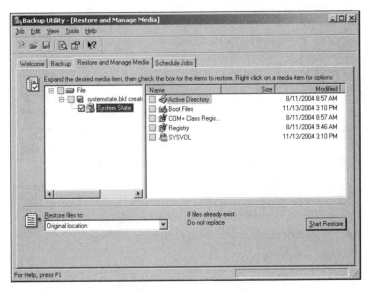

Figure 14-7   Restoring a System State backup

18. Ensure that the Restore files to drop-down list box is set to **Original location** and then click **Start Restore**.

19. A message box warns you that the current System State will be overwritten. Click **OK**.

20. In the Confirm Restore dialog box, click **Advanced**. Note the options that are selected by default.

NOTE

When you restore a domain controller from backup, FRS attempts to fully re-sync the SYSVOL data with another domain controller the next time the domain controller is restarted in normal mode. However, if there is only one domain controller in the domain, there is no other domain controller to replicate with and thus FRS never allows the domain controller to fully start. If you are restoring the only domain controller in a domain or the first of multiple domain controllers (that is, when a domain has multiple domain controllers and all of a domain's domain controllers need to be restored from backup), you need to perform what is called a primary restore. To perform a primary restore, check the "When restoring replicated data sets, mark the restored data as the primary data for all replicas" option. What this does is instructs FRS not to perform the full re-sync after a domain controller has been restored from backup. Note that it is very important you only use this option when restoring the only or first domain controller in a domain—do not use this option if there are already domain controllers in the domain.

21. Click **Cancel** to discard any accidental changes.

22. In the Confirm Restore dialog box, click **OK**.

23. Once the restore process is complete, click **Close** on the Restore Progress dialog box. Click **No** when prompted if you want to restart now.

24. Close the Backup Utility.

NOTE   At this point, if you were performing a non-authoritative restore, you would simply restart the server in normal mode. Restarting at this point allows all changes from other domain controllers to update the domain controller that was just restored. However, to restore deleted objects, you must perform an authoritative restore. You must perform the following steps (before restarting the server in normal mode) to complete the authoritative restore process.

25. Click **Start** and then click **Command Prompt**.

26. Type **Ntdsutil** and then press **Enter**.

27. Type **Authoritative restore** and then press **Enter**.

28. Type **Restore Subtree "OU=North America XX,DC=childZZ,DC=supercorp,DC=net"** (where *XX* is the number of your server and *ZZ* is the number of the forest root domain for which your server is a domain controller), all on one line, and then press **Enter**.

29. When prompted if you are sure you want to perform this Authoritative Restore, click **Yes**. The authoritative restore is then performed, as shown in Figure 14-8.

```
Command Prompt - Ntdsutil                                    _ □ ×
C:\>Ntdsutil
Ntdsutil: Authoritative restore
authoritative restore: Restore Subtree "OU=North America 01,DC=child01,DC=superc
orp,DC=net"

Opening DIT database... Done.

The current time is 11-13-04 17:13.42.
Most recent database update occured at 11-06-04 10:30.31.
Increasing attribute version numbers by 800000.

Counting records that need updating...
Records found: 0000000023
Done.

Found 23 records to update.

Updating records...
Records remaining: 0000000000
Done.

Successfully updated 23 records.

Authoritative Restore completed successfully.
authoritative restore: _
```

Figure 14-8   Using Ntdsutil to mark objects as authoritative

30. Type **Quit** and then press **Enter**.

31. Type **Quit** again and then press **Enter**.

32. Close the Command Prompt window.

33. Restart your server in normal mode.

34. Use Active Directory Users and Computers to confirm that the previously deleted objects appear. If you wish, you can also use Active Directory Sites and Services to manually initiate replication with your partner's server and then confirm that the restored objects still exist.

35. Close all open windows and shut down your server.

Authoritatively Restoring SYSVOL

Although you can use Ntdsutil to authoritatively restore Active Directory objects, you may also need to authoritatively restore files in SYSVOL. For example, you may need to restore a previous version of a group policy object—part of which is stored as a group policy template in SYSVOL. As another example, you may need to restore the previous version of a logon script.

When you restore a System State backup, the domain controller's local SYSVOL folder is overwritten. However, the next time the domain controller restarts in normal mode, FRS attempts to perform a full re-sync of the SYSVOL folder (assuming the When restoring replicated data sets, mark the restored data as the primary data for all replicas option was not selected during the restore). When a full re-sync occurs, FRS moves all the existing files and folders inside the SYSVOL*domainname* folder into a folder named NtFrs_PreExisting__ See_EventLog. FRS then pulls a new copy of the domain's SYSVOL files and folders from another domain controller in the domain.

In order to use the older version of a SYSVOL file or folder from a System State backup, you must perform a few additional steps. (1) First, start by authoritatively restoring any necessary Active Directory objects as described in Activity 14-5. For example, this would include the group policy container for any group policy objects (which are located in the CN=Policies,CN=Systems,*DC=domainname*... container) you want to restore. Once you have restarted the domain controller in normal mode, allow FRS to fully replicate SYSVOL (you can tell when this is done by looking for an event in the FRS event log indicating the process was completed). (2) Next, open the Restore and Manage Media tab of the Backup Utility. From the Restore and Manage Media tab, select the System State backup you want to restore. Then, in the Restore files to drop-down list box (which is visible at the bottom of Figure 14-7), select the Alternate location option, specify an alternate location to restore the files such as C:\\sstemp, and then start the restore process. Once the restore process has completed, copy the file(s) you want to authoritatively restore from the alternate restore location to the actual SYSVOL folder.

14

NOTE In the preceding paragraph, you only have to perform the first set of steps (1) if there are actually Active Directory Objects that need to be restored. For example, if you only need to restore an older version of a logon script, you only need to perform the second half of the preceding steps (2). In contrast, a GPO is made up of both files and folders in SYSVOL and Active Directory objects, so you must perform both sets of steps.

By copying the files from the alternate location to the actual SYSVOL folder, the files' modification date is changed to the current date and time. Thus, the next time SYSVOL replication occurs; the files copied from the alternate location to the actual SYSVOL folder will have the most recent modification date and will be replicated to all other domain controllers.

Reinstalling Active Directory

Another option for fixing Active Directory corruption is reinstalling Active Directory if you do not have a backup. This is only a valid option if there is at least one other domain controller that can supply the current contents of Active Directory by replication, or if you are willing to completely rebuild your domain. There are two, and possibly three, steps involved in reinstalling Active Directory. The first is to run DCPROMO to demote the domain controller with the corrupt database to a member server. If you are unable to demote the domain controller by just running DCPROMO, you need to forcibly demote the domain controller and then clean up the server's metadata in Active Directory. Finally, run DCPROMO again to promote the server to a domain controller.

TIP For more information on forcibly demoting a domain controller and cleaning up the server's metadata in the Directory, see knowledge base articles 332199 and 216498 at *support.microsoft.com*.

Repairing Active Directory

If you do not have a second domain controller to replicate a current copy of the Active Directory database or a current backup, one final option available is performing a repair of the database. In Active Directory terminology, repair has a specific meaning. A repair performs a low-level rebuild of the Active Directory database and deletes any data that is not valid (that is, data that cannot be correctly read). The repair command can only fix data that it can find; data that is missing or incomplete cannot be repaired.

CAUTION Practice extreme caution when using the repair option. The repair option does not apply any recent changes from the transaction logs. Additionally, a repair of the database could result in major data loss. You should only perform a repair as a last resort.

To perform the repair operation, start by restarting the server in Directory Services Restore Mode. At the command prompt, start the NTDSUTIL tool by typing NTDSUTIL and then press enter. Once at the NTDSUTIL prompt, type FILES, press enter, type REPAIR, and then press enter. After the repair process is complete, you should perform a semantic integrity check as described earlier. Restart the server when finished.

CREATING A DISASTER RECOVERY PLAN

Because Active Directory has built-in fault tolerance (because multiple copies of the directory exist), creating a disaster recovery plan is a little different for Active Directory than a file or database server. While the plan contains the same type of general information, the backup strategy you use may be quite different. In this section, you will learn what needs to be backed up, when backups should be performed, where backups should be stored, and finally how to create and implement a disaster recovery plan.

Determining What to Back Up

The goal when determining what to back up is to back up every directory partition that exists in the forest. Now, this does not mean that every *copy* of a given partition must be backed up. What you must have, at a minimum, is one copy of the schema partition, one copy of the configuration partition, one copy of the domain partition for each domain, and one copy of each application partition in the forest.

In Windows 2000 Server, a backup of a single domain controller from each domain covered all the necessary partitions. However, new application partitions in Windows Server 2003 may require that additional domain controllers be backed up. For example, to have a backup of the ForestDnsZones application partition, you must back up at least one domain controller in the forest that is also a Windows Server 2003 DNS server. Similarly, to have a backup of the DomainDnsZones application partition for each domain, you must back up at least one domain controller in each domain that is also a Windows Server 2003 DNS server. You still may only need to back up one domain controller for each domain; however, you should make sure that the domain controller contains all the required application partitions.

Something to notice is that you do not have to back up every domain controller in the forest. At a minimum, one copy of each partition is sufficient to restore the directory in the event of a disaster. This raises some questions, however; such as, what domain controller should be the one that gets backed up in each domain? Or, are there instances when backing up multiple domain controllers is preferable?

To answer the first question, the optimal domain controller to back up is one that is centrally located on the network. Because updates from remote sites propagate to the central part of the network before being sent to other remote sites, the central part of the network is most likely to have the most current updates. However, if possible, you should avoid selecting an FSMO role holder to be the only domain controller that is backed up (that is, if you only

14

back up a single domain controller). For example, if an object is deleted from the directory, you must take the domain controller offline in order to restore the directory on that server. While having to take an FSMO role holder offline temporarily is not the end of the world, it could cause network interruptions. Additionally, there is the potential for data loss if an FSMO role holder does not have a chance to replicate recent changes to one of its replication partners before it is restored.

TIP   Remember that a global catalog server contains a partial copy of every object in the forest. Because of this, backups of global catalog servers are typically larger and take longer to make. In a large, multi-domain forest, you can speed up the time it takes to back up and reduce the size of backups by avoiding global catalog servers. Be aware, however, if you ever need to rebuild a global catalog server, the data needs to be replicated from another global catalog server or from a domain controller in each domain.

As for the second question, one domain controller is only a minimum. For a small directory that is less than 50 MB (although in this case, most of the backup's size will be made up of other items that are part of the System State backup) and only has three domain controllers, backing up all three domain controllers makes sense. The directory is so small and there are so few domain controllers, the extra backup time is negligible. If any of the domain controllers become corrupted, performing a nonauthoritative restore is much faster than having to rebuild the domain controller from scratch. Plus, in the event one of the backups fails, there is another backup available.

On the other hand, in a large multi-domain forest with thousands of objects, dozens of domain controllers, and a directory of several gigabytes for each domain, backing up each domain controller is not practical. It is still a good idea to make a backup of two domain controllers in the event one backup does not work correctly, but any more than two is not absolutely required.

One other issue to take into consideration is convenience. In most cases, the reason for restoring a domain controller is the result of having to recover a deleted object. If the only backups of the network are from a single site, administrators in other sites that need to restore deleted objects have to contact the site with the backups in order to get something restored. Instead, by backing up a server in each major site, administrators can use the backup taken from their own site to restore a local server and in turn restore the deleted objects. In addition, by making the backups at different sites, if one site is destroyed by a natural disaster, the second site still has backups of everything.

NOTE   These guidelines assume the server is only a domain controller. If the domain controller is also providing other services that require backups, you must also consider those services.

Determining When to Back Up

Determining when to back up depends on the environment, but there are some general rules that you should follow. First, you should manually back up the directory after any major event. For example, adding a new domain to the forest or creating a large number of user accounts are examples of major events. Major events also include when a domain controller's hardware or software configuration changes. Basically, a major event includes anything that would take you a substantial amount of time to redo in the event something goes wrong.

In addition to backing up after major events, it is important to back up on a regular schedule. For most directories, this means backing up once every evening. Backing up every evening is a good compromise between the potential for lost data and the resources needed to make the backup. In the worst possible case scenario (that is, all domain controllers are destroyed), only one day of work is lost. In a small number of circumstances, this rule of thumb may require tweaking—such as when a custom application uses Active Directory as its store, and makes a large number of changes throughout the day.

Once you have decided the number of times to back up, you must decide at what time of the day to back up. Again, in the vast majority of situations, backups are taken sometime in the evening or night after most or all users are gone. When selecting the exact time, you should keep the replication schedule of your network in mind. For example, if you have two sites that replicate at 6:00 p.m., the best solution is to schedule a backup sometime after 6:30 (or even later if the link is extremely slow). By backing up after replication occurs, the backup will contain the latest updates from both sites.

14

Determining Where to Back Up

After determining what domain controllers to back up and when to back up, you must now decide to where you should back up. The two major options available are to back up to a file on a hard drive (either in the same or another server) or to back up to removable media such as a tape. Looking at each option's weaknesses and strengths, each lends themselves to specific scenarios. The major benefit of a file backup to a hard drive is speed. In most cases, a hard drive is going to be much faster than any removable media (unless you use a removable hard drive as your media, of course). Additionally, file backups are typically always online and a few clicks away. The down side to hard drive backups is they are susceptible to data loss just like the rest of the directory files. A virus or natural disaster could take the hard drive backups out just as easily as it could the Active Directory database itself.

Backing up to media, on the other hand, is just about an exact opposite of a hard drive backup. By backing up to media, you can store your backups off site. Additionally, backups made to media are typically removed from the network shortly after they are made, reducing the chance the backup could be destroyed by a virus. The downside to media backups is they are typically slower. This may not be an issue with smaller directories, but it can be with larger ones. Another downside to media backups is they may not always be quickly available. Because media backups can be stored offsite, someone may have to go retrieve the media if it is ever needed.

A third solution is to combine hard drive and removable media backups. First, back up the file to the hard drive. This allows for quick access to the file in the event it must be restored. Next, make a backup copy of the backup file onto removable media. Now you have a copy of the backup that can be stored offsite for safe keeping.

CAUTION

If someone has access to your tapes, you might as well give them access to your server. Keep all backups stored on removable media secure at all times.

Creating and Testing the Plan

Having decided how often to back up, where to back up, and where to store the backups, what's left in a disaster recovery plan? Quite a lot, but most of it is highly dependent on your environment. The first step is to document, document, and document. Get a folder and dedicate it to your disaster recovery plan. Here are some things that you should include in your plan:

- Server hardware specifications
- Network layout
- Active Directory physical layout
- Active Directory logical layout
- Server software configurations
- Active Directory file layout (store and log file locations)
- Label your removable media and include a backup and rotation description.

The next step is to start thinking about, and write down, what should happen if a failure occurs. Keep in mind when you start to write out the plan, you should assume that you are not on-site and are unable to come to the rescue. You should also assume that the person restoring the server does have technical knowledge about Active Directory, but knows nothing about your particular setup. Think about such things as:

- Who should be contacted if something goes wrong?
- Where are the backups stored?
- Where are the software and driver disks stored?
- Are there any tech support numbers available?
- If new hardware is required, what should be done?
- Is there any other information that may be useful?

Once you have completed documenting what should happen if a disaster occurs, there is one final step that you must complete: testing your plan. Having a plan is not enough; you have to test to see if your plan has all the necessary information, if your backups work correctly, and if everyone knows what to do. In order to do this, you should set up a fake disaster. Now, don't go lighting your servers on fire (everyone knows how tempting that can be sometimes!), but use some extra hardware to test your plan. Don't worry about getting exactly the same hardware setup; you need just enough to run the services and any client applications. When testing, you should follow your disaster recovery plan and see if all the information is available in the plan. If you left anything out, or something was wrong, now is the time to make corrections and additions. By using the test hardware, you not only get a feel for what information needs to be in your plan, but you are also able to test your backups by restoring Active Directory from backup.

CHAPTER SUMMARY

- Although Active Directory has built-in fault tolerance when multiple domain controllers are used, it is still important to back up the directory. Backups are required to restore deleted objects, restore the directory in the event of a major disaster where all domain controllers are lost, and restore the directory in the extremely rare event that the entire directory becomes corrupted.

- Active Directory is backed up as part of the System State on a domain controller. The Active Directory database can be backed up while it's online.

- The Backup Utility included with Windows Server 2003 is unable to back up the System State of a remote server. Additionally, the Backup Utility must back up all components of the System State at once—you cannot back up individual items of the System State independently. Third-party utilities are available, however, that do allow these two types of operations.

- You cannot restore backups that are older than the tombstone lifetime due to data consistency issues. By default, the tombstone lifetime is 60 days, which means you can restore backups up to 60 days from the date the backup was taken.

- To check the Active Directory file integrity, you can perform a low-level integrity check. To check the Active Directory database integrity, you can perform a higher-level semantic check. Both an integrity check and a semantic check require that you restart the domain controller in Directory Services Restore Mode.

- Soft recovery is automatically performed when a domain controller is shut down incorrectly, but you can also manually initiate it in Directory Services Restore Mode by using NTDSUTIL.

- When a non-authoritative restore of Active Directory is performed, the restored data is overwritten with newer changes from other domain controllers. Non-authoritative restores are used to replace a corrupted database on a domain controller, not changed or deleted objects in Active Directory.

14

❏ An authoritative restore overwrites objects on other domain controllers. This is used to replace accidentally deleted or corrupted objects and is accomplished by incrementing the objects' USNs by 100,000 for each day between the backup and restore dates.

❏ If more than one domain controller exists in a domain, reinstalling Active Directory (on the effected domain controller) is a possible solution in the event a domain controller becomes corrupted. If a domain only has one domain controller, reinstalling Active Directory requires the directory manually be rebuilt.

❏ Repairing the Active Directory database is a final solution in the event a second domain controller is not available from which to replicate changes and no current backups exist. Data loss is possible when performing a repair operation, so it should only be used as a last resort.

KEY TERMS

authoritative restore — An Active Directory restore that allows you to restore deleted or modified objects and have those changes replicated to other domain controllers in the domain.

Backup Utility — The tool included with Windows Server 2003 used to back up and restore files and System State information.

differential backup — A backup type that only backs up those files that have changed since the last normal or incremental backup took place, but does not clear the archive attribute associated with those files.

incremental backup — A backup type that only backs up those files that have changed since the last normal or incremental backup took place, and clears the archive attribute associated with those files.

least privilege — The concept that users are only given the permissions they need to do their jobs and nothing more.

Non-authoritative restore — A restore of Active Directory used to restore a damaged database. Updates made after the backup was taken are replicated from other domain controllers in the domain.

normal backup — A backup type that backs up all selected files and folders, and clears the archive attribute on these files and folders.

recover — To repair a database; to return it to a consistent state; to fix corruption therein.

restore — To replace the current copy of a database (or part of it) with a back-up copy made previously.

System State — A group of critical operating system files and components that can be backed up as a single group on a Windows Server 2003 system. System State data always includes the Registry, COM+ Registration database, boot files, and system files. On a domain controller, it also includes Active Directory and the SYSVOL directory. Other components that are included (assuming their associated services are installed) are the Certificate Services database, the Cluster Service, and the IIS Metadirectory.

REVIEW QUESTIONS

1. Which of the following actions could you perform to restore a deleted Active Directory object?

    a. a non–authoritative restore

    b. an authoritative restore

    c. soft recovery

    d. Use the undelete feature of Active Directory Users and Computers.

2. Which of the following is not backed up as part of the System State?

    a. registry

    b. SYSVOL

    c. user's home folders

    d. system files

3. Which type of check examines the directory database at a low level?

    a. data check

    b. integrity check

    c. semantic check

    d. security check

4. When performing an authoritative restore, the restored objects' USNs are incremented by which of the following for each day between the date the backup was taken and the date it is restored?

    a. 1

    b. 10

    c. 1000

    d. 100,000

5. To use the new install from media feature, which of the following must you do?

    a. Use the CVSDE utility to export Active Directory.

    b. Use the LDIFDE utility to export Active Directory.

    c. Create a System State backup of an existing domain controller.

    d. Create a .dit file using the Install From Media Export Wizard.

6. A low-level rebuild of the Active Directory database is called which of the following?

    a. repair

    b. soft recovery

    c. hard recovery

    d. defragmentation

14

7. Which type of check examines the directory database, ensuring that every object has a valid security descriptor?

   a. data check

   b. integrity check

   c. semantic check

   d. security check

8. The Backup Utility included with Windows Server 2003 can back up the System State of another server remotely. True or False?

9. Which of the following commands would you use when promoting a domain controller using the install from media feature?

   a. DCPROMO /m

   b. DCPROMO /m:C:\backupfilename.bak

   c. DCPROMO /media:C:\backupfilename.bak

   d. DCPROMO /adv

10. You can't restore a backup that is older than the _____ lifetime.

11. At an absolute minimum, you should back up which of the following?

    a. at least one domain controller per site

    b. at least one domain controller per domain

    c. at least one domain controller per forest

    d. every domain controller in the forest

12. The Backup Utility included with Windows Server 2003 is unable to back up the individual components of the System State independently. True or False?

13. System State backups are always made using which of the following methods?

    a. normal backup

    b. differential backup

    c. incremental backup

    d. copy backup

14. Which of the following naming contexts cannot be authoritatively restored?

    a. domain

    b. configuration

    c. schema

    d. application

15. You must be in Directory Services Restore Mode to back up the Active Directory database. True or False?

16. Assuming that replication occurs at 9:00 p.m. every evening between two sites, what time would be the best to schedule a backup?

    a. 8:00 p.m.

    b. 8:30 p.m.

    c. 9:00 p.m.

    d. 9:30 p.m.

17. Which of the following operations should you only perform as a last resort?

    a. a soft recovery of the Active Directory database

    b. a repair of the Active Directory database

    c. a restore of the Active Directory database

    d. a reinstallation of the Active Directory database

18. If resources are available to only back up one domain controller per domain, which of the following domain controllers would be the best choice to back up?

    a. a domain controller located centrally on the network

    b. a domain controller located in the same site as the schema master

    c. a domain controller located in the same site as the domain naming master

    d. the RID master for the domain

19. Which of the following utilities can you use to perform an authoritative restore?

    a. NETDOM

    b. NTDSUTIL

    c. DSMOD

    d. LDIFDE

14

20. If a domain has more than one domain controller for redundancy, it is not necessary to back up the domain. True or False?

CASE PROJECTS

CASE
PROJECTS

Case Project 14-1: Designing a Disaster Recovery Plan

Super Corp has asked you to create a disaster recovery plan that will allow the company to continue operating in the event of an IT disaster. The goal of the disaster recovery plan is to:

1. Ensure all domains can be restored from backup.

2. Ensure all application partitions used by the Windows Server 2003 DNS server are backed up.

3. Minimize the time it takes to restore a backup.

4. Minimize the size of backups.

5. Outline the steps you would take to ensure that these goals are met.

Case Project 14-2: Possibility of Data Loss

Super Corp began experiencing random power outages, causing a domain controller with a bad UPS to shut down unexpectedly. The staff is worried that changes they made to data in Active Directory will be lost the next time the power fails and the domain controller turns off unexpectedly.

What can you tell them regarding Active Directory to eliminate their fears?

A

Exam Objectives Tracking for MCSE Certification Exam #70-294: Planning, Implementing, and Maintaining a Microsoft Windows Server 2003 Active Directory Infrastructure

PLANNING AND IMPLEMENTING AN ACTIVE DIRECTORY INFRASTRUCTURE

Objective	Chapter: Section	Activity
Plan a strategy for placing global catalog servers. • Evaluate network traffic considerations when placing global catalog servers. • Evaluate the need to enable universal group caching.	Chapter 1: Introduction to Windows Server 2003 Active Directory Chapter 6: Planning and Designing the Physical Structure	Activity 6-6
Plan flexible operations master role placement. • Plan for business continuity of operations master roles. • Identify operations master role dependencies.	Chapter 8: Forest-wide Roles Chapter 8: Domain-wide Roles	Activity 8-1 Activity 8-2 Activity 8-3
Implement an Active Directory directory service forest and domain structure. • Create the forest root domain. • Create a child domain. • Create and configure Application Data Partitions. • Install and configure an Active Directory domain controller. • Set an Active Directory forest and domain functional level based on requirements. • Establish trust relationships. Types of trust relationships might include external trusts, shortcut trusts, and cross-forest trusts.	Chapter 1: Introduction to Windows Server 2003 Active Directory Chapter 5: Choosing a DNS Name for Active Directory Chapter 5: Designing Forests Chapter 5: Designing Domains Chapter 5: Understanding and Implementing Trust Relationships Chapter 5: Upgrading Windows NT or Windows 2000 Domains Chapter 13: Working with Application Directory Partitions	Activity 1-4 Activity 5-1 Activity 5-2 Activity 5-3 Activity 5-5 Activity 5-6 Activity 5-7 Activity 13-6 Activity 13-7 Activity 13-8

Objective	Chapter: Section	Activity
Implement an Active Directory site topology. • Configure site links. • Configure preferred bridgehead servers.	Chapter 1: Introduction to Windows Server 2003 Active Directory Chapter 6: Active Directory Physical Objects Chapter 6: Planning and Designing the Physical Structure Chapter 7: Determining Replication Topology Chapter 7: Controlling Replication Frequency	Activity 6-3 Activity 6-5 Activity 7-3 Activity 7-4
Plan an administrative delegation strategy. • Plan an organizational unit (OU) structure based on delegation requirements. • Plan a security group hierarchy based on delegation requirements.	Chapter 3: Ownership Roles Chapter 3: Making Active Directory Design Decisions Chapter 5: Designing Organizational Units Chapter 10: Planning and Administering Groups	Activity 3-2 Activity 3-3 Activity 3-5

MANAGING AND MAINTAINING AN ACTIVE DIRECTORY INFRASTRUCTURE

Objective	Chapter: Section	Activity
Manage an Active Directory forest and domain structure. • Manage trust relationships. • Manage schema modifications. • Add or remove a UPN suffix.	Chapter 4: Active Directory Schema Chapter 5: Understanding and Implementing Trust Relationships Chapter 10: Planning and Administering User Accounts	Activity 4-1 Activity 4-2 Activity 4-3 Activity 4-4 Activity 10-1
Manage an Active Directory site. • Configure replication schedules. • Configure site link costs. • Configure site boundaries.	Chapter 1: Introduction to Windows Server 2003 Active Directory Chapter 6: Active Directory Physical Objects Chapter 6: Planning and Designing the Physical Structure Chapter 7: Controlling Replication Frequency	Activity 6-1 Activity 6-2 Activity 6-4 Activity 6-5 Activity 7-4
Monitor Active Directory replication failures. Tools might include Replication Monitor, Event Viewer, and support tools. • Monitor Active Directory replication. • Monitor File Replication Service (FRS) replication.	Chapter 7: Identifying Data to Replicate Chapter 7: Monitoring and Troubleshooting Replication Chapter 7: SYSVOL	Activity 7-2 Activity 7-5
Restore Active Directory directory services. • Perform an authoritative restore operation. • Perform a nonauthoritative restore operation.	Chapter 14: Recovering Active Directory	Activity 14-5

A

Objective	Chapter: Section	Activity
Troubleshoot Active Directory. • Diagnose and resolve issues related to Active Directory replication. • Diagnose and resolve issues related to operations master role failure. • Diagnose and resolve issues related to the Active Directory database.	Chapter 4: Active Directory Physical Database Storage Chapter 7: Identifying Data to Replicate Chapter 7: Determining Replication Topology Chapter 7: Monitoring and Troubleshooting Replication Chapter 8: Transferring and Seizing Roles Chapter 14: Identifying Active Directory Corruption	Activity 7-5 Activity 8-4 Activity 8-5 Activity 14-2 Activity 14-3

PLANNING AND IMPLEMENTING USER, COMPUTER, AND GROUP STRATEGIES

Objective	Chapter: Section	Activity
Plan a security group strategy.	Chapter 10: Planning and Administering Groups	Activity 10-6 Activity 10-7
Plan a user authentication strategy. • Plan a smart card authentication strategy. • Create a password policy for domain users.	Chapter 9: Active Directory Authentication Chapter 11: Security Management with Group Policy	Activity 9-3 Activity 11-7

Objective	Chapter: Section	Activity
Plan an OU structure. • Analyze the administrative requirements for an OU. • Analyze the Group Policy requirements for an OU structure.	Chapter 3: Ownership Roles Chapter 3: Making Active Directory Design Decisions Chapter 5: Designing Organizational Units Chapter 10: Organizing Objects in the Directory	Activity 3-2 Activity 3-3 Activity 3-5
Implement an OU structure. • Create an OU. • Delegate permissions for an OU to a user or to a security group. • Move objects within an OU hierarchy.	Chapter 5: Designing Organizational Units Chapter 9: Active Directory Authorization Chapter 10: Organizing Objects in the Directory	Activity 5-4 Activity 9-4

PLANNING AND IMPLEMENTING GROUP POLICY

Objective	Chapter: Section	Activity
Plan Group Policy strategy. • Plan a Group Policy strategy by using Resultant Set of Policy (RSoP) Planning mode. • Plan a strategy for configuring the user environment by using Group Policy. • Plan a strategy for configuring the computer environment by using Group Policy.	Chapter 11: Group Policy Chapter 11: Group Policy Processing Chapter 12: Preparing Software Deployment	

Objective	Chapter: Section	Activity
Configure the user environment by using Group Policy. • Distribute software by using Group Policy. • Automatically enroll user certificates by using Group Policy. • Redirect folders by using Group Policy. • Configure user security settings by using Group Policy.	Chapter 11: Desktop Management with Group Policy Chapter 11: Security Management with Group Policy Chapter 12: Configuring Software Deployment	Activity 11-1 Activity 11-2 Activity 11-3 Activity 11-4 Activity 11-5 Activity 11-6 Activity 12-2 Activity 12-4
Deploy a computer environment by using Group Policy. • Distribute software by using Group Policy. • Automatically enroll computer certificates by using Group Policy. • Configure computer security settings by using Group Policy.	Chapter 11: Desktop Management with Group Policy Chapter 11: Security Management with Group Policy Chapter 12: Configuring Software Deployment	Activity 11-1 Activity 11-2 Activity 11-3 Activity 11-4 Activity 11-5 Activity 11-8 Activity 11-9

Managing and Maintaining Group Policy

Objective	Chapter: Section	Activity
Troubleshoot issues related to Group Policy application deployment. Tools might include RSoP and the gpresult command.	Chapter 11: Troubleshooting Group Policy Chapter 12: Troubleshooting Software Deployment	Activity 11-11
Maintain installed software by using Group Policy. • Distribute updates to software distributed by Group Policy. • Configure automatic updates for network clients by using Group Policy.	Chapter 12: Maintaining Deployed Software	Activity 12-5 Activity 12-6
Troubleshoot the application of Group Policy security settings. Tools might include RSoP and the gpresult command.	Chapter 11: Troubleshooting Group Policy	Activity 11-11

B

DETAILED LAB SETUP GUIDE

HARDWARE

Classroom PCs should be configured as follows:

- Pentium 233 MHz processor or faster
- At least 128 MBs of random access memory (RAM)
- At least 1.5 GBs of available hard disk space
- CD-RW or DVD-RW drive
- Keyboard and mouse or some other compatible pointing device
- Video adapter and monitor with Super VGA (800 × 600) or higher resolution
- Sound card for the Instructor PC
- Self-powered/amplified speakers for the Instructor PC
- Internal or external fax/modem
- Two Ethernet network interface controllers per PC
- 3.5-inch floppy disk drive
- An Ethernet hub or switch with at least as many ports as there are PCs in the classroom
- One twisted-pair Category 5 straight-through cable per PC

Other equipment that may be needed:

- An additional Instructor PC that will be used as an additional domain controller
- A generic printer
- A crossover cable for each PC

Consumable items that students should bring to class:

- Five blank CD-R disks
- Five blank 3.5-inch disks

SOFTWARE

The following software is needed:

- Microsoft Windows Server 2003 Enterprise Edition operating system (1 CD media per student)
- Adobe Acrobat Reader (version 4 or greater)
- Microsoft Virtual PC (*www.microsoft.com/windows/virtualpc*) (optional)
- The latest Windows Server 2003 service pack (if available) (optional)

SETUP INSTRUCTIONS

To work on the Activities and Case Projects in this book, students need to have administrative privileges over their respective PCs. In a classroom setting, students should have the freedom to make administrative-level configuration errors. Normally such errors can render a PC unbootable or otherwise unusable for participation in the classroom. However, a student's mistakes should never impede completion of lab assignments. In this light, the lab should have a data recovery system and working backups that are both easy to use and reliable.

Ensure that all hardware used in the classroom is compatible with Windows Server 2003. To do this, it may be necessary to perform a test installation. Once the installation process is complete, use Device Manager to ensure that all devices are functioning correctly and that the appropriate drivers are installed. If a device has a driver that is not functioning, it may be necessary to go to the manufacturer's Web site and see if there is a device for Windows Server 2003.

The instructor computer should be set up as a domain controller for the supercorp.net domain. The domain administrator password should be set to Password01. The instructor computer should also run Network Address Translation (NAT) to provide student computers with access to the Internet. A good practice would be to label the two network connections as Classroom and External for whichever network they are plugged into. Each student will need to have a user account created in Active Directory with a name of AdminXX (where XX is the server number of their server). The password for the student accounts should also be Password01. Students will be creating child domains to the instructor's forest root domain using ChildXX (where XX is the server number of their server) as the name of their domain.

Because students will have administrative control of their computers, you may need to perform data recovery if a student cannot recover from a configuration change. The most straightforward method of data recovery is the reinstallation of the operating system from the Microsoft factory CDs. However, having to reinstall the operating system from the factory CD every time a student corrupts his or her system can prove to be time consuming and frustrating. There are no activities in the book that go over a Windows Server 2003 install. This leaves some flexibility for the instructor to decide on how the students should install Windows Server 2003. Therefore, to ensure rapid and reliable data recovery, consider the following guidelines when setting up the lab:

- Microsoft's Virtual PC provides quick access to an operating system from a previous state. The ability to use undoable disks will give students the opportunity to restore their computers to the state before the lab. Students will have to Save State in Virtual PC after each successful lab. Virtual PC is very resource intensive and the student computers should exceed the hardware requirements previously stated if used.

- If using an imaging product, such as Norton Ghost, a single image file that contains all of the data stored on the reference installation is created. This image file even contains the partition table of the hard disk drive, along with the master boot record. Restoring data from such an image will bring the machine back to its original state at the time the backup was created.

- When creating a reference image file, it is important to remember that the image file will be an exact copy of the reference PC's hard disk drive. This means that data such as Network Basic Input/Output System (NetBIOS) computer names and security identifiers (SIDs) will be preserved as they were on the reference PC. This also means that unless further steps are taken, all PCs that are imaged from this reference image will have the *same* NetBIOS computer name, SID, and perhaps even Internet Protocol (IP) address (if the IP addresses are set up statically). However, you do *not* want a classroom where all the PCs have the same NetBIOS name or IP address. You may be able to get away with all the SIDs being the same for a while, but this should not be a permanent state. You especially do not want identical SIDs in an environment that employs the use Active Directory domains.

- In order to make a classroom of uniquely identifiable PCs, utilities such as Microsoft's SysPrep, Norton Ghost Walker, or REMBO Toolkit (the NTChange-Name command) may be executed on each PC. The easiest to use is Ghost Walker; it is an MS-DOS program that not only changes the NetBIOS computer name but also creates a randomly generated SID in one easy step. If you don't feel the need to change the SID, you can manually change the NetBIOS name by simply right-clicking the My Computer icon, clicking Properties, clicking the Computer Name tab, clicking the Change button, and typing the desired NetBIOS computer name in the Computer name field. Click OK when finished.

Keep the following in mind if imaging or Virtual PC is not available:

- The instructor needs to decide on the following key points and make them available to all students during their installs:

  - Computer naming convention

  - IP addressing (default gateways, Domain Name System (DNS), and Windows Internet Naming Service (WINS), if necessary)

  - Workgroup/domain names

- Students should install Windows Server 2003 Enterprise Edition from the CD

EXPANDED CHAPTER SUMMARIES

CHAPTER 1 SUMMARY

Windows Server 2003 is a network operating system (NOS). Active Directory is one of the core services that Windows Server 2003 provides. Active Directory is a directory service, which is a service used to catalog information on the network. This allows users to easily find information such as e-mail addresses, phone numbers, and network resources.

The most important step in the deployment of Active Directory is the initial step, which is planning. Failure to appropriately plan the installation can quickly result in disaster. Active Directory maintenance is the most routine task for an administrator. This includes regularly monitoring Active Directory to prevent performance degradation.

Active Directory enhances security because it requires authentication; to access the network, users must identify themselves. Group Policy, a feature of Active Directory, grants administrators the ability to control many aspects of the end-user experience, including password policies, desktop configuration, and communication standards.

Active Directory is not the only administrative model supported. Windows Server 2003 supports workgroups as well. This is a logical group of computers and is ideally limited to fewer than 10 hosts on the network. A limit is suggested because the workgroup's decentralized management model works best with a smaller number of network hosts.

Domains are included with Active Directory, and they permit centralized management with a centralized security database. In addition, within Active Directory, servers act as domain controllers. Last, note that member servers are computers that run Windows Server 2003 and that belong to a domain.

Active Directory consists of many parts. The items stored in Active Directory are objects. These can include printers, user accounts, and computers. The logical structure of Active Directory includes domains and organizational units (OUs), which are used to group objects such as user accounts and printers. A group of domains with a contiguous namespace is called a tree. A group of trees with a common root domain is a forest. The domains in a forest do not have a contiguous namespace, unlike the domains of a tree, which all have a contiguous namespace.

In Active Directory, the creation of a child domain creates a trust. A trust is a two-way transitive relationship between the child and parent domains. Adding a tree to a forest also creates a trust between the forest root domain and the root domain of the new tree.

Active Directory relies on a standard protocol for communication. That protocol is Lightweight Directory Access Protocol (LDAP). LDAP uses a naming path, which has two main parts: the distinguished name (DN) and the relative distinguished name (RDN). The DN is a unique name for the object in Active Directory. The RDN is a portion of the DN that is a unique identifier for an object in a specified container.

The physical component of Active Directory is called a site. A site is used to control replication and is defined by the administrator. It is a group of well-connected computers. Computers are well-connected when they have a connection speed of 10 Mbps or faster.

A Global Catalog is an index, or replica, of the information in Active Directory. Global Catalogs are consulted during user searches for data and objects in Active Directory. They allow users to locate information, as well as provide universal group membership information. Global catalogs also provide authentication services for users in another domain. Certain applications that are Active Directory-aware, such as Exchange 2000 and 2003, also query the global catalog for information.

Windows Server 2003 also provides new features in Active Directory that were not implemented in Windows 2000. Active Directory has been improved to be easier to deploy and manage in large enterprises. Tools such as the Active Directory Migration Tool (ADMT) 2.0, have been improved to make migration to Windows 2003 easier. Domains can also now be renamed, and the schema can be modified more easily than in Windows 2000. These capabilities give administrators more options and flexibility in managing their environment.

Security has also been improved. Windows Server 2003 includes a stronger default configuration. Administrators also have a new tool, the Credential Manager, to aid in managing user authentication and user credentials. Software restriction policies have been added to control the software that is allowed to run on a computer as well.

Finally, performance and dependability have been enhanced. Features such as Universal group caching allows branch offices to have quicker authentication, and they generate less traffic over wide area network (WAN) links. Application directory partitions allow the fine-grained control of Active Directory data. Finally, Active Directory data can be replicated to newly installed domain controllers through a copy on media, which saves network bandwidth and can speed up the process.

CHAPTER 2 SUMMARY

Information travels through the Internet and Transmission Control Protocol/Internet Protocol (TCP/IP) with Internet Protocol (IP) addresses as destinations; however, IP addresses are easy for computers—not people—to remember. Fortunately, a DNS server can resolve IP addresses to domain names.

A NetBIOS name is a 16-character long name. The first 15 characters can be specified, and the last character is reserved as an identifier. The characters are not case sensitive.

Hosts can use broadcasts for NetBIOS name resolution. In addition, Windows Internet Naming Service (WINS) can also supply name resolution services. When queried for a NetBIOS name, WINS servers will respond with an IP address.

Unlike WINS, which resolves NetBIOS names, DNS works in a hierarchical system and resolves fully qualified domain names (FQDNs) to IP addresses. Because it's hierarchical, the load of resolution can be deployed to multiple servers.

An FQDN has two parts: the hostname, such as www or server01, and the domain suffix, such as Microsoft.com or supercorp.net. The DNS server contains a record for a specific hostname and the corresponding IP address.

The root of the hierarchy is the root domain, represented by a single period (.). In the FQDN *www.microsoft.com.*, the rightmost period represents the root domain. The next level of the hierarchy is the top-level domain (TLD). In our example, that is the *com* portion of the domain name.

TLDs can represent a country, as in .us for the United States and .ca for Canada. These are country code TLDs (ccTLDs). Other TLDs are not country specific. The most familiar ones include .com, .net, .org, .edu, .gov, and .mil. Newer TLDs include .name, .info, and .biz.

Records for DNS resolution can be broken down into several different types. The basic record is the address (A) record, which maps a host name to a specific host. Other Resource Records (RRs) exist. These include mail exchanger (MX) records, name server (NS) records, and start of authority (SOA) records.

All records are stored in a zone, which is a text file or database of records that is typically for a specific subdomain. A DNS server with information regarding a specific zone is called an authoritative server for that subdomain. When information is kept on separate servers for the same zone, one server is the primary server and another server is the secondary server. The transferring of zone information is a zone transfer. To be more efficient, servers can send only the new or changed information. This is known as an incremental zone transfer.

The DNS name resolution process takes place as a DNS client queries a DNS server to find the mapping of IP address to host name. There are two types of queries that may be carried out during this process: the recursive query and the iterative query. The recursive query has the DNS server that was contacted by the client. This server contacts other DNS servers to resolve the host name for the client. An iterative query has the client contact the respective appropriate DNS servers.

Resource record errors are incorrect pieces of information stored in a resource record. Fortunately, with graphical tools and modern software, these are infrequent. Delegation errors, which are defined as errors in delegating authority between DNS servers, can be avoided with careful planning. Weak authority errors result when a machine is supposed to be authoritative but isn't, or vice versa.

An FQDN is made up of a host name and a suffix. For instance, *www.microsoft.com* consists of the hostname www and the suffix microsoft.com. A DNS server's role is to resolve the FQDN to an IP address for the client.

DNS is a required service for Active Directory. With older Windows NT 4.0 networks, DNS was not a required service. Note also that Microsoft relies solely on DNS starting with Windows 2000 for DNS name resolution.

Active Directory uses the same hierarchical naming structure as DNS. Locating services and resources in Active Directory relies on a new type of resource record, called a service locator (SRV) record. This record allows a client to look for a computer, such as a domain controller or primary domain controller (PDC) emulator, that provides a specific service. A client also uses the records to find Global Catalog servers and to start the Kerberos authentication process.

For Active Directory, you can install a Windows 2000- or Windows Server 2003-based DNS server, or you can use a Berkeley Internet Name Domain (BIND) DNS server. If you are using BIND, you can use BIND version 4.9.7. However, version 8.2.2 or later is recommended.

Using a Windows-based server allows you to use Active Directory integrated zones. These zones must reside on a DNS server, which is also a domain controller. These zones store DNS information in Active Directory and allow more effective zone transfers.

CHAPTER 3 SUMMARY

Active Directory is the directory service in a Windows Server 2003 domain. It can provide an enterprise-wide directory, an e-mail directory, and a "white pages" directory for the corporation, as well as an e-commerce authentication system.

In addition, there are various ownership roles in an Active Directory environment. All objects have an object owner. These are referred to as data owners. Service owners hold the second ownership role. They are sometimes referred to as directory owners or directory administrators. Their responsibilities include creating or removing domains, implementing schema changes, and managing domain controllers.

Active Directory design must be taken seriously and given due thought. Security should also be at the forefront of the design process. Active Directory terminology includes frequent use of the word "trust." Trust includes not only the traditional transitive trusts in domains, but also the clients, users, and administrators on the network. Physical security of your domain controllers is paramount, and protecting them is critical to your network.

In the Active Directory design process, there can be several factors that drive the design. A design should be made to meet the organization's goals. This is a primary goal of any directory design process. With any design process, it is also important to involve executive management throughout the process. Management sponsorship builds support for the project and helps ensure that it can be carried out with success.

Additionally, designing for the future should be a goal. Not only should the Active Directory design process include current considerations, but projected plans and growth should also be factored in as well. This reduces the likelihood that major redesign projects will need to be undertaken in the future.

Windows Server 2003 also includes the capability to split administrative responsibilities. This delegation of authority allows for more granular management of Active Directory objects and resources. This capability should be considered during the design process so that it can be used most effectively.

Part of this design process will therefore include Group Policy considerations and the design of Active Directory to incorporate the needs of the environment based on policy application. Departments that require different policies can be separated into different organizational units (OUs) to aid in policy application.

To start the design project, there are several different frameworks that can be considered. The two most common are the Microsoft Solutions Framework (MSF) and the Microsoft Operations Framework (MOF).

The MSF is well-suited for businesses whose goals include creating and publishing software. The framework breaks apart the process into the envisioning phase, which gives the project vision and scope. The planning phase occurs next, and it incorporates a detailed plan of what the resulting Active Directory structure will look like. This phase ends with a document called the functional specification. This includes a project schedule as well.

The developing phase, which is the third phase, takes the planning phase's results and works toward making them a reality. It involves extensive testing, configuration of domain controllers, and testing that may continue into the next phase as well, which is the stabilizing phase. During this phase, the details of the design are complete. When this is complete, the project is considered ready for use during the final phase, which is the deploying phase. During this phase, there may be continued testing and stabilizing, especially if this is a migration project.

MOF is designed around the operations of an information technology (IT) infrastructure. It includes guidelines and best practices to maximize the performance of the network.

The need for vision in the Active Directory design process is very important. As a team is created, it is important to remember these key concepts. Business goals should be communicated to the design team, and everyone on the design team should know the big picture. Ownership roles should be defined and key data owners should be a part of the design process. The Active Directory infrastructure's role should be understood by the design team, and executive management should be represented on the team.

CHAPTER 4 SUMMARY

Active Directory is made up of several different layers, which make up the directory service. Key layers include the Extensible Storage Engine (ESE), the database layer, and the Directory System Agent (DSA).

The ESE is an essential part of Active Directory. The Active Directory store is a transactional database driven by the ESE. All modifications to Active Directory are called transactions, which are first logged to a file for recovery purposes before changes are actually made to data. It uses advanced database features, such as the transaction log that it keeps, as well as checkpoints to ensure that data integrity is maintained.

Several files are important in Active Directory. These include NTDS.DIT, EDB.LOG, EDBXXXXX.LOG, EDB.CHK, RES1.LOG and RES2.LOG, and TEMP.EDB. Specifics about these files include the following:

- NTDS.DIT is the actual Active Directory store. All objects and their attributes that are located in Active Directory are stored in this file.

- The EDB.LOG is the current transaction log file used by Active Directory and the ESE. In the event of a system failure, the EDB.LOG file can be used to determine what changes were in progress in Active Directory, and they then can be completed.

- When the EDB.LOG file is refilled, it is renamed to EDBXXXXX.LOG, where XXXXX is a hex number. A new EDB.LOG file is created and the old EDBXXXXX.LOG files are deleted every 12 hours.

- EDB.CHK works in conjunction with the log file. It provides information regarding the changes in the EDB.LOG file that have actually been committed to Active Directory. These are noted by checkpoints, which the EDB.CHK file tracks.

- The RES1.LOG and RES2.LOG files are placeholders that reserve disk space. These each reserve 10 MB of space in case there is a lack of disk space on the server and information can't be written.

- TEMP.EDB is a temporary storage space for the ESE.

When working with Active Directory, the primary protocol in use is Lightweight Directory Access Protocol (LDAP). It is important to understand LDAP naming paths. LDAP uses a distinguished name (DN) and a relative distinguished name (RDN). An object's name consists of three parts: the domain component, which is part of the domain name; the organizational unit (OU) in which it resides, and the common name (CN), which is typically the object's name.

The Active Directory schema defines all the objects and attributes available in Active Directory. There are several aspects of the Active Directory schema. Each object class and attribute in the schema must have a unique CN, an LDAP display name, and an Object Identifier (OID).

Object classes define the groupings of objects in Active Directory. Common object classes include the User object class. These are templates for the creation of additional objects, for instance, user accounts, in that object class. There are four types of object classes: Structural, Abstract, Auxiliary, and 88 classes.

The schema contains a list of all possible attributes for a class, including mandatory and optional attributes. Attributes also include syntax. These are predefined. Common syntaxes include Boolean, Integer, and various string syntaxes.

Active Directory uses indexing. This is a method to improve the speed of searches for information in Active Directory. It is similar to the index stored in the back of a book. The index allows attributes to be found quickly. Using indexes, however, can also slow down the creation process of objects as well as object modification.

Active Directory effectively manages replication by using partitions. Partitions divide the database into groups. Each partition, or naming context, is replicated independently of the others. The most commonly referenced partition is the domain partition. This partition contains computers, users, and OUs.

The schema for Active Directory is stored on its own partition, which is called the schema partition. The partition holds class and attribute definitions. The configuration partition is used to store replication topology information. Replication topology determines how domain controllers determine replication partners. The domain partition holds the objects, such as users, computers, groups, and the OUs that are located in Active Directory. It is typically the most frequently modified partition. The final partition is the application partition, which can be used by developers when storing data in Active Directory.

CHAPTER 5 SUMMARY

An important aspect of setting up Active Directory revolves around choosing a name. The name should be meaningful and scalable. The name chosen becomes part of the name of each child domain. To be practical, therefore, the name should be representative of the company and allow for future growth.

DNS names are used typically for two purposes: one is for Active Directory namespace definition, and the other is to identify the company to the rest of the world for services such as e-mail, the company Web site, and other communications.

There are a few variations in how DNS can be set up. The same DNS name can be used for both, different names can be used for both, or a subdomain of your Internet name can be used for Active Directory. Each has advantages and disadvantages.

If you use the same DNS name for each, complicated steps are required to keep confidential data off of the public Internet. This is typically not a recommended configuration. It can also expose all of your internal DNS records to the public. Separate DNS servers must be maintained as well, and this can require manual management of records.

Using completely different names addresses those concerns. You must ensure that internal clients can resolve internal names as well as access external resources. Clients can query the internal servers for this if they are configured to use a forwarder or recursion. If a client is not configured correctly, they may have trouble accessing resources.

The third option creates a subdomain based on the Internet presence domain name. This allows the creation of separate Active Directory domains. It tends to be simple to administer and works well for companies with existing Berkeley Internet Name Domain (BIND) DNS servers or other UNIX software.

Choosing a DNS name for your organization should be given careful consideration. Microsoft encourages several practices. All domain controllers should also typically run DNS. In a small branch office, you can choose not to set up a DNS server on a domain controller. This will limit replication traffic.

Forest design is also a consideration for administrators. Active Directory design should start at the forest level and work toward the domain level. This allows you to view things from an enterprise-wide level and keeps you from getting bogged down in smaller operational decisions that may not impact the big picture.

A forest has several fundamental characteristics. A single forest represents a single implementation of Active Directory. A forest is a collection of domains linked together running Active Directory, and a forest can exist on a single or multiple domain controllers. Most organizations need only a single forest. However, there are reasons to have multiple forests. If different parts of an organization require different schemas, or complete separation of administrative capabilities, then separate forests are in order. Additionally, if part of a company cannot join the complete trust model, a separate forest must be created.

Domains are a part of the forest. They are also replication boundaries. Domains represent authentication stores where user and group information is kept. Policy-based administration is carried out at the domain level, and account policies must all be the same for a domain. It is sometimes considered a security boundary because of these factors; however, information can be sent outside the domain, so be careful with this reference.

Active Directory no longer has the Windows NT size limitation, so theoretically, a single domain is sufficient. It is easier to manage and delegate authority, and it requires less hardware. Multiple domains allow multiple sets of administrators, however. Additional domains are required if using the dedicated forest root model. In this model, the first domain is the forest root. A single subdomain is created beneath it to manage all user and resource objects. This allows the greatest flexibility for supporting growth and change.

You may also choose to use a dedicated forest root. The first domain in an Active Directory forest is the forest root. It has a few special characteristics not held by other domains. It contains the Enterprise Admins group and the Schema Admins group. It is the central point of trust relationships in the forest. It cannot be deleted without completing removing Active Directory. The recommendation by Microsoft is to dedicate the forest root domain to the management of Active Directory.

Trust relationships in Active Directory allow users in one domain to access resources in another domain without supplying their credentials. The credentials initially used to log in are presented to the second domain for authentication and to approve access to resources. Trusts in Windows Server 2003 domains that are part of a tree are, by default, transitive. This simply means that if Domain A trusts Domain B, and Domain B trusts Domain C, then Domain A trusts Domain C. Trusts in a forest are considered two-way transitive trusts, which means that in addition to being transitive, if Domain A trusts Domain B, Domain B trusts Domain A.

Shortcut trusts are trusts between domains that may not have a direct connection between them. This allows for quicker authentication and is useful when users in a remote domain require frequent access to resources in a different domain.

One-way trusts, unlike two-way trusts, allow resource access in a single direction: one-way trusts allow users in one domain the ability to access resources in another domain. By creating the trust, however, access is not automatically granted; it must still be specifically assigned to the user or group accounts.

Organizational units (OUs) are another tool of administrators. OUs are flexible and easy to implement and restructure as necessary. They can also be nested within one another;

however, they should not be nested more than 10 levels deep, because this may start slowing down Group Policy object processing. They allow administrators to logically group Active Directory objects, such as user accounts, into departments or geographic regions for easier management, delegation of authority, and application of Group Policy.

When integrating Windows Server 2003 into an existing domain, there are several considerations. Active Directory includes functional levels. These define a feature base, which grants capabilities depending on the operating system in use on domain controllers.

In Windows 2000, there were two different functional levels: mixed mode and native mode. Native mode required all Windows 2000 domain controllers, and mixed mode allows older NT 4.0 domain controllers to participate in the domain. Since Windows 2000, two new levels have been added: Windows Server 2003 interim and Windows Server 2003. Also, forest functional levels have been created. These are Windows 2000, Windows Server 2003 interim, and Windows Server 2003. These affect forest-wide functions. When domains are initially created, they are Windows 2000 mixed modes. It has the most limited functionality of all the levels.

Windows 2000 native domains add additional features, such as group nesting, universal groups, remote access policies for dial-up and VPN access, as well as security identifier (SID) histories for domain migration purposes.

The newest Windows Server 2003 interim forests add features such as replication of logon timestamps, schema additions, and the ability to rename a domain controller.

The Windows Server 2003 interim forest also increases capabilities. They add linked value replication as well as improved Intersite Topology Generator (ISTG) algorithms, which benefit the replication process. Finally, a Windows Server 2003 forest adds enhancements, including trusts between forests, domain renaming, and schema modification. Schema modifications include deactivation of schema attributes and classes.

When moving from an existing NT domain to a new Windows Server 2003 domain, several options are available. These options include keeping the existing infrastructure or creating a new one. Keeping the existing structure simplifies the process. A new domain structure should be used when the existing structure is not sufficient. The Active Directory Migration Tool (ADMT) tool can be used to aid with this. It allows for password migration, is scriptable, and works from the command line. A trust relationship between domains must also be created: the source must trust the target, and the target domain, if desired, may trust the source. This can allow for easier configuration.

CHAPTER 6 SUMMARY

In the Windows Server 2003 implementation of Active Directory, we have a logical structure that comprises the forests, trees, and domains. We also have a physical structure related to the physical objects. For instance, a site is one or more well-connected Internet Protocol (IP) subnets. Sites represent a single physical area of the network, which could be a single office floor, an entire building, a city, or a geographic region, depending on how well connected the networks are.

Site objects are well connected, which typically means they are connected at local area network (LAN) speeds instead of at wide access network (WAN) speeds (WAN speeds tend to be slower). In most offices, computers on a network are connected to a 10/100 Ethernet switch. These switches provide excellent communications speed and are considered well connected and sufficient to be a single site.

When Active Directory is initially installed, a site is created by default. This site is called the Default-First-Site-Name. It can be set up as the first site in use by the Active Directory infrastructure. Sites allow computers to access servers that are in close proximity. This helps ensure that computers use local services, as opposed to remote services over expensive WAN links, which improves cost and performance. Services that use site information are considered site-aware. Some site-aware services include domain controllers, global catalog servers, and the distributed file systems (DFSs).

Subnet objects are objects in Active Directory. The purpose of subnet objects is to identify subnets on your network. When a subnet is created, it can be associated with a site. This determines which computers belong to a specific site that has been defined on the network.

Site link objects are also part of the site topology. The site link that is created automatically by Active Directory is called DefaultIPSiteLInk. Site links represent connections to other networks. Parameters, such as cost and transport protocol, can be defined for the links. Site links can then be used to control replication and determine which servers should be used for specific clients.

Domain controllers are Windows servers that contain a copy of the domain database. By using the Active Directory Installation Wizard (DCPROMO), a new domain controller is placed in the correct site, based on its IP address. If the appropriate site cannot be determined, it is placed in the Default-First-Site-Name site. Client computers will determine their appropriate site each time they start; however, a domain controller determines this only upon promotion to being a domain controller.

Your planning process for designing the physical structure should include a diagram of the proposed installation. Included should be cable types, approximate paths of cable routing, and server maps. The server maps should also include the server's role, IP address, name, and domain membership (if any), as well as the owner's name and contact information.

Other devices should also be represented on your map, including peripheral devices, such as printers, as well as hubs and switches. Proxy servers, firewall servers, and remote access modems and wireless access points should also be represented, along with the roles they play in the network. Finally, include any WAN connections and Internet service provider (ISP) information, and the number of users and computers at each location. Any nonstandard implementations or special considerations should be noted as well.

Your site topology should be defined by and based on the network diagram you created. It should model the available bandwidth between sites. Cost should also be associated with the links that you defined. Costs are arbitrary values and are not necessarily directly correlated with the actual dollar cost of the WAN link. Sites use the path of least cost to determine which path clients should take to remote resources.

Sites can be used to control replication and load by manipulating the cost. For instance, a slower connection may be the preferred connection for client access to remote services, so it can be given a lower cost. However, if performance is poor over the slower link, and better performance is required, a more expensive link can be given a lower cost value and that link will be the preferred link.

To assist an administrator in controlling replication, the replication schedule can be set. The schedule defines the hours that a link is available. The transport protocol is the final parameter to define. The options are Remote Procedure Call (RPC) over Transmission Control Protocol/Internet Protocol (TCP/IP) and Simple Mail Transfer Protocol (SMTP). A high-quality link that is reliable should use RPC over TCP/IP. If a quality link is not available, then SMTP is recommended.

Transport protocols also come into play with traffic over links. The options include RPC over TCP/IP and SMTP. Within a site, replication always uses RPC over TCP/IP. If sites have a good fast link between them, it is a good idea to use RPC over TCP/IP. However, if sites have an intermittent link, then SMTP is usually the preferred protocol for replication.

Site link bridges come into play when sites are not in a fully routed IP environment. The status of not-fully-routed can be determined if a PC in one environment is not able to ping a computer in another location in the same network. In such a situation, a site link bridge may be required to bridge connectivity and ensure replication takes place as needed.

Other aspects of the design include designating roles to physical servers. For instance, each domain in the forest should have two domain controllers, even if there are only a few users. The redundancy provided for authentication and other directory service access can be critical. When there are remote offices, it may be wise to put a domain controller in the remote site as well. This gives users faster access to directory services and eliminates unnecessary WAN link authentication traffic.

Global catalog servers are used by end users to query Active Directory. It is recommended that a global catalog server be located at each site. Large sites should typically designate at least two domain controllers to be global catalog servers. For branch offices, a global catalog server may or may not be required. It is typically a good idea, unless the WAN link is at capacity or there are only a few users at the remote site.

CHAPTER 7 SUMMARY

Replication is an important component of Active Directory. It ensures all domain controllers have current data. Active Directory uses multimaster replication, as opposed to NT 4.0, which used single-master replication. This means that, unlike in NT 4.0 where only one domain controller had a writeable copy of the database, all Windows Server 2003 domain controllers have writeable copies of the Active Directory database.

Replicated data updates come in two forms: originating updates and replicated updates. An originating update is an Active Directory change made on the local domain controller. If the update is a new user account that was created on domain controller 1 (DC1), then it is an originating update on DC1. Replicated updates are changes that come from other domain controllers. The new user on DC1 would be a replicated update on domain controller 2 (DC2).

All updates to object changes are tracked using Update Sequence Numbers (USNs). Each DC maintains its own USN number. If a change is made, the domain controller independently updates its USN number. Because changes do not happen simultaneously on all domain controllers, different domain controllers can have different information on a single object. This is caused by latency. As replication occurs, all information on all domain controllers is synchronized. This is called convergence.

There are several identifiers for a domain controller, and for our purposes, three are important to you. The first is the Settings Server object, which can be viewed using Active Directory Sites and Services. The second is the server globally unique identifier (GUID). It is used to identify replication partners. The third is the database GUID. It is used by domain controllers to identify other domain controllers during replication requests.

The USN is a 64-bit number. It is an attribute of objects in Active Directory maintained by the domain controller. It is updated when the object is modified. USNs are maintained independently of other domain controllers. For this reason, it is useless to compare USNs between domain controllers.

Each domain controller keeps track of the high-watermark value. This is the highest USN associated with an object. It is used to reduce the number of objects that need to be considered for replication. The up-to-dateness vector also helps reduce replication traffic by reducing the number of attributes that need to be replicated. Propagation dampening is used when there are multiple paths between domain controllers. It is designed to help prevent endless looping in replication.

However, conflict resolution may still be needed so that a domain controller can determine how to handle conflicting updates. With attribute updates, a conflict can occur when the same attribute is changed on two different domain controllers. In this case, the version number, timestamp, and originating Directory System Agent (DSA) GUID are used to resolve the conflict. The version number is checked first, and the attribute change with the higher version number is used. If these are the same, then the most recent timestamp, and then the highest DSA GUID are used to determine which is kept.

There can be circumstances where, for instance, an administrator deletes a container, such as an organizational unit (OU), on one domain controller, while another administrator creates an object in that OU on a second domain controller. In this instance, the OU is gone; however, the object is stored in Active Directory Users and Computers under lost and found. This container can be viewed by enabling the Advanced view.

If two objects are created simultaneously on different domain controllers with the same name, the object with the higher version number keeps its name, while the lower version numbered object will be renamed.

Replication topology is a combination of paths that are available for Active Directory updates. The domain controllers that a DC uses to replicate are connection objects. These are unidirectional. Replication can be either intrasite or intersite replication. Intrasite replication takes place between domain controllers in a single site. Intersite replication takes place between domain controllers in different sites. Connection objects are created in one of two ways: either automatically using the Knowledge Consistency Checker (KCC) and Intersite Topology Generator (ISTG), or manually by the administrator.

There are two types of source replicas: master and read-only replicas. Domain controllers have a master replica, which is both readable and writeable. Global catalog servers contain a partial read-only replica. Replication requires that master replicas be created from other master replicas, and a read-only replica can be sourced from either a master or another read-only replica.

Intrasite replication is handled by the KCC. It creates the replication topology that is used. It determines a bidirectional ring, providing fault tolerance and reliability. Intersite replication relies on the ISTG. The ISTG is the oldest server in a site by default. Its job is to create connection objects with domain controllers in other sites. If it becomes unavailable for an hour, then another DC takes over the role. The ISTG cannot be designated manually.

The bridgehead server is a domain controller designated for replication purposes. Active Directory domain information is replicated to the bridgehead server. It is responsible for replicating the information it receives to other domain controllers at its same site. The bridgehead server is chosen by the ISTG, or an administrator can manually specify one.

Intrasite replication occurs on a notify-pull basis. As changes are made and a domain controller receives notification, it pulls the changes down. Replication intervals and notifications in Windows Server 2003 have been reduced from their values in Windows 2000. This should be kept in mind in a mixed domain controller environment.

Intersite replication is time-based. Replication occurs at set intervals. By default this is every three hours. An administrator can adjust these times, taking into consideration traffic on wide area network (WAN) links.

Certain changes are replicated more frequently within a site due to their importance. Account lockouts, for instance, should be replicated as quickly as possible. Other similar situations involve certain policies, such as domain password policies, the Local Security Authority (LSA) secret change, and the relative identifier (RID) master role. Password replication is another instance of an urgent change. Password changes are replicated to the primary domain controller (PDC) emulator to facilitate logins.

Replication is a critical factor in Active Directory. Therefore, it is important to monitor and troubleshoot replication regularly. This helps ensure Active Directory works properly. Replication problems typically result in login failures as well as inconsistencies in Active Directory information between domain controllers. The Active Directory Replication Monitor allows you to monitor replication traffic between domain controllers, as well as force a replication and view the replication topology.

In addition to Active Directory replication, the SYSVOL folder is also a consideration. It contains policies and user scripts processed during logon. It is replicated using the File Replication service (FRS). If SYSVOL doesn't seem to be replicating properly, then Event Viewer can be checked for errors generated by the FRS. You should also ensure that name resolution via fully qualified domain name (FQDN) is occurring properly. You can restart the FRS as necessary. Last, always ensure that there is sufficient disk space for the files that are generated while using these folders and services.

CHAPTER 8 SUMMARY

In Active Directory there are several roles served by domain controllers in the forest. These roles are called Flexible Single Master Operation (FSMO) roles, and they are held by a single computer in the entire forest. These two forest-wide roles are the schema master and the domain naming master.

Modifying the schema is a critical process. Because merging schema modifications is extremely complicated, a single domain controller has the responsibility of managing the schema and changes to it. This domain controller is the schema master. This role is assigned automatically to the first domain controller installed in the forest. It is recommended that this role always stay in the forest root domain.

If the server becomes unavailable, then users will be unlikely to notice an impact on Active Directory. Network administrators also may not notice any problems unless they are modifying the schema. Additions or modifications to the schema are not possible until the schema master has been returned to service.

Like the schema master, the domain naming master is also assigned by default to the first domain controller in the forest. As new domains are added to the forest, the domain naming master ensures that each of the domain names are unique. Only one domain controller in the entire forest can hold this role, and this ensures that the domain names throughout the forest stay unique. The load of this computer is minimal, as domains are not frequently added to the forest. If the functional level of the domain is Windows 2000, then the domain naming master must reside on a global catalog server. However, if the functional level is set to Windows Server 2003, residing on the global catalog server is not a requirement.

If this server is unavailable, as with the schema master, typically no impact is felt. If domains are being added or removed from the forest, then these actions will not be successful until the domain naming master is back online. Otherwise, Active Directory performance continues as usual.

Along with the forest-wide roles, there are domain-wide roles. These are the primary domain controller (PDC) emulator, relative identifier (RID) master, and infrastructure master. Each role can be assigned to only a single domain controller at a time. However, a single domain controller can have multiple FSMO roles, both domain-wide and forest-wide, at the same time.

The PDC emulator acts as a Windows NT 4.0 primary domain controller. This server will replicate changes and information to Windows NT 4.0 backup domain controllers (BDCs). It also handles password changes and other updates for older clients, such as NT 4.0 and Windows 98 computers. This role is assigned to the first domain controller in the domain by default. Clients use it frequently, so it should be a domain controller that is highly available. If this server becomes unavailable, users will be directly affected if they are using older Windows NT and Windows 98 clients without the Active Directory client software. They may experience authentication problems and errors when changing passwords.

The RID master ensures that a user's domain security identifier (domain SID) and the RID are unique for every security principle in the domain. It also is responsible for moving objects between domains to prevent object duplication. The first domain controller in the domain is assigned this role, and if it is unavailable, typically, users will not notice the impact. Administrators who are moving objects between domains will notice they are unable to move objects until the RID master is back online.

The final FSMO role is the infrastructure master. Its role is to update object references in its domain that point to objects located in another domain. It updates references if an object is moved or deletes the reference if the object is deleted. The infrastructure master should not be located on a global catalog server in a forest with multiple domains. This will result in no updates. If there is only a single domain, however, it can be located on the same server.

Roles may occasionally need to be moved to new domain controllers in a transfer operation. A transfer operation is a preferred method for moving roles. The need to transfer can occur as a result of changes in the network or failure of a domain controller. The process of transferring a role occurs when both servers are still online.

If a server is offline in a disaster recovery situation, you may not be able to bring it back into production. If it held a FSMO role, then the role may need to be seized by another server. This is a drastic step and should not be taken lightly. If a role has been seized, the old role holder should never be placed back on the network unless Windows has been reinstalled.

CHAPTER 9 SUMMARY

Authentication is a key part of Windows. Authentication ensures that only authorized users are on your network. Authentication relies on a security identifier (SID). Objects in Active Directory that have a SID are called security principals. The ObjectSID is a binary value that specifies a user's SID. Typically, however, the SID is represented in Security Descriptor Definition Language (SDDL). In this format, a SID might look like this: S-1-5-21-606252524-532625125-1421435136-3485.

SIDs are the primary identifiers of accounts. Part of a SID is the domain identifier. The domain identifier is the fifth, sixth, and seventh portions of the previous example: S-1-5-21-606252524-532625125-1421435136-3485. Portions of the SID are separated by dashes, and there are eight sections of the entire SID. Note that 32 bits, or the last four digits, are used to identify the object uniquely within the domain. This is the relative identifier (RID).

When a user authenticates to the domain, an access token is created. This access token contains several pieces of information, including the user's SID and the SID of all groups to which the user belongs.

Permissions and rights are granted based on the access token. Permissions are rules associated with access to an object. For instance, permissions indicate whether a user can read a file or write to a folder, or print to a specific printer. These rules are contained in an object's discretionary access control list (DACL). Rights are often referred to interchangeably with permissions. However, they are not the same. Rights indicate the tasks or operations a user can perform on a computer or on the domain. They are not associated with a specific object such as a file or printer. For instance, the ability to log into a domain controller and the ability to change a computer's time fall under the realm of rights and privileges. Privileges are tasks that you can perform once you are logged into the network.

Active Directory authentication can be done using one of two methods. The older method is NT LAN Manager (NTLM) authentication. The newer, more secure option is Kerberos, which was introduced with Windows 2000.

NTLM authentication is used for backward compatibility. It is used in various situations with older NT clients. It is based on LAN Manager authentication, which is older and less secure. NTLM is an improvement on LAN Manager, but it is still not as secure as Kerberos. To improve NTLM, a new version was released, NTLM v2. This is available to Windows NT 4.0 if Service Pack 4 is installed; it is available for Windows 95 and 98 clients with the Active Directory Client Extension installed.

NTLM authentication is the second authentication option. In this option, a user authenticates in Windows Server 2003. NTLM is older than Kerberos and is used under specific conditions. It is less secure than other options, and it is not preferred.

Kerberos v5 authentication is the default for all Windows Server 2003, Windows XP, and Windows 2000 computers. Kerberos is based on Request for Comment (RFC) 1510 and is a standard. Windows Kerberos can operate successfully with other RFC-compliant implementations; however, most implementations do vary somewhat from the standard.

Kerberos involves three components: the security principal requesting access, the Key Distribution Center (KDS), which is the Active Directory domain controller, and the server holding the resource or service that is being requested.

The KDC provides two main services: an authentication service and a ticket-granting service. Each is required to gain access to a resource. The first ticket is a ticket-granting ticket. It is issued when a user successfully logs on. The ticket-granting ticket (TGT) allows a user to receive a session ticket. Session tickets are used to allow a user access to a network resource or service, and they are presented to that resource or network service.

The Kerberos authentication process involves many steps. Initially, a user logs in and provides this authentication information: a username and password. Additionally, a ticket granting ticket is requested. After the user is authenticated by a key distribution center, the KDC gives him or her the TGT. The TGT then allows the user to request a service ticket. The service ticket can be used to initiate a session with a server.

Older clients are referred to as down-level clients. Windows 95, 98, and NT 4.0 clients create a security concern because they use weaker authentication. However, the authentication is improved by using the Directory Services Client. It is an add-on component that enables NTLM v2 support on the older clients on Windows 2000/2003 networks. It also grants Active Directory Site awareness, allows Active Directory searches, and allows password changes on any domain controller instead of just the primary domain controller (PDC) emulator.

To further strengthen authentication, two-factor authentication is recommended. Two-factor authentication contains two of the following three methods of authentication: something you know, such as a password; something you have, such as a key or smart card; and something you are, such as a fingerprint, signature, or voice. The more factors you use, the stronger your authentication mechanism.

One method of adding a factor is the use of smart cards. Smart cards and certificates are part of a public/private key infrastructure (PKI). This hierarchical structure uses certificates for security. Two different keys are used to protect information: a public key and a private key. The public key is available to everyone; however, the private key must never be disclosed except to the owner. Otherwise, the data is compromised.

Active Directory uses several methods to secure data. One of these is the DACL, which relies on access control entry (ACE) to determine authorization to access information. ACEs can allow or deny access to a resource.

Groups are a management tool for applying security in Windows 2003. Groups hold users, computers, and other groups to create a single security principal that can be used to assign permissions or privileges on the network. Groups can be used with the Delegation of Control Wizard to grant access to organizational units (OUs) and to delegate administrative responsibility.

To keep track of security on the network, auditing can be used. Auditing will record information in the Windows 2003 security log. Successful and failed actions on the network can be recorded. Auditing can occur on objects in the network, logon events, directory service access, privilege use, policy changes, and process tracking. This allows administrators to monitor the network for security violations.

Data can be protected using the NT File System (NTFS). It allows granular permissions such as read and write permission to an object. Other network resources can have access controlled by permissions as well. Printing documents, managing the printer, and managing documents are all levels of control for a printer that can be set for a user or group. File shares can also be controlled by using file share permissions, which are Full Control, Change, and Read.

Registry keys are a repository of information for the operating system. These keys hold configuration information. The registry is separated into hives, which are collections of keys.

Applications are increasingly making use of Active Directory. Applications such as Exchange can store information in Active Directory. Applications can use Active Directory for authentication purposes as well as authorization, depending on the applications needs.

CHAPTER 10 SUMMARY

User accounts have two different user names, which users can use to log into the domain. In Active Directory Users and Computers, the first name is the user logon name, which is also known as a user principal name (UPN). The second reference is the user logon name (pre-Windows 2000), which is also referred to as the sAMAccountName.

Good planning for Active Directory includes planning a naming convention. When choosing a naming convention, consider all the possibilities of possible names in your organization. Large companies especially need to have a plan for identical names created by a naming convention.

A new consideration in Windows Server 2003 is a forest trust creation, which is the creation of name resolution across forests. Name suffix routing routes authentication requests to the correct forest. It also requires that a unique name suffix exists only in a single forest. If the suffix exists in more than one forest, that suffix is disabled for name suffix routing. Conflicts can also occur when the DNS name is already in use, the NetBIOS name is already in use, or the domain security identifier (SID) conflicts with another name suffix SID.

New users in Active Directory are created with the Active Directory Users and Computers console. The New Object – User dialog box allows entry of basic information regarding the user, such as the first, last, and full name.

Initial security options include setting the password and forcing the user to change the password at next logon. You can also specify that the password cannot be changed, that it never expires, and that the account is disabled upon creation.

Additional tabs on the user account properties allow for other attributes to be set. There are dozens of settings available for users. Active Directory is extensible. This means that the schema can be modified. Additional settings are possible, but implementations of the Active Directory Users and Computers console may not be identical to one another.

Tabs with the Properties dialog box are available for general and business information, such as phone numbers and addresses. In addition, account and profile settings that affect the user's environment upon login are available. For instance, group membership for the user can be added on the Member of tab. Terminal services options are available via the Terminal Services profile tab, the Remote Control tab, and the Sessions tab. These tabs allow options such as setting up the users available resources, enabling remote control for administrative purposes, and handling the length of sessions.

Other actions that can be taken through the Active Directory Users and Computers console include resetting passwords and creating account templates. Account templates are precon- figured user accounts that retain settings such as group membership and organization information when they are copied. This allows quick creation of several accounts all based on a common standard.

Other options for creating and managing accounts include command-link utilities, such as DSADD, DSMOD, and DSQUERY, for adding accounts, modifying accounts, and querying Active Directory for specific objects.

Bulk management of accounts can be done through two tools: CSVDE and LDIFDE. CSVDE is a command-line tool that supports bulk import and export of data from Active Directory using comma-separated-value files. They can be easily edited in a tool like Excel or even in a text editor. LDIFDE is similar to CSVDE; however, it uses a file format known as Lightweight Directory Access Protocol (LDAP) Interchange Format, which is an industry standard that defines the format in which the file should be. It can be used to extend the Active Directory schema. The files can be managed with any text editor.

User accounts can also be created and modified through automated methods. These methods include scripts and programs. They also include Microsoft Metadirectory Services (MMS).

A scripting interface you can use is the Active Directory Service Interface (ADSI). ADSI can be used through advanced programming languages, such as C#. Most network administra- tors, however, use Windows Scripting Host (WSH) and VBScript.

A group is a way to organize user accounts. Windows Server 2003 includes two main types of groups: security groups and distribution groups. Security groups are the most flexible of the two, as they can play both the role of a security group and that of a distribution group. Security groups allow the assignment of permissions to resources and can be used in conjunction with group policy as. Security groups can also be used as a distribution group.

Distribution groups, however, cannot be used to assign permissions or access to resources. The primary function of a distribution group is to distribute information; for example, a distribution group could be a mailing list group for e-mails. Sending an e-mail message to a distribution group sends the e-mail message to all members of that group. If the user accounts on a distribution list will never be needed to assign permissions, it should be created as a distribution group.

If you have created a group and need to change its type, you are limited by the domain's functional level. If a domain is in Windows 2000 native mode or Windows Server 2003 mode, then the group type can be changed. It can not be changed if the functional level is different, however.

Group scopes determine where a group can be used in a forest. They also determine the types of objects a forest can contain. A group can have one of four different scopes, as follows:

- The first type of group scope is a local group scope. This group can only be used to assign resource access to resources on the local machine. It cannot be used on remote machines because the remote machine will not be familiar with the group.

- A domain local group scope is domain-based. It can be used to assign access only to those resources that are located in the domain in which the domain local group was created. It can, however, contain members from other domains, including user accounts, global groups, and universal groups. The difference between a domain local group and a local group is that the domain local group can be used throughout the domain in which it was created, whereas the local group can be used only on the single machine where it was created.

- A global group scope is in some ways just the opposite of a domain local group. A domain local group can have members from any domain, but can access only those resources that are in its own domain. A global group, on the other hand, can have members only from its own domain. However, it can be used to assign access to resources in any domain.

- The last group type is the universal group scope. It is available only in Windows 2000 native mode functional levels and above. It does not have the limitations imposed on the domain local or global group; a universal group can have members from any domain, and it can access resources in any domain.

Microsoft recommends the AGDLP strategy when implementing groups:

1. Place accounts into global groups.
2. If you use universal groups, place global groups into the appropriate universal group.
3. Add universal or global groups to domain local groups.
4. Assign permissions to access resources to the domain local groups.

Group nesting is a feature available based on a domain's functional level. If the domain is either Windows 2000 native or Windows Server 2003 functional level (at the minimum), you are able to nest groups. Nesting groups is the placement of groups within other groups. For instance, you might place a sales global group and a marketing global group within a third global group to ease the administrative task of assign permissions.

Built-in groups are created upon the installation of Active Directory. The Builtin container holds several of these domain local group accounts. These groups are intended to fulfill basic administrative needs.

The Users container contains domain local and global group accounts. These include groups such as DnsAdmins, which is used to administer the DNS Service, and Domain Admins, which has far-reaching power over the entire domain.

Special identity groups are special in that no one can assign membership to these groups. Membership is based upon interaction with the network. For instance, the Everyone group includes all users. The Interactive group includes those that log in while sitting at the keyboard or using Terminal services, and the Network group includes those who access a resource over the network (instead of interactively).

Creating your own groups can be accomplished using Active Directory Users and Computers. You can right-click a container, click New, and then click Group to launch the wizard.

Changing group membership can be accomplished by using the Add button on the Members tab of the Group properties window. You can use the Remove button to remove members of the group as well.

Just like users, computers also have accounts on the domain. If a computer does not have an account, then no users can log into the domain from that computer.

Publishing resources is a way to make them easily findable when users search Active Directory. Shared folders and Printers are commonly published items. Other Active Directory-enabled applications may use published information to locate resources as well.

Objects can be organized using organizational units. These are created by an administrator and can contain objects. These objects, such as user accounts, can be managed collectively through tools such as Group Policy. Objects can also be moved easily between organizational units using the drag and drop method.

CHAPTER 11 SUMMARY

In Windows NT 4.0 domains, policies were applied through the System Policy Editor and the system policies it created. These were stored in the netlogon share, and the settings were applied to computers in the domain. The settings in the configuration file would permanently change the setting in the registry. The shortcomings of this system occurred when changes needed to be rolled back. Simply removing the policy left the changes in place.

Fortunately, Group Policy can now be used instead. It allows an administrator to easily and consistently apply policies and configurations for multiple computers. Group Policy was an improvement because policies did not permanently change the registry. In addition, there are more settings available to administrators to allow more control over the end user's environment.

Most policies that are implemented are based on administrative templates, which are files with the .adm extension. These templates contain the registry settings that can be modified through a policy.

Client-side extensions are a feature of Group Policy as well. They provide more advanced configuration options. These options include Encryption File System (EFS), folder redirection, Internet Explorer maintenance, Internet Protocol (IP) security, disk quotas, and software installation.

Group policies are stored locally on clients in hidden folders. These policies are known as local computer policies and work well for a workgroup environment. However, typically, group policies are managed at the domain or forest level and are stored as part of Active Directory. A portion of the Group Policy is stored in the Active Directory database, and another portion is stored in the SYSVOL share.

Group Policy Objects (GPOs) have two parts: a user configuration and a computer configuration. They are linked to sites, domains, and organizational units (OUs) using GPO links. To understand how policies are set up, it is important to understand their processing order. The first policy applied is the local computer policy. The next policy is a site policy, followed by domain policies, and then OU policies.

Note that higher-level, parent OU policies are applied before lower-level, child OU policies. Note that a conflict occurs when a setting is enabled in one policy, for instance, and disabled in another. If there is a conflict in settings between policies, the default behavior is that the most recently applied setting will be the applicable setting. Within a single site, domain, or OU, if multiple policy objects are applied, then they are processed from the last in the list to the first, with the last one applied taking precedence if there is a conflict.

To further control how settings are applied, an administrator has three options available: No Override, Block Policy Inheritance, and Loopback Processing Mode. No Override enforces a setting if a conflict occurs later in processing. This setting takes priority over other options. If there are conflicting settings, a policy with the No Override option will override the other conflicting setting. Block Policy Inheritance will prevent higher-level GPO settings from being applied to the OU, unless administrators have set the No Override option on the higher level GPO. No Override overrides a Block Policy Inheritance setting. Block Policy Inheritance prevents other settings from a higher-level GPO from being applied to the location of the Block Policy Inheritance GPO. Loopback Processing Mode controls user-based Group Policy settings. It ensures that settings are processed based on the computer's location in Active Directory.

Group Policy applications can be controlled through permissions. GPOs are not linked to groups; they are applied to users by linking the GPO to an OU containing user accounts. GPOs can be prevented from affecting a user or group by denying the Apply Group Policy permission to a user or group.

Windows Management Instrumentation (WMI) filters can be used to control the application of Group Policies as well. They can be used to control the application of a GPO. The control can be based, for example, on hardware configuration, file existence, or free hard drive space.

When policies are being applied over a slow link, link speed can be determined so that portions of Group Policy that are bandwidth-intensive are not applied. By not applying these portions, the administrator ensures that the user's experience is not degraded.

Group Policy can be used for desktop management and for control of the end user environment. For instance, Windows features can be restricted. Options such as proxy server settings for Internet Explorer can be locked down so that they cannot be changed.

Other features of Group Policy include redirecting common folders. These folders include the Application data, Desktop, My Documents, and Start menu folders. Folder redirection is accomplished by using the User Configuration portion of Group Policy. Basic folder redirection affects all users, while Advanced redirection allows more refined direction based on the user's security group membership.

Scripts can be created for logon, logoff, startup, and shutdown scenarios. These scripts can be batch files or they can be written in a scripting language such as VBScript or JScript.

Security management through Group Policy can be accomplished through Account Policies, which allow the definition of Password Policies, including password age settings, lockout settings, and password complexity requirements. Password history options remember users' last passwords so that they cannot be reused. Password ages options control how often a user is able to change his or her password, as well as how often they must change it. Password complexity options ensure that a user creates stronger passwords using alphanumeric characters, symbols, and upper and lowercase letters.

Group Policy also allows the creation of restricted groups, which cannot have their membership modified once the group is defined as such. This prevents user accounts from accidentally or maliciously being added or removed as members.

In addition, system services on local computers can be managed, and registry keys can be secured. NT File System (NTFS) permissions on the file system can be set, and wireless network policies can be defined. Taken as a group, all of these can increase security for you and your network.

Public-key policies control features such as the Encrypting File System (EFS). This section of group policy allows the setting of recovery agents. You can also configure clients to automatically request certificates with the Automatic Certificate Request Settings node. Software restriction policies work only in Windows Server 2003 and Windows XP systems. They allow software and application control by dictating which software applications are allowed to run.

Security templates are predefined policy settings. They can be used to as a baseline to compare against the computer's settings. They can also be used to define and enforce common standards throughout an organization. The default template is the Setup Security. inf file. There are also incremental templates, which modify settings incrementally.

To manage settings, administrators can use the Group Policy Management Console. It is available as a free download, and it brings together several different tools into a single console for group policy management.

To troubleshoot group policy application, check the No Override settings as well as Block Policy Inheritance settings, which modify the way group policy is applied. The Loopback Processing feature may be enabled as well, so that should be checked. Newly created GPOs will need time to replicate in the domain. If there is a slow link, portions of the GPO may be disabled.

Additional troubleshooting tools include the Resultant Set of Policy (RSoP) tool, Gpresult, Gpupdate, and Dcgpofix. All of these except for RSoP are command-line tools. RSoP can be used to determine how policies are applied in hypothetical situations. Gpresult offers similar capabilities and can be scripted. Gpupdate forces group policy replication, and Dcgpofix resets domain controller group policies back to their default configuration.

Chapter 12 Summary

Software management is an ongoing task in most departments. It can be broken down into four phases: preparation, deployment, maintenance, and removal.

The first step is the preparation phase. This includes preparing the software and setting up distribution points on the network. Additionally, users and computers that require the software should be identified.

When using Group Policy to distribute software, the Windows Installer service is used. It runs on Windows 2000, XP, and Server 2003 computers. It allows for the complete automation of the installation and configuration process. Benefits of this service include the customization of the installation, repair of any corrupted file of an installation, privilege elevation, clean removal of the software, and if necessary, rollback of the installation.

To use Group Policy, you need a Windows Installer package (.msi) file. It allows for the installation and removal of a software package. It includes a list of all required files, their locations, the registry information, and summary information regarding the application.

Many software vendors are now supplying Microsoft Installer packages (MSIs) with their applications. Older software packages that lack an MSI package can have one created using third-party utilities, such as WinINSTALL from Veritas. You can also use a ZAP file, which is a text-based file. It has limitations, however; software deployed with a ZAP file can be published, but it is not resilient and cannot self-repair. In addition, they are installed with the permissions of the logged-in user.

Distribution points for the software have to be prepared. You should use a single distribution point or a distribution point based on Dfs, which is site-aware. Distribution points should have appropriate NT File System (NTFS) permissions, including allowing only administrators to have write and modify permissions on the distribution point. It should also typically be a hidden share.

The scope of the installation includes determining the users and computers that should receive the application. This should be based on the need for installation of the application throughout the domain. Keep in mind that different needs for the application and its configuration may require different Group Policy Objects (GPOs).

There are two methods of configuring software deployment: assignment of an application and publication of an application. Assignment of an application to a computer will cause an application to be installed the next time the computer is started, and it is available to all users of the computer. When it is assigned to a user, however, the application is advertised on the Start menu. Note, however, that it is not installed until the application is started or a document associated with that application is opened. This action is known as documentation invocation. When an application is assigned to a user, it can be installed on any computer on which the user logs.

Publishing applications can be done only with users, not computers. Publishing an application makes it available through Add or Remove Programs in Control Panel. The user can also use document invocation to install the application.

To configure an application for deployment, a GPO must be created or modified to deploy the specific application. Then, the specific deployment options can be set. This component allows administrators to publish or assign applications, for instance. In addition, transform files can be created. These allow for the installation of different feature sets, for instance, for different departments. A complete installation of Office could be accomplished for one organizational unit (OU), while another OU may only receive Word and Excel.

Document invocation can be configured as well. Associated extensions for packages can be set up, and a preference order for applications with the same extensions can be set up as well. This allows, for instance, different versions of the same application to be given different priorities when document invocation is invoked.

Deployment options include auto-installation by file extension, as well as uninstalling the application when the computer or user is no longer under management by the GPO that is assigned. Packages can be prevented from appearing as an Add or Remove option in Control Panel, and applications can be installed at logon as well.

Once an application is deployed, it still requires maintenance. Mandatory upgrades can be used when a new major version of the application is created and you want to ensure all users upgrade to the new version. The old package is removed under such conditions. Optional upgrades can also be created, which are not required. To install the upgrade, the Add or Remove Programs option in Control Panel must be used.

Redeployment of an application is the reinstallation of an application everywhere it is currently installed. This may be done to distribute a hot fix or service pack. A new .msi file may be provided, or you can use a .msp file, which is a Windows Installer patch file to update the existing .msi package.

Automatic updates to the operating system can be accomplished through Group Policy for Windows 2000, Windows XP Professional, and Windows Server 2003. Computers can be configured to update automatically from the Microsoft Windows Update Web site or through Software Update Services, a free update tool provided by Microsoft. It allows updates to be stored locally so that computers do not need to download updates over a wide area network (WAN) link.

The last step is removal of deployed software. Software can be set up for forced or optional removal. Forced removal uninstalls the application from all computers. Optional remove does not remove copies and it does not perform future installations either. If a user uninstalls the application, it cannot be reinstalled.

The issues that occur with software deployment are varied. For instance, applications that may not appear on the Start menu as expected are often published instead of assigned, and this requires GPO reconfiguration. You may also have Group Policy application problems. In addition, applications that are not visible in Add or Remove programs may not have the option enabled properly, so the Group Policy should be examined. It also may not have been applied to the user. Last, if applications are visible where they should be, but do not install, there may be problems with the distribution point or the installation files. There may be an older application installed that is not uninstalling properly, or files may have become corrupted.

Chapter 13 Summary

Administering and maintaining Active Directory includes monitoring the performance of Active Directory. As with other monitoring of your server, the Performance console is a primary tool. The Performance console consists of two tools: System Monitor and Performance Logs and Alerts.

System Monitor allows an administrator to carry out several tasks. With this tool, an administrator can monitor the server's performance and examine how it behaves under a load. System Monitor can also be used for problem diagnosis by finding bottlenecks and for capacity planning so that future upgrades can be planned. Additionally, configuration changes can be checked to gauge their impact on the system.

Information in System Monitor can be displayed in one of three views. The graph display shows a continuous graph that displays updates in real time. The histogram view shows counter information as a histogram, with information updated in real time. The report view shows a text-based view of counters, with information updated in real time.

The information displayed depends on the performance objects and counters selected. Server performance measurements typically include several common counters that provide a good indicator of how the server is doing. The counters include the following:

- *%Processor time*—This is the time that the processor spends executing an active thread.
- *%Interrupt time*—This counter measures hardware interrupts of the processor.

- *Pages/second*—This counter measures the number of pages read in or out to disk for resolution of hard page faults.

- *Page Faults/second*—This memory counter indicates the number of hard and soft page faults each second.

- *%Disk Time*—This counter measures the percentage of time that the disk is busy, for both the logical and physical disk.

- *Average Disk Queue Length*—This counter indicates the length of the queue for outstanding read or write requests for a volume or partition.

Maintaining the Active Directory database involves several responsibilities. Just like with a fragmented hard drive, the Active Directory database can become fragmented. Defragmentation is done in both offline and online modes to improve performance.

When an object is deleted from Active Directory, it is not immediately removed. It is marked as being tombstoned. This allows other domain controllers to be notified of the object's state of pending deletion and allows the other domain controllers to plan for deletion of the object. Tombstoning ensures that a deleted object is not simply replicated back to the domain controller, which would be the case without tombstoning.

The time that an object spends in the tombstoned state is its tombstone lifetime. The default is 60 days, but it can be modified as needed. Every 12 hours, a process known as garbage collection occurs. This process deletes objects from Active Directory that are still present past the tombstone lifetime period.

Active Directory online defragmentation is a process that occurs as part of the garbage collection process, every 12 hours by default. During this time, Active Directory is still available to users. Data is reorganized for optimum performance and space is reclaimed from deleted objects; however, the size of the database is not decreased by this process. If reduction of the overall size of the database is desired, then an offline defragmentation must be performed. An offline defragmentation is accomplished by using Active Directory's Directory Services Restore Mode.

You should also optimize the location of your Active Directory files. Because the files are accessed frequently, all files ideally would be on separate drives. However, this is typically not a possibility. Most often, many of the files all reside on the same partition. One option is to separate the log files from the page file and the Active Directory store. Log files are typically smaller than the other files and do not require as much disk space. To move log files to different drives, you must be in Active Directory's Directory Services Restore Mode.

Another optimization feature is an application directory partition. This gives an administrator granular control over where data is replicated, allowing the amount of replication data to be decreased. Application partitions can be created using a tool that may come with the application and that is provided by the application vendor. Alternatively, the Ntdsutil utility can be used to create the partition.

Practice Exam

70-294 Planning, Implementing, and Maintaining a Microsoft Windows Server 2003 Active Directory Infrastructure

Name:_____

Date:_____

1. Which of the following is *not* a function of a domain in Active Directory?
   a. providing a security boundary
   b. providing an administrative boundary
   c. providing a unit of replication
   d. none of the above

2. To which of the following is the domain directory partition replicated in Active Directory?
   a. all domain controllers in the forest
   b. all domain controllers in the same domain
   c. all member servers in the domain
   d. all domain controllers within the same site

3. Which operations master is responsible for updating references to objects in another domain in the forest?
   a. PDC Emulator
   b. RID Master
   c. Infrastructure Master
   d. Schema Master
   e. Domain Naming Master

4. Which of the following is forest wide? (Choose all that apply.)
   a. PDC Emulator
   b. RID Master
   c. Infrastructure Master
   d. Schema Master
   e. Domain Naming Master

5. Which of the following statements regarding global catalog servers is correct? (Choose all that apply.)
   a. A global catalog server must be a domain controller.
   b. The global catalog server contains all attributes for all objects in the forest.
   c. The global catalog server is used to verify universal group memberships during logon.
   d. There can only be one global catalog server per forest.

6. Which of the following is an Active Directory requirement for a DNS server? (Choose all that apply.)
   a. It must support SRV resource records.
   b. It must support dynamic updates.
   c. It must support incremental zone transfers.
   d. It must support secure dynamic updates.

7. What minimum group membership is required to rename a domain controller in Windows Server 2003?
   a. Enterprise Admin
   b. Schema Admin
   c. Domain Admins
   d. Server Operator

8. **Which of the following domain controllers can be renamed in Windows Server 2003?**
   a. Windows NT 4.0 domain controller
   b. Windows 2000 domain controller
   c. Windows Server 2003 domain controller
   d. all of the above

9. **What is the name of the Active Directory database file?**
   a. ntds.dit
   b. ad.dit
   c. ad.ebd
   d. ntds.edb
   e. ntad.dit

10. **Which of the following is an Active Directory forest functional level? (Choose all that apply.)**
   a. Windows 2000 mixed
   b. Windows 2000 native
   c. Windows 2003 Server
   d. Windows 2003 interim

11. **Which group membership is required to change the forest functional level?**
   a. Enterprise Admin
   b. Schema Admin
   c. Domain Admin
   d. Server Operator

12. **By default, all trusts between domains in a forest are _____ . (Choose all that apply.)**
   a. one-way
   b. two-way
   c. transitive
   d. nontransitive

13. **In the Windows Server 2003 functional level, a global group can be a member of a _____ . (Choose all that apply.)**
   a. global group from any trusted domain
   b. domain local group from any trusted domain
   c. global group from the same domain
   d. domain local group from the same group
   e. universal group from any trusted domain

14. **What domain functional level supports universal distribution groups in a Windows Server 2003 domain? (Choose all that apply.)**
   a. Windows 2000 mixed
   b. Windows 2000 native
   c. Windows 2003 Server
   d. Windows 2003 interim

15. **When is an object assigned a new GUID?**
    a. when the object is moved from one OU to another in the same domain
    b. when the object is moved to another domain within the same forest
    c. when the object is moved to another tree in the forest
    d. when the object is moved to another forest

16. **By default, to which operations master does the Group Policy Management console connect?**
    a. PDC Emulator
    b. RID Master
    c. Infrastructure Master
    d. Schema Master
    e. Domain Naming Master

17. **By default, Group Policy Slow Link Detection considers links slower than _____ to be slow.**
    a. 56 Kbps
    b. 128 Kbps
    c. 256 Kbps
    d. 500 Kbps
    e. 600 Kbps

18. **By default, how long will a Windows Server 2003 domain controller wait after the last change to notify the other domain controllers in the site?**
    a. 0 seconds
    b. 1 second
    c. 2 seconds
    d. 15 seconds
    e. 30 seconds

19. **Users are complaining that it takes a very long time to be authenticated by another child domain in another tree. What type of trust can you create to speed up authentication between the two child domains in the forest?**
    a. shortcut trust
    b. realm trust
    c. forest trust
    d. external trust

20. **Which of the following tools can be used to create OUs? (Choose all that apply.)**
    a. CSVIDE
    b. DSADD
    c. LDIFDE
    d. Windows Scripting Host

21. **Which protocol is used by ADSI to communicate with Active Directory?**
    a. SNMP
    b. LDAP
    c. Kerberos
    d. API

22. As part of the process to decentralize user administration, you want to be able to grant a user (Steve) the ability to reset user passwords for all users in Accounting. How should you organize Active Directory to accomplish this?

    a. Create a separate domain for Accounting.

    b. Create a universal group for Accounting and grant Steve permissions to reset passwords for the group.

    c. Create an OU called Accounting and grant Steve permissions to reset passwords for the Accounting OU.

    d. Assign Steve as a member of the Account Operators group.

23. Which of the following tools can be used only for creating new accounts and does *not* allow for editing existing accounts?

    a. LDIFDE

    b. CSVDE

    c. ADSI

    d. Windows Scripting Host

24. With the Active Directory Users and Computers snap-in, you can move an object _____ . (Choose all that apply.)

    a. from one OU to another OU in the same domain

    b. from one domain to another domain in the tree

    c. from one domain to another domain in the forest

    d. between forests

25. You have created an account policy for the root domain that specified a minimum password length. To what will that policy be applied?

    a. all domains in the forest

    b. all child domains of the root domain

    c. all sites containing the root domain

    d. the root domain only

26. When securing the account, which of the following *cannot* be accomplished?

    a. disabling the account

    b. renaming the account

    c. deleting the account

    d. all of the above

27. Which of the following groups replicates changes in membership in Active Directory?

    a. Global

    b. Domain local

    c. Local

    d. Universal

28. Which of the following objects can be stored in Active Directory? (Choose all that apply.)

    a. domain user accounts

    b. computer accounts

    c. shared folders

    d. shared printers

    e. local user accounts

29. **What is the purpose of sites in Active Directory? (Choose all that apply.)**
    a. They control logon traffic.
    b. They control replication.
    c. They function as security boundaries.
    d. They control broadcast traffic.

30. **What component is responsible for replication within a site?**
    a. Site Connector
    b. Knowledge Consistency Checker
    c. Relpmon
    d. USN

31. **What type of replication topology does the KCC create?**
    a. linear bus
    b. star
    c. ring
    d. mesh

32. **Which of the following statements regarding intrasite replication is correct? (Choose all that apply.)**
    a. Intrasite replication traffic is compressed.
    b. Intrasite replication is based on time intervals.
    c. Intrasite replication is notification based.
    d. Intrasite replication uses a replication schedule.
    e. Intrasite replication traffic is uncompressed.

33. **Which of the following statements regarding SMTP replication protocol is incorrect? (Choose all that apply.)**
    a. SMTP can be used only for intrasite replication.
    b. SMTP can be used only for replication between sites in different domains.
    c. SMTP cannot be used to replicate domain data.
    d. SMTP can be used only if there is permanent connectivity between the sites.

34. **You want to configure replication between two sites to occur as often as possible. What is the maximum replication interval you can configure?**
    a. every minute
    b. every 5 minutes
    c. every 10 minutes
    d. every 15 minutes
    e. every 30 minutes

35. **What component is responsible for creating the replication topology between sites?**
    a. KCC
    b. ISTG
    c. Site Link
    d. Schema

36. By default, how often does the KCC check the replication topology to ensure that it is up to date?
    a. every 15 minutes
    b. every 60 minutes
    c. every 3 hours
    d. every 12 hours
    e. every 24 hours

37. Which of the following FSMO roles can be transferred using the Active Directory Users and Computers snap-in? (Choose all that apply.)
    a. PDC Emulator
    b. Infrastructure Master
    c. Schema Master
    d. Domain Naming Master
    e. RID Master

38. Which of the following client operating systems is allowed when the domain is upgraded to Windows Server 2003 functional level? (Choose all that apply.)
    a. Windows 95
    b. Windows 98
    c. Windows NT 4.0 Professional
    d. Windows 2000 Professional
    e. Windows XP Professional

39. You want to replace the NTFS permission on a folder and all its subfolders using the CACLS command. What switch is used to replace permissions on all subfolders?
    a. /T
    b. /S
    c. /C
    d. /D
    e. /E

40. When assigning GPOs on multiple levels, which GPO will be processed first?
    a. domain
    b. site
    c. OU
    d. local

41. How often will a domain controller refresh its group policy settings?
    a. every minute
    b. every 2 minutes
    c. every 5 minutes
    d. every 60 minutes
    e. every 24 hours

42. Which of the following statements regarding ZAP files is correct? (Choose all that apply.)
    a. ZAP files can be published only to users.
    b. ZAP files are self-repairing.
    c. ZAP files do not require user intervention.
    d. ZAP files cannot install using elevated permissions.

43. When are published applications installed?
    a. when the computer is restarted
    b. when the group policy is refreshed
    c. when the user manually installs the application using Add/Remove Programs
    d. when the user starts the application on the Start Menu

44. You want to assign a new application using a GPO to all computers for all clients in the organization. Which operating system supports assigning applications? (Choose all that apply.)
    a. Windows 95
    b. Windows 98
    c. Windows NT 4.0
    d. Windows 2000 Professional
    e. Windows XP

45. You have assigned an application to all users in the organization. However, the application is not being installed on Sue's Windows XP computer. What tool can you use to verify that the proper GPO is being applied?
    a. GPResult
    b. DCDIAG
    c. SECEDIT
    d. NSLOOKUP

46. A user has called informing you that he has uninstalled an application from his computer. The application is assigned to the user using a GPO. What should the user do to reinstall the application?
    a. Restart his or her computer.
    b. Log back on to the domain.
    c. Run the GPResult utility.
    d. Reinstall the application using Add/Remove Programs.

47. You have created a GPO to assign an application to all computers in the organization. When will the application be installed?
    a. when the computer is restarted
    b. when the applications desktop icon is double-clicked
    c. when the user manually installs the application from Add/Remove Programs
    d. when the user double-clicks the application's associated file extension

48. Which of the following statements about links in a Site Link Bridge is true?
    a. Each link must use the Transport protocol.
    b. Each link must have the same network connectivity speed.
    c. Each site link must be assigned the same cost.
    d. The site links must be in the same site.

49. Due to a hardware failure, the global catalog server is not available on the domain. The domain is set to Windows 2000 native functional level. What happens when a new user attempts to log on to the domain?

    a. A domain controller in the same site as the user will authenticate the user.
    b. A random domain controller will authenticate the user.
    c. The user will be able to log on to the domain using cached credentials.
    d. The user will not be able to log on to the domain.

50. You are attempting to create a new user on a domain controller, but are unsuccessful. You also cannot create groups or computers. What FSMO role is unavailable?

    a. PDC Emulator
    b. RID Master
    c. Schema Master
    d. Domain Naming Master

Glossary

Abstract classes — Used as templates for Structural classes and other Abstract classes, but cannot be directly instantiated.

access control entry (ACE) — An entry in a DACL or SACL that lists a security principal (by SID), a type of action (such as read or write), and whether that SID is allowed or denied the action (or if it should be audited in the case of a SACL).

access token — A binary structure that lists the identity, rights, and group membership of a user on the network. An access token contains, among other items, the user's SID and the SID of each group to which the user belongs.

account policies — Configuration settings for passwords, account lockouts, and Kerberos. They must be linked to the domain to affect settings for the domain.

Active Directory (AD) — Microsoft's directory service included with Windows Server 2003 that provides a single point of administration, and storage for user, group, and computer objects.

Active Directory integrated zones — A DNS zone in which data is stored as objects in Active Directory. Available only on Microsoft DNS servers running on domain controllers.

Active Directory Migration Tool (ADMT) — A tool that migrates user accounts, groups, and computer accounts from one domain to another.

Active Directory Replication Monitor — A tool used to monitor, troubleshoot, and verify Active Directory replication.

Active Directory schema — Contains the definitions of all object classes and attributes used in the Active Directory database.

Active Directory store — The NTDS.DIT database file in which all Active Directory objects are stored. The Active Directory store is a transactional database based on the Extensible Storage Engine (ESE).

address (A) record — An address (A) resource record maps a hostname to an IP address.

administrative templates — Files containing settings used by the GPO Editor to define the registry key that should be changed, the options, and a description of the effects.

ADPREP.EXE /domainprep — A command run on the infrastructure master of the domain to prepare Active Directory before installing the first Windows Server 2003 domain controller in the domain.

ADPREP.EXE /forestprep — A command run on the schema master of the forest to prepare Active Directory before installing the first Windows Server 2003 domain controller in the forest.

assigned — Applications can be assigned to either computers or users. When assigned to computers, applications are installed when the computer starts. When assigned to users, applications are installed the first time the user runs the application by default.

attributes — Used to define the characteristics of an object class within Active Directory.

authentication — The process of identifying a user by using a set of credentials. Typically a user name and password are provided as credentials.

authoritative restore — An Active Directory restore that allows you to restore deleted or modified objects and have those changes replicated to other domain controllers in the domain.

authorization — Determines if a user is allowed access to a particular resource. Authorization can only occur after a user has been identified through authentication.

Auxiliary classes — Contains a list of attributes that are included in another classes' definition.

Backup Utility — The tool included with Windows Server 2003 used to back up and restore files and System State information.

baseline — A performance benchmark that is used to determine what is normal server performance under a specific workload.

best practices — A preferred way of doing something, defined either by an authority or by common practice in well-run companies.

Block Policy Inheritance — A setting in the Group Policy configuration for a domain or organizational unit that prevents settings from GPOs higher in the tree from being inherited.

bridgehead server — A domain controller that is configured to perform replication to and from other sites.

checkpoints — An event where ESE writes all completed transactions to the copy of the Active Directory store on the hard drive. Checkpoints shorten the amount of time needed to recover the Active Directory store, because ESE only needs to reapply the transactions that were made after the last checkpoint.

child domain — A domain that is connected to another domain (its parent) in an Active Directory tree. The child domain uses a subdomain of the parent domain's DNS name in a contiguous DNS namespace. Child.parent.company.com is a child domain of parent.company.com. Parent and child domains are connected with a two-way, transitive trust.

closed sets — When intra-forest migration is performed, all groups of which a user is a member must be migrated when the user is migrated. In addition, when a group is migrated, all users that are members of that group must be migrated.

computer account — An account that is stored in the domain database and provides a way for a domain member computer to securely identify itself to the domain.

connection object — A connection between two domain controllers that is used for replication.

convergence — The state when all replicas of a database have the same version of the data. (In Active Directory, this means that all domain controllers have the same set of information.)

country code TLD (ccTLD) — A top-level domain assigned by ISO country codes on a geo-political basis, such as .us for the United States.

CSVDE — A command-line utility that can be used to import and export data to and from Active Directory in a comma-separated file format.

data owner — A person or team responsible for managing the content of a part of the directory, not maintaining the directory service itself. Data owners usually create objects and edit their attributes.

Database layer — A functional layer of Active Directory that provides an object-oriented hierarchical view of the objects contained in the Active Directory store. It presents a set of application programming interfaces (APIs) to the Directory System Agent (DSA) so that DSA does not communicate directly with the Extensible Storage Engine (ESE).

Dcgpofix — A command-line utility that recreates the Default Domain Policy and the Default Domain Controllers Policy.

Default-First-Site-Name — The site that is automatically created when you promote the first domain controller in the forest.

DEFAULTIPSITELINK — The site link that is automatically created when you promote the first domain controller in the forest.

defragmentation — The process of reorganizing the data inside of the Active Directory store in order to improve performance.

delegation of control — Refers to assigning permissions on Active Directory objects so that data owners can manage their own objects. The Delegation of Control Wizard assists with setting permissions for common tasks.

differential backup — A backup type that only backs up those files that have changed since the last normal or incremental backup took place, but does not clear the archive attribute associated with those files.

directory service (DS) — A network application or database, usually integrated as a core component of a network operating system, that provides information about users, computers, resources, and other network elements.

Directory Service Agent (DSA) — A functional layer of Active Directory that is responsible for enforcing the semantics that govern how objects in Active Directory are created and manipulated.

disabled — An account is disabled or enabled by an administrator. Disabled accounts cannot be used. See also locked out.

discretionary access control list (DACL) — A list of ACEs used to control access to an object or resource.

distinguished name (DN) — An LDAP component used to uniquely identify an object throughout the entire LDAP hierarchy by referring to the relative distinguished name, domain name, and the container holding the object.

distributed file system (DFS) — A distributed service that integrates file shares located on multiple servers into a single logical namespace.

distribution groups — Groups that can be used for tasks such as sending e-mail to a list of users and contacts. It cannot be used to control security.

distribution point — A file share on the network that provides the files necessary to install an application.

DNS namespace — The entire map of valid names in the domain name system.

document invocation — Allows users to open a file and have the appropriate application installed automatically based on the file's extension.

domain — A logically structured organization of objects, such as users, computers, groups, and printers, that are part of a network and share a common directory database. Domains are defined by an administrator and administered as a unit with common rules and procedures.

domain controller — A Windows Server 2003 system explicitly configured to store a copy of the Active Directory database, and service user authentication requests or queries about domain objects.

domain identifier — Three 32-bit numbers that are statistically unique and identify a particular domain.

domain local group — Can only be assigned permissions to a resource available in the domain in which it is created. However, group membership can come from any domain within the forest. Created on domain controllers within the domain.

Domain Name System (DNS) — A highly available, scalable, and dispersed system that provides name resolution on the Internet or private networks.

domain naming master — The forest-wide operations master that controls the addition and removal of domains in the forest.

down-level client — Clients older than the current operating system that lack some functionality. Usually refers to Windows products released prior to Windows 2000.

DSADD — A command-line utility used to add objects to Active Directory.

DSMOD — A command-line utility used to modify Active Directory objects.

DSMOVE — A command-line utility used to move or rename Active Directory objects.

DSQUERY — A command-line utility used to query for Active Directory objects.

DSRM — A command-line utility used to delete Active Directory objects.

dynamic linking of auxiliary classes — Linking a class to a single instance of an object to add attributes, rather than all instances of a class.

Extensible Storage Engine (ESE) — The Active Directory database engine; it is based on an improved version of the Jet database engine that Microsoft Exchange Server 5.5 uses. ESE uses transactions to ensure that data can be recovered even in the event of an unexpected system failure.

File Allocation Table (FAT) — An older file format used by down-level clients and DOS. FAT disks do not support file-based permissions, auditing, or journaling.

File Replication Service (FRS) — A multi-threaded, multi-master replication engine that replaces the LMREPL service in Microsoft Windows NT 4.0.

Folder redirection — A user configuration setting that redirects folders from the local user profile to the server. Basic redirection redirects all users' folders to the same path (although you can use variables such as *%USERNAME%*). Advanced redirection allows completely different paths based on security group memberships.

forced removal — A removal where all existing installations of the software are removed and no new installations are performed.

forest — A collection of Active Directory domains that do not necessarily share a contiguous DNS naming convention but do share a common global catalog and schema.

forest root domain — The first domain created within the Active Directory structure.

Fully Qualified Domain Names (FQDN) — A host name that includes all parts necessary to resolve a name to an IP address from the host name to the root domain, including any subdomains or TLDs, such as myhost.mysubdomain.mycompany.com.

fully routed IP environment — A network where computers from one site can communicate with all other sites on the network.

functional specification — The document created at the end of the planning stage that describes the Active Directory design.

garbage collection — The process of purging deleted objects from Active Directory. By default, garbage collection occurs every 12 hours.

generic TLDs (gTLD) — A top-level DNS domain that is not assigned to a specific country, and is directly delegated by the root servers .aero, .biz, .com, .coop, .edu, .gov, .info, .int, .mil, .museum, .name, .net, .org, and .pro.

Global catalog — An index of the objects and attributes used throughout the Active Directory structure. It contains a partial replica of every Windows Server 2003 domain within Active Directory, enabling users to find any object in the directory.

global group — A group that is mainly used for organizing other objects into administrative units. A global group can be assigned permissions to any resource in any domain within the forest. The main limitation of a global group is that it can only contain members of the same domain in which it is created.

globally unique identifier (GUID) — A 16-byte value generated by an algorithm and should be different from every other GUID generated anywhere in the world. A GUID is used to uniquely identify a particular device, component, item, or object.

GPO link — GPOs are assigned to a site, domain, or OU by linking them. You can link a single GPO to multiple locations.

Gpresult — A command-line utility that is equivalent to RSoP.

Gpupdate — A command-line utility that forces the update of Group Policy on a workstation or server. It replaces the portion of the secedit command that was used to refresh Group Policy in Windows 2000.

group — A container object that is used to organize a collection of users, computers, contacts, or other groups into a single object reference.

Group Policy — The Windows Server 2003 feature that allows for policy creation that affects domain users and computers. Policies can be anything from desktop settings to application assignment to security settings and more.

group policy container (GPC) — The collection of objects in Active Directory that holds GPOs and their settings.

Group Policy objects (GPOs) — A set of specific group policy settings applied in Active Directory.

group policy template (GPT) — A set of files and folders in the SYSVOL folder that holds settings and files for a GPO.

group scope — Groups can have the following scopes: local (also called machine local), domain local, global, or universal. A group's scope determines who can be a member of the group and where the group can be assigned permissions.

group types — Groups can be either security groups or distribution groups. Distribution groups cannot be included in SACLs or DACLs.

incremental backup — A backup type that only backs up those files that have changed since the last normal or incremental backup took place, and clears the archive attribute associated with those files.

incremental zone transfer — A process whereby a secondary DNS server can request changes made only to zone data, not the entire zone.

inetOrgPerson — An object used by most LDAP applications to represent users.

infrastructure master — The operations master for a domain that updates references to objects in other domains.

inheritance — The concept that a security setting on one object can be inherited by objects lower (that is, deeper) in the hierarchy. Examples include folders inheriting settings from parent folders, or OUs inheriting settings from parent OUs.

instantiation — The process of creating an instance of an object from an object class.

inter-forest migration — The migration of objects between two domains in different forests. Migration from a Windows NT domain is also inter-forest migration.

Inter-site replication — Replication occurring between sites.

Inter-Site Topology Generator (ISTG) — A process that runs on one domain controller in every site and is responsible for creating the replication topology between its site and other sites.

Internet presence — In the context of DNS, the Internet presence refers to the DNS subdomain name used by the public to reach an organization's e-mail or Web servers. The term can also be used generically, as in "our company needs an Internet presence."

intra-forest migration — The migration of objects from one domain to another domain in the same forest. Users and groups are moved in closed sets.

Intra-site replication — Replication occurring within a site.

IP security policies — Security policy settings relating to IPSec configuration.

JScript (.js) — A scripting language that you can use to write logon, logoff, startup, and shutdown scripts. It is similar to JavaScript.

Kerberos — An authentication protocol first developed at MIT to allow for a wide-area, distributed method of securely authenticating users before they are allowed to access network resources.

Key Distribution Center (KDC) — A network service that is made up of an Authentication Service and Ticket-granting Service. The Authentication Service authenticates users and issues TGTs. The Ticket-granting Service issues session tickets for access to network resources. All domain controllers in Active Directory are KDCs by default.

Knowledge Consistency Checker (KCC) — A process that runs on each DC to create the replication topology within a site.

lastLogonTimestamp — A user attribute used to track the last time a user logged on to the network. It is replicated to all domain controllers in the domain and is only available if the domain is at the Windows Server 2003 functional level.

latency — The delay or "lag time" between a change made in one replica being recognized in another.

LDIFDE — A command-line utility that can be used to import and export data to and from Active Directory using the LDAP Interchange Format.

least privilege — The concept that users are only given the permissions they need to do their jobs and nothing more.

Lightweight Directory Access Protocol (LDAP) — An access protocol that defines how users can access or update directory service objects.

local computer policy — A GPO that is stored on the local computer, and is only available on the local computer. It is sometimes called the local GPO.

local group — Can only be assigned permissions to a resource available on the local machine in which it is created.

local policies — A wide variety of settings for auditing, user rights, and security options.

locked out — An account can be locked out automatically by the system after too many failed log-on attempts. A locked-out account cannot be used. See also disabled.

logoff script — A script that runs when a user logs off.

logon script — A script that runs when a user logs on.

Loopback Processing Mode — A computer configuration setting that changes the processing of user configuration settings. When in effect, user settings from the GPOs that apply to the computer are used rather than user settings from the GPOs that apply to the user.

mail exchanger (MX) record — A mail exchanger (MX) resource record specifies the host that can receive SMTP mail for the subdomain.

mandatory upgrade — An upgrade that is performed automatically the next time a computer starts or the user runs the application (by default). All existing installations are upgraded to the new version and no new installations of the old version are performed.

member server — A Windows Server 2003 system that has a computer account in a domain, but is not configured as a domain controller.

Microsoft Operations Framework (MOF) — A set of documents, guidelines, and models developed by Microsoft to help companies increase reliability, availability, and ease of management and support. MOF provides guidance for the operation of systems, particularly Microsoft infrastructure systems in large enterprises. Visit *www.microsoft.com/mof.*

Microsoft Solutions Framework (MSF) — A set of documents, guidelines, and models developed by Microsoft to help companies improve the effectiveness of software or infrastructure development projects. Visit *www.microsoft.com/msf.*

Movetree — A tool to move objects from one domain to another within the same forest.

Multi-master replication — A replication model in which any domain controller accepts and replicates directory changes to any other domain controller. This differs from other replication models in which one computer stores the single modifiable copy of the directory and other computers store backup copies.

multi-valued — An attribute that can hold multiple values of the same syntax.

name server (NS) record — A name server (NS) resource record is used to delegate authority for a subdomain to another zone or server.

naming contexts — A category or division of information within Active Directory. Each naming context is replicated separately.

NETDOM.EXE — A command-line utility used to rename domain controllers, create trusts, and join computers to a domain.

netlogon share — A default share that is available on all NT 4.0 domain controllers. It is commonly used to hold logon scripts and system policies.

network operating system (NOS) — A computer operating system that is designed primarily to support workstations on a local area network (LAN).

No Override — A link setting that prevents policies linked at a lower level from having priority over the settings in the GPO.

Non-authoritative restore — A restore of Active Directory used to restore a damaged database. Updates made after the backup was taken are replicated from other domain controllers in the domain.

nontransitive trust — A trust between two domains, realms, or forests where trust does not extend outside of the two domains/forests between which the trust exists.

normal backup — A backup type that backs up all selected files and folders, and clears the archive attribute on these files and folders.

NT File System (NTFS) — Known almost exclusively by its initials, NTFS is the robust file system used by Windows NT, Windows 2000, Windows XP, and

Windows Server 2003. NTFS supports the ability to control and audit access, and uses a journaling system to minimize corruption.

NT LAN Manager (NTLM) — More commonly known by its initials, NTLM is the older network authentication protocol used by Windows systems prior to Windows 2000. It is still used with Windows 2000, Windows XP, and Windows Server 2003 in certain circumstances.

object — A collection of attributes that represent items within Active Directory, such as users, groups, computers, and printers.

object classes — Define which types of objects can be created within Active Directory, such as users, groups, and printers.

object owner — Specifically, each object in the directory has an identified owner. More generically, sometimes used to mean data owner.

objectSID — The Active Directory attribute that stores a security principal's security identifier (SID).

offline defragmentation — A defragmentation process that occurs with Active Directory offline. An offline defragmentation can do everything an online defragmentation can, plus an offline defragmentation can shrink the file size of the Active Directory store.

one-way trust — A trust relationship where security principals in the trusted domain can use resources in the trusting domain, but not vice versa. Two one-way trusts in opposite directions are equivalent to a two-way trust.

online defragmentation — A defragmentation process that occurs with Active Directory online. Online defragmentation can reclaim space used by deleted objects and reorganize data to optimize performance. However, online defragmentation cannot shrink the file size of the Active Directory store.

operations masters — Domain controllers that manage specific changes to Active Directory that would be impractical to manage using a multi-master replication model. (Also called Flexible Single Master Operations roles, or FSMO.)

optional removal — A removal where existing installations are not removed, but no new installations are performed.

optional upgrade — An upgrade that users can run manually at their discretion. Existing installations of the old version are not removed; however, no new installations of the old version are performed.

organizational unit (OU) — An Active Directory logical container used to organize objects within a single domain. Objects such as users, groups, computers, and other organizational units can be stored in an organizational unit container.

originating updates — A change to Active Directory made by an administrator on the local domain controller.

partitions — See naming contexts.

PDC emulator — An operations master for a domain that simulates a Windows NT 4.0 PDC for backward compatibility with older Windows clients and servers. It also is used for time synchronization, and it receives preferential replication of password changes.

Performance console — A predefined MMC that includes both the System Monitor and Performance Logs and Alerts tools.

physical objects — Active Directory objects that have an equivalent physical structure or component in the real world. Physical objects include sites, site links, and domain controllers.

possible superiors — A list of other classes in which a given class's objects can be contained.

primary name server — The only DNS server where changes can be made to zone data.

printer object — An object in Active Directory that represents a print queue (which in Windows NT, 2000, and 2003 is also referred to as a "printer").

private/public key pair — A set of two mathematically related keys used in public key cryptography (or asymmetric encryption). If a message is encrypted with one key, it can only be decrypted with the other. The public key is widely distributed; the private key is closely guarded.

propagation dampening — The process of preventing a domain controller from replicating an update to another domain controller that already has the update.

Public Key Infrastructure (PKI) — An organized system that issues and manages certificates and key pairs to support the use of public key cryptography in an organization.

publish — A published application appears in Add or Remove Programs and must be installed manually by the user or through document invocation. Applications cannot be published to computers.

Recover — To repair a database; to return it to a consistent state; to fix corruption therein.

redeployment — Forces an application to be reinstalled the next time the computer starts or a user runs the application (by default).

registry hives — Major sections of the Windows registry that contain a set of related registry keys.

registry keys — One or more related settings stored in the Windows registry. A key is similar to a folder in the file system; it can contain other keys or values.

relative distinguished name — An LDAP component used to identify an object within the object's container.

Relative Identifier (RID) — A 32-bit number, unique within the domain, that makes up part of a security principal's SID.

replica — An instance of an Active Directory naming context stored on a domain controller.

replicated updates — Changes to Active Directory that were made through replication from another domain controller.

replication — The process of updating Active Directory on all domain controllers on the network.

replication boundary — A set of data that is replicated to only specific replicas, or a barrier (physical or logical) that prevents replication. In the case of Active Directory, it is used to describe the fact that domain information is not replicated to other domains (except for attributes sent to the global catalog).

replication partner — A domain controller that replicates with another domain controller.

replication topology — The set of connections used by domain controllers to replicate directory updates among domain controllers in both the same and different sites.

resources — Any shared piece of equipment or information made available to users on the network, such as file shares and printers.

Restore — To replace the current copy of a database (or part of it) with a back-up copy made previously.

Restricted groups — A security policy setting that defines group membership.

Resultant Set of Policy (RSoP) — A tool used to show how settings are applied, and which GPO supplied a particular setting.

reverse lookup — The process of looking up a host's FQDN using its IP address, which is the reverse of the normal process.

RID master — The operations master for a domain that allocates blocks of RIDs to domain controllers for use when creating security principles such as users, groups, and computer accounts.

root domain — The top of the DNS hierarchy, which delegates authority for all TLDs.

sAMAccountName — A unique attribute of a user object that specifies the username used to log on to the domain. Active Directory domains can use the sAMAccountName or the userPrincipalName.

schema master — The forest-wide operations master that controls changes to the Active Directory schema.

secondary name server — An authoritative DNS server that has a read-only copy of zone data that has been transferred from a primary name server.

Security Accounts Manager (SAM) database — The local security and account database on a Windows Server 2003 stand-alone or member server.

security descriptor — A package of binary information associated with an object or a resource, which contains the DACL, SACL, object owner, and related security information. For Active Directory objects, the security descriptor is an attribute of all objects and is called ntSecurityDescriptor.

Security Descriptor Definition Language (SDDL) — A format that efficiently describes SIDs. SDDL is both reasonably compact and easily read by humans.

security groups — A group that can be used as a distribution group and can also be included in SACLs and DACLs to control access and auditing.

Security Identifier (SID) — A binary number that uniquely represents a security principal. For most security principals, the two key components are a domain identifier and a RID that are unique within the domain.

security policy — The collection of user configuration and computer configuration settings located in Windows Settings, Security Settings. You can update these using security templates.

security principals — An object in the directory to which resource permissions can be granted. In Active Directory, security principals are user objects (including inetOrgPerson objects), computer objects, and security group objects.

security template — An .inf file that contains settings for some or all of the computer settings in a security policy.

Security Templates snap-in — An MMC snap-in that edits existing security templates or creates new ones.

service locator (SRV) record — The service locator (SRV) resource record provides a method to locate servers offering specific services in specific sites by using the Domain Name System.

service owner — A person or team responsible for maintaining and operating the directory service as a whole. The service owner manages domain controllers and the site structure.

service principal name (SPN) — The name by which a client uniquely identifies an instance of a service on the network.

service ticket (ST) — A Kerberos ticket presented to a resource server allowing it to authenticate the user.

shared folder object — An object in Active Directory that represents a shared folder (a share folder) on the network.

shortcut trusts — A manually created trust that improves the efficiency of inter-domain authentications within a forest.

shutdown script — A script that runs when a computer is shut down.

SIDhistory — A user attribute that is enabled only in domains at the Windows 2000 native or Windows Server 2003 functional level. It is used to track the previous SIDs of migrated users and groups.

single sign-on — The concept that a user only has to identify himself or herself with a single set of credentials once to access all resources that he or she has been authorized to use throughout the entire network.

site — A combination of one or more Internet Protocol (IP) subnets connected by a high-speed connection.

site link — A low-bandwidth or unreliable/occasional connection between sites. The site links can be adjusted for replication availability, bandwidth costs, and replication frequency. They enable control over replication and logon traffic.

site link bridge — An object that exists in Active Directory to define which site links can communicate with one another on an IP network that is not fully routed.

site-aware — A service that can use site information in Active Directory to locate the closest server based on the cost of site links.

special permissions — A specific, granular permission available from the Advanced dialog box when setting permissions.

split administration model — The concept that service ownership and data ownership can be divided.

stand-alone server — A Windows Server 2003 system that is configured as part of a workgroup.

standard permissions — Permissions shown on the main Security tab in an object's properties that represent the most common permissions granted to users. A standard permission represents several related special permissions.

start of authority (SOA) records — A start of authority (SOA) resource record provides information about the zone data.

startup script — A script that runs when a computer starts up.

Structural classes — Classes that can have objects instantiated from them. A Structural class can be derived from other Structural classes or an Abstract class.

subdomain — A subdivision of a DNS domain name.

subnet objects — An Active Directory object that is used to define an IP subnet. Subnet objects are associated with sites and in turn allow computers to determine in which site they are located.

symmetric keys — Encryption keys that can be used to encrypt or decrypt a message. The same key is used for both encryption and decryption.

syntax — Defines the type of data an attribute can store.

system access control list (SACL) — A list of ACEs used to determine which actions are audited or logged for a particular object or resource.

system policies — Collections of registry entries that are used to control Windows 9x and Windows NT workstations.

System State — A group of critical operating system files and components that can be backed up as a single group on a Windows Server 2003 system. System State data always includes the Registry, COM+ Registration database, boot files, and system files. On a domain controller, it also includes Active Directory and the SYSVOL directory. Other components that are included (assuming their associated services are installed) are the Certificate Services database, the Cluster Service, and the IIS Metadirectory.

tattooing the registry — The normally undesired effect of leaving permanent changes in the Windows registry, even after the policy no longer applies.

ticket-granting ticket (TGT) — A Kerberos ticket used to request service tickets from a KDC.

tombstone — A marker in the Active Directory database that indicates an object has been deleted.

tombstone lifetime — The time period after which deleted objects' tombstones are removed from Active Directory. The default is 60 days.

top-level domain (TLD) — A division of the DNS namespace that is divided directly off the root domain. It includes ccTLDs and gTLDs.

transaction — A modification to the Active Directory store including the creation and deletion of objects or the modification of attributes.

tree — A group of one or more domains in a forest that have a contiguous DNS namespace.

trust relationship — A link between two domains that allows security principals from one domain to be recognized by the other.

two-factor authentication — Authentication systems that require possession of a physical object (or present a biometric identification) and a password or PIN.

two-way, transitive trust — A trust relationship between two domains that can also be used by any other domains trusted by either of the domains. For example if A trusts B, and B trusts C, then A also trusts C.

universal group — Can be assigned permissions to any resource in any domain within the forest. Universal groups can consist of any user or group object except for local groups.

Update Sequence Number (USN) — A unique number assigned to every object and attribute in Active Directory to track changes. Each domain controller maintains its own set of USNs.

user account template — A user account configured with attributes that can be copied in order to simplify the creation of user accounts with common attributes.

user logon name (pre-Windows 2000) — The Active Directory Users and Computers property that maps to the sAMAccountName attribute.

user logon name — The Active Directory Users and Computers property that maps to the userPrincipalName attribute.

user objects — Objects in Active Directory that represent users in your domain. A user is a security principal and may be a person or a network service.

User Principal Name (UPN) — A user-account naming convention that includes both the user name and domain name in the format user@domain.com.

userPrincipalName — A unique attribute of a user object that specifies the username that can be used to log on to the domain from clients that support Active Directory.

VBScript (.vbs) — A scripting language that you can use to write logon, logoff, startup, and shutdown scripts. It is based on Visual Basic and is sometimes called Visual Basic Scripting Edition.

Windows Installer package (.msi) file — A file that contains all of the information needed to install an application using the Windows Installer service.

Windows Installer patch (.msp) file — An update to a Windows Installer package that usually contains bug fixes or new functionality.

Windows Installer service — A service that can be used to fully automate the software installation and configuration process.

Windows Installer transform (.mst) file — Customized settings for a Windows Installer package that are applied during installation.

Windows Management Instrumentation (WMI) — The Windows implementation of Web-Based Enterprise Management (WBEM) that uses a common set of interfaces to present information about a computer system in a consistent way across a variety of tools and platforms.

WINNT32.EXE /checkupgradeonly — A command run on an existing Windows server to determine upgrade compatibility.

Wireless network (IEEE 802.11) policies — Security policy settings that configure settings for wireless access.

workgroup — A logical group of computers characterized by a decentralized security and administration model.

X.509 digital certificate — A specially structured electronic document that describes the identity of a person or service. The certificate is digitally signed by its issuer.

ZAP (.zap) file — A text file that is used by Group Policy to deploy applications for which a Windows Installer package cannot be created.

zone — A file or database containing DNS records for a subdomain.

zone transfer — The process by which a primary DNS server sends copies of the zone data to secondary DNS servers.

Index